INFORMATION INDIA : 1991-92

CONCEPTS IN COMMUNICATION INFORMATICS & LIBRARIANSHIP (CICIL)

For a list of titles in this series, see pp. 577-80 at the end of the book

---

S.P. AGRAWAL (*b.* 1929) was Director, National Social Science Documentation Centre, ICSSR, and Member Secretary, Indian Association of Social Science Institutions. He was also the Vice-Chairman of the Asia and Pacific Information Network in Social Sciences (APINESS). In 1988 he was awarded the degree of Doctor of Philosophy in Education (*Honoris Causa*) by International University Foundation. Presently, he is Member, Round Table on Research in Reading, IFLA, and Member, International Committee for Social Science Information and Documentation. He is also Member of Board of Studies of National Archives of India and Hindi Advisory Committee, Ministry of Coal, Government of India. Born and brought up in the cradle of freedom movement which he joined at the tender age of twelve, he gained an insight into political problems and developed a sense of responsibility which bore fruit as an information scientist committed to Gandhiji's philosophy and action-plan in the field and its social concept. He has written extensively on various aspects of education, Indian Polity and library and information science.

J.C. AGGARWAL (*b.* 1928), former Deputy Director of Education/Executive Director of Delhi Bureau of Textbooks, Delhi Administration has a varied experience in the field of education. He has singly/jointly authored about 130 books on Education, Social Sciences and Current Problems. In collaboration with S.P. Agrawal, he has written *Documentation Encyclopaedia of UNESCO and Education* (in two Parts); *Women's Education in India*; *National Policy on Education: Agenda for India 2001*; *Indian Writings on Education, 1979 to 1986*; and *Vocational Education in India*.

His other recent publications include: *Yearbook of Indian Education, 1991: World Overview*; *Ramamurti Report 1990 on National Policy on Education in India*; and *Survey of Educational Documents in the World Since 1983*, etc.

Concepts in Communication
Informatics & Librarianship No. 47

General Editor. **S.P. Agrawal**

INFORMATION INDIA : 1991-92

Global View

S.P. AGRAWAL
Former Director
National Social Science Documentation Centre, ICSSR, New Delhi

J.C. AGGARWAL
Former Executive Director
Delhi Bureau of Textbooks, Delhi Administration

CONCEPT PUBLISHING COMPANY, NEW DELHI 110059

ISBN 81-7022-308-3

First Published 1993

S.P. **Agrawal** (*b. 1929*)
J.C. **Aggarwal** (*b. 1928*)

Published and Printed by
Ashok Kumar Mittal
Concept Publishing Company
A/15-16, Commercial Block, Mohan Garden
NEW DELHI 110059 (India)

Lasertypeset by
Microtech Advance Printing Systems (Pvt.) Ltd.
H-13, **Bali Nagar**
NEW DELHI 110015

General Editor's Introduction

Information India was first brought out in 1989 by the Publisher under CICIL series which covers a wide range of disciplines—interrelated but at the same time including a very wide stretch of topics for investigation, research and study. It is of great consolation that previous editions of *Information India* placed in the hands of the discerning readers as also reviewers have been received well. In all humility, we assume that these annuals have fulfilled a long felt need.

The focus of the present volume is on India as it was in 1991. As many as 28 out of the total of 39 chapters, under suitable divisions, are devoted to various aspects of the country. The chapters are, by and large, a combination of descriptive accounts and vital statistics.

S.P. AGRAWAL

Preface

In this compilation it has been endeavoured to give all important facets of not only of India but also of the world as a whole.

A comparative study of the indicators of development with regard to 170 countries including populous and less populous countries, as also developed, developing and under-developed countries has been included.

Relating to India also, it has been attempted to provide almost all embracing facts and figures with regard to various sectors of development since 1947. A detailed account has been given about eight important aspects —, Census 1991, Election 1991 (May-June), Education, State of Economy, Fiscal Measures, Inflation, Balance of Payments and Monetary Trends. Other chapters provide information about Agricultural Development, Culture, Defence, Energy Conservation, Health, AIDS, Environmental Protection, Industries, Scheduled Castes, Scheduled Tribes and Other Backward Classes, as well as other topical areas which are of significance in any discussion on India.

As a matter of fact, the book includes a panoramic view of almost everything important that happened in India during the period under review.

It is observed that data collected by various national and international organisations from different sources and also used here, do not necessarily relate to the same year in a few cases.

S.P. AGRAWAL
J.C. AGGARWAL

CONTENTS

Part-II : India 1991-92

Appendices

PART ONE

WORLD OVERVIEW

1

ENVIRONMENT AND DEVELOPMENT

1.1 Earth Summit : United Nations Conference on Environment and Development

The first-ever "Earth Summit"—the United Nations Conference on Environment and Development (UNCED)—will take place in Rio de Janeiro, Brazil, from 1 to 12 June 1992.

The primary goal of the Summit will be to lay the foundation for a global partnership between developing and more industrialized countries, based on mutual need and common interests, to ensure the future of the planet.

A highlight of the Conference will be the observance of World Environment Day on 5 June 1992, the twentieth anniversary of the opening of the United Nations Conference on the Human Environment, held in Stockholm, Sweden, in 1972.

In Stockholm environment was placed on the world agenda. The Brazil Summit will ensure that the issue becomes central to policy-making and implementation in almost every sector of economic life. It will seek agreement on concrete measures to reconcile economic activities with the need to protect the planet and ensure a sustainable future for all people.

The General Assembly has decided that Member States should be represented at the Conference by Heads of State or Government. It is expected to be the largest summit meeting to date. International organizations, non-governmental groups and private-sector interests will also take part in an unprecedented attempt to mobilize people to set a new and more hopeful course for the future of humanity.

The relationship between economic development and environmental impact was recognized at the Stockholm Conference. It was also the focus *Our Common Future,* the 1987 report of the United Nations World Commission on Environment and Development.

However, between 1972 and 1987, too little was done to integrate, in practical terms, concerns for development and the environment in economic planning and decision-making. Progress was made in specific instances but overall the environment of the planet deteriorated. Ozone depletion, global warming and other major environmental problems grew more serious.

In December 1989, the United Nations called for a conference that would take steps to reverse trends and establish the basis for a sustainable way of life on the planet as we move into the twenty-first century.

Issues at Stake

In an effort to maintain the quality of the environment and achieve environmentally sound, sustainable development in all countries, the Conference will address:

— protection of the atmosphere (climate change, depletion of the ozone layer, transboundary air pollution);
— protection of land resources (combating deforestation, soil loss, desertification and drought);
— conservation of biological diversity;
— protection of fresh water resources;
— protection of oceans, seas and coastal areas, and the rational use and development of their living resources;
— environmentally sound management of biotechnology and hazardous wastes (including toxic chemicals);
— prevention of illegal traffic in toxic products and wastes;
— improvement in the quality of life and human health;
— improvement in living and working conditions of the poor by eradicating poverty and stopping environmental degradation.

The Conference will look at underlying patterns of development which cause stress to the environment. Poverty in developing countries, levels of economic growth, unsustainable patterns of consumption, demographic pressures and the impact of the international economy are development issues that will be addressed.

Objectives

The Conference is expected to produce:

— an Earth Charter that will embody basic principles which must govern the economic and environmental behaviour of peoples and nations to ensure "our common future";
— Agenda 21, a blueprint for action in all major areas affecting the relationship between the environment and the economy. It will focus on the period up to the year 2000 and extend into the twenty-first century;
— the means to carry out the agenda by making available to developing countries the additional financial resources and environmentally sound technologies they require to participate fully in global environmental cooperation and to integrate environmental considerations into development policies and practices;
— agreement on strengthening institutions in order to implement these measures;
— conventions on climate change, biological diversity and, perhaps, forestry may be negotiated prior to the Conference and signed or agreed to in Brazil.

1.2 Direction for Agenda*

United Nations Conference on Environment and Development (UNCED)

---

* *Based on a lecture given by Mohamed, T. El-Ashry, Environment Director of the World Bank and the then Senior Vice-President at the World Resources Institute (WRI) in Washington DC, before the Norwegian Academy of Science and Letters.*

(June 1-12, 1992) offers the world a chance to move beyond rhetoric to real action on international cooperation for sustainable development. So far, however, the debate throughout the conference's preparatory process has been a bi-polar one, and the list of issues on its agenda is still long and divisive. All but the most essential issues must be set aside so that the 1992 conference can result in actions rather than just discussion, in binding agreements rather than simple declarations.

I would like to propose *six* major areas for formulating high priority conference initiatives. Three of these issues are sectoral and three of them cut across sectors. All six encompass many of the issues of the Preparatory Committee's long list, and together they form the basis for a new agenda for international cooperation.

On the sectoral side, the first need is for *Integrated Land Resources Management.* Land and water degradation, declining agricultural productivity, unsustainable and uses, rural poverty, and hunger are interrelated and can best be addressed by actions aimed at the entire range of land resources. This includes: the land itself (soils, water and biota); the uses of land resources and competition between uses; the use of natural resources as inputs to the development process; and government policies as they affect land resources.

The second sectoral agenda item is *Sustainable Energy Strategies.* A worldwide push towards the rational development and use of energy would go a long way towards mitigating global warming, local and transboundary air pollution, the developmental needs of the South as well as the continued growth needs of the North. Improved energy efficiency—which confers immediate environmental and economic benefits—must become the cornerstone of all national energy plans. But, as important as an increase in energy efficiency is, it must be complemented by a massive shift to renewable sources of energy and non-fossil transportation technologies.

The third sectoral area is *Forests and Biological Diversity.* The loss of the world's living resources—its species, genes, habitats, and ecosystems—is accelerating at an alarming rate, despite recent action plans and conservation strategies. An all-fronts assault on the root causes of deforestation and biological impoverishment requires transforming the way that people and societies treat the world's biotic wealth. We need new management regimes that integrate the conservation of living resources with development goals, that use natural resources to simultaneously serve short- and long-term local, national, and international goals. We also need the institutional and economic tools to promote sustainable management of forest resources.

As for the cross-cutting initiatives, the first area is *International Finance* including the related areas of debt and trade. A significant increase in new financing to the South is essential if these countries are to address their sustainable development needs. It is also essential that their external debt burdens be greatly reduced. In Latin America, Africa, and Asia the burden of servicing the $1.3 trillion external debt (which represents almost half of their collective GNP) is lowering per capita income and keeping environmental problems of the agenda.

Developed countries should also revamp their trade policies to remove the impediments to sustainable development that poor countries now face. These trade barriers are costing developing countries an estimated $100 billion a year in foregone income.

Despite this pessimism, some progress on international finance was made last year —namely the Multilateral Fund for implementing the Montreal Protocol and the Global Environment Facility (GEF) established at the World Bank with United Nations Development Programme (UNDP) and United Nations Environment Programme (UNEP). These are excellent models for future international cooperation towards sustainable development.

The second cross-cutting area is *International Technology Transfer;* who pays how much for what and on what terms and conditions. Few developing countries have the information, capital, institutions, and public policies needed to make widespread use of existing technologies for preventing pollution and improving energy efficiency. Transfer of emerging commercial technologies is clouded by unresolved questions of intellectual property rights. To solve this thorny issue, international institutions (or intermediaries) could buy international rights to commercial technologies and then make them available to developing countries, either free or at a nominal charge. Last but not least is the cross-cutting issue of *Institutions.* The United Nations (UN) and other international governmental and non-governmental organizations can play a critical role in bringing about a new era of international cooperation. UN has played a leading role in dealing with global environmental issues, as demonstrated by the Montreal Protocol and the Intergovernmental panel on Climate Change. But we need new thinking and new approaches to devise interdisciplinary mechanisms and innovative structures for cooperation that can meet the challenges of the twenty-first century.

The UN system can tackle these challenges only if the mandates of its component institutions are clarified and their capacities strengthened. UNEP, for instance, should be strengthened organizationally and financially as the environmental conscience of the UN system and as the primary source of policy leadership. Similarly, the environmental and financial capabilities of (UNDP) should be strengthened so it can be the sustainable development voice of the UN system by better integrating environmental guidelines and concerns into programmes and projects.

Our collective actions over the eleven months leading to the 1992 conference, the conference itself, and what we do after it, will determine whether we continue on the road to over-exploitation and abuse of our natural resources, or take the high road towards sustainable development and alleviating poverty and environmental degradation. The decade of the 1990s is our last chance in this century to take the necessary steps to sustain the Earth on which our survival depends.

Source : *Network*, July 1991.

1.3 **Student Sector and Earth Summit**

The challenges the world faces to reach a sustainable society will require an enormous intellectual effort combined with dedication and creativity. The young and bright students of today will become the leaders in tomorrow's society. Student awareness must happen so that these creative and intelligent students can focus their energies towards solutions for a better world.

Students and Youth

AIESEC International, the representative of the Student Sector on the IFC, geared its activities towards the Earth Summit and beyond. Since cooperation between the different independent sector is vital, AIESEC International will aim to have the student sector cooperate closely with the youth sector. (In order to make the distinction between students and youth it is important to note that Students are defined as students at universities or institutes of higher education.) Concretely we will seek to cooperate with the Canadian Youth Working Group on Environment and Development in the preparation of an international Youth Forum to be held in Costa Rica, and the Worldlink Foundation for their Global Youth Summit in Rio de Janeiro.

Students, Academia and Business Community

The visionaries in academia are expressing the importance of incorporating environmental management and awareness of environment and development issues in the curricula. However, this cannot remain only a vision among the few. A rapid and broad implementation of environment and development in the curricula is needed in order to close the gap between what will be expected of companies in the years to come and the education that students get today. Therefore, AIESEC will promote discussions between the student sector, the leaders of academia (i.e. Ministers of Education, University Presidents) and the leaders of the business community on how to implement education on environment and development so that it is relevant to both the students and the educational institutions as well as to the ultimate recipients of the output, the business community. Of course this will have to be done at the National level, but if we share our experiences, our frustrations and the fruits of our progress, we can hopefully attain positive result more quickly. Other international student associations assistance in this area will be crucial to reaching the necessary impact. In order to link to the business community we will seek to cooperate with the International Chamber of Commerce and the Business Council for Sustainable Development.

AIESEC Contribution

AIESEC hosted a World Conference on the theme "A Youth Perspective on Sustainable Development —The Role of Economics and Education" in Tokyo August 1990. At that conference 150 students from 50 countries met with business executives, government representatives and experts from the scientific and academic communities to outline the environment and development problems, identify some possible solutions to these problems, and finally create concrete action plans to implement these solutions. The output of the conference, which has been turned into a book, has a strong focus on what youth thinks it can contribute to the issue of sustainable development.

The success of the Tokyo conference is being followed up by throughout the globe. They continue to create awareness about socio-economic issues linked to development within the framework of the new AIESEC Global Theme Programme. The theme this year, until the next Global Theme Conference in August of 1992 will be "Entrepreneurship and Corporate Responsibility —New

Opportunities for Global Development." Key areas within this theme are: Entrepreneurial Development, Business Ethics (where environmental and social responsibilities are central) and International Cooperation (North South, East-West) and the role these factors play in development.

World will be looking towards Brazil, to see what will happen at the Earth Summit. Everyone seems to be focussed on the work being done up until this very important meeting, but if we don't start looking at what will happen after UNCED it will take another mobilizing effort after the meeting to implement the resolutions of the conference. In this respect, AIESEC's Global Theme Conference is strategically placed in late August, early September of 1992. This conference will take place in Rome and will bring together 400 delegates from over 70 countries and there will be substantial participation from the Student and Youth sectors, Development NGOs, the Business Community and Governments. Over and above discussing issues specifically related to the theme, the conference in Rome will provide a forum for analysis of the findings and resolutions of the Earth Summit. This will be the channel for the results of UNCED to be turned into action in many sectors, especially among Youth and Students.

Source : Bjurström, Lennart and Skreta, Marek, *Network*, July, 1991.

2

HUMAN DEVELOPMENT

Measuring Human Development

There is a need for a means of measuring human development as well as economic progress. According to UNICEF there is a need for an agreed method of measuring the level of child well-being and its rate of change.

The under five mortality rate (U5MR) is used in Table 2.1 as the principle indicator of such progress.

U5MR has several advantages. First, it measures an end result of the development process rather than an 'input' such as school enrolment level, per capita calorie availability, or the number of doctors per thousand population — all of which are means to an end.

Second, the U5MR is known to be the result of a wide variety of inputs: the nutritional health and the health knowledge of mothers; the level of immunization and ORT use: the availability of maternal and child health services (including pre-natal care); income and food availability in the family; the availability of clean water and safe sanitation; and the overall safety of the child's environment.

Third, U5MR is less susceptible than, say, per capita GNP to the fallacy of the average. This is because the natural scale does not allow the children of the rich to be one thousand times as likely to survive, even if the man-made scale does permit them to have one thousand times as much income. In other words, it is much more difficult for a wealthy minority to affect a nation's U5MR, and it therefore presents a more accurate, if far from perfect, picture of the health status of the majority of children (and of society as a whole).

For these reasons, the U5MR is chosen by UNICEF as its single most important indicator of the state of a nation's children. That is why the statistical annex lists the nations of the world not in ascending order of their per capita GNP but in descending order of their under five mortality rates.

Measuring Rate of Progress

The speed of progress in reducing the U5MR can be measured by calculating its average annual reduction rate (AARR). Unlike the comparison of absolute changes, the AARR reflects the fact that the limits to U5MR are approached only with increasing difficulty. As lower levels of under mortality are reached, for example, the same absolute reduction obviously represents a great percentage of reduction. The AARR therefore, shows a higher rate of progress for, say,a ten point reduction if that reduction happens at a lower level of under five mortality. (A fall in U5MR of 10 points from 100 to 90 represents a reduction of 10 per cent, whereas the same 10-point fall from 20 to 10 represents a reduction of 50 per cent).

When used in conjunction with GNP growth rates, the U5MR and its reduction rate can therefore give picture of the progress being made by any county or region, and over any period of time, towards the satisfaction of some of the most essential of human needs.

As Table 2.1 shows, here is no fixed relationship between the annual reduction rate of the U5MR and the annual rate of growth in per capital GNP. Such comparisons help to throw the emphasis on to the policies, priorities, and other factors which determine the ratio between economic and social progress.

Finally, the Table 2.1 gives the total fertility rate for each country and its average annual rate of reduction. It will be seen that many of the nations which have achieved significant reductions in U5MR have also achieved significant reduction in fertility.

Source : *The State of the World's Children 1992,* UNICEF, New York, 1992.

TABLE 2.1 Rate of Progress : Country Profile

	Under 5 mortality rate						GNP per capita average annual growth rate (%)		Total fertility rate				
				average annual rate of reduction (%)								average annual rate of reduction(%)	
	1960	1980	1990	1960-80	1980-90	required** 1990-2000	1965-80	1980-89	1960	1980	1990	1960-80	1980-90
1	2	3	4	5	6	7	8	9	10	11	12	13	14
Very high U5MR countries (over 140) Median	**302**	**238**	**189**	**1.3**	**1.7**	**9.9**	**0.8**	**—1.1**	**6.7**	**6.6**	**6.6**	**—0.1**	**0.0**
1 Mozambique	331	268	297	1.1	—1.0	14.5	—	—6.0	6.3	6.5	6.3	—0.2	0.3
2 Afghanistan	381	320	292	0.9	0.9	14.3	0.6	—	6.9	7.1	6.9	—0.1	0.3
3 Angola	344	261	292	1.4	—1.1	14.3	—	—	6.4	6.4	6.4	0.0	0.0
4 Mali	369	325	284	0.6	1.3	14.0	2.1	1.0	7.1	7.1	7.1	0.0	0.0
5 Sierra Leone	385	300	257	1.2	1.5	13.0	0.7	—3.2	6.2	6.5	6.5	—0.2	0.0
6 Malawi	366	299	253	1.0	1.7	12.8	3.2	—0.1	6.9	7.6	7.6	—0.5	0.0
7 Guinea-Bissau	336	290	246	0.7	1.6	12.6		1.5	5.1	5.7	5.8	—0.6	—0.2
8 Guinea	336	275	237	1.0	1.5	12.2	1.3	—	7.0	7.0	7.0	0.0	0.0
9 Burkina Faso	363	266	228	1.6	1.5	11.8	1.7	2.3	6.7	6.5	6.5	0.2	0.0
10 Niger	321	259	221	1.1	1.6	11.5	—2.5	—5.0	7.1	7.1	7.1	0.0	0.0
11 Ethiopia	294	260	220	0.6	1.7	11.5	0.4	—1.1	6.7	6.8	6.8	—0.1	0.0
12 Chad	325	254	216	1.2	1.6	11.3	—1.9	3.9	6.0	5.9	5.8	0.1	0.2
13 Somalia	294	247	215	0.9	1.4	11.2	—0.1	—1.3	6.6	6.6	6.6	0.0	0.0
14 Mauritania	321	249	214	1.3	1.5	11.2	—0.1	—2.2	6.5	6.5	6.5	0.0	0.0
15 Liberia	310	245	205	1.2	1.8	10.7	0.5	5.2	6.6	6.8	6.8	—0.1	0.0

**The average annual reduction rate required to achieve an under five mortality rate in all countries of 70 per 1000 live births or of two-thirds the 1990, rate, whichever is less.

Contd.

TABLE 2.1 *Contd.*

	1	2	3	4	5	6	7	8	9	10	11	12	13	14
16	Rwanda	248	231	198	0.4	1.5	10.4	1.6	—1.9	7.5	8.5	8.1	—0.6	0.5
17	Cambodia	218	330	193	—2.1	5.4	10.1	—	—	6.3	4.6	4.6	1.6	0.0
18	Burundi	260	225	192	0.7	1.6	10.1	2.4	1.6	6.8	6.8	6.8	0.0	0.0
19	Bhutan	298	222	189	1.5	1.6	9.9	—	7.8	6.0	5.6	5.5	0.3	0.2
20	Nepal	298	222	189	1.5	1.6	9.9	0.0	2.1	5.8	6.4	5.7	—0.5	1.2
21	Yemen	378	235	187	2.4	2.3	9.8	—	—	7.5	7.7	7.7	—0.1	0.0
22	Senegal	299	232	185	1.3	2.3	9.7	—0.5	0.0	7.0	6.9	6.3	0.1	0.9
23	Bangladesh	262	212	180	1.1	1.6	9.4	—0.3	0.7	6.7	6.4	5.3	0.2	1.9
24	Madagascar	364	216	176	2.6	2.0	9.2	—0.4	—2.6	6.6	6.6	6.6	0.0	0.0
25	Sudan	292	210	172	1.6	2.0	9.0	0.8	—1.8	6.7	6.6	6.4	0.1	0.3
26	Tanzania	249	202	170	1.0	1.7	8.9	0.8	—1.6	6.8	7.1	7.1	—0.2	0.0
27	Central African Rep.	308	213	169	1.8	2.3	8.8	0.8	—1.5	5.6	6.0	6.2	—0.3	—0.3
28	Namibia	263	202	167	1.3	1.9	8.7	—	—	6.0	6.1	5.9	—0.1	0.3
29	Nigeria	316	198	167	2.3	1.7	8.7	4.2	—3.6	6.8	6.9	6.8	—0.1	0.1
30	Gabon	287	194	164	2.0	1.7	8.5	5.6	—2.6	4.1	4.4	5.2	—0.4	—1.7
31	Uganda	223	186	164	0.9	8.5	8.3	—2.2	—1.0	6.9	7.2	7.3	—0.2	—0.1
32	Bolivia	282	207	160	1.5	2.6	8.3	1.7	—3.5	6.7	6.3	5.9	0.3	0.7
33	Pakistan	276	193	158	1.8	2.0	8.1	1.8	2.9	6.9	7.0	6.2	—0.1	1.2
34	Laos	233	190	152	1.0	2.2	7.8	—	0.0	6.2	6.7	6.7	—0.4	0.0
35	Cameroon	275	175	148	2.3	1.7	7.5	2.4	0.7	5.8	6.7	6.9	—0.7	—0.3
36	Benin	310	176	147	2.8	1.8	7.4	—0.3	—1.8	6.9	7.1	7.1	—0.1	0.0
37	Togo	305	184	147	2.5	2.2	7.4	1.7	—2.4	6.6	6.6	6.6	0.0	0.0
38	India	282	181	142	2.2	2.4	7.1	1.5	3.2	5.9	4.8	4.2	1.0	1.3

Contd.

TABLE 2.1 *Contd.*

	1	2	3	4	5	6	7	8	9	10	11	12	13	14
	High U5MR countries (71-140) Median	**229**	**133**	**90**	**2.5**	**2.9**	**4.1**	**2.8**	**—0.7**	**6.9**	**6.0**	**5.2**	**0.6**	**1.3**
39	Ghana	224	166	140	1.5	1.7	6.9	—0.8	—0.8	6.9	6.5	6.3	0.3	0.3
40	Côte d'Ivoire	264	167	136	2.3	2.1	6.6	2.8	—3.0	7.2	7.4	7.4	—0.1	0.0
41	Haiti	270	163	130	2.5	2.3	6.2	0.9	—0.7	6.3	5.3	4.9	0.9	0.8
42	Zaire	269	163	130	2.5	2.3	6.2	—1.3	—1.6	6.0	6.1	6.1	—0.1	0.0
43	Lesotho	208	161	129	1.3	2.2	6.1	6.8	—0.5	5.8	5.8	5.8	0.0	0.0
44	Zambia	228	146	122	2.2	1.8	5.6	—1.2	—3.8	6.6	7.2	7.2	—0.4	0.0
45	Peru	233	144	116	2.4	2.2	5.1	0.8	—1.6	6.9	5.0	3.8	1.6	2.7
46	Libyan Arab Jamahiriya	269	150	112	2.9	2.9	4.7	0.0	—9.9	7.1	7.3	6.8	—0.1	0.7
47	Morocco	265	153	112	2.7	3.1	4.7	2.7	1.3	7.2	5.7	4.5	1.2	2.4
48	Congo	241	132	110	3.0	1.8	4.5	2.7	0.1	5.9	6.3	6.3	—0.3	0.0
49	Kenya	208	133	108	2.2	2.1	4.3	3.1	0.4	8.0	8.0	6.9	0.0	1.5
50	Algeria	270	147	98	3.0	4.1	4.1	4.2	0.0	7.3	6.8	5.1	0.4	2.9
51	Indonesia	225	138	97	2.4	3.5	4.1	5.2	3.6	5.5	4.4	3.3	1.1	2.9
52	Guatemala	230	130	94	2.9	3.2	4.1	3.0	—2.6	6.9	6.3	5.6	0.5	1.2
53	Saudi Arabia	292	131	91	4.0	3.6	4.1	4.0	—5.9	7.2	7.3	7.1	—0.1	0.3
54	South Africa	192	120	88	2.4	3.1	4.1	3.2	—0.8	6.5	4.9	4.3	1.4	1.3
55	Myanmar	230	118	88	3.3	2.9	4.1	1.6	—	6.0	4.8	3.9	1.1	2.1
56	El Salvador	207	122	87	2.6	3.4	4.1	1.5	—1.1	6.8	5.5	4.7	1.1	1.6
57	Zimbabwe	181	116	87	2.2	2.9	4.1	1.7	—0.8	7.5	6.4	5.6	0.8	1.3
58	Iraq	222	110	86	3.5	2.5	4.1	—	—	7.2	6.8	6.1	0.3	1.1

Contd.

TABLE 2.1 *Contd.*

	1	2	3	4	5	6	7	8	9	10	11	12	13	14
59	Egypt	301	172	85	2.8	7.0	4.1	2.8	2.8	7.0	5.2	4.3	1.5	1.9
60	Botswana	173	110	85	2.3	2.6	4.1	9.9	6.7	6.8	7.1	6.7	—0.2	0.6
61	Turkey	258	139	85	3.1	4.9	4.1	3.6	3.0	6.3	4.3	3.5	1.9	2.1
62	Mongolia	185	112	84	2.5	2.9	4.1.	—	—	6.0	5.4	4.9	0.5	1.0
63	Honduras	232	141	84	2.5	5.2	4.1	1.1	—1.2	7.3	6.4	5.2	0.7	2.1
64	Ecuador	184	107	83	2.7	2.5	4.1	5.4	—0.5	6.9	5.1	4.1	1.5	2.2
65	Brazil	159	103	83	2.2	2.2	4.1	6.3	0.9	6.2	4.0	3.3	2.2	1.9
66	Papua New Guinea	248	112	80	4.0	3.4	4.1	—	—0.7	6.3	5.7	5.0	0.5	1.3
67	Nicaragua	209	133	78	2.3	5.3	4.1	—0.7	—4.7	7.3	6.1	5.3	0.9	1.4
68	Dominican Rep.	199	103	78	3.3	2.8	4.1	3.8	—0.1	7.4	4.5	3.5	2.5	2.5
	Middle U5MR countries (21-70) Median	**134**	**53**	**35**	**4.5**	**3.7**	**4.1**	3.7	—0.2	6.3	3.8	**3.0**	**2.1**	**1.8**
69	Philippines	134	87	69	2.2	2.3	4.1	3.2	—1.8	6.9	4.9	4.1	1.7	1.8
70	Vietnam	232	103	65	4.1	4.6	4.1	—	—	6.1	5.2	3.9	0.8	2.9
71	Tunisia	254	103	62	4.5	5.1	4.1	4.7	0.6	7.1	5.3	3.7	1.5	3.6
72	Paraguay	134	70	60	3.2	1.5	4.1	4.1	—1.5	6.8	4.9	4.5	1.6	0.9
73	Syria	217	88	59	4.5	4.0	4.1	5.1	—2.1	7.3	7.3	6.5	0.0	1.2

Contd.

TABLE 2.1 *Contd.*

	1	2	3	4	5	6	7	8	9	10	11	12	13	14
74	Iran, Islamic Rep. of	254	114	59	4.0	6.6	4.1	2.9	—	7.2	5.8	5.0	1.1	1.5
75	Lebanon	91	62	56	1.9	1.0	4.1	—	—	6.3	4.0	3.6	2.3	1.1
76	Jordan	217	81	52	4.9	4.4	4.1	5.8	–3.0	7.7	7.1	5.8	0.4	2.0
77	Colombia	157	65	50	4.4	2.6	4.1	3.7	0.9	6.8	3.8	3.0	2.9	2.4
78	Mexico	140	68	49	3.6	3.3	4.1	3.6	–1.5	6.8	4.5	3.3	2.1	3.1
79	Oman	378	110	49	6.2	8.1	4.1	9.0	5.3	7.2	7.2	7.1	0.0	0.1
80	Mexico	114	50	43	4.1	1.5	4.1	2.3	–2.3	6.5	4.3	3.6	2.1	1.8
81	China	203	56	42	6.4	2.9	4.1	4.1	8.2	5.7	2.6	2.4	3.9	0.8
82	Albania	151	57	37	4.9	4.3	4.1	—	—	5.9	3.8	2.9	2.2	2.7
83	Argentina	75	47	35	2.3	2.9	4.1	1.7	–1.6	3.1	3.3	2.9	–0.3	1.3
84	Korea, Dem.	120	44	35	5.0	2.3	4.1	—	—	5.7	3.1	2.5	3.0	2.2
85	Sri Lanka	114	53	35	3.8	4.1	4.1	2.8	2.4	5.3	3.5	2.6	2.1	3.0
86	Thailand	149	60	34	4.5	5.7	4.1	4.4	4.5	6.4	3.9	2.4	2.5	4.9
87	Romania	82	36	34	4.1	0.6	4.1	—	—	2.3	2.4	2.1	–0.2	1.3
88	USSR	53	37	31	1.8	1.8	4.1	—	—	2.7	2.3	2.3	0.8	0.0
89	Panama	105	43	31	4.5	3.3	4.1	2.8	–2.1	5.9	3.8	3.0	2.2	2.4
90	United Arab Emirates	105	43	30	8.6	3.6	4.1	—	–8.4	6.9	5.4	4.6	2.2	2.4
91	Korea, Rep.	120	44	30	5.0	3.8	4.1	7.3	8.8	5.7	2.6	1.7	3.9	4.2
92	Malaysia	105	42	29	4.6	3.7	4.1	4.7	1.9	6.8	4.2	3.8	2.4	1.0
93	Mauritius	104	42	28	4.5	4.1	4.1	3.7	5.3	5.9	2.8	1.9	3.7	3.9
94	Chile	143	43	27	6.0	4.7	4.1	0.0	1.0	5.3	2.9	2.7	3.0	0.7
95	Uruguay	57	43	25	1.4	5.4	4.1	2.5	–0.8	2.9	2.7	2.4	0.4	1.2
96	Yugoslavia	113	37	23	5.6	4.8	4.1	5.2	–0.7	2.8	2.1	1.9	1.4	1.0
97	Costa Rica	121	31	22	6.8	3.4	4.1	3.3	0.4	7.0	3.7	3.1	3.2	1.8

Contd.

TABLE 2.1 *Contd.*

	1	2	3	4	5	6	7	8	9	10	11	12	13	14
	Low U5MR countries (20 and under) Median	**39**	**16**	**10**	**4.7**	**4.4**	**4.1**	**3.3**	**1.9**	**2.9**	**2.0**	**1.8**	**2.1**	**0.6**
98	Jamaica	89	28	20	5.8	3.4	4.1	—0.1	—1.7	5.4	3.8	2.5	1.8	4.2
99	Kuwait	128	34	19	6.6	5.8	4.1	0.6	—2.1	7.3	5.4	3.7	1.5	3.8
100	Poland	70	25	18	5.1	3.3	4.1	—	1.8	3.0	2.3	2.2	1.3	0.4
101	Bulgaria	69	24	18	5.3	2.9	4.1	—	—	2.2	2.1	1.9	0.2	1.0
102	Trinidad and Tobago	67	26	17	4.7	4.2	4.1	3.1	—7.3	5.2	3.2	2.8	2.4	1.3
103	Hungary	57	26	16	3.9	4.9	4.1	5.1	1.4	2.0	2.0	1.8	0.0	1.1
104	Portugal	112	31	16	6.4	6.6	4.1	4.6	2.1	3.1	2.2	1.7	1.7	2.6
105	Cuba	87	25	14	6.2	5.8	4.1	—	—	4.2	2.0	1.9	3.7	0.5
106	Czechoslovakia	33	20	13	2.5	4.3	4.1	—	—	2.5	2.2	2.0	0.6	1.0
107	New Zealand	26	16	12	2.4	2.9	4.1	1.7	0.9	3.9	2.1	2.0	3.1	0.5
108	Israel	39	19	11	3.6	5.5	4.1	3.7	1.4	3.9	3.3	2.9	0.8	1.3
109	Greece	64	23	11	5.1	7.4	4.1	4.8	0.6	2.2	2.1	1.7	0.2	2.1
110	USA	29	15	11	3.3	3.1	4.1	1.8	2.2	3.5	1.9	1.8	3.1	0.5
111	Italy	50	18	10	5.1	5.9	4.1	3.2	2.1	2.5	1.7	1.4	1.9	1.9
112	Norway	22	10	10	3.9	0.0	4.1	3.6	3.5	2.9	1.8	1.7	2.4	0.6
113	Australia	24	13	10	3.1	2.6	4.1	2.2	1.8	3.3	2.0	1.8	2.5	1.1
114	Spain	57	16	10	6.4	4.7	4.1	4.1	2.4	2.8	2.2	1.6	1.2	3.2
115	Belgium	35	14	9	4.6	4.4	4.1	3.6	1.7	2.6	1.7	1.6	2.1	0.6
116	Austria	43	17	9	4.6	6.4	4.1	4.0	1.9	2.7	1.6	1.5	2.6	0.6
117	United Kingdom	27	15	9	2.9	5.1	4.1	2.0	2.9	2.7	1.8	1.8	2.0	0.0

Contd.

TABLE 2.1 *Contd.*

	1	2	3	4	5	6	7	8	9	10	11	12	13	14
118	Singapore	49	16	9	5.6	5.8	4.1	8.3	5.7	5.5	1.8	1.8	5.6	0.0
119	France	34	12	9	5.2	2.9	4.1	3.7	1.6	2.8	1.9	1.8	1.9	0.5
120	Switzerland	26	12	9	3.9	2.9	4.1	1.5	1.8	2.4	1.5	1.5	2.4	0.0
121	Denmark	25	10	9	4.6	1.1	4.1	2.2	2.2	2.6	1.6	1.5	2.4	0.6
122	Ireland	36	14	9	4.7	4.4	4.1	2.8	0.8	3.8	3.2	2.4	0.9	2.9
123	Germany	40	15	9	4.9	5.1	4.1	3.0	2.4	2.4	1.5	1.5	2.4	0.0
124	Canada	33	13	9	4.7	3.7	4.1	3.3	2.6	3.8	1.7	1.7	4.0	0.0
125	Netherlands	21	11	9	3.2	2.0	4.1	2.7	1.3	3.1	1.5	1.6	3.6	—0.6
126	Hong Kong	64	15	7	7.3	7.6	4.1	6.2	5.7	5.0	2.1	1.4	4.3	4.1
127	Finland	28	9	7	5.7	2.5	4.1	3.6	2.9	2.7	1.7	1.7	2.3	0.0
128	Sweden	20	9	7	4.0	2.5	4.1	2.0	2.0	2.3	1.7	1.9	1.5	—1.1
129	Japan	39	11	6	6.3	6.1	4.1	5.1	3.5	2.0	1.8	1.7	0.5	0.6

Notes:

Bhutan	GNP per capita growth rate 1980-88
Botswana	GNP per capita growth rate 1980-88
Egypt	GNP per capita growth rate 1980-88
Germany	GNP per capita growth rate former Fed. Rep. of Germany only
Jordan	GNP per capita growth rate 1970-80
Kuwait	GNP per capita growth rate 1965-86
Laos	GNP per capita growth rate 1980-88
Liberia	GNP per capita growth rate 1980-88
Libya	GNP per capita growth rate 1980-88
Mali	GNP per capita growth rate 1967-80
Nicaragua	GNP per capita growth rate 1980-88
Saudi Arabia	GNP per capita growth rate 1965-86
Sudan	GNP per capita growth rate 1980-88

Source: The State of the World's Children 1992, UNICEF, New York, 1992.

3

ADVANCEMENT OF WOMEN: SOME HIGHLIGHTS

Illiteracy

Between 1970 and 1985 the number of illiterate women rose by 54 million — to almost half a billion.

Marriage

Women now spend less of their lives married and fewer years bearing and rearing children. Couples are marrying later and separating or divorcing more. This changing structure of families is profoundly affecting women. Women now head more than a fifth of all households in Africa, the developed regions, and Latin America and the Caribbean. Most often, households headed by women are poorer than those headed by men.

Child-bearing

The world over, women are having fewer children than 20 years ago. In developed regions, the average is 1.8 births per woman. In developing regions, where three-quarters of the world's women live, child-bearing rates dropped from a range of 5-7 births per woman in 1970 to 3-6 in 1990. But maternal mortality rates in Africa and southern Asia are still more than 30 times those in developed countries.

Work and pay

Women everywhere work as much as men or more, as much as 13 hours more each week in Asia and Africa. Even when women do the same work as men, they typically receive less pay — 30 to 40 per cent less throughout the world.

Women's living conditions — and their contributions to the family, the economy and the household — have generally been statistically invisible. Many statistics have been defined, in terms that portray men's conditions and contributions — not women's — or that simply ignore gender. What women do is, therefore "often unrecorded, undervalued or not valued at all".

Despite these shortcomings, women everywhere contribute significantly to economic production. As officially measured, 828 million or 41 per cent of the world's women aged 15 and above are economically active. Another 10 to 20 per cent are economically productive but not counted as part of the labour force because of inadequate measurement.

Source : *The World's Women 1970-1990*, United Nations, 1991.

Women Work Harder

Women in many regions work longer hours than men. Women everywhere earn less than men and, in addition, it is men who are more likely to have regular full-time work and to receive greater seniority benefits.

In Cyprus, Japan and the Republic of Korea, women's wages are the lowest, about half those for men, among the countries for which data are available. Even in Canada, where women have made inroads into traditionally male-dominated high paying jobs, their earnings are still only 71 per cent of men's.

Most working women are engaged in agriculture in much of the developing world, particularly in Africa and Asia, but this, once again, is an area where their contribution remains invisible in official statistics and continues to be poorly estimated or ignored. According to some studies conducted in developing countries, women today "may have become even more important in food production" than a few years ago "as a result of men's increased migration" to cities and towns.

This gives rise to an increase in the number of women-headed households, a growing worldwide phenomenon. One in every five households in Africa, Latin America and the Caribbean is headed by a woman. Asia has the lowest proportion of such women-headed households, but that rate is comparatively high at 14 per cent.

Women who have chosen to remain in rural areas but whose husbands migrate to urban centres find themselves with even more family and economic responsibilities. Only a few receive remittances. Most do not, making them widows in all but name. In Lesotho, one survey showed, fewer than half of the women staying home received any money from their husbands working in cities. Research in India and Pakistan showed that migrant men actually sent remittances home, but to their fathers rather than to their wives. Here again, women turned out losers.

The global illiteracy rate is declining but the absolute numbers of illiterates continue to grow. In 1985, there were about 949 million illiterates, an increase of 58 million from 1970. Of this increase, 54 million or 93.1 per cent were women. Lower levels of functional literacy make it more difficult for many of the rural women to understand the need for family planning and the importance of primary health care for young children.

In many developing countries, child-bearing still exposes women to an array of health risks. Maternal mortality stemming from pregnancy is 80 to 600 times higher than in the developed regions.

Adolescent pregnancy — sometimes the cause of early marriage and sometimes the result of it — is very common in developing countries. Teenage mothers have a higher risk for both maternal and infant mortality, twice the threat on mothers aged 20 to 24.

"Such pregnancy can limit a young girl's chances for education and a paying job," "continuing the cycle of disadvantaged mothers passing on their vulnerability to their daughters, and their daughters to theirs."

Developed Regions

These and other major problems and difficulties facing women are no monopoly of developing countries.

Throughout the developed regions, the health of women is generally good and their fertility is low. "But in other fields," "indicators of the status of women show mixed results."

Women's participation in economic activity is high in eastern Europe and the erstwhile Soviet Union, northern Europe and North America. In Australia, Japan and New Zealand, as well as in southern and western Europe, however, it remains low. In political participation, women held no ministerial-level positions during 1987-1988 in nine countries: Belgium, Czechoslovakia, France, Japan, Luxembourg, Malta, Spain, the Soviet Union and Yugoslavia.

Statistics show that only 3.5 per cent of the World's cabinet ministers are women. Of the 159 member states of the United Nations, only six or 3.8 per cent were headed by women at the end of 1990: Dominica, Iceland, Ireland, Nicaragua, Norway and the Philippines.

Investing in the Future

The world community should take collective initiatives to advance women's interests and to broaden their opportunities. Investing in wider opportunities for women —in health, in education, in formal and informal work and in decision-making at all levels — is far more than an investment in women alone. Rather, it is an investment in their families and societies.

"It is a way to lift people out of poverty." "It is a way to slow population growth. It is a way to protect the environment. And it is a way to get onto a path of equitable, sustainable development."

The cost of these changes, especially when weighed against the benefit, would be small. Many of the policy changes usually cost nothing. "Many of the required investments are small in relation to a country's gross domestic product — and in relation to military spending."

Casualties from wars for which the arms race is often responsible are increasingly civilians, a "growing" proportion being women and children. "Although there are no wide-scale statistics on women's involvement in disarmament movements, they are affected by decisions regarding military policies and expenditures."

Source: *Development Forum*, July-August, 1991.

TABLE 3.1: Data on Women

	Item	Year	India	Country with best position	Number of countries for which data available	India's position in the world
1.	Adult Literacy Rate as % of Males	1990	**55**	—	Information of many advanced countries not available	
2.	% Pregnant Women Immunised against Tetanus	1989-90	**77**	Korea - 99 D.R.G. - 99	Information of many countries not available	
3.	% Contraceptive Prevalence	1980-90	**34**	U.K. 83	100	67

4

CHILD WELFARE AND DEVELOPMENT

4.1 Goals for the 2000

The following is the full list of goals, to be attained by the year 2000, which were adopted by the *World Summit for Children* on September 30, 1990.

Overall goals

— A one-third reduction in under-five death rates (or a reduction to below 70 per 1,000 live births whichever is less).
— A halving of maternal mortality rates.
— A halving of severe and moderate malnutrition among the world's under-fives.
— Safe water and sanitation for all families.
— Basic education for all children and completion of primary education by at least 80 per cent .
— A halving of the adult illiteracy rate and the achievement of equal educational opportunity for males and females.
— Protection for the many millions of children in especially difficult circumstances and the acceptance and observance, in all countries, of the recently adopted Convention on the Rights of the Child. In particular, the 1990s should see rapidly growing acceptance of the idea of special protection for children in the time of war.

Protection for girls and women

— Family planning education and services to be made available to all couples to empower them to prevent unwanted pregnancies and births which are 'too many and too close' and to women who are 'too young or too old'.
— All women to have access to pre-natal care, a trained attendant during childbirth and referral for high-risk pregnancies and obstetric emergencies.
— Universal recognition of the special health and nutritional needs of females during early childhood, adolescence, pregnancy and lactation.

Nutrition

— A reduction in the incidence of low birth weight (less than 2.5 kg) to less than 10 per cent .
— A one-third reduction in iron deficiency anaemia among women.
— Virtual elimination of vitamin A deficiency and iodine deficiency disorders.
— All families to know the importance of supporting women in the task of ex-

clusive breastfeeding for the first four to six months of a child's life and of meeting the special feeding needs of a young child through the vulnerable years.

- Growth monitoring and promotion to be institutionalized in all countries.
- Dissemination of knowledge to enable all families to ensure household food security.

Child health

- The eradication of polio.
- The elimination of neonatal tetanus (by 1995).
- A 90 per cent reduction in measles cases and a 95 per cent reduction in measles deaths, compared to pre-immunization levels.
- Achievement and maintenance of at least 90 per cent immunization coverage of one-year-old children and universal tetanus immunization for women in the child-bearing years.
- A halving of child deaths caused by diarrhoea and a 25 per cent reduction in the incidence of diarrhoeal diseases.
- A one-third reduction in child deaths caused by acute respiratory infections.
- The elimination of guinea worm disease.

Education

- In addition to the expansion of primary school education and its equivalents, today's essential knowledge and life skills could be put at the disposal of all families by mobilizing today's vastly increased communications capacity.

Source : *World Summit for Children, 1990,* UNICEF, New York.

TABLE 4.1: Mortality Rate

Item	Year	India	Country with best position	Number of countries for which data available	India's position in the world
Infant Mortality Rate under I	1990	94	Japan 05	129	92
Under 5 Mortality Rate	1990	142	Japan 6	129	93

5

ECONOMY: GLOBAL PERSPECTIVE

5.1 World Bank Report

Developing countries experienced a drop in their per capita gross domestic product (GDP) in 1990, and another year of decline appears to be in prospect.

Improvement has to wait till 1992, and even in that, sub-Sahara will do poorly.

The only region that has been and is expected to remain a good performer is Asia.

In sub-Saharan Africa, per capita GDP was down 1.1 per cent in 1980-89 and 1.7 per cent in 1990. In 1991, it is expected to be down 1 per cent and in 1992, by 0.3 per cent.

Asia has kept growing. Per capita GDP in Asia was up 5 per cent in 1980-89 and 4 per cent in 1990. It is expected to be up 3.5 per cent in 1991 and 3.9 per cent in 1992.

In Europe, West Asia and North Africa, per capita GDP was up 0.6 per cent in 1980-89, but dipped 2.5 per cent in 1990. It is expected to be down 5.1 per cent in 1991 and go up by 0.9 per cent in 1992.

In Latin America and the Caribbean, per capita GDP was down 0.4 per cent in 1980-89 and 2.5 per cent in 1990. It is expected to be up 0.3 per cent in 1991 and 1.2 per cent in 1992.

In all developing countries taken together, per capita GDP grew 1.6 per cent in 1980-89, but dipped 0.1 per cent in 1990. In 1991, it is expected to be down 0.2 per cent. However, in 1992, it should be up 2 per cent.

Poor Performance

The production losses in eastern Europe was in some cases due to 1990's poor performance.

Poor performance in Brazil, Iraq, Poland, Romania and Yugoslavia had a large, negative impact on the developing world's overall 1990 growth rate.

Per capita income declined in most of the sub-Saharan Africa, with weak demand for the region's exports and continuing hostilities in a number of countries are further depressing growth. The severe impact of the AIDS epidemic does not bode well for a number of sub-Saharan countries in the medium term.

Source : *World Bank News*, World Bank, New York, as reported in, *Times of India*, October 17, 1991.

5.2 Organisation for Economic Cooperation and Development (OECD) Forecast

Economic recovery in industrialised countries should get on track in the first half of 1992, making 3 per cent annual growth possible in 1993.

OECD's 1992-93 economic outlook for its 24-member nations slashed growth predictions for the second half of this year to 1.0 per cent from an estimated 2.4 per cent projected in July.

Next year's growth projections were also pared from July's estimates. Growth was set at 2.2 per cent in the first half of 1992 and 3.1 per cent in the second, down from earlier projections of 3.0 per cent and 3.2 per cent, respectively.

The sluggish economic recovery was traced to excessive expectations of the Persian Gulf war boosting the economy and continued low levels of corporate and consumer confidence.

The framework for economic recovery has been put in place by the marked fall in the interest rates around the globe, especially in recession-hit Britain and the United States. OECD economic growth should reach an annual rate of 3.3 per cent in 1993.

The report raised substantially the 1991 annual growth forecast for Japan from the July forecast and warned against signs of slow to more sustainable levels in 1992 before returning to a recovery stage.

Japan's real gross national product (GNP) growth should slow from 4.5 per cent in 1991 to 2.4 per cent in 1992, but will turn up in 1993 to 3.5 per cent, a level that is in line with Japan's growth potential.

With Japan's projected current account surplus remaining largely unchanged at $69.8 billion in 1991, $81.8 billion in 1992, and $80.4 billion in 1993. Japan will continue to be the only member of the group of seven industrial nations to maintain a surplus.

Japan's trade surplus could be a potential source of intensified trade frictions and heightened protectionism by trade partners.

But despite that risk, the surplus is not, by itself, indicative on conditions that require correction, especially when there is concern in many other parts of the world about adequacy of the flow of funds available for investment.

In Germany, meanwhile, the costs of unification should result in a continued current account deficit.

Inflation in Germany should peak in the second half of this year at 5.3 per cent, after which inflationary pressures should subside.

Inflation among the OECD member states as a whole should remain at a low level of 3.3 per cent in 1993, slowing from 4.2 per cent in 1991 and 3.7 per cent in 1992.

Unemployment is expected to remain a problem in Europe, where it could reach as high as 9.3 per cent in 1993. Unemployment for all OECD members should peak at 7.4 per cent in 1992.

There are no signs of recovery in central and eastern European output.

In the politically disintegrating Soviet Union, falling production and exports, as well as hoarding of convertible currencies, are making it more difficult to maintain debt service and purchase imported inputs.

The economic disintegration has accelerated since August's failed coup as flows of raw materials and final products between republics have been disrupted further.

The collapse of the Soviet Union as an export market has complicated the difficult situation already facing east European countries as they are trying to move toward a market economy.

Nonetheless, all have made advances, even if none is yet on a path of economic expansion. Poland, Hungary and more recently Czechoslovakia have set most prices free and made impressive progress in shifting exports to other markets.

Source : *Hindustan Times*, December 21, 1991.

5.3 **Morgan Guaranty Trust Co. (New York Bank) Report**

With the US economy mired in recession, experts predict a spreading slowdown in Japan, Germany and other industrialised nations in 1992.

The global outlook seems to be stagnation in the short term, with improved prospects by late 1992.

"Now that the Japanese and German expansions are fading, economic growth will be sluggish across all industrial countries well into next year."

"Inflation will fall nearly everywhere in 1992". "Interest rates will drop still more, and enable global economic growth revival later in the year."

Willard Workman, vice-president of the US Chamber of Commerce, predicted global economic growth will be a scant one per cent in 1992, the lowest level since the worldwide recession of 1982.

Much depends on the US economy, where the Federal Reserve (the Central Bank) has tried vainly to bolster consumer confidence with a series of interest rate cuts.

In 1991, the world started out on two main roads in search of prosperity — private enterprise and regional free trade associations.

There was one major problem: while regional groups made progress, world trade talks among the 108 members of the General Agreement on Tariffs and Trade in Brussels have remained stymied since December 1990.

The dispute between the European Community and the United States over subsidised EC farm exports remained the main sticking point into the final days of 1991.

Europe's biggest economies slowed going into 1992, when the European Community plans to complete a common market of 325 million people.

Europe's main economic engines — Germany, France, Britain and Italy — are sputtering. Unemployment is rising relentlessly,

One hopeful sigh is that the 12-nation European Community and the 7-nation European Free Trade Association (EFTA) are forming a 19-nation free trade zone from the Arctic to the Mediterranean by January 1, 1993. The accord will create the world's biggest market, comprising 380 million consumers accounting for 46 per cent of global trade.

The EC is also looking to expand the trading zone to Hungary, Czechoslovakia and Poland, the three strongest economies of formerly communist Eastern Europe. These three might conceivably join the EC by the year 2000.

In January 1992 the EC plans to begin trade discussions with Bulgaria and Romania.

But Eastern Europe is currently languishing, and the EC has pumped more than 20 billion US dollars to the region, in hopes of starving off a flood of refugees from economic chaos.

The disintegrating Soviet Union, faced a winter of shortages and even hunger, and was another source of potential economic refugees into Western

Europe. In 1991, according to Soviet President Mikhail Gorbachev, national income dropped 15 per cent. The country was headed for catastrophe, if the seceding Republics did not join in common economic policies. Prospects of this seemed hazy under the new Commonwealth of Independent States led by Russian President Boris Yeltsin.

The G-7 group of the world's seven top industrial nations offered to help by deferring Soviet debt payments and offering US $1 billion in aid. One condition was that the individual Republics shoulder their proportionate share of Soviet debts but only some Republics assented.

In the Far East the Japanese economy slowed after years of phenomenal expansion. The International Monetary Fund (IMF) estimated Japan's growth in 1992 at a very modest 2.5 to 3.4 per cent.

South Korea, Taiwan, Singapore, Hong Kong and Malaysia have brighter growth prospects for 1992, but Australia is currently enduring its worst recession since the great depression of the 1930s.

Source : *Hindustan Times*, December 23, 1991.

5.4 **Economic Environment**

International Action on debt, aid, and trade should create an environment in which economic reform in the developing world can succeed in allowing its people to earn a decent living.

Although average incomes had risen substantially in Asia (including China and India), the 1980s were nonetheless a disastrous decade for the majority of countries in the developing world. Average incomes fell by approximately 10 per cent in Latin America (and by much more among the poorest) and by 25 per cent in Africa (where incomes were already the lowest in the world).

In 1990, this uneven pattern continued. In the 18 countries of East Asia, per capita incomes rose by over 4 per cent in 1990; in the eight countries of South Asia (including Bangladesh, India and Pakistan) per capita incomes rose by just over 2 per cent . But in the two most debt-ridden continents, the decline of the 1980s has continued; per capita incomes fell again by over 2 per cent in Africa and by over 2.5 per cent in Latin America (and even more steeply in countries such as Argentina, Brazil, and Peru, which have extremely high levels of debt).

It is particularly important to address those difficulties at the present time. Shaken into a new realism by the harsh economic ride of the 1980s, and aware of the experience of Central and Eastern Europe, many if not most developing nations have begun to adopt the kind of economic reforms that could bring increasing prosperity to their peoples in the years ahead. This change in attitude and economic thinking has passed almost unnoticed in a world preoccupied by more dazzling change (although some commentators have noted that these changes represent a *quiet revolution* with a *potential for advancing human welfare that can scarcely be exaggerated.*) But it is an opportunity not to be missed.

At the moment, it is unlikely that this potential will be fulfilled because too many of the factors which brought disaster in the 1980s are still present in the 1990s. Even if economic policy and management were to improve, the problems of external debt, of declining terms of trade, of protectionism in the rich world's markets, and of excessive military spending, still remain. In other words, the developing world will find it difficult to find a place in a new world order because it is still chained to the mistakes of the old.

World prices for raw materials, on which so many developing countries are dependent, remain at their lowest levels since the depression of the 1930s. In the last decade alone, the price that Africa is paid for its primary products has fallen by approximately 30 per cent in relation to the price it has to pay for its imports.

The degree of dependence on such commodities, and the steady deterioration in their real value, is one of development's most intransigent problems. And it is going to get worse. As new technologies, synthetics, and management systems continue to increase manufacturing efficiency, fewer raw materials will be needed. And in the years ahead, the increasing use of biotechnology could further undermine the trading position of agricultural raw materials.

It seems that there is little the developing world can do to prevent this steady erosion of its prices and markets. It can attempt to coordinate production, at least regionally, to avoid depressing prices further by overproduction. It can also attempt to strengthen its own research and development capacity for processing more of its own raw materials into semi-manufactured or manufactured goods. But at the same time, it must attempt to diversify its exports to reduce its dependence on a crumbling economic base.

The problem with diversification of exports is that the industrialized world, which so enthusiastically urges free market policies on the developing world, protects its own producers by surrounding itself with tariffs, quotas, and subsidies which effectively close the rich world's markets to a whole range of possible exports from the developing world (including a wide range of agricultural and tropical produce, steel, textiles, clothing, leather goods and footwear).

Estimates of the cost of such protectionism to the developing world vary widely, but the total is not less than $55 billion a year — more than all the aid received. A dismantling of those tariff and non-tariff barriers would, according to IMF managing director, Michael Camdessus, raise the growth rate of developing countries by nearly 3 percentage points, so yielding benefits equal to twice the aid they receive.

Dismantling such trade barriers, through a successful completion of the present Uruguay round of talks under the General Agreement on Tariffs and Trade, would therefore provide much needed oxygen to the process of economic reform in the developing world.

Source : *The State of the World's Children 1992*, UNICEF, New York, 1992

5.5 **Economic Survey**

This year, for the first time since the Second World War, total production and income in the world have fallen.

In every other year, the economic downturns in some countries were offset by economic growth in others. However, this year, economic decline is so widespread — and so deep in eastern Europe and the former Soviet Union, now known as the Commonwealth of Independent States — that it fully negates the positive impact of the more dynamic economies such as China, Japan, and several other Asian and Latin American countries.

Some of the world's economies have been severely disrupted by war and its aftermath or civil strife, as in Western Asia, Yugoslavia and a number of African countries. In addition, the economic dislocations or countries in transition from centrally planned to market economies are causing large declines in output.

The unemployment rate is of almost seven per cent in the United States and that of Canada, which now exceeds 10 per cent. In the other major economy in outright recession, the United Kingdom and Northern Ireland, the unemployment rate rose above eight per cent this summer.

Source : 1991 World Economic Survey update as reported in *UN Newsletter*, January 18, 1992.

6

DEVELOPMENT AND GROWTH IN ASIA AND THE PACIFIC

6.1 **Overall Economic Expansion**

Most of Asia's rapidly developing economies lost their dynamism in the year just passed, but regional economic growth remained the strongest in the world, averaging 6.4 per cent.

With the exceptions of Hong Kong and Taiwan, Asia's dynamic economics did not perform well in 1991, compared to 1990.

The overall economic expansion rate in the region's developing nations in 1991 was slightly better than that of the previous year (6.1%).

As a sharp contrast to the region, the world economy grew less that one per cent in 1991, while the combined average of all the developing countries was 2.4 per cent.

Despite several obstacles from global economic difficulties, developing Asia-Pacific economies showed resilience and had good prospects "to remain relatively strong".

In Asia, China, Nepal and Pakistan did creditably well in 1991, as did Papua New Guinea, Samoa, Tonga and Vanuatu in the Pacific.

Economic growth in India and Sri Lanka fell slightly from five and 6.2 per cent in 1990 to 4.5 and five per cent respectively last year.

The rapidly industrialising Republic of Korea and Singapore saw their growth rates drop—although still remaining at a relative high—to 8.5 and 7.5 per cent in 1991, from mine and 8.3 per cent in the year before.

Economic growth in the other pair of the "four tigers" (Hong Kong and Taiwan) moved ahead from 2.8 and 5.1 per cent in 1990 to 4.5 and 7.1 per cent respectively last year.

Of the six members of the Association of South East Asian Nations (ASEAN), the Philippines showed the worst growth record at 0.8 per cent, the lowest among the region's developing countries.

6.2 **Comparative Data on Economic Growth,** 1991-92

Sl. No.	Country	Growth of GDP in % in 1991	Projected figure of GDP in % in 1992	Annual rate of inflation in % in 1991	Projected rate of inflation in % in 1992
1.	China	7.5	4.6	9.0	7.0
2.	**India**	**3.0**	**4.9**	**12.0**	**11.0**
3.	Indonesia	5.6	6.6	6.5	7.0
4.	Malaysia	8.1	8.9	3.7	4.5
5.	Pakistan	5.6	5.0	14.0	11.5
6.	Thailand	8.6	9.3	6.0	5.3

Source for 6.1 and 6.2: *Report, Economic and Social Commission for Asia and the Pacific,* 1991.

6.3 Growth of GDP Per Capita, 1960-90

(*in percentage*)

	1960-70	1970-80	1980-90
Indonesia	1.0	4.8	3.1
Korea	6.0	7.7	8.4
Malaysia	3.5	5.4	2.2
Thailand	5.2	4.3	5.1
China	3.6	3.3	8.3
India	**1.3**	**1.0**	**3.3**
Bangladesh	1.0	0.9	0.8
Lao, People's Dem. Rep.	—	—	0.4
Myanmar	0.1	2.4	—1.0
Nepal	0.7	0.1	2.1
Papua New Guinea	4.2	—0.2	—0.3
Philippines	1.9	3.5	—1.7
Sri Lanka	2.0	3.1	2.5
Pacific Islands	1.8	2.4	—0.5
Asia	2.4	3.2	5.1
Other developing countries	2.7	3.0	—0.4

Source : *World Bank. Finance and Development*, September 1991.

6.4 Projected GDP and Per Capita Income for 1992

Sl. No.	Name of the country	Projected GDP for 1992 in billion $	Projected Per Capita income for 1992 in $
1.	China	360	305
2.	**India**	**232**	**270**
3.	Indonesia	114	605
4.	Malaysia	50	2755
5.	Pakistan	51	425
6.	Thailand	102	1763

6.5 International Trade and Balance of Payments, 1990-1992

Although the international trade and the balance of payments situation in the Asia and Pacific region during the 1990-91 period has been one of mixed impacts, it was far from being a story of gloom.

In general exports (in US dollar terms) within the region performed reasonably well, despite the Gulf War and the continuing global economic recession.

China's exports grew well in 1990, but lost some momentum in 1991. In the Newly Industrialized Economies (NIEs) exports dropped in 1990 but picked up again during 1991, with the exception of Singapore, which showed an apparent slowdown in 1991. In Indonesia, Malaysia, the Philippines and Thailand, there were marked decelerations in exports between 1989 and 1991.

South Asia, with the exception of India and Pakistan experienced substantial export growth in 1990. In India, there was a steady drop up to 1991, while Pakistan recorded strong export growth in 1991. Exports from the Pacific Islands economies decline further in 1990, but for 1991 there appears to have been an appreciable turnaround which is expected to continue into 1992.

Imports were a different matter. For the Republic of Korea and Taiwan province of China, imports dipped in 1990, whereas Singapore recorded a big rise in 1990 followed by a drop in 1991. By contrast, Hong Kong experienced a steady rise throughout the 1990-91 period.

Indonesia, Malaysia and Thailand recorded substantial import rises in 1990, followed by a slowdown in 1991. The Philippines, however, saw import values remain constant through 1990 and 1991. There was a noticeable drop in Pacific Islands imports in 1990, but the level picked up again the next year.

In South Asia, the overall import level grew slightly in 1990 due mainly to increases in India and Sri Lanka; in India the level showed an apparent drop in 1991. Bangladesh experienced a decline in imports in 1990, and then notably rose the following year, while Nepal's imports increased substantially in 1990 and eased back in 1991.

With regard to the 1990-91 current account deficits in the balance of payments of the developing countries, sharp increases were recorded. For 1991-92, with the exception of Japan, only a handful of ESCAP countries are expected to achieve substantial current account surpluses, including China, Taiwan province of China, Hong Kong and Singapore. In the Republic of Korea, however, the current account deficit was expected to increase in 1991, a trend that has been projected to continue in 1992. Overall, projections indicate that the magnitude of the combined current account surpluses of the NIEs will be reduced almost fourfold between 1989 to 1992.

Following several years of concerted efforts to solve the debt crisis, some improvement became evident in 1990-91. In general, the overall debt — GNP ratios in the ESCAP region have been declining since 1990 in the small low-income economies, in countries with recent debt-servicing difficulties and 15 heavily indebted countries. In the case of individual countries, however, the situation has been diverse. In Indonesia, Malaysia, the Philippines and Sri Lanka, the ratios have remained comparatively high. For others such as India, while the ratios still remained comparatively low, there have recently been noteworthy increases.

Debt servicing also appears to have stabilized in several countries. In the developing countries of the region as a whole, the debt service ratio dropped to 14 per cent in 1990, compared to a 1986 peak of 20 per cent. In 1991, however, the ratio is expected to rise to 16 per cent.

In part, Asia's debt servicing ratio is the lowest among the developing countries of the world, and is slightly less than half of the global average. But taken individually within Asia, the ratios vary widely. For the four NIEs it is slightly over 3 per cent for 1991, while Indonesia recorded 30 per cent and the Philippines, almost 28 per cent. Malaysia and Thailand, however, experienced moderate ratios of 8.5 and 15 per cent, respectively.

Source : Review of Economic Performance and Prospects in the ESCAP Region at the End of 1991, as reported in *UN Newsletter*, January 11, 1992

7

ECONOMIC AND SOCIAL DEVELOPMENT: COMPARATIVE COUNTRY PROFILE (OTHER THAN TRADE)

The tables given in this chapter cover a wide range of economic and social statistics on the nations of the world providing a comparative study of various facets of life. The data derived by United Nations Children Fund (UNICEF) from following international agencies, among others assume a special significance (i) United Nations Population Division, (ii) United Nations Statistical Office, (iii) World Bank, (iv) United Nations Educational Scientific and Cultural Organization (UNESCO), (v) World Health Organisation (WHO), (vi) Food and Agricultural Organisation of the United Nations (UNO), (vii) International Monetary Fund (IMF), (viii) Organisation for Economic Cooperation and Development (OECD), besides UNICEF's own divisions and offices.

Where possible only comprehensive or representative national data have been used. The data for infant mortality rates, life expectancy, crude birth and death rates, etc. are part of the regular work on estimates and projection undertaken by the United Nations Population Division. These and other internationally produced estimates are revised periodically, which explains why some of the data will differ from those found in earlier other publications. In the case of GNP per capita and ODA, the data are the result of a continuous process of revising and undating by the World Bank and OECD respectively. The tables include extensive revisions to the data on literacy, underweight, wasting, stunting, access to water and maternal mortality.

The value of 70 under five deaths per 1000 live births used to delineate the two higher U5MR groups of countries from the two lower groups reflects the World Summit for Children mortality goal target. The U5MR goal aims at a reduction of the under five mortality rate in all countries during the 1990s by one-third or to 70 per 1000 live births, whichever is less. Hence, if all countries achieve the under five mortality goal, by the end of the 1990s all countries should belong to the two lowest U5MR groups.

Following signs have been generally used.

NA Data not available
* UNICEF estimate
T Total(as opposed to a median)
x See footnote at the end of the tables
y UNICEF estimate; see footnote at the end of the tables.

TABLE 7.1: Basic Data

		Under 5 mortality rate		Infant mortality rate (under 1)		Total popul-tion (milli-ons)	Annual no. of births (thous-ands)	Annual no. of under 5 deaths (thous-ands	GNP per capita (US $)	Life expect-ancy at birth (years)	Total adult literacy rate	% of age group enrolled in primary school Total	% share of house-hold income 1980-1988	
		1960	1990	1960	1990	1990	1990	1990	1989	1990	1990	1986-1989	lowest 40%	highest 20%
	1	2	3	4	5	6	7	8	9	10	11	12	13	14
	Very high U5MR countries (over 140) Median	302	189	184	116	1536T	58458T	9774T	290	50	35	63	NA	NA
1	Mozambique	331	297	190	173	15.7	699	208	80	48	33	68	NA	NA
2	Afghanistan	381	292	215	167	16.6	888	260	280[x]	43	29	25	NA	NA
3	Angola	344	292	208	173	10.0	472	138	610	46	42	93	NA	NA
4	Mali	369	284	210	164	9.2	472	134	270	45	32	23	NA	NA
5	Sierra Leone	385	257	219	149	4.2	201	52	220	42	21	53	NA	NA
6	Malawi	366	253	207	144	8.8	494	125	180	48	NA	72	NA	NA
7	Guinea-Bissau	336	246	200	146	1.0	41	10	180	43	NA	53	NA	NA
8	Guinea	336	237	203	140	5.8	294	70	430	44	24	30	NA	NA
9	Burkina Faso	363	228	205	133	9.0	426	97	320	48	18	32	NA	NA
10	Niger	321	221	191	130	7.7	401	89	290	46	28	30	NA	NA
11	Ethiopia	294	220	175	130	49.2	2424	534	120	46	NA	36	NA	NA
12	Chad	325	216	195	127	5.7	249	54	190	47	30	51	NA	NA
13	Somalia	294	215	175	127	7.5	360	77	170	46	17[x]	15	NA	NA
14	Mauritania	321	214	191	122	2.0	94	20	500	47	34	52	NA	NA
15	Liberia	310	205	184	134	2.6	122	25	450[x]	54	40	34	NA	NA

Contd.

TABLE 7.1 *Contd.*

	1	2	3	4	5	6	7	8	9	10	11	12	13	14
16	Rwanda	248	198	146	117	7.2	368	73	320	50	50	67	NA	NA
17	Cambodia	218	193	146	123	8.2	322	62	NA	50	35	NA	NA	NA
18	Burundi	260	192	153	115	5.5	261	50	220	49	50	59	NA	NA
19	Bhutan	298	189	187	123	1.5	58	11	190^{x}	49	38	26	NA	NA
20	Nepal	298	189	187	123	19.1	725	137	180	52	26	86	13^{x}	59^{x}
21	Yemen	378	187	214	114	11.7	602	113	650	51	32^{y}	87	NA	NA
22	Senegal	299	185	172	84	7.3	328	61	650	48	38	59	NA	NA
23	Bangladesh	262	180	156	114	115.6	4796	866	180	52	35	70	24	37
24	Madagascar	364	176	220	115	12.0	547	96	230	55	80	97	NA	NA
25	Sudan	292	172	170	104	25.2	1111	191	420^{x}	51	27	49	NA	NA
26	Tanzania	249	170	147	102	27.3	1378	235	130	54	91^{y}	66	NA	NA
27	Central African Rep.	08	169	183	100	3.0	138	23	390	50	38	67	NA	NA
28	Namibia	263	167	155	102	1.8	76	13	1030	58	NA	NA	NA	NA
29	Nigeria	316	167	190	101	108.5	5183	865	250	52	51	66	NA	NA
30	Gabon	287	164	171	99	1.2	49	8	2960	53	61	NA	NA	NA
31	Uganda	223	164	133	99	18.8	985	161	250	52	48	77	NA	NA
32	Bolivia	282	160	167	102	7.3	309	50	620	55	78	91	12*	58*
33	Pakistan	276	158	163	104	122.6	5451	863	370	58	35	40	19	46
34	Laos	233	152	155	104	4.1	187	28	180	50	NA	110	NA	NA
35	Cameroon	275	148	163	90	11.8	566	83	1000	54	54	111	NA	NA
36	Benin	310	147	185	88	4.6	229	34	380	47	23	63	NA	NA
37	Togo	305	147	182	90	3.5	158	23	390	54	43	101	NA	NA
38	**India**	**282**	**142**	**165**	**94**	**853.1**	**26985**	**3835**	**340**	**59**	**48**	**99**	**20**	**41**

Contd.

TABLE 7.1 *Contd.*

	1	2	3	4	5	6	7	8	9	10	11	12	13	14
	High U5MR countries (71-140) Median	229	90	143	66	793T	25837T	2510T	885	62	68	97	12	55
39	Ghana	224	140	132	86	15.0	665	93	390	55	60	73	17	45
40	Cote d'Ivoire	264	136	165	92	12.0	603	82	790	53	54	70	13	53
41	Halti	270	130	182	92	6.5	233	30	360	56	53	83	6*	48*
42	Zaire	269	130	158	79	35.6	1626	211	260	53	72	76	NA	NA
43	Lesotho	208	129	149	95	1.8	72	9	470	57	NA	112	NA	NA
44	Zambia	228	122	135	76	8.5	433	53	390	54	73	97	11X	61X
45	Peru	233	116	142	82	21.6	647	75	1010	63	85	122	13	52
46	Libyan Arab Jamahiriya	269	112	160	75	4.5	199	22	5310	62	64	NA	NA	NA
47	Morocco	265	112	163	75	25.1	858	96	880	62	50	67	23	39
48	Congo	241	110	143	69	2.3	105	12	940	54	57	NA	NA	NA
49	Kenya	208	108	124	68	24.0	1132	122	360	60	69	93	9X	60X
50	Algeria	270	98	168	68	25.0	877	86	2230	65	57	96	NA	NA
51	Indonesia	225	97	139	71	184.3	5091	494	500	61	77	119	21	41
52	Guatemala	230	94	125	54	9.2	367	34	910	63	55	77	14	55
53	Saudi Arabia	292	91	170	65	14.1	594	54	6020	65	62	71	NA	NA
54	South Africa	192	88	135	67	35.3	1108	98	2470	62	NA	NA	NA	NA
55	Myanmar	230	88	153	65	41.7	1252	111	220X	61	81	103	NA	NA
56	El Salvador	207	87	143	59	5.3	191	17	1070	64	73	80	8*	66*
57	Zimbabwe	181	87	110	61	9.7	399	35	650	60	67	128	NA	NA
58	Iraq	222	86	139	63	18.9	789	68	2340X	65	60	96	NA	NA

Contd.

TABLE 7.1 *Contd.*

1		2	3	4	5	6	7	8	9	10	11	12	13	14
59	Egypt	301	85	179	61	52.4	1727	148	640	60	48	90	21*	41*
60	Botswana	173	85	119	63	1.3	61	5	1600	60	74	117	9	59
61	Turkey	258	80	190	69	55.9	1579	134	1370	65	81	117	11*	55*
62	Mongolia	185	84	128	64	2.2	77	7	780^{X}	63	NA	102	NA	NA
63	Honduras	232	84	144	63	5.1	198	17	900	65	73	106	12*	59*
64	Ecuador	184	83	124	60	10.6	338	28	1020	66	86	117	NA	NA
65	Brazil	159	83	116	60	150.4	4115	341	2540	66	81	104	8	63
66	Papua New Guinea	248	80	165	56	3.9	131	10	890	55	52	73	NA	NA
67	Nicaragua	209	78	140	56	3.9	156	1	830^{X}	65	NA	99	12*	58*
68	Dominican Rep.	199	78	125	61	7.2	214	17	790	67	83	101	NA	NA
	Middle U5MR countries (21-70) Median	134	35	86	30	2048T	45680T	1909T	1775	70	88	105	14	51
69	Philippines	134	69	80	43	62.4	1988	138	710	64	90	110	14*	52*
70	Viet Nam	232	65	156	49	66.7	2076	134	240^{X}	63	88	101	NA	NA
71	Tunisia	254	62	159	48	8.2	239	15	1260	67	65	113	NA	NA
72	Paraguay	134	60	86	41	4.3	146	9	1030	67	90	104	NA	NA
73	Syria	217	59	135	44	12.5	550	33	980	66	65	110	NA	NA
74	Iran, Islamic Rep. of	254	59	169	46	54.6	1830	36	3200	66	54	116	NA	NA
75	Lebanon	91	56	68	44	2.7	85	5	2150^{X}	66	80	125	NA	NA
76	Jordan	217	52	135	40	4.0	157	8	1640	67	80	99	NA	NA
77	Colombia	157	50	99	39	33.0	878	44	1200	69	87	114	13	53
78	Mexico	140	49	92	40	88.6	2466	122	2010	70	87	117	13*	NA

Contd.

TABLE 7.1 *Contd.*

	1	2	3	4	5	6	7	8	9	10	11	12	13	14
79	Oman	378	49	214	37	1.5	67	3	5220	66	NA	100	NA	NA
80	Venezuela	114	43	81	35	19.7	582	25	2450	70	88	106	14	51
81	China	203	42	150	30	1139.1	24288	1010	350	70	73	134	22*	38*
82	Albania	151	37	112	31	3.2	74	3	NA	72	NA	100	NA	NA
83	Argentina	75	35	61	31	32.3	670	24	2160	71	95	111	NA	NA
84	Korea, Dem.	120	35	85	26	21.8	530	18	970[x]	70	NA	100	NA	NA
85	Sri Lanka	114	35	71	26	17.2	369	13	430	71	88	107	13	56
86	Thailand	149	34	103	26	55.7	1158	39	1220	66	93	96	15[x]	50[x]
87	Romania	82	34	69	27	23.3	358	12	1620[x]	71	NA	97	NA	NA
88	USSR	53	31	38	23	288.6	5065	159	4550[x]	71	NA	105	NA	NA
89	Panama	105	31	69	22	2.4	63	2	1760	72	88	106	NA	NA
90	United Arab Emirates	239	30	145	24	1.6	34	1	18430	70	48*	104	NA	NA
91	Korea, Rep.	120	30	85	23	42.8	670	20	4400	70	96	108	20*	42*
92	Malaysia	105	29	73	22	17.9	538	16	2160	70	78	102	14	51
93	Mauritius	104	28	70	22	1.1	19	1	1990	70	NA	105	12*	46*
94	Chile	143	27	114	20	13.2	306	8	1770	72	93	100	13*	54*
95	Uruguay	57	25	51	22	3.1	54	1	2620	72	96	109	18*	44*
96	Yugoslavia	113	23	92	20	23.8	339	8	2920	73	93	95	17	43
97	Costa Rica	121	22	84	18	3.0	81	2	1780	75	93	100	12	55

Contd.

TABLE 7.1 *Contd.*

	1	2	3	4	5	6	7	8	9	10	11	12	13	14
	Low U5MR countries (20 and under) Median	39	10	32	8	896T	11829T	126T	14485	76	NA	102	18	40
98	Jamaica	89	20	63	16	2.5	56	1	1260	73	98	103	15	49
99	Kuwait	128	19	89	17	2.0	55	1	16150	73	73	93	NA	NA
100	Poland	70	18	62	16	38.4	588	11	1790	72	NA	101	24	35
101	Bulgaria	69	18	49	14	9.0	112	2	2320	73	NA	104	13^{x}	50^{x}
102	Trinidad and Tobago	67	17	54	15	1.3	32	1	3230	72	NA	100	13^{x}	50^{x}
103	Hungary	57	16	51	15	10.6	123	2	2590	71	NA	97	26	32
104	Portugal	112	16	81	13	10.3	137	2	4250	74	85	127	NA	NA
105	Cuba	87	14	62	11	10.6	188	3	1170^{x}	75	94	104	NA	NA
106	Czechoslovakia	33	13	27	11	15.7	217	3	3450	72	NA	96	NA	NA
107	New Zealand	26	12	23	10	3.4	55	1	12070	75	NA	107	16	45
108	Israel	39	11	33	10	4.6	99	1	9790	76	NA	95	18^{x}	40^{x}
109	Greece	64	11	53	10	10.0	117	1	5350	76	93	106	NA	NA
110	USA	29	11	26	9	249.2	3634	40	20910	76	NA	100	16	42
111	Italy	50	10	44	9	57.1	587	6	15120	76	97	95	19	41
112	Norway	22	10	19	8	4.2	53	1	22290	77	NA	95	19	38
113	Australia	24	10	21	8	16.9	246	2	14360	77	NA	106	16	42
114	Spain	57	10	47	8	39.2	486	5	9330	77	95	113	19	40
115	Belgium	35	9	31	8	9.8	118	1	16220	75	NA	100	22^{x}	36^{x}
116	Austria	43	9	37	8	7.6	88	1	17300	75	NA	101	NA	NA
117	United Kingdom	27	9	23	8	57.2	786	7	14610	76	NA	106	17^{x}	40^{x}

Contd.

TABLE 7.1 *Contd.*

	1	2	3	4	5	6	7	8	9	10	11	12	13	14
118	Singapore	49	9	36	8	2.7	47	0	10450	74	NA	109	15	49
119	France	34	9	29	8	56.1	761	7	17820	76	NA	113	18ˣ	41ˣ
120	Switzerland	26	9	22	7	6.6	78	1	29880	77	NA	NA	17	45
121	Denmark	25	9	22	8	5.1	57	1	20450	76	NA	99	17	39
122	Ireland	36	9	31	8	3.7	67	1	8710	75	NA	100	NA	NA
123	Germany	40	9	34	7	77.6	863	8	20440ˣ	75	NA	105	20ˣ	39ˣ
124	Canada	33	9	28	7	26.5	356	3	19030	77	NA	105	18	40
125	Netherlands	21	9	18	7	15.0	192	2	15920	77	NA	115	20	38
126	Hong Kong	64	7	44	7	5.9	72	1	10350	77	NA	106	16	47
127	Finland	28	7	22	6	5.0	60	0	22120	75	NA	101	18	38
128	Sweden	20	7	16	6	8.4	109	1	21570	77	NA	100	21	37
129	Japan	39	6	31	5	123.5	1390	9	23810	79	NA	102	22ˣ	38ˣ

TABLE 7.2: Demographic Data

		Population (millions) 1990		Population annual growth rate (%)		Crude death rate		Crude birth rate		Life expectancy		Total ferti-lity rate	% pop-lation urbani-zed	Average annual growth rate of urban population (%)	
		under 16	under 5	1965-80	1980-90	1960	1990	1960	1990	1960	1990	1990	1990	1965-80	1980-90
	1	2	3	4	5	6	7	8	9	10	11	12	13	14	15
	Very high U5MR countries (over 140) Median	655T	241T	2.5	2.8	26	16	48	47	39	50	6.6	27	5.4	5.6
1	Mozambique	7.2	2.8	2.5	2.6	26	18	47	45	37	48	6.3	27	11.8	9.7
2	Afghanistan	7.3	3.0	2.4	0.3	30	23	52	51	33	43	6.9	18	6.0	1.8
3	Angola	4.7	1.8	2.8	2.6	31	19	50	47	33	46	6.4	28	6.4	5.6
4	Mali	4.5	1.8	2.1	2.9	29	20	52	51	35	45	7.1	19	4.9	4.0
5	Sierra Leone	1.9	0.8	2.0	2.4	33	23	48	48	32	42	6.5	32	4.3	5.1
6	Malawi	4.4	1.8	2.9	3.5	28	20	54	56	38	48	7.6	12	7.8	6.0
7	Guinea-Bissau	0.4	0.2	1.2	1.9	29	22	40	43	34	43	5.8	20	1.7	3.5
8	Guinea	2.8	1.1	1.9	2.5	31	21	53	51	34	44	7.0	26	6.6	5.5
9	Burkina Faso	4.2	1.6	2.0	2.6	28	18	52	47	36	48	6.5	9	3.4	5.1
10	Niger	3.9	1.5	2.7	3.2	29	20	53	52	35	46	7.1	19	6.9	7.1
11	Ethiopia	23.5	9.3	2.7	2.4	28	20	51	49	36	46	6.8	13	6.6	4.5
12	Chad	2.6	1.0	2.0	2.4	30	19	46	44	35	47	5.8	30	9.2	6.2
13	Somalia	3.7	1.4	2.7	3.4	28	19	49	49	36	46	6.6	36	6.1	5.7
14	Mauritania	0.9	0.4	2.3	2.7	28	18	48	46	35	47	6.5	47	12.4	7.4
15	Liberia	1.2	0.5	3.0	3.2	25	15	50	47	41	54	6.8	46	6.2	5.9

Contd

TABLE 7.2 *Contd.*

	1	2	3	4	5	6	7	8	9	10	11	12	13	14	15
16	Rwanda	3.7	1.5	3.3	3.4	22	16	50	51	42	50	8.1	8	6.3	7.7
17	Cambodia	3.0	1.4	0.3	2.5	21	16	45	39	42	50	4.6	12	1.9	3.8
18	Burundi	2.6	1.0	1.9	2.8	23	17	46	47	41	49	6.8	6	1.8	5.4
19	Bhutan	0.6	0.2	1.6	2.0	25	16	43	38	38	49	5.5	5	3.7	5.0
20	Nepal	8.5	3.1	2.4	2.5	26	14	46	38	38	52	5.7	10	5.1	7.0
21	Yemen	6.1	2.4	2.3	3.5	28	15	53	52	36	51	7.7	29	6.4	7.1
22	Senegal	3.5	1.3	2.5	2.8	27	17	50	45	37	48	6.3	38	4.1	3.7
23	Bangladesh	53.5	19.0	2.7	2.7	23	15	47	41	40	52	5.3	16	8.0	6.5
24	Madagascar	5.7	2.2	2.5	3.1	24	13	48	45	41	55	6.6	24	5.7	5.8
25	Sudan	11.9	4.5	3.0	3.0	25	15	47	44	39	51	6.4	22	5.1	4.1
26	Tanzania	14.0	5.6	3.3	3.7	24	13	51	50	41	54	7.1	33	8.7	10.6
27	Central African Rep.	1.4	0.6	1.8	2.7	26	17	43	45	39	50	6.2	47	4.8	4.7
28	Namibia	0.9	0.3	1.0	3.1	23	11	46	43	42	58	5.9	28	1.9	5.1
29	Nigeria	53.8	21.1	2.5	3.2	25	15	52	48	40	52	6.8	35	4.8	5.9
30	Gabon	0.4	0.2	3.5	3.7	24	16	31	41	41	53	5.2	46	4.2	6.2
31	Uganda	9.7	3.9	2.9	3.6	21	15	50	52	43	52	7.3	10	4.1	5.4
32	Bolivia	3.4	1.3	2.5	2.7	22	13	46	42	43	55	5.9	51	2.9	4.2
33	Pakistan	58.4	23.0	3.1	3.6	24	12	49	44	43	58	6.2	32	4.3	4.9
34	Laos	1.9	0.7	0.6	2.6	23	16	45	45	40	50	6.7	19	4.8	5.8
35	Cameroon	5.8	2.3	2.7	3.1	25	14	44	47	39	54	6.9	41	8.1	5.8
36	Benin	2.3	0.9	2.7	2.9	33	19	47	49	35	47	7.1	38	10.2	4.7
37	Togo	1.7	0.6	3.0	3.0	26	13	48	45	39	54	6.6	26	7.2	6.2
38	**India**	**329.0**	**114.4**	**2.3**	**2.1**	**21**	**11**	**43**	**32**	**44**	**59**	**4.2**	**27**	**3.6**	**3.7**

Contd.

TABLE 7.2 *Contd.*

	1	2	3	4	5	6	7	8	9	10	11	12	13	14	15
	High U5MR countries (71-140) Median	326T	114T	2.8	2.8	20	9	49	38	46	62	5.2	46	4.7	4.4
39	Ghana	7.1	2.8	2.2	3.4	19	13	48	44	45	55	6.3	33	3.4	4.1
40	Cote d'Ivoire	6.0	2.4	4.2	3.8	25	14	53	50	39	53	7.4	40	8.7	5.3
41	Halti	2.8	1.0	2.0	1.9	24	13	42	36	42	56	4.9	28	4.0	3.7
42	Zaire	17.2	6.6	2.8	3.0	23	14	47	46	41	53	6.1	39	7.2	4.5
43	Lesotho	0.8	0.3	2.3	2.8	24	12	43	41	42	57	5.8	20	14.6	6.8
44	Zambia	4.3	1.8	3.1	3.9	23	13	50	51	42	54	7.2	50	7.1	6.1
45	Peru	8.6	2.9	2.8	2.2	19	8	47	30	48	63	3.8	70	4.1	3.1
46	Libyan Arab Jamahiriya	2.2	0.8	4.6	4.0	19	9	49	44	47	62	6.8	70	9.7	6.2
47	Morocco	10.7	3.8	2.5	2.6	21	9	50	34	47	62	4.5	48	4.2	4.1
48	Congo	1.1	0.4	2.7	3.1	23	14	45	46	42	54	6.3	40	3.5	4.3
49	Kenya	12.6	4.7	3.6	3.7	23	11	53	47	45	60	6.9	24	9.0	7.5
50	Algeria	11.5	3.8	3.1	2.9	20	8	51	35	47	65	5.1	52	3.8	4.6
51	Indonesia	70.0	22.8	2.3	2.0	23	9	44	28	41	61	3.3	31	4.7	5.2
52	Guatemala	4.4	1.6	2.8	2.8	20	8	49	40	46	63	5.6	39	3.6	3.4
53	Saudi Arabia	6.7	2.5	4.6	4.1	23	7	49	42	44	65	7.1	77	8.5	5.6
54	South Africa	13.8	4.9	2.4	2.2	17	9	42	31	49	62	4.3	59	2.6	3.4
55	Myanmar	16.4	5.6	2.3	2.1	21	9	42	30	44	61	3.9	25	2.8	2.4
56	El Salvador	2.5	0.8	2.7	1.5	16	8	49	36	51	64	4.7	44	3.5	2.2
57	Zimbabwe	4.6	1.7	3.1	3.1	20	10	53	41	45	60	5.6	28	7.5	5.4
58	Iraq	9.2	3.4	3.4	3.5	20	7	49	42	49	65	6.1	71	5.3	4.3

Contd.

TABLE 7.2 *Contd.*

	1	2	3	4	5	6	7	8	9	10	11	12	13	14	15
59	Egypt	21.7	7.6	2.4	2.5	21	10	45	33	46	60	4.3	47	2.9	3.1
60	Botswana	0.7	0.3	3.5	3.7	21	11	52	46	46	60	6.7	28	15.4	9.7
61	Turkey	20.5	7.1	2.4	2.3	18	8	45	28	50	65	3.5	61	4.3	5.7
62	Mongolia	1.0	0.3	3.0	2.8	18	8	43	35	47	63	4.9	52	4.5	2.9
63	Honduras	2.4	0.9	3.2	3.4	19	8	51	39	46	65	5.2	44	5.5	5.3
64	Ecuador	4.4	1.5	3.1	2.6	15	7	46	32	53	66	4.1	56	5.1	4.4
65	Brazil	56.1	19.0	2.4	2.1	13	8	43	27	55	66	3.3	75	4.5	3.4
66	Papua New Guinea	1.7	0.6	2.3	2.3	23	11	44	34	41	55	5.0	16	8.4	4.2
67	Nicaragua	1.9	0.7	3.1	3.3	18	7	51	40	47	65	5.3	60	4.6	4.5
68	Dominican Rep.	2.9	1.0	2.7	2.3	16	7	50	30	52	67	3.5	60	5.3	4.1
	Middle U5MR countries (21-70) Median	**634T**	**214T**	**2.5**	**2.0**	**13**	**6**	**43**	**26**	**57**	**70**	**3.0**	**54**	**4.0**	**3.2**
69	Philippines	26.4	9.2	2.9	2.6	15	7	46	32	53	64	4.1	43	4.0	3.9
70	Viet Nam	27.7	9.3	1.0	2.2	23	9	42	31	44	63	3.9	22	4.1	3.4
71	Tunisia	3.3	1.1	2.1	2.5	19	7	47	29	48	67	3.7	54	4.2	2.9
72	Paraguay	1.8	0.7	2.8	3.1	9	7	43	34	64	67	4.5	47	3.2	4.4
73	Syria	6.3	2.4	3.4	3.5	18	6	47	44	50	66	6.5	50	4.5	4.3
74	Iran, Islamic Rep. of	25.2	8.2	3.2	3.4	21	7	47	34	50	66	5.0	57	5.5	4.7
75	Lebanon	1.0	0.4	1.6	0.1	14	8	43	31	60	66	3.6	84	4.6	1.1
76	Jordan	1.9	0.7	2.6	3.2	23	6	50	39	47	67	5.8	68	5.3	4.4
77	Colombia	12.6	4.1	2.2	2.0	13	6	45	27	57	69	3.0	70	3.5	2.9
78	Mexico	35.1	11.6	3.1	2.3	12	6	46	28	57	70	3.3	73	4.5	3.2

Contd.

TABLE 7.2 *Contd.*

	1	2	3	4	5	6	7	8	9	10	11	12	13	14	15
79	Oman	0.7	0.3	3.6	4.2	28	7	51	44	40	66	7.1	11	8.1	7.9
80	Venezuela	8.0	2.7	3.5	2.7	10	5	45	30	60	70	3.6	90	4.5	3.6
81	China	324.3	112.3	2.2	1.3	19	7	37	21	47	70	2.4	33	2.6	6.7
82	Albania	1.1	0.4	2.5	1.9	10	6	41	23	62	72	2.9	35	3.4	2.4
83	Argentina	10.3	3.2	1.6	1.4	9	9	24	21	65	71	2.9	86	2.2	1.8
84	Korea, Dem.	6.7	2.4	2.7	1.8	13	5	42	24	54	70	2.5	60	4.6	2.3
85	Sri Lanka	6.0	1.8	1.8	1.5	9	6	36	22	62	71	2.6	21	2.3	1.4
86	Thailand	19.4	5.7	2.7	1.8	15	7	44	21	52	66	2.4	23	4.6	4.4
87	Romania	5.8	1.7	1.1	0.5	9	11	20	15	65	71	2.1	53	3.4	1.2
88	USSR	77.9	25.3	0.9	0.8	7	10	24	18	68	71	2.3	66	2.2	1.3
89	Panama	0.9	0.3	2.6	2.1	10	5	41	26	61	72	3.0	53	3.4	2.8
90	United Arab Emirates	0.5	0.2	16.1	4.5	19	4	46	22	53	70	4.6	78	18.9	4.1
91	Korea, Rep.	11.9	3.3	1.9	1.2	14	6	43	16	54	70	1.7	72	5.7	3.5
92	Malaysia	7.2	2.6	2.5	2.6	15	5	44	30	54	70	3.8	43	4.5	4.8
93	Mauritius	0.3	0.1	1.6	1.1	10	6	44	18	59	70	1.9	40	4.0	0.7
94	Chile	4.3	1.5	1.8	1.7	13	6	37	23	57	72	2.7	86	2.6	2.2
95	Uruguay	0.9	0.3	0.4	0.6	10	10	22	17	68	72	2.4	85	0.7	0.8
96	Yugoslavia	5.7	1.7	0.9	0.7	10	9	24	14	63	73	1.9	56	3.0	2.8
97	Costa Rica	1.1	0.4	2.6	2.8	10	4	47	27	62	75	3.1	47	3.7	3.7

Contd.

TABLE 7.2 *Contd.*

	1	2	3	4	5	6	7	8	9	10	11	12	13	14	15
	Low U5MR countries (20 and under) Median	192T	59T	0.8	0.5	9	10	20	13	69	76	1.8	76	1.9	1.2
98	Jamaica	0.9	0.3	1.5	1.4	10	6	39	23	63	73	2.5	52	3.4	2.5
99	Kuwait	0.8	0.3	7.0	3.9	10	2	44	27	60	73	3.7	96	8.2	4.5
100	Poland	10.3	3.0	0.8	0.8	8	10	24	16	67	72	2.2	62	1.8	1.4
101	Bulgaria	1.9	0.6	0.5	0.2	9	12	18	13	68	73	1.9	68	2.8	1.2
102	Trinidad and Tobago	0.5	0.2	1.3	1.7	9	6	38	25	64	72	2.8	69	5.0	3.6
103	Hungary	2.3	0.6	0.4	-0.1	10	13	16	12	68	71	1.8	61	1.8	1.2
104	Portugal	2.4	0.7	0.6	0.5	11	10	24	13	63	74	1.7	34	2.0	1.8
105	Cuba	2.6	0.9	1.5	0.9	9	7	31	18	64	75	1.9	75	2.7	1.9
106	Czechoslovakia	3.9	1.1	0.5	0.2	10	12	17	14	70	72	2.0	77	1.9	1.6
107	New Zealand	0.8	0.3	1.3	0.9	9	8	26	16	71	75	2.0	84	1.5	0.9
108	Israel	1.5	0.5	2.8	1.7	6	7	27	22	69	76	2.9	92	3.5	2.0
109	Greece	2.1	0.6	0.7	0.4	8	10	19	12	69	76	1.7	62	2.5	1.2
110	USA	56.9	18.3	1.0	0.9	9	9	23	15	70	76	1.8	75	1.2	1.1
111	Italy	10.4	2.8	0.6	0.1	10	10	18	10	69	76	1.4	69	1.0	0.4
112	Norway	0.9	0.3	0.6	0.3	9	11	18	13	73	77	1.7	75	5.0	0.9
113	Australia	4.0	1.2	1.8	1.4	9	8	22	15	71	77	1.8	85	0.2	1.3
114	Spain	8.5	2.3	1.0	0.4	9	9	21	13	69	77	1.6	78	2.4	1.2
115	Belgium	1.9	0.6	0.3	0.0	12	12	17	12	70	75	1.6	97	0.5	0.2
116	Austria	1.4	0.4	0.3	0.0	13	12	18	12	69	75	1.5	58	0.1	0.7
117	United Kingdom	11.6	3.8	0.2	0.2	12	12	17	14	71	76	1.8	89	0.5	0.2

Contd.

TABLE 7.2 *Contd.*

	1	2	3	4	5	6	7	8	9	10	11	12	13	14	15
118	Singapore	0.7	0.2	1.6	1.2	8	5	38	17	65	74	1.8	100	1.6	1.2
119	France	12.1	3.8	0.7	0.4	12	10	18	14	70	76	1.8	74	2.7	0.5
120	Switzerland	1.2	0.4	0.5	0.4	10	10	18	12	71	77	1.5	60	1.2	0.9
121	Denmark	0.9	0.3	0.5	0.0	9	11	17	11	72	76	1.5	87	1.1	0.4
122	Ireland	1.1	0.3	1.2	0.9	12	9	22	18	70	75	2.4	57	2.2	1.2
123	Germany	13.2	4.3	0.2	-0.1	12	12	17	11	70	75	1.5	85	0.9	0.2
124	Canada	5.9	1.8	1.3	1.0	8	8	26	14	71	77	1.7	77	1.5	1.2
125	Netherlands	2.9	0.9	0.9	0.6	8	9	21	13	73	77	1.6	89	1.5	0.6
126	Hong Kong	1.3	0.4	2.1	1.5	7	6	35	13	66	77	1.4	94	2.3	1.8
127	Finland	1.0	0.3	0.3	0.4	9	10	19	12	68	75	1.7	60	2.5	0.4
128	Sweden	1.6	0.5	0.5	0.2	10	12	15	13	73	77	1.9	84	1.0	0.3
129	Japan	24.7	6.8	1.2	0.6	8	7	18	11	68	79	1.7	77	2.1	0.7

Note: Nations are listed in descending order of their 1990 under five mortality rates (see table 1).

TABLE 7.3: Economic Data

		GNP per capita (US $)	GNP per capita average annual growth rate (%)		Rate of inflation (%)	% of population below absolute poverty level (1980-89)		% of central government expenditure allocated to (1986-90)			ODA inflow in millions US $	ODA inflow as % of recipient-GNP	Debt service as % of exports of goods and services	
		1989	1965-80	1980-89	1980-89	Urban	rural	health	education	defence	1989	1989	1970	1989
	1	2	3	4	5	6	7	8	9	10	11	12	13	14
	Very U5MR Countries (over 140) Median	290	0.8	-1.1	8	36	61	5	12	16	320	13	4	14
1	Mozambique	80	NA	-6.0	35	50*	67*	5*	10*	35*	759	64	NA	17
2	Afghanistan	280X	0.6	NA	NA	18X	36X	NA	NA	NA	95	NA	NA	NA
3	Angola	610	NA	NA	NA	NA	NA	6*	15*	34*	140	2	NA	NA
4	Mali	270	2.1X	1.0	4	27X	48X	4*	17*	17*	470	22	1	10
5	Sierra Leone	220	0.7	-3.2	54	NA	65X	6	13	3	99	12	11	6X
6	Malawi	180	3.2	-0.1	15	25	85	7	11	7	394	27	8	17
7	Guinea-Bissau	180	NA	1.5	NA	NA	NA	NA	NA	NA	102	59	NA	27
8	Guinea	430	1.3	NA	NA	NA	NA	3*	11*	29*	346	15	NA	13
9	Burkina Faso	320	1.7	2.3	5	NA	NA	5	14	18	284	10	7	8
10	Niger	290	-2.5	-5.0	3	NA	35X	NA	NA	NA	296	13	4	9
11	Ethiopia	120	0.4	-1.1	2	60	65	NA	NA	NA	702	12	11	34
12	Chad	190	-1.9	3.9	2	30X	56X	8*	8*	NA	NA	NA	4	2
13	Somalia	170	-0.1	-1.3	43	40X	70X	1*	2*	38*	440	43	2	18
14	Mauritania	500	-0.1	-2.2	9	NA	NA	4*	23*	NA	195	20	3	16
15	Liberia	450X	0.5	5.2X	NA	NA	23X	7	16	9	58	NA	8	NA

Contd.

TABLE 7.3 *Contd.*

	1	2	3	4	5	6	7	8	9	10	11	12	13	14
16	Rwanda	320	1.6	-1.9	4	30^{X}	90^{X}	5*	26*	NA	238	11	1	14
17	Cambodia	NA	NA	NA	NA	NA	NA	NA	NA	NA	25	NA	NA	NA
18	Burundi	220	2.4	1.6	4	55^{X}	85^{X}	4*	16*	16*	198	17	2	30
19	Bhutan	190^{X}	NA	7.8^{X}	NA	NA	NA	5*	8*	NA	40	NA	NA	NA
20	Nepal	180	0.0	2.1	9	55^{X}	61^{X}	6	9	7	488	15	3	14
21	Yemen	650	NA	NA	NA	NA	NA	NA	NA	NA	338	5	NA	17
22	Senegal	650	-0.5	0.0	7	NA	NA	NA	NA	NA	652	14	3	21
23	Bangladesh	180	-0.3	0.7	11	86^{X}	86^{X}	10	11	10	1791	9	NA	13
24	Madagascar	230	-0.4	-2.6	18	50^{X}	50^{X}	NA	NA	NA	320	13	4	37
25	Sudan	420^{X}	0.8	-1.8^{X}	34^{X}	NA	85^{X}	NA	NA	NA	760	NA	11	5
26	Tanzania	130	0.8	-1.6	26	NA	NA	6	8	16	918	30	5	13
27	Central African Rep.	390	0.8	-1.5	7	NA	NA	NA	NA	NA	189	17	5	6
28	Namibia	1030	NA	NA	13	NA	NA	14*	18*	5*	44	NA	NA	NA
29	Nigeria	250	4.2	-3.6	14	NA	NA	1	3	3	339	1	4	21
30	Gabon	2960	5.6	-2.6	-1	NA	NA	NA	NA	NA	134	4	6	9
31	Uganda	250	-2.2	-1.0	108	NA	NA	2	15	26	397	9	3	45
32	Bolivia	620	1.7	-3.5	392	NA	NA	1	12	6	432	10	11	26
33	Pakistan	370	1.8	2.9	7	32^{X}	29^{X}	1	3	30	1119	3	24	16
34	Laos	180	NA	0.0^{X}	NA	NA	NA	NA	NA	NA	141	20	NA	11
35	Cameroon	1000	2.4	0.7	7	15^{X}	40^{X}	4	13	8	470	4	3	7
36	Benin	380	-0.3	-1.8	8	NA	NA	NA	NA	NA	247	14	2	5
37	Togo	390	1.7	-2.4	5	42^{X}	NA	5	20	11	182	13	3	12
38	**India**	**340**	**1.5**	**3.2**	**8**	**29***	**33***	**2**	**3**	**19**	**1874**	**1**	**22**	**19^{X}**

Contd.

TABLE 7.3 *Contd.*

	1	2	3	4	5	6	7	8	9	10	11	12	13	14
	High U5MR countries 71-140) Median	885	2.8	-0.7	12	31	51	7	15	11	227	4	7	17
39	Ghana	390	-0.8	-0.8	44	59*	37*	9	26	3	543	10	6	22
40	Cote d'Ivoire	790	2.8	-3.0	3	30	26	4	21	4	409	4	7	10
41	Haiti	360	0.9	-0.7	7	65	80	NA	NA	NA	198	8	59	6
42	Zaire	260	-1.3	-1.6	59	NA	80[X]	4	6	14	637	7	4	4
43	Lesotho	470	6.8	-0.5	13	50[X]	55[X]	7	16	10	118	14	5	3
44	Zambia	390	-1.2	-3.8	38	25	NA	7	9	NA	388	13	6	11
45	Peru	1010	0.8	-1.6	160	46*	83*	6	16	20	300	1	12	4
46	Libyan Arab Jamahiriya	5310	0.0	-9.9[X]	0	NA	NA	NA	NA	NA	11	0	NA	NA
47	Morocco	880	2.7	1.3	7	28[X]	45[X]	3	17	15	443	2	9	26
48	Congo	940	2.7	0.1	0	NA	NA	NA	NA	NA	91	4	12	23
49	Kenya	360	3.1	0.4	9	10[X]	55[X]	5*	19*	8*	967	11	6	19
50	Algeria	2230	4.2	0.0	5	20[X]	NA	NA	NA	NA	153	0	4	68
51	Indonesia	500	5.2	3.6	8	20*	16*	2	10	8	1830	2	7	27
52	Guatemala	910	3.0	-2.6	13	17*	5'1*	8*	13*	19*	256	3	7	16
53	Saudi Arabia	6020	4.0[X]	-5.9	-4	NA	NA	NA	NA	NA	16	0	NA	NA
54	South Africa	2470	3.2	-0.8	14	NA	NA	NA	NA	NA	NA	NA	NA	NA
55	Myanmar	220[X]	1.6	NA	NA	40[X]	40[X]	8	12	19	220	NA	12	29
56	El Salvador	1070	1.5	-1.1	17	20	32	7	17	26	446	8	4	13
57	Zimbabwe	650	1.7	-0.8	11	NA	NA	8	23	16	266	4	2	20
58	Iraq	2340	NA	NA	30[X]	NA	NA	NA	NA	NA	5	NA	NA	NA

Contd.

TABLE 7.3 *Contd.*

	1	2	3	4	5	6	7	8	9	10	11	12	13	14
59	Egypt	640	2.8	2.8^{X}	11	34^{X}	34^{X}	3	12	20	1578	5	38	17
60	Botswana	1600	9.9	6.7^{X}	12	40	55	6	18	8	162	8	1	4
61	Turkey	1370	3.6	3.0	41	NA	NA	2	13	10	122	0	22	28
62	Mongolia	780^{X}	NA	NA	NA	NA	NA	NA	NA	NA	4	NA	NA	NA
63	Honduras	900	1.1	-1.2	5	31	70*	NA	NA	NA	256	6	3	10
64	Ecuador	1020	5.4	-0.5	34	40	65	7	25	12	162	2	9	29
65	Brazil	2540	6.3	0.9	228	NA	NA	6	3	3	189	0	13	19
66	Papua New Guinea	890	NA	-0.7	6	10^{X}	75^{X}	9	15	4	334	10	1	16
67	Nicaragua	830^{X}	-0.7	-4.7^{X}	87^{X}	21^{X}	19^{X}	11*	9*	50*	227	NA	11	NA
68	Dominican Rep.	790	3.8	-0.1	19	45^{X}	43^{X}	8*	10*	5*	141	3	4	7
	Middle U5MR countries (21-70) Median	1775	3.7	-0.2	14	18	20	5	14	8	91	0	11	15
69	Philippines	710	3.2	-1.8	15	52*	64*	4	17	13	831	2	8	20
70	Viet Nam	240^{X}	NA	NA	NA	NA	NA	NA	NA	NA	NA	NA	NA	NA
71	Tunisia	1260	4.7	0.6	8	20^{X}	15^{X}	6	15	6	247	2	20	21
72	Paraguay	1030	4.1	-1.5	23	19^{X}	50^{X}	3	12	12	91	2	12	10
73	Syria	980	5.1	-2.1	15	NA	NA	2	10	40	139	1	11	19^{X}
74	Iran, Islamic Rep. of	3200	2.9	NA	14	NA	NA	6	20	14	89	NA	NA	NA
75	Lebanon	2150^{X}	NA	NA	NA	NA	NA	NA	NA	NA	132	NA	NA	NA
76	Jordan	1640	5.8^{X}	-3.0	2^{X}	14^{X}	17^{X}	4	14	30	280	5	4	15
77	Colombia	1200	3.6	0.9	24	32*	70*	NA	NA	NA	62	0	12	38
78	Mexico	2010	3.6	-1.5	73	NA	NA	1	7	1	97	0	24	26

Contd.

TABLE 7.3 *Contd.*

	1	2	3	4	5	6	7	8	9	10	11	12	13	14
79	Oman	5220	9.0	5.3	-7	NA	NA	5	11	38	4	0	NA	NA
80	Venezuela	2450	2.3	-2.3	16	NA	NA	10	20	6	21	0	3	20
81	China	350	4.1	8.2	6	NA	13*	NA	NA	8*	2227	1	NA	8
82	Albania	NA	NA	NA	NA	NA	NA	NA	NA	NA	9	NA	NA	NA
83	Argentina	2160	1.7	-1.6	335	NA	NA	2	6	7	215	0	22	23
84	Korea, Dem.	970^x	NA	NA	NA	NA	NA	NA	NA	NA	50	NA	NA	NA
85	Sri Lanka	430	2.8	2.4	11	NA	NA	6	11	7	558	8	11	13
86	Thailand	1120	4.4	4.5	3	10*	25*	6	19	19	697	1	3	8
87	Romania	1620^x	NA	NA	NA	NA	NA	1	2	5	NA	NA	NA	24^x
88	USSR	4550^x	NA	NA	NA	NA	NA	NA	NA	NA	NA	NA	NA	NA
89	Panama	1760	2.8	-2.1	3	21^x	30^x	20	19	8	17	0	8	0
90	United Arab Emirates	18430	NA	-8.2	1	NA	NA	7	14	44	-6	0	NA	NA
91	Korea, Rep.	4400	7.3	8.8	5	18^x	11^x	2	19	27	-9	0	20	7
92	Malaysia	2160	4.7	1.9	2	13	38	5*	NA	NA	139	0	4	12
93	Mauritius	1990	3.7	5.3	9	12^x	12^x	9	14	1	57	3	3	6
94	Chile	1770	0.0	1.0	21	12*	20*	4*	12*	NA	61	0	19	15^x
95	Uruguay	2620	2.5	-0.8	59	22*	NA	4	9	8	38	0	22	20
96	Yugoslavia	2920	5.2	-0.7	97	NA	NA	NA	NA	55	43	0	10	8
97	Costa Rica	1780	3.3	0.4	25	8*	20*	17*	13*	3*	224	5	10	15

Contd.

TABLE 7.3 *Contd.*

	1	2	3	4	5	6	7	8	9	10	11	12	13	14
	Low U5MR (20 and under) median	14485	3.3	1.9	6	NA	NA	11	9	7	NA	NA	NA	NA
98	Jamaica	1260	-0.1	-1.7	19	NA	80	7*	11*	8*	258	9	3	16
99	Kuwait	16150	0.6^{x}	-2.1	-3	NA	NA	8	14	14	4	0	NA	NA
100	Poland	1790	NA	1.8	38	NA	NA	NA	NA	NA	NA	NA	NA	NA
101	Bulgaria	2320	NA	NA	1	NA	NA	NA	NA	NA	NA	NA	NA	9
102	Trinidad and Tobago	3230	3.1	-7.3	6	NA	39^{x}	NA	NA	NA	6	0	5	11
103	Hungary	2590	5.1	1.4	8	NA	NA	2	2	5	NA	NA	NA	23^{x}
104	Portugal	4250	4.6	2.1	19	NA	NA	NA	NA	NA	79	0	7	17
105	Cuba	1170^{x}	NA	NA	NA	NA	NA	23*	10*	NA	27	NA	NA	NA
106	Czechoslovakia	3450	NA	NA	2	NA	NA	NA	NA	NA	NA	NA	NA	NA
107	New Zealand	12070	1.7	0.9	11	NA	NA	12	11	5	NA	NA	NA	NA
108	Israel	9790	3.7	1.4	117	NA	NA	4	10	27	1192	3	3	NA
109	Greece	5350	4.8	0.6	18	NA	NA	NA	NA	NA	33	0	9	26^{x}
110	USA	20910	1.8	2.2	4	NA	NA	13	2	25	NA	NA	NA	NA
111	Italy	15120	3.2	2.1	10	NA	NA	10	8	3	NA	NA	NA	NA
112	Norway	22290	3.6	3.5	6	NA	NA	11	9	8	NA	NA	NA	NA

Contd.

TABLE 7.3 *Contd.*

	1	2	3	4	5	6	7	8	9	10	11	12	13	14
113	Australia	14360	2.2	1.8	8	NA	NA	10	7	9	NA	NA	NA	NA
114	Spain	9330	4.1	2.4	9	NA	NA	13	6	6	NA	NA	NA	NA
115	Belgium	16220	3.6	1.7	5	NA	NA	2	13	5	NA	NA	NA	NA
116	Austria	17300	4.0	1.9	4	NA	NA	13	9	3	NA	NA	NA	NA
117	United Kingdom	14610	2.0	2.9	6	NA	NA	13	2	13	NA	NA	NA	NA
118	Singapore	10450	8.3	5.7	2	NA	NA	4	19	21	95	0	1	NA
119	France	17820	3.7	1.6	7	NA	NA	21	8	6	NA	NA	NA	NA
120	Switzerland	29880	1.5	1.8	4	NA	NA	13	3	10	NA	NA	NA	NA
121	Denmark	20450	2.2	2.2	6	NA	NA	1	9	5	NA	NA	NA	NA
122	Ireland	8710	2.8	0.8	8	NA	NA	13	11	3	NA	NA	NA	NA
123	Germany	20440[X]	3.0[X]	2.1[X]	3[X]	NA	NA	NA	NA	NA	NA	NA	NA	NA
124	Canada	19030	3.3	2.6	5	NA	NA	6	3	7	NA	NA	NA	NA
125	Netherlands	15920	2.7	1.3	2	NA	NA	11	12	5	NA	NA	NA	NA
126	Hong Kong	10350	6.2	5.7	7	NA	NA	8*	17*	NA	23	0	NA	NA
127	Finland	22120	3.6	2.9	7	NA	NA	11	14	5	NA	NA	NA	NA
128	Sweden	21570	2.0	2.0	7	NA	NA	1	9	7	NA	NA	NA	NA
129	Japan	23810	5.1	3.5	1	NA	NA	NA	NA	NA	NA	NA	NA	NA

TABLE 7.4: Educational Data

		Adult literacy rate				No. of sets per 100 population 1988		Primary school enrolment ratio						% of grade 1 enrolment reaching final grade of primary school	Secondary school enrolment ratio 1986-89 (gross)	
		1970		1990				1960 (gross)		1986-89 (gross)		1986-89 (net)				
		Male	Female	Male	Female	Radio	Television	Male	Female	Mele	Female	Mele	Female	1985-87	male	female
	1	2	3	4	5	6	7	8	9	10	11	12	13	14	15	
	Very high U5MR countries (over 140)															
	Median	27	8	49	24	93	6	35	16	70	50	52	38	50	19	9
1	Mozambique	29	14	45	21	39	1	60	36	76	59	49	41	34	7	4
2	Afghanistan	13	2	44	14	102	8	15	2	33	17	NA	NA	78	10	7
3	Angola	16	7	56	29	50	6	NA	NA	101	85	NA	NA	24	17	9
4	Mali	11	4	41	24	38	NA	14	6	29	17	23	14	40	9	4
5	Sierra Leone	18	8	31	11	218	9	30	NA	65	40	NA	NA	NA	23	11
6	Malawi	42	18	NA	NA	242	NA	NA	45	79	65	56	47	31	5	3
7	Guinea-Bissau	13	6	50	24	38	NA	NA	NA	69	37	52	29	19	9	3
8	Guinea	21	7	35	13	34	3	44	16	42	19	31	15	43	13	4
9	Burkina Faso	13	3	28	9	25	5	12	5	41	24	34	20	68	8	4
10	Niger	6	2	40	17	63	4	7	3	38	21	NA	NA	75	8	3

Contd.

TABLE 7.4 *Contd.*

	1	2	3	4	5	6	7	8	9	10	11	12	13	14	15	
11	Ethiopia	8	NA	NA	NA	193	2	11	3	44	28	31	22	50	18	12
12	Chad	20	2	42	18	235	1	29	4	73	29	52	23	78	10	2
13	Somalia	5	1	27x	9x	40	0	13	13	20	10	14	8	33*	NA	NA
14	Mauritania	NA	NA	47	21	143	1	13	3	61	43	NA	NA	78	23	10
15	Liberia	27	8	50	329	225	18	45	18	43	24	NA	NA	NA	NA	NA
16	Rwanda	43	21	64	37	57	NA	NA	NA	67	64	63	63	46	7	5
17	Cambodia	NA	NA	48	22	107	8	NA	NA	NA	NA	NA	NA	50*	45	20
18	Burundi	29	10	61	40	56	0	27	9	68	50	52	37	87	6	3
19	Bhutan	NA	NA	51	25	15	NA	5	NA	31	20	NA	NA	NA	7	2
20	Nepal	27	3	38	13	33	2	19	1	112	57	84	35	27*	35	17
21	Yemen	14	3	47y	21y	44	12	NA	NA	132	39	NA	NA	31y	42	7
22	Senegal	18	5	52	25	111	34	36	NA	70	49	59	41	85	19	10
23	Bangladesh	36	12	47	22	41	4	66	26	76	64	67	44	20	24	11
24	Madagascar	56	43	88	73	196	6	58	45	99	95	67	65	48*	23	19
25	Sudan	28	6	43	12	233	53	35	14	58x	41x	23x	17x	76	23	17
26	Tanzania	48	18	93y	88y	20	1	33	18	67	66	50	51	71	5	3
27	Central African Rep.	26	6	52	25	62	3	53	12	83	51	59	39	56	17	6
28	Namibia	NA	NA	NA	NA	125	11	NA	NA	NA	NA	NA	NA	NA	NA	NA
29	Nigeria	35	14	62	40	164	6	46	27	68	63	NA	NA	63*	28	18
30	Gabon	43	22	74	49	135	23	NA	NA	NA	NA	NA	NA	44	NA	NA

Contd.

TABLE 7.4 *Contd.*

	1	2	3	4	5	6	7	8	9	10	11	12	13	14	15	
31	Uganda	52	30	62	35	99	6	NA	32	76	63	43	38	76	16	9
32	Bolivia	68	46	85	71	574	77	78	50	97	85	88	78	60	40	35
33	Pakistan	30	11	47	21	86	13	46	13	51	28	NA	NA	49y	26	11
34	Laos	37	28	NA	NA	124	3	34	16	122	98	NA	NA	38*	23	22
35	Cameroon	47	19	66	43	126	12	87	43	119	102	85	74	70	32	21
36	Benin	23	8	32	16	76	4	38	15	83	43	66	34	36	23	9
37	Togo	27	7	56	31	179	6	63	24	124	78	87	59	52	36	12
38	**India**	47	20	62	34	78	7x	80	40	114	83	NA	NA	40*	50	29
	High U5MR countries (71-140) Median	55	37	76	60	164	55	68	52	100	92	84	80	67	35	35
39	Ghana	43	18	70	51	294	13	52	25	81	66	NA	NA	NA	49	30
40	Cote d'Ivoire	26	10	67	40	128	54	68	24	82	58	NA	NA	73	26	12
41	Halti	26x	17x	59	47	40	4	50	42	86	80	44	42	32	20	17
42	Zaire	61	22	84	61	99	1	88	32	86	65	NA	NA	60	32	14
43	Lesotho	49	74	NA	NA	68	1	63	102	101	123	NA	NA	52	20	30
44	Zambia	66	37	81	65	74	15	51	34	102	92	NA	NA	80	NA	NA
45	Peru	81	60	92	79	241	85	95	71	125	120	NA	NA	70	68	61
46	Libyan Arab Jamahiriya	60	13	75	50	223	70	92	24	NA	NA	NA	NA	82	NA	NA
47	Morocco	34	10	61	38	207	55x	67	27	80	53	65	46	67	43	30
48	Congo	50	19	70	44	122	3	103	53	NA	NA	NA	NA	71	37*	14*

Contd.

TABLE 7.4 *Contd.*

	1	2	3	4	5	6	7	8	9	10	11	12	13	14	15	
49	Kenya	44	19	80	59	91	6	64	30	95	91	NA	NA	51	27	19
50	Algeria	39	11	70	46	229	71	55	37	105	87	97	81	90	61	53
51	Indonesia	66	42	84	62	146	41	86	58	121	117	100	97	80	53	43
52	Guatemala	51	37	63	47	63	37	50	39	82	NA	NA	36	21	19	
53	Saudi Arabia	15	2	73	48	280	269	22	NA	78	65	64	48	90	52	35
54	South Africa	NA	NA	NA	NA	323	98	94	85	NA	NA	NA	NA	NA	NA	NA
55	Myanmar	85	57	89	72	79	2	61	52	106	100	NA	NA	33*	25	23
56	El Salvador	61	53	76	70	402	84	NA	NA	79	81	71	62	31	27	31
57	Zimbabwe	63	47	74	60	85	22	NA	NA	130	126	100	100	74	49	42
58	Iraq	50	18	70	49	200	68	94	36	104	87	90	82	73	60	37
59	Egypt	50	20	63	34	312	84	80	52	100	79	NA	NA	95	79	58
60	Botswana	37	44	84	65	134	7	35	48	114	120	94	100	89	31	36
61	Turkey	69	34	90	71	161	172	90	58	121	113	NA	NA	97	57	34
62	Mongolia	87	74	NA	NA	130	32	79	78	100	103	NA	NA	NA	88	96
63	Honduras	55	50	76	71	383	68	68	67	104	108	89	94	43	28	36
64	Ecuador	75	68	88	84	293	81	87	79	118	116	NA	NA	63	55	57
65	Brazil	69	63	83	80	371	194	97	93	NA	NA	NA	NA	22	32	42
66	Papua New Guinea	39	24	65	38	64	2	59	7	79	67	78	NA	62	16	10
67	Nicaragua	58	57	NA	NA	246	61	65	66	94	104	74	79	35	29	58
68	Dominican Rep.	69	65	85	82	166	81	99	98	99	103	NA	78	35	NA	NA

Contd.

TABLE 7.4 *Contd.*

	1	2	3	4	5	6	7	8	9	10	11	12	13	14	15	
	Middle U5MR countries (21-70) Median	83	74	90	86	241	110	100	92	106	104	94	89	87	57	58
69	Philippines	84	81	90	90	135	37	98	93	109	111	97	94	75	66	71
70	Viet Nam	NA	NA	92	84	103	34	NA	NA	107	94	NA	NA	57*	44	41
71	Tunisia	44	17	74	56	180	69	88	43	121	105	100	89	72	46	38
72	Paraguay	85x	75x	92	88	166	24	105	90	106	102	91	84	50	30	29
73	Syria	60	20	78	51	244	59	89	39	115	104	100	94	89	69	47
74	Iran, Islamic Rep. of	40	17	65	43	237	53	56	27	123	109	99	89	87	57	44
75	Lebanon	79x	58x	88	73	773	302	105	99	105	95	NA	NA	NA	57	56
76	Jordan	64	29	89	70	238	70	94	59	98	99	88	88	96	80	78
77	Colombia	79	76	88	86	170	110	77	77	112	115	72	74	57	55	56
78	Mexico	78	69	90	85	241	124	82	77	118	115	NA	NA	69	54	53
79	Oman	NA	NA	NA	NA	649	740	NA	NA	105	95	85	77	92	46	34
80	Venezuela	79	71	87	90	428	147	100	100	NA	107	107	88	90	48	59
81	China	NA	NA	84	62	184	24	NA	NA	142	126	100	95	77*	50	37
82	Albania	NA	NA	NA	NA	168	83	102	86	100	99	NA	NA	NA	80	71
83	Argentina	94	92	96	95	666	217	98	99	107	114	.	NA	NA	69	78
84	Korea, Dem.	NA	NA	NA	NA	111	12	NA	NA	100	100	NA	NA	99	100	100
85	Sri Lanka	85	69	93	84	191	32	100	90	108	105	100	100	94	63	74
86	Thailand	86	72	96	90	177	104	88	79	98	94	NA	NA	64*	32	28
87	Romania	96	91	NA	NA	291	174*	101	95	NA	NA	NA	NA	NA	79	80
88	USSR	98	97	NA	NA	686	319	100	100	106	104	NA	NA	98	NA	NA

Contd.

TABLE 7.4 *Contd.*

	1	2	3	4	5	6	7	8	9	10	11	12	13	14	15	
89	Panama	81	81	88	88	222	164	98	94	108	104	90	89	82	56	63
90	United Arab Emirates	24	7	58*	38*	321	107	NA	NA	104	104	93	89	88	55	68
91	Korea, Rep.	94	81	99	94	986	203	99	89	107	108	100	99	99	91.	83
92	Malaysia	71	48	87	70	438	142	108	83	102	102	NA	NA	99	59	57
93	Mauritius	77	59	NA	NA	264[X]	188[X]	103	93	104	105	94	95	98	53	53
94	Chile	90	88	94	93	338	183	111	107	101	99	NA	NA	85	72	78
95	Uruguay	93[X]	93[X]	97	96	595	173	111	111	110	108	NA	NA	86	68	76
96	Yugoslavia	92	76	97	88	195[X]	179[X]	113	108	95	94	NA	NA	98	82	79
97	Costa Rica	88	87	93	93	259	80	97	95	100	97	85	85	76	40	43
	Low U5MR countries (20 and under) Median	95	89	NA	NA	586	379	105	103	102	102	97	97	95	86	87
98	Jamaica	96	97	98	99	401	110	92	93	102	105	96	99	82	62	68
99	Kuwait	65	42	77	67	329	262	131	102	94	91	NA	77	90	86	79
100	Poland	98	97	NA	NA	294[X]	263[X]	110	107	101	101	99	99	93	78	82
101	Bulgaria	94	89	NA	NA	224[X]	189[X]	94	92	105	103	NA	NA	86	75	76
102	Trinidad and Tobago	95	89	NA	NA	458	297	NA	NA	99	100	87	88	84	80	85

Contd.

TABLE 7.4 *Contd.*

	1	2	3	4	5	6	7	8	9	10	11	12	13	14	15	
103	Hungary	998	98	NA	NA	590	404	103	100	97	97	94	96	92	69	70
104	Portugal	78	65	89	82	215	160[X]	132	129	131	123	NA	NA	NA	47	56
105	Cuba	86	87	95	93	337	203	109	109	107	101	97	94	91	85	96
106	Czechoslovakia	NA	NA	NA	NA	274[X]	395	93	93	95	96	NA	NA	93	27	49
107	New Zealand	NA	NA	NA	NA	917	372	110	106	107	106	100	100	NA	84	86
108	Israel	93	83	NA	NA	468	265	99	97	94	97	NA	NA	NA	79	87
109	Greece	93	76	98	89	415	175[X]	104	101	106	106	91	92	99	89	80
110	USA	99	99	NA	NA	2120	812	NA	NA	101	100	97	97	NA	98	99
111	Italy	95	93	98	96	790	419	112	109	NA	NA	97	98	100	76	76
112	Norway	NA	NA	NA	NA	795	350[X]	100	100	95	95	97	97	100	92	97
113	Australia	NA	NA	NA	NA	1273	484	103	103	106	105	97	98	NA	96	99
114	Spain	93	87	97	93	302	380	106	116	113	113	98	98	98	97	107
115	Belgium	99	99	NA	NA	466[X]	320[X]	111	108	99	100	82	83	78	99	100
116	Austria	NA	NA	NA	NA	627	487	106	104	102	101	NA	NA	95	78	81
117	United Kingdom	NA	NA	NA	NA	1146	435	92	92	105	106	97	97	NA	82	85

Contd.

TABLE 7.4 *Contd.*

	1	2	3	4	5	6	7	8	9	10	11	12	13	14	15
118	Singapore	92	55	NA	NA	307^{X}	360	121	113	110	107	100	100	95	70 71
119	France	99	98	NA	NA	895	399	144	143	114	113	100	100	94	89 96
120	Switzerland	NA	NA	NA	NA	401^{X}	408	118	118	NA	NA	NA	NA	99	NA NA
121	Denmark	NA	NA	NA	NA	452^{X}	526	103	103	98	99	NA	NA	100	106 107
122	Ireland	NA	NA	NA	NA	581	260	107	112	100	100	NA	NA	NA	91 101
123	Germany	NA	NA	NA	NA	895	378^{X}	NA	NA	103	102	NA	NA	99	92 88
124	Canada	NA	NA	NA	NA	960	586	108	105	106	104	97	97	NA	104 104
125	Netherlands	NA	NA	NA	NA	912	478	105	104	114	116	85	88	94	105 103
126	Hong Kong	90^{X}	64^{X}	NA	NA	634	247	93	79	106	105	NA	95	98^{X}	71 76
127	Finland	NA	NA	NA	NA	997	486	100	95	102	101	NA	NA	98	98 114
128	Sweden	NA	NA	NA	NA	875	395^{X}	95	96	100	100	NA	NA	100	90 92
129	Japan	99	99	NA	NA	863	589	103	102	102	102	100	100	100	95 97

TABLE 7.5: Health Data

		% of population with access to safe water 1988-90			% of population with access to health service 1985-90			Percentage fully immunized 1981/1989-90					ORT use rate 1987-89
								one-year-old children				pregnant women	
		Total	Urban	Rural	Total	Urban	rural	TB	DPT	Polio	Measles	Tetanus	
	1	2	3	4	5	6	7	8	9	10	11	12	13
	Very high U5MR countries (over 140) Median	42	66	34	46	88	38	24/85	14/55	8/54	23/55	5/44	27
1	Mozambique	24	44	17	39	100	30	46/59	56/46	32/46	32/58	NA/23	30
2	Afghanistan	21	39	17	29	80	17	8/30	3/25	3/25	6/20	3/ 3	11
3	Angola	35	75	19	30X	NA	NA	NA/47	NA/23	NA/23	NA/38	NA/26	12
4	Mali	41	53	38	15	NA	NA	19/82	NA/42	NA/42	NA/43	1/31	41
5	Sierra Leone	42	83	22	NA	NA	NA	35/98	15/83	13/83	28/75	10/77	55
6	Malawi	56X	97X	50X	80	NA	NA	86/97	66/81	68/79	65/80	NA/82	14
7	Guinea-Bissau	25	18	27	NA	NA	NA	NA/92	NA/38	NA/38	NA/42	NA/44	5
8	Guinea	32	55	24	47	100	40	4/53	NA/17	NA/17	15/18	5/10	63
9	Burkina Faso	69	44	72	49X	51X	48X	16/84	2/37	2/37	23/42	11/76	16
10	Niger	61	100	52	41	99	30	28/50	6/13	6/13	19/21	3/44	54
11	Ethiopia	19	70	11	46	NA	NA	10/57	6/44	7/44	7/37	NA/43	32
12	Chad	NA	NA	NA	30	NA	NA	NA/59	NA/20	NA/20	NA/32	NA/42	10
13	Somalia	37	50	29	27X	50X	15X	3/31	2/18	2/18	3/30	5/ 5	38
14	Mauritania	66	67	65	40	NA	NA	57/75	18/28	18/28	45/33	1/40	54
15	Liberia	55	93	22	39	50	30	87/62X	39/28X	26/28X	99/55X	60/20X	9

Contd

TABLE 7.5 *Contd.*

	1	2	3	4	5	6	7	8	9	10	11	12	13
16	Rwanda	50^{x}	79^{x}	48^{x}	27^{x}	40^{x}	25^{x}	51/92	17/84	15/83	42/83	5/87	24
17	Cambodia	3^{x}	10^{x}	2^{x}	53	80	50	NA/54	NA/40	NA/40	NA/34	NA/NA	6
18	Burundi	38	100	34	61	NA	NA	65/97	38/86	6/86	30/75	25/56	30
19	Bhutan	32	60	30	65	NA	NA	36/99	13/95	11/95	21/89	NA/63	40
20	Nepal	37	66	34	NA	NA	NA	32/97	16/79	1/78	2/67	4/28	14
21	Yemen	38^{x}	56^{x}	30^{x}	38	NA	NA	14/71	21/53	21/53	33/45	NA/ 8	7
22	Senegal	54^{x}	79^{x}	38^{x}	40	NA	NA	NA/92	NA/60	NA/66	NA/59	NA/45	27
23	Bangladesh	81	39	89	45	NA	NA	1/86	1/62	1/62	NA/54	1/74	26
24	Madagascar	22	62	10	56	NA	NA	25/67	40/46	NA/46	NA/33	NA/60	11
25	Sudan	46	56	43	51	90	40	3/73	1/62	1/62	1/57	1/14	36
26	Tanzania	56	75	46	76^{x}	99^{x}	72^{x}	78/93	58/85	49/82	76/83	36/42	37
27	Central African Rep.	12	13	11	45	NA	NA	NA/96	NA/82	NA/82	NA/82	NA/87	20
28	Namibia	NA	NA	NA	NA	NA	NA	NA/85	NA/53	NA/53	NA/41	NA/50	NA
29	Nigeria	NA	NA	54	66	85	62	23/96	24/57	24/57	55/54	11/58	35
30	Gabon	68	90	50	90^{x}	NA	NA	NA/96	NA/78	NA/78	NA/76	NA/86	10
31	Uganda	21	43	18	61^{x}	90^{x}	57^{x}	18/99	9/77	8/77	22/74	20/31	15
32	Bolivia	53	77	27	63	90	36	30/48	13/41	15/50	17/53	NA/20	60
33	Pakistan	56	80	45	55	99	35	11/98	3/96	3/96	2/97	1/87	42
34	Laos	29	47	25	67	NA	NA	4/26	7/18	7/26	7/13	2/10	30
35	Cameroon	44	50	39	41	44	39	8/76	5/56	5/54	16/56	NA/63	22

Contd

TABLE 7.5 *Contd.*

	1	2	3	4	5	6	7	8	9	10	11	12	13
36	Benin	54	66	46	18	NA	NA	NA/92	NA/67	NA/67	NA/70	NA/83	45
37	Togo	71	100	61	61	NA	NA	44/94	9/61	9/61	47/57	57/81	33
38	**India**	75	79	73	NA	NA	NA	12/97	31/92	7/93	NA/87	24/77	13
	High U5MR countries (71-140) Median	61	85	41	75	97	50	61/83	42/75	42/76	33/73	10/48	45
39	Ghana	57	93	39	60	92	45	67/81	22/57	25/56	23/60	11/33	21
40	Cote d'Ivoire	NA	NA	NA	30^{x}	61^{x}	11^{x}	70/63	42/48	34/48	28/42	25/63	16
41	Haiti	36	59	27	50	NA	NA	60/72	14/41	3/40	NA/31	NA/23	24
42	Zaire	33	59	17	26	40	17	34/65	18/32	18/31	23/31	NA/29	40
43	Lesotho	48	59	45	80	NA	NA	81/97	56/76	54/75	49/76	NA/NA	68
44	Zambia	60	76	43	75^{x}	100^{x}	50^{x}	72/97	44/79	77/78	21/76	NA/68	87
45	Peru	61	78	22	75^{x}	NA	NA	63/83	18/72	18/73	24/64	4/ 9	25
46	Libyan Arab Jamahiriya	94	100	80	NA	NA	NA	55/90	55/84	55/84	57/70	6/ 6	60
47	Morocco	61	100	25	70	100	50	NA/96	43/81	45/81	NA/79	NA/64	14
48	Congo	38	92	2	83	97	70	92/90	42/79	42/79	49/75	NA/60	13
49	Kenya	31^{x}	61^{x}	21^{x}	NA	NA	NA	NA/80	NA/74	NA/71	NA/59	NA/37	80
50	Algeria	71^{x}	85^{x}	55^{x}	88	100	80	59/99	33/89	30/89	17/83	NA/27	26
51	Indonesia	46	60	40	80	NA	NA	55/93	NA/87	NA/91	NA/86	10/41	39
52	Guatemala	61	91	41	34	47	25	29/62	42/66	42/74	8/68	1/48	24
53	Saudi Arabia	94	100	74	97	100	88	49/99	53/94	52/94	12/90	NA/62	45

Contd

TABLE 7.5 *Contd.*

	1	2	3	4	5	6	7	8	9	10	11	12	13
54	South Africa	NA	NA	NA	NA	NA	NA	NA/85	NA/67	NA/69	NA/63	NA/NA	NA
55	Myanmar	33	43	29	33	100	11	15/66	5/61	NA/61	NA/44	6/56	19
56	El Salvador	48	84	19	56	80	40	47/60	42/76	38/76	44/75	20/12	45
57	Zimbabwe	66	31	80	71	100	62	64/71	39/73	38/72	56/69	NA/60	77
58	Iraq	92	100	72	93	97	78	76/96	13/75	16/75	33/62	4/67	70
59	Egypt	73x	92x	56x	NA	NA	NA	71/88	82/87	84/87	65/86	10/63	83
60	Botswana	54x	84x	46x	89x	100x	85x	80/92	64/86	71/82	68/78	32/62	66
61	Turkey	78x	95x	63x	NA	NA	NA	42/NA	64/74	69/74	52/67	NA/15	NA
62	Mongolia	65	78	50	NA	NA	NA	53/92	99/84	99/85	NA/86	NA/NA	59
63	Honduras	73	89	60	66	80	56	46/71	38/84	37/87	38/90	11/51	66
64	Ecuador	58	75	37	75	92	40	82/88	26/68	19/67	31/61	4/8	70
65	Brazil	97	100	86	NA	NA	NA	62/78	47/81	99/93	73/78	NA/62	45
66	Papua New Guinea	34	93	23	96	NA	NA	64/89	50/69	32/69	NA/67	NA/70	46
67	Nicaragua	54	78	19	83	100	60	65/81	23/65	52/86	20/82	NA/25	38
68	Dominican Rep.	63	86	28	80	NA	NA	34/68	27/69	42/90	17/96	26/24	22
	Middle U5MR countries (21-70) Median	77	91	60	81	98	78	65/95	52/90	51/90	46/87	6/53	51
69	Philippines	81	93	72	NA	NA	NA	61/97	51/89	44/88	NA/85	37/47	25
70	Viet Nam	42	50	40	80	100	75	NA/90	NA/87	NA/87	NA/87	NA/18	65
71	Tunisia	68	100	31	90x	100x	80x	65/99	36/90	37/90	65/87	2/40	63
72	Paraguay	34	65	7	61	NA	NA	42/90	28/78	26/76	16/69	6/58	52
73	Syria	70	90	50	75x	92x	60x	36/92	14/90	14/90	14/87	3/84	67

Contd

TABLE 7.5 *Contd.*

	1	2	3	4	5	6	7	8	9	10	11	12	13
74	Iran, Islamic Rep. of	89	98	76	80	95	65	6/95	29/93	47/91	48/83	2/47	71
75	Lebanon	NA	NA	NA	NA	NA	NA	NA/NA	NA/82	NA/82	NA/39	NA/NA	10
76	Jordan	99	100	98	97	98	95	NA/NA	81/92	87/92	40/87	2/23	68
77	Colombia	88	88	87	60	NA	NA	57/95	20/87	22/93	26/82	6/40	40
78	Mexico	71	79	49	78	80	60	41/70	41/66	85/96	33/78	NA/42	72
79	Oman	47	87	42	91	100	90	49/93	9/96	9/96	6/96	27/97	19
80	Venezuela	90^{x}	93^{x}	65^{x}	NA	NA	NA	77/63	54/63	75/72	43/62	NA/NA	49
81	China	74	87	68	90	100	80	NA/99	NA/97	NA/98	NA/98	NA/NA	40
82	Albania	NA	NA	NA	NA	NA	NA	93/94	94/94	92/96	90/96	NA/NA	NA
83	Argentina	65	73	17	71	80	21	63/99	46/85	38/89	73/95	NA/NA	70
84	Korea, Dem.	NA	NA	NA	NA	NA	NA	52/99	52/98	51/99	31/99	NA/99	52
85	Sri Lanka	60	80	55	93^{x}	NA	NA	58/88	45/90	49/90	NA/83	48/60	58
86	Thailand	74	67	76	70	85	80	71/99	52/92	22/92	NA/80	27/79	40
87	Romania	NA	NA	NA	NA	NA	NA	NA/NA	NA/96	NA/95	NA/79	NA/NA	NA
88	USSR	NA	NA	NA	NA	NA	NA	NA/92	95/68	95/75	95/85	NA/NA	NA
89	Panama	84	100	66	80^{x}	95^{x}	64^{x}	77/97	49/86	50/86	53/99	NA/27	29
90	United Arab Emirates	NA	NA	NA	90^{x}	NA	NA	18/96	45/85	45/85	42/75	NA/NA	24
91	Korea, Rep.	79	91	49	93	97	86	42/72	61/74	62/74	5/95	NA/NA	NA
92	Malaysia	79	96	66	NA	NA	NA	91/99	54/91	61/90	NA/90	20/71	20
93	Mauritius	95	100	92	100	100	100	87/94	82/90	82/90	NA/84	1/94	7
94	Chile	89	100	21	97	NA	NA	100/97	97/99	96/99	93/98	NA/NA	1
95	Uruguay	73	85	5	82	NA	NA	76/99	57/88	58/88	95/82	18/13	86
96	Yugoslavia	NA	NA	NA	NA	NA	NA	99/89^{x}	90/91^{x}	95/92^{x}	95/93^{x}	NA/NA	NA
97	Costa Rica	92	100	84	80^{x}	100^{x}	63^{x}	81/92	83/95	85/95	71/90	NA/90	78

Contd

TABLE 7.5 *Contd.*

	1	2	3	4	5	6	7	8	9	10	11	12	13
	Low U5MR countries (20 and under) Median	NA	NA	NA	NA	NA	NA	95/91	85/90	90/94	70/85	NA/NA	NA
98	Jamaica	71	95	46	90	NA	NA	NA/98	39/86	37/87	NA/74	50/NA	15
99	Kuwait	100	100	NA	100	NA	NA	NA/NA	54/94	76/94	66/98	30/22	3
100	Poland	NA	NA	NA	NA	NA	NA	95/95	95/96	95/96	65/95	NA/NA	NA
101	Bulgaria	NA	NA	NA	NA	NA	NA	97/99X	97/99X	98/99X	98/99X	98/NA	NA
102	Trinidad and Tobago	98X	100X	95X	99	NA	NA	NA/NA	52/82	55/87	NA/70	NA/NA	60
103	Hungary	NA	NA	NA	NA	NA	NA	99/99	99/99	98/99	99/99	NA/NA	NA
104	Portugal	NA	NA	NA	NA	NA	NA	74/87	75/92	16/92	70/100	NA/NA	NA
105	Cuba	NA	NA	NA	NA	NA	NA	97/98	67/92	82/94	49/94	NA/88	75
106	Czechoslovakia	NA	NA	NA	NA	NA	NA	95/99	95/99	95/99	95/91	NA/NA	NA
107	New Zealand	97	100	82	NA	NA	NA	NA/10X	72/69X	NA/75X	NA/67X	NA/NA	NA
108	Israel	NA	NA	NA	NA	NA	NA	70/NA	84/87X	91/93X	69/86X	NA/NA	NA
109	Greece	NA	NA	NA	NA	NA	NA	95/NA	95/83X	95/98X	NA/82X	NA/NA	NA
110	USA	NA	NA	NA	NA	NA	NA	NA/NA	NA/97X	NA/97X	96/98X	NA/NA	NA
111	Italy	NA	NA	NA	NA	NA	NA	NA/NA	NA/85X	NA/85	NA/50	NA/NA	NA
112	Norway	NA	NA	NA	NA	NA	NA	NA/NA	NA/87	NA/84	NA/84	NA/NA	NA

Contd

TABLE 7.5 *Contd.*

	1	2	3	4	5	6	7	8	9	10	11	12	13
113	Australia	NA	NA	NA	NA	NA	NA	NA/NA	NA/93	NA/95	NA/85	NA/NA	NA
114	Spain	NA	NA	NA	NA	NA	NA	NA/NA	NA/73^x	NA/73^x	NA/84^x	NA/NA	NA
115	Belgium	NA	NA	NA	NA	NA	NA	NA/NA	95/80	99/95	50/75	NA/NA	NA
116	Austria	NA	NA	NA	NA	NA	NA	90/90^x	90/90^x	90/90^x	90/60^x	NA/NA	NA
117	United Kingdom	NA	NA	NA	NA	NA	NA	NA/75	44/75	71/87	52/80	NA/NA	NA
118	Singapore	100	100	NA	100	100	NA	83/99	87/85	88/85	57/87	NA/NA	NA
119	France	NA	NA	NA	NA	NA	NA	80/80	79/95	80/95	NA/60	NA/NA	NA
120	Switzerland	NA	NA	NA	NA	NA	NA	NA/NA	NA/90	NA/98	NA/90	NA/NA	NA
121	Denmark	NA	NA	NA	NA	NA	NA	95/NA	85/99	97/100	NA/80	NA/NA	NA
122	Ireland	NA	NA	NA	NA	NA	NA	NA/80	36/77	76/72	NA/68	NA/NA	NA
123	Germany	NA	NA	NA	NA	NA	NA	54/84	58/95	83/95	50/60	NA/NA	NA
124	Canada	NA	NA	NA	NA	NA	NA	NA/NA	NA/85^x	NA/85^x	NA/85^x	NA/NA	NA
125	Netherlands	NA	NA	NA	NA	NA	NA	NA/NA	97/94	97/94	93/93	NA/NA	NA
126	Hong Kong	100	100	96	99^x	NA	NA	99/99	84/88	94/96	NA/41	NA/NA	NA
127	Finland	NA	NA	NA	NA	NA	NA	90/91	92/90	90/90	70/95	NA/NA	NA
128	Sweden	NA	NA	NA	NA	NA	NA	NA/14^x	99/99^x	99/98^x	56/94^x	NA/NA	NA
129	Japan	NA	NA	NA	NA	NA	NA	85/85	NA/87	NA/93	NA/77	NA/NA	NA

TABLE 7.6: Nutrition Data

	% of infants with low birth-weight 1980-88	% of mothers breast-feeding 1980-91			% of children (1980-91) suffering from:				Average index of food production per capita (1979-81= 100) 1990	Daily per capita calorie supply as % of requirements 1988	% of household income (1980-85) spent on:	
		3 months	6 months	12 months	underweight (0-4 years) moderate & severe	severe	wasting (12-23 months) moderate & severe	stunting (24-59 months) moderate &severe			all food	cereals
1	2	3	4	5	6	7	8	9	10	11	12	13
Very high U5MR countries (over 140) Median	17	93	90	82	33	6	14	43	90	92	54	22
1 Mozambique	20*	99*	96*	NA	NA	NA	NA	NA	85	70	NA	NA
2 Afghanistan	20	NA	94[X]	61[X]	NA	NA	NA	NA	NA	94[X]	NA	NA
3 Angola	17	NA	NA	NA	NA	NA	NA	NA	77	73	NA	NA
4 Mali	17*	91	95	82	31[X]	9[X]	16	34[X]	96	93	57	22
5 Sierra Leone	17*	99*	98*	92*	23[X]	2[X]	14[X]	NA	88	79	56	22
6 Malawi	20*	NA	NA	96*	24[X]	NA	8	61	80	87	55	28
7 Guinea-Bissau	13	100	100	98	23[X]	NA	NA	NA	101	92	NA	NA
8 Guinea	25*	100*	90*	85*	NA	NA	NA	NA	87	88	NA	NA
9 Burkina Faso	21[X]	98*	98*	97*	NA	NA	NA	NA	108	87	NA	NA
10 Niger	15	65	30	15	49	NA	23[X]	38[X]	73	100	NA	NA
11 Ethiopia	8	NA	97*	95*	38[X]	NA	19[X]	43[X]	85	71	50	24
12 Chad	NA	NA	NA	NA	NA	NA	NA	NA	94	78	NA	NA
13 Somalia	NA	92*	78*	54*	NA	NA	NA	NA	96	75	NA	NA
14 Mauritania	11	91	86	67	31	NA	24[X]	37[X]	85	109	NA	NA
15 Liberia	NA	87	75	61	NA	NA	NA	NA	72	98	NA	NA

Contd.

TABLE 7.6 *Contd.*

	1	2	3	4	5	6	7	8	9	10	11	12	13
16	Rwanda	NA	97*	97*	74*	33^{x}	4^{x}	1^{x}	34^{x}	73	77	30	11
17	Cambodia	NA	100*	93*	72*	NA	NA	NA	NA	160	98^{x}	NA	NA
18	Burundi	9^{x}	NA	95*	90*	38^{x}	10^{x}	10	60^{x}	89'	97	NA	NA
19	Bhutan	NA	NA	NA	NA	38^{x}	NA	4^{x}	56^{x}	86	NA	NA	NA
20	Nepal	NA	92^{x}	92^{x}	82^{x}	NA	NA	NA	NA	109	94	57	39
21	Yemen	NA	74^{x}	66^{x}	34^{x}	53^{x}	NA	15^{x}	61^{x}	79	92	NA	NA
22	Senegal	11	95	91	86	22^{x}	6^{x}	8	28^{x}	100	84	50	15
23	Bangladesh	47	91^{x}	86^{x}	82^{x}	66^{x}	27^{x}	28	66	99	83	59	36
24	Madagascar	10*	95	95	85	33^{x}	8^{x}	17	56^{x}	90	93	59	26
25	Sudan	15*	93	90	79	NA	NA	13^{x}	32^{x}	67	85	60	NA
26	Tanzania	14	100*	90*	70*	48*	6*	NA	NA	85	93	64	32
27	Central African Rep.	15*	NA	NA	NA	NA	NA	NA	NA	95	88	NA	NA
28	Namibia	NA	98^{x}	88^{x}	73^{x}	29^{x}	6^{x}	9^{x}	30^{x}	95	83	NA	NA
29	Nigeria	20*	98	97	92	36	12	16	60	113	86	52	18
30	Gabon	NA	NA	NA	NA	NA	NA	NA	NA	80	102	NA	NA
31	Uganda	NA	92	88	85	23	5	4	25^{x}	90	86	NA	NA
32	Bolivia	12*	92	84	67	13^{x}	3^{x}	2	51^{x}	105	87	33	NA
33	Pakistan	25*	87*	74*	70*	52^{x}	10^{x}	17^{x}	42^{x}	105	95	54	17
34	Laos	39	NA	99^{y}	93^{y}	37	NA	20	44	130	119	NA	NA
35	Cameroon	13^{x}	92^{x}	90^{x}	77^{x}	17^{x}	NA	2^{x}	43^{x}	88	93	24	8

Contd.

TABLE 7.6 *Contd.*

	1	2	3	4	5	6	7	8	9	10	11	12	13
36	Benin	8*	90	90	76	NA	NA	NA	NA	115	93	37	12
37	Togo	20*	95	87	84	24	6	10	37^{x}	96	93	NA	NA
38	India	30	NA	NA	NA	61^{x}	9^{x}	NA	NA	118	95	52	18
	High U5MR countries (71-140) Median	14	90	82	76	16	2	4	34	94	105	40	12
39	Ghana	17*	90	92	87	27	6	15	39	102	96	66	NA
40	Cote d'Ivoire	14^{x}	87	84	78	12	1	17	20	92	102	40	14
41	Haiti	17^{x}	92*	80*	NA	37^{x}	3^{x}	17^{x}	51^{x}	89	85	NA	NA
42	Zaire	13	100*	100*	86*	NA	NA	NA	NA	95	92	55	15
43	Lesotho	11	93^{x}	89^{x}	76^{x}	16	2	7	23	76	101	NA	NA
44	Zambia	NA	NA	NA	93*	25^{x}	5^{x}	10^{x}	59^{x}	86	88	37	8
45	Peru	9*	85	76	58	13^{x}	2^{x}	3	43	90	97	35	8
46	Libyan Arab Jamahiriya	NA	NA	NA	NA	NA	NA	NA	NA	102	143	NA	NA
47	Morocco	NA	87	77	59	16^{x}	4^{x}	6	34^{x}	124	117	40	12
48	Congo	16*	100*	98	90*	24	NA	13	33	92	113	42	19
49	Kenya	15	94	92	82	NA	NA	10^{x}	41^{x}	108	85	39	16
50	Algeria	9*	NA	NA	NA	10^{x}	NA	4^{x}	13^{x}	94	114	NA	NA
51	Indonesia	14	95	87	79	51^{x}	1^{x}	NA	NA	132	124	61	18
52	Guatemala	14*	95	79	80	34^{x}	8^{x}	3	68^{x}	95	107	36	10
53	Saudi Arabia	6	91*	52*	NA	NA	NA	NA	NA	252	117	NA	NA

Contd.

TABLE 7.6 *Contd.*

	1	2	3	4	5	6	7	8	9	10	11	12	13
54	South Africa	12	NA	NA	NA	NA	NA	NA	NA	85	124	26	NA
55	Myanmar	16*	90	90	90	38x	NA	17	75x	96	119	NA	NA
56	El Salvador	15*	85	77	55	15	NA	3	36	94	105	33	12
57	Zimbabwe	NA	95	92	88	12x	2x	2	31x	92	93	40	9
58	Iraq	9*	76	45	19	NA	NA	NA	NA	92	123	NA	NA
59	Egypt	5	90	83	68	13x	3x	2	32x	123	128	50	10
60	Botswana	8*	97	90	73	15	NA	NA	51*	75	98	35	13
61	Turkey	7*	98*	72*	63*	NA	NA	NA	NA	98	122	40	8
62	Mongolia	10	70*	NA	NA	NA	NA	NA	NA	88	101	NA	NA
63	Honduras	20*	73*	55*	NA	21	4	2x	34x	89	96	39	NA
64	Ecuador	11*	84	73	57	17	0	4	39	107	102	30	NA
65	Brazil	8*	66x	37x	34x	7	1	3	16	105	113	35	9
66	Papua New Guinea	25x	NA	NA	NA	35	NA	NA	NA	105	98	NA	NA
67	Nicaragua	15	NA	NA	NA	11	1	0	22	62	105	NA	NA
68	Dominican Rep.	16*	70	47	25	13x	2x	3	26x	91	104	46	13
	Middle U5MR countries (21-70) Median	8	81	57	38	19	3	7	23	99	120	35	7
69	Philippines	18*	NA	74*	NA	34	5	14	45	88	100	51	20
70	Viet Nam	17*	96*	93*	49*	42	14	12x	49x	123	103	NA	NA
71	Tunisia	8*	92	76	58	10x	2x	4	23x	102	124	37	7
72	Paraguay	7	85	69	45	4	1	0	17	120	122	30	6
73	Syria	11*	81*	72*	NA	NA	NA	NA	NA	82	128	NA	NA
74	Iran, Islamic Rep. of	5	91*	73*	51*	43*	NA	23x	55x	97	129	37	10

Contd.

TABLE 7.6 *Contd.*

	1	2	3	4	5	6	7	8	9	10	11	12	13
75	Lebanon	10	50*	40*	15*	NA	NA	NA	NA	NA	125	NA	NA
76	Jordan	5^{X}	93	80	61	NA	NA	NA	NA	108	118	35	NA
77	Colombia	8*	80	56	36	10	2	5	18	111	110	29	NA
78	Mexico	12*	71	50	33	14	NA	6^{X}	22^{X}	97	135	35	NA
79	Oman	7*	75*	55*	20*	NA	NA	NA	NA	NA	NA	NA	NA
80	Venezuela	9	50^{X}	40^{X}	30^{X}	6^{X}	NA	4^{X}	7^{X}	92	103	38	NA
81	China	9*	65*	55*	NA	21^{X}	3^{X}	8^{X}	41^{X}	138	112	61	NA
82	Albania	7	NA	NA	NA	NA	NA	NA	NA	93	114^{X}	NA	NA
83	Argentina	NA	66	36	14	NA	NA	NA	NA	92	133	35	4
84	Korea, Dem.	NA	NA	NA	NA	NA	NA	NA	NA	107	135	NA	NA
85	Sri Lanka	25*	94	80	72	38^{X}	9^{X}	19	34^{X}	89	104	43	18
86	Thailand	12	89	69	67	26^{X}	4^{X}	10	28^{X}	101	103	30	7
87	Romania	6	NA	NA	NA	NA	NA	NA	NA	91	127	NA	NA
88	USSR	6	NA	NA	NA	NA	NA	NA	NA	112	133^{X}	NA	NA
89	Panama	8	62	53	55	16	NA	7	24	90	107	38	7
90	United Arab Emirates	6*	NA	NA	NA	NA	NA	NA	NA	NA	NA	NA	NA
91	Korea, Rep.	9	58^{X}	40^{X}	27^{X}	NA	NA	NA	NA	89	122	35	14
92	Malaysia	10	88	NA	NA	NA	NA	NA	NA	159	120	30	NA
93	Mauritius	9*	79	55	40	24	NA	16^{X}	22^{X}	105	118	24	7
94	Chile	7	81*	57*	20*	3^{X}	NA	1	10^{X}	118	106	29	7
95	Uruguay	8*	50*	43*	NA	7^{X}	2^{X}	NA	16^{X}	113	104	31	7
96	Yugoslavia	7	NA	NA	NA	NA	NA	NA	NA	88	138	27	NA
97	Costa Rica	6*	85*	60*	24*	6	NA	3	8	92	124	33	8

Contd.

TABLE 7.6 *Contd.*

	1	2	3	4	5	6	7	8	9	10	11	12	13
	Low U5MR countries (20 and under) Median	6	47	25	NA	NA	NA	NA	NA	103	132	16	2
98	Jamaica	8*	95	82	43	7	1	6	7	89	115	39	NA
99	Kuwait	5*	47[x]	32[x]	12[x]	6	NA	2	14	NA	NA	NA	NA
100	Poland	8	32[x]	25[x]	NA	NA	NA	NA	NA	108	132	29	NA
101	Bulgaria	6	NA	NA	NA	NA	NA	NA	NA	95	145	NA	NA
102	Trinidad and Tobago	NA	84	49	27	7[x]	0[x]	5	4[x]	69	122	NA	NA
103	Hungary	10	86	NA	NA	NA	NA	NA	NA	107	137	25	NA
104	Portugal	5	29	12	• 7	NA	NA	NA	NA	121	138	34	NA
105	Cuba	8	NA	NA	NA	NA	NA	NA	NA	98	135	NA	NA
106	Czechoslovakia	6	NA	NA	NA	NA	NA	NA	NA	121	144	NA	NA
107	New Zealand	5	NA	NA	NA	NA	NA	NA	NA	99	131	12	2
108	Israel	7	NA	NA	NA	NA	NA	NA	NA	99	122	22	NA
109	Greece	6	NA	NA	NA	NA	NA	NA	NA	95	148	30	NA
110	USA	7	33	24	NA	NA	NA	NA	NA	96	139	13	2
111	Italy	NA	NA	NA	NA	NA	NA	NA	NA	94	142	19	2
112	Norway	4	NA	NA	NA	NA	NA	NA	NA	100	121	15	2

Contd.

TABLE 7.6 *Contd.*

	1	2	3	4	5	6	7	8	9	10	11	12	13
113	Australia	6^{x}	56	40	10	NA	NA	NA	NA	95	125	13	2
114	Spain	1	NA	NA	NA	NA	NA	NA	NA	114	144	24	3
115	Belgium	5	NA	NA	NA	NA	NA	NA	NA	119	146^{x}	15	2
116	Austria	6	41	NA	NA	NA	NA	NA	NA	105	132	16	2
117	United Kingdom	7	26	22	NA	NA	NA	NA	NA	109	129	12	2
118	Singapore	6	NA	NA	NA	14^{x}	NA	NA	NA	94	126	19	NA
119	France	5	NA	NA	NA	NA	NA	NA	NA	99	131	16	2
120	Switzerland	5^{x}	NA	NA	NA	NA	NA	NA	NA	103	132	17	NA
121	Denmark	6	NA	NA	NA	NA	NA	NA	NA	138	133	13	2
122	Ireland	4	NA	NA	NA	NA	NA	NA	NA	114	147	22	4
123	Germany	6	NA	NA	NA	NA	NA	NA	NA	114	NA	NA	NA
124	Canada	6	53	30	NA	NA	NA	NA	NA	115	130	11	2
125	Netherlands	NA	33^{x}	NA	NA	NA	NA	NA	NA	119	125	13	2
126	Hong Kong	5	NA	NA	NA	NA	NA	NA	NA	67	127	12	1
127	Finland	4	NA	7^{x}	NA	NA	NA	NA	NA	115	117	16	3
128	Sweden	4	47	23	NA	NA	NA	NA	NA	104	112	13	2
129	Japan	5	NA	NA	NA	NA	NA	NA	NA	95	122	16	4

TABLE 7.7: Women Data

		Life expectancy females as a percentage of males 1990	Adult literacy rate females as a percentage of males 1990	Enrolment ratios females as a percentage of males 1986-89		Contraceptive prevalence (%) 1980-90	Pregnant women immunized against Tetanus 1989-90	% of births attended by trained health personnel 1983-90	Maternal mortality rate 1980-90
				Primary school	Secondary school				
	1	2	3	4	5	6	7	8	9
	Very high U5MR countries (over 140) Median	106.3	48	65	50	5	44	28	570
1	Mozambique	106.5	47	78	57	4	25	28	300
2	Afghanistan	102.4	32	52	70	2^{x}	3	9^{x}	640^{x}
3	Angola	106.8	52	84	53	1^{x}	26	15	NA
4	Mail	109.3	59	59	44	3	31	27	2000
5	Sierra Leone	110.0	35	62	48	4*	77	25	450
6	Malawi	104.3	NA	82	60	7	82	45	170
7	Guinea-Bissau	107.3	48	54	33		44	NA	700^{x}
8	Guinea	102.3	37	45	31	1^{x}	10	25	800*
9	Burkina Faso	106.4	32	59	50	1	76	30	810
10	Niger	106.8	43	55	38	1^{x}	44	47	700
11	Ethiopia	106.8	NA	64	67	2	43	14	NA
12	Chad	106.7	43	40	20	1^{x}	42	24^{x}	960*
13	Somalia	109.1	33^{x}	50	NA	NA	5	2	1100
14	Mauritania	108.9	45	70	43	1	40	20	NA
15	Liberia	105.7	58	56	NA	6	20^{x}	87	NA

Contd.

TABLE 7.7 *Contd.*

	1	2	3	4	5	6	7	8	9
16	Rwanda	106.3	58	96	71	10	87	22	210^x
17	Cambodia	106.3	46	NA	44	NA	NA	47*	500
18	Burundi	106.4	66	74	50	7	56.	19	NA
19	Bhutan	96.0	49	65	29	NA	63	7	1310
20	Nepal	98.1	34	51	49	14	28	6	830
21	Yemen	102.9	45^y	30	17	NA	8	12	NA
22	Senegal	104.3	48	70	53	5	45	41	600
23	Bangladesh	100.0	47	84	46	25	74	5	600
24	Madagascar	105.7	83	96	83	NA	60	62	570
25	Sudan	104.0	28	71^x	74	9	14	60	550
26	Tanzania	107.7	95^y	99	60	1^x	42	60	340^x
27	Central African Rep.	110.6	48	61	35	NA	87	66	600
28	Namibia	105.4	NA	NA	NA	NA	50	NA	370^y
29	Nigeria	106.0	65	93	64	6	58	40^x	800
30	Gabon	105.9	66	NA	NA	NA	86	80	190
31	Uganda	108.0	56	83	56	5	31	38	300
32	Bolivia	109.6	84	88	88	30	20	42	600
33	Pakistan	100.0	45	55	42	8	87	40*	500
34	Laos	106.3	NA	80	96	NA	10	NA	NA
35	Cameroon	105.8	65	86	66	2^x	63	10	430

Contd.

TABLE 7.7 *Contd.*

1	2	3	4	5	6	7	8	9
36 Benin	108.9	50	52	39	9	83	45	160^{x}
37 Togo	107.7	55	63	33	12	81	15*	420*
38 India	**100.0**	**55**	**73**	**58**	**34**	**77**	**33**	**460**
High U5MR countries (71-140) Median	106.3	75	94	86	33	48	50	200
39 Ghana	107.5	73	81	61	13	33	55*	1000
40 Cote d'Ivoire	105.8	60	71	46	3	63	20	NA
41 Haiti	105.6	80	93	85	7	23	40	340*
42 Zaire	107.8	73	76	44	1^{x}	29	NA	800*
43 Lesotho	117.0	NA	122	150	5^{x}	NA	40	NA
44 Zambia	105.7	80	90	NA	1^{x}	68	39*	150
45 Peru	106.6	86	96	90	46	9	78*	300
46 Libyan Arab Jamahiriya	106.7	67	NA	NA	NA	6	76	80^{x}
47 Morocco	106.7	62	66	70	36	64	29^{x}	300^{x}
48 Congo	109.8	63	NA	38*	NA	60	NA	900*
49 Kenya	106.9	74	96	70	27	37	28	170^{x}
50 Algeria	103.1	66	83	87	7^{x}	27	15	140^{x}
51 Indonesia	105.0	74	97	81	48	441	49	450
52 Guatemala	108.2	75	85	90	23	48	34	200*
53 Saudi Arabia	104.8	66	83	67	NA	62	88*	NA

Contd.

TABLE 7.7 *Contd.*

1		2	3	4	5	6	7	8	9
54	South Africa	110.2	NA	NA	NA	48	NA	NA	83x
55	Myanmar	105.0	81	94	92	5	56	57	460
56	El Salvador	111.5	92	103	115	47	12	50	NA
57	Zimbabwe	105.2	81	97	86	43	60	60	NA
58	Iraq	103.1	70	84	62	NA	67	50*	120
59	Egypt	105.1	54	79	73	38	63	47	320
60	Botswana	110.5	77	105	116	33	62	78*	200*
61	Turkey	104.7	79	93	60	77*	15	77*	150
62	Mongolia	104.9	NA	103	109	NA	NA	99	140*
63	Honduras	106.3	93	104	129	35	51	66	220
64	Ecuador	106.3	95	98	104	44	8	56*	170*
65	Brazil	107.9	96	NA	131	66	62	95	200
66	Papua New Guinea	103.7	58	85	63	4	70	20	900
67	Nicaragua	104.8	NA	111	200	27	25	41x	NA
68	Dominican Rep.	106.2	96	104	NA	50	24	90	NA
Middle U5MR countries (21-70) Median		107.1	94	98	98	54	53	88	80
69	Philippines	106.5	100	102	108	45	47	57	100
70	Viet Nam	108.3	91	88	93	20	18	95*	120
71	Tunisia	103.0	76	87	83	50	40	68	50*
72	Paraguay	106.2	96	96	97	45	58	30	300
73	Syria	106.3	65	90	68	20x	84	61	140

Contd.

TABLE 7.7 *Contd.*

1	2	3	4	5	6	7	8	9
74 Iran, Islamic Rep. of	101.5	66	89	77	23[x]	47	70*	120
75 Lebanon	106.3	83	90	98	NA	NA	NA	NA
76 Jordan	106.2	79	101	98	26	23	83	48[x]
77 Colombia	109.1	98	103	102	65	40	71	200
78 Mexico	110.6	94	97	98	53	42	94	110*
79 Oman	106.3	NA	90	74	NA	97	60	NA
80 Venezuela	109.0	103	NA	123	49[x]	NA	69	NA
81 China	104.3	74	89	74	74	NA	94	95[x]
82 Albania	107.1	NA	99	89	NA	NA	99	NA
83 Argentina	108.8	99	107	113	74	NA	NA	140
84 Korea, Dem.	109.0	NA	100	100	NA	99	100	41
85 Sri Lanka	105.8	90	97	117	62	60	94	80
86 Thailand	106.3	94	96	88	66	79	71	NA
87 Romania	108.8	NA	NA	101	58[x]	NA	100[x]	150
88 USSR	113.6	NA	98	NA	NA	NA	NA	21
89 Panama	107.1	100	96	113	58	27	89	60
90 United Arab Emirates	107.2	66*	100	124	NA	NA	99	NA
91 Korea, Rep.	109.0	95	101	91	77*	NA	89	26
92 Malaysia	105.9	80	100	97	51	71	82	59
93 Mauritius	107.5	NA	101	100	75	94	85	99

Contd.

TABLE 7.7 *Contd.*

1	2	3	4	5	6	7	8	9
94 Chile	110.3	99	98	108	43^{x}	NA	98	67
95 Uruguay	110.1	99	98	112	NA	13	97^{x}	36
96 Yugoslavia	108.6	91	99	96	55^{x}	NA	86^{x}	8
97 Costa Rica	105.5	100	97	108	70	90	97	36
Low U5MR countries (20 and under) Median	108.4	NA	100	103	73	NA	99	8
98 Jamaica	105.6	101	103	110	52	NA	90	120
99 Kuwait	105.6	87	97	92	NA	22	99	6
100 Poland	111.8	NA	100	105	75^{x}	NA	100^{x}	11
101 Bulgaria	108.6	NA	98	101	76^{x}	NA	100	9
102 Trinidad and Tobago	107.2	NA	101	106	53	NA	98	110
103 Hungary	111.9	NA	100	101	73	NA	99^{x}	15
104 Portugal	108.5	92	94	119	66^{x}	NA	87^{x}	10
105 Cuba	104.1	98	94	113	60	88	99	39
106 Czechoslovakia	111.8	NA	101	181	95^{x}	NA	100	10
107 New Zealand	108.3	NA	99	102	70^{x}	NA	99	13
108 Israel	105.4	NA	103	110	NA	NA	99	3
109 Greece	105.4	91	100	90	NA	NA	97^{x}	5
110 USA	109.7	NA	99	101	68	NA	99	8
111 Italy	108.2	98	NA	100	78^{x}	NA	NA	4
112 Norway	108.1	NA	100	105	71^{x}	NA	NA	3

Contd.

TABLE 7.7 *Contd.*

	1	2	3	4	5	6	7	8	9
113	Australia	109.6	NA	99	103	67[X]	NA	99[X]	3
114	Spain	108.1	96	100	110	59	NA	96	5
115	Belgium	109.7	NA	101	101	81[X]	NA	100	3
116	Austria	109.9	NA	99	104	71[X]	NA	NA	8
117	United Kingdom	108.2	NA	101	104	83	NA	100[X]	8
118	Singapore	108.5	NA	97	101	74	NA	100*	10
119	France	111.1	NA	99	108	79[X]	NA	99[X]	9
120	Switzerland	109.5	NA	NA	NA	71[X]	NA	99[X]	5
121	Denmark	108.2	NA	101	101	NA	NA	100[X]	3
122	Ireland	106.9	NA	100	111	NA	NA	NA	2
123	Germany	109.4	NA	99	96	NA	NA	99[X]	NA
124	Canada	109.5	NA	98	100	73	NA	99	5
125	Netherlands	109.5	NA	102	98	76	NA	100[X]	10
126	Hong Kong	106.7	NA	99	107	72	NA	100*	6*
127	Finland	109.7	NA	99	116	80[X]	NA	100[X]	11
128	Sweden	106.7	NA	100	102	78	NA	100[X]	5
129	Japan	106.6	NA	100	102	64	NA	100	11

TABLE 7.8: Basic Data on Less Populous Countries

		Under 5 mortality rate		Infant mortality rate		Total popul-tion (thous-ands)	Annual no. of births (thous-ands)	Annual no. of under 5 deaths (thous-ands)	GNP per capita (US $)	Life expect-ancy at birth (years)	Total adult literacy rate	% of age group enrolled in primary school Total	% of children immunized against measles
		1960	1990	1960	1990	1990	1990	1990	1989	1990	1985-90	1986-89	1989-90
	1	2	3	4	5	6	7	8	9	10	11	12	13
1	Gambia	375	238	213	138	861	39.7	9.0	240	44	27	61	73
2	Equatorial Guinea	316	206	188	122	352	15.5	3.0	330	47	50	108X	88
3	Swaziland	226	167	152	113	789	37.2	6.0	900	57	55X	105	85
4	Djibouti	NA	164	186	117	409	18.9	3.0	1210X	48	12*	46	85
5	Comoros	279	151	165	94	551	26.2	4.0	460	55	48X	80	87
6	Vanuatu	NA	91	NA	69	159	6.0	1.0	860	65	53X	84y	66
7	Kiribati	NA	88	NA	58	66	2.0	0.2	700	56	96	100y	63
8	Maldives	NA	85	NA	61	215	8.4	NA	420	62	95*	87*	89
9	Guyana	126	71	100	52	796	20.4	1.0	340	64	92X	79	73
10	Samoa	NA	59	NA	46	169	5.0	0.3	700	66	98*	91y	82
11	Cape Verde	164	56	110	41	370	15.3	1.0	780	67	37X	110	79
12	Sao Tome and Principe	NA	55	NA	43	121	4.0	0.2	340	66	57X	NA	57
13	St. Christopher-Nevis	NA	44	NA	37	44	1.0	0.0	2860X	70	90*	100	99
14	Tuvalu	NA	NA	NA	34y	10	NA	NA	650X	NA	90*	NA	79
15	Suriname	95	38	70	31	422	11.2	0.4	1900	70	95	125	65

Contd.

TABLE 7.8 *Contd.*

	1	2	3	4	5	6	7	8	9	10	11	12	13
16	Grenada	NA	38	NA	31	85	2.5	0.1	1900	70	96^x	88^x	85
17	Solomon Islands	NA	NA	NA	30	321	12.2	NA	580	70	15*	65^y	70
18	Montserrat	NA	36	NA	30	13	0.0	0.0	3330^x	71	97^x	100^y	99
19	Qatar	239	36	145	29	368	10.8	0.4	15500	69	76	117	79
20	British Virgin Islands	NA	NA	NA	27	13	0.2	NA	2100^x	69^y	98^x	NA	99
21	Fiji	97	31	71	26	765	19.6	1.0	1650	65	79^x	129	84
22	Turks and Caicos Islands	NA	NA	NA	25	10	0.2	NA	780^x	NA	98^x	NA	81
23	Bahamas	NA	NA	NA	25	254	5.1	NA	11320	72	70^x	NA	87
24	Belize	NA	29	NA	23*	188	7.0	0.2	1720	68	93*	90	81
25	Fed. States of Micronesia	NA	28	NA	23	99	3.5	0.1	NA	74	63^x	101^y	12
26	St. Vincent & the Grenadines	NA	27	NA	23	116	3.0	0.1	1200^x	70	82*	95^x	96
27	Palau	NA	NA	NA	23*	18	0.6*	NA	790^y	74*	75	98^y	98
28	Marshall Islands	NA	NA	NA	23*	40	1.3*	NA	NA	74*	76^x	107*	25^x
29	Tonga	NA	26	NA	22	95	3.0	0.1	910	67	78*	100^y	63
30	Antigua	NA	24	NA	20	77	1.0	0.0	3880^x	74	95*	100	89

Contd.

TABLE 7.8 *Contd.*

	1	2	3	4	5	6	7	8	9	10	11	12	13
31	Saint Lucia	NA	23	NA	19	151	4.0	0.1	1810	71	82X	95y	82
32	Seychelles	NA	21	NA	18	69	2.0	0.0	3010	70	88*	102y	89
33	Dominica	NA	20	NA	17	83	2.0	0.0	1670X	75	94X	100	88
34	Cook Islands	NA	NA	NA	15	18	0.4	NA	1550X	NA	75*	100	100
35	Bahrain	208	17	130	14	516	13.7	0.2	6360X	71	77	110	86
36	Malta	42	14	37	11	353	4.9	0.1	5830	73	88	108	86
37	Cyprus	36	13	30	11	701	12.4	0.2	7040	76	89X	104	76
38	Barbados	90	12	74	11	255	4.1	0.1	6350	75	98*	110X	87
39	Brunei Darussalam	NA	NA	NA	9	266	6.4	NA	20760X	74	78X	NA	99X
40	Luxembourg	41	8	33	7	373	4.4	0.1	24980	75	NA	NA	71X
41	Iceland	22	5	17	4	254	4.1	0.0	21070	78	NA	102	99

Note: Nations are listed in descending order of their 1990 infant mortality rate where no under five mortality rate is available.

Notes :

NA= Data not available
* = UNICEF Estimate
T = Total (as opposed to a median)
x = See footnotes at the end of the tables
y = UNICEF estimate; see footnote at the end of the tables.

Footnotes to Tables

1. Basic Data: Data for following countries are as indication below:

Afghanistan	GNP per capita	1987
Belgium	Household income	1978-79
Bhutan	GNP per capita	1988
Cuba	GNP per capita	1987
France	Household income	1979
Germany	GNP per capita	former Fed. Rep. of Germany only
	Household income	former Fed. Rep. of Germany only
Iraq	GNP per capita	1987
Israel	Household income	1979
Japan	Household income	1979
Kenya	Household income	1976
Korea, Dem. Rep. of	GNP per capita	1987
Lebanon	GNP per capita	1987
Liberia	GNP per capita	1987
Mongolia	GNP per capita	1987
Myanmar	GNP per capita	1987
Nepal	Household income	1976-77
Nicaragua	GNP per capita	1987
Romania	GNP per capita	1990
Somalia	Adult literacy	1985
Sudan	GNP per capita	1988
Tanzania	Adult literacy	1986
Thailand	Household income	1976
Trinidad & Tobago	Household income	1976
USSR	GNP per capita	1980
United Kingdom	Household income	1979
Viet Nam	GNP per capita	1987
Yemen	Adult literacy	1985
Zambia	Household income	1976

3. Economic: Data for following countries are as given below:

Afghanistan	GNP per capita	1987
	Poverty level	1977
Algeria	Poverty level	1977
Bangladesh	Poverty level	1976-77
Bhutan	GNP per capita	1988
	GNP per capita growth rate	1980-88
Botswana	GNP per capita growth rate	1980-88
Burundi	Poverty level	1978
Cameroon	Poverty level	1979
Chad	Poverty level	1976
Chile	Debt service	1988
Cuba	GNP per capita	1987
Dominican Republic	Poverty level	1978
Egypt	GNP per capita growth rate	1980-88
Germany	GNP per capita	former Fed. Rep. of Germany only
	GNP per capita growth rate	former Fed. Rep. of Germany only
	Inflation rate	former Fed. Rep. of Germany only

Greece	Debt service	1988
Hungary	Debt service	1988
India	**'Debt service**	**1988**
Iraq	GNP per capita	1987
	Inflation rate	1980-87
Jordan	GNP per capita growth rate	1970-80
	Inflation rate	1980-88
	Poverty level	1977
Kenya	Poverty level	1977
Korea, Dem. Rep. of	GNP per capita	1987
Korea, Rep.	Poverty level	1978
Kuwait	GNP per capita growth rate	1965-86
Laos	GNP per capita growth rate	1980-88
Lebanon	GNP per capita	1987
Lesotho	Poverty level	1979
Liberia	GNP per capita	1987
	GNP per capita growth rate	1980-88
	Poverty level	1977
Libya	GNP per capita growth rate	1980-88
Madagascar	Poverty level	1977
Mali	GNP per capita growth rate	1967-80
	Poverty level	1975
Mauritius	Poverty level	1979
Mongolia	GNP per capita	1987
Morocco	Poverty level	1979
Myanmar	GNP per capita	1987
	Poverty level	1978
Nepal	Poverty level	1979
Nicaragua	GNP per capita	1987
	GNP per capita growth rate	1980-88
	Inflation rate	1980-88
	Poverty level	1977
Niger	Poverty level	1978
Pakistan	poverty level	1979
Panama	Poverty level	1978
Papua New Guinea	Poverty level	1979
Paraguay	Poverty level	1978
Romania	GNP per capita	1990
	Debt service	1988
Rwanda	Poverty level	1977
Saudi Arabia	GNP per capita growth rate	1965-86
Sierra Leone	Poverty level	1977
	Debt service	1988
Somalia	Poverty level	1978
Sudan	GNP per capita	1988
	GNP per capita growth rate	1980-88
	Inflation rate	1980-88
	Poverty level	1975
Syria	Debt service	1988
Togo	Poverty level	1978
Trinidad & Tobago	Poverty level	1977
Tunisia	Poverty level	1977
USSR	GNP per capita	1980

Viet Nam	GNP per capita	1987
Zaire	Poverty level	1975

4. Educational: Data for following countries are as given below:

Belgium	Radio sets	Licences only
	TV sets	Licences only
Bulgaria	Radio sets	Licences only
	TV sets	Licences only
Czechoslovakia	Radio sets	Licences only
Denmark	Radio sets	Licences only
Germany	TV sets	Licences only
Greece	TV sets	Licences only
Haiti	Adult literacy (1970)	1971
Hong Kong	Adult literacy (1970)	1971
	Reaching final grade	1980
India	**TV sets**	**Licences only**
Lebanon	Adult literacy (1970)	Age 10 years and older
Mauritius	Radio sets	Licences only
	TV sets	Licences only
Morocco	TV sets	Licences only
Norway	TV sets	Licences only
Pakistan	Reaching final grade	1981
Paraguay	Adult literacy (1970)	1972
Poland	Radio sets	Licences only
	TV sets	Licences only
Portugal	TV sets	Licences only
Romania	TV sets	Licences only
Singapore	Radio sets	Licences only
Somalia	Adult literacy	1985
Sudan	Primary enrolment	1985
Sweden	TV sets	Licences only
Switzerland	Radio sets	Licences only
Tanzania	Adult literacy	1986
Uruguay	Adult literacy (1970)	1975
Yemen	Adult literacy	1985
	Reaching final grade	1983
Yugoslavia	Radio sets	Licences only
	TV sets	Licences only

5. Health: Data for following countries are as given below:

Algeria	Access to safe water	1985
Angola	Access to health services	1980
Austria	TB, DPT, Polio, Measles	1988
Botswana	Access to safe water	1985
	Access to health services	1980
Bulgaria	TB, DPT, Polio, Measles	1988
Burkina Faso	Access to health services	1980
Cambodia	Access to safe water	1985
Canada	DPT, Polio, Measles	1987-88
Costa Rica	Access to health services	1980
Cote d'Ivoire	Access to health services	1980
Egypt	Access to safe water	1985
Gabon	Access to health services	1983
Greece	DPT, Polio, Measles	1988
Hong Kong	Access to health services	1984
Israel	DPT, Polio, Measles	1988
Italy	DPT	DT only
Kenya	Access to safe water	1985

Liberia	TB, DPT, Polio, Measles, Tetanus	1988
Malawi	Access to safe water	1985
New Zealand	TB, DPT, Polio, Measles	1987-88
Panama	Access to health services	1980
Paraguay	Access to health services	1980
Peru	Access to health services	1980
Rwanda	Access to safe water	1985
	Access to health services	1980
Senegal	Access to safe water	1985
Somalia	Access to health services	1980
Spain	DPT, Polio, Measles	1988
Sri Lanka	Access to health services	1980
Sweden	TB, Polio, Measles	1988
	DPT	1988; DT only
Syrian Arab Rep.	Access to health services	1980
Tanzania	Access to health services	1980
Trinidad and Tobago	Access to safe water	1985
Tunisia	Access to health services	1983
Turkey	Access to safe water	1985
USA	DPT, Polio, Measles	1988
Uganda	Access to health services	1980
United Arab Emirates	Access to health services	1980
Venezuelä	Access to safe water	1985
Yemen	Access to safe water	Northern 80% of country
Yugoslavia	TB, DPT, Polio, Measles	1988
Zambia	Access to health services	1980

6. Nutrition: Data for following countries are as given below:

Afghanistan	Breast-feeding	Kabul only
	Calorie supply	1984-86
Albania	Calorie supply	1984-86
Algeria	Underweight	0-72 months
	Wasting	12-24 months
	Stunting	24-48 months
Australia	Low birth weight	1979
Bangladesh	Breast-feeding	1975-76
	Underweight	6-59 months
Belgium	Calorie supply	1984-86
Bhutan	Underweight	0-60 months
	Wasting	0-60 months
	Stunting	0-60 months
Bolivia	Underweight	3-36 months
	Stunting	24-36 months
Botswana	Stunting	Clinic data
Brazil	Breast-feeding	North-East only
Burkina Faso	Low birth weight	1979
Burundi	Low birth weight	Bujumbura only
	Underweight	3-36 months
	Stunting	24-36 months
Cambodia	Calorie supply	1984-86
Cameroon	Low birth weight	Yaounde only
	Breast-feeding	1978
	Underweight	1978; 3-47 months
	Wasting	1978
	Stunting	1978; 24-47 months
Chile	Underweight	0-71 months
	Stunting	24-71 months
China	Underweight	9 provinces
	Wasting	9 provinces

	Stunting	9 provinces
Cote d'Ivoire	Low birth weight	1975; Abidjan only
Cuba	Wasting	Lowest 3 percentiles; 12-59 months
Djibouti	Wasting	0-59 months
Dominican Rep.	Underweight	6-36 months
	Stunting	24-36 months
Egypt	Underweight	3-36 months
	Stunting	24-36 months
Ethiopia	Underweight	Data from 9 zones
	Wasting	Data from 9 zones
	Stunting	Data from 9 zones
Finland	Breast-feeding	1972
Guatemala	Underweight	3-36 months
	Stunting	24-36 months
Guinea-Bissau	Underweight	1978-80
Haiti	Low birth weight	1978
	Underweight	1978; Gomez; 3-59 months
	Wasting	1978
	Stunting	1978
Honduras	Wasting	0-59 months
	Stunting	0-59 months
India	**Underweight**	**Gomez; 12-72 months; 8 States**
Indonesia	Underweight	Moderate & severe <80% median Severe <60% median
Iran, Islamic Rep. of	Underweight	National rural
	Wasting	National rural
	Stunting	National rural
Jordan	Low birth weight	1979
Kenya	Stunting	National rural
	Wasting	National rural
Korea, Rep. of	Breast-feeding	1978
Kuwait	Breast-feeding	1978-79
Lao People's Dem. Rep.	Breast-feeding	1979; 5 provinces only
Lesotho	Breast-feeding	1977
Madagascar	Underweight	0-23 months
	Stunting	12-23 months
Malawi	Underweight	6-59 months
Mali	Underweight	3-36 months
	Stunting	24-36 months
Mauritania	Wasting	13-24 months
	Stunting	25-59 months
Mauritius	Wasting	0-59 months
	Stunting	0-59 months
Mexico	Wasting	0-59 months
	Stunting	0-59 months
Morocco	Underweight	0-36 months
	Stunting	24-36 months
Myanmar	Underweight	0-36 months
	Stunting	24-35 months
Namibia	Breast-feeding	Northern areas
	Underweight	6-60 months; Northern areas
	Wasting	6-60 months; Northern areas
	Stunting	6-60 months; Northern areas
Nepal	Breast-feeding	1976
Netherlands	Breast-feeding	Excluding Amsterdam & Rotterdam
Niger	Wasting	0-59 months
	Stunting	0-59 months
Pakistan	Underweight	Gomez
	Wasting	<80% median; 13-24 months
	Stunting	<90% median; 25-60 months

Papua New Guinea	Low birth weight	1979
Peru	Underweight	0-71 months
Poland	Breast-feeding	1977
Rwanda	Underweight	Mod. & severe <80% median; rural
		Severe <60% median; rural
	Wasting	<80% median; 13-24 months; rural
	Stunting	<90% median; 25-60 months; rural
Senegal	Underweight	6-36 months
	Stunting	24-36 months
Sierra Leone	Underweight	1977-78
	Wasting	1977-78
Singapore	Underweight	0-72 months
Sri Lanka	Underweight	3-36 months
	Stunting	24-36 months
Sudan	Wasting	0-59 months; Northern Sudan
	Stunting	0-59 months; Northern Sudan
Switzerland	Low birth weight	1979
Thailand	Underweight	3-36 months
	Stunting	24-36 months
Togo	Stunting	24-36 months
Trinidad and Tobago	Underweight	3-36 months
	Stunting	24-36 months
Tunisia	Underweight	3-36 months
	Stunting	24-36 months
USSR	Calorie supply	1984-86
Uganda	Stunting	24-60 months
Uruguay	Underweight	0-71 months
	Stunting	0-71 months
Venezuela	Breast-feeding	1977
	Underweight	0-60 months
	Wasting	13-24 months
	Stunting	25-60 months
Viet Nam	Wasting	0-59 months; eight rural regions
	Stunting	0-59 months; eight rural regions
Yemen	Breast-feeding	1979
	Underweight	1979-83; combined estimate
	Wasting	1979-83; combined estimate
	Stunting	1979-83; combined estimate
Zambia	Underweight	Rural only
	Wasting	Rural only
	Stunting	Rural only
Zimbabwe	Underweight	3-60 months
	Stunting	24-60 months

Gomez: moderate & severe— below 75 per cent of median weight for age of reference population; severe— below 60 per cent of median weight for age of reference population

---

7. Women: Data for following countries are as given below:

Afghanistan	Contraceptive prevalence	1976
Algeria	Contraceptive prevalence	1977
	Maternal mortality	1978
Angola	Contraceptive prevalence	1977
Australia	Contraceptive prevalence	1970
	Births attended	1982
Austria	Contraceptive prevalence	Marriage cohorts of 1974 & 1978

Belgium	Contraceptive prevalence	Flemish population
Benin	Maternal mortality	Hospital data only
Bulgaria	Contraceptive prevalence	1976
Cameroon	Contraceptive prevalence	1978
Chad	Contraceptive prevalence	1977
	Births attended	1980-82
Chile	Contraceptive prevalence	1978
China	Maternal mortality	30 provinces
Czechoslovakia	Contraceptive prevalence	1977; ever used while married
Denmark	Births attended	1979
Finland	Contraceptive prevalence	1977
	Births attended	1979
France	Contraceptive prevalence	1978
	Births attended	1976
Germany	Births attended	1977-79
Greece	Births attended	1978
Guinea	Contraceptive prevalence	1977
	Maternal mortality	Hospital data only
Hungary	Births attended	1982
Iran	Contraceptive prevalence	1978
Italy	Contraceptive prevalence	1979; since last pregnancy
Jordan	Maternal mortality	1979, hospital data only
Kenya	Maternal mortality	1977
Lesotho	Contraceptive prevalence	1977
Liberia	Tetanus	1988
Libyan Arab Jamahiriya	Maternal mortality	1978
Morocco	Births attended	1980
	Maternal mortality	1974
Namibia	Maternal mortality	Northern areas only
Netherlands	Births attended	1978
New Zealand	Contraceptive prevalence	1976
Nicaragua	Births attended	Institutional deliveries only
Niger	Contraceptive prevalence	1977
Nigeria	Births attended	1980
Norway	Contraceptive prevalence	1977; during past 4 weeks
Poland	Contraceptive prevalence	1977
	Births attended	1980
Portugal	Contraceptive prevalence	1979
	Births attended	1978
Romania	Contraceptive prevalence	1978
	Births attended	1979
Rwanda	Maternal mortality	All hospitals
Somalia	Adult literacy	1985
South Africa	Maternal mortality	From 267 hospitals
Sudan	Primary enrolment	1985
Sweden	Births attended	1976
Switzerland	Contraceptive prevalence	Marriage cohorts of 1970-79
	Births attended	1976
Syrian Arab Rep.	Contraceptive prevalence	1978
Tanzania	Adult literacy	1986
	Contraceptive prevalence	1977
	Maternal mortality	From 48 hospitals; all regions
United kingdom	Births attended	1978
Uruguay	Births attended	Institutional deliveries only
Venezuela	Contraceptive prevalence	1977
Yemen	Adult literacy	1985
Yugoslavia	Contraceptive prevalence	1976; during last 6 months
	Births attended	1979
Zaire	Contraceptive prevalence	1977
Zambia	Contraceptive prevalence	1977

8. Basic Data on Less Populous Countries: Data for following countries are as given below:

Antigua	GNP per capita	1988
Bahamas	Adult literacy	1981
Bahrain	GNP per capita	1988
Barbados	Primary enrolment	1984
British Virgin Islands	GNP per capita	1983
	Life expectancy	1980
	Adult literacy	1970
Brunei Darussalam	GNP per capita	1987
	Adult literacy	1981
	Measles	1988
Cape Verde	Adult literacy	1970; aged 14 and over
Comoros	Adult literacy	1980
Cook Islands	GNP per capita	1987
Cyprus	Adult literacy	1976
Djibouti	GNP per capita	1987
Dominica	GNP per capita	1988
	Adult literacy	1970
Equatorial Guinea	Primary enrolment	1983
Fed. States of Micronesia	Adult literacy	1982
	Primary enrolment	1982
Fiji	Adult literacy	1976
Grenada	Adult literacy	1984
	Primary enrolment	1984
Guyana	Adult literacy	1970
Kiribati	Primary enrolment	1985
Luxembourg	Measles	1988
Marshall Islands	Adult literacy	1982
	Measles	1988
Montserrat	GNP per capita	1987
	Adult literacy	1970
	Primary enrolment	1982
Palau	GNP per capita	1986
	Primary enrolment	1982
Saint Lucia	Adult literacy	1970
	Primary enrolment	1980
Saint Vincent	GNP per capita	1988
	Primary enrolment	1982
Samoa	Primary enrolment	1985
Sao Tome and Principe	Adult literacy	1981
Seychelles	Primary enrolment	1982
Solomon Islands	Primary enrolment	1983
St. Christopher-Nevis	GNP per capita	1988
Swaziland	Adult literacy	1976
Tonga	Primary enrolment	1984
Turks & Caicos Islands	GNP per capita	1987
	Adult literacy	1970
Tuvalu	Infant mortality rate	1985
	GNP per capita	1987
Vanuatu	Adult literacy	1979
	Primary enrolment	1984

Source: *The State of the World's Children 1992*, UNICEF, New York

8

WORLD TRADE: RECENT DEVELOPMENTS

8.1 Background Recovery and Forecasts

The world economy has weakened for the third consecutive year but some improvement is in sight. World output growth in 1991 was forecast to halve to a mere 0.7 per cent and world trade to expand by only about 3 per cent. By the end of the year, however, a recovery is expected to be under way, gathering strength as growth trends converge and yielding overall gains in 1992 of 2.3 per cent in output and 6 per cent in trade. On the other hand the projected recovery is rather modest and its extent in doubt, in part due to increased financial fragility in some major industrial countries.

Recovery

The indications are that most regions will experience a healthier economic performance in the coming year, albeit in varying degrees (Table 8.1). For developing countries as a whole, GDP growth should pick up slightly in 1991 and accelerate in 1992. Even non-oil exporting countries in Latin America, the only major group that registered substantial output losses in 1990, are expected to recover. Prospects remain good for the oil exporting countries in the region too, as a result of sustained efforts at policy reform and increased oil revenues.

The African region will be among the most affected by the slowdown in world economic activity in 1991 through its corollaries of lower commodity prices, higher interest rates and reduced demand from developed countries. The Report warns that medium-term prospects for the majority of African countries depend on the successful implementation of domestic policy reforms and support for them by the international community. Among the policies identified in the former category it mentions the need to attract more development capital, to encourage the creation of small businesses and to make further progress in price and trade liberalization.

With regard to the 42 least developed countries (LDCs), of which 29 are situated in Africa, there may be continuing increases in oil bills and contractions of demand for commodity exports in most cases. A further worsening of trade and current account balances is likely, though a minor improvement in their GDP is possible.

The Asian experience is expected to remain mixed this year, an improved performance in East Asia being offset in West Asia by the economic impact of the Gulf crisis, with highly trade-oriented countries continuing to suffer from reduced export demand and domestic capacity constraints. For South Asian countries the full effects of the Gulf crisis including higher import bills for oil, a decline in remittances from overseas workers and lower tourist revenues, will be felt. In China, on the other hand, the recent economic momentum is expected to continue in the next two years, resulting in a growth rate of around 6 per cent.

A major factor which influences the economic prospectus of developing countries, is the prices of non-fuel primary commodities. In 1990, the combined index of prices for the principal commodities exported by these countries fell in current dollar terms for the first time since 1985. The fall, which continued in the first half of 1991, was even more pronounced in real terms. With production outpacing consumption, high stock levels have been a major depressing influence on prices. It is only with the modest recovery expected in 1992 that real prices of non-fuel primary commodities are likely to stabilize.

Every single country in Central and Eastern Europe experienced negative growth in 1990 and new destabilising social and political factors, including the dismantling of COMECON, have added to the difficulties inherent in the transition. As regards the Russia, "whatever economic policies are followed, the lowest point of the economic crisis is, almost certainly, not yet past, and depressed conditions are likely to continue over the next few years". The Hungarian economy is considered to have the best prospects in the region, with a probable return to modest growth in 1992. Cautious optimism for Poland while the Czech and Slovak Federal Republic, with its relatively low level of indebtedness and high industrial potential, is also seen as likely to make a quick transition to a market economy. Bulgaria, on the other hand, may face one of the most difficult years in its economic history because of the severe consequences of the Gulf crisis and the disintegration of its traditional economic links with the Russia. After a disappointing performance in 1990, immediate prospects for Romania are seen as uncertain.

In the industrialized world, the steady deceleration in overall growth since 1988 coupled with increasingly divergent performances among major economies should give way to a modest, but convergent recovery by the end of 1991, resulting in an overall growth rate of about 0.9 per cent for the year and of 2.7 per cent in 1992. Continental Europe and Japan are expected to post a significant economic slowdown this year, but some improvement is likely in 1992. In North America, the United Kingdom and most of the Nordic countries, however, the recession may bottom out in the second half of 1991. Easier money in the United States and a revival of consumer confidence are having positive effects on the economy, but on the other hand, the country is facing its highest unemployment levels since 1986 and capacity utilization has fallen considerably. Moreover, the significant improvement in the current account deficit in 1991 may be reversed in 1992 if the projected economic recovery entails a renewed surge in imports. Prospects for Western Europe are affected by sluggish investment, a slowdown in intra-European trade, resistant high inflation rates and high unemployment.

Financial Fragility

While the premises for a global recovery exist, its pace could be slowed by a number of factors which are eroding the financial strength of banks and depressing lending, notably in the United States and Japan. It explains how financial innovation and deregulation of financial markets have made interest rates and asset prices more variable and the supply of finance less predictable, thus increasing the potential for instability. Governments have reacted to the resulting weaknesses in bank balance sheets by requiring increases in the capital base of banks and other improvements. However, a slump in the prices of assets held by banks, primarily real estate in the United States and direct capital market investments in commercial and property companies in Japan, has had the opposite effect to that intended by the authorities' actions. Indeed, the increased incidence of defaults and of impaired loans have not only made it difficult for banks to meet the new standards of capital adequacy, but they have also effectively ruled out the possibility of raising capital directly. As a result, the only way to achieve higher capital ratios is to cut lending.

TABLE 8.1: World Output, 1980-1990 and Forecast for 1991 and 1992

(Percentage change)[a]

	Actual		Estimated	Forecast	
Country group	1980-1985	1985-1990	1990	1991	1992
World	2.6	3.2	1.8	0.7	2.3
Development market-economy countries	2.4	3.2	2.3	0.9	2.7
Central and Eastern Europe[b]	2.9	1.1	-4.8	-8.9	-8.5 [c]
China	9.8	7.5	4.8	5.8	6.3
Developing countries	2.0	3.1	2.5	2.9	4.6
of which:					
Latin America	1.1	1.6	-0.5	1.6	3.7
Africa	1.8	2.3	3.5	3.8	2.8
Asia	2.7	4.4	4.2	4.1	5.9
Memo Item:					
Least developed countries	2.4	3.2	2.5	2.7	2.9

Source: UNCTAD secretariat, based on national and international sources and SIGMA forecasts.

a Percentage change — Annual average or change over previous year.

b Net material product. Estimated GDP weights used for purposes of aggregation.

c It is assumed that the decline in Soviet NMP will be the same as in 1991.

The resultant impaired ability of banks to extend credit for investment purposes will represent a major factor affecting the strength of the recovery in the developed market economies. Thus, while current recessionary conditions will not be deep, they are likely to be persistent and cumulative. A process of balance sheet recovery for both financial institutions and households will be required before real, sustained expansion can take place. This process has dominated 1991, and may well persist well into 1992.

Current economic conditions together with the weakened state of financial markets suggest that there will not be a rapid opening and expansion of developed economies' markets to the exports of developing countries, nor will there be substantial additional flows of finance to developing countries. More active measures will, therefore, need to be taken to assure the basic conditions necessary for the successful functioning of the debt recovery programmes through increased institutional lending. Since the impediments are on the side of finance for development, rather than in terms of a lack of real savings, there is considerable merit in the Japanese proposal for a new SDR allocation of $20 billion to take place over 10 years. Under this scenario, developed countries would contribute their allocation to the IMF, thus boosting the institution's capacity for lending to developing countries.

Debt Indicators and Overhang

The access of most developing countries to these markets, other than a few in South and South-East Asia, has remained restricted by unfavourable perceptions of creditworthiness and by continuing difficulties with the servicing of external debt. Though there have been some welcome improvements in debt indicators generally, their incidence has been uneven. The debt burden of sub-Saharan African debtors remains particularly heavy.

The bilateral official debt of developing countries now accounts for about one third of their total debt stock. This is attributed to increase in higher new borrowing, to the protracted nature of the problems of many debtor countries and to the shortcomings of past Paris Club rescheduling arrangements is welcomed.

There is ample scope to reduce military spending. The cost of investment goods has been falling sharply, thanks to rapid technical progress, especially in computing. Moreover, "household saving behaviour has not in realty been worsening, despite some appearances to the contrary". Besides, as long as the world's production potential is not being fully utilised — which is likely to be the case for some time — investment can be stepped up with increased bank lending, without governments and households having first to cut their consumption, since the investment itself will create the required savings by generating additional income. The constraint on financing development will not be the supply of real resources but the institutional capacity to generate finance. One way of tackling the problem would be, as the Japanese have proposed, to renew SDR allocations and link them to development finance.

Conditions for Liberalisation

However, even with better access to external finance, developing countries will still need to reform their own financial systems considerably in order to mobilise domestic resources and to allocate and utilise them to maximum effect. Liberalisation can bring benefits, provided that certain other conditions are also met, as the experience of countries like the Republic of Korea has shown. First it should be "adopted only when considerable industrial advance has already been achieved, and strong institutions and markets and competitive industries are in place". Second, it has to be undertaken from a position of relative financial strength, because liberalisation would not succeed in the context of domestic financial disorder. That would not aggravate the financial difficulties of firms and further weaken the balance sheets of financial institutions. Third, it should be undertaken gradually and be accompanied by strong measures to ensure financial stability and to strengthen market institutions. Finally, it implies a role for the state since it is important to have strong prudential regulations and effective supervision. Without them, there would be a likelihood of widespread speculation, excessive risk-taking, fraud and irregularities.

The intervention cannot be dispensed with as long as there are no institutions, in particular private institutions, capable of providing long-term finance. In most developing countries these are weak or even absent, while business firms tend to be undercapitalised. Consequently entrepreneurship is stymied, and businessmen have to operate with very short time horizons, and hold back from learning by doing when the pay-off, though high, is distant. All developing countries that have industrialised successfully, have improvised techniques consciously to direct credit according to government priorities. It is also important that government does not become a prisoner of vested interests; "it should ensure that any support it extends to enterprises (whether private or public) is fully matched by good performance, and withdraw it when obsolete."

Financing Development

The best way for most developing countries to generate investment finance, until they achieve substantial economic advance, is through a system of bank-based finance combining investment banking with deposit taking. in this case, investment banks could raise funds in the capital markets and onlend them to the corporate sector. Subject to adequate precautions, this may be deemed to be more appropriate than a financial system based on the Anglo-Saxon model which gives a key role to capital markets.

The experience of Germany and Japan where banks have successfully played a leading role in financing business growth may be mentioned. One of the reasons is that, because the banks have greater access than capital markets to information about corporate performance and prospects and can monitor more closely corporate decision-making, they have been able to provide capital at lower cost. At the same time, the Report observes, firms have also enjoyed greater confidence regarding the continued availability of funds for expansion and have therefore been able to take a long-term view in designing their business strategies. When firms depend instead on equity markets for outside finance, they are at the mercy of their share prices, which are especially volatile in developing countries, so that management focuses on short-term financial results rather than on long-term profitability.

While all countries continue to express a commitment to freer trade, the fact is that protectionism has continued unabated in developed countries. The latter, moreover, increasingly manage their trade relations in a selective and discriminatory way, thus eroding the most-favoured-nation (MFN) principle. This applies especially to non-tariff measures (NTMs): even if their proliferation has levelled off somewhat, NTMs cover a larger proportion of developed countries' imports today than they did at the launching of the Uruguay Round.

There have been some trade liberalisation moves recently in the major industrialised countries. But these moves have also been selective both in product coverage and in geographical scope, with the greatest beneficiaries being in Eastern Europe. At the same time, protectionism is becoming more pervasive, with "voluntary" export restraints (VERs) and anti-dumping investigations now being directed even against very small countries with marginal markets.

Within the developing world the prevailing trend is in the opposite direction.

Regional Trading Arrangements

Regional trading arrangements can help rationalise production and promote growth, but they cannot substitute for a properly functioning multilateral trading system. If the world market becomes more segmented, the present diversity and complexity of restrictions on trade in individual markets is likely to increase, further exacerbating difficulties of market access. Overall, there is a danger that existing regional trading arrangements, even if they do not become more inward-looking, will contribute to a further marginalisation of the developing countries unable to participate in them. Moreover, because of their weak negotiating leverage, these countries could gain more from an improvement in the multilateral system than from participation in a geographically limited trading group.

While this or that group of countries may obtain temporary gains from preferential access to one of the main markets, in the long run all countries will lose if the international trading system is split up into a few large economic blocks characterised by managed imports. On a practical level, two elements may be noted that militate against the formation of such blocks: the heavy dependence of the emerging groupings on extra-regional markets; and the internationlisation of production on a world scale through foreign direct investment.

Nevertheless the establishment of a system of international review of the functioning of such groups in order to protect the interests of both weaker members and of non-participants may be advocated. Such a system would help to ensure that regional trading arrangements do not act as stumbling blocks but rather as building blocks of a revitalised multilateral trading system that fully takes into account the needs of the developing countries. This would require the concomitant reduction of barriers, including selective ones, towards non-participating countries.

Source : *Trade and Development Report, 1991*, United Nations Conference on Trade and Development Geneva, 1991.

8.2 **UNCTAD**

The United Nations Conference on Trade and Development (UNCTAD) was set up by the General Assembly in 1964 as one of its permanent organs, mandated to promote international trade, particularly that of developing countries, with a view to accelerating their economic development. UNCTAD has evolved into a universal forum with a development perspective, in which member States review the interdependence of economies and of issues in trade, money and finance. UNCTAD is composed of 171 member States, including the 166 members of the United Nations; many intergovernmental and non-governmental organisations have observer status. The Conference normally meets every four years at ministerial level to establish policy guidelines. Between sessions, work is carried out by the Trade and Development Board and its standing committees dealing with commodities, manufactures, tariff preferences, development finance and insurance, shipping, transfer of technology and economic co-operation among developing countries, and by other subsidiary bodies. The problems of the least developed countries and of Africa's economic recovery receive special attention in UNCTAD's work.

The *UNCTAD Bulletin* is published six times a year in English and French.

UNCTAD in a Changing World

UNCTAD was born when, an overwhelming majority of member States of the United Nations shared a common belief that a co-operative effort was required to bring about a more just world economic order in which the developing countries would participate more fully in, and thus benefit from, a prospering world economy. Since that development consensus was forged, a number of developing countries have achieved a degree of progress which is remarkable by historical standards. Meanwhile, however, many other countries have fared poorly and systemic asymmetries and inequities in the world economy persist. Indeed, the vast majority of developing countries are today burdened with a general loss of economic dynamism after a decade in which more than two thirds of them experienced a decline in per capita incomes. A major challenge for the 1990s must, therefore, be the revitalisation of economic growth and social development in the developing world.

After UNCTAD became a Participating and Executing Agency of the United Nations Development Programme (UNDP) in 1968, technical co-operation assumed an increasingly important role. The level of activity increased steadily from 1972 to a peak in 1981 when expenditures totalled $ 15.3 million. The programme contracted somewhat in the early 1980s, but since 1986 it has been growing rapidly. Activity doubled over the four years to 1990, when 230 projects were financed at a cost of $ 22 million.

Following an established pattern, the 1990 programme was characterised by: a predominance of projects in the areas of international trade, resources for development and data management, an emphasis on intercountry activities and a focus on human resource development.

8.3 Foreign Trade Profile

TABLE 8.2: Foreign Trade Profile: Exports

		1988	1989	1990	1991 June	1991 July
1	2	3	4	5	6	7
IFS World Total		**2,694.3**	**2,906.6**	**3,311.2**	—	—
DOTS World Total	**001**	**2,693.6**	**2,913.9**	**3,334.6**	**273.2**	**284.9**
Industrial Countries	**110**	**1,958.4**	**2,117.3**	**2,441.0**	**195.6**	**203.2**
United States	111	430.02	457.91	494.02	39.30	41.33
Canada	156	100.76	110.82	116.93	10.24	9.83
Australia	193	33.02	38.58	37.58	2.99	3.23
Japan	158	164.51	186.37	210.00	16.38	18.05
New Zealand	196	6.24	7.44	7.94	.62	.60
Austria	122	36.92	38.52	47.16	3.81	4.06
Belgium-Luxembourg	126	97.90	104.18	125.25	9.75	9.76
Denmark	128	25.54	25.97	30.79	2.46	2.31
Finland	172	19.99	22.28	24.18	1.38	1.46
France	132	171.88	189.06	228.25	18.11	18.27
Germany	134	233.48	246.31	317.20	28.35	30.25

Contd.

TABLE 8.2 *Contd.*

1	2	3	4	5	6	7
Greece	174	14.04	16.11	19.04	1.62	1.63
Ireland	178	15.14	16.79	19.81	1.48	1.63
Italy	136	124.68	135.93	163.56	12.89	13.23
Netherlands	138	117.04	124.38	145.48	10.68	12.14
Norway	142	20.24	20.08	23.76	2.08	1.72
Portugal	182	16.08	18.26	22.91	2.16	2.07
Spain	184	56.96	66.06	79.99	6.96	7.44
Sweden	144	42.20	45.42	50.70	3.35	3.02
Switzerland	146	59.88	63.02	72.97	5.61	5.40
United Kingdom	112	170.50	182.41	201.95	15.24	15.66
Developing Countries	**200**	**689.85**	**743.26**	**838.46**	**74.08**	**78.16**
Africa	605	64.50	64.68	74.00	6.10	6.28
Algeria	612	7.27	7.96	9.33	.64	.69
Cameroon	622	1.11	1.18	1.30	.09	.10
Cote d'Ivoire	662	1.80	1.86	1.75	.15	.15
Gabon	646	.83	.73	.76	.07	.08
Ghana	652	1.00	1.10	1.32	.12	.11
Kenya	664	2.18	2.26	2.35	.19	.20
Morocco	686	5.25	5.62	6.90	.55	.55
Nigeria	694	4.69	4.59	5.77	.64	.64
Senegal	722	1.07	1.08	1.26	.10	.10
South Africa	199	13.28	12.00	11.96	1.06	1.12
Sudan	732	1.38	1.11	1.10	.08	.10
Tanzania	738	.99	.96	1.06	.07	.08
Tunisia	744	3.27	3.88	5.17	.53	.46
Zaire	636	2.26	1.36	1.77	.08	.11
Zambia	745	.59	.71	.74	.05	.04
Asia	**505**	**342.14**	**381.51**	**434.21**	**39.98**	**42.19**
China, People's Rep.	924	52.23	52.20	49.62	5.36	5.62
Hong Kong	532	63.58	70.12	81.15	7.88	8.38
India	**534**	**21.70**	**22.07**	**23.16**	**1.29**	**1.62**
Indonesia	536	10.34	12.51	18.03	1.41	1.53
Korea	542	44.63	51.24	58.24	5.50	5.54
Malaysia	548	16.36	20.57	25.31	2.89	3.08
Pakistan	564	7.33	7.31	7.88	.74	.73
Philippines	566	9.32	11.64	13.39	1.00	1.08
Singapore	576	38.96	46.02	55.61	4.89	4.94
Thailand	578	17.56	22.56	30.32	2.70	2.94
Europe	**170**	**80.14**	**82.86**	**94.61**	**7.16**	**7.27**
Hungary	944	9.90	9.90	10.43	.92	.82
Poland	964	14.13	14.43	14.05	1.36	1.26
Romania	968	7.96	8.04	8.57	.42	.66
Turkey	186	14.26	14.86	20.51	1.58	1.70
Yugoslavia	188	14.10	15.27	19.72	1.22	1.12
Middle East	**405**	**99.02**	**100.03**	**107.28**	**9.61**	**10.35**
Bahrain	419	2.31	3.03	3.77	.27	.30
Egypt	469	10.78	10.45	12.07	.97	1.30
Iran, I.R. of	429	7.91	8.75	12.97	1.39	1.54
Iraq	433	8.48	8.75	6.13	.02	—
Israel	436	11.68	11.25	12.98	1.14	1.17
Kuwait	443	5.37	5.64	3.58	.20	.27
Libya	672	5.63	4.98	5.20	.42	.50
Saudi Arabia	456	23.39	22.88	24.52	2.67	2.72

Contd.

TABLE 8.2 *Contd.*

1	2	3	4	5	6	7
Syrian Arab Republic	463	2.06	2.01	2.25	.18	.18
Western Hemisphere	**205**	**104.05**	**114.17**	**128.35**	**11.23**	**12.08**
Argentina	213	5.41	4.44	4.99	.51	.60
Bahamas, The	313	1.89	1.83	2.30	.21	.13
Brazil	223	16.12	19.42	21.63	1.53	1.90
Chile	228	4.67	6.19	6.86	.60	.65
Colombia	233	4.61	4.91	5.47	.37	.43
Ecuador	248	1.77	1.80	1.78	.17	.19
Jamaica	343	1.56	1.86	1.80	.15	.15
Mexico	273	27.30	34.22	39.80	3.92	3.98
Netherlands Antilles	353	1.20	2.24	2.56	.19	.24
Panama	283	6.08	6.48	7.08	.56	.63
Peru	293	2.49	2.13	2.33	.21	.23
Trinidad and Tobago	369	.80	1.06	1.02	.09	.09
Venezuela	299	10.40	6.52	7.29	.80	.82
U.S.S.R. and selected other countries n.i.e.	**910**	**81.67**	**86.93**	**74.25**	**4.87**	**4.74**
Minus adjustment for trade of U.S.S.R. and selected other countries n.i.e.	**980**	**-76.98**	**-78.01**	**-64.48**	**-3.96**	**-4.42**
Memorandum Items						
Oil Exporting Countries	999	96.56	97.92	109.19	9.88	10.42
Non-Oil Developing Countries	201	593.29	645.35	729.27	64.20	67.74

TABLE 8.3: Foreign Trade Profile: Imports

		1988	1989	1990	1991 June	1991 July
1	2	3	4	5	6	7
IFS World Total		**2,767.6**	**3,005.6**	**3,448.8**	—	—
DOTS World Total	**001**	**2,772.3**	**3,000.3**	**3,440.2**	**281.4**	
Industrial Countries	**110**	**2016.1**	**2,160.2**	**2,496.3**	**203.8**	**215.1**
United States	111	328.55	370.61	408.28	36.43	37.35
Canada	156	114.00	122.95	129.56	10.95	10.36
Australia	193	35.35	39.96	43.16	3.55	3.53
Japan	158	278.70	293.91	310.70	26.95	29.03
New Zealand	196	9.39	9.66	10.29	.90	.92
Austria	122	32.70	34.01	42.05	3.34	3.57
Belgium-Luxembourg	126	92.92	98.88	117.52	9.43	9.56
Denmark	128	27.35	28.24	34.63	2.86	2.65
Finland	172	23.71	24.77	28.05	1.46	1.91
France	132	167.31	179.49	218.45	18.17	19.20

Contd.

TABLE 8.3 *Contd.*

1	2	3	4	5	6	7
Germany	134	318.32	330.47	399.76	30.32	32.91
Greece	174	8.11	8.98	9.48	.71	.78
Ireland	178	18.20	19.75	23.06	1.95	1.91
Italy	136	128.69	139.93	169.38	13.91	15.87
Netherlands	138	107.23	113.65	136.96	10.64	11.00
Norway	142	23.42	27.49	33.59	2.47	2.57
Portugal	182	11.33	13.28	17.24	1.27	1.53
Spain	184	40.51	43.71	53.87	4.49	5.00
Sweden	144	49.55	51.74	58.51	4.67	4.11
Switzerland	146	60.74	62.38	75.18	5.55	5.53
United Kingdom	112	138.52	145.27	174.75	13.66	15.60
Developing Countries	**200**	**746.49**	**832.12**	**932.38**	**76.63**	**84.97**
Africa	605	66.14	73.65	85.44	6.58	6.87
Algeria	612	8.78	9.83	13.30	.98	.89
Cameroon	622	1.89	2.06	2.49	.22	.25
Cote d'Ivoire	662	3.06	2.94	3.40	.28	.27
Gabon	646	1.36	.172	2.72	.20	.19
Ghana	652	1.15	1.14	1.46	.12	.12
Kenya	664	1.16	1.21	1.28	.10	.11
Morocco	686	4.15	4.29	5.45	.39	.48
Nigeria	694	8.30	11.19	14.11	.97	1.06
Senegal	722	.67	.70	.74	.06	.05
South Africa	199	14.47	14.53	14.81	1.19	1.34
Sudan	732	.59	.60	.54	.04	.04
Tanzania	738	.43	.52	.45	.04	.04
Tunisia	744	2.38	2.98	3.75	.35	.45
Zaire	636	2.04	1.94	1.93	.16	.17
Zambia	754	1.19	1.44	1.47	.13	.15
Asia	**505**	**362.81**	**403.39**	**451.44**	**40.88**	**46.85**
China, People's Rep.	924	60.27	73.13	87.67	8.39	9.46
Hong Kong	532	44.79	46.47	50.82	5.08	7.27
India	534	15.41	18.38	20.80	1.63	1.79
Indonesia	536	20.53	23.32	26.94	2.13	2.34
Korea	542	58.56	59.15	59.34	4.87	5.50
Malaysia	548	26.66	29.44	34.27	3.16	3.52
Pakistan	564	4.50	4.75	5.48	.56	.51
Philippines	566	8.56	8.99	9.68	.82	.99
Singapore	576	29.33	35.86	44.00	4.14	4.46
Thailand	578	16.43	20.84	24.03	2.20	2.44
Europe	**170**	**84.62**	**85.77**	**84.70**	**6.28**	**6.94**
Hungary	944	11.23	11.30	11.04	.90	.89
Poland	964	15.45	15.69	18.90	1.28	1.46
Romania	968	11.96	10.72	5.87	.49	.52
Turkey	186	12.09	13.30	14.56	.98	1.08
Yugoslavia	188	15.79	16.75	18.41	1.23	1.62
Middle East	**405**	**103.04**	**124.49**	**154.04**	**10.36**	**10.56**
Bahrain	419	1.56	1.76	2.06	.17	.21
Egypt	469	3.95	4.67	5.35	.40	.36
Iran, I.R. of	429	9.09	12.62	17.08	1.14	1.54
Iraq	433	10.57	13.40	11.50	—	—
Israel	436	9.29	9.98	11.38	.89	.98
Kuwait	443	8.38	11.12	7.84	.01	.01
Libya	672	7.22	7.88	11.66	.83	.81

Contd.

TABLE 8.3 *Contd.*

1	2	3	4	5	6	7
Saudi Arabia	456	31.29	35.66	51.13	3.99	3.82
Syrian Arab Republic	463	1.49	3.01	4.58	.46	.43
Western Hemisphere	**205**	**129.88**	**144.83**	**156.76**	**12.53**	**13.75**
Argentina	213	10.55	11.64	13.80	1.17	1.40
Bahamas, The	313	.67	1.13	1.09	.05	.08
Brazil	223	36.90	37.55	36.14	2.77	3.19
Chile	228	7.41	8.88	9.89	.77	.79
Colombia	233	5.51	6.03	7.02	.50	.58
Ecuador	248	2.60	2.82	2.87	.27	.23
Jamaica	343	1.02	1.31	1.48	.14	.13
Mexico	273	32.38	36.99	40.95	3.54	3.44
Netherlands Antilles	353	.85	.95	1.10	.13	.11
Panama	283	2.24	2.80	2.41	.12	.28
Peru	293	3.10	3.96	3.79	.31	.31
Trinidad and Tobago	369	1.36	1.51	1.93	.16	.14
Venezuela	299	10.74	13.51	17.51	1.14	1.47
U.S.S.R. and Selected other countries n.i.e.	**910**	**78.32**	**78.95**	**67.55**	**4.02**	**4.60**
Minus adjustment for trade of U.S.S.R. and selected other countriesn.i.e.	**980**	**-95.49**	**-101.09**	**-83.92**	**-5.33**	**-5.18**
Memorandum Items						
Oil Exporting Countries	999	132.49	159.90	199.10	13.44	14.09
Non-Oil Developing Countries	201	614.00	672.22	733.29	63.19	70.88

Notes:

1. DOTS = Direction of Trade Statistics
2. IFS = International Financial Statistics
3. The term 'Country' does not in all cases refer to a territorial entity that is a state as understood by international law and practice; the term also covers some territorial entities that are not states but for which statistical data is maintained and provided internationally on a separate and independent basis.
4. As from July 1990 (or Third Quarter) the data for Germany covers the area of United Germany.
5. On May 22, 1990, the Yemen Arab Republic and the People's Democratic Republic of Yemen became unified single state.

Source: *Direction of Trade Statistics*, December 1991.

9

WORLD OUTLOOK: DIVERSE ISSUES

9.1 A New World Order

The world order which has dominated the political and economic life of the 20th century is visibly dying.

In the blink of an historical eye, the world has witnessed the beginning of the end for apartheid, the liberation of Central and Eastern Europe, the ending of the 40-year cold war, the beginning of significant reductions in arms expenditure, the virtual abandonment of the idea of state economic monopoly, the narrowing of ideological divides, the strengthening of the economic heartbeat of Asia, the turn away from dictatorship in virtually every republic of Latin America, and a new impulse towards democracy, pluralism, and economic reform in Africa.

The period of history that is most difficult to understand is always one's own, but the suddenness and scale of these changes, in a landscape previously considered glacial in its rate of progress, suggests that we are living through a revolution. If so, it is a revolution significantly different from revolutions past. It is different, first of all, in that its principal agent is not violence but communication. And as ends are often inherent in means, it is also different in that it is a revolution which appears to be transferring power not to the few but to the many.

These are profound differences in the process of historical change, differences which give a new meaning to the idea of the communications revolution. For in the many countries where political and economic change is now unfolding, it is the power of communication that is allowing the judgements, provoking the comparisons, heightening the frustrations and posing the alternatives. After years of somewhat empty talk about the global village, it is as if the first village meeting were being held and people were voting almost unanimously to reject the political and economic autocracies which have deprived them of choice without meeting their needs.

There have been unpleasant reminders of the vulnerability of this process of change, but recent events in the Soviet Union, and particularly on the streets of Moscow and St. Petersburg in August of 1991, have sent a message of courage to peoples all over the world. In many capital cities today, there is an almost tangible sense that some vital balance may be shifting, that the contours of the possible may be changing, that people are finding a new confidence in their own rights and abilities to participate in the management of their own affairs. And it may also be, although it should be said only tentatively, that there is a new nervousness, a new hesitancy, among those who might be tempted to suppress those rights.

This advance for democracy is not exclusively led by, or confined to, Eastern and Central Europe. Ten years ago, most of the 22 republics of Central and

South America were gripped by dictatorship; today, all but one have an elected government. It also appears that Africa may now be embarked on a gradual political transformation. The shock waves from Eastern Europe and the Soviet Union are reverberating through that continent with a particular resonance because they are coinciding with the sudden and painful realization of the moral and financial inadequacies of many of its existing economic and political systems. Simultaneously, the ending of the cold war is raising new hopes that the destinies of many nations in Africa, and in other parts of the developing world, may now be detached from the superpower rivalries which have so distorted international relationships in the post-war era. Those rivalries have had much to do with the over-militarization of the developing world and with the perpetuation of the kind of regimes which, in so many countries and for so many decades, have denied human rights and crushed human hopes.

Despite an international agenda that is crowded with pressing political, economic, and environmental problems, there is therefore more cause for hope on the human horizon than perhaps at any other time in this century. It may be that the years ahead will show such optimism not to have been justified; but what is not in doubt is that a new order is emerging in our times. The threat of war, have diverted our physical and financial resources, our science and technology, our ingenuity and imagination, and our human capacity and concern. That threat is receding. The time has therefore come for the world to recommit itself to the task of ending the age-old evils of absolute poverty, malnutrition, illiteracy, and preventable disease and to build again towards a new world order which will reflect mankind's brightest hopes rather than its darkest fears.

Source : *The State of the World's Children, 1992,* UNICEF, New York

9.2 **AIDS Virus**

New Clues to Treatment

The finding of a research team of United States published in the proceedings of the National Academy of Sciences (U.S) yields important clue in understanding how the virus disables the body's ability of fight of disease.

The AIDS virus stimulates the body's lymphocytes to produce a hormone, corticotropin, which suppresses part of the immune that system, hormone, once it gets in the bloodstream, becomes another hormone, melanotropin, which has a similar but more potent effect.

The research does not lead directly to a therapy, but it may eventually contribute to a strategy that would inhibit the effects of the hormones.

The discovery that high doses of antibodies can prevent HIV infections in chimps may give doctors a new tool for preventing the spread of AIDS from mothers to babies.

Scientists from the New York Blood Centre purified the anti-bodies and found that they prevented two chimpanzees from getting HIV infections despite large doses of the virus.

The antibodies, called HIV immune globulin, or HIVIG, are derived from the blood of outwardly healthy people with AIDS infections. They are concentrations of antibodies that kill the AIDS virus in a test tube. There is a possibility that HIVIG might be used to protect babies born to infected mothers when given to the baby and perhaps also to the mother.

The national institutes of health in United States plan to begin a major study of infected pregnant women to see if the treatment protects their babies from HIV.

Pregnant women infected with HIV, the AIDS virus, face about a 1-in-3 risk of passing the virus to their babies during or before birth. An estimated 1,500 to 2,000 babies get the virus this way each year.

The study will be conducted on 400 women at about 20 hospitals across the United States. The women will be randomly chosen to take either HIVIG or ordinary antibodies for several months before they give birth. Their babies also will receive one of the two treatments.

The goal is to provide extremely high doses of antibodies that naturally hunt down the virus and kill it. Doctors hope this will prevent infection if given at the same time as exposure to the virus.

A key step to the AIDS treatment was learning to produce high doses of antibodies that are not tainted with the AIDS virus. If the technique proves to work in people. Researchers will probably try to mass produce them using monoclonal antibodies, which do not require handling infected blood.

Source : *Times of India,* January 1, 1992

9.3 **Book Trade**

International Publishers Association Meet, January, 1992

While inaugurating the 24th Congress of the International Publishers Association, Vice President of India, Shri S.D.Sharma urged several hundred publishers gathered from different parts of the world that they must make translations available not only of scientific texts but also those on humanities, culture and other subjects. He wanted the congress to discuss whether the copyright matter facilitated large scale translation, and said that in India we are moving in the direction of laying greater emphasis on translations as it was a country of diverse languages. In India, there is no doubt that by the end of the century the number of reading public would reach at least 800 million and the publishers should utilise this great opportunity.

As the world is coming together with growth of science and technology publishers have a great role to play in seeing that "humanity may survive and prosper." Spread of literature from one part of the world to another will only help knitting together humanity as people notice their basic oneness, he added.

The publishers belonged to the fraternity of Emperor Ashoka, the first publisher who published his message of tolerance 2,300 years ago on rocks. A free publishing is part of Indian Constitution under Article 19 A.

President of Portugal, Mario Soares said that in the spreading of culture, books play a role similar to the one played by energy in economic development. This is so because books are not only an indispensable instrument for the aesthetic treatment of the word, its expression as literary art; books are also, and will always be, the least expensive and easiest to handle, a collection of information, a reference means and the repository of learning.

More than 20 years ago Mac Luhan prophesied the end of the Gutenberg Galaxy as the audio-visual means would create a new communication system, likely to bring our secular system based on books and the press to an end. However, it is precisely during the past 23 years — while television has reached every household — that books have undergone an unprecedented boom, so much so that in several countries the number of titles and copies have doubled. In my opinion this explosion is not only the result of economic growth, the increase of schools, growth of population or the progressive urbanisation; this increase is essentially due to the permanency of books as a favoured instrument for the furtherance of culture and as such an indispensable element of cultural development.

The theme chosen for the 24th publishers congress was "breaking the barrier, and indeed as contemporaries we are witnessing and living through a stupendous breaking of barriers in all senses of the term. It was not only the Berlin Wall that has been broken in a symbolic way or the Iron Curtain which has vanished along with the divisions of a traditionally bipolar world nor even other political and ideological barriers.

President of International Publishers Association, Mr. Andrew H. Neilly said that he would not subscribe to the view that in today's unstable world publishers and copyright — the doctrine that makes our profession possible — are obsolete and that IPA itself is an exercise in futility.

Our markets have become truly international. We have said this for years but rarely acted as if it were true. Intellectual property is finally recognised as a major asset to national economies and often their largest export. Trade agreements now being negotiated recognise the need to protect patents and copyrights as national or international assets, a striking departure from past practice.

Dr. Karan Singh, former Ambassador to US said that publishers have a crucial role to play in restructuring of our minds and concept towards seeing the world as one which was a dream earlier.

Mr. David Hartridge, Director GATT Negotiations Group said that draft agreement on trade related aspects of intellectual property rights including trade in counterfeit goods was one of the three subjects on the agenda of the Uruguay Round package which were new to GATT and it is no secret that the first two years of negotiation were very difficult. Yet the negotiators have produced what is certainly the most comprehensive agreement of intellectual property of this century establishing agreed international discipline across the full range of intellectual property rights and providing for the first time rules to ensure that rights can be effectively enforced in all member countries.

Source : *Hindustan Times*, January 28, 1992

World Book Fair

The 10th World Book Fair, a nine day affair was opened on 1 February 1992 in New Delhi at Pragati Maidan. It was considered to be the largest book fair ever held in India. Millions of books in English, Hindi and other Indian and Foreign languages were exhibited by more than 800 publishers and booksellers in India and from abroad. The Indian languages were represented by 269 participants. Foreign participants included from France, Germany, Japan, America, Iran, New Zealand, Italy, China, the Netherlands, Switzerland, Singapore, Malaysia, Egypt, Bangladesh and Pakistan. Most British and American publishers were represented through their Indian distributors.

For promoting translation of books, a Rights Hall had been set-up in a Hall.

Three types of exhibits of select books had been set-up:

(1) Select children's books of 1989 and 1990 — ninety seven children's books in Indian languages, including English, selected out of more than 1,700 titles published in 1989 and 1990.

(2) Award winning books of Indian languages — In this exhibit, 107 titles of 12 Indian languages, awarded by the Sahitya Akademi and Bharatiya Jnanpith are displayed to promote their translation into foreign languages.

(3) Books recommended for translation — In this section, the National Book Trust has placed more than 700 books in Indian languages including English which have been recommended by experts for translation.

The nine-day fair was spread over nearly 24,000 sq. metres of Pragati Maidan. The Trust had booked 20,000 sq. metres and it had 4,000 display racks in its stock. Yet it ran out of space and equipment. An additional 1500 display racks were manufactured while the booking was eventually closed at 25 per cent more than 1990.

9.4 Cultural Development

New Sites on World Heritage List

The World Heritage Convention which met in Carthage, Tunisia in the second week of December 1991 selected 6 natural and 17 cultural sites in 16 countries round the world from among the 30 proposals that were submitted.

There are now 360 sites inscribed on the List; of these 262 are cultural, 84 natural and 14 of both natural and cultural significance. Other new comers include: Shark Bay (Australia), Sucre (Bolivia), Serra de Capivara (Brazil), Suomenlinna (Finland), Old Rauma (Finland), Banks of the Seine, the Cathedral of Notre Dame, Saint-Remi Abbey and the Palace of Tau of Reims (France), the Abbey and Altenmunster of Lorsch (Germany), temple of Borobodur, Komodo National Park, Prambanan and the Ujung Kulon National Park (Indonesia), Morelia (Mexico), Ilha de Mozambique (Mozambique), Air-Tenere (Niger), the Historic Centre of Limba (Peru), Danube Delta (Romania), Poblet Monastery (Spain), the Golden Rock Temple of Dambulla in Sri Lanka, Palace of Drottningholm (Sweden) and the historic sites of Ayuddhya, Sukothai and their associated towns and the Thungyai-Haui Kha Khaeng Wildlife Sanctuary (Thailand).

The Convention on the World Heritage was established by UNESCO in 1972 to protect the cultural and natural heritage of mankind. The list is established by the Committee in cooperation with ICOMOS (International Council on Monuments and Sites) and IUCN (The World Conservation Union). The two organizations are consulted regarding nominations of cultural and natural sites, monitoring and on requests for international assistance.

Next year the Convention will celebrate its 20th anniversary with special events in different parts of the world, including national days on heritage, films and exhibitions. UNESCO will host a large exhibition on the World Heritage next summer as well as special events celebrating the heritage of different countries.

There is more than celebration on the agenda for next year. The Convention and its activities will be re-evaluated with the aim of preparing a new strategy. The study will examine how representative the list is, if the monitoring is efficient and try to determine what UNESCO can do to help countries deal with the negative effects of tourism on World Heritage sites.

Source : *UN Newsletter*, January 11 1992

9.5 **Drug Abuse**

Situation and Control

Interlocking criminal trafficking organisations, well-financed and heavily armed are engaged in joint venture organisations in South America, Western Europe and South-East Asia to smuggle heroin and cocaine. As a result, abuse of heroin is soaring in a number of regions, and cocaine, once abused mainly in the Americas and Europe, now also threatens Africa, the Near and Middle East, South and South-East Asia and Oceania.

International Narcotics Control Board reiterates its 1990 call for even stronger, more comprehensive, more innovative response to the drug menace, stating that despite some encouraging developments and resolute pursuit of counteraction by countries at the community, national, regional, bilateral and multilateral levels, the drug abuse situation world-wide remains grim.

In this overall assessment of the international drug situation, the Board in its 1991 annual report reiterates the disturbing tendencies pointed out in the Board's previous annual report of the continued threat of illicit production, trafficking and abuse, along with drug-related violence and corruption, not only to public health but to political institutions, economic development and the environment. The report also makes a special reference to the spreading danger to human immuno deficiency virus (HIV) infection as a result of intravenous drug abuse.

Positive Developments

Nevertheless, the report notes some positive developments in 1991. Surveys indicate that in a number of countries the abuse of certain drugs continue to show stabilisation or even decline, and action by citizens at the community level in some countries to turn the tide against drug abuse is beginning to show results.

Traffickers are shifting their activities to new regions and areas as a consequence of stepped-up national and international counteraction, putting heavy pressure on traffickers. The Board makes special note of the fact that that relentless pressure had led to the arrest of kingpin traffickers and had crippled a major and ruthless cartel in Colombia.

As a new positive development, the Board draws attention to the fact that the newly created United Nations International Drug Control Programme is developing an International Drug Abuse Assessment System to provide a comprehensive overview and analysis of drug abuse and programmes being pursued by governments and national organisations to prevent and reduce such abuse, including epidemiology, prevention, education, treatment, rehabilitation and social integration.

Also on the positive side, the Board notes an increase in 1991 in the number of parties to the three drug control treaties (the 1961 Single Convention on Narcotic Drug, amended by the 1972 Protocol; the 1971 Convention on Psychotropic Substances; and the 1988 United Nations Conventions Against Illicit Trafficking in Narcotic Drugs and Psychotropic Substances). Several countries have also adopted new or strengthened legislation and measures for the effective implementation of those Conventions.

Weaknesses in Control

However, despite those developments, the Board draws attention to existing weaknesses in internal control mechanisms. One of those remains the lack of effective co-ordination between services involved in drug control efforts at the national level: health, customs, and law enforcement, in particular. Another weakness continues to be the lack of stringent controls on psychotropic substances and on precursors and chemicals used to manufacture illicit drugs, as well as on drug destined for export. The Board notes with concern that 20 years after conclusion of the 1971 Convention, Austria, Belgium, Ireland, the Netherlands and Switzerland have not become parties.

In terms of action to be taken on the international level, the Board reaffirms its belief that special emphasis should be accorded by the international community to enacting and vigorously pursuing comprehensive measures to contain and reduce the illicit demand for drugs. Unless progress can be made towards that end, sustained success in other dimension of the drug education can only be temporary. The Board stresses the need to provide, in response to requests of States under attack by traffickers, full assistance including security services, weapons, aircraft, ships and training.

To counter illicit cultivation of drugs, the report calls on the international community to afford States access to modern technology and for producing countries to themselves employ methods to permit the location and environmentally safe destruction of narcotic drugs.

A new element, the report points out, is the increased security problem posed by the mounting stocks of seized drugs. This is underscored by instances of their re-diversion into the illicit market. Security is, therefore, best guaranteed by the prompt destruction of drugs following seizure.

Alternative Crops

In addition to detection and eradication, the Board also acknowledges the need for providing large-scale integrated rural development assistance to enable cultivators of illicit crops to make their living through licit agricultural or other enterprise. In order to do so, the Board reiterates its call for expanding marketing possibilities and establishing fair export prices for alternative economic activities, stating that without those measures containment and progressive reduction of drug crops cannot succeed. Thus, the Board welcomes the action taken by the European Economic Community (EEC) to include Bolivia, Colombia, Ecuador and Peru into its preferential customs system for a number of agricultural and industrial products.

To counter illicit trafficking effectively, the Board stresses that priority should be accorded to exchanging information promptly to facilitate the apprehension, arrest and prosecution of traffickers; to prevent traffickers from acquiring precursors, arms, sophisticated weaponry, aircraft, ships and the like; and to deny traffickers the opportunity to launder their ill-gotten gains through legitimate enterprises and financial institutions. In that regard, the Board notes as an important step the establishment of the Chemical Action Task Force by the Group of Seven major industrialised countries to recommend effective procedures to ensure that precursors are not diverted from legitimate commerce for use in the illicit manufacture of drugs.

Source : *Annual Report*, International Narcotics Control Board, 1991, as reported in *UN Newsletter*, February 1, 1992.

9.6 **Educational Survey**

The total world expenditure on formal education increased to over a trillion dollars in 1988 — equivalent to around 5.5 per cent of the world's GNP of this, only one eighth was spent in the developing countries of Asia, Africa and Latin America, which, nevertheless, account for three fourth of the total world enrolment in formal education.

Contrary to the popular belief that a large portion of Indian students opt for science, medicine and engineering, it is the study of law, social science and the humanities that predominates in the country. Thirty-eight per cent of students choose the humanities and 23 per cent law and social science as against 29 per cent who take the natural sciences, engineering and agriculture and only 4 per cent who go in for medicine.

In 1988, India spent 8.5 per cent of the total government expenditure on education. Among the 24 Asian countries out of 41 for which figures are available, only Sri Lanka and Laos fared worse.

Source : *World Education Report 1991*, UNESCO, Paris, 1992

9.7 **European Community Accord**

The European Community (EC) leaders have agreed to a historic political and monetary union treaty in Maastricht (Netherlands) on December 11, 1991 that will give western Europe a single currency by 1999 and a stronger joint voice in world affairs.

The breakthrough came when 11 members agreed to implement a social charter enshrining basic workers' rights outside the EC; legal framework, enabling the U.K., which vehemently opposed it, to sign a comprehensive treaty on the other issues.

"The compromise represents a significant progress. With this Maastricht decision Europe has certainly achieved the decisive breakthrough", said a beaming German Chancellor, Mr. Helmut Kohl, who brokered the key deal. Under the deal a single currency, the ECU, managed by an independent European Central Bank, will be introduced as early as 1997 if seven EC states meet strict economic criteria, and at the latest by 1999.

Britain obtained a special protocol allowing it to postpone a decision on whether and when to join the monetary union, but it failed to prevent the others from going ahead.

The treaty opened the prospect of a common European defence, with the western European union military pact eventually implementing decisions of the EC political union. Member states agreed that their defence policy would be compatible with the U.S. led NATO alliance, which defended western Europe for the 40 years of the cold war.

9.8 International Peace and Security

Security Council Summit Meeting, January 31, 1992

The following is the text of the statement read out by British Prime Minister John Major at the end of the firstever Security Council summit-level meeting called by him as the President of the 15-nation UN Security Council at the level of Heads of State and Government on January 31, 1991.

The members of the Security Council have authorised me to make the following statement on their behalf.

The Security Council met at the headquarters of the United Nations in New York on January 31, 1992, for the first time at the level of Heads of State and Government.

The members of the Council considered, within the framework of their commitment to the United Nations Charter, "the responsibility of the Security Council in the maintenance of international peace and security."

The members of the Security Council consider that their meeting is a timely recognition of the fact that there are new favourable international circumstances under which the Security Council has begun to fulfil more effectively its primary responsibility for the maintenance of international peace and security.

A Time of Change

This meeting takes place at a time of momentous change. The ending of the cold war has raised hopes for a safer, more equitable and more humane world. Rapid progress have been made in many regions of the world towards democracy and responsive forms of Government, as well as towards achieving the purposes set out in the Charter. The completion of the dismantling of apartheid on South Africa would constitute a major contribution to these positive trends, including to the encouragement of respect for human rights and fundamental freedoms.

Last year, under the authority of the United Nations, the international community succeeded in enabling Kuwait to regain its sovereignty and territorial integrity, which it had lost as a result of Iraqi aggression. The resolutions adopted by the Security Council remain essential to the restoration of peace and stability in the region and must be fully implemented. At the same time, the members of the Council are concerned by the humanitarian situation of the innocent civilian population of Iraq.

The members of the Council support the West Asia peace process, facilitated by the Russian Federation and the United States, and hope that it will be brought to a successful conclusion on the basis of Council Resolution 242 (1967) and 338 (1973).

They welcome the role, the United Nations has been able to play under the

Charter in progress towards settling long-standing regional disputes, and will work for further progress towards their resolution. They applaud the valuable contribution being made by United Nations peace-keeping forces now operating in Asia, Africa, Latin America and Europe.

The members of the Council note that United Nations peace-keeping tasks have increased and broadened considerably in recent years. Election monitoring, human rights verification and the repatriation of refugees at the request or with the agreement of the parties concerned, have been integral parts of the Security Council's efforts to maintain international peace and security. They welcome these developments.

The members of the Council also recognise that change, however welcome, has brought new risks for stability and security. Some of the most acute problems result from changes to state structures. The members of the Council will encourage all efforts to help achieve peace, stability and cooperation during these changes.

The international community therefore faces new challenges in the search for peace. All member states expect the United Nations to play a central role at this crucial stage. The members of the Council stress the importance of strengthening and improving the United Nations to increase its effectiveness. They are determined to assume fully their responsibilities within the United Nations Organisation in the framework of the Charter.

The absence of war and military conflicts amongst states does not in itself ensure international peace and security. The non-military sources of instability in the economic, social, humanitarian and ecological fields have become threats to peace and security. The United Nations membership as a whole needs to give the highest priority to the solution of these matters.

Commitment to Collective Security

The members of the Council pledge their commitment to international law and to the United Nations Charter. All disputes between states should be peacefully resolved in accordance with the provision of the Charter. The members of the Council reaffirm their commitment to the collective security system of the Charter to deal with threats to peace and to reverse acts of aggression.

The members of the Council express their deep concern over acts of international terrorism and emphasise the need for the international community to deal effectively with all such acts.

To strengthen the effectiveness of these commitments, and in order that the Security Council should have the means to discharge its primary responsibility under the Charter for the maintenance of international peace and security, the members of the Council have decided on the following approach.

Peacemaking and Peace-keeping

They invite the Secretary-General to prepare, for circulation to the members of the United Nations by July 1, 1992, his analysis and recommendations on ways of strengthening and making more efficient within the framework and provisions of the Charter the capacity of the United Nations for preventive diplomacy, for peace-making and for peace-keeping.

The Secretary-General's analysis and recommendations could cover the role of the United Nations in identifying potential crises and areas of instability as well as the contribution to be made by regional organisations in accordance with Chapter VIII of the United Nations Charter in helping the work of the Council.

They could also cover the need for adequate resources, both material and financial. The Secretary-General might draw lessons learned in recent United Nations peace-keeping missions to recommend ways of making more effective secretariat planning and operations. He could also consider how greater use might be made of his good offices, and of his other functions under the United Nations Charter.

The members of the Council, while fully conscious of the responsibilities of other organs of the United Nations in the fields of disarmament, arms control and non-proliferation, reaffirm the crucial contribution which progress in these areas can make to the maintenance of international peace and security. They express their commitment to take concrete steps to enhance the effectiveness of the United Nations in these areas.

Disarmament, Arms Control and Weapons of Mass Destruction

The members of the Council underline the need for all member States to fulfil their obligations in relation to arms control and disarmament to prevent the proliferation in all its aspects of all weapons of mass destruction, to avoid excessive and destabilising accumulations and transfers of arms and to resolve peacefully in accordance with the Charter any problems concerning these matters threatening or disrupting the maintenance of regional and global stability. They emphasise the importance of the early ratification and implementation by the States concerned of all international and regional arms control arrangements, especially the START and CFE Treaties.

The proliferation of all weapons of mass destruction constitutes a threat to international peace and security. The members of the Council commit themselves to working to prevent the spread of technology relayed to the research for or production of such weapons and to take appropriate action to that end.

On nuclear proliferation, they note the importance of the decision of many countries to adhere to the Non-Proliferation Treaty and emphasise the integral role in the implementation of that treaty of fully effective IAEA safeguards, as well as the importance of effective export controls. The members of the Council will take appropriate measures in the case of any violations notified to them by the IAEA.

On chemical weapons, they support the effort of the Geneva conference with a view to reaching agreement on the conclusion, by the end of 1992 of a universal convention, including a verification regime, to prohibit chemical weapons.

On conventional armaments, they note the General Assembly's vote in favour of the United Nations register of arms transfers as a first step, and in this connection recognise the importance of all States providing all the information called for in the General Assembly's resolution.

In conclusion the members of the Security Council affirm their determination to build on the initiative of their meeting in order to secure positive advances in promoting international peace and security. They agree that the United Nations Secretary-General has a crucial role to play. The members of the Council express their deep appreciation to the outgoing Secretary-General, His Excellency Mr. Javier Perez de Cuellar, for his outstanding contribution to the work of the United Nations, culminating in the signature of the El Salvador peace agreement. They welcome the new Secretary-General, His Excellency Dr. Boutros Boutros-Ghali, and note with satisfaction his intention to strengthen and improve the functioning of the United Nations. They pledge their full support to him, and undertake to work closely with him and his staff in fulfilment of their shared objectives, including a more efficient and effective United Nations system.

The members of the Council agree that the world now has the best chance of achieving international peace and security since the foundation of the United Nations. They undertake to work, in their own efforts and in close cooperation with other United Nations member States to achieve this, as well as to address urgently all the other problems, in particular those of economic and social development, requiring the collective response of the international community. They recognise that peace and prosperity are indivisible and that lasting peace and stability require effective international cooperation for the eradication of poverty and the promotion of a better life for all in larger freedom.

Source : *Hindustan Times*, February 1, 1992.

9.9 **Korean Agreement**

The agreement signed in Seoul by the Premiers of North and South Korea, Mr. Yon Hyong Muk and Mr. Chung Won Shik, on December 13, 1991 called for reconciliation and non-aggression in the last theatre of the cold war. The agreement calls upon Seoul and Pyongyang to relax their military rivalry, respect each other's political system, permit free travel between the two Koreas and cooperate on economic exchanges.

The agreement reaffirmed the principle of peaceful unification pledged in the 1972 joint statement. It also stipulated an end to abuse and slander, non-intervention in domestic affairs and the establishment of a standing liaison office in the border village of Panmunjom.

The 1972 pact had called for the peaceful unification of the peninsula and promised exchange and cooperation on newspapers, television and radio, contact between people and the promotion of mutual visits by divided families. But these talks had ended in a stalemate.

The new agreement marks the culmination of 15 months of monumental changes in inter-Korean relations, spurred along by the collapse of communism in Eastern Europe and Soviet Union and the end of the cold war.

It may be recalled that Korea was divided into two parts after the Second World War in 1945.

9.10 **Military Expenditures**

Developing countries continue to allocate, on average, over 5 per cent of their GDP and up to 20 per cent of central government expenditures for the military, a major drain on their financial resources.

TABLE 9.1: Average military spending around the world: Adjusted SIPRI data, 1972-88

	In percent of[1]		
	GDP 1972-88	World military expenditure 1972-88	Central government expenditure[2] 1972-88
Industrial countries[3]	3.8	52.7	14.3
Eastern Europe	9.2	25.4	20.7
Developing countries	5.9	22.0	20.0
Asian developing	6.3	8.1	27.2
Middle East	11.6	8.0	23.1
North Africa	9.6	1.8	17.1
Sub-Saharan Africa	3.7	1.5	12.8
Latin America and Caribbean	2.3	2.5	8.6
Total	4.9	100.0	16.5
Developing country groupings:			
Net creditor nations	9.4	5.4	25.0
Heavily indebted	2.8	3.5	10.9
Small low-income economies	3.6	0.6	12.2

1 These are weighted averages derived by converting annual figures into US dollars, using official exchange rates, and then averaging the yearly ratios.

2 This column shows SIPRI military expenditures as per cent of central government expenditures; adjusted SIPRI military expenditures to central government would be higher.

3 The country categories are derived from the IMF *World Economic Outlook*, with major modifications to reflect the entire time period covered in this study.

Sources: Daniel P. Hewitt's, Estimates, based on SIPRI and ACDA data as reported in *Finance and Development*, September 1991.

9.11 **Nuclear Disarmament**

The US initiative was announced by the President, Mr. George Bush, on 28 September, 1991 following consultations with members of the North Atlantic Treaty Organisation (NATO). The Soviet response was announced in a television address by the Soviet President, Mr. Mikhail Gorbachev, on 5 October 1991 after talks with the Russian President, Mr. Boris Yeltsin, and other republican leaders.

U.S.'s Initiative

Speaking on 28 September, President Bush said that the pace of history had created an unparalleled opportunity to change the nuclear posture of the United States and the Soviet Union. "The prospect of a Soviet invasion into Western Europe, launched with little or no warning, is no longer a realistic threat. The Warsaw Pact has crumbled. In the Soviet Union, the advocates of democracy triumphed over a coup that would have restored the old system of repression." The events during August 'not only permit, but indeed demand swifter, bolder, action'.

Calling for the Soviet Union to match his initiatives, the President Bush said that the United Sates would:

— destroy all its ground-launched, short-range nuclear weapons;
— withdraw all tactical nuclear weapons from US warships, submarines, and land-based naval aircraft, and destroy many of them; and
— cancel the replacement programme for the nuclear short-range attack missile used by strategic bombers.

On US strategic nuclear weapons, Mr. Bush announced that he would:

— stand down immediately from their alert status all US strategic bombers;
— stand down from alert immediately all intercontinental ballistic (ICBMs) scheduled for destruction under the strategic arms reduction talks (START) treaty.
— accelerate the planned elimination of these systems once the treaty had been ratified by the US Congress;
— cancel the development of a mobile ICBM; and
— streamline US command and control procedures into one Strategic Command, which would allow US strategic nuclear forces to be more effectively managed.

Other proposals included:
— an early US-Soviet agreement to eliminate all ICBMs carrying multiple warheads;
— joint steps to permit the limited deployment of non-nuclear defences to protect against ballistic missile attack, while not undermining the credibility of existing deterrent forces; and
— an intensification of efforts to curb nuclear and missile proliferation.

Discussions with the Soviet Union were suggested on storage, movement, dismantling and destruction of nuclear warheads; improved security and safety arrangements for nuclear weapons; and more protection against their unauthorised or accidental use.

Soviet Proposals

The then President Gorbachev responding to the US initiative on 5 October, 1991 said that the Soviet Union would:

— eliminate all its nuclear artillery shells and nuclear warheads for tactical missiles;
— remove nuclear warheads from anti-aircraft missiles for storage in central bases;
— eliminate all its nuclear mines;
— remove tactical nuclear weapons from ships, submarines and naval aircraft; and
— eliminate some of these weapons.

In addition, the Soviet Union would:

— take Soviet heavy bombers off combat alert (storing their nuclear weapons at army warehouses);

— stop the development of a modified nuclear short-range missile for heavy bombers and of a small mobile ICBM;
— remove from alert status over 500 ICBMs (including 134 ICBMs with multiple individually targeted warheads);
— freeze the number of launchers for rail-deployed ICBMs with multiple warheads and halt the modernisation of these missiles; and
— remove from service three more nuclear-missile submarines.

Other unilateral commitments announced by Mr Gorbachev included:

— a reduction in the number of strategic nuclear weapons to 5,000, 1,000 below the limit of 6,000 set out in the START treaty; and
— a one-year moratorium on nuclear weapons testing.

Further ideas were put forward for new negotiations, including discussions on an additional 50 per cent reduction in strategic nuclear weapons. The Soviet Union would also be ready to discuss with the United States the latter's proposals on non-nuclear anti-missile defence systems. It also wanted to talk about the development of safe ways of storing and transporting nuclear warheads, and to reach an agreement with the United States on ending the production of fissionable material for nuclear weapons. The Soviet armed forces would be reduced by 700,000 (from 3.7 million).

Source : *Survey of Current Affairs*, October, 1991.

9.12 **Population and Output: Regionwise: 1989-92**

	Population 1990 (millions)	Population growth rate (annual %)	Rates of change of gross domestic product (annual %)			
			1989	1990[a]	1991[b]	1992[b]
1	2	3	4	5	6	7
World	5292	1.8	3.0	1.0	0.0	2.1
Developed market economics	813	0.6	3.3	2.4	1.4	3.0
North America	276	0.8	2.5	1.0	1.0	3.1
West Europe	358	0.2	3.4	2.7	1.2	2.3
Developed Asia	144	0.5	4.6	5.0	3.1	4.1
Eastern Europe and the Soviet Union[c]	405	0.6	1.4	-6.3	-9.5	-4.5
Developing countries	4074	2.1	3.4	2.9	3.5	5.0
Western hemisphere	432	2.1	1.1	-0.7	1.5	3.0
Africa	606	3.1	3.3	3.4	3.0	3.0
West Asia	130	3.0	2.4	0.0	-0.5	7.0
South and East Asia	1686	2.2	6.0	6.1	5.5	6.0
China[c]	1139	1.5	3.3	4.8	5.5	6.0
Mediterranean	81	1.5	1.0	-0.7	2.0	4.0

Contd.

1	2	3	4	5	6	7
Memorandum Items						
Heavily indebted countries	612	2.3	1.5	-0.8	1.5	—
Sub-Saharan Africa[d]	383	3.2	2.7	1.9	3.0	—

a Preliminary estimates.
b Forecast, based on project LINK and Secretariat estimates. For the groups of developing countries, estimates are rounded to the nearest half percentage point. Eastern Europe and the Soviet Union excludes former German Democratic Republic, which in included in Western Europe; there is therefore a break in the series after 1990 for the developed market economies and Eastern Europe and the Soviet Union.
c Net material product; data for 1989 are government estimates.
d Excluding Nigeria.
Source : *World Population Prospects*, 1990, United Nations, New York, 1991; *Development Forum*, July-August, 1991.

9.13 RUSSIA

USSR's Disintegration and Emergence of Independent Republics/States

Fall of Gorbachev

Mr. Mikhail Gorbachev, the man who changed the face of the Soviet Union and the world, resigned as President of the U.S.S.R. on December 25, 1991, officially bringing to a close the Soviet chapter of history. His resignation ended the existence of the once mighty Super Power and pledged to work for the success of the Commonwealth of Independent States (CIS) formed by 11 former Republics on the ruins of the world's first socialist state.

In a nationally televised address, Mr. Gorbachev, 60, who bowed out of office after nearly seven tumultuous years, said he was leaving "with concern but also with confidence." The first and the last President and the eighth and final leader of the now defunct Soviet Union, said he was "ceasing the activities as President of the U.S.S.R."

Shortly after stepping down as the last President of the Soviet Union, Mr. Gorbachev handed over to the Russian Federation President, Mr. Boris Yeltsin, the black briefcase with the Red Button — the ultimate control of 30,000 Soviet nuclear weapons.

Commonwealth of Independent States

Alma-Ata Declaration

Following is the text of the Alma-Ata declaration, signed by the heads of the 11 states.

The independent states —

The Azerbaijani Republic, the Republic of Armenia, the Republic of Byelorussia, the Republic Kazakhstan, the Republic of Kirghizia, the Republic of Moldavia, the Russian Federation, the Republic of Tadzhikistan, Turkmenistan, the Republic of Uzbekistan and Ukraine.

Seeking to build democratic law-governed states, the relations between which will develop on the basis of mutual recognition and respect for state sovereignty and sovereign equality, the inalienable right to self-determination, principles of equality and non-interference in the internal affairs, the rejection of the use of force, the threat of force and economic and any other methods of pressure, a peaceful settlement of disputes, respect for human rights and freedoms, including the rights of national minorities, a conscientious fulfilment of commitments and other generally recognised principles and standards of international law.

Believing that the strengthening of the relations of friendship, good neighbourliness and mutually advantageous cooperation, which has deep historic roots, meets the basic interests of nations and promotes the cause of peace and security.

Being aware of their responsibility for the preservation of civilian peace and inter-ethnic accord.

Being loyal to the objectives and principles of the agreement on the creation of the commonwealth of independent states, are making the following statement:

Cooperation between members of the commonwealth will be carried out in accordance with the principle of equality through coordinating institutions formed on a parity basis and operating in the way established by the agreements between members.

Independent Republics/States

1. *Russia*: Population: 147.7 mil. Largest republic. 52 per cent of population. Oil 90 per cent , wheat 50 per cent , textiles 50 per cent , minerals 75 per cent , key defence units. Problem of port.
2. *Ukraine*: Population: 51.7 mil (21 per cent of Russians). Sugar 60 per cent , Corn 56 per cent , wheat 25 per cent , iron ore 50 per cent , coal 30 per cent , meat 25 per cent .
3. *Uzbekistan*: Population: 19.6 mil. Cotton 75 per cent , exports.
4. *Kazakhstan*: Population: 16.5 mil (41 per cent Russians). 2nd largest republic. Wheat 30 per cent , power 15 per cent , coal 20 per cent , wool 30 per cent.
5. *Byelorussia*: Population: 10.1 mil. Fertilisers 50 per cent . Major exporter of consumer goods.
6. *Azerbaijan*: Population 6.9 mil. Oil equipment 70 per cent , major cotton grower.
7. *Georgia*: Population: 5.3 mil. Tea & citrus fruits 95 per cent .
8. *Tajikistan*: Population: 5 mil. (23 per cent Uzbeks).
9. *Moldavia*: Population: 4.2 mil. Major centre for machine tools, tobacco and grapes. Big exporter.
10. *Kirghizia*: Population: 4.2 mil. (26 per cent Russians). World's third largest wool producer. Major source of coal.
11. *Lithuania*: Population: 3.7 mil. Industrial hub of consumer goods, ship building and electronics.
12. *Armenia*: Population: 3.5 mil. Major gold and copper supplier. Exports computers.
13. *Turkmenistan*: Population: 3.5 mil. Rich in coal and sulphur.

14. *Latvia*: Population: 2.7 mil. (33 per cent Russians). Makes 50 per cent of mopeds, 35 per cent washing machines.
15. *Estonia*: Population: 1.6 mil. (28 per cent Russians). 95 per cent of shale oil. Has Tallinn port.

Russia-U.S. Cooperation Declaration

The U.S. President, Mr. George Bush, and the Russian President, Mr. Boris Yeltsin signed a joint declaration at Camp David, a U.S. presidential retreat in Maryland, to begin a new phase of friendship and cooperation between their nations.

Their joint declaration said: "Russia and the United States do not regard each other as potential adversaries. From now on, the relationship will be characterised by friendship and partnership founded on mutual trust and respect, and a common commitment, to democracy and economic freedom."

Source: *Times of India*, February 3, 1992.

9.14 SAARC Summit, December 21, 1991

South Asian Association for Regional Cooperation (SAARC) summit in Colombo on December 21, 1991 agreed to liberalise trade in the region.

The Heads of Governments also decided to closely examine the proposal to establish a SAARC preferential trade arrangement by 1997. They also decided to establish an independent South Asian committee on poverty alleviation, consisting of eminent persons from SAARC member states to conduct an in-depth study of diverse experiences of the seven nations of the grouping.

The declaration, laying stress on promoting primary education in the region, agreed to share the member countries' expertise and technical know-how so as to achieve by the year 2000 total primary education for children.

At the sixth summit of the SAARC, the participating nations expressed faith in greater regional cooperation in solving pressing problems.

9.15 United Nations in 1992

General Assembly

The General Assembly is composed of all 166 United Nations Member States. These are:

Afghanistan, Albania, Algeria, Angola, Antigua and Barbuda, Argentina, Australia, Austria, Bahamas, Bahrain, Bangladesh, Barbados, Belarus, Belgium, Belize, Benin, Bhutan, Bolivia, Botswana, Brazil, Brunei DaruSalam, Bulgaria, Burkina Faso, Burundi, Cambodia, Cameroon, Canada, Cape Verde, Central African Republic, Chad, Chile, China, Colombia. Comoros, Congo, Costa Rica, Cote d'Ivoire, Cuba, Cyprus, Czechoslovakia, Democratic People's Republic of Korea, Denmark, Djibouti, Dominica, Dominican Republic, Ecuador, Egypt, El Salvador, Equatorial Guinea, Estonia, Ethiopia, Federated States of Micronesia, Fiji, Finland, France, Gabon, Gambia, Germany, Ghana, Greece, Grenada, Guatemala, Guinea, Guinea Bissau, Guyana, Haiti, Honduras, Hungary, Iceland, India, Indonesia, Iran, Iraq, Ireland, Israel, Italy, Jamaica, Japan, Jordan, Kenya, Kuwait, Lao People's Democratic Republic, Latvia, Lebanon, Lesotho Liberia, Libya, Liechtenstein, Lithuania, Luxembourg, Madagascar, Malawi, Malaysia, Maldives, Mali, Malta, Marshall Islands, Mauritania, Mauritius, Mexico, Mongolia, Morocco, Mozambique, Myanmar, Namibia, Nepal, Netherlands, New Zealand, Nicaragua, Niger, Nigeria, Norway, Oman, Pakistan, Panama, Papua New Guinea, Paraguay, Peru, Philippines, Polland, Portugal, Qatar, Republic of Korea, Romania, Russian Federation, Rwanda, Saint Christopher and Nevis, Saint Lucia, Saint Vincent and the Grenadines, Samoa, Sao Tome and Principe, Saudi Arabia, Senegal Seychelles, Sierra Leone, Singapore, Solomon Islands, Somalia, South Africa, Spain, Sri Lanka, Sudan, Suriname, Swaziland, Sweden, Syria, Thailand, Togo, Trinidad and Tobago, Tunisia, Turkey, Uganda, Ukraine, United Arab Emirates, United Kingdom, United Republic of Tanzania, United States, Uruguay, Vanuatu, Venezuela, Viet Nam, Yemen, Yugoslavia, Zaire, Zambia, Zimbabwe.

Security Council

The Security Council has 15 members. The Charter designates five States as Permanent Members, and General Assembly elects 10 other members for two-year terms.

The five permanent members of the Council are: China France, Russian Federation, United Kingdom and the United States.

The Union of Soviet Socialist Republics was an original member of the United Nations from 24 October 1945. In a letter dated 24 October, 1991, Boris Yeltsin, President of the Russian Federation, informed the Secretary-General, Javier Perez de Cuellar, that the membership of the Soviet Union in the Security Council and all other United Nations organs was being continued by the Russian Federation with the support of the countries of the Commonwealth of Independent States. According to President Yeltsin, the Russian Federation remains responsible in full for all the rights and obligations of the former Soviet Union under the United Nations Charter.

Economic and Social Council

The Economic and Social Council has 54 members, elected for three-year terms by the General Assembly. In 1992, the Council is composed of the following States:

Algeria, Angola, Argentina, Australia, Austria, Bahrain, Bangladesh, Belarus (former Byelorussia), Belgium Benin, Botswana, Brazil, Bulgaria, Burkina Faso, Canada, Chile, China, Colombia, Ecuador, Ethiopia, Finland, France, Germany, Guinea, India, Iran, Italy, Jamaica, Japan, Kuwait, Madagascar, Malaysia, Mexico, Morocco, Pakistan, Peru, Philippines, Poland, Romania, Russian Federation, Rwanda, Somalia, Spain, Suriname, Swaziland, Sweden, Syria, Togo, Trinidad and Tobago, Turkey, United Kingdom, United States, Yugoslavia and Zaire.

Trusteeship Council

The Trusteeship Council has five members. One member, the United States, administers Palau, one of the remaining four entities which constituted the original Trust Territory of the Pacific Islands, the only territory that still remained under the trusteeship system. On 22 December 1990, the Security Council terminated the Trusteeship Agreement for three of the entities: the Federated States of Micronesia and the Marshall Islands (now United Nations Member States), which had drawn up Covenant with the administering authority. Palau, however, has not yet determined the nature of its future status with the administering authority and therefore remains under the Trusteeship Agreement.

The non-administering members of the Trusteeship Council are the other four Permanent Members of the Security Council (China, France, Russian Federation and United Kingdom).

International Court of Justice

The International Court of Justice has 15 members, elected by both the General Assembly and the Security Council. Judges hold nine-year terms.

As of 5 February 1992, the composition of the 15-member Court will be as follows: Roberto Ago, of Italy; Andres Aguilar Mawdsley, of Venezuela; Mohammed Bedjaoui, of Algeria; Bola Ajibola, of Nigeria; Jens Evensen of Norway; Gilbert Guillaume, of France; Sir Robert Yewdall Jennings, of the United Kingdom; Manfred Lachs, of Poland; Ni Zhengyu, of China; Shigeru Oda, of Japan; Raymond Ranjeva, of Madagascar; Stephen M. Schwebel, of the United States; Mohammed Shahabdeen, of Guyana; Nikolai K. Tarassov, of the Russian Federation and Christopher S. Weeramantry, of Sri Lanka.

Source: *UN Newsletter*, January 25, 1992.

Mr. Boutros Ghali, New Secretary General of the United Nations

Boutros Boutros-Ghali, the Deputy Prime Minister of Egypt, was appointed by the General Assembly on 3 December, 1991 the sixth Secretary-General of the United Nations, for a five-year term beginning on 1 January 1992. In a statement to the Assembly, Mr. Boutros-Ghali said that, in the name of every African, he wished to express appreciation for the opportunity afforded to Africa, through his election, to take part in the service of the international community and that Africa feels ready to make its contribution by virtue of its creative ability and recent achievements in the international arena.

He went on to say that because he belonged to Egypt, an Arab African State that bordered the Mediterranean Sea, which throughout the ages had been a crossroad for many cultures, it was his fervent desire to communicate cultural legacy through mutual cooperation, and to raise the banner of peace wherever there was underdevelopment, conflict and tension in the world.

He was well aware, he stated, that the organization faced the need for fundamental readjustments in response to a world in constant transformation. A number of basic issues confronted the international community. Outlining those issues, Mr Boutros-Ghali cited the need for strengthening of United Nations peace-keeping and peace-making, narrowing of the gap between the North and the South and the strengthening of the fundamental freedoms and democratic institutions as well as democracy on the international level.

Statement of Perez de Cuellar

In his statement to the Assembly, Secretary-General Javier Perez de Cuellar expressed his satisfaction with the unanimous decision of the General Assembly. He said he was happy to leave his delicate post in the hands of an Egyptian of "notable skill and courage," who was also endowed with "the vision and pragmatism necessary in the times to come." He was also happy that, as he left his post, the Organization was no longer on the sidelines, but was at the hub of world affairs. Only in one respect - financial insolvency, not due to poor management - was there a problem.

The Secretary-General-designate holds several positions related to his background in law, international affairs and political science, among them, his membership in the Institute of International Law, the International Studies and the Academice des Sciences Morales et Politique (Academie Francaise) Paris.

He has participated in many conferences, meetings and symposia over the last four decades. They deal, among other things, with international law, human rights, economic and social development, decolonization, the Middle East question, non-alignment, and Afro-Arab cooperation.

In September 1978, Mr. Boutros-Ghali attended the Camp David Summit Conference and had a role in negotiating the Camp David accords between Egypt and Israel, which were signed in 1979. He has led many delegations of his country to, among others, meetings of the Organization of African Unity (OAU) and the movement of non-aligned countries, as well as to the Summit Conference of the French and the African Heads of State. He has similarly headed Egypt's delegation to the General Assembly sessions in 1979, 1982 and 1990.

Source: *UN Newsletter*, December 7, 1991.

10

SIGNIFICANT INTERNATIONAL EVENTS

April 1991

30 Several thousand people killed in Bangla cyclone.
— Hundreds killed in Georgian earthquake.

May

1 The Cambodian Prime Minister, Mr. Hun Sen, agrees for cease-fire.
2 Pakistan lifts martial law.
5 Foreign Ministers of six Gulf Cooperation Council call upon UN to impose economic sanction against Iraq.
14 The Nepalese Prime Minister, Shri K.P. Bhattarai resigns.
16 The Soviet Union and China sign border agreement. The first French women Prime Minister Ms. Edith Cresson assumes office.
21 The Ethiopian President flees to Zimbabwe
29 G.P. Koirala Ministry sworn in Nepal

June

12 Shri Boris Yeltsin's victory as Russian Federation's first President
25 The UN team finds chemical weapon's site in Iraq.
The Yugoslavia republics of Slovenia and Croatia declare independence.

July

10 The US President Shri George Bush lifts sanctions against South Africa.
23 PLO announces Parliament in exile.
31 Shri Mikhail Gorbachev and Shri George Bush sign pact to reduce long range nuclear weapons at Moscow summit.

August

19 National state of emergency declared in the Soviet Union.
19 Removal of Shri Mikhail Gorbachev as President by communist junta.
21 Shri Gorbachev's return to Moscow after the failure of the coup.
24 Resignation of Shri Gorbachev as communist party chief.
30 Azerbaijan declares independence.
31 Uzbekistan and Kirqizia declare independence.

September

2 The US recognises Baltic republics.
3 The Soviet republic of Tadzhikistan declare independence.
21 Armenia votes for independence.
26 The Romanian Premier, Shri Petre Roman resigns following violent street protests.
30 The Haitian President Shri Jean Bertrand Aristide is ousted.

October

1 Twelve Soviet republics agree to a new Economic Union.

14 Nobel peace prize for Myanmar's pro-democracy leader, Smt. Aung San Suer Kyi.

17 NATO decides to cut nuclear arsenal in Europe by 80 per cent.

18 The Soviet Union and Israel restore diplomatic ties after twenty-four years.

November

1 Shri Kenneth Kaunda concedes defeat in Zambia's Presidential election.

5 Kichi Miyazawa becomes Japanese Prime Minister.

22 Shri Boutros Ghali of Egypt elected next UN Secretary-General.

December

1 Republic of Ukrainians votes for independence.

5 Russia, Ukraine and Byelorussia form Commonwealth of Independent States and declare the Soviet Union defunct.

17 Shri Mikhail Gorbachev and Shri Boris Yeltsin agree to dissolve the Soviet Union and proclaim new Commonwealth by year end.

19 The Australian Prime Minister Shri Bob Hawke loses power.

21 Eleven former Soviet Republics sign a Commonwealth agreement.

25 Shri Mikhail Gorbachev resigns as the Soviet President.

January 1992

1 Mr. Boutros Ghali takes over as the Secretary General of the UN.

2 The Georgian opposition leaders announce the formation of a military council to replace President Zviad Gamsakhurdia.

6 Georgian President toppled.

21 Eighty-six dead in French Air Crash.
Sixty securitymen killed in Sri Lanka.

24 China establishes ties with Israel.

29 US President Bush announces N-arms cut.
Russian President Yeltsin also announces N-arms cut.

31 Prime Minister P.V. Narasimha Rao suggests wider representation to Security Council.

February 1992

20 The Negotiating Group of General Agreement on Tariffs and Trade (GATT) held two meetings from February 20 to February 28.

26 Two missions commissioned by a Washington Conference of UNO, visited the New Independent States of the Soviet Union and found that health care institutions were deteriorating rapidly.

March 1992

2 The fourth and final session of the Preparatory Committee for the Earth Summit, June 1992, was held from March 2 to March 31, 1992.

17 A referendum was held in South Africa which endorsed the reform programme of the South African President, M.F.W. de Klerk.

15 UN's largest Peace Keeping Operation began in Cambodia.

19 Britain and other European Community countries welcomed the result of the referendum held in South Africa.

PART TWO

INDIA 1991-92

11

LAND AND ITS PEOPLE

India that is Bharat covering a land area 32,87,263 sq.km is the seventh largest and the second most populous country of the world. It stretches 3,214 km from North to South between the extreme latitudes and 2,933 km from East to West between the extreme longitude. On this 2.4 per cent of earth's surface live 15 per cent (88 crore people) of world's population.

11.1 **Population**

Over 160 million people are added annually to our population (President's Republic Day Speech, 25th January, 1989). Since 1881, the Census in India has been taken regularly after ten years. According to 1991 Census, the total population of India (including the projected population of Assam) is 8,43,930,861. As compared to 1981 census, it showed an increase of 23.50 per cent. According to 1991 Census, the growth of urban population in the country during the decade 1981-1991, slowed down by about ten per cent as compared to the earlier decade of 1971-81. However, the number of cities and towns has been consistently increasing. The urban population at present in 25.72 per cent.

11.2 **Density**

The average density of population per km^2 in 1991 is 267. It varies considerably from State to State.

11.3 **Sex Ratio**

According to 1991 Census (Provisional) there are 43.7 crore males and 40.6 crore females; thus for every 1,000 males India has 929 females. Only Kerala has more women than men, i.e., 1,040 per 1,000 men. The lowest female ratio among the State is in Haryana, i.e., 874 for 1000 men and the lowest female ratio among the Union Territories is in Chandigarh where it is 733 per thousand.

11.4 **Literacy**

According to 1991 Census, the literacy percentage is 52.11. Out of this 63.86 per cent of males and 39.42 per cent of females are literate.

11.5 **Major Religions and Persuasions, 1981**

TABLE 11.1: Major religions and persuations, 1981 (exluding Assam)

Religion Community	Population	Percentage of Total Population
1	2	3
Hindus	54,97,24,717	82.63
Muslims	7,55,71,514	11.36

Contd.

1	2	3
Christians	1,61,74,498	2.43
Sikhs	1,30,78,146	1.96
Buddhists	47,19,900	0.71
Jains	31,92,572	0.48
Other persuasions	27,66,285	0.42
Religion not stated	60,217	0.01

11.6 Languages

The detailed data from the 1981 Census (data for 1991 not yet available) which were made available only in 1988, enumerates the main languages spoken in the household and not the mother tongue and groups related languages under a dominant language. By this count, 106 languages are separately recognised. Of these 94 are spoken by 10,000 or more people.

There were 1562 mother tongues, 10 writing system, and 67 languages as used in the school system out of 2000 codified languages.

Fifteen languages have been specified in the Eighth Schedule of the Constitution. These are: Assamese, Bengali, Gujarati, Hindi, Kannada, Kashmiri, Malayalam, Marathi, Oriya, Punjabi, Sanskrit, Sindhi, Tamil, Telugu and Urdu.

11.7 National Flag

The National Flag is horizontally tricolour with deep saffron (*Kesari*) at the top, white in the middle and dark green at the bottom in equal proportion. The ratio of the width of the flag to its length is two to three. In the centre of the white band is a wheel, in navy blue, which represents the *Charkha*. Its design is that of the wheel (*Chakra*) which appears on the abacus of the Sarnath Lion Capital of Ashoka. Its diameter approximates to the width of the white band and it has 24 spokes.

The design of the National Flag was adopted by the Constituent Assembly of India on 22nd July, 1947. Its use and display are regulated by a code.

11.8 State Emblem

The State Emblem of India is an adaptation from the Sarnath Lion Capital of Ashoka as preserved in the Sarnath Museum. In the original, there are four lions, standing back to back, mounted on an abacus with a frieze carrying sculptures in high relief of an elephant, a galloping horse, a bull and a lion separated by intervening wheels (*Chakras*) over a bell-shaped lotus. Carved out of a single block of polished sandstone, the Capital is crowned by the Wheel of the Law (*Dharma Chakra*).

In the State Emblem adopted by the Government of India on 26th January, 1950, only three lions are visible, the fourth being hidden from view. The wheel appears on relief in the centre of the abacus with a bull on the right and a horse on the left and the outlines of the other wheels on the extreme right and left. The bell-shaped lotus has been omitted. The words *Satyameva Jayate* from the *Mundaka Upanishad,* meaning 'Truth alone Triumphs', are inscribed below the abacus in Devanagri script.

11.9 National Anthem

The song *Jana-gana-mana,* composed by Rabindranath Tagore (1861-1941) was adopted by the Constituent Assembly as the National Anthem of India on 24th January, 1950. It was first sung on 27th December, 1911 at the Calcutta Session of the Indian National Congress. The complete song consists of five stanzas. The first stanza constitutes the full version of the National Anthem. It reads:

Jana-gana-mana-adhinayaka, jaya he
Bharata-bhagya-vidhata
Punjab-Sindhu-Gujarat-Maratha-
Dravida-Utkala-Banga
Vindhya-Himachala-Yamuna-Ganga
Uchchala-jaladhi-taranga.
Tava shubha name jage,
tava shubha asisa, mage,
gahe tava jaya-gatha,
Jana-gana-mangala-dayaka jaya he
Bharata-bhagya-vidhata.
Jaya he, jaya he, jaya he,
Jaya jaya jaya, jaya he !

Playing time of the full version of the National Anthem is approximately 52 seconds. A short version consisting of the first and last lines of the stanza (playing time approximately 20 seconds) is also played on certain occasions. The following is Tagore's English rendering of this stanza:

Thou art the ruler of the minds of all people,
dispenser of India's destiny.
Thy name rouses the hearts of Punjab, Sind, Gujarat and Maratha.
Of the Dravida and Orissa and Bengal;
it echoes in the hills of the Vindhyas and Himalayas,
mingles in the music of Jamuna and Ganges
and is chanted by the waves of the India Sea.
They pray for thy blessings and sing thy praise.
The saving of all people waits in thy hand,
thou dispenser of India's destiny.
victory, victory, victory to thee.

11.10 National Song

The song *Vande Mataram,* composed by Bankimchandra Chatterji (1838-1894) was a source of inspiration to the people in their struggle for freedom. It has an equal status with *Jana-gana-mana.* The first political occasion on which it was sung was the 1896 session of the Indian National Congress. The following is the text of its first stanza:

Vande Mataram!
Sujalam, suphalam, malayaja shitalam,

Shasyashyamalam, Mataram!
Shubhrajyotsna pulakitayaminim,
Phullakusumita drumadala shobhinim,
Suhasinim sumadhura bhashinim,
Sukhadam, Varadam, Mataram!

The English translation of the stanza rendered by Sri Aurobindo (1872-1950) in prose* is:

I bow to thee, Mother,
richly-watered, richly-fruited,
cool with the winds of the south,
dark with the crops of the harvests,
the Mother!
Her nights rejoicing in the glory of the moonlight,
her lands clothed beautifully with her trees in flowering bloom,
sweet of laughter, sweet of speech,
the Mother, giver of boons, giver of bliss.

11.11 National Calendar

A uniform National Calendar based on the *Saka Era* with *Chaitra* as its first month and a normal year of 365 days was adopted from 22 March, 1957 (along with the Gregorian calendar) for the following official purposes in particular :

(i) *Gazette of India*
(ii) news broadcast by All India Radio,
(iii) calendars issued by the Government of India, and
(iv) government communications addressed to members of the public.

The dates of the National Calendar have a permanent correspondence with the dates of the Gregorian calendar; *Chaitra* 1 falling on 22 March normally and on 21 March in a leap year.

Chaitra 1 of Saka Era 1012 is the New Year Day. *Saka Era* was established in AD 78 by Emperor Kanishka of the Saka dynasty, who ruled in the North and North-Western India in the first century of the Christian era. The day, which has been chosen to become the first day of the New Year, is *vernal equinox* when the day and the night are of equal duration throughout the world. *Saka* calendar is based on Solar *Chaitra* and not no Lunar *Chaitra*. *Chaitra Shukla Pratipada* which is celebrated as New Year Day, in many parts of the country, is called differently. It is *Gudi Padwa* in Maharashtra and *Yugadi* in Karnataka based on lunar calendar, etc. April 13, *Baishakhi* in Punjab, *Pongal* on April 14 in Tamil Nadu and *Paila Baishakh* in West Bengal are based on solar calendar. In solar calendar this discrepancy of 22 or 23 days (between March 22 and April 13/14) has been caused by an astronomical phenomenon called the precession of the equinoxes.

* As published in *Sri Aurobindo Birth Centenary Library*, Popular edition, 1972, Vol. 8.

11.12 **National Animal**

The majestic tiger (*Panthera tigris*) (Linnaeus), the national animal of India for its rich colour, illusive design and formidable power, has always been held in high esteem in India. Among the carnivores, the tiger if very gorgeous and attractive with roaring voice as symbol of power. Out of eight races of the species known the world over, the Indian race is the Bengal tiger. The Royal Bengal Tiger is found throughout the country and also in Nepal, Bhutan and Bangladesh. As shrinkage of habitat in India dwindled its population to only 1,827 in 1972, the Project Tiger was launched on Ist April, 1973. Since then there is a gradual increase in its population estimated to be 4,230 in April 1986.

11.13 **National Bird**

The Indian peacock (*Pavo cristatus*) (Linnaeus), the national bird of India, is one of the most beautiful birds, particularly the males having the glistering blue neck, breast, fanshape crest and long magnificent tail. The courtship dance of the male by fanning up the tail before the female is most spectacular. From time immemorial, this bird has found a profound place in Indian literature, folklore and legends.

The Indian peafowl, as the peacock is called, is widely found in the country in south and east of Indus, Jammu and Kashmir, east Assam, south of Mizoram and the whole of Indian Peninsula. It is fully protected under the Indian Wild Life (Protection) Act, 1972.

Source : *India 1988-89*

11.14 **Presidents of India**

January 26, 1950 — May 13, 1962	Rajendra Prasad
May 13, 1962 — May 13, 1967	S. Radhakrishnan
May 13, 1967 — May 3, 1969	Zakir Husain
May 3, 1969 — July 20, 1969	V.V. Giri (Acting)
July 20, 1969 — August 21, 1969	M. Hidayatullah (Acting)
August 24, 1969 — August 24, 1974	V.V. Giri
August 24, 1974 — February 11, 1977	Fakhruddin Ali Ahmed
February 11, 1977 — July 25, 1977	B.D. Jatti (Acting)
July 25, 1977 — July 25, 1982	N. Sanjeeva Reddy
July 25, 1982 — July 25, 1987	Zail Singh
July 25, 1987 —	R. Venkataraman

11.15 **Vice Presidents of India**

1952-1962	S. Radhakrishnan
1962-1967	Zakir Husain
1967-1969	V.V. Giri
1969-1974	G.S. Pathak
1974-1979	B.D. Jatti
1979-1984	M. Hidayatullah
1984-1987	R. Venkataraman
1987-1992	S.D. Sharma

11.16 **Prime Ministers of India**

August 15, 1947 — May 27, 1964	Jawaharlal Nehru
May 27, 1964 — June 9, 1964	Guljari Lal Nanda (Acting)
June 09, 1964 — January 11, 1966	Lal Bahadur Shastri
January 11, 1966 — January 24, 1966	Guljari Lal Nanda (Acting)
January 24, 1966 — March 24, 1977	Indira Gandhi
March 24, 1977 — July 28, 1979	Morarji Desai
July 28, 1979 — January 14, 1980	Charan Singh
January 14, 1980 — October 31, 1984	Indira Gandhi
October 31, 1984 — December 1, 1989	Rajiv Gandhi
December 2, 1989 — November 7, 1990	V. P Singh
November 9, 1990 — June, 20, 1991	Chandra Shekhar
June 20, 1991 —	P.V. Narasimha Rao

11.17 **Speakers of the Lok Sabha**

1952-1956	G.V. Mavlankar
1956-1962	Ananthasayanam Ayyangar
1962-1967	S. Hukam Singh
1967-1969	N. Sanjeeva Reddy
1969-1975	G.S. Dhillon
1975-1977	B.R. Bhagat
March 1977—July 1977	N. Sanjeeva Reddy
1977-1979	K.S. Hegde
1980-1989	Balram Jakhar
November 19, 1989— June 1991	Rabi Ray
July 10, 1991—	Shivraj Patil

11.18 **Important Days**

National Youth Day	January 12
Army Day	January 15
Republic Day	January 26
International Customs Day	January 26
Martyrs' Day	January 30
National Science Day	February 28
International Women's Day	March 8
World Disabled Day	March 15
World Forestry Day	March 21
National Maritime Day	April 5
World Health Day	April 7
May Day (Worker's Day: International Labour Day)	May 1
World Red Cross Day	May 8
Commonwealth Day	May 24
World Environment Day	June 5

Hiroshima Day	August 6
Quit India Day	August 9
Nagasaki Day	August 9
Independence Day	August 15
Teacher's Day	September 5
World Literacy Day	September 8
World Tourism Day	September 27
Mahatma Gandhi Birthday	October 2
World Habitat Day	October 5
Air Force Day	October 8
Post Office Day	October 19
World Standard Day	October 14
World Food Day	October 16
UN Day	October 24
National Re-dedication Day	October 31
Children's Day	November 14
National Integration Day	November 19
Navy Day	December 4
Flag Day	December 7
Human Rights Day (UN)	December 10
Kisan Day	December 23

12

INDIA SINCE INDEPENDENCE

12.1 Achievements

Going back, India that is Bharat was the richest and the most prosperous country in the world. It was then known as the 'Golden sparrow'. The standard of living of the common man was reasonably high. Articles of everyday needs were available in plenty. A common man could get easily things like milk, butter, ghee and foodgrains. Literally speaking 'Rivers of milk flowed'. Indian handicrafts and industrial products were known for their excellence of design and quality all over the world. From the richness of this land and from the labour and wisdom of its people had sprung great wealth, great ideas, great skills and arts. Naturally, therefore, foreigners were tempted to come to India for learning, as well as loot and plunder.

The well-knit economic organisation of the country received a serious setback with the advent of invaders and especially with the British rulers who were primarily concerned with the governance of the country, not its growth. They were greatly interested in draining out wealth from India. Industrial crafts, industries and agriculture, all suffered heavily. As a result, India became a poor country. People remained underfed, ill-housed and scantily dressed.

The statement 'A rich country inhabited by the poor people' seems paradoxical and strange. But it is still true to a considerable extent though since independence we have made a spectacular progress in different fields. The giant irrigation dams at Bhakra, Hirakud and Nagarjunasagar; the huge steel mills at Bhilai, Bokaro, Rourkela and Durgapur; the fertiliser factories at Sindri and Nangal; the 1000-tonne per day ammonia plant (said to be the largest in the world) at Tuticorin; the aircraft factories at Bangalore, Hyderabad and Nasik; the locomotive factory at Chittaranjan; the atomic reactor at Trombay; the rocket launching station at Sriharikota; the ISRO's establishment like Vikram Sarabhai Space Centre, Trivandrum and Space Application Centre, Ahmedabad; launching of Indian Satellite Bhaskara and Rohini; three axis-stabilised Geostationary Communication Satellite; APPLE (Ariane Passenger Payload Experiment), establishment of Indian National Satellite System (INSAT); participation of an Indian Cosmonaut in a joint Indo-Soviet Space Flight; nuclear explosion at Pokaran, etc., are the prized possessions of the Indian Nation.

November 21, 1988 marked the 25th anniversary of Indian Space Programme. The Silver Jubilee Year saw the launching of three major programmes; IRS-1A, ASLV-02 and INSAT-1A (see relevant Chapter for details). Militarily we are among the first five countries in the world.

India is the sixth country to successfully detonate a nuclear device as part of its successful experiment for peace purposes.

We have the third largest reservoir of highly skilled scientific and technical manpower in the world.

India is the fifth nation to have its remote sensing satellite.

We have achieved self-sufficiency in foodgrains.

India is the third largest producer of books in English, next to the U.S.A. and U.K.

The problem of eradication of poverty of the masses became the first consideration of the government soon after we achieved independence. We decided to adopt the system of planned development for tackling our problem of poverty which was linked with rising prices, low production, unemployment and inequalities of income.

To frame a development plan for independent India, the Planning Commission was set up in March 1950, by a resolution of the Government of India. The aims of planning as defined by the resolution were, 'to promote a rapid rise in the standard of living of the people by efficient exploitation of the resources of the country, increasing production and offering opportunities to all for employment in the service of the community'.

The First Five Year Plan was initiated in April 1951. This covered the period 1951-1956. So far we have had seven Five Year Plans and three Yearly Plans. The Eighth Five-Year Plan, which is under consideration, will cover the period 1992 to 1996.

The most important achievement of planning in the post-independence period is our self-sufficiency in foodgrains. Now we need not import foodgrains for domestic requirements as we did till a few years ago. The production is expected to touch a high figure of about 176 million tonnes in 1991-92 as against 51 million tonnes in 1950-51.

As a result of many multipurpose projects, area under irrigation increased from 226 lakh hectares in 1950 to 860 lakh hectares in 1990-91.

Our industry has many strengths: a wide range of products, a demonstrable ability to absorb and operate high technology, a large entrepreneurial capability and ample managerial and technical skills.

During the Plans, industrial production has made rapid strides, both in terms of quality and quantity. As per the index of industrial production, the growth rates achieved in the industrial sector as a whole were 8.6 per cent in 1984-85, 8.7 per cent in 1985-86, 9.1 per cent in 1986-87, 7.3 per cent in 1987-88, 8.7 in 1988-89, 8.6 in 1989 and 8.1 in 1990-91. However, there was a setback in 1991-92. There was a (—)0.9 per cent decline (April-November).

In the year 1950-51, there were only two major units producing iron and steel. Now we have eleven relevant major steel plants. Steel production rose from about one million tonnes in 1950-51, to about 13.40 million tonnes in 1990-91.

Cotton textile industry holds the second place in the production of cloth in the world. At present there are about 700 textile mills in the country.

In 1951, we had 138 sugar mills in the country. This number increased to 351 in 1987. About half the mills are in the public sector.

The production of cement increased from 2.69 million tonnes in 1951 to 10.7 million tonnes in 1990-91 (provisional).

The generation of electric power registered a twenty-fold increase.

Public sector in the field of industries has witnessed a very significant rise. In 1951, we had only 5 public undertakings whereas there were 244 public undertakings in 1991, in the Central Sector.

By 1985, the road network in the country had become very elaborate system of national highways, state and district roads, and rural roads totalling about

18 lakh km. This four and a half times the figure of 4 lakh km of roads in 1950-51.

Between 1950-51 and 1984-85, the number of trucks rose from 82,000 to 7,63,000 and buses from 34,000 to 2,06,000.

Per capita income increased from Rs. 246 in 1950-51 to about Rs. 5,700 in 1990 at current prices.

Prior to Independence, average life span of an Indian was 32 years. Today it has lengthened to 58 years.

Our Constitution can be described as a charter of freedom. It enshrines the supremacy of the will of the people and their resolve to secure for all citizens: justice, social economic and political; Equality of status and opportunity, and to promote among them all Fraternity assuring the dignity of the individual and the unity of the nation. The will of the people is exercised through universal adult franchise and a parliamentary democracy. Election to Parliament and State legislature are open contests for all political parties, and independent candidates also enjoy full scope to express themselves.

Notwithstanding various problems and the magnitude of the task of conducting elections, we have all general elections with significant success. Barring the period, March 1977 to July 15, 1979 and December 1989 to May 1991 when the Janata Party and National Front were in power at the Centre, the Congress had held the reigns of the Government since the first General Election in 1951-52.

Many political changes accompanied by government changes, especially in States have taken place in the country since Independence, through peaceful and constitutional means. Transfer of power from one party to another has taken place as a natural course and in an orderly manner.

Another historic step in the development of democracy in the country was the inauguration of Panchayati Raj in October 1959. The Panchayati Raj aims at giving authority and responsibility to the village people and helping them play an active role in local development through the Panchayats. There are over 228,500 Village Panchayats in the country covering partially the entire population of India.

With the Panchayati Raj, we now have parliamentary democracy in operation from the Gram Sabha to the Lok Sabha.

We have got an established judicial system.

12.2 **Tasks Ahead**

A large part of our population still remains backward. There is a wide gulf between the rich and the poor. Unemployment is on the increase. National integration is our urgent need. Erosion in the standard of values, in fact, is the topmost blockade, which requires to be checked and a crusade for 'Clean Life, Clean Politics and Clean Administration' is to be given first priority.

India is on the move. The tasks before us are very challenging and tremendous. But there is no cause for despair. By harnessing all our resources and working unitedly and sincerely, we can usher in an era of peace, progress and prosperity.

The 21st century beckons us holding forth new hopes. We, the people of India, must march ahead as an integrated resurgent.

As Gurudev Rabindranath Tagore would advise, we must "hold the faith firm", surely "the day will dawn".

13

CENSUS OF INDIA, 1991

13.1 Conduct of Census

The Indian Census is carried out under the Census Act, 1948. This Act makes it obligatory for a persons assigned with census duties to perform the same faithfully and diligently. It also makes it obligatory for the public to answer all the census questions correctly and fully. It guarantees the confidentiality of the information and total non-identification of the individual. While according to the Census Act, the census is taken by the Central Government, the census machinery is provided by the State Governments and Union Territory Administrations. The census enumerators are mostly drawn from among local school teachers and also from other Central and State Government staff and employees of local bodies.

The 1991 census included India's population at sunrise on March 1, 1991. It was the fifth census after independence and the thirteenth as reckoned from 1872. The population of India according to 1991 census stood at 843,930,861. The preparation for the 1991 census began in 1987. In the first place, up-to-date list of villages and towns as also the latest maps at State/and Union Territory/District/Tehsil/town level were prepared, after taking into account the various jurisdictional changes that had taken place since the 1981 census. Draft questionnaires were prepared and presented at the First Data Users Conference which was held during April 18-20, 1988. The Data Users Conference was attended by representatives of the various Ministeries of the Government of India, Planning Commission, State Governments, Universities, Demographic and Population institutions and individual experts and scholars. The questionnaires were modified in the light of the deliberations of the Conference and placed before the Advisory Committee on Technical issues related to the holding of the 1991 census. The Advisory Committee representing various groups was appointed by the Government of India on August 31, 1988. The Census questionnaires vetted by the Advisory Committee were tested in selected areas during November 1988. As a result of this first pretest, certain changes were incorporated in the questionnaires which were again submitted to the Advisory Committee for their opinion. Again census questionnaires were tested in selected enumeration blocks in June-July 1989. The Advisory Committee again considered the modified questionnaires in November 1989. Thereafter, the Government of India developed the following questionnaires.

1. The Household Schedule
2. The Individual Slip
3. The House List Questionnaire

The census enumeration began from February 9 and ended on February 28 with the census reference point of time being the sunrise of March 1, 1991.

Source: *Census of India*, 1991.

13.2 India's Position in World Population

TABLE 13.1: India's Position in World Population

Country	Reference data	Population
China*	1.7.90	1,160,017,381
India	1.3.91	843,930,861
U.S.A.*	1.4.90	248,909,873
U.S.S.R.*	12.2.89	286,730,817

* Source: United Nations Statistical Office.

In absolute terms, the population of India has grown by 16.06 crore during the decade 1981-91. This is almost equal to the population added during the three decades 1931-41, 1941-51 and 1951-61. The absolute addition to the population during the decade 1981-91 is more than the total population of Japan.

It is interesting to note that every 10 years we added to our population the equivalent of two times of Britain, three times of France, five times of Canada, or half of U.S.A.

13.3 Demographic and Literacy Data at a Glance

TABLE 13.2: Demographic and Literacy Data India, 1991

Population	
Total	843,930,861
Males	437,597,929
Females	406,332,932
Decennial Population Growth 1981-91	
1. Absolute	160,606,764
2. Percentage	+ 23.50
Density of Population	267 per sq.km.
Sex Ratio	929 Females per 1,000 Males
Literacy Rate:	
Total	52.11 per cent
Males	63.86 per cent
Females	39.42 per cent

Notes: 1. Population of India includes projected population of Jammu and Kashmir where the 1991 Census is yet to be held.
2. Density has been worked out on comparable data.
3. Literacy rates relate to population aged seven years and above.
4. Literacy rates exclude Jammu and Kashmir.

TABLE 13.3: India 1961 and 1991

	1981	1991
1. Total Population	683,929,097	843,930,861
2. Sex Ratio		
Females per 1,000 males	934	929
3. Density of Population	216	267
4. Literacy Rate	43.56	52.11 per cent
(i) Males	56.37	63.86 per cent
(ii) Females	29.75	39.42 per cent

TABLE 13.4: Population, Percentage to Total Population, Decadal Population Growth and Density of States and Union Territories

Sl. No.	State/ Union Territory	Population 1991	Percentage to total population 1991	1981	Decadal Population growth 1981—1991	Density
1	2	3	4	5	6	7
1.	Uttar Pradesh	138,760,417	16.44	16.22	25.16	471
2.	Bihar	86,338,853	10.23	10.23	23.49	497
3.	Maharashtra	78,706,719	9.33	9.19	25.36	256
4.	West Bengal	67,982,732	8.06	7.99	24.55	766
5.	Andhra Pradesh	66,304,854	7.86	7.84	23.82	241
6.	Madhya Pradesh	66,135,862	7.84	7.64	26.75	149
7.	Tamil Nadu	55,638,318	6.59	7.08	14.94	428
8.	Karnataka	44,817,398	5.31	5.43	20.69	234
9.	Rajasthan	43,880,640	5.20	5.01	28.07	128
10.	Gujarat	41,174,060	4.88	4.99	20.80	210
11.	Orissa	31,512,070	3.73	3.86	19.50	202
12.	Kerala	29,011,237	3.44	3.72	13.98	747
13.	Assam	22,294,562	2.64	2.64	23.58	284
14.	Punjab	20,190,795	2.39	2.46	20.26	401
15.	Haryana	16,317,715	1.93	1.89	26.28	369
16.	Delhi	9,370,475	1.11	0.91	50.64	6,319
17.	Jammu and Kashmir	7,718,700	0.91	0.88	28.92	76
18.	Himachal Pradesh	5,111,079	0.61	0.63	19.39	92
19.	Tripura	2,744,827	0.32	0.30	33.69	262
20.	Manipur	1,826,714	0.22	0.21	28.56	82
21.	Meghalaya	1,760,626	0.21	0.19	31.80	78
22.	Nagaland	1,215,573	0.14	0.11	56.86	73
23.	Goa	1,168,622	0.14	0.15	15.96	316
24.	Arunachal Pradesh	858,392	0.10	0.09	35.86	10
25.	Pondicherry	789,416	0.09	0.09	30.60	1,605
26.	Mizoram	686,217	0.08	0.07	38.98	33
27.	Chandigarh	640,725	0.08	0.07	41.88	5,620
28.	Sikkim	403,612	0.05	0.05	27.57	57
29.	Andaman and Nicobar Islands	277,989	0.03	0.03	47.29	34
30.	Dadra and Nagar Haveli	138,542	0.01	0.01	33.63	282
31.	Daman & Diu	101,439	0.01	0.01	28.43	906
32.	Lakshadweep	51,681	0.01	0.01	28.40	1,615
	All India	843,930,861	—		23.50	267

13.4 Most Populous Indian States

The six most populous States in the country are Uttar Pradesh, Bihar, Maharashtra, West Bengal, Andhra Pradesh and Madhya Pradesh. These States alone accounted for 59.10 per cent of India's population ten years ago. Together they have contributed 62.49 per cent of the increase during the past decade 1981-91. In contrast are the States of Tamil Nadu, Goa, Karnataka, Gujarat, Orissa, Kerala, Punjab and Himachal Pradesh. The share of these States to the total population has reduced. Some States have shown a relatively lower absolute increase in population during the decade 1981-91 as compared to similar figures for 1971-81. These are Goa, Gujarat, Karnataka, Kerala,

Sikkim and the Union Territory of Chandigarh.

A comparative picture of the population of various States can be had from Table 13.4. It will be seen that Sikkim, as a State, has the minimum population among the State with just 403,612 people. Mizoram is second from the bottom with population registering at 686,217. Among the Union Territories, Delhi tops with 9,370,475 people while Lakshadweep stood at the bottom of the list with a population as low as 51,681 persons.

TABLE 13.5: Growth Rate in Population of India : 1901-1991

Year	Population	Decadal Growth		Average annual exponential growth rate (per cent)	Progressive growth rate over 1901 (per cent)
		Absolute	Per cent		
1	2	3	4	5	6
1901	238,396,327	—	—	—	—
1911	252,093,390	+13,697,063	+ 5.75	0.56	+ 5.75
1921	251,321,213	- 772,177	- 0.31	-0.03	+ 5.42
1931	278,977,238	+27,656,025	+ 11.00	1.04	+ 17.02
1941	318,660,580	+39,683,342	+ 14.22	1.33	+ 33.67
1951	361,088,090	+42,420,485	+ 13.31	1.25	+ 51.47
1961	439,234,771	+77,682,873	+ 21.51	1.96	+ 84.25
1971	548,159,652	+108,924,881	+ 24.80	2.20	+129.94
1981	683,329,097	+135,169,445	+ 24.66	2.22	+186.64
1991	843,930,861	+160,601,764	+ 23.50	2.11	+254.00

*Notes:*1. In 1981, census was not conducted in Assam. Based on the 1971 Census and the provisional results of the 1991 Census the population of Assam as on March 1, 1981 has been interpolated.

2. As a consequence of the revised estimate for Assam for the year 1981, the total population of India as of 1981 has been estimated as 683,329,097 as against the earlier published figure of 685,184,692.
3. The 1991 Census has not yet been conducted in Jammu and Kashmir. The provisional population figures for India include the population figure for Jammu and Kashmir projected by the Standing Committee of Experts on Population Projections.
4. The 1971 Census was conducted with April, 1, 1971 as the reference date. In both the 1961 and 1981 Censuses the reference data was March 1. The average annual exponential growth rate presented in the statement takes into account this difference. No such adjustment has been made while calculating decadal growth rate.
5. In working out 'decade variation' and 'percentage decade variation' for India for 1941-51 and 1951-61, the 1951 population of Tuensang district of Nagaland i.e., 7,025 and 1961 population of Tuensang (83,501) and Mon (5,774) districts have not been taken into account as these areas were censused for the first time in 1951 and these figures are not comparable.
6. In Arunachal Pradesh the census was conducted for the first time in 1961. While working in the decadal growth, both absolute as well as per cent, for 1951-61, 1961 Census population of Arunachal Pradesh has been excluded.

13.5 Decennial Growth Rate

The decennial growth rate of population is 23.50 per cent during 1981-91. The decennial growth rate in the decade 1971-81 was 24.66 per cent. There has, therefore, been a decrease by 1.16 percentage points in the growth rate during 1981-91 compared to 1971-81. The growth rate of population in India from 1901 onwards is indicated in Table 13.6.

TABLE 13.6: Decennial growth rate—1901-11 to 1981-91

Decade	Decadal growth rate in per cent
1901-11	+ 5.75
1911-21	- 0.31
1921-31	+ 11.00
1931-41	+ 14.22
1941-51	+ 13.31
1951-61	+ 21.51
1961-71	+ 24.80
1971-81	+ 24.66
1981-91*	+ 23.50

* Provisional.

The average annual exponential growth rate has decreased from 2.22 per cent during 1971-81 to 2.11 per cent during 1981-91.

13.6 Density of Population

The density of population in the country according to the 1991 Census is 267 per square kilometre as against 216 at the 1981 Census. There has, therefore, been an increase of 51 persons per square kilometre in the country during the decade 1981-91. The densities from 1901 onwards in India are indicated below in Table 13.7:

TABLE 13.7 Density of Population 1901 to 1991

Census year	Density per square kilometre
1901	77
1911	82
1921	81
1931	90
1941	103
1951	117
1961	142
1971	177
1981	216
1991	267*

* Provisional

13.7 Sex Ratio

The sex ratio, i.e, number of females per 1000 males, as recorded at this Census is 929 as against 934 at the 1981 Census. The sex ratio has, therefore, declined in the country during the decade 1981-91. The sex ratios in India from 1901 onwards are indicated in Table 13.8.

13.8 Brief Notes on Provisional Results of 1991 Census

1. The Census of India 1991 is the fifth Census since Independence

2. The first phase of the 1991 Census namely, the House-listing Operations, were conducted during April-September, 1990 in different States and Union Territories according to a calendar. The House-listing Operations which included house numbering and listing of buildings, houses and households provided an inventory for organising the census enumeration on a scientific basis.
3. In the second phase, the enumeration was conducted all over the country except Jammu and Kashmir, from February 9 to February 28, 1991 with a revisional round from March 1 to 5, 1991. The population figures are with reference to the Sunrise of March 1, 1991. It proposed to conduct the census in Jammu and Kashmir during August-October 1991. In certain pockets of the country which are inaccessible during February-March when they are snow-bound, the enumeration had been carried out a little early.
4. The figures for Jammu and Kashmir included in the provisional totals are the projections of the Standing Committee of Expert on Population Projections appointed by the Planning Commission.

TABLE 13.8: Sex Ratio 1901 to 1991

Census year	Sex ratio
1901	972
1911	964
1921	955
1931	950
1941	945
1951	946
1961	941
1971	930
1981	934
1991	929*

* Provisional.

13.9 **Urban Population Growth**

The growth of urban population in the country during the decade (1981-91) slowed down by about ten per cent, as compared to the earlier decade of 1971-81. During 1971-81, the growth of urban population was recorded as 46.14 per cent, and between 1981-91, it went down to 36.19 per cent.

This is notwithstanding the fact that the number of cities and towns has been consistently increasing — there were 3,126 cities and towns in 1971, and the figure went up to 4,029 in 1981 and it now stood at 4,689. The urban population in the country was now 25.72 per cent of the country's more than 84.43 crore population.

With the change of growth pattern, the big four cities, which were earlier classified as metropolitan cities, are no longer metros; they have "graduated" into "mega cities" now. The four mega cities, with a population of more than five million are Bombay, Calcutta, Delhi and Madras. Then comes metros, which are now 23, with each having a population of between one and five million. These included Hyderabad, Bangalore, Ahmedabad, Pune, Kanpur, Ludhiana, Bhopal, Surat, Jaipur, Indore, Baroda, Patna, Varanasi and Nagpur.

TABLE 13.9: Distribution of Population, Sex Ratio and Density of Population

State/Union	Persons	Population 1991		Sex Ratio		Density		Growth rate	
		Males	Females	1981	1991	1981	1991	1971-81	1981-91
1	2	3	4	5	6	7	8	9	10
INDIA	843,930,861	437,597,929	406,332,932	934	929 *	216	267	24.66	23.50
Andhra Pradesh	66,304,854	33,623,738	32,681,116	975	972	195	241	23.10	23.82
Arunachal Pradesh	858,392	461,242	397,150	862	861	8	10	35.15	35.86
Assam	22,294,562	11,579,693	10,714,869	NA	925	230	284	23.36	23.58
Bihar	86,338,853	45,147,280	41,191,573	946	912	402	497	24.06	23.49
Goa	1,168,622	593,563	575,059	975	969	272	316	26.74	15.96
Gujarat	41,174,060	21,272,388	19,901,672	942	936	174	210	27.67	20.80
Haryana	16,317,715	8,705,379	7,612,336	870	874	292	363	28.75	26.28
Himachal Pradesh	5,111,079	2,560,894	2,550,185	973	996	77	92	23.71	19.39
Jammu & Kashmir	7,718,700	4,014,100	3,704,600	892	923	59	76	29.69	28.92
Karnataka	44,817,398	22,861,409	21,955,989	963	960	194	234	26.75	20.69
Kerala	29,011,237	14,218,167	14,793,070	1,032	1,040	655	747	19.24	13.98
Madhya Pradesh	66,135,862	34,232,048	31,903,814	941	932	118	149	25.27	26.75
Maharashtra	78,706,719	40,652,056	38,054,663	937	936	204	256	24.57	25.36
Manipur	1,826,714	931,511	895,203	971	961	64	82	32.46	28.56
Meghalaya	1,760,626	904,308	856,318	954	947	60	78	32.04	31.80

Contd.

TABLE 13.9 (*Contd.*)

1	2	3	4	5	6	7	8	9	10
Mizoram	686,217	356,672	329,545	919	924	23	33	48.55	38.98
Nagaland	1,215,573	643,273	572,300	863	890	47	73	50.05	56.86
Orissa	31,512,070	15,979,904	15,532,166	981	972	169	202	20.17	13.50
Punjab	20,190,795	10,695,136	94,956,659	879	888	333	401	23.89	20.26
Rajasthan	43,880,640	22,935,895	20,944,745	919	913	100	128	32.97	28.07
Sikkim	403,612	214,723	188,889	835	880	45	57	50.77	27.57
Tamil Nadu	55,638,318	28,217,947	27,420,371	977	972	372	428	17.50	14.94
Tripura	2,744,827	1,410,545	1,334,282	946	946	136	262	31.92	33.69
Uttar Pradesh	138,760,417	73,745,994	65,014,423	885	882	377	471	25.49	25.16
West Bengal	67,982,732	35,461,898	35,520,834	911	917	615	766	32.17	31.55
A & N Islands	277,989	152,737	125,52	760	820	23	34	67.33	47.23
Chandigarh	640,725	357,411	283,314	769	733	3,961	5,520	75.55	41.88
Dadra & Nagar Haveli	138,542	70,927	67,615	974	953	211	282	39.78	33.63
Daman & Diu	101,439	51,452	49,987	1,062	972	705	806	36.07	38.12
Delhi	9,370,475	5,120,733	4,243,742	808	830	4,194	6,319	57.00	50.61
Lakshadweep	51,681	26,582	25,099	975	944	1,258	1,615	26.53	28.40
Pondicherry	789,416	398,324	391,092	985	982	1,229	1,605	28.15	30.60

Notes: 1. In 1981, Census was not conducted in Assam. Based on the 1971 Census and the 1991 Census provisional results the population as of 1981 has been interpolated.

2. As a consequence of the revised estimates for Assam for the year 1981, the total population of India as of 1981 has been estimated as 683, 329, 097 as against earlier published figures of 685, 184, 692.

3. As a consequence of the revised figures the decadal growth rate for India during 1971-81 has been estimated as 24.66.

4. 1991 Census has not yet been conducted in J&K. The figures are as per projections prepared by the Standing Committee of Experts.

* Provisional.

The growth of urban population has, however, been uneven. If on one extreme is Haldia, where the population growth recorded during the last decade was about 374 per cent, Vanparai in Tamil Nadu represented the other extreme with a minus eight per cent in growth.

Big cities (class I) in 15 States like West Bengal, Andhra Pradesh, Maharashtra, Madhya Pradesh, Uttar Pradesh and Tamil Nadu had more than 50 per cent of urban population. Again, in the two States of Maharashtra and West Bengal, the share of population was very high, viz. 77.85 per cent and 81.71 per cent, respectively. About two-thirds of the urban population in Gujarat, Karnataka and a few other States lived in class one cities.

In several States like Gujarat, Tamil Nadu, Karnataka and Punjab, the level of urbanisation has been higher than the national average of 25.72 — varying between 26 and 34 per cent.

Another interesting point brought out in the just released census report (which is follow-up of the one on population released a few months ago) is that the "tempo" of urbanisation has slowed down. The annual growth has declined from 3.83 per cent during 1971-81 to 3.09 per cent during the next decade (1981-91).

Among the States, Mizoram has recorded a growth rate in urban population of 160.27 per cent.

Delhi has, however, shown a rapid increase in its population over the years. In 1911, its population was about 2.38 lakh, the year when Delhi became the national Capital. By 1951, it recorded a very large growth of 106.58 per cent. But later the tempo of the growth rate started slowing down from 1961 onwards — from 54.57 per cent during 1961-71 to 46.18 per cent during 1981-91.

Source: *Report of the Registrar General and Census Commissioner on Rural-Urban Distribution of the Country's Population* (Paper-2)

13.10 **Workers' Distribution**

The number of people engaged in agriculture has gone down in 16 States during the last decade (1981-91), and there has been a sharp increase in the number of those working as agriculture labourers in as many as 24 States and Union Territories. This shift in the "work-pattern", from cultivation to farm labour is perhaps indicative of drop in the number of land owners or share-croppers, and a drop in land-holdings in those States.

Nagaland and Madhya Pradesh were the only two States which witnessed the reverse trend, that of increase in the proportion of cultivators during the last decade. While in Nagaland, the jump was quite substantial (nearly 68%), in the case of Madhya Pradesh it was only marginal. This trend of drop in cultivators was also significant in the case of two union territories of Chandigarh (8.54%) and Delhi (12.25%). An interesting feature of this shift in work-pattern was that people in rural areas did not migrate to city centres, but got absorbed in some other work in the villages itself.

The 1991 Census data, showed that the proportion of women cultivators registered a slight increase (1.64%) and that of women engaged as farm labour went down by 1.53 per cent, at the end of 1991, as compared to the 1981 census figures. The number of women cultivators in Punjab went up significantly by

18.31 per cent during the last decade, where as the share in agriculture labour in Chandigarh dropped by 11.70 per cent.

The Census Commissioner's report defined a "cultivator" as the one who is the owner of land, or employees others in production, or holds land from the Government or a private person for payment in money, kind or share. A person who has given out his or her land for cultivation to others for money or kind is not a cultivator. Nor a person engaged in growing fruits, vegetables, tea-plantation or coffee and rubber plantation are not cultivators; only those who produce cereals and millet crops and cash crops are counted in that category.

A person who works on another person's land for money is termed as agriculture labourer. A person who runs or works in a household production activity, not registered as a factory, is treated as a household worker for purposes of census enumeration. The Government employees, teachers, construction labour, plantation workers and others are put in a separate category of "other work".

The States where cultivators and household workers have declined and agriculture labour has gone up are Andhra Pradesh, Gujarat, Haryana, Punjab, Tamil Nadu and Karnataka. The places where "other workers" have increased are Goa and Chandigarh. While the overall drop in cultivators (male) was of 3.42 per cent, it was as high as 9.47 per cent in Manipur, over six per cent in Andhra Pradesh and Tamil Nadu and nearly six per cent in Haryana and Uttar Pradesh. The number of agriculture labour went up by 2.29 per cent in the country, but it was higher in States like Andhra Pradesh (5.83%), Haryana (4.37%), Tamil Nadu (4.94%), and Haryana (4.37%). Among the Union Territories, however, the number of farm labour went down — in Chandigarh by 1.54 per cent, Pondicherry by 4.02 per cent and Delhi by 2.22 per cent.

In the case of other workers (rural), the figure went up in 24 State and Union Territories, including Andhra Pradesh, Gujarat, and West Bengal. But the increase was quite big in Chandigarh (10.83%) and Daman (21%). Another interesting point in the report was that the number of males in urban areas engaged in "other work" also went down in 22 States and Union Territories — perhaps indicates the fall in government jobs and other similar areas. The number of males engaged in household industry in city areas, however, went up in 22 States and UTs — the highest being in Bihar (2.80%).

A fairly large number of men in urban areas in Uttar Pradesh are engaged in household industry (9.18%). In Bihar, it was nearly 6 per cent, 5.39 per cent in Rajasthan and 5.03 per cent in Haryana. Those engaged in "other work" (including white-collar jobs) in cities constituted 90 per cent in 13 States and UTs, and between 50 and 80 per cent in other States. In UP, those engaged in such work formed 75.60 per cent and in Bihar urban are as it came to 74.30 per cent. The overall percentage of people engaged in "other work" in the country was 84.85 per cent, as compared to 85.97 per cent in the 1981 census.

The number of women in the household industry was much higher than those of men — 46.13 per cent women and 29.41 per cent men. The share of women in household industry was even higher in villages — 40.83 per cent as compared to men (17.96%).

Source : Report of the Registrar General and Census Commissioner on Workers and their Distribution in the Country, as reported in *Hindustan Times*, December 29, 1991.

14

ELECTIONS: 1991, MAY-JUNE

14.1 Statutory Provisions and Their Operation

The conduct of elections in India is governed by specific Constitutional provisions. Art. 324 provides that the superintendence, direction and control of elections is to be vested in an Election Commission. The Commission is headed by a Chief Election Commissioner who is appointed by the President. The Election Commission has the responsibility for preparation of electoral rolls and for elections to the offices of the President and Vice-President besides all elections to Parliament and to the Legislature of every State. There is also provision for appointment of Election Commissioners and Regional Commissioners to assist the Chief Election Commissioner.

Article 325 of the Constitution reinforces the spirit of Universal Adult Suffrage. 'No person shall be ineligible for inclusion in any such roll (general electoral roll for every territorial constituency for election to either House of Parliament or to the House or either House of the Legislature of a State) or claim to be included in any special electoral roll for any such constituency on grounds only of religion, race, caste, sex or any of them. . . .' Every person who is a citizen of India and who is not less than 18 years of age on such date as may be fixed in that behalf and is not otherwise disqualified under this Constitution shall be entitled to be registered as a voter.

Laws relating to matters concerning elections to either House of Parliament (Lok Sabha and Rajya Sabha) or either House of the Legislature of a State (Vidhan Sabha and Vidhan Parishad) including the preparation of electoral rolls, the delimitation of constituencies and all matters necessary for securing the due constitution of such House or Houses are to be made by the Parliament. Where such provisions do not exist, Legislature of the State has the power to make provision with respect to elections to such Legislature.

The courts are barred from interference so far laws relating to delimitation of constituencies or the allotment of seats to such constituencies is concerned. The elections to either House of Parliament or to the House or either House of the Legislature can be called in question only by an election petition.

With a view to ensure free and fair elections, a number of Corrupt Practices have been identified. An election can be declared void by the competent authority, if it is established that the person had committed any Corrupt Practice during the course of election. The person can also be disqualified for future elections up to six years and can also be prosecuted.

(The voting age was lowered from 21 to 18 by the Constitution [Sixty-first Amendment] Act 1988). The number of voters for the 1991 election was 514,126,380, an increase of about 15 million over the 1989 figures. Men outnumbered the women voters at the National level. Kerala and Manipur are exceptions where women voters outnumbered their male counterparts. The largest number of voters were in the State of Uttar Pradesh and the lowest in the Union

Territory of Lakshadweep.

The details of the electorate in different States and Union Territories are given in Table 14.1.

TABLE 14.1: Electorate: Sexwise and Statewise

State/U.T.	Men	Women	Total
Andhra Pradesh	21,433,197	21,314,665	42,747,682
Arunachal Pradesh	279,308	239,921	519,229
Assam	6,323,078	5,538,279	11,861,357
Bihar	28,124,164	24,521,071	52,645,235
Goa	389,054	379,019	768,073
Gujarat	12,801,439	12,070,532	24,871,971
Haryana	5,233,092	4,464,311	9,697,403
Himachal Pradesh	1,554,891	1,518,035	3,072,926
Karnataka	14,724,709	14,010,406	28,735,115
Kerala	9,688,768	9,920,177	19,608,945
Madhya Pradesh	19,432,452	18,266,911	37,699,363
Maharashtra	25,434,433	23,230,322	48,664,755
Manipur	615,188	616,455	1,231,643
Meghalaya	474,945	466,617	941,562
Mizoram	208,480	205,347	413,827
Nagaland	455,476	359,260	814,836
Orissa	10,606,570	9,191,028	19,797,598
Punjab	7,077,864	6,029,160	13,107,024
Rajasthan	14,041,298	12,445,948	26,487,246
Sikkim	104,799	96,440	201,239
Tamil Nadu	20,165,453	19,660,956	39,826,409
Tripura	796,288	761,930	1,558,218
Uttar Pradesh	44,190,361	36,012,524	80,202,885
West Bengal	22,107,328	19,242,852	41,350,180
Andaman and N.I.	93,642	68,089	161,731
Chandigarh	202,365	154,702	357,067
Dadra and N.H.	38,086	36,870	74,956
Daman and Diu	28,713	28,572	57,285
Delhi	3,309,145	2,719,539	6,028,684
Lakshadweep	16,135	14,578	30,713
Pondicherry	305,350	285,693	591,043
Total	270,256,171	243,870,209	514,126,380

14.2 Allocation of Seats in Lok Sabha

The total number of seats in the Lok Sabha is 545. Art. 331 of the Constitution provides for special representation for the Anglo-Indian Community and to that end, the President is empowered to nominate not more than two members, in case the community is not adequately represented in the Lok Sabha. That leaves 543 seats to be filled up by election. Constitutional provision also exists for distribution of the 543 seats between the States and Union Territories. The 25 States elect 530 M.Ps while the remaining 13 are from the Union Territories.

Provision also exists for reserved seats for the Scheduled Castes and Scheduled Tribes. Out of the total of 543 elected seats, 79 are reserved for the Scheduled Castes and another 41 for the Scheduled Tribes. The Statewise distribution of seats for the 10th Lok Sabha is shown in Table 14.2.

TABLE 14.2: Statewise Distribution of Seats for 10th Lok Sabha

Sl No.	State/Union Territory	Lok Sabha Total	General	SC	ST
1.	Andhra Pradesh	42	34	6	2
2.	Arunachal Pradesh	2	2	—	—
3.	Assam	14	11	1	2
4.	Bihar	54	41	8	5
5.	Goa	2	2	—	—
6.	Gujarat	26	20	2	4
7.	Haryana	10	8	2	—
8.	Himachal Pradesh	4	3	1	—
9.	Jammu and Kashmir	6	6	—	—
10.	Karnataka	28	24	4	—
11.	Kerala	20	18	2	—
12.	Madhya Pradesh	40	25	6	9
13.	Maharashtra	48	41	3	4
14.	Manipur	2	1	—	1
15.	Meghalaya	2	2	—	—
16.	Mizoram	1	1	—	—
17.	Nagaland	1	—	—	1
18.	Orissa	21	13	3	5
19.	Punjab	13	10	3	—
20.	Rajasthan	25	18	4	3
21.	Sikkim	1	1	—	—
22.	Tamil Nadu	39	32	7	—
23.	Tripura	2	1	—	1
24.	West Bengal	42	32	8	2
25.	Uttar Pradesh	85	67	18	—
26.	Andaman and Nicobar Islands	1	1	—	—
27.	Chandigarh	1	1	—	—
28.	Dadra and Nagar Haveli	1	—	—	1
29.	Daman and Diu	1	1	—	—
30.	Delhi	7	6	1	—
31.	Lakshadweep	1	—	—	1
32.	Pondicherry	1	1	—	—
	Total	543	433	79	41
	Nominated	2			
	Grand Total	545			

14.3 1991 Election Manifestoes: Comparative Study

On the eve of a national election, major political parties come out with their Election Manifestoes. These manifestoes are a plethora of platitudes and promises about what will be done should the party come in power. Every party makes it a point to say something on everything that may be agitating people's minds. No manifesto bothers as to how these promises can be achieved or how will the resources be raised to fulfill the promises. Often the promises are contradictions in themselves e.g. promising more subsidies and lesser taxation in the same breath.

This time also every political party made it a point to say something about the Mandal Commission, the Ram Janambhoomi, terrorism, emancipation of women, labour welfare, etc. In addition, all manifestoes included homilies on topics such as nationalism, secularism, federalism etc. without any reference to how these issues were perceived in the past when the party was in power at one time or the other and somewhere or the other.

Agriculture and Rural Development

The BJP promised an allocation of 60 per cent plan outlay under this head. The farmers were promised pass books and implementation of the land laws. Its major appeal to the agriculture based voter lay in promising parity of prices between agricultural and industrial products.

The Communists could promise only 50 per cent allocation. (The BJP manifesto had come subsequent to the issue of the Communist manifesto). It was however equally emphatic about remunerative prices for the peasant's produce.

The CPI (M) went a step further. It promised a comprehensive legislation to protect the rights of workers. The insistence on implementation of Land Reforms Acts was common. JD (S) promised 4500 ideal villages. While it also promised reduction in regional disparities, remunerative prices for farm products was also emphasised.

The Indian National Congress stood for the highest national priority to Agriculture with a promise of far more remunerative price for farm produce.

The National Front was yet more emphatic and precise. Apart from formulation of National Policy on Agriculture, it promised equal distribution of land. Other items that found place in the manifesto included Format of a Commodities Management Service and an offer of minimum support prices for agricultural produce.

Centre-State Relations

The BJP has always maintained that Art. 370 of the Constitution needs to be repealed so that Jammu and Kashmir fall in line with the other States of India. Formation of smaller States found favour with the party and it also promised implementation of the Sarkaria Committee Report on Centre-State Relations.

Both CPI and CPI (M) agreed to get Article 356 of the Constitution abrogated. The National Front, however, promised only a review of the same.

Cow Slaughter

Only the BJP manifesto had demanded a total ban on the slaughter of cows.

Economy

The BJP promised a White Paper on the Indian Economy. For the consumer, there was the promise of holding the price line.

The Communists were for a Planned development with curbs on monopoly houses.

The Indian Congress expressed its concern for vigorous export promotion and restoration of fiscal balances. It made a specific mention of the problem of parallel economy and promised measure to curb the menace of black money in the economic life of the country.

The National Front was for rationalisation of tax structure to bring down disparities in income.

Education

The JD (S) promised total literacy by 1995. The BJP felt that allocation to education needed to be raised to reach 6 per cent of the G.N.P. The CPI (M) was for ending the National Policy on Education formulated in 1986.

In contrast, the Indian National Congress promised vigorous implementation of the New Education Policy, as also the implementation of the three language formula.

The National Front was for consideration of the recommendations made by the Ramamurti Report.

Elections

The BJP was for Public Auditing of party funds. Every one else thought this was best understood as impractical.

Defence Force

The BJP stood for providing Nuclear Teeth to the country's Defence Forces. A National Security Council has been proposed to be set up for institutionalising forward planning. It assured servicemen of implementing the policy of one pension for one rank and also assuring the Jawans that the retirement age would be enhanced to 58. The promise of one rank-one pension was also reiterated by the CPI and CPI (M) The Indian National Congress was relatively less emphatic. It only talked of finding a solution to the proposal of one rank-one pension. The National Front offered provision of meaningful post-retirement employment to defence personnel.

Foreign Policy

BJP felt that the country needed a Policy Planning Committee of experts to formulate a long-term foreign policy for India. The CPI advocated peace, disarmament and anti-colonialism. CPI (M) was worried about US blackmail and wanted protection against it. The Congress, as usual insisted on Non-alignment.

Government Employees

The BJP promised 'Time Scale' promotions and raising the income tax exemption limit to Rs.48000.

Industrial Policy

The BJP was of the view that there was too much regulation. It promised encouragement to people's initiative in public service undertakings.

The CPI (M) stuck to its felt posture. It was for workers participation in management of industries.

The Indian National Congress, while promising encouragement to entrepreneurship, also upheld the promise of simplifying the regulatory system. For the National Front Industrial Development was the right tool for maximising employment.

Language Policy

The BJP was for implementation of the three language formula. The Communists also supported that/but in addition made specific mention of the recommendations of the Gujral Committee on the status of Urdu with Muslim voters in mind. The National Front too did not lag behind in its offer to the Muslim Community.

Panchayati Raj

The BJP promised Constitutional status to local bodies. The Janata Dal (S) was, however, content with just mentioning the need for streamlining Panchayati Raj. Congress promised Nagar Palika Constitution Amendment Bills and the Revival of Panchayati Raj. The National Front was vague and only talked about decentralisation and democratisation in general terms.

Price Stability

No party wanted to ignore the fixed income and salaried voter. The Communists were of the opinion that the wholesale trade in grains needed to be taken over by the State. The Janata Dal (S) was for parity between the prices of agricultural and industrial commodities. Indian National Congress promised stern action against black marketing as its proposed strategy for arresting price rise.

Public Life

The promise of setting an example in simple living came from the BJP. Congress, chose not to be specific about it.

Public Sector

The BJP proposed throwing open some of the public sector unit to people's participation. The Communists accorded priority to Worker's participation. Indian National Congress realised that more autonomy was needed in the sector as less government interference could make them more efficient.

Ram Janambhoomi

The BJP talked of a Grand National Reconciliation by righting the wrongs of history. Ram Janambhoomi was to be restored in Ayodhya. The Communists wanted status quo in matters relating to place of religious worship, the cut-off date being August 15, 1947. Janata Dal (S) offered to restore peacefully through dialogue and cooperation. The CPI (M) was also for a negotiated settlement of the dispute or alternatively adherence to court verdict. The Congress vied with the Communists for a status quo and so did the National Front.

Reservations

Considering the number of OBCs, no party could disown the Mandal Commission report. The BJP wanted the reservation base broadened beyond the Mandal Commission OBCs, to include other classes on the basis of their economic condition. Even among the OBCs, preference was promised to the poorest among them. The CPI endorsed all that Mandal Commission stood for and went a step beyond that offering 10 per cent reservation for weaker sections among the so called forward castes. The CPI (M) talked of the implementation of Karpoori Thakur Formula. The JD (S) promised a constructive approach to the problems highlighted by the Mandal Commission. The Congress avoided any mention of the Mandal Report and such but promised legislation for establishing a Backward Classes Development Corporation. The National Front reiterated its stand on 27 per cent reservation and even promised five to ten per cent similar facilities for the economically backward not covered by the Mandal Commission.

States

Deletion of Article 370 had been a matter of faith with the BJP and the party stood for the same in its 1991 Manifesto so far Kashmir was concerned. For Punjab, it proposed creation of a kilometre deep Security Zone. In respect of North East, the party wanted an electrified barbed wiring. The Communists talked about multi-pronged political initiatives at all levels.

CPI (M) wanted that the demands of the people should be conceded when they were genuine and within the frame of Indian unity. Firm action was proposed against secessionist forces in Assam and J and K. For Punjab, the struggle against terrorism was to continue.

The National Front had a stand opposed to delete Article 370. It wanted restoration of faith of the people in the democratic process.

Status of Women

The BJP thought of women who could be preferred for employment as primary school teachers.

The Communists were for a 30 per cent while JD (S) talked of employment for women. Congress pleaded for a vigorous implementation of the National Perspective Plan for Women. Setting up of the National Commission on Women was promised by the National Front. A 30 per cent reservation was promised to women in the local bodies.

Time-Bound Programmes

Congress Party if elected will:

In first 100 days—

* Reintroduce and pass the Constitution Amendment Bills on Panchayati Raj and Nagarpalika for devolving powers on units of local self-Government.
* Reservation for women 30 per cent seats or positions in all statutory

bodies and committees including Panchayats and Nagarpalikas.

* Arrest price-rise in essential commodities and, in particular, roll back prices to levels obtaining in July, 1990 in the case of —

  (i) Diesel;
  (ii) Kerosene;
  (iii) Salt;
  (iv) Edible oils;
  (v) Cycles and two-wheelers;
  (vi) Electric bulbs;
  (vii) Cotton sarees and *dhotis* of 40s count or below;
  (viii) Stoves including smokeless *chulhas*;
  (ix) Newsprint;
  (x) Postcards, Inland Letters and Envelopes.

* Maintain a stable tax rates through the fiscal year in respect of customs and excise duties.
* Exempt profits from taxation if they are reinvested in:

  (i) Low and middle income group houses;
  (ii) Highways, roads and bridges;
  (iii) Non-conventional energy generation;
  (iv) School buildings;
  (v) Drinking water supply.

* Increase interest rates for small savings.
* Establish a composite Rapid Action Force to quell communal riots.
* Introduce and pass a Bill to maintain the status quo as on 15th August 1947 in respect of all places of worship and to foreclose any new controversy.
* Establish a Backward Classes Development Corporation.

In first 365 days —

* Fund every village panchayat under Jawahar Rozgar Yojana.
* Hand over Primary Health Centres to Panchayat bodies at Taluka/Samiti levels and provide funds directly.
* Generate 1000 million man-days of guaranteed rural employment every year.
* Create 10 million new jobs every year, adding up to 100 million new jobs before the year 2000.
* Offer stock of public sector companies to workers and small and medium investors among the general public.
* Reduce waste in government expenditure — cut non-development expenditure by 10 per cent in the first year and maintain the same level of expenditure in the second and third years.
* Dismantle selected regulatory agencies, beginning with at least 5 agencies in the first year.
* Establish one Free-Investment Industrial Centre in every declared Backward District with immunity for investments made within the first 365 days.

* Throw open construction of toll-highways and toll-bridges to private and joint sectors.
* Allow the establishment of new mutual funds, particularly pension funds, in the private sector.
* Allow public and private sector banks to raise offshore funds.
* Implement a new formula for determining agricultural prices.
* Construct one million irrigation wells every year.
* Replace hand-pulled rickshaws by cycle rickshaws on ownership basis to the rickshaw driver.
* Build 1000 urban night-shelters and Sulabh Shauchalayas every year.
* Establish by law a Human Rights Commission to investigate and adjudicate violations of human rights, particularly the civil rights of groups or classes of people.
* Make statutory provision for grant of compensation to victims of riots.
* Set up Special Courts to protect tribals' rights and interests.
* Guarantee tuition fees and maintenance allowance to every SC/ST student admitted to any university for a maximum period of six years.
* Build one million dwelling units every year for Scheduled Castes and Scheduled Tribes.
* Build one million dwelling units every year for poor Backward Classes in villages.
* Offer broadcasting and telecasting rights to public corporations to compete with Prasar Bharati.
* Appoint a Commissioner for Women's Rights.
* Appoint Judges to all vacancies in the High Courts.
* Establish a Pension Trust Fund for Central Government Employees.
* Find an innovative solution to the Ex-Servicemen's demand for one rank one pension.
* Restore fairness and justice in the selection and placement of All India Services Officers through the mechanism of the Civil Services Board.
* Fill all vacancies at Board level in public sector enterprises.

In first 730 days —

* Decentralise Planning and take Planning to the District and Block levels through Panchayati Raj bodies and Nagarpalikas.
* Introduce comprehensive crop and cattle insurance schemes.
* Abolish the monopoly of any sector or any individual enterprise in any field of manufacture (except on strategic or military considerations) and throw them open to competition.
* Promote in the private sector or the joint sector the establishment of a multi-discipline, high-quality Institute of Medical Sciences with Hospital in every State capital.
* Legislate on Freedom of Information.
* Establish and enforce standards for Noise Pollution.

In first 1000 days —

* Oversee the gradual withdrawal of the public sector from areas where the private and joint sectors have developed capabilities.

* Run Inter-city fast trains inter-connecting major cities/towns served by the Railways in every State.
* Instal one public telephone in every post office.
* Set up one Navodaya Vidyalaya in every District with reservations for SC/ST and Other Backward Classes and preference for poorer sections.
* Launch and complete a special drive to enroll SC/ST and Other Backward Class students in schools.
* Establish the National Mid-day Meal programme.
* Revamp and strengthen the Public Distribution System all over the country to make foodgrains and other items available at reasonable prices.
* Draft retired High Court judges and ensure disposal of five year old civil and criminal appeals within three years.

Other Parties did not give any such schedule.

14.4 **Position after Elections** *Lok Sabha*

TABLE 14.3: Statewise Electorate and Percentage of Votes Polled in 1991

State	Men	Women	Total	Votes Polled	Percentage
Andhra Pradesh	21,433,197	21,314,665	42,747,862	24,088,530	56.35
Arunachal Pradesh	279,308	239,921	519,229	258,901	49.86
Assam	6,323,078	5,538,279	11,861,357	5,698,340	48.04
Bihar	28,124,164	24,521,071	52,645,235	23,956,361	45.50
Goa	389,054	379,019	768,073	318,988	41.53
Gujarat	12,801,439	12,070,532	24,871,971	10,206,715	41.03
Haryana	5,233,092	4,464,311	9,697,403	5,622,591	57.98
Himachal Pradesh	1,554,891	1,518,035	3,072,926	1,760,721	57.29
Karnataka	14,724,709	14,010,406	28,735,115	13,858,862	48.22
Kerala	9,688,768	9,920,177	19,608,945	14,497,498	73.93
Madhya Pradesh	19,432,452	18,266,911	37,699,363	15,772,918	41.83
Maharashtra	25,434,433	23,230,322	48,664,755	23,314,979	47.90
Manipur	615,188	616,455	1,231,643	726,258	58.96
Meghalaya	474,945	466,617	941,562	342,921	36.42
Mizoram	208,480	205,347	413,827	230,122	55.60
Nagaland	455,476	359,260	814,836	622,831	76.43
Orissa	10,606,570	9,191,028	19,797,598	9,799,269	49.49
Punjab	7,077,864	6,029,160	13,107,024	—	—
Rajasthan	14,041,298	12,445,948	26,487,246	12,068,972	45.56
Sikkim	104,799	96,440	201,239	111,101	55.20
Tamil Nadu	20,165,453	19,660,956	39,826,409	24,182,453	60.71
Tripura	796,288	761,930	1,558,218	979,688	62.87
Uttar Pradesh	44,190,361	36,012,524	80,202,885	33,855,484	42.21
West Bengal	22,107,328	19,242,852	41,350,180	30,251,329	73.15
And. & Nic. Islands	93,642	68,089	161,731	107,336	66.36
Chandigarh	202,365	154,702	357,067	203,486	56.98
Dadra & N.H.	38,086	36,870	74,956	47,925	63.93
Daman & Diu	28,713	28,572	57,285	28,129	49.10
Delhi	3,309,145	2,719,539	6,028,684	2,811,316	46.63
Lakshadweep	16,135	14,578	30,713	25,321	82.44
Pondicherry	305,350	285,693	591,043	447,251	75.67
Total	263,178,307	237,841,049	501,019,356	256,196,596	51.13

The 10th Lok Sabha was constituted on June 20, 1991. The Congress Party secured 225 seats and emerged as the largest party, although it did not command an absolute majority. Shri P.V. Narasimha Rao of the Congress assumed office of the Prime Minister on June 21, 1991. The occasion marked the return of Congress to power at the Centre after a lapse of one and a half years. Shri Narasimha Rao was not a member of Parliament when he became the Prime Minister. Subsequently he was elected from the Nandyal constituency in the by-election held on November 16, 1991. It was for the first time that a non-MP was elected as its leader by the Congress. Shri Narasimha Rao was elected to the Lok Sabha by a record margin of 5,80,297 votes and made all his rivals lose their security deposits. 1991 Elections were held on account of the resignation of Shri Chandra Shekhar from the Office of the Prime Minister. It may be recalled he had assumed office in December 1989 after the defeat of Shri V.P. Singh who had formed the Government at the Centre having been elected on the National Front Ticket in December 1989. Shri Chandra Shekhar also of the National Front who had formed a split group with about 60 members and with the outside support of the Congress had become the Prime Minister on November 10, 1990. On March 3, 1991, he resigned but continued as care-taker Prime Minister till June 20, 1991.

TABLE 14.4: Party Position as on June 24, 1991

States	T.S.	CMN	D.S.	INC	BJP	JD	SJP	CPM	CPI	Other	Ind
Andhra Pradesh	42	1	41	24	1	—	—	1	1	14	—
Arunachal Pradesh	2	—	2	2	—	—	—	—	—	—	—
Assam	14	—	14	8	2	—	—	1	—	2	1
Bihar	54	5	46	—	5	27	—	1	7	6	—
Goa	2	—	2	2	—	—	—	—	—	—	—
Gujarat	26	1	25	4	20	—	—	—	—	1	—
Haryana	10	—	10	9	—	—	—	—	—	1	—
Himachal Pradesh	4	—	4	2	2	—	—	—	—	—	—
Karnataka	28	1	26	21	4	—	1	—	—	—	—
Kerala	20	—	20	13	—	—	—	3	—	4	—
Madhya Pradesh	40	—	40	27	12	—	—	—	—	1	—
Maharashtra	48	1	47	37	5	—	—	1	—	4	—
Manipur	2	—	2	1	—	—	—	—	—	1	—
Meghalaya	2	—	2	2	—	—	—	—	—	—	—
Mizoram	1	—	1	1	—	—	—	—	—	—	—
Nagaland	1	—	1	—	—	—	—	—	—	1	—
Orissa	21	1	20	12	—	6	—	1	1	—	—
Rajasthan	25	—	25	13	12	—	—	—	—	—	—
Sikkim	1	—	1	—	—	—	—	—	—	1	—
Tamil Nadu	39	—	39	28	—	—	—	—	—	11	—
Tripura	2	—	2	2	—	—	—	—	—	—	—
Uttar Pradesh	85	3	82	5	50	22	4	—	1	—	—
West Bengal	42	—	42	5	—	—	—	27	3	7	—
Andaman & Nicobar	1	—	1	1	—	—	—	—	—	—	—
Chandigarh	1	—	1	1	—	—	—	—	—	—	—
Dadra & Nh	1	—	1	1	—	—	—	—	—	—	—
Daman and Din	1	—	1	—	1	—	—	—	—	—	—
Delhi	7	—	7	2	5	—	—	—	—	—	—
Lakshadweep	1	—	1	1	—	—	—	—	—	—	—
Pondicherry	1	—	1	1	—	—	—	—	—	—	—
National	524	13	507*	225	119	55	5	35	13	54	1

Outstanding Seats=4

Results awaited: 3 from Bihar and 1 from Karnataka

Note: T.S. = Total Seats, CMN = Countermanded, D.S. = Declared Seats. The 'NC tally includes one UCPI nominee who contested on Hand Symbol in Tamil Nadu.

Note: For results as on November 24, 1991, i.e.. after the by-elections see Chapters 2 and 19.

National UNI — Indchem Poll Analysis — 1991.

TABLE 14.5: Party Position in the Tenth Lok Sabha as on 22.2.92 (after Punjab Lok Sabha Polls)

Party	Seats	Party	Seats
Congress	243	AIFB	3
BJP	119	BSP	3
Janata Dal	55	Shiv Sena	2
CPI (M)	35	Muslim League	2
CPI	14	Ind. & others	11
Telugu Desam	13	Unattached	6
AIADMK	11	Nominated	2
JMM	5	Vacancies	11
Janata Party	5	Total	544
RSP	4	Speaker	1

Note: (Election not held in J.& K).

States

In Assam, Congress President Hiteswar Saikia was elected leader of the Congress Legislature Party and sworn in as the Chief Minister on June 29, 1991.

In Haryana, Shri Bhajan Lal took over as Chief Minister of the State for the second time.

At Trivandrum (Kerala) Shri K. Karunakaran was elected leader of the Kerala Congress Legislature Party and sworn in as Chief Minister of the Congress-led U.D.F.

In Pondicherry, Shri V. Vaidyalingam, of Congress (I) was elected as the leader of the Legislature Party.

In Tamil Nadu Ms. Jayalalitha was sworn in as the Chief Minister on June 24. She headed a government voted to power with Congress (i) in alliance.

In Uttar Pradesh, Shri Kalyan Singh was unanimously elected as the leader of the Bharatiya Janata Party in Vidhan Sabha. He took over as the Chief Minister on June 24.

In West Bengal, Shri Jyoti Basu became the Chief Minister for a record 4th term.

Shri Sudhir Rao Naik replaced Shri Sharad Pawar as Chief Minister of Maharashtra consequent to Shri Sharad Pawar moving to Delhi to join the Union Council of Ministers.

Elections were held in Punjab in February 1992. Almost all the Akali factions boycotted the elections. The Congress party won an absolute majority in the State Assembly and Shri Beant Singh became the Chief Minister. (The Congress won 12 Lok Sabha seats and one went to the Bahujan Samaj Party)

15

FIVE-YEAR PLANS

15.1 Planning Commission and Planning Process

The Planning Commission is a high powered Central Agency which was constituted in March 1950 to prepare a blue-print for development of the country. It has been entrusted with the task of assessing the resources of the country, drawing up Plans for the development and utilisation of resources within the framework of specified national priorities and determining conditions, modalities and adjustments needed for the success of the planning process. The commission also appraises the progress of the Plans from time to time.

The Prime Minister is the Chairman of the Commission. In order to achieve co-ordination among the States in implementing the Plans and to achieve targets set in the Plans, an advisory body called National Development Council (NDC) was set up in 1952, with the Prime Minister as Chairman and Chef Minister of all the States and Administrators of the Union Territories as members.

Broadly speaking the national Plans are formulated and finalised in three stages. In the *First* stage, the rough projections and estimates, prepared by the Planning Commission in consultation with the Central Ministries and State Governments against the background of the long-term perspective, are approved and modified, if necessary, by the NDC in the form of preliminary instructions.

In the *Second* stage, State Governments/Union Territories prepare their own Plans and send them to the Planning Commission, which dovetails these schemes, programmes and projects into an integrated Plan called the "Draft Plan". The Draft Plan is then released for public discussion.

The *Third* stage consists of prolonged discussions between the members of the Planning Commission and the representatives of different Central Ministries, State Governments and Union Territories, for arriving at an agreement on the nature and the size of the Plans.

These tentative agreements are sent to the NDC after examination by the Union Cabinet. In the light of the recommendations of the NDC, the Planning Commission gives the final shape to the Plan, which is placed before the Parliament for approval and subsequently becomes the official national Plan.

Till date, the Planning Commission has drawn up seven Five-Year Plans in addition to Annual Plans and Perspective Plans. Each Five-Year Plan covers period to five years, beginning from the 1st April of the concerned year and ending on the 31st March of the fifth year. The 8th Plan is expected to be finalised by March 31, 1992.

Planning in India derives its objectives and social content from the Directive Principles of State Policy, which are enumerated in the Constitution. The basic objective of the Five-Year Plans has been to secure a rapid and sustained economic growth and radical expansion of employment through most effective and balanced utilisation of country's resources. Its aim has been to ensure a fast reduction of disparities in income and wealth, thereby preventing concentration of economic power among a small number of people. It seeks to improve the living standards and working conditions of the toiling and denuded masses. It is the kingpin of a comprehensive strategy designed to bring about total self-reliance.

In the scheme of Indian Planning, the concept of mixed economy has been followed wherein the public and private sectors are considered complementary to each other. Social gains rather than personal enrichment form the crux of this philosophy.

15.2 Five Year Plans

The *First Plan (1951-52 to 1955-56)* was a 'ground preparing' exercise which gave its primary attention to the achievement of economic stability and elimination of shortages of food and basic resources. Accordingly it accorded top priority to agriculture of which irrigation and power were deemed essential ingredients. About 44.6 per cent of the total outlay was earmarked for the agricultural sector. The annual growth targeted in this Plan was 2.1 per cent of the national income.

The Plan also aimed at increasing the rate of investment from five per cent to about seven per cent of the national income.

The Second Plan (1956-57 to 1960-61) aimed, among other things, at 25 per cent increase in the national income, rapid industrialisation with particular emphasis on development of basic and heavy industries, large expansion of employment opportunities, and reduction of inequalities in income and wealth and more even distribution of economic power. The Plan laid special stress on fastening industrialisation with the aim of strengthening the capital base and productive capacity.

The Plan also aimed at increasing the rate of investment from about seven per cent of the national income to eleven per cent by 1960-61.

The Third Plan (1961-62 to 1965-66) aimed at securing a marked advance towards self-sustaining growth. Its immediate-objectives were to (a) secure an increase in national income of over 5 per cent per annum and a simultaneous evolution of a pattern of investment capable of sustaining this rate of growth during subsequent Plan period; (b) achieve self-sufficiency in foodgrains (the target of foodgrains production stood at 100 million tonnes) and increased agricultural production to meet the requirement of industry and exports; (c) expand basic industries like steel, chemicals, fuel and power and establish machine building capacity; (d) utilise fully manpower resources and ensure a substantial expansion of employment opportunities; and (e) establish greater equality of opportunity and bring about reduction in disparities of income and wealth and more equitable dispersal of economic power. The Plan sought to increase the national income by about 30 per cent from Rs. 14,500 crore in 1960-61 to about Rs. 19,000 crore by 1965-66 (at 1960-61 prices) and per capita income by about 17 per cent from Rs. 300 to Rs. 385 during the same period.

The finalisation of the Fourth Plan was delayed on account of the situation created by the Indo-Pakistan War in 1965, two successive years of severe drought, devaluation of currency, general rise in prices and erosion of resources available for Plan purposes. Therefore, three Annual Plans were formulated between 1966 and 1969.

The Fourth Plan (1969-70 to 1973-74) aimed at accelerating the tempo of development in conditions of stability and reducing the fluctuations in agricultural production as well as the impact uncertainties in foreign aid.

It sought to raise the standard of living and promote equality and social justice. The Plan laid particular emphasis on improving the conditions of the less-privileged and weaker sections of society through gainful employment and education and on diluting the concentration through wider diffusion of wealth, income and economic power. The average annual rate of growth envisaged was 5.7 per cent.

The Fifth Plan (1974-75 to 1977-78) aimed at achieving self-reliance and adoption of measures to boom consumption standards of the people living below the poverty line. The Plan also gave high priority to bringing inflation under control and achieving stability of the economic front. The Plan targeted an annual growth rate of 5.5 per cent in national income and better capacity utilisation of industries, developing renewable sources of energy, and integration of science and technology into the mainstream of development.

The Sixth Plan (1980-81 to 1984-85) assigned the highest priority to the removal of poverty. The strategy was essentially to strengthen the infrastructure for both agriculture and industry so as to create conditions for a sustained and accelerated growth in investment output and exports. It aimed at meeting the minimum basic needs of the people through special programmes and creating increased opportunities for employment, especially in the rural areas and the unorganised sector. Stress was laid on greater management efficiency and intensive monitoring in all sectors and involvement of people in formulation and speedy implementation of schemes at the local level.

The Seventh Plan (1985-86 to 1989-90) gives highest priority to food, employment and productivity. Faster movement towards the objective of self-reliance with social justice is the core idea of the Plan. The salient features of the Plan are: decentralised Planning, maximum employment generation, self-sufficiency in food at higher levels of consumption export-import balance, modernisation and upgradation of technology. The Seventh Plan lays down an average annual growth rate target of 5 per cent. It also aims at a 8.7 per cent annual growth rate for industries. The Seventh Plan outlay for Minimum Needs Programme is Rs. 11800.94 crores. The expenditure is likely to be within the outlay except in the Educational Sector where new programmes have been taken up for implementing the National Policy on Education.

The Eighth Plan, which was to commence from 1990-91, could not keep the schedule on account of political changes in the last two years. The policy of fiscal correction initiated by the Government and the momentous changes taking place in the World necessitated a reorientation in the planning process. The Eighth Five Year Plan is now being formulated in this background. The National Development Council (NDC) approved the objectives and the document on Thrusts and Macro-Economic Dimensions of the Eighth Plan at its meeting held on December 23-24, 1991. The Plan will commence from April 1, 1992.

The Plan will give priority to the following objectives.:

(i) Generating adequate employment to achieve near full employment by the turn of the century;

(ii) Containing population growth through people's active cooperation and an effective scheme of incentives and disincentives;

(iii) Universalisation of elementary education and complete eradication of illiteracy among people in the age group 15 to 35 years;

(iv) Provision of safe drinking water and primary health care accessible to all villages and entire population and complete elimination of scavenging;

(v) Growth and diversification of agriculture to achieve self-sufficiency in food and generate surplus for exports; and

(vi) Strengthening of infrastructure (energy, transport, communication, irrigation) in order to support growth process on a sustainable basis.

The Eighth Plan will focus on these objectives keeping in view the need for (a) continued reliance on domestic resources for financing investment; (b) increasing, technical capabilities for the development of science and technology; and (c) modernisation and competitive efficiency so that the Indian economy can keep pace with and take advantage of global developments.

Human resource development will be the main focus of the Eighth Plan. It is towards this ultimate goal that employment generation, population control, literacy, education, health, drinking water and provision of adequate food and basic infrastructure are considered as the priorities of th Plan. Provision of the basic elements which help development of human capital will remain the primary responsibility of the Government.

The Eighth Plan aims at an average growth of 5.6 per cent per annum and Incremental Capital-output Ratio (ICOR) is assumed to remain more or less at the same level as in the Seventh Plan. For achieving the targeted growth, the average rate of domestic savings required during the Eighth Plan will be 21.6 per cent of GDP. The corresponding investment rate will be 23 per cent of GDP. A total investment of Rs. 7,92,000 crore at 1991-92 prices is envisaged for the Eighth Plan out of which the share of public sector investment will amount to Rs. 3,42,000 crore or 43.2 per cent of the total investment as compared with 45.7 per cent realised in the Seventh Plan. This allows a larger scope for the private sector than that given hitherto. Public Sector outlay is Rs. 4,00,000 crore inclusive of the current outlay component. The Plan envisages a perceptible change in the manner of financing practised so far, which was neither envisaged nor healthy for the economy. Draft on foreign savings is estimated at 1.4 per cent of GDP amounting to Rs. 49,000 crore. The public sector investment will be financed to the extent of 70 per cent from household savings, 20 per cent from own savings and 10 per cent from the rest of the world. Determined efforts are called for on the part of the Central and State Governments and their enterprises to make their respective contributions to savings, so that the projected public sector outlay of Rs. 4,00,000 crore is realised.

It is also considered necessary to reorient the process of planning so as to:

(a) weed out projects which are not economically sound;

(b) rationalise plan expenditure by a process of consolidation and coordination of schemes;

(c) generate net additional resources to the extent possible through non-inflationary measures, particularly in the sectors which claim higher outlays; and

(d) divert some funds from the sectors which have surplus largely due to the government policies (administered prices), to the needy sectors, which cannot raise resources out of their own activities.

TABLE 15.1: Annual Plan Outlays by Heads of Development: Centre, States and Union Territories

	Amount (Rs.crore)		Percentage distribution	
	Annual Plan 1990-91	Annual Plan 1991-92	Annual Plan 1990-91	Annual Plan 1991-92
1	2	3	4	5
I. Agricultural and allied activities	3395.7	4473.1	5.5	6.2
II. Rural development	4120.9	4442.3	6.7	6.1
III. Special area programmes	1027.1	1142.9	1.7	1.6
IV. Irrigation and flood control	3837.2	4699.0	6.2	6.5
V. Energy	17998.5	21302.3	29.3	29.5
1. Power	11334.4	13678.0	18.4	18.9
2. Petroleum	4130.1	4917.3	6.7	6.8
3. Coal and lignite	2391.8	2520.0	3.9	3.5
4. Non-conventional sources of energy	142.2	187.1	0.2	0.3
VI. Industry and minerals	8239.7	8617.7	13.4	11.9
1. Village and small scale industries	906.6	1186.9	1.5	1.6
2. Other industries	7333.1	7430.8	11.9	10.3
VII. Transport	8695.8	9916.3	14.1	13.7
1. Railway	4916.0	5325.0	8.0	7.4
2. Others	3779.8	4519.3	6.1	6.3
VIII. Communication	3040.0	3385.1	4.9	4.7
IX. Science, technology and environment	787.0	1017.4	1.3	1.4
X. General economic services	1032.5	1265.7	1.7	1.8
XI. Social services	9104.2	11790.1	14.8	16.3
1. Education	2062.7	2603.4	3.4	3.6
2. Medical and public health	960.9	1185.5	1.6	1.6
3. Family welfare	784.9	749.0	1.3	1.0
4. Housing	559.8	925.2	0.9	1.3
5. Urban development	693.2	823.1	1.1	1.1
6. Other social services	4042.7	5503.9	6.5	7.7
XII. General services	239.5	264.9	0.4	0.3
XIII. Total (I to XII)	61518.1 (61523.1)	72316.8	100.0	100.0
(a) Central Plan	38052.3	42968.8	61.9	59.4
(b) State Plans	22452.4 (22457.4)	28062.5	36.5	38.8
(c) Union Territory Plans	1013.4	1285.5	1.6	1.8

Notes: 1. As per revised budget classification.
2. Figures in brackets are inclusive of expenditure on works financed by central assistance for relief against natural calamities (Rs. 5.0 crore in 1990-91).

Source: *Economic Survey*, 1991-92.

16

STATE OF INDIAN ECONOMY

16.1 **Policy Directions**

The year 1991-92 was a year of revolutionary changes in economic, fiscal and monetary policies, etc. An overall picture of these reforms is available from the Finance Minister Manmohan Singh's letter dated November 11, 1991 placed in the table of Parliament on February 26, 1992 addressed to World Bank President L.T. Preston. The letter throws light on the following: —

1. Programme for Structural Reform
2. Restoring Macroeconomic Stability.
3. Fiscal Policy
4. Monetary Policy
5. Industrial Policy
6. Enhancing the Efficiency of Financial Intermediation
7. Public Enterprise Reform
8. Strengthening Social Sectors and Safety Nets.

Matters listed at serial Numbers 3 to 8 have been dealt with separately in relevant chapters.

Source : *Times of India*, February 27, 1992.

16.2 **Programme for Structural Reform**

1. The government of India has recently initiated a comprehensive programme of macroeconomic stabilisation and structural adjustment. In support of the initial phase of its programme the government requests the assistance of the World Bank in the form of a structural adjustment loan credit (SAL/SAC). The programme aims at restoring macroeconomic balance and economic growth, regaining external creditworthiness and preparing the Indian economy to respond effectively to emerging global challenges and opportunities. It is inspired by the vision that India can grow faster as part of the world economy. However, the programmes is also being formulated at a time when the Indian economy faces a balance of payments crisis of unprecedented severity.

2. The new government which assumed office in June, 1991 inherited a situation with foreign exchange reservers at an all time low, drying up of normal external commercial borrowing, and a continuing withdrawal of foreign currency deposits by Non-Resident Indians (NRIs). Meanwhile severe import compression introduced earlier had begun to constrict industrial production and exports. The government moved rapidly to formulate a strategy for restoring viability in the external payments situation. The strategy relied upon restoration of macroeconomic stability through strict control over the fiscal deficit, tightening of

monetary policy, an adjustment in the exchange rate, and the announcement of major structural reforms in industrial and trade policies. These measures are bold and challenging. Through strenuous efforts, India has successfully met all its international payment obligations during a very difficult period.

3. Committed to the pursuit of equity and social justice, and blessed with a political system with a proven capability to provide both governance and freedom, the government's key economic objective is to restore sustained high growth which is essential to alleviate poverty and raise the standard of living. In pursuit of these objectives, the government's reform strategy, seen over the course of the next five years, aims at achieving: (i) a liberalised trade regime characterised by tariff rates comparable to other industrialising development countries and the absence of discretionary import licensing (with the exception of a small negative list); (ii) an exchange rate system which is free of allocative restrictions for trade; (iii) a financial system operating in a competitive market environment and regulated by sound prudential norms and standards; (iv) an efficient and dynamic industrial sector subject only to regulations relating to environmental security, strategic concerns, industrial safety, and unfair trading and monopolistic practices; and (v) an autonomous, competitive, and streamlined public sector geared to the provision of essential infrastructure goods and services, the development of key natural resources and areas of strategic concern. These objectives can be realised if sufficient financing is secured to enable the adjustment process to take place in an environment in which the momentum of growth is sustained.

4. Effective management of structural change in India, as in any other democratic society, requires not only the formulation of a consistent package of economic reforms, but also a broad social and political consensus. Building consensus involves articulation of the need for reform, and securing the cooperation and support of political parties as well as various interests group on the ends and means of reform. It also involves taking every step necessary to ensure that the burden of adjustment is fairly distributed and that the very poor are protected. As a first step in this direction, the government has established a National Renewal Fund (NRF) to provide a social safety net in order to ensure that the cost of adjustment does not fall on the workers. The NRF will provide ameliorative measures of workers affected in the course of structural changes, as well as financing their retraining, so that they will remain active productive partners in the process of adjustment.

5. Due to the initiatives taken over the past four decades, India now has a prosperous agriculture and a strong and diversified industrial base; it has capital markets and institutions which are on par with those of many advanced industrial nations; it has a large well-trained and skilled labour force; and is endowed with a vigorous and growing private sector. Over the course of the decades since Independence, our country has successfully dealt with many difficult situations arising out of droughts, wars and international oil shocks. The economy's performance was particularly impressive in the decade of the 1980s. Stimulated by the liberalisation initiatives of Shri Rajiv Gandhi's administration, GDP growth accelerated to 5.6 per cent per annum, compared to an average of 3.5 per cent during the previous three decades. This resulted in an increase in real per capita income by 40 per cent in the 1980s, compared to less than 30 per cent over the previous two decades combined. Despite the many disruptions of 1990-91, overall GDP grew by five per cent and manufacturing by eight per cent.

6. It is on the strength of these achievements, and with a firm commitment to removing the constraints on growth originating from the present macro-economic imbalances and long-standing structural impediments, that the government has initiated a comprehensive programme of macro-economic stabilisation and structural reform. The thrust of the programme would initially be on easing the country's extremely tight external payments situation and reducing inflation. The emergency measures taken in April-July 1991, including a severe compression of imports through tight credit policy, adjustments in the foreign exchange value of the rupee and mobilising part of the country's gold stocks, have had some success in meeting these initial objectives. Further, to stabilise expectations and to consolidate the gains from the recent exchange rate adjustment, the government intends to pursue a stable exchange rate policy geared to maintain the rupee constant in nominal terms and to rely on fiscal adjustment accompanied by a tight monetary policy to contain inflation.

7. There are long-term causes underlying the current macro-economic imbalances, some of which are structural in nature. These include the low productivity of investment, in particular the poor rates of return on past investments. Moreover, the excessive and often indiscriminate protection provided to industry has not only worked to the disadvantage of the rural economy, and accentuated disparities in income and wealth, but has also weakened the incentives to develop a vibrant export sector. Hence, stabilisation by itself is not enough. As the traditional demand impulses originating from fiscal policy will remain constrained in the next two to three years, the main impetus for sustainable economic growth has to originate with efficiency and productivity growth brought about through the expansion of investment and exports. Underpinning such a path of growth must be a consistent and comprehensive structural reform strategy designed to promote exports, to improve the relationship between the return on investment and the cost of capital, and to increase the degree of competition between firms in the domestic and external markets so that there are adequate incentives for upgrading of technology, improving efficiency and reducing costs. The key features of such a strategy are described below.

Restoring Macro-economic Stability

8. The macro-economic objectives of the government centre on the restoration of internal and external balance consistent with sustained economic growth. There is one basic direction of economic policy required to achieve these objectives. A substantial change in the composition of aggregate demand and supply must be engineered. Public sector consumption needs to be reduced in favour of higher domestic saving, while investment and net exports need to grow in relation to GDP. Fiscal consolidation, particularly measures to increase public sector saving, is a key requirement for this adjustment. These measures must be supported by reform measures aimed at removing structural rigidities in the economy arising from the regulatory system, which needs to be revamped in light of the new strengths and capabilities of the economy. Thus, measures to restore macro-economic stability are being supported by structural reforms in the areas of investment, trade, taxation, financial markets, and public enterprises.

9. The key macro-economic targets of the government are (i) a rapid recovery of GDP growth from about 3.5 per cent in 1991-92 to about six per

cent by the mid 1990s; (ii) an inflation rate of about 9 to 10 per cent (as measured by changes in the GDP deflator) in 1991-92, falling to 7.5 per cent in 1992-93 and to six per cent by 1995-96; and (iii) an easing of the present critical payments situation and a rebuilding of foreign exchange reserves from the low level of US $ 2.1 billion as of November 1, 1991 to US $ 2.3-2.5 billion (about 1 month's imports cover) by the end of 1991-92. Over the next few years, foreign exchange reserves would be built up to about 2-3 months' worth of imports. The external current account deficit is expected to decline from about 3.5 per cent of DGP in 1990-91 to about 2.7 per cent of GDP in 1991-92, falling gradually to about 1.5 per cent of GDP by 1995-96 as export growth strengthens under the influence of improved competitiveness and a recovery of demand in world markets.

10. The macro-economic policy framework within which these targets are to be achieved stresses the role of fiscal adjustment buttressed by appropriate monetary policies, especially in the net term. It is only such a prudent management of macro-economic policy that would enable us to curb the exponential growth in internal and external debt, and limit the burden of debt servicing for the government and the country to manageable levels. Moreover, this framework will place a new emphasis on the role of market institutions and incentives in the management of economic policy. The progress already achieved in introducing greater flexibility and autonomy in the determination of interest rates will be extremely important in this regard, as will the substitution of quantitative restrictions applying to intermediate and capital goods imports by a marketable import entitlement (Eximscrip).

16.3 **Economic Survey, 1991-92**

The Economic Survey, 1991-92 was presented to the Parliament on February 27, 1992, by Finance Minister, Manmohan Singh.

The pre-budget survey released two days prior to the presentation of the annual budget underlined the need for sustained correct action in 1992-93 to contain inflation and overcome the balance of payments problem. The survey asserted that although the twin problems of balance of payment and inflation had not been overcome, they were more "manageable." A considerable better economic performance was also within reach provided policy directions of the recent months were continued.

Highlights

* Modest growth in GDP of about 2.5 per cent
* Inflation rate down to 11.8 per cent
* Foreign exchange reserves to touch $ 4.4 billion
* Good performance by infrastructure
* Agricultural growth static — at best negligible
* Negative growth in industrial production
* Highest priority to balance of payments and containing inflation
* Calls for reduction of subsidies and elimination of open-ended cross-subsidisation
* Reduction of external support to production enterprises to make them responsive to price and demand changes
* Four-point adjustment strategy to boost exports.

16.4 **State of Economy at a Glance**

1. *GDP: Fall in Growth Rate*

TABLE 16.1: Growth Rate

Year	Per cent growth
1987-88	4.2
1988-89	10.5
1989-90	6.0
1990-91	5.6
1991-92	2.5

2. *Agriculture : Zero % Growth*

TABLE 16.2: Agriculture Production Growth

Agricultural Production	Per cent Growth
1987-88	—0.8
1988-89	21.0
1989-90	2.1
1990-91	2.6
1991-92	00

3. *Trade gap: Narrowing Down*

TABLE 16.3: Trade Gap

Year	Trade gap (Rs. Hundred crores)
1987-88	65.7
1991-92	
(April-September 1991)	23.6

4. *Industry : Negative Growth (per cent)*

TABLE 16.4: Industry Group

Year	
1987-88	7.3
1988-89	8.7
1989-90	8.6
1990-91	8.5
1991-92 (April-November 91)	—0.9

5. *Inflation*

TABLE 16.5: Rate of Inflation

Year and Month	Rate of Inflation
1990 (August-September)	7 %
1991 (February)	13.7%
1991 (August)	16.7%
1992 (January)	11.8%
*February 23 1992	12.10%

Source: *Economic Survey, 1991-92*; *Hindustan Times*, March 9, 1992

6. *Foreign Exchange Reserves*

The Foreign Exchange Reserves increased from Rs. 4,388 crore at the end of March 1991 to Rs. 41,424 crore on February 22, 1992.
Source: Minister of State for Finance in Rajya Sabha, March 3, 1992.

7. *Foreign Exchange on Imports*

Foreign exchange on imports during the financial year between April 1991 to December 1991 was Rs. 34,238 crore ($ 14,277 million) compared with Rs. 31,734 crore ($ 17,962 million) during the corresponding year last year. (Minister of State for Finance in Rajya Sabha, March 3, 1992)

8. *Debt Services*

India had to pay Rs. 5,367 crore towards the servicing of external debts during 1991-92. The interest paid on foreign debt was Rs. 412 crore in 1980-81 and Rs. 1,592 crore in 1985-86.
(Minister of State for Finance in Rajya Sabha, March 3, 1992).

9. *Consumer Price Index*

The increase in consumer prices continued.

TABLE 16.6: Consumer Price Index

	Sept '91	Aug '91	Sept '90	% change over month	year
Industrial workers (1982=100)	221	217	191	1.84	15.70
Urban non-manual Workers (1984-85=100)	184	183	159	0.54	15.72

10. *Wholesale Price Index*

The wholesale price index for all commodities on a year-on-year basis was up 13.97 per cent. This increase was mainly because of the sharp increase in the prices of primary articles. However, in the case of manufactured products the increase had been only 11.1 per cent over the year.

TABLE 16.7: Wholesale Price Index

(1981-82=100)

	23 Nov '91	26 Oct '91	24 Nov '91	% Change Over month	year
All commodities	211.2	209.2	185.3	0.95	13.97
Primary articles	226.8	221.8	187.4	2.25	21.02
Manufactured products	204.7	204.1	184.1	0.29	11.18

On 23.2.92, the Wholesale Price Index was 215.0 as against 191.8 on 23.2.91.

11. *Bullion Prices and Stockmarket Index*

TABLE 16.8: Bullion Prices and BSE Index

	24 Dec. '91	23 Nov. '91	22 Dec. '90	% Change over month	year
Gold (Bombay)	4920	4762	3480	3.3	41.37
Silver (Bombay)	7875	7206	6495	9.2	21.24
BSE Index (1978-79=100)	1908.85	1886.56	1035	1.10	84.42

(Price of gold is in rupees per 10 gms and silver in rupees per kg.)

12. *Industrial Production and Infrastructure*

TABLE 16.8A: Industrial Production Index

	Latest month 1991	Previous month 1991	Year ago 1990	% change over month	year
Industrial Production Index	201. 1(9)	198.5	200.3	1.30	0.39
Railway freight (million tonnes)	25.80(9)	26.36	23.80	-2.12	8.40
Crude oil production (1000 tonnes)	2503(11)	2581	2697	-3.02	-7.19
Power generation (million units/day)	831.4(10)	786.4	(703.7)	5.72	18.14
Coal production (lakh tonnes/day)	6.6(11)	5.86	6.6	12.62	—
Steel production (1000 tonnes)	858.1(11)	885	834.9	3.03	2.77
Cement production (1000 tonnes)	4305(11)	4310	3859	0.11	11.55

Note: *(Figures in brackets indicate month).*

13. *Money and Banking (Scheduled Commercial Banks)*

TABLE 16.9: Money and Banking

	29 Nov '91	25 Oct '91	30 Nov '90	% change over month	year
Broad Money (M3)	2,98,520	2,92,343	2,53,339	2.11	20.81
Aggregate deposits	2,17,884	2,14,528	1,83,973	1.56	18.42
Bank credit	1,70,031	1,19,958	1,07,859	0.06	11.28
Food credit	4,547	4,257	4,383	6. 8	3.74
Credit/Deposit ratio	55.09	55.92	58.63		

Source: *Business India*, January 6-19, 1992.

14. *Poverty Line*

It was estimated that there were 23.77 crore persons below the poverty line in 1987-88. The annual income with regard to poverty line is proposed to be increased from Rs. 6,400 to Rs. 11,000 because of the increase in the cost of living.

Source: (Rajya Sabha, March 9, 1992.)

16.5 **Extract from the Economic Survey**

Performance and Prospects

The year 1991-92 has been an exceptionally difficult year for the economy with the deepening of the crisis which began in 1990-91. The balance of payments problems, which emerged in 1990-91, had reached crisis proportions by June 1991. A severe import squeeze, introduced in the course of 1990-91 in response to the shortage of foreign exchange, disrupted industrial production, which began to decline early in the year 1991-92. Inflation, which had begun to accelerate in 1990-91, reached a peak level of 16.7 per cent in August 1991. Growth of real GDP decelerated sharply and is likely to be no more than 2.5 per cent this year.

The new Government which assumed office in June 1991 took a series of corrective measures to bring the situation under control. These included short-term measures aimed at crisis management as well as long-term measures of structural reform, aimed at improving efficiency and productivity and putting the economy back on the path of sustainable growth with equity and social justice.

1. *Growth Performance*

The growth of the economy slowed down substantially in 1991-92, partly because of a slowdown in agriculture and partly because of a deceleration in industrial growth. Industrial growth, which had been buoyant in earlier years, had already slowed down considerably in the second half of 1990-91 before turning into a decline by the beginning of 1991-92. The index of industrial production in April-June 1991 was 2.3 per cent lower than a year earlier.

2. *Payment Crisis*

The first signs of the current payments crisis became evident in the second half of 1990-91 when the Gulf War led to a sharp increase in oil prices. Foreign exchange reserves began to decline from September 1990. The rapid loss of reserves had prompted the government to take a number of counter-measures in the second half of the 1990-91.

The Outcome

The early results of the crisis management effort in 1991-92 have been encouraging: foreign currency assets, which had declined to $1.1 billion at their lowest point in June 1991, had risen to about $4.4. billion by 19 February 1992. In addition to the build-up of foreign exchange reserves, the Government was able to bring back the gold pledged to the Bank of England and the Bank of Japan in July. The value of this gold was approximately $600 million. $1.605 billion was received on India Development Bonds, which is held by the State Bank of India. Thus there was an increase in external assets of about $4.6 billion, against which must be placed an increase in foreign liabilities of about $3.2 billion. (These figures are preliminary and are given only to indicate order of magnitude).

3. *Inflation*

The current inflationary spiral began in October 1990. In August and September 1990, the annual rate of inflation, as measured by the wholesale price index on a point-to-point basis, was only about 7 per cent. From October onwards it rose rapidly to reach 13.7 per cent in February 1991. After a brief slowing down in April and May, this process of accelerating inflation, peaking in the fourth week of that month at 16.7 per cent. Since then the rate of inflation has declined; by 8 February it had gone down to 11.8 per cent.

4. *Growth and Equity*

The crisis of last summer has been brought under control. This does not mean that the problems have been overcome: the balance of payments will continue to be critical in the coming year, and there is some way to go before we can say that inflation has been contained. But both problems have been made more manageable; the Government can now give a creditable assurance that if we continue in the policy directions worked out in recent months, a considerably better economic performance is within reach, and with it, better living and working conditions for the people.

5. *Conclusion*

When a country is in such a grave crisis, it is tempting for the Government to stave off collapse, to take short cuts, to live through the present and let the future take care of itself. The economic policies of the Government have been designed to tackle the immediate crisis, but they emanate from a vision of a future, from the promise of a better life for our people. The crisis has involved hardship for the people. The Government has tried to ameliorate it, but not enough. The resources of the Government are limited, and more needs to be done to ensure that they are used efficiently and for the benefits of the most deserving. But the immediate options are limited. It is important to broaden them, and that is where the vision comes in.

The basis of this vision is self-reliance. It has been the foundation of our economic policy for over four decades. Even if anyone wished to abandon self-reliance, India is too large a country for the rest of the world to look after. There is thus no alternative to self-reliance.

This means that our achievements depend on our own efforts. Our standards of living depend on our productivity, the only fruits we can enjoy are the fruits of our labour. Our hard work, creativity, enterprise and intelligence—they will decide how well our children live. We must build a society that cares for the people today and builds for their tomorrows.

But self-reliance does not mean isolation. We live in a world of great variety— of people, resources, of knowledge and behaviour. It is there for us to cooperate with, trade with, learn from and contribute to. It is there for us to measure ourselves against. From it we must derive our standards of excellence—standards to equal and surpass. To it we must contribute care—care for the weak and the unfortunate.

The Government has tried to expand the economic space in which the people can exercise their initiative and ingenuity. It hopes to do more to expand their opportunities, to enhance their potential. But what shape the economy takes ultimately depends on what the people make of it. In that sense, the future is in their hands.

TABLE 16.10: Key Indicators

(Percentage change over previous year)

	1980-81	1981-82	1982-83	1983-84	1984-85	1985-86	1986-87	1987-88	1988-89	1989-90	1990-91 (P)	1991-92 (P)
1	2	3	4	5	6	7	8	9	10	11	12	13
1. Gross national product[1]	7.3	5.8	2.6	7.9	3.8	4.1	4.0	4.0	10.5	6.1	5.8	2.5 to 3
2. Gross domestic product[1]	7.2	6.1	3.1	8.2	3.8	4.1	4.3	4.2	10.5	6.0	5.6	2.5 to 3
3. Agricultural production	15.6	5.6	-3.8	13.7	-1.2	2.5	-3.7	-0.8	21.0	2.1	2.6	0.0*
4. Foodgrains production	18.1	2.9	-2.9	17.7	-4.5	3.4	-4.7	-2.1	21.0	0.6	3.0	-1.5*
5. Industrial production[2]	4.0	9.3	3.2	6.7	8.6	8.7	9.1	7.3	8.7	8.6	8.5	-0.8[3]
6. Electricity generated	5.9	10.2	6.7	7.6	11.9	8.6	10.2	7.6	9.5	10.8	7.8	9.0[4]
7. Wholesale price index[5]	16.7	2.4	7.2	7.2	6.0	4.8	5.1	10.7	5.7	9.1	12.1	11.8[6]
8. Consumer price index[7] for industrial workers	12.6	8.8	9.8	8.6	5.3	8.3	6.2	10.9	8.5	6.6	13.6	13.1[4]
9. Money supply(M3)	18.1	12.5	16.1	18.1	18.9	15.9	18.6	15.9	17.8	19.4	14.9	14.9[8]
10. Imports at current prices (in Rupees)	37.3	8.4	5.0	10.8	8.2	14.7	2.2	10.7	26.9	25.4	22.0	7.0[9]

Contd.

TABLE 16.10 (*Contd.*)

1	2	3	4	5	6	7	8	9	10	11	12	13
11. Imports at current prices (in US dollars)	40.5	-4.4	-2.5	3.5	-5.9	11.5	-2.2	9.1	13.6	9.1	13.2	-20.7[9]
12. Exports at current prices (in Rupees)	4.6	16.3	12.8	11.0	20.2	-7.2	14.3	25.9	29.1	36.8	17.6	28.1[9]
13. Exports at current prices (in US dollars)	7.0	2.6	4.6	3.8	4.5	-9.8	9.4	24.0	15.6	19.0	9.1	-5.0[9]
14. Foreign currency assets (Rupee crore)	4822	3355	4265	5498	6817	7384	7645	7287	6605	5787	4388	11410[10]
15. Foreign currency assets (US $ million)	5850	3582	4281	5099	5482	5972	5924	5618	4226	3368	2236	4395[10]

* Anticipated. (P) Provisional.

1. New series at 1990-91 prices.
2. Based on old index (1970-71 = 100) for 1980-81 and new index (1980-81 = 100) thereafter
3. April-October 1991.
4. April-December 1991.
5. Old index (1970-71 = 100) up to 1981-82 and revised index (1981-82 = 100) thereafter to 1981-82
6. April 1991-January 25, 1992
7. Old index (1960 = 100) up to 1982-83 and revised index (1982 = 100) thereafter.
8. April 1991-January 19, 1992.
9. April-November 1991.
10. As on February 20, 1992 for 1991-92 and at the end of March for past years.

Source: *Economic Survey*, 1991-92.

TABLE 16.11: Gross National Product and Net National Product

Year	Gross national product at factor cost (Rs. crore)		Net national product at factor cost (Rs. crore)		Per capita net national product (Rs.)		Index numbers (1950-51=100) Net national product		Index numbers (1950-51=100) Per capita NNP	
	At current prices	At 1980-81 prices	At current prices	At 1980-81 prices	At current prices	At 1980-81 prices	At current prices	At 1980-81 prices	At current prices	At 1980-81 prices
1	2	3	4	5	6	7	8	9	10	11
1950-51	8938	42644	8574	40454	238.8	1126.9	100.0	100.0	100.0	100.0
1951-52	9445	43730	9034	41443	247.5	1135.4	105.4	102.4	103.6	100.8
1952-53	9324	45002	8882	42613	238.8	1145.5	103.6	105.3	100.0	101.7
1953-54	10161	47768	9696	45293	255.8	1195.1	113.1	112.0	107.1	106.1
1954-55	9534	49750	9023	47111	233.8	1220.5	105.2	116.5	97.9	108.3
1955-56	9707	51119	9161	48288	233.1	1228.7	106.8	119.4	97.6	109.0
1956-57	11583	54002	10972	50955	273.6	1270.7	128.0	126.0	114.6	112.8
1957-58	11839	53304	11177	50051	273.3	1223.7	130.4	123.7	114.4	108.6
1958-59	13231	57311	12459	53869	298.1	1288.7	145.3	133.2	124.8	114.4
1959-60	13877	58434	13035	54775	306.0	1285.8	152.0	135.4	128.1	114.1
1960-61	15182	62532	14242	58602	328.2	1350.3	166.1	144.9	137.4	119.8
1961-62	15999	64359	14946	60168	336.6	1355.1	174.3	148.7	141.0	120.3
1962-63	17104	65657	15947	61165	351.3	1347.2	186.0	151.2	147.1	119.5
1963-64	19559	69006	18258	64216	393.5	1384.0	212.9	158.7	164.8	122.8
1964-65	22836	74121	21373	68942	450.9	1454.5	249.3	170.4	188.8	129.1
1965-66	23899	71338	22247	65734	458.7	1355.3	259.5	162.5	192.1	120.3
1966-67	27159	72092	25215	66089	509.4	1335.1	294.1	163.4	213.3	118.5
1967-68	31929	77845	29745	71519	587.8	1413.4	346.9	176.8	246.1	125.4
1968-69	33688	79945	31311	73285	604.5	1414.8	365.2	181.2	253.1	125.5
1969-70	37057	85149	34421	78177	650.7	1477.8	401.5	193.2	272.5	131.1

Contd.

TABLE 16.11 (*Contd.*)

1	2	3	4	5	6	7	8	9	10	11
1970-71	39424	89465	36503	82211	674.7	1519.6	425.7	203.2	282.5	134.8
1971-72	41957	90281	38717	82675	698.9	1492.3	451.6	204.4	292.7	132.4
1972-73	46171	89997	42510	81991	749.7	1446.0	495.3	202.7	313.9	128.3
1973-74	56629	94395	52362	86010	902.8	1482.9	610.7	212.6	378.1	131.6
1974-75	66748	95885	61290	87116	1033.6	1469.1	714.8	215.3	432.8	130.4
1975-76	70946	104660	64623	95433	1064.6	1572.2	753.7	235.9	445.8	139.5
1976-77	76303	105996	69523	96253	1121.3	1552.5	810.9	237.9	469.6	137.8
1977-78	87118	113903	79749	103670	1257.9	1635.2	930.1	256.3	526.8	145.1
1978-79	93724	120302	85298	109466	1316.3	1689.3	994.8	270.6	551.2	149.9
1979-80	102595	114379	92324	102937	1390.4	1550.3	1076.8	254.5	582.2	137.6
1980-81	122772	122772	110685	110685	1630.1	1630.1	1290.9	273.6	682.6	144.7
1981-82	143256	129928	128797	117140	1855.9	1687.9	1502.2	289.6	777.2	149.8
1982-83	158761	133299	141875	119704	2001.1	1688.3	1654.7	295.9	838.0	149.8
1983-84	185779	143861	166550	129392	2300.4	1787.2	1942.5	319.8	963.3	158.6
1984-85*	207153	149292	185062	133844	2504.2	1811.2	2158.4	330.9	1048.7	160.7
1985-86*	232047	155399	205810	139059	2726.0	1841.8	2400.4	343.7	1141.5	163.4
1986-87*	257250	160975	227427	143682	2953.6	1866.0	2652.5	355.2	1236.9	165.6
1987-88*	291647	167703	257961	149408	3286.1	1903.3	3008.6	369.3	1376.1	168.9
1988-89*	349105	185543	310015	166200	3875.2	2077.5	3615.8	410.8	1622.8	184.4
1989-90@	392524	195237	346994	174798	4252.4	2142.1	4047.0	432.1	1780.7	190.1

* Provisional

@ Quick estimates. Estimates for 1990-91 were not available at the time of printing.

Source: *Economic Survey*, 1991-92.

TABLE 16.12: Net State Domestic Product at Current Prices (New Series)

(*Rs. crore*)

		1980-81	1981-82	1982-83	1983-84	1984-85	1985-86	1986-87	1987-88	1988-89 (P)	1989-90 (Q)
1	2	3	4	5	6	7	8	9	10	11	12
1	Andhra Pradesh	7324	8974	9702	11516	11962	13412	14242	16598	19793	—
2	Arunachal Pradesh	97	129	148	167	196	237	268	284	337	342
3	Assam	2356	2978	3398	3766	3725	5118	5476	5993	6563	7699
4	Bihar	6077	7002	7830	9178	11086	12008	13732	14848	17348	17824
5	Goa	315	343	418	442	542	555	657	731	796	851
6	Gujarat	6594	8247	8745	11385	11866	11507	13429	13614	19328	21668
7	Haryana	3032	3498	4004	4351	4747	5643	5935	6629	8693	10032
8	Himachal Pradesh	721	844	894	1019	1024	1228	1353	1509	1780	1999
9	Jammu and Kashmir	974	1098	1269	1417	1640	1803	2013	1873	2422	—
10	Karnataka	5866	6735	7413	8984	10072	10510	12124	13870	16447	18012
11	Kerala	3782	4008	4662	5465	6078	6436	7321	8085	8934	9991
12	Madhya Pradesh*	6122	6784	7732	9641	9454	11136	11621	14625	17002	18000

Contd.

TABLE 16.12 (*Contd.*)

1	2	3	4	5	6	7	8	9	10	11	12
13	Maharashtra	15113	16966	18277	21152	23084	26530	28157	32642	38990	45613
14	Manipur	201	243	258	307	354	377	428	506	600	618
15	Meghalaya	180	206	227	263	302	341	380	462	512	551
16	Mizoram	62	70	78	95	122	157	194	259	—	—
17	Nagaland	105	132	161	194	231	261	294	338	361	—
18	Orissa	3225	3677	3765	4893	4801	5936	6206	6521	8433	9416
19	Punjab	4451	5240	5808	6400	7307	8315	9209	10784	12408	14311
20	Rajasthan	4126	4850	5531	7043	6983	7669	8254	8977	12253	—
21	Sikkim	49	55	65	75	95	113	135	156	177	189
22	Tamil Nadu	7218	8677	8821	10222	12028	13682	15125	18105	20084	21562
23	Tripura	268	290	352	360	441	485	512	599	667	716
24	Uttar Pradesh	14102	15156	17757	19704	21658	24785	27413	30289	35626	40719
25	West Bengal	8637	9777	10688	12832	14778	15602	17397	19252	22791	25944

P Provisional.
Q Quick estimates.
— Not available (The figures have not been supplied by the concerned State Governments).
* Based on old (1970-71) series.
Note: Owing to differences in source material used, the figures for different States are not strictly comparable.
Source: *Economic Survey*, 1991-92.

TABLE 16.13: Per Capita Net State Domestic Product at Current Prices (New Series)

(*Rupees*)

		1980-81	1981-82	1982-83	1983-84	1984-85	1985-86	1986-87	1987-88	1988-89 (P)	1989-90 (Q)
1	2	3	4	5	6	7	8	9	10	11	12
1	Andhra Pradesh	1380	1657	1756	2046	2086	2296	2394	2741	3211	—
2	Arunachal Pradesh	1561	2011	2240	2455	2793	3274	3579	3679	4236	4176
3	Assam	1200	1474	1641	1777	2182	2313	2420	2589	2772	3179
4	Bihar	878	989	1083	1242	1468	1558	1744	1846	2111	2122
5	Goa	3145	3365	4003	4127	4931	4927	5702	6209	6619	6939
6	Gujarat	1951	2390	2484	3162	3233	3077	3525	3509	4893	5404
7	Haryana	2370	2664	2967	3133	3325	3849	3950	4321	5537	6265
8	Himachal Pradesh	1698	1948	2025	2264	2233	2630	2848	3122	3622	4005
9	Jammu and Kashmir	1649	1817	2050	2237	2528	2716	2966	2701	3420	—
10	Karnataka	1596	1790	1926	2285	2508	2564	2900	3254	3787	4075
11	Kerala	1494	1559	1782	2050	2238	2328	2603	2828	3076	3389
12	Madhya Pradesh*	1183	1284	1432	1746	1675	1931	1973	2433	2772	2878

Contd.

TABLE 16.13 (*Contd.*)

1	2	3	4	5	6	7	8	9	10	11	12
13	Maharashtra	2427	2669	2813	3185	3403	3835	3997	4558	5363	6184
14	Manipur	1430	1684	1742	2018	2265	2354	2611	3008	3480	3502
15	Meghalaya	1361	1516	1625	1831	2046	2250	2437	2893	3112	3250
16	Mizoram	1289	1383	1471	1724	2139	2658	3165	4077	—	—
17	Nagaland	1383	1666	1941	2251	2579	2800	3034	3361	3464	—
18	Orissa	1231	1380	1388	1772	1707	2072	2128	2194	2793	3066
19	Punjab	2675	3082	3343	3605	4028	4486	4862	5572	6274	7081
20	Rajasthan	1222	1392	1544	1914	1849	1978	2074	2197	2923	—
21	Sikkim	1571	1701	1926	2136	2635	3023	3472	3886	4254	4396
22	Tamil Nadu	1498	1776	1777	2024	2341	2620	2851	3362	3677	3894
23	Tripura	1323	1390	1641	1640	1962	2108	2177	2494	2722	2866
24	Uttar Pradesh	1286	1349	1547	1682	1812	2032	2201	2382	2444	3072
25	West Bengal	1564	1735	1860	2189	2473	2561	2803	3046	3542	3963

P Provisional

Q Quick estimates.

— Not available (The figures have not been supplied by the concerned State Governments).

* Based on old (1970-71) series.

Note: Owing to differences in source material used, the figures for different States are not strictly comparable.

Source: *Economic Survey*, 1991-92.

16.6 Growth Rate

The Reserve Bank of India (RBI) forecasts a GDP growth rate of 3 per cent in the financial year ending March 1991-92. It has been predicted that economic difficulties such as inflation, trade deficits and foreign exchange drain the "short term" would continue.

The fall in GDP growth rate from 5 per cent in 1990-91 to 3 per cent in the current fiscal year will be largely caused by a slowdown in industrial growth from 8.4 per cent to 6 per cent in the same period under review. The projected 3 per cent rate of growth also depends crucially on the RBI forecast of a one per cent increase in agricultural output. A shortfall in this could lead to an even lower GDP growth rate.

Particularly hard hit will be sectors which depend on "public sector subventions" and large public sector demand. In effect, RBI is forecasting a slowdown in growth of core public sector industries and private sector industries which depend on supplies to public sectors units.

Restrictive Policies

This will be the result of the severely restrictive import and credit policies initiated for a short-term by the authorities. To some extent measures aimed at restraining the aggregate expenditure may also affect production. While efforts should be made to minimise such adverse effects, the overall compulsion to contain expenditures cannot be avoided until the balance of payments moves to a more sustainable level.

An adverse BoP situation as the most important difficulty facing policy-makers in the last one year is identified . Because of this, "although monetary policy is usually framed against the background of recent trends in money supply, prices and output, in the current financial year, monetary policy responses have been framed almost exclusively against the background of a difficult balance of payments situation".

Describing the recent devaluation as "appropriate", the RBI obliquely hints that even that may not be enough. The more important measure of competitiveness is the real effective exchange of rupee. And, "the real effective exchange rate of rupee in the more recent period had begun to appreciate". According to the report, while countries such as China and Indonesia depreciated their currencies more than the rupee, inflation in those countries was lower than in India.

For the devaluation and other policy measures to have any positive impact, "it is necessary to ensure that the domestic prices do not rise to wipe out the price advantage provided by depreciation". In this context, the present tight monetary policy can be reversed only when there is a significant improvement in the balance of payments situation and strong inflationary pressures have begun to slow down.

Categories

In a detailed analysis of the measures, RBI distinguishes two broau categories. One of them is directly aimed at import containment. The cash margins for imports which has been raised to 200 per cent is one of the more important measures in this category. The second category is restrictive monetary policies which too are ultimately aimed at containing the current account deficit in the balance of payments.

With a candid approach RBI comes down heavily on profligate government measures. "It is imperative to ensure that the deficit remains within budget levels. In the recent period a recurring features has been that actual deficits have turned out to be much higher than the budgeted deficits. To the extent there is any shortfall in revenue, it will have to be compensated by a combination of appropriate measures of expenditure reductions and resource mobilisation".

RBI severely criticises the debt waiver schemes which have been initiated by successive governments. "While there are time tested procedures for affording relief to borrowers affected by natural calamities, across the board loan and or interest waivers have seriously impaired credit discipline. . . . Such a situation cannot but inflict irretrievable damage to the financial system".

On the issue of financial system reforms, branches of banks should henceforth be opened only after assessing their financial viability. It also calls for special tribunals to deal exclusively with industrial sickness expeditiously so that profitability of the banking sector improves. In a major move, the RBI has also supported the commercial banks view point with regard to mutual funds.

Two other major reviews of RBI has asked for are the operation of the statutory liquidity ratio and the interest rate structures. The level of interest should reflect the scarcity of capital. There should also be a flexible interest rate policy.

While these are reforms with a medium term perspective, the containment of inflation is the immediate aim of monetary policy.

Source : *Annual Report*, 1990-91, Reserve Bank of India, Bombay, as reported in *Times of India,* September 10, 1991.

17

POVERTY ALLEVIATION AND EMPLOYMENT

17.1 Poverty: Incidence and Alleviation

Alleviation of poverty has been a primary objective of our planning process particularly after the Fourth Five Year Plan and several special programmes have been in operation over the last two decades focussing on the poor as the target group. As a result, the extent of incidence of absolute poverty has significantly declined over the years. The overall improvement in human resources as evident from the estimates of incidence of poverty made by the Planning Commission is given in the Table 17.1

TABLE 17.1: Estimates of incidence of Poverty

(*Percentage*)

	1972-73	1977-78	1983-84	1987-88
1	2	3	4	5
Rural	54.1	51.2	40.1	33.4
Urban	41.2	38.2	28.1	20.1
All India	51.5	48.3	37.4	29.9

TABLE 17.2: Unemployed Persons

Year	No in million
1981	17.8
1983	22.0
1985	26.3
1986	30.1
1989	30.3
1990 end March	33.4

Note: Number of persons on live registers of employment exchanges
Source: *India To-day*, March 31, 1991

17.2: Employment Programmes

A number of Special Employment Programmes have over the years sought to supplement employment generation by the growth process.

Programmes for the rural poor are the Integrated Rural Development Programme (IRDP) and its two sub-programmes: Training for Rural Youth for Self Employment (TRYSEM) and Development of Women and Children in Rural Areas (DWCRA) and the wage employment programmes — the National Rural Employment Programme (NREP) and the Rural Landless Employment Guarantee Programme (RLEGP), later merged to form the Jawahar Rozgar

Yojana (JRY) in 1989-90. IRDP seeks to promote self-employment by providing productive assets and inputs to the rural poor through a mix of subsidy and bank credit. TRYSEM provides training in technical skills to poor rural youth to enable them to take up self-employment or wage employment and DWCRA seeks to promote economic activities among groups of poor rural women. JRY is designed to generate additional gainful employment for the rural unemployed and under employed by taking up works for creating productive economic assets. During the Seventh Plan period, 18.2 million families were assisted under IRDP and the wage employment programmes (NREP/RLEGP and JRY) generated 3,497 million mandays of employment. Details of the self employment and wage employment generated are given in Table 17.3.

The Self-Employment Programmes for the Urban Poor (SEPUP), Scheme for Self-Employment to the Educated Urban Youth (SEEUY) and Nehru Rozgar Yojana (NRY) are programmes initiated for the urban poor.

SEPUP was launched in September 1986 and covers all cities and towns with a population of 10,000 and above and areas not covered by IRDP. Under the scheme, loans upto Rs.5,000 are provided by banks to the urban poor for taking up useful economic ventures with Central Government providing a capital subsidy of 25 per cent of the total loan. Available provisional figures show that during the years 1986-87 to 1989-90, 14.37 lakh beneficiaries were sanctioned loans amounting to Rs.516.02 crore. During 1990-91, 1.19 lakh beneficiaries were covered and the amount of loan sanctioned was Rs.50.44 crore. The scheme is being continued during the financial year 1991-92. However, from the year 1992-93 SEPUP is being merged with the Scheme of Urban Enterprises (SUME) under Nehru Rozgar Yojana (NRY).

Source: *Economic Survey*, 1991-92.

TABLE 17.3: Achievements of Special Employment Programmes (In Rural Areas)

	Seventh (1985-90)		1990-91		1991-92* (Upto November, 91)	
	Target	Achievement	Target	Achievement	Target	Achievement
(i) IRDP —Number of families assisted (Million)	16.04	18.2	2.37	2.90	2.25	1.22
(ii) TRYSEM —Number of rural youth trained (Million)	—	1.0	0.43	0.24	0.43	0.10 **
(iii) DWCRA —(a) Number of groups formed	35,000	28,000	7,500	7,139	10,000	3,670
—(b) Number of members	—	4,68,383	—	1,09,557	—	45,257
(iv) JRY (NREP & RLEGP) — Number of man-days of employment generated (Million)	2180	3497	929	874	816	406@

*Provisional
** Up to October, 1991
@ Up to December, 1991

TABLE 17.4: Employment in Public Sector by Industry

(Lakh, as on 31 March)

	1977	1978	1979	1980	1981	1983	1984	1985	1986	1987	1988	1989*
1	2	3	4	5	6	7	8	9	10	11	12	13
A. By branch												
1. Central Government	30.82	30.96	31.34	31.78	31.95	32.66	33.11	33.29	33.46	33.50	33.81	33.89
2. State Governments	50.20	51.60	53.09	54.78	56.76	60.38	61.54	62.80	64.73	66.66	67.81	68.90
3. Quasi-Governments	36.75	39.29	41.70	43.43	45.76	50.40	52.74	54.96	56.74	57.95	59.48	59.99
4. Local bodies	19.89	20.15	20.63	20.80	20.37	21.11	21.30	21.64	21.90	22.14	22.11	22.38
Total	137.66	142.00	146.76	150.79	154.84	164.55	168.69	172.69	176.83	180.25	183.21	185.16
B. By industry												
0. Agriculture, hunting etc.	3.66	3.87	4.08	4.31	4.63	4.76	4.89	4.98	5.26	5.57	5.54	5.65
1. Mining and quarrying	7.57	7.58	7.71	7.97	8.18	8.84	9.27	9.74	9.66	9.42	9.56	9.57
2.& 3 Manufacturing	12.26	13.55	14.16	14.46	15.02	16.34	17.17	17.61	18.15	18.62	18.67	18.48
4. Electricity, gas and water	5.63	5.99	6.34	6.61	6.83	7.21	7.33	7.60	7.85	7.89	8.49	8.66
5. Construction	10.09	9.98	10.32	10.68	10.89	11.20	11.20	11.46	11.81	11.85	12.14	11.80
6. Wholesale and retail trade	0.76	0.83	0.99	1.10	1.17	1.18	1.24	1.31	1.31	1.34	1.39	1.44
7. Transport, storage and Communications	24.67	25.20	25.97	26.51	27.09	28.26	28.64	28.94	29.29	29.70	30.11	30.26
8. Finance, insurance, real estate etc.	5.34	5.80	6.47	6.91	7.48	8.72	9.14	9.83	10.30	10.56	10.95	11.16
9. Community, social and personal services	67.69	69.18	70.71	72.24	73.55	78.06	79.81	81.23	83.21	85.29	86.35	88.13
Total	137.67	141.98	146.75	150.79	154.84	164.57	168.69	172.70	176.84	180.24	183.20	185.15

*Provisional

Source: *Economic Survey*, 1991-92

TABLE 17.5: Employment in Private Sector By Industry+

(*Lakh, as on March*)

	1977	1978	1979	1980	1981	1983	1984	1985	1986	1987	1988	1989*
1	2	3	4	5	6	7	8	9	10	11	12	13
0. Agriculture, hunting etc.	8.38	8.53	8.41	8.60	8.58	8.47	8.19	8.07	8.22	8.48	8.44	8.70
1. Mining and quarrying	1.30	1.27	1.24	1.25	1.30	1.20	1.13	1.13	1.11	0.91	0.93	0.97
2.&3. Manufacturing	41.65	43.21	44.33	44.17	45.45	46.56	44.73	44.21	44.48	44.10	43.95	43.89
4. Electricity, gas and water	0.35	0.34	0.34	0.34	0.35	0.37	0.39	0.39	0.40	0.40	0.41	0.41
5. Construction	0.83	0.83	0.83	0.73	0.72	0.68	0.66	0.70	0.69	0.58	0.50	0.64
6. Wholesale and retail Trade	2.75	2.74	2.81	2.74	2.77	2.75	2.76	2.77	2.77	2.77	2.83	2.86
7. Transport, storage & communications	0.71	0.61	0.71	0.71	0.60	0.59	0.57	0.54	0.54	0.52	0.51	0.51
8. Finance, insurance, real estate etc.	1.86	1.80	2.01	2.06	1.96	2.07	2.14	2.19	2.21	2.29	2.38	2.43
9. Community, social & personal services	10.86	11.10	11.40	11.67	12.22	12.83	12.89	13.09	13.32	13.59	13.97	14.29
Total	68.69	70.43	72.08	72.27	73.95	75.52	73.46	73.09	73.74	73.64	73.92	74.70

* Provisional.

\+ Relates to non-agricultural establishments in the private sector employing 10 or more persons.

Note: Coverage in construction, particularly on private account is known to be inadequate.

Source: *Economic Survey*, 1991-92

18

INFLATION, PRICE POLICY AND PUBLIC DISTRIBUTION

18.1 Prices

The prices which had risen rapidly in 1990-91, continued their rise in 1991-92. The wholesale price index (WPI) registered 11.7 per cent increase from April 1990 to February 1, 1992 and the consumer price index (CPI) for industrial workers increased by 11.9 per cent from April to December, 1991. The annual rate of inflation was 12.1 per cent in terms of WPI as on the February 1, 1992 and 13.1 per cent in terms of CPI for industrial workers in December, 1991.

The major concern about inflation during the current year, as in 1990-91, is that it is concentrated in primary commodities including items such as foodgrains, vegetables, sugar and edible oils. Prices have tended to rise even in respect of commodities which are not in short supply.

Some pressure on prices may have arisen because of increase in the prices of administered items such as coal, petroleum products (other than diesel and kerosene), fertilizer, and electricity. However, the impact of these changes is small and in any case a failure to adjust these prices would have meant a large deficit and correspondingly higher price pressure elsewhere in the system. A steep increase in prices was also observed in respect of raw cotton.

The build-up of inflationary pressures is mainly attributable to excess demand arising from the large and persistent fiscal deficits over the years, resulting in excessive growth in money supply and a liquidity overhang. There have also been supply and demand imbalances in sensitive commodities such as pulses, edible oils, etc. due to shortfalls in domestic production and constraints in importing desired quantities due to the severe foreign exchange crunch. A sharp increase in procurement prices of cereals, and consequent rise in the issue prices, has set the trends for open market prices. Exchange rate adjustments in early July, 1991, led to increase in import costs which contributed to some cost pressure in import intensive industries. The uneven progress of monsoon until the end of August, 1991, also generated some inflationary expectations in the economy, exacerbating the pressure on prices.

In order to check the inflationary pressures in the economy and to bring down the prices, particularly that of essential commodities, a number of measures have been initiated by the Government. A major element in the strategy to combat inflation is the massive effort to correct the fiscal imbalances by reducing the fiscal deficit from 8.4 per cent of GDP in 1990-91 to 6.5 per cent in 1991-92. The growth of aggregate demand has been contained by restraining the growth of broad money (M_3) and bank credit to the Government. The selective credit controls on bank advances against price-sensitive essential commodities such as rice, paddy, cotton and kapas, and pulses have been tightened. Steps have been taken to revamp the Public Distribution System

(PDS), and its reach has been extended to 1,700 blocks in far-flung and disadvantaged areas. Allocation of sugar, rice and wheat, etc. under the PDS has been increased for the lean period. Stocks of wheat and rice have been offloaded in the market to bring about a sobering effect on prices. Steps have been initiated to improve domestic supply of critical items such as edible oils, cotton and wheat through imports. Action against blackmarketeers and hoarders has been intensified to flush out the hoarded goods. Efforts have been made to remove transport bottlenecks and other infrastructural constraints in the movement of coal, raw materials and finished goods which had earlier led to a sharp increase in the prices of some commodities. State Governments have also been requested to ensure availability of essential commodities at reasonable and affordable price and to regularly monitor and review the price situation at the highest level. These measures, together with other economic reforms, have begun to show results. The rate of increase in prices has fallen after September, 1991. A downturn in the annual rate of inflation has also set in; the annual rate of inflation in 1st February, 1992 is lower than at the same point in the previous year.

Trends in WPI and CPI over the years 1985-86 to 1991-92 are shown in Table 18.1.

Source: *Economic Survey*, 1991-92.

Wholesale Prices

Variations in the WPI of major commodity groups/sub-groups and important commodities during 1991-92 are given in Table 18.2. The major contributors to the rising trend in prices during the current year are primary articles though the increase is less as compared to that of last year. Manufactured products also exhibited a marginally higher increase in prices than in the previous year. Though fuel, power, light and lubricants recorded a rise in the price index, the magnitude of its increase is lower than that in the previous year. Under *primary articles*, the real impetus to inflation was provided by food articles, such as cereals (especially rice and coarse cereals), fruits, eggs, fish and meat, condiments and spices and non-food articles (primarily raw cotton), rape and mustard seeds. Prices of gram, onion, coffee and raw jute slightly offset the price rise by registering modest to steep decline. Primary articles as whole, with a weight of 32.3 per cent in the general index, contributed 46.9 per cent to the total price rise compared with 47.2 per cent in the corresponding period last year.

TABLE 18.1: Trends in WPI and CPI

Items/Groups	Weight (%)	Changes during Financial year							Annual rate of inflation (Point-to-Point)						
		85-86	86-87	87-88	88-89	89-90	90-91	91-92*	85-86	86-87	87-88	88-89	89-90	90-91	91-92
1	2	3	4	5	6	7	8	9	10	11	12	13	14	15	16
(A) Whole Price Index (1981-82 = 100)															
ALL COMMODITIES	**100.0**	**4.8**	**5.1**	**10.7**	**5.7**	**9.1**	**12.1**	**11.7**	**4.7**	**5.8**	**9.4**	**6.3**	**8.1**	**13.5**	**12.1***
(a) Primary articles	32.30	4.4	5.5	15.7	-0.2	6.4	17.1	16.6	0.7	8.7	14.1	2.2	3.6	18.9	16.3*
(b) Fuel, power, light & lubricants	10.66	12.1	2.2	5.3	5.1	6.3	14.4	10.6	15.3	2.9	5.7	4.2	2.3	19.2	11.2*
(c) Manufactured products	57.04	4.1	5.3	8.9	9.2	11.1	8.9	9.0	4.8	5.2	8.8	7.9	11.8	9.6	9.7*
(B) Consumer Price Index (1982 = 100) (For Industrial Workers)															
GENERAL INDEX	**100.00**	**8.3**	**6.2**	**10.9**	**8.5**	**6.6**	**13.6**	**11.9**	**6.7**	**7.8**	**10.9**	**8.5**	**5.4**	**13.7**	**13.1$**
(a) Food index	57.00	10.0	7.6	9.9	8.3	5.3	16.3	15.5	7.4	9.9	9.7	9.5	2.3	16.9	15.5$
(b) Pan, supari, tobacco and intoxicants	3.15	17.2	10.2	6.4	9.8	15.3	10.3	10.1	16.4	10.1	8.5	7.9	16.7	8.5	16.5@
(c) Fuel & light	6.28	8.0	4.4	8.5	8.5	4.8	14.4	2.0	9.1	6.1	5.7	8.8	6.8	12.2	5.2@
(d) Housing	8.67	11.3	7.0	13.9	5.8	7.9	7.9	3.1	13.0	7.4	13.7	6.7	7.5	8.2	7.0@
(e) Clothing, bedding and footwear	8.54	6.7	5.4	5.1	8.9	11.2	7.4	7.5	4.9	6.5	5.2	8.3	10.7	7.6	10.3@
(f) Miscellaneous	16.36	5.9	8.0	11.1	8.7	9.2	10.1	9.2	5.1	7.3	11.4	8.2	7.5	10.5	13.2@

* = WPI up to February 1, 1992 (Provisional); @ = CPI up to November, 1991 and $ = CPI up to December, 1991.

TABLE 18.2: Price Variations of Selected Items

(*Base : 1981-82 = 100*)

Items/Groups	Weight in WPI	1990-91				1991-92		
		Whole Years (April-March)		End-March to Feb.2 (44th WK)		End-March to Feb.1 (44th WK)		Annual rate of inflation as on Feb. 1 1992
	(%)	% change	% share	% change	% share	% change	% share	(per cent)
(1)	(2)	(3)	(4)	(5)	(6)	(7)	(8)	(9)
ALL COMMODITIES	**100.00**	**12.10**	**100.00**	**11.69**	**100.00**	**11.68**	**100.00**	**12.09**
I. Primary Articles	**32.30**	**17.14**	**44.63**	**17.50**	**47.16**	**16.62**	**46.86**	**16.27**
(A) Food articles	17.39	18.89	28.14	20.25	31.22	19.31	31.60	17.96
(a) Foodgrains	7.92	22.72	13.89	24.53	15.52	25.19	17.47	23.37
1. Cereals	6.82	25.35	12.68	26.46	13.71	28.26	16.38	27.12
(i) Rice	3.69	13.36	3.94	13.48	4.11	28.27	8.73	28.13
(ii) Wheat	2.25	48.91	7.32	53.85	8.34	21.13	4.35	17.24
2. Pulses	1.09	10.81	1.19	15.93	1.81	9.46	1.07	4.62
(b) Fruits & vegetables	4.09	22.83	7.55	22.65	7.75	11.29	4.24	11.45
(i) Fruits	2.80	25.04	5.68	20.16	4.73	19.36	5.08	24.22
(ii) Vegetables	1.29	17.68	1.83	28.20	3.03	-7.05	-0.79	-14.68
(c) Milk	1.96	8.85	1.69	5.29	1.05	9.09	1.75	12.78
(d) Eggs, fish & meat	1.78	10.47	1.63	11.08	1.79	20.41	3.25	19.75
(e) Condiments & spices	0.95	32.25	3.57	31.22	3.57	37.85	5.11	38.94
(f) Other food articles	0.69	-1.96	-0.18	15.93	1.48	-3.10	-0.25	-18.06
(B) Non-food articles	10.08	19.33	16.61	18.03	16.03	14.87	14.09	16.14
1. Fibers	1.79	24.46	3.42	10.99	1.59	25.06	4.04	40.23
2. Oilseeds	3.86	26.60	8.30	30.25	9.77	19.45	7.10	16.11
(C) Minerals	4.83	-0.46	-0.12	-0.46	-0.12	5.14	1.21	5.14

Contd.

TABLE 18.2 (*Contd*)

(1)	(2)	(3)	(4)	(5)	(6)	(7)	(8)	(9)
II. Fuel, Power, Light & Lubricants	**10.66**	**14.37**	**12.20**	**13.77**	**12.10**	**10.60**	**9.25**	**11.19**
III. Manufactured Produced	**57.04**	**8.93**	**42.99**	**8.19**	**40.78**	**8.99**	**43.54**	**9.74**
(A) Food products	10.14	13.17	10.87	13.05	11.15	10.85	9.37	10.97
1. Sugar, khandsari & gur	4.06	0.07	0.02	-0.07	-0.02	7.67	2.05	7.82
(i) Sugar	2.01	0.42	0.06	1.76	0.25	19.68	2.52	18.11
2. Edible oils	2.45	32.67	7.34	32.46	7.55	8.06	2.22	8.23
3. Oilcakes	0.43	4.56	0.17	7.29	0.28	29.91	1.08	26.61
Others								
1. Textiles	11.55	5.27	4.97	3.79	3.70	7.88	7.22	9.42
2. Cement	0.86	14.06	0.95	12.45	0.87	4.76	0.34	6.25
Administered Items	19.70	9.86	14.23	9.42	14.07	9.34	13.68	9.77
1. Petroleum crude & natural gas	4.27	-0.40	-0.08	-0.40	-0.09	1.91	0.36	1.91
2. Petroleum products (Mineral oils)	6.67	20.55	9.34	20.55	9.67	7.88	3.99	7.88
3. Coal mining	1.26	0.04	0.01	0.04	0.01	26.82	3.51	26.82
4. Electricity	2.74	11.38	2.89	9.29	2.44	7.73	2.02	9.79
5. Fertilisers	1.75	0.00	0.00	0.00	0.00	37.44	2.90	37.44
6. Iron & steel	2.44	6.00	1.38	6.00	1.43	1.84	0.41	1.84
7. Non-ferrous metals (other than aluminium)	0.57	9.42	0.69	8.08	0.62	6.56	0.49	7.89
1. Administered items	19.70	9.86	14.23	9.42	14.07	9.34	13.68	9.77
2. Seasonal items	34.41	18.03	52.28	18.35	55.05	16.14	51.03	15.83
3. Raw materials	14.91	14.79	16.49	13.79	15.91	12.93	15.29	13.93

* Provisional

Consumer Prices

All the three Consumer Price Indices (CPI) for industrial workers, urban non-manual employees and agricultural labourers, exhibited accelerated rates of inflation during the third quarter of the current year due to relatively higher increase in the prices of food articles and food products which have a much higher weight in the Consumer Price Index than the Wholesale Price Index. Among the three consumer price indices, the CPI for agricultural labourers has witnessed the highest rate of inflation. Upward movement in the wholesale prices of these commodities have been transmitted to the retail prices of these commodities in around a month's time. The comparable movements in the rates of inflation in terms of the WPI and CPI during the current year are given below:

TABLE 18.3: Annual Rates of Inflation on a Point-to-Point Basis in WPI and the CPI during 1991

(*per cent*)

Month	WPI (1981-82=100)	CPI for industrial workers (1982=100)	CPI for urban non-Manual Employees (1984-85=100)	CPI for agricultural labourers (1960-61=100)
March	12.7	13.6	13.4	16.6
April	11.6	12.2	12.6	14.7
May	11.8	12.1	11.8	13.7
June	12.2	13.0	12.3	15.4
July	13.1	13.2	13.3	15.9
August	16.1	14.2	15.1	18.3
September	16.3	15.7	15.7	23.1
October	14.7	14.4	14.2	23.1
November	13.7(P)	13.6	14.0	21.2
December	13.1(P)	13.1	13.3	21.7

P=Provisional

18.2 Factors underlying Inflation and Anti-inflationary Measures

The buildup of inflationary pressure is mainly attributable to excess demand arising from the large and persistent fiscal deficits over the years, resulting in excessive growth in money supply and a liquidity overhang. There have also been supply and demand imbalance in sensitive commodities such as pulses, edible oils, etc. due to shortfalls in domestic production and constraints in importing desired quantities due to the severe foreign exchange crunch. Exchange rate adjustments in early July, 1991, led to increase in import costs which contributed to some cost pressure in the import intensive-industries. The uneven progress of monsoon until the end of August, 1991 also generated some inflationary expectations in the economy, exacerbating the pressure on prices.

The acceleration in the rate of inflation is a cause for serious concern; equally worrisome is the rise in prices even of commodities which are not in short supply in the market. Fairly good monsoons for four years in a row leading to very good harvests in the last three years and prospects of a good crop during this year have not been able to contain the pressure on prices. The offtake of foodgrains from the PDS has also been higher this year compared to the previous year. Selective credit control measures have been tightened on bank advances against foodgrains, cotton and kapas, oilseeds and edible oils; and the lending rates and margin money for such advances have been increased substantially this year.

With an improvement in the balance of payments situation, imports of essential commodities in short supply in the domestic market are being arranged. Due attention is also being given to the building up of adequate stocks of these commodities to contain prices in the lean season. The continuance of tight monetary policy, judicious fiscal corrections, improvement in the foreign exchange reserves and regular supplies of critical commodities to the needy population would have salutory impact in bringing down the prices.

Anti-inflationary Measures

A number of reforms in the spheres of fiscal and monetary policies, trade and industry, and external sector of the economy have been initiated which, among other things, are expected to check the inflationary pressures in the economy. Improvement in the foreign exchange reserves would facilitate a more effective management of supply through imports of essential commodities which are in short supply. A number of monetary measures have been introduced during the year to moderate the expansion of liquidity and to curtail effective demand. These were supplemented by a number of fiscal measures such as reduction in fiscal deficit of the Central Government by about 2 percentage points from 8.4 per cent of GDP in 1990-91 to 6.5 per cent of GDP in 1991-92.

18.3 Public Distribution System (PDS)

The Government is supplying six key essential commodities through the PDS : wheat, rice, sugar, imported edible oils, kerosene and soft-coke. They are supplied at reasonable (below market) rates to consumers, the access to the system being universal. While the Central Government procures or allocates and supplies these commodities to the States or UTs, the latter, in turn, are responsible for the allocation and distribution within the State/UT and allied implementational activities. The PDS aims at insulating the consumer from the impact of rising prices of these commodities and maintaining the minimum nutritional status of our population. The PDS supplies have a stabilising effect on open market prices by increasing availability, removing scarcity psychosis and deterring speculative tendencies.

The network of the PDS has been expanded over the years, the number of fair price shops having increased to 3.75 lakhs now from about 3.12 lakhs in 1984. About 75 per cent of these shops are located in the rural areas. More than 15 million tonnes of foodgrains, i.e. about 9-10 per cent of total production, are supplied through the PDS per year. As PDS supplies are made at concessional rates, the Central Government has to spend over Rs. 2,000 crores on subsidising distribution of wheat and rice alone. Despite shortcomings, the PDS has established its relevance, and the pressures are mounting for its expansion both in the urban and rural areas to protect the poorest sections of the population from the general inflationary situation.

The Government has initiated, in consultation with the State Governments and the UT administrations, steps to revamp the Public Distribution System to improve its reach on the basis of an area approach and to eliminate leakages and malpractices that have crept into this system. Preference is now being given to the population living in the most difficult areas of the country, such as the drought prone areas, desert areas, tribal areas, certain designated hilly areas and the urban slum areas. About 1,700 blocks have been covered in these areas under the revamped PDS. Ration cards are being issued to all those who have not been issued such cards so far. Additional fair price shops are being opened where needed. Supply of additional items is being arranged through the PDS outlets. Beneficiaries are being involved in monitoring the functioning of the PDS. The Government has initiated steps to create infrastructural and other facilities necessary to support these operations.

Off Take under PDS

Foodgrains supplies under the PDS have increased in recent years. During 1990-91 a total quantity of nearly 16.0 million tonnes of foodgrains (rice, wheat and coarse grains) was distributed against 15.7 million tonnes in the previous year. During the first nine months of the current year (up to December 1991), 15.53 million tonnes of foodgrains (rice 8.7 million tonnes, and wheat 6.6 million tonnes and coarse grains 0.23 million tonnes) have been distributed under the PDS.

Source: *Economic Survey*, 1991-92.

19

FISCAL POLICY AND BUDGET 1992-93

19.1 Introduction

The fiscal situation, which was under strain throughout the 1980s, reached a critical situation in 1990-91 with a sharp deterioration in the revenue deficit. Fiscal deficits generate pressures on inflation as well as on the balance of payments. The gross fiscal deficit of the Central Government, which measures the total resource gap, has been more than 8 per cent of GDP since 1985-86, as compared with 6 per cent at the beginning of 1980s and 4 per cent in the mid-1970s. Such fiscal deficits are unsustainable and would lead the country into a debt-trap. The unabated growth of non-plan expenditure and poor returns from investments made in the public sector have been the main contributory factors in the fiscal crisis.

A particularly disquieting feature of the Centre's finances has been growing deficits on revenue account. The ratio of the revenue deficit to GDP reached 3.5 per cent in 1990-91 (provisional actuals) as compared with 1.5 per cent in 1980-81. There has been a steady decline in the share of capital formation in Central Government expenditure. The gross savings of the Government, which turned negative for the first time in 1984-85, continued to remain so. The fiscal imbalance also manifested in a sharp increase in internal debt and resultant increase in interest payments.

The regular Budget for 1991-92 presented on July 24, 1991, initiated a major effort towards correcting the fiscal imbalance. It envisaged a reduction in the fiscal deficit by nearly two percentage points of GDP, from 8.4 per cent in 1990-91 (RE) to 6.5 per cent in 1991-92 (based on projections of GDP at that time; the latest GDP estimate yields 6.2 per cent). It aimed at containing Government expenditure and augmenting revenues; reversing the downward trend in the share of direct taxes in total tax revenues; curbing conspicuous consumption; encouraging indigenous industry and improving competitiveness of the industrial sector, particularly export-oriented industries. The important policy initiatives comprised reduction in fertiliser subsidy, abolition of Cash Compensatory Support for exports, abolition of subsidy on sugar, divestment of 20 per cent of Government equity in selected public sector undertakings to mutual funds, a 20 per cent increase in the prices of motor spirit and adjustment of tax rates to yield an additional net revenue of Rs. 2005 crore to the Centre. The provision of non-plan expenditure, excluding interest payments, in the current year represents a reduction of 4.5 per cent compared with the provisional actuals for 1990-91.

Aggregate resources of the Central Government, including internal and extra-budgetary resources of Central public enterprises, were to be about 11.3 per cent higher in 1991-92 (BE) than the revised estimates for 1990-91. Aggregate disbursements were 8 per cent higher than the revised estimates for 1990-91. The containment of disbursements through various measures was aimed at limiting the budgetary deficit to Rs.7719 crore. Aggregate receipts of the Centre, States and Union Territories, including internal and extra-budgetary resources of their enterprises, were budgeted to increase by 11.7 per cent over 1990-91 (RE) while aggregate expenditure was estimated to increase by 10.4 per cent.

The Annual Plan for 1991-92 provided for a total outlay of Rs.72,317 crore for the Centre, States and Union Territories, an increase of 17.6 per cent over the revised estimates for 1990-91. The allocation for the Central Plan was Rs.42,969 crore.

The working of both the departmental and non-departmental commercial undertakings of States and Union Territories deteriorated in 1990-91.

Sustained corrective action on the part of the Centre and the State Government over the next few years is required to correct the fiscal imbalance.

Source: *Economic Survey, 1991-92*, Ministry of Finance, (Economic Division) Government of India, New Delhi, 1992.

19.2 **Fiscal Policy***

11. Our medium term objective is to reduce substantially the Central Government fiscal deficit within the broader context of an adjustment of the overall public sector deficit. The fiscal deficit target of the Union Government budget introduced on July 24, 1991 is 6.5 per cent of GDP — a reduction of about two and-a-half percentage points of GDP from the estimated 1990-91 outcome. Since interest payments are projected to rise from 4.3 per cent of GDP to 4.7 per cent in 1991-92, achieving this deficit reduction requires an even bigger adjustment in the primary deficit, from 4.8 per cent of GDP to 1.8 per cent. In keeping with the targeted path of overall public sector adjustment the Central Government deficit is targeted to fall to 5 per cent of GDP in 1992-93, with further improvements thereafter. Reducing the overall public sector deficit will require increased financial discipline by the state governments as well and the Central Government will encourage the state governments to take steps to improve their fiscal performance and to streamline the working of their enterprises. As a result of these efforts to improve efficiency and profitability, we expect the internal resource generation of the central public enterprises to improve significantly beginning in 1991-92.

12. The fiscal adjustment outlined in the 1991-92 budget provides for a rough balance between expenditure and revenue measures. Total expenditures and net lending are targeted to decline from 20.1 per cent of GDP to 19.1 per cent, thanks to cuts equivalent to 1.2 per cent of GDP in non-interest current expenditures, notably fertiliser and export subsidies, transfers to central public enterprises, and a moderation in defence spending. On the revenue side. Central Government revenue and grants are projected to rise by one percentage point to 12.6 per cent of GDP. Average petroleum product prices were raised by seven per cent (on top of increases of 24 per cent in October 1990 and 11 per cent in last year's budget) to offset the effect of the recent exchange

---

* *Note*: Paras refer to paras of the Finance Minister's letter of November 11, 1991.

rate adjustment on the budget. Corporation tax was also increased, depreciation allowances were lowered, some tariffs were lowered, and plans tc transfer assets of some public enterprises to financial institutions (expected to yield proceeds equal to about 0.1 per cent of GDP this year) were confirmed.

13. The targeted reduction of the fiscal deficit is central to the success of the overall programme. The main strengths of the new 1991-92 budget are its primary deficit reduction, the balance between current expenditure cuts and revenue measures, and the relative protection given to investment and social development outlays. However, given the very short time the new government had for preparing the budget (only eight months remained in the fiscal year at the time of budget presentation), there are naturally a number of areas which will require follow up. The government intends to take additional measures as necessary, on both the revenue and expenditure sides, to ensure that the targeted reduction of the Central Government fiscal deficit is achieved.

14. The government realises the necessity of strengthening budgetary control mechanisms and setting in place a fiscal framework that would be supportive of the structural reforms being introduced. Proposals for a comprehensive reform of the tax system are being formulated by a high level committee of exports. The terms of reference of the committee focus on the need for specific recommendations that will lead to (i) an improvement in the elasticity of tax revenues, in part through the identification of new areas for taxation, and an increase in the share of direct taxes as a proportion of total tax revenues and of GDP; (ii) a more equitable and broad-based system particularly with regard to commodity taxation and personal taxation; (iii) the removal of anomalies that distort economic incentives, including a simplification and rationalisation of customs tariffs with a view to reducing the multiplicity and dispersion of rates and the elimination of exemptions, as well as a reduction in the average level of tariffs; and, finally (iv) improved compliance of direct taxes and strengthened enforcement. The initial recommendations of this committee will be introduced in the 1992-93 Union government budget.

15. The government efforts at fiscal consolidation would include a major thrust for a more efficient expenditure control system. A thorough review of the existing system would be undertaken to remove existing deficiencies and to significantly strengthen its effectiveness. Particular scrutiny would be given to transfers and loans to public enterprises. There is also need for further rationalisation and reduction of subsidies, particularly in light of the desirability of moving to a more objective system of administered prices that takes into account world market developments and domestic supply conditions.

Exchange Rate Policy

16. The adjustment in the exchange rate of the rupee by 23 per cent (in terms of rupees per dollar) in early July 1991 provides for a significant real depreciation which will improve export incentives and international competitiveness. The exchange rate adjustment is also expected to check speculation, as well as making for a more orderly compression of imports. The government intends to keep the nominal effective exchange rate stable by relying on appropriate fiscal and monetary policies to maintain competitiveness and ensure the balance of payments objectives.

Monetary Policy

17. There has already been a significant tightening of credit and monetary policies through higher interest rates and higher cash reserve requirements. Consistent with our foreign exchange reserve target and the anticipated slow-down in GDP growth, broad money expansion is targeted to decline to a rate of 13 per cent in 1991-92, with a further declaration in 1992-93. In the context of a rapidly declining recourse on financial savings by the government, this should permit a steady increase in the volume of domestic credit to the private sector, for investment. However, the government is committed to a further tightening of monetary policy if necessary to defend the external position. Monetary policy affects the pace of aggregate supply as well as aggregate demand. This dictates that monetary policy should be pursued flexibly and prudently to avoid the risk of weakening the economy's productive capacity, including its capacity to export. In its application, the government would judiciously balance the stance of monetary policy to control inflation with its possible adverse impacts on the supply side.

*Enhancing the Efficiency of Financial Intermediation**

31. Since independence India has witnessed the growth of a well diversified and comprehensive financial infrastructure. In terms of financial sector size the financial system ranks in the top quarter among developing countries. The capital market is broad and active and in recent years has found the public increasingly receptive. In 1990-91 non-government companies were able to raise Rs. 25.27 billion through new issuance of equity and debentures as compared to Rs. 11.04 billion in 1985-86. The government's ownership of the financial and banking institutions is dominant. This has enabled it to achieve multiple objectives including mobilisation of resources, integration of the rural population into the financial mainstream, enhancement of availability of long-term loans to all levels of industry and agriculture and increased access to credit to small industrialists, farmers and weaker sections of society.

32. However, there are weaknesses and imbalances. The Statutory Liquidity Ratio (SLR) and Cash Reserve Ratio levels are high, which implies low returns for commercial banks on their funds; it also reduces the resources available to and raise the costs for non-priority borrowers.

33. To move closer to a market-based operation of financial institutions, interest rates on term loans have been decontrolled (subject to a floor of 15 per cent) while all regulated deposit interest rates were increased by one percentage point. Interest rates on commercial bank loans had been decontrolled earlier (with a floor of 18.5 per cent) set for non-priority sector loans, now raised to 20 per cent). Measures have also been taken to strengthen capital markets: interest rates for debentures (except for tax-free bonds for the public sector) have been freed, mutual funds are being opened up to the private sector, and full statutory powers are to be given to an independent agency to regulate security markets. Finally, a high level committee (Narasimham Committee) has been es-

---

* *Note*: Paras refer to paras of the Finance Minister's letter of November 11, 1991.

tablished to review the structure and overall functioning of the financial system and to advise the government on reforms by end-November 1991.

34. In line with the recommendations of the Narasimham Committee, further reforms of the financial sector will be formulated and implemented. The aim would be to increase the efficiency of financial intermediation through a well sequenced programme for (i) deregulation of the interest rate structure; (ii) enhancement in the flexibility and autonomy of financial institutions and banks to adjust resource flows to emerging needs and priorities; (iii) strengthening the prevailing prudential regulatory framework applying particularly to capital adequacy norms and assessment of bad and doubtful debt in banks' portfolios; and (iv) enabling expansion of private and cooperative sector banks (including foreign banks) in the banking sector. The measures required to meet these objectives would principally involve a phased reducation of involuntary financing of budget targeting of priority lending scheme towards the most deserving groups, and eventual elimination of the subsidies involved, formulation of prudential norms and standards to guide efforts in recapitalisation of the banking sector, and full decontrol of deposit rates. It is also recognised that improved prudential standards are important for the healthy development of India's already sizeable and rapidly growing securities markets.

Fiscal Imbalance

A more complete measure of macro-economic imbalance used internationally is the concept of gross fiscal deficit, which reckons the total resource gap in terms of excess of total Government expenditure over revenue receipts and grants. This concept fully reflects the indebtedness of the Government. The trends in various indicators of fiscal imbalance over the eighties are given in Table 19.1. The gross fiscal deficit of the Central Government has been more than 8 per cent of GDP since 1985-86, as compared with 6 per cent at the beginning of 1980s and 4 per cent in the mid-1970s.

TABLE 19.1: Budget Deficit, Revenue Deficit, Monetised Deficit and Gross Fiscal Deficit of the Central Government.

(*per cent of GDP at current market prices*)

	Budget Deficit	Revenue Deficit	Monetised Deficit	Gross Fiscal Deficit
1975-76	0.5	1.1	0.3	4.1
1980-81	1.9	1.5	2.6	6.2
1981-82	0.9	0.2	2.0	5.4
1982-83	0.9	0.7	1.9	6.0
1983-84	0.7	1.2	1.9	6.3
1984-85	1.6	1.8	2.6	7.5
Average Sixth Plan	1.2	1.1	2.2	6.3
1985-86	2.0	2.2	2.4	8.3
1986-87	2.8	2.7	2.4	9.0
1987-88	1.7	2.7	2.0	8.1
1988-89	1.4	2.7	1.6	7.8
1989-90	2.4	2.6	3.1	7.9
Average Seventh Plan	2.1	2.6	2.3	8.2
1990-91 (R.E.)	2.0	3.3	2.8	8.2
1990-91 (Prov.Act.)	2.1	3.5	2.8	8.4
1991-92 (B.E.)	1.3	2.3	1.3	6.2

Note: GDP at current market prices is estimated to grow at 15 per cent in 1991-92.

The important policy initiatives introduced in the Budget for correcting the fiscal imbalance are briefly listed below.

(i) Reduction in the fertiliser subsidy by increasing the average prices of fertilisers by 30 per cent (except for marginal and small farmers);
(ii) Abolition of Cash Compensatory Support for exports;
(iii) Abolition of subsidy on sugar distributed through the Public Distribution System by increasing the price by 85 paise per kg to Rs. 6.10 per kg;
(iv) Offering of upto 20 per cent of Government equity in selected public sector undertakings to mutual funds and investment institutions in the public sector. This is estimated to fetch the Governments Rs. 2,500 crore;
(v) A 20 per cent increase in the prices of motor spirit, domestic LPG and aviation turbine fuel for domestic use; and
(vi) Adjustment of tax rates to yield an additional net revenue of Rs. 2,005 crore to the Centre.

While revenue receipts grew on an average by 16.6 per cent per annum during 1980-81 to 1990-91 (RE), the growth in revenue expenditure was 17.1 per cent. The revenue deficit — GDP ratio reached 3.3 per cent in 1990-91 (RE) as compared with 1.5 per cent in 1980-81 shown in Table 19.2.

Contued.

TABLE 19.2: Centre's Revenue Receipts and Revenue Expenditure (As per cent of GDP)

	1980-81	1983-84	1984-85	1985-86	1986-87	1987-88	1988-89	1989-90	1990-91 (R.E.)	1991-92 (B.E.)
1. Tax revenue (Net of States'share)	**6.9**	**7.5**	**7.6**	**8.1**	**8.3**	**8.4**	**8.6**	**8.5**	**8.4**	**8.6**
2. Non-Tax revenue	**2.5**	**2.4**	**2.9**	**3.1**	**3.4**	**3.1**	**2.9**	**3.5**	**2.8**	**2.9**
3. Total current revenue (1+2)	**9.4**	**9.9**	**10.5**	**11.1**	**11.7**	**11.5**	**11.4**	**12.0**	**11.2**	**11.5**
4. Total current expenditure	**10.9**	**11.1**	**12.3**	**13.3**	**14.4**	**14.2**	**14.1**	**14.6**	**14.5**	**13.8**
(a) Interest payments	2.0	2.3	2.6	2.9	3.2	3.4	3.6	3.9	4.1	4.5
(b) Subsidies	1.2	1.3	1.6	1.8	1.9	1.8	2.0	2.4	2.0	1.4
(c) Defence expenditure	2.6	2.7	2.8	2.9	3.4	3.0	2.9	2.6	2.4	2.1
(d) Grants to States and UTs	2.1	2.1	2.3	2.7	2.6	2.8	2.6	1.9	2.5	2.5
(e) Others	3.2	2.5	3.1	3.1	3.3	3.3	3.0	3.8	3.5	3.2
5. **Revenue Account surplus (+)/deficit (-) [3-4]**	-1.5	-1.2	-1.8	-2.2	-2.7	-2.7	-2.7	-2.6	-3.3	-2.3

Note: Figures may not add up to total because of rounding.

TABLE 19.3: Budgetary Transactions of the Central and State Governments and Union Territories
(Including extra-budgetary resources of public sector undertakings for financing their Plans)

(*Rs. Crore*)

	1980-81	1984-85	1985-86	1986-87	1987-88	1988-89	1989-90	1990-91 (BE)	1990-91 (RE)	1991-92 (BE)
I. Total Outlay	**36845**	**72825**	**83961**	**100790**	**112169**	**130048**	**158107**	**176191**	**179443**	**198160**
	27.1	31.5	32.0	34.4	33.7	33.0	35.1	33.3	33.9	32.5
(a) Developmental	24426	48085	53397	63778	68801	79548	98501	107993	107945	116726
(b) Non-Developmental	12419	24740	30564	37012	43368	50500	59606	68198	71498	81434
II. Current Revenue	**24563**	**47098**	**56773**	**64823**	**73485**	**85714**	**103115**	**117855**	**112273**	**132412**
	18.1	20.4	21.6	22.1	22.1	21.7	22.9	22.3	21.2	21.7
(a) Tax Revenue	19844	35813	43267	49540	56976	66925	77693	89183	89303	102896
	14.6	15.5	16.5	16.9	17.1	17.0	17.2	16.8	16.9	16.9
(i) Direct Taxes	3268	5329	6252	6890	7483	9757	11165	13047	13397	15338
(ii) Indirect Taxes	16576	30484	37015	42650	49493	57168	66528	76136	75906	87558
(b) Non-Tax Revenue	4719	11285	13506	15283	16509	18789	25422	28672	22970	29516
III. (Gap I-II)	**12282**	**25727**	**27188**	**35967**	**38684**	**44334**	**54992**	**58336**	**67170**	**65748**
	9.0	11.1	10.4	12.3	11.6	11.2	12.2	11.0	12.7	10.8
Financed By:										
(i) Domestic Capital Receipts	7161	18765	21899	24439	29415	36172	40812	45010	50517	50424
(ii) Net External Assistance	1670	1857	1850	2378	3765	3060	3567	4327	4806	4378
(iii) Budgetary Deficit	3451	5105	3439	9150	5504	5102	10613	8999	11847	10946
	2.5	2.2	1.3	3.1	1.7	1.3	2.4	1.7	2.2	1.8

Notes: Figures in decimals are percentages to new series of GDP at current market prices released by CSO and, therefore, will differ from the figures given in the earlier issues of Economic Survey.

19.3 **Budget 1992-93***

TABLE 19.4: Budget at a Glance

(in crores of rupees)

	1990-91 Actuals	1991-92 Budget Estimates	1991-92 Revised Estimates	1992-93 Budget Estimates
1. **Revenue Receipts**	**54954**	**67529**	**66549**	**75688**
2. Tax Revenue (Net to Centre)	42978	52500	50006	56456
3. Non-Tax Revenue	11976	15029	16543	19232
4. **Capital Receipts**	**39015**	**38174**	**39521**	**38010**
5. Recoveries of Loans	5712	5666	6261	6491
6. Other Receipts	—	2500	2500	2500
7. Borrowings and Other Liabilities	33303	30008	30760	29019
8. **Total Receipts (1+4)**	**93969**	**105703**	**106070**	**113698**
9. Non-Plan Expenditure	76198	79697	80070	84475
10. On Revenue Account	60850	64315	66696	71233
11. On Capital Account	15348	15382	13374	13242
12. **Plan Expenditure**	**29118**	**33725**	**33032**	**34612**
13. On Revenue Account	12666	17068	16934	18337
14. On Capital Account	16452	16657	16098	16275
15. **Total Expenditure (9+12)**	**105316**	**113422**	**113102**	**119087**
16. Revenue Expenditure (10+13)	73516	81383	83630	89570
17. Capital Expenditure (11+14)	31800	32039	29472	29517
18. **Revenue Deficit (1-16)**	**18562**	**13854**	**17081**	**13882**
19. **Budgetary Deficit (8-15)**	**11347**	**7719**	**7032**	**5389**
20. **Fiscal Deficit [(1+5+6) -15=7+19]**	**44650**	**37727**	**37792**	**34408**
21. Increase in net RBI Credit to Central Government*	14745	7719	8800	5389 **

* Including other variations in Reserve Bank of India's credit to Central Government.
** Not independently estimated.

TABLE 19.5: Outlay for Sectors

Sectors	1991-92*	1992-93**	% change
Agriculture	1,735	1,879	8.29
Rural Development	2,356	2,610	10.8
Irrigation and Flood Control	217	231	6.5
Energy	12,269	14,998	22.2
Industry and Minerals	6,690	8,198	22.2
Transport	7,415	9,129	22.5
Communications	3,630	4,890	34.7
Science, Technology & Environment	841	935	11.2
Social Services	4,565	5,128	12.3
Others	454	409	-9.9
Total	40,172	48,407	20.5

*Revised estimates **Budget estimates

* *Note*: Budget presented by the Finance Minister Manmohan Singh in Parliament on February 29, 1992.

19.4 Tax Proposals at a Glance

Direct Taxes

* Exemption limit for income tax raised by Rs.6,000 to Rs. 28,000.
* !-T rate slabs reduced from four to three.
  — 20 per cent tax on income upto Rs.50,000; 30 per cent on income upto Rs. 1 lakh; 40 per cent on income exceeding Rs. 1 lakh.
* Standard deduction for women with income upto Rs. 75,000 hiked by Rs.3,000 to Rs.15,000
* 12 per cent surcharge on I-T for income exceeding Rs. 1 lakh
* Tax deductions under section 80 L, 80 CC (A) and 80 CC (B) abolished. But prospective beneficiaries of saving schemes under these provisions allowed tax rebate under Section 88 of I-T Act.
* Norms for computing income from houses tightened.
* Presumptive I-T on traders with turnover exceeding Rs 5 lakh.
* Presumptive tax on certain trades such as liquor withdrawn.
* Income of children to be clubbed with parents to plug revenue leakages.
* Inflation indexing of capital gains. Standard deduction withdrawn. 20 per cent tax on long-term capital gains for individuals and 40 per cent for companies and other organisations.
* 10 per cent tax rebate for persons over 65 years and with a income below Rs. 50,000.
* Tax deduction for persons maintaining handicapped dependents doubled to Rs 12,000.
* Tax deduction for medical insurance doubled to Rs. 6000.
* Tax exemption for employees opting for voluntary retirement extended to private sector.
* Tax deduction at source in respect of interest on bank deposits and commission payments withdrawn.
* Wealth tax on productive assets such as shares withdrawn and limited to non-productive assets such as houses at a rate of one per cent.
* Mutual funds exempted from I-T.
* Expenditure tax on air-conditioned restaurants withdrawn and its range narrow in the case of hotels.
* Cooperative sector banks exempted from Interest Tax Act.
* Corporate tax reforms deferred and confined to marginal tightening of set off of carried forward depreciation and investment. Allowable expenditure on entertainment and services relating to tax proceedings increased.

Indirect Taxes

Excise

* 5 to 15 per cent hike in special excise on all goods, excluding specified essential commodities such as sugar and petroleum products and specified consumer durables such as TVs.
* Duty on cigarettes increased.
* Duty on watches doubled to 10 per cent .

* Duty on viscose staple fibre, acrylic fibre and filament yarn hiked.
* Duty on polyester staple fibre and yarn and nylon filament yarn slashed.
* Uniform duty on polypropylene filament yarn imposed on the higher side.
* Duty on cotton yarn not containing any synthetic staple fibre rationalised on the higher side but with differential rates for cooperative and other users.
* Duty on blended yarn containing polyester and on cellulosic spun yarn not containing any synthetic staple fibre rationalised.
* Duty on cocoa and cocoa-based products increased by 10 to 25 per cent
* Duty on specified pesticide intermediates removed.
* Duty on white cement reduced by 5 to 35 per cent but increased on portland cement.
* Duty on paints hiked by 5 per cent .
* Duty on specified bulk plastics increased by 10 to 40 per cent .
* Duty on PTA, the intermediate for polyester manufacture, hiked by 10 to 30 per cent .
* 30 per cent duty slapped on plastic insulated wares.
* Duty on pig iron and iron products hiked by Rs 100 per tonne.
* Duty of Rs 400 per tonne imposed on sponge iron.
* Duties on certain specified iron and steel items hiked.
* Duty on doors, windows, kitchenware and other household items made from iron and steel withdrawn.
* 10 per cent duty imposed on specified copper products and duty increased in case of copper sheets and circles produced in a rolling mill.
* 10 per cent duty on specified lead and zinc products.
* 15 per cent duty on two-wheelers of engine capacity upto 75 CC and 25 per cent on of higher capacity.
* Duty on light commercial vehicles of payload not exceeding 4,000 kg up from 10 to 15 per cent
* 30 per cent duty imposed on vacuum flasks.
* Duty on specified malt off.

Customs

* Import duty on items presently attracting duty higher than 110 per cent reduced to 110 per cent except on baggage and alcoholic beverages.
* Auxiliary customs duty rationalised unspecified in unspecified number of cases.
* Additional countervailing duty on account on hike in special excise on all products except specified items.
* Duty on general projects reduced by 20 to 60 per cent.
* Duty on project imports, specified capital goods, etc cut by 10 per cent to 50 per cent .
* Duty on general machinery slashed by 20 per cent to 60 per cent .
* Duty on certain other machinery with a duty rate of 80-110 per cent reduced by 10 per cent and on items with a duty rate of 60-79 to 60 per cent .
* Duty on asbestos sheet reduced by 15 to 25 per cent.
* Duty on petrochemical intermediates viz. butadiene, benzene, ethyl benezene, styrene, caprolactum, butene-1 and pure octanes reduced by

varying rates.

* Duty on specified technical grade pesticides and specified pesticide intermediates reduced substantially.
* Duty on specified intermediates for methyl dopea drug slashed 70 to 25 per cent .
* Auxiliary duty on colour negatives of cinematograpic films unexposed reduced by 20 to 30 per cent .
* Duty on glazed newsprint withdrawn.
* Duty on raw silk reduced by 25 to 30 per cent .
* Duty on synthetic and woolen rags raised by 75 per cent to 110 per cent .
* Import duty of 40 per cent prescribed on rice planters and specified equipment required for making fly ash and phos gypsum bricks prescribed.
* Duty on components of motor vehicles rationalised.
* Uniform duty of 40 per cent on certain raw materials and piece parts with a existing duty rate of 50-70 per cent prescribed and existing concession duty of 50-70 per cent on certain other such items withdrawn.
* Duty of 50 per cent on non-electronic parts for specified telecom equipment and computer peripherals with present duty rate of 70-85 per cent .
* Duty of Rs 450 prescribed per ten grams of gold imported as baggage by returning Indians and NRIs.
* Duty on coal mining projects and petroleum refinery projects slashed by 50 to 30 per cent .

Rupee: How it will come and go

	Rupee will come Item	Paisa		Rupee will go Item	Paisa
1.	Excise	23	1.	Interest	23
2.	Customs	18	2.	States share of taxes and duties	14
3.	Internal borrowings	18	3.	Central Plan	13
4.	Non-tax revenue	14	4.	Defence	13
5.	Corporation tax	6	5.	State and Union Territory Plan Assistance	12
6.	Income tax	6	6.	Other non-plan expenditure	12
7.	Other capital receipts	6	7.	Subsidies	7
8.	Borrowings from Reserve Bank of India (91 days Treasury Bills)	4	8.	Non-plan assistance to State and Union Territory Governments	6
9.	External borrowings	3			
10.	Other taxes	2			

Income-tax rates

TABLE 19.6: Slabs of income with rates in the case of individuals, Hindu undivided families (other than those covered by Table 19.7), associations of persons, bodies of individuals, etc.

Income slab	Existing rates*	Income slab	Proposed rates*
Upto Rs.22,000	Nil	Upto Rs.28,000	Nil
Rs.22,001—Rs.30,000	20%	Rs.28,001—Rs.50,000	20%
Rs.30,001—Rs.50,000	30%	Rs.50,001—Rs.1,00,000	30%
Rs.50,001—Rs.1,00,000	40%	Above Rs.1,00,000	40%
Above Rs. 1,00,000	50%		

TABLE 19.7: Slabs of income with rates in the cases of Hindu undivided families having one or more members with independent income exceeding the exemption limit

Income slab	Existing rates*	Income slab	Proposed rates@
Upto Rs. 12,000	Nil	Upto Rs.18,000	Nil
Rs. 12,001—Rs. 20,000	25%	Rs.18,001—Rs.1,00,000	30%
Rs. 20,001—Rs. 40,000	30%	Above Rs.1,00,000	40%
Rs. 40,001—Rs. 60,000	40%		
Rs. 60,001—Rs. 1,00,000	50%		
Above Rs. 1,00,000	55%		

*Rates as specified in Part 1 of the Bill
@Rates as specified in Part III of the First Schedule to the Bill

TABLE 19.8: Excise Duties and Customs

(*In Rs. crore*)

1986-87	1987-88	1988-89	1989-90	1990-91	1991-92	1992-93
Union Excise Duties						
14,470	16,426	18,841	22,406	24,500	27,696	32,211
Customs						
11,475	18,702	15,805	18,036	20,800	22,896	25,212

19.5 Extracts from Finance Minister's Budget Speech

Part A

The fiscal year now drawing to a close has been a difficult one by any standards. It has been a year of crisis and of crisis management. It has also been a year of great economic challenges and bold new initiatives.

When the new government assumed office eight months ago, we inherited an economy on the verge of collapse. Inflation was accelerating rapidly. The balance of payments was in serious trouble. The foreign exchange reserves were barely enough for two weeks of imports. Foreign commercial banks had stopped lending to India. Non-Resident Indians were withdrawing their deposits. Shortages of foreign exchange had forced a massive import squeeze, which had halted the rapid industrial growth of earlier years and had produced negative growth rates from May 1991 onwards.

Challenge

Our first and immediate challenge was to arrest the slide and restore India's credibility both domestically and in the eyes of the world. To achieve this objective we had to take immediate measures to avert a default in international payments and also take steps to restore macro-economic balance in the economy in the short run, with a view to controlling inflation and reducing the balance of payments deficit to a manageable level. Our medium term objective was to place the economy back on the path of high and sustainable growth.

The new Government took several initiatives in pursuit of these objectives. We took emergency measures to prevent a default in external payments, which would have been highly disruptive. The previous Government had already decided to use a part of the gold held by the Reserve Bank of India to mobilise temporary liquidity abroad. We did not consider it prudent to reverse this decision. But we promised to redeem the gold at the earliest opportunity and we have kept our word. We began the process of restoring macro-economic balance by seeking to reduce the fiscal deficit which had grown very large in the previous year. We also embarked on a medium term programme of structural reform, including new initiatives in trade policy and industrial policy aimed at improving the efficiency, productivity and international competitiveness of Indian industry. Our longer term objective is to evolve a pattern of production which is labour intensive and generates larger employment opportunities in productive higher income jobs, and reduces the disparities in income and wealth between rural and urban areas.

Stabilisation and structural adjustment are never painless or quick, especially when we are dealing with imbalances and structural rigidities which have built up over several years. It will take sustained effort, over at least three years, to bring the economy back to a path of rapid and sustainable growth. A firm commitment to austerity, the pursuit of excellence and the promotion of efficiency and productivity for the benefit of the common people has to be an integral part of this effort. Given our limited resources, our people cannot afford to copy the soulless consumerism and the wasteful life styles of the affluent countries of the West. Conspicuous consumption has to be actively discouraged. The virtues of thrift have to be emphasised. The owners of wealth, as Gandhiji used to say, must learn to regard themselves as trustees of society. We cannot postpone structural reform and adjustment, but we must ensure that the burden of adjustment on the poorer and weaker sections of our society is ameliorated to the maximum possible extent. We are travelling through difficult and uncharted terrain, where no action is without attendant risks, and success will not always be immediate. We need patience, perseverance and national cohesion if we are to succeed.

Gold Bonds

I propose to introduce a scheme under which citizens can obtain a gold Bond in return for gold. The bond would be for a period of five to seven years and would be liquidated by return of gold, or equivalent value, at the option of the holder. It would enjoy a small interest, which will not attract income-tax. The bonds will also be free of wealth tax and gift tax. As an added incentive, holders of such bonds will not be asked any questions about the source of the gold holding. The Reserve Bank of India is preparing a detailed proposal along these lines.

One of the initiatives of the new Industrial Policy is a new approach towards foreign investment.

Deficit

The Budget deficit in the Revised Estimates for 1991-92 is Rs 7,032 crores which is lower than the Budget Estimates of Rs 7,719 crores, and much lower than in 1990-91, when the Budget deficit reached Rs.11,347 crores. The fiscal deficit, which takes into account all borrowings, is Rs. 37,792 crores in the Revised Estimates. This is almost identical to the figure of Rs. 37,727 crores in Budget Estimates, and is much lower than Rs. 44,650 crores in 1990-91. With this, we have successfully reduced fiscal deficit from about 8.4 per cent of GDP in 1990-91 to around 6.5 per cent in 1991-92.

The reduction in the deficit was made possible by enforcement of strict discipline on the expenditure side. Certain additional expenditure provisions became necessary after the Budget was presented. The most notable of these were the additional requirement for fertiliser subsidy, consequent on the decision to restrict the price increase from 40 per cent proposed initially to only 30 per cent, and also the fact that the rupee cost of imported fertilisers was higher than assumed in the Budget Estimates. As a result, the provision for fertiliser subsidy has been increased from Rs. 4,000 crores in the Budget Estimates to Rs. 4,800 crores in the Revised Estimates. Even this amount does not fully cover the subsidy claims for 1991-92 and some amount will spill over into the next year as is normal commercial practice. A separate provision of Rs. 405 crores has been included in the Revised Estimates for the scheme for supplying fertilisers to small farmers at the pre-revised prices.

I have also had to increase the Budget provision for food subsidy by Rs. 250 crores on account of the delay in increasing issue prices. An extra amount of Rs. 550 crores has also been provided for the export subsidy. This subsidy was abolished on 3rd July 1991, but the claims in the pipeline appear to be much more than was originally anticipated. These demands for additional expenditure have however been offset by savings located within the sanctioned Budgets of various Ministries.

The House will be happy to note that even though the Central Government's own expenditure in the Revised Estimates is below the Budget Estimates, the total transfer to the States by way of share of taxes, and Central Plan assistance is higher than the Budget Estimates by Rs. 1,683 crores. This more than offsets the shortfall in small savings loans of Rs. 1,365 crores. We have not allowed our fiscal difficulties to come in the way of meeting our obligations to the States in any way.

Defence

For the Defence Services I am providing Rs. 17,500 crores, an increase of 7 per cent over the provision of Rs. 16,350 crores in the current year. Combined with some economies and tight expenditure control, I am confident that this allocation will enable our armed forces to fulfil their responsibilities in ensuring the security and defence of the nation.

In the Election Manifesto of our party, we had committed ourselves to find an innovative solution to the long standing demand of Defence pensioners for "One Rank One Pension". An Empowered Committee, under the chairmanship of *Raksha Mantri* and comprising ex-servicemen and Members of Parliament representing the major political parties has looked into the issue and its recommendations have been accepted by the Government. Accordingly, Government has sanctioned ad hoc increase in the pension rates applicable to Defence personnel. This decision effective from January 1, 1992 will benefit over six lakh Armed Forces pensioners of all ranks, of whom over two lakhs are Jawans, some of whom retired after January 1, 1986. Government has also ordered grant of ex-gratia Family Pension to the families of deceased Reservists not in receipt of Family Pension. These benefits will entail an expenditure of over Rs. 120 crore per annum at current rates of dearness relief.

Subsidies

Subsidies are another important component in non-Plan expenditure. Last year, Food, Fertiliser and Export subsidies were the three major subsidies and their rapid growth has been one of the main factors behind the unchecked growth of non-Plan expenditure. We made an important change this year by abolishing export subsidies. However, some subsidy payments still remain in the pipeline, and I am providing Rs. 480 crores on this account.

Food subsidy is a part of our system of food security for the poorer and weaker sections of our population and is a basic element in our social policy. I am providing an allocation of Rs. 2,500 crores on this account which should be sufficient for the normal requirements of the system. The revamped Public Distribution System being implemented in 1,700 backward blocks will require an additional allocation of Rs. 250 crores on account of the additional subsidy and also the cost of constructing a large number of godowns with a capacity of 3 lakh tonnes. The allocation for these items will be augmented in the course of the year to meet the requirements fully.

This brings me to fertiliser subsidy which has grown into the largest single subsidy in our system. There is no doubt that fertiliser is an essential ingredient for agricultural production, and agricultural development is vital not only for economic growth in general, but also to ensure rising levels of income and employment in rural areas. In 1980-81, the fertiliser subsidy was 12 per cent the total allocation in the Central and the State Plans taken together for Agriculture, Rural Development, Special Area Programmes and Irrigation and Flood Control. It increased to 33 per cent in 1991-92. A Parliamentary Committee is currently looking intc the whole issue of fertiliser pricing and subsidy including alternatives for restructuring the subsidy. I propose to wait for the report of this committee and take a view, on this matter later in the year. Taking all factors into account, I am making a provision of Rs. 5,000 crores for fertiliser subsidy in 1992-93.

Concluding Remarks

Our nation will remain eternally grateful to Jawaharlal Nehru for his vision and insistence that the social and economic transformation of India had to take place in the framework of an open society, committed to parliamentary democracy and the rule of law. India's development is of tremendous significance for the future of the developing world. To realise our development potential, we have to unshackle the human spirit of creativity, idealism, adventure and enterprise that our people possess in abundant measure. We have to harness all our latent resources for a second industrial revolution and a second agricultural revolution. Our economy, polity and society have to be extraordinarily resilient and alert if we are to take full advantage of the opportunities and to minimise the risks associated with the increasing globalisation of economic processes. We have to accept the need for reform if we are to avoid an increasing marginalisation of India in the evolving world economy. The economic policy changes brought about by our Government in the last eight months are inspired by this vision. Our party is an inheritor of great traditions of national service. True to this heritage, we commit ourselves to providing a firm and purposeful sense of direction to the reform process so that this ancient land of India regains its glory and rightful place in the comity of nations. This budget represents a contribution to the successful implementation of this great national enterprise, of building an India free from the fear of war, want and exploitation, an India worthy of the dreams of the founding fathers of our republic. We shall pay any price, bear any burden, make any sacrifice to realise those dreams. India is on the move again. We shall make the future happen.

19.6 Estimates Committee Report on Fiscal Policy

The Estimates Committee, headed by Shri Manoranjan Bhakta, submitted its report to the Parliament on February 28, 1992.

In its twelfth report fiscal policy-management of deficit, external and internal, the committee said over the decade, total government expenditure had multiplied at a compounds growth rate of 17.6 per cent, from Rs. 24,383 crore in 1981-82 to Rs. 1,06,717 crore in 1990-91 and was estimated to reach Rs. 1,13,422 crore.

It said throughout the 1980s, the share of non-Plan expenditure had continued to outstrip Plan expenditure. Among others, three major items, interest payments, defence and subsidies constituted 68 per cent of non-Plan expenditure.

It said defence expenditure which topped the list a couple of years ago had now been relegated to a secondary position with the alarming rise in interest burden.

The report has, however, cautioned the government against hasty and indiscriminate measures to cut expenditure to raise revenue and has called for a balance between measures for economic restructuring, expenditure contraction and revenue augmentation.

Government Cautioned

It focussed attenticn on the dangers of inflation and unemployment which together could obliterate the possible benefits of economic restructuring as levels of public dissatisfaction rise. It cautioned the government against abruptly doing away with subsidies which affect the poorest people living in remote hilly, tribal regions. In this regard, it has called for better targeting of subsidies on food as well as fertilisers.

About defence expenditure, it has drawn attention to the various areas of saving and income generation and has called for an early action on the recommendations of the Arun Singh Committee report on the defence expenditure.

On the burgeoning borrowings of the government, the Estimates Committee has favoured a ceiling on borrowing and called for a flexible approach in determining the figure at which savings should be imposed year after year, after due discussion and voting in the Parliament.

It has also stressed the need to ensure definitional clarity in regard to depiction of deficit in the budget document as lack of such clarity in the past had left to soft focussing of the widening gap between revenue receipt and revenue expenditure. Thus, it has called for definition of deficits in all its connotations, namely, fiscal deficit, primary deficit and monetary deficit.

Referring to the public sector, the Committee has advocated case to case approach in closing unviable public sector units. The need for adequate social security to the affected employees and workers has also been suggested.

It also underlined the need for wider acceptance of financial discipline in the entire public sector of the economy including state governments and asked the government to actively work in this direction.

Project Completion

The committee has asked the government to lay emphasis on the completion of existing projects before starting new ones and said instead of an across-the-board cut in expenditure, the Government should identify the areas of unproductive expenditure while taking steps to reduce Government spending.

It also underlined the need to evolve a comprehensive approach to the problem of unaccounted income and wealth and said the recent tax amnesty and immunity scheme has not yielded the desired results. As such, there should not be any hesitation on the part of the government to take stern measures against hoarders, blackmarketeers, smugglers and other habitual tax evaders to unearth the ill-gotten unaccounted wealth.

As exports depend crucially on imports,the committee said in view of the improvement in foreign exchange reserves position, import restrictions imposed by the RBI during the last six months should be lifted immediately for all those items which form an input for exports.

The Committee said the government should repay short-term debts, particularly commercial borrowings from the international money market, at the earliest opportunity in order to reduce the interest burden.

Source: *Times of India,* February 29, 1992.

19.7 **Chelliah Committee Report on Tax Reforms: Highlights**

Following are the highlights of the main summary from the interim report of the tax reform committee headed by Dr Raja Chelliah, placed in the Lok Sabha on February 29, 1992 by the Finance Minister, Dr Manmohan Singh:

* A single-rate income-tax — the simplest both for compliance and administrative reasons, marginal rates of tax (inclusive of surcharge) 20 per cent for total income in the range of Rs. 28,000 to Rs. 50,000: 27.5 per cent for total income in the range of Rs. 50,000 to Rs. 2 lakh and 40 per cent for total income exceeding Rs. 2 lakh.
* For local authorities, tax should be at a flat rate of 30 per cent.
* In the case of domestic companies, the marginal rates of tax should be 40 per cent as in the case of individuals.
* Tax incentives under sections 80-HH, 80-HHA, 80-T, 80-IA, 80-JJ, 80-QQ, and 80-QQA to be abolished.
* Provisions of Sections 35-AC, 35-CCA, 35-CCB and 80-GGA should be amalgamated.
* Provisions of clause (134) section 10 of the I.T. Act, providing for exemption

of house rent allowance as per rule 2A should be abolished.

* Allowances to legislators should be fully subjected to tax.
* Existing provisions seeking to restrict the deductionability of certain expenses in business be reviewed and limits prescribed should be revised.
* Withdrawal of deductions of Rs. 3,600 in respect of each residential unit forming part of a building for a period of five years from the date of completion of such a building proposed.
* An amount equal to one-fifth of the annual value of the property to be allowed as a statutory standard deduction for the aggregate expense on repair of the house property.
* For partnership firms, scheme of registration of firms proposed to be abolished.
* Traders and manufactures operating on a small-scale but enjoying taxable income to be brought under presumptive tax scheme.
* Tax on wealth should be abolished in all items other than those which was unproductive.
* The first Rs. 15 lakhs of the net value of the taxable items of wealth not to attract tax. Any excess of net value over that level to bear tax at one per cent of value.
* Restructuring of import tariff to be progressively achieved so that by 1998-99 average tariff rates be reduced to around 25 per cent and the maximum rate to 50 per cent.
* A switch over to value added tax for domestically produced goods and services proposed.
* Under the value added tax system, such services as advertising, stock brokers, automobile insurance to attract 10 per cent tax of the value of the transaction.
* Creation of a directorate of valuation proposed.
* A tariff guide giving the classification of all commodities manufactured in the country to be made available.

20

BALANCE OF PAYMENTS AND FOREIGN TRADE

20.1 **Balance of Payments (BOP)**

The domestic political developments and the Gulf crisis during 1990-91 in the context of fragile balance of payments situation culminated in payments crisis of unprecedented dimension in the first quarter of 1991-92. Its prime manifestations were difficulty in financing current imports and in meeting debt service obligations together with the erosion of confidence of short-term lenders and NRI depositors. Short-term credits became difficult to obtain and inflows into non-resident deposits became outflows of an alarming magnitude. This brought the country to a near-default in July, 1991. Default would have entailed widespread shortages of essential imported commodities and led to a cutback in industrial output, layoffs and inflation. India's brush with default was the outcome of an uncertain and disturbed situation in the domestic policy which made it difficult to execute a medium-term balance of payments strategy. Besides, the trade deficit widened during 1990-91 as a result of surge in import bill and a deceleration in export growth.

During the current year, trade deficit has shrunk largely because of severe compression in imports arising out of import tightening effected in the recent past. Given the large current account deficit and the consequent need to finance it through large-scale external borrowing, it became essential to restore international confidence. To this end, a new balance of payments strategy was put in place by the new Government which assumed office towards the end of June, 1991. It laid emphasis on exchange rate adjustment, fiscal correction and structural reforms in industrial and trade policy. Besides, recourse to exceptional financing from the IMF of the order US $ 2.3 billion was negotiated under the stand-by arrangement. This was necessitated by the need to provide foreign exchange as an immediate means of support to the balance of payments. As a result of the balance of payments adjustment strategy adopted there has been a distinct improvement in the external payments position within a short period as reflected in the steady build-up in the reserves during the later half of the current year. Foreign currency assets, which had plummeted to US $ 1.1 billion in June 1991, rose to about US $ 4.2 billion by the middle of February, 1992. However, a lasting improvement in the balance of payments position depends upon a strong revival in the exports. Export performance in 1991-92 has been adversely affected by the disruption of trade with the erstwhile Soviet Union and continuing recession in industrialised countries.

BOP and Foreign Exchange Reserves

Table 20.1 shows the evolution of key BOP indicators during the Sixth (1980-85) and the Seventh (1985-90) Plan periods and also for the years 1989-90 and 1990-91 (quick estimates).

TABLE 20.1: Key Indicators of India's Balance of Payments (As per cent of GDP)

Year/Period	Exports	Imports	Net invisibles	Trade balance	Current A/c balance
Average 1980-85	5.0	8.4	2.2	-3.4	-1.3
Average 1985-90	5.1	8.2	1.0	-3.2	-2.2
1989-90	6.3	9.0	0.6	-2.8	-2.2
1990-91 (QE)	6.3	9.1	0.4	-2.9	-2.5

Note: The ratios have been computed on the basis of balance of payments data as given in Appendix Table 6.2 and the CSO estimates of GDP at current market prices. Official grant receipts and US embassy expenditure in India out of PL-480 Rupee funds are taken as current account receipts in conformity with the balance of payments statistics published by the RBI.

QE : Quick estimates.

Source: *Economic Survey*, 1991-92.

20.2 Trade Policy*

Moving Towards a More Open Trade Regime

18. The government recognises that trade reform is an essential element in securing supply responses to facilitate the overall restructuring of the economy and to restore external payments viability. Rapid export growth is crucial for regaining access to international capital markets, and providing for external debt service. The thrust of trade reform is therefore to aim at a quick revival of the momentum of exports and to expose domestic industry to greater external competition.

19. There are five key medium-term objectives in the government's trade policy agenda. First, the broadening and simplification of export incentive measures and the removal of restrictions of exports; second, the elimination of quantitative restrictions (QRs) on all imports; third, substantial reductions in tariff rates; fourth, the decanalisation of exports and imports with the exception of a few items; and finally; moving to a foreign exchange system which is free of allocative restrictions for trade.

20.In support of these objectives, the government announced a package of trade policy reforms on July 4 and August 13, 1991. Several changes in trade policy were introduced aimed at strengthening export incentives and eliminating a substantial proportion of import licensing requirements. Essential imports of sensitive items such as oil and petroleum products and fertilisers are fully protected, but other imports of raw materials and components were lined to exports through an enlargement and restructuring of the replenishment licensing (REP) system. REP licences have been replaced by a new instrument named Eximscrip which is issued to exporters at higher rates and is freely tradable. Under this new regime the range of items which can be imported without discretionary licensing has been substantially widened. The system of cash compensatory support (CCS) for exports was abolished consequent on the downward

* *Note*: Paras refer to the paras of the Finance Minister's letter of November 11, 1991.

adjustment of the exchange rate of the rupee in July 1991. A high level committee has been appointed to formulate proposals for reform of the tariff system in the context of a broader tax reform. To promote exports, the system of advance licensing permitting duty-free import of raw materials, components and consumables at international prices was simplified, made more automatic and the issue of licences under the scheme was made time-bound. The export processing zones scheme and 100 per cent EOUs scheme which create duty-free enclaves were simplified and made more attractive, especially in the matter of allowing exports of upto 25 per cent of production to the domestic tariff area at preferential rates of customs duty (50 per cent of the normal rate).

21. In addition to the trade reform measures already taken, further actions are planned by the government along the following lines.

(i) The government recognises that the temporary restrictions on imports which had to be imposed earlier in the year by the Reserve Bank of India as part of its effort to manage the acute balance of payments situation need to be relaxed. Recently, the RBI has eliminated the cash margins on certain export-related imports, provided all exporters with a margin free window for imports of items on OGL of upto 40 per cent of the previous year's exports (upto Rs. 10 crore), and has also relaxed prior approval requirements for exporters. The remaining restrictions that affect exporters will be eliminated as a first priority, to be followed as soon as possible by the elimination of such restrictions that affect all other importers.

(ii) The Eximscrip scheme is intended to act as a transitional mechanism for the equilibration of the trade account. It is the intention of the government to integrate the Eximscrip scheme with OGL as soon as feasible and, in any event, not later than mid-1995.

(iii) Since the promotion of exports is one of the key objectives in the government's trade strategy, the government will review the export licensing and canalisation systems with a view to the removal of these impediments to exports. The government will remove export licensing and minimum export prices except for a small negative list, and decanalise and allow private participation in the export of major agricultural and mineral products. The government has already decontrolled and decanalised several export items. It will establish modalities and a timetable for the decontrol and decanalisation of the remaining items with a view to complete liberalisation by the end of 1995.

(iv) At present a number of items are exclusively or principally imported by specified public sector agencies (canalising agencies). The government recognises that there is a strong case for decanalising imports. The role of state monopoly agencies in foreign trade will be substantially reduced, and greater private sector participation will be permitted. Firstly, all remaining canalised imports will be decanalised, except for a small negative list of "sensitive" products and products canalised for health and security reasons, by April 1992. Secondly, with the aim of removing dual pricing for canalised imports, the amount of official foreign exchange allocated to canalising agencies will be progressively reduced and eventually phased out.

(v) As part of the government's strategy to allow greater flexibility in the import regime, the "Actual User" requirement, which has already been relaxed as a result of the Eximscrip scheme, will be abolished by April 1992.

(vi) It is the policy of the government to move to a situation where imports, including ultimately final goods, are regulated through appropriate tariffs. Therefore, import bans, discretionary import licensing, and other barriers are to be eliminated and replaced by a tariff-based protection system. In support of this objective, and as a first step, such of the intermediate items in the restricted list of imports, the production of which is at least one third of the total production of all intermediate items in the list, would be importable against the Eximscrip of OGL by November 1991. The government proposes to rationalise the list further by shifting more such intermediate items for about two-thirds of the total production covered by the restricted list for import against the Eximscrip of OGL at the time of issue of import policy for 1992-93 (April 1992). Capital goods corresponding to 50 per cent of domestic production covered by the restricted list (Quantitative Restrictions) will also be made freely importable under either Eximscrip or OGL by May 1992. In addition, the import of all unlisted capital goods will be permitted with the use of Eximscrips by April 1992.

(vii) The government recognises the need to introduce greater transparency into the trade regime. To that end, a computerised list corresponding to customs tariff HS classification giving the import control status of each product will be released by October 1991. This will reduce the scope for discretionary decision-making at lower levels and introduce greater transparency in import policy. In addition, a negative list principle will be established under which all products not on the restricted lists, the canalised list or importable under OGL will be importable with the use of Eximscrip scheme by May 1992.

(viii) Despite the reduction in peak advalorem tariff rates in the 1991-92 budget to a maximum of 150 per cent, current tariff levels are very high in comparison with other industrialising developing countries and this raises domestic production costs and renders many Indian industries non-competitive by international standards. However, customs revenues account for about 50 per cent of total current government revenue in 1991-92. The objective of tariff reduction therefore has to be achieved hand in hand with the broader objective of fiscal policy reform which includes mobilisation of an adequate amount of resources. To that end, the government has set-up a committee on tax reform which will undertake a comprehensive review of customs tariffs. With a view towards enhancing India's international competitiveness, the committee has been mandated to recommend ways and means for the following. First, the average level of tariffs would be reduced substantially to internationally comparable levels. Second, the maximum level of tariffs will be progressively reduced in a sequence of yearly adjustments over the next five years. Third, the structure of tariff rates would be simplified with a view to substantially reducing their variability and the incidence of exemptions and partial exemptions. Fourth, the use of specific tariffs will be minimised. The committee has been asked to make recommendations as to the phasing of the introduction of the new customs tariffs within a relatively short period of time of no longer than five years. It will also recommended alternative revenue sources to compensate for any reduction in total government revenues which is likely to follow from the tariff reform. The government proposes to take action on the basis of the committee's recommendations in the 1992-92 budget.

20.3 **Trade Deficit**

As a percentage of GDP, the current account deficit is estimated to have gone up to 2.5 per cent in 1990-91 from 2.2 per cent in 1989-90. The results of the quick estimates prepared by the RBI place the current account deficit in 1990-91 at Rs. 13088 crore (US $ 7295 million) as compared to Rs. 9824 crore (Us $ 5900 million) during 1989-90. This sharp increase in the current account deficit of Rs. 3264 crore (US $ 1395 million) during 1990-91 is made up for a larger trade deficit coupled with a smaller net invisible receipts. Trade deficit during 1990-91 on a payments basis stood at Rs. 15142 crore (US $ 8440 million), higher by Rs. 2729 crore (US $ 985 million) over the preceding year's (1989-90) level of Rs. 12413 crore (US $ 7455 million). The trade deficit on a payments basis as reported by the RBI is higher compared with the trade deficit reported by the DGCI&S based on customs valuation owing to differences in the timing, coverage and valuation of the trade data. Estimates of other net invisible receipts showed a decline to Rs. 1200 crore (US $ 669 million) from Rs. 1686 crore (US $ 1013 million) in 1989-90.

Movements in the country's foreign exchange reserves given in Table 20.2 manifest the net result of transactions in the external sector since 1980-81. Among the three components of foreign exchange reserves, the foreign currency assets of the RBI declined by Rs. 1399 crore (US$ 1132 million) in 1990-91 as against a decline of Rs. 818 crore (US$ 858 million) in 1989-90. As a result of the BOP adjustment strategy, there has been a distinct turnaround in BOP situation as reflected in the steady build-up in the foreign currency assets of the RBI. These have risen to Rs. 10958 crore (US $ 4243 million) on February 14, 1992 and were higher by Rs. 6570 crore (US $ 2007 million) over the end-March 1991 level.

20.4 **Merchandise Trade**

Overall trends in merchandise trade, on customs basis, during the recent years, both in Rupee and dollar terms, are given in Table 20.3.

This performance is marked by a high trade deficit, about $ 5.4 billion per annum during the last five years. The capacity of exports to finance imports (export/import ratio) declined in 1990-91 to about 75 per cent from around 78 per cent in the previous year, in the face of a fall in the growth of exports and sizeable growth in imports. However, during the first half of the current financial year, the trade deficit has been curtailed by nearly sixty per cent (in dollar terms) due to a sharp reduction in imports.

Imports

The high rate of growth in imports witnessed during the previous three years continued in 1990-91 when imports increased by 13.2 per cent in dollar terms or 22 per cent in Rupee terms. The acceleration in 1990-91 was mainly attributable to higher oil imports as POL imports in dollar terms increased by 60 per cent as a result of both a hike in world oil prices following the Gulf crisis as well as increased volume of oil imports as domestic production was impaired by supply difficulties. Non-oil imports during the year rose by only 3.1 per cent (in dollar terms). The compression on non-oil imports resulted from a series of measures taken by the Government and the RBI in view of acute scarcity of foreign exchange reserves.

Table 20.4 shows imports by major categories and commodities for 1990-91 and April-September 1991-92 along with growth rates for 1990-91 and the first half of 1991-92.

Exports

There was a major slowdown in export growth during 1990-91 signalling a reversal of the buoyancy witnessed in earlier years. During 1986-87 to 1989-90, exports grew at 17.0 per cent per annum in dollar terms or 26.5 per cent in Rupee terms. In contrast, export growth in 1990-91 was modest at 9.1 per cent in dollar terms or 17.6 per cent in Rupee terms. This deceleration in exports was caused by a number of factors, such as, (i) a slowdown in the expansion of world trade (volume of world trade decelerated from 7.3 per cent in 1989 to 4.2 per cent in 1990 and further to 0.9 per cent in 1991) and recessionary conditions in some major industrial economies; (ii) loss of export markets in the Middle East due to the Gulf crisis; (iii) political and economic upheavals in Eastern Europe, which earlier provided a sheltered market to Indian exports; (iv) import curbs introduced during 1990-91 in response to the foreign exchange shortage and intensified after the Gulf crisis, affecting export-related imports; (v) movement in the exchange rate which was broadly supportive of exports since 1986-87 becoming adverse thus affecting competitiveness of exports; and (vi) internal law-and-order problems in some states.

TABLE 20.2. Movements in Foreign Exchange Reserves

(*In Rupees Crore and U.S. Dollar Million*)

Year	Foreign currency assets of RBI at the end of year		Foreign exchange reserves at the end of the year @		Movements in foreign exchange reserves		Net drawals on IMF	
1	2	3	4	5	6	7	8	9
	Rs.crore	$ million	Rs. crore	$ million	Rs. crore	$ million	Rs. crore	$ million
1980-81	4822	5850	5544	6823	—390	—538	814*	1029*
1981-82	3355	3582	4024	4390	—1520	—2433	637	639
1982-83	4265	4281	4782	4896	758	506	1893	1958
1983-84	5498	5099	5972	5649	1190	753	1342	1298
1984-85	6817	5482	7243	5952	1271	303	63	53
1985-86	7384	5972	7820	6520	577	568	—327*	—267*
1986-87	7645	5924	8151	6574	331	54	—840*	—690*
1987-88	7287	5618	7687	6223	—464	—351	—1388*	—1123*
1988-89	6605	4226	7040	4802	—647	—1421	—1749*	—1175*
1989-90	5787	3368	6251	3962	—789	—840	—1688*	—1035*
1990-91	4388	2236	11416 +	5834	5165 +	1872 +	—2043*	—1183*
1991-92 (up to end-Jan.)	9766	3774	19392 ++	7501 ++	7976 ++	1667 ++	2169	794

@ Includes foreign currency assets of RBI, gold holdings of RBI and SDR holdings of Government.

* Includes Trust loan drawals and repayments.

\+ Effective October, 17, 1990 gold is revalued close to international market price at the end of every month. For earlier periods gold is valued at official rate of Rs. 84.39 per 10 grammes.

++ Includes purchase of gold of Rs. 494 crore and US $ 191 million from Government of India on December 21, 1991 and January 7, 1992.

TABLE 20.3: Trends in Foreign Trade

Year	Imports	Exports	Trade balance	Changes in imports	Changes in exports	Trade balance as % of exports
	Rupees hundred crore			*Per cent*		
1986-87	201.0	124.5	—76.4	2.2	14.3	61.4
1987-88	222.4	156.7	—65.7	10.7	25.9	41.9
1988-89	282.4	202.3	—80.0	26.9	29.1	39.6
1989-90	354.2	276.8	—77.3	25.4	36.8	27.9
1990-91	431.9	325.5	—106.4	22.0	17.6	32.7
1991-92*	210.7	187.1	—23.6	9.0	23.9	12.6
	Billion US Dollars			*Per cent*		
1986-87	15.7	9.7	—6.0	—2.1	9.4	
1987-88	17.2	12.1	—5.1	9.1	24.0	
1988-89	19.5	14.0	—5.5	13.6	15.6	
1989-90	21.3	16.6	—4.6	9.1	19.0	
1990-91	24.1	18.1	—5.9	13.2	9.1	
1991-92*	9.1	8.1	—1.0	—17.5	—6.2	

Data for 1989-90 and April-September, 1991-92 are provisional.
* April-September, 1991-92.
Source: *Economic Survey,* 1991-92.

TABLE 20.4: Imports by Major Commodity Groups

Item	1990-91	1991-92 April-Sept (P)	1990-91	1991-92 April-Sept (P)	Per cent change (Rs. terms) 1990-91 / 1989-90	Per cent change (Rs. terms) April-Sept.91 / April-Sept.90	Per cent change ($ terms) 1990-91 / 1989-90	Per cent change ($ terms) April-Sept.91. / April-Sept.90
	(Rs. hundred crore)		(Billion US Dollars)					
1	2	3	4	5	6	7	8	9
I. *Bulk imports* **200.2**	**94.9**	**11.1**	**4.1**	**35.9**	**15.0**	**26.1**	—13.0	
(a) *Essential imports*	**141.9**	**70.1**	**7.9**	**3.0**	**43.5**	**22.2**	33.1	—7.5
1. POL (Petroleum Oil and Lubricants)	108.2	53.8	6.0	2.3	72.4	35.4	60.0	2.4
2. Cereals etc.	1.8	0.7	0.1	0.0	—51.8	—20.1	—55.3	—39.6
3. Edible oils	3.3	0.6	0.2	0.0	54.5	—66.4	43.4	—74.6
4. Fertilisers	17.7	11.6	1.0	0.5	—0.6	19.8	—7.8	—9.3
5. Non-ferrous metals	11.0	3.4	0.6	0.1	—12.1	—35.7	—18.4	—51.3
(b) *Other bulk imports*	**58.3**	**24.8**	**3.2**	1.1	**20.4**	—1.4	**11.7**	**—25.4**
6. Pulses	4.8	1.4	0.3	0.1	111.2	—38.5	95.9	—53.4
7. Coal	7.9	4.2	0.4	0.2	40.5	23.8	30.3	—6.3
8. Iron and steel	21.1	10.9	1.2	0.5	—8.3	19.3	—14.9	—9.8
9. Paper, board and pulp	9.1	4.1	0.5	0.2	38.1	—4.2	28.2	—27.6
10. Ores and metal scrap	15.3	4.2	0.8	0.2	41.0	—31.0	30.8	—47.8

Contd.

TABLE 20.4 (*Contd.*)

1	2	3	4	5	6	7	8	9
II. *Non-bulk imports*	**203.5**	**102.0**	**11.3**	**4.4**	**11.1**	**7.6**	**3.1**	**—18.6**
(a) Capital goods	**104.7**	**48.7**	**5.8**	**2.1**	**18.5**	**9.5**	**10.0**	**—17.2**
(b) Mainly export-related imports	**66.0**	**38.7**	**3.7**	**1.7**	**—2.9**	**12.7**	**—9.9**	**—14.8**
(1) Pearls and precious stones	37.4	21.7	2.1	0.9	—11.9	28.7	—18.2	—2.6
(2) Chemicals	22.9	14.4	1.3	0.6	7.2	0.4	—0.5	—24.1
(3) Textiles yarn, fabrics, etc.	4.4	1.8	0.2	0.1	26.8	—21.3	17.6	—40.5
(4) Cashewnuts	1.3	0.8	0.1	0.0	74.8	—6.0	62.2	—28.9
(c) *Other non-bulk items*	**32.8**	**14.7**	**1.8**	**0.6**	**22.0**	**—8.5**	**13.2**	**—30.8**
(1) Professional instruments etc.	10.6	4.6	0.6	0.2	19.6	—19.6	11.0	—39.2
(2) Chemicals	9.2	2.5	0.5	0.1	44.4	—34.9	34.0	—50.8
(3) Plastics and resins	10.9	6.6	0.6	0.3	9.9	26.3	2.0	—4.4
(4) Non-metallic minerals	2.0	1.0	0.1	0.0	20.8	—20.2	12.1	—39.6
III. *Unclassified* **28.3**	**13.7**	**1.6**	**0.6**	**19.7**	**—14.1**	**11.1**	**—35.0**	
IV. Total	**431.9**	**210.7**	**24.1**	**9.1**	**22.0**	**9.0**	**13.2**	**—17.5**

(P)-Provisional.

Notes: 1. Item I (a) 4 includes fertiliser crude, manufactured and fertiliser material.
2. Item II (b) 2 includes organic and inorganic chemicals.
3. Item II (c) 2 relates to materials and products including pharmaceutical and dyeing and colouring material.
4. A zero in column 5 indicates a negligible amount.

TABLE 20.5 Exports by Major Commodity Groups

Commodity	1990-91	1991-92 April-Sept (P)	1990-91	1991-92 April-Sept (P)	Per cent change (Rs. terms)		Per cent change ($ terms)	
	(Rs. hundred crore)		(Billion US Dollars)		1990-91/ 1989-90	April-Sept.91/ April-Sept.90	1990-91/ 1989-90	April-Sept.91/ April-Sept.90
1	2	3	4	5	6	7	8	9
I. *Agriculture and allied products*	**63.2**	**36.7**	**3.5**	**1.6**	**29.5**	18.8	20.1	—10.1
1. Cashew kernels	4.5	3.5	0.2	0.2	21.6	46.9	12.8	11.1
2. Coffee	2.5	1.3	0.1	0.1	—27.3	2.8	—32.6	—22.2
3. Marine products	9.6	6.0	0.5	0.3	39.7	54.8	29.6	17.1
4. Oil meals	6.1	3.5	0.3	0.1	—0.3	19.5	—7.5	—9.6
5. Raw cotton	8.5	2.9	0.5	0.1	558.9	—45.2	511.4	—58.6
6. Rice	4.6	2.5	0.3	0.1	8.2	23.6	0.4	—6.5
7. Species	2.3	1.7	0.1	0.1	—15.5	42.7	—21.6	8.0
8. Sugar	0.4	0.6	0.0	0.0	15.6	140.3	7.2	81.8
9. Tea & mate	10.7	4.8	0.6	0.2	16.7	—10.2	8.3	—32.1
10. Tobacco	2.6	2.4	0.1	0.1	50.5	77.4	39.6	34.2
II. *Ores and minerals*	**15.0**	**8.8**	**0.8**	**0.4**	**9.8**	**47.6**	**1.9**	**11.7**
11. Iron ore	10.5	5.9	0.6	0.3	13.1	50.4	5.0	13.8

Contd.

TABLE 20.5 (*Contd.*)

1	2	3	4	5	6	7	8	9
III. *Manufactured goods*	**237.4**	**137.4**	**13.2**	**6.0**	**14.9**	**25.3**	**6.6**	**—5.2**
12. Engineering goods	38.8	21.3	2.2	0.9	17.9	18.2	9.4	—10.6
13. Chemicals	25.4	16.0	1.4	0.7	18.7	38.7	10.1	5.0
14. Textiles	21.0	14.2	1.2	0.6	39.3	58.9	29.3	20.2
15. Jute manufactures	3.0	1.4	0.2	0.1	0.7	—12.8	—6.6	—34.0
16. Leather and mfrs.	25.7	13.6	1.4	0.6	31.6	15.6	22.1	—12.5
17. Readymade garments	40.1	21.5	2.2	0.9	24.3	20.0	15.4	—9.2
18. Handicrafts	61.7	38.1	3.4	1.7	—0.0	32.7	—7.2	0.4
of which:								
Gems and jewellery	52.5	31.6	2.9	1.4	—0.9	28.5	—8.1	—2.8
IV. *Mineral fuels and lubricant*	**9.5**	**3.9**	**0.5**	**0.2**	**28.2**	**—1.1**	**18.9**	**—25.2**
19. POL	9.4	3.7	0.5	0.2	34.6	—6.0	24.9	—28.9
V. *Others*	**0.6**	**0.3**	**0.0**	**0.0**	**37.3**	**—44.3**	**27.4**	**—57.9**
Total	**325.5**	**187.1**	**18.1**	**8.1**	**17.7**	**23.9**	**9.1**	**—6.2**

(P)-Provisional

Notes:
1. Item 12 includes Machinery, Transport equipment, meal manufactures (including iron and steel), electronic goods and computer software.
2. Group IV includes coal.
3. The group totals pertaining to I, II, III, IV & V are provisional tentative estimates based on preliminary details.
4. Item 13 excludes rubber, glass, paints and other products.
5. Item 14 includes cotton yarn, fabrics, made up etc.
6. Item 18 includes handicrafts, carpet (handmade) and gems and jewellery.
7. Group totals may not add up to the total due to errors and omissions.
8. Others include errors and omissions.
9. A zero in column 5 indicates a negligible amount.

TABLE 20.6: Foreign Exchange Reserves

(*Rs. crore*)

	Reserves			Transactions with IMF		
	Gold	SDRs (in millions of SDRs)	Foreign exchange	Drawings	Repurchases#	Outstanding repurchase obligations
1	2	3	4	5	6	7
1950-51	117.8	—	911.4	—	—	48
1951-52	117.8	—	746.6	—	—	48
1952-53	117.8	—	763.3	—	—	48
1953-54	117.8	—	792.2	—	17.3	30
1954-55	117.8	—	774.1	—	17.2	13
1955-56	117.8	—	784.6	—	7.1	6
1956-57	117.8	—	563.3	60.7	6.0	61
1957-58	117.8	—	303.4	34.5	—	95
1958-59	117.8	—	261.1	—	—	95
1959-60	117.8	—	245.1	—	23.8	71
1960-61	117.8	—	185.8	—	10.7	61
1961-62	117.8	—	179.5	119.1	60.7	119
1962-63	117.8	—	177.3	11.9	—	131
1963-64	117.8	—	188.0	—	23.8	107
1964-65	133.8	—	115.9	47.6	47.6	107
1965-66	115.9	—	182.1	65.5	35.7	137
1966-67	182.5	—	295.9	89.3	43.1	313
1967-68	182.5	—	356.1	67.5	43.1	338
1968-69	182.5	—	391.2	—	58.5	279
1969-70	182.5	122.7	546.4	—	125.3	154
1970-71	182.5	148.9	438.1	—	153.8	—
1971-72	182.5	247.7	480.4	—	—	—
1972-73	182.5	246.5	478.9	—	—	—
1973-74	182.5	244.9	580.8	62.0	—	59
1974-75	182.5	234.9	610.5	484.7	—	557
1975-76	182.5	202.8	1491.7	207.1	—	804
1976-77	187.8	187.4	2863.0	—	302.8	492
1977-78	193.1	161.6	4499.8	—	248.6	210
1978-79	219.5	364.9	5219.9	—	206.9	—
1979-80	224.7	529.1	5163.7	—	55.1 $	—
1980-81	225.6	490.5	4822.1	274.4 @	5.1 $$	268
1981-82	225.6	425.1	3354.5	636.8 @@	—	901
1982-83	225.6	270.2	4265.3	1892.8 @@	—	2867
1983-84	225.6	216.4	5497.9	1413.7 @@	72.1 (A)	4444
1984-85	245.8	146.5	6816.8	218.8 @@	155.9 (B)	4888
1985-86	274.3	115.1	7384.4	—	253.0 (C)	5285
1986-87	274.3	139.4	7645.2	—	672.2 (D)	5548
1987-88	274.3	69.7	7287.1	—	1208.9 (E)	4732
1988-89	274.3	79.5	6604.6	—	1547.3 (F)	3696
1989-90	280.7	81.9	5787.2		1459.6 (G)	2572

Contd.

TABLE 20.6 (*Contd.*)

1	2	3	4	5	6	7
1990-91	6828.3	75.9	4388.1	2858.7 @@@	1155.9 (H)	5132
June	280.7	89.1	5356.2	—	251.1	2405
Sept.	280.7	343.3	4511.6	—	344.8	2243
Dec.	6584.9	222.1	2152.4	—	238.9	2034
March	6828.3	75.9	4388.1	2858.7 @@@	321.1	5132
1991-92 (I)						
April	6960.6	134.1	2527.1	—	112.5	5185
May	7160.2	47.7	2677.4	—	103.6	5252
June	7410.8	47.7	2382.7	—	—	5206
July (P)	9105.8	88.4	3312.9	570.4 *	241.5	6748
Aug. (P)	8882.6	36.8	2964.8	—	86.3	6716
Sept. (P)	8658.4	134.5	4441.6	1262.2 **	—	8525
Oct. (P)	8909.7	105.3	6032.5	—	102.6	8422
Nov. (P)	8945.4	32.3	7015.8	228.8	134.0	8706
Dec. (P)	9489.6	32.3	9286.7	—	—	8993

* Drawal of Rs. 570.41 crores under Compensatory and Contingency Financing Facility.

** Drawal of Rs. 1262.19 crores under Compensatory and Contingency Financing Facility.

P Provisional.

@ Excludes Rs. 544.53 crores drawn under Trust Fund.

@@ Drawals under Extended Fund Facility (EFF).

@@@ Drawals of Rs. 1615.2 crores under Compensatory and Contingency Financing Facility and Rs. 1243.5 crores under First Credit Tranche of Stand-by Arrangement.

$ Includes voluntary repurchases of (Rs. 199 crores) and sales of rupees by the IMF under its General Resources Account (Rs. 35.2 crores).

$$ Sales of rupees by the Fund.

\# Additionally, SDRs 59.9 million in May 1979, SDRs 7.3 million in July 1980 and SDRs 34.5 million in March 1982 were used for voluntary repurchases of rupees.

(A) SDRs 66.50 million were used for repurchases of drawals under Compensatory Financing Facility.

(B) SDRs 33.25 million and Rs. 117.85 crores in foreign currencies were used for repurchases of drawals under CFF.

(C) SDRs 66.5 million and SDRs 131.25 million were used for repurchases of drawals under CFF and EFF, respectively.

(D) SDRs 431.25 million were used for repurchases of drawals under EFF.

(E) SDRs 704.17 million were used for repurchases of drawals under EFF.

(F) SDRs 804.18 million were used for repurchases of drawals under EFF.

(G) SDRs 681.25 million were used for repurchases of drawals under EFF.

(H) SDRs 468.75 million were used for repurchases of drawals under EFF.

(I) SDRs 204.16 million were used for repurchases of drawals under EFF during April-October, 1991-92.

Notes

1. Figures after 1965-66 are not comparable with those of the earlier years due to devaluation of the Rupee in June 1966.
2. Also figures for July 1991 onwards are not comparable with those of earlier periods due to the downward adjustment of the rupee effected on July 1&3, 1991.
3. The outstanding repurchase obligations are calculated at the ruling rates of exchange.
4. Gold is valued at Rs. 53.58 per 10 grams upto May 1966 and at Rs. 84.39 per 10 grams upto September 1990 and closer to international market price w.e.f. October 17, 1990.
5. Foreign exchange includes (a) Foreign assets of the Reserve Bank of India and (b) Government balances held abroad upto 1955-56.

Source: *Economic Survey*, 1991-92

TABLE 20.7: Balance of Payments

	1960-61		1970-71		1980-81		1985-86	
	Rs. crore	U.S. $ million	Rs. crore	U.S. $ million	Rs. crore	U.S. $ million	Rs. crore	U.S. $ million
1	2	3	4	5	6	7	8	9
1. Imports (c.i.f.)	1105.7	2322.9	1826.1	2434.8	12543.6	15862.3	21163.6	17297.7
(a) PL 480 Title I	185.1	388.9	49.9	66.5	—	—	—	—
(b) Others	920.6	1934.0	1776.2	2368.3	12543.6	15862.3	21163.6	17297.7
2. Exports (f.o.b.)	630.5	1324.6	1404.5	1872.7	6576.4	8316.3	11577.6	9462.7
3. Trade balance (2-1)	—475.2	—998.3	—421.6	—562.1	—5967.2	—7546.0	—9586.0	—7835.0
4. Non-monetary gold movement (net)	—	—	13.1	17.5		—	28.5	23.3
5. Invisibles								
(a) Receipts	259.9	546.0	496.1	661.1	5890.2	7448.6	7875.2	6436.7
(b) Payments	177.1	372.1	533.0	710.7	1579.6	1997.5	4245.0	3469.6
(Of which: Interest and service payments on loans and credits)	(33.8)	(71.0)	(203.8)	(271.7)	(282.4)	(357.1)	(1371.5)	(1120.9)
(c) Net	82.8	173.9	—36.9	—49.2	4310.6	5451.1	3630.2	2967.1
6. Current account (net)	—392.4	—824.4	—445.4	—593.8	—1656.6	—2094.9	—5927.3	—4844.6
7. Capital transactions								
(a) Private								
(i) Receipts	51.5	108.2	79.9	106.5	162.6	205.6	2566.9	2098.0
(ii) Payments	35.0	73.5	59.6	79.5	65.5	83.0	212.6	173.7
(iii) Net	16.5	34.7	20.3	27.0	97.1	122.6	2354.3	1924.3

Contd

TABLE 20.7 (*Contd.*)

1	2	3	4	5	6	7	8	9
(b) Government miscellaneous								
(i) Receipts	147.0	308.8	323.7	431.6	1010.9	1278.4	2233.2	1825.3
(ii) Payments	42.0	88.2	353.3	471.0	1246.8	1576.7	895.8	732.2
(iii) Net	105.0	220.6	—29.6	—39.4	—235.9	—298.3	1337.4	1093.1
(c) Amortisation payments (Gross)	—37.6	—79.0	—231.8	—309.1	—691.1	—874.1	—1465.3	—1197.6
(d) Repurchases from IMF	—10.7	—22.5	—154.0	—205.3	—7.5	—9.5	—253.0	—206.8
(e) Banking capital (net)	9.7	20.4	0.1	0.1	12.7	16.1	186.1	152.1
8. Errors and omissions	—6.3	—13.2	—66.9	—89.2	—158.0	—199.7	580.1	474.1
9. Total Surplus (+)/ Deficit (-) (6 to 8)	—315.8	—663.4	—907.3	—1209.7	—2639.5	—3337.8	—3187.7	—2605.4
FINANCED BY:								
10. External assistance loans	256.6 @	539.1	743.3 @	991.1	1728.7 **	2186.0	2481.2	2028.0
11. Drawings from IMF (Gross)	—	—		—	274.3	346.9	—	—
12. Allocation of SDRs	—	—	75.4	100.5	120.5	152.4	—	—
13. Decline (+)/ increase (-) in Reserves	59.2	124.3	88.6	118.1	516.0	652.5	706.5	577.4
TOTAL (10 to 13)	315.8	663.4	907.3	1209.7	2639.5	3337.7	3187.7	2605.4

Contd.

TABLE 20.7 (*Contd.*)

	1986-87		1987-88		1988-89		1989-90	
	Rs. crore	U.S. $ million	Rs. crore	U.S. $ million	Rs. crore	U.S. $ million	Rs. crore	U.S. $ million
1	10	11	12	13	14	15	16	17
1. Imports (c.i.f.)	22668.9	17740.3	25692.5	19815.6	43202.3	23617.6	40642.4	24411.0
(a) PL 480 Title I	—	—	—	—	—	—	—	—
(b) Others	22668.9	17740.3	25692.5	19815.6	34202.3	23617.6	40642.4	24411.0
2. Exports (f.o.b.)	13315.0	10420.1	16396.4	12645.9	20646.7	14257.1	28229.0	16955.2
3. Trade balance (2-1)	—9353.9	—7320.2	—9296.1	—7169.7	—13555.6	—9360.5	—12413.4	—7455.8
4. Non-monetary gold movement (net)	—	—	—	—	—	—	6.4	3.8
5. Invisibles								
(a) Receipts	8274.4	6475.4	9278.5	7156.1	10926.3	7544.9	12483.9	7498.2
(b) Payments	4750.5	3717.7	6275.0	4839.6	7780.7	5372.8	9900.7	5946.7
(Of which: Interest and service payments on loans and credits)	(1533.3)	(1199.9)	(1948.8)	(1503.0)	(2560.2)	(1767.9)	(3536.2)	(2123.9)
(c) Net	3523.9	2757.7	3003.5	2316.5	3145.6	2172.1	2583.2	1551.5
6. Current account (net)	—5830.0	—4562.5	—6292.6	—4853.2	—10410.2	—7188.4	—9823.8	—5900.5
7. Capital transactions								
(a) Private								
(i) Receipts	3141.4	2458.4	3880.5	2992.9	6261.4	4323.6	9816.2	5895.9
(ii) Payments	514.2	402.4	966.3	745.3	2520.7	1740.7	6191.4	3718.7
(iii) Net	2627.2	2056.0	2914.2	2247.6	3740.7	2582.9	3624.8	2177.2

Contd.

TABLE 20.7 (*Contd.*)

1	10	11	12	13	14	15	16	17
(b) Government miscellaneous								
(i) Receipts	5386.9	4215.7	8499.1	6555.0	9465.5	6536.2	12015.3	7216.7
(ii) Payments	2060.9	1612.8	4837.9	3731.3	3571.3	2466.4	6153.3	3695.8
(iii) Net	3326.0	2602.9	3661.2	2823.7	5893.8	4069.8	5862.0	3520.9
(c) Amortisation payments (Gross)	—3039.9	—2378.9	—3611.0	—2785.0	—3924.3	—2709.8	—3773.4	—2266.4
(d) Repurchases from IMF	—672.3	—526.1	—1209.0	—932.5	—1547.3	—1068.4	—1459.6	—876.7
(e) Banking capital (net)	—70.1	—54.9	74.8	57.7	—265.2	—183.1	59.2	35.6
8. Errors and omissions	—129.3	—101.2	—947.7	—730.9	203.4	140.5	—720.0	—432.5
9. Total Surplus (+)/ Deficit (-) (6 to 8)	—3788.4	—2964.7	—5410.1	—4172.6	—6308.9	—4356.5	—6230.8	—3742.4
FINANCED BY:								
10. External assistance loans	3056.2	2391.7	4453.9	3435.1	4859.6	3355.7	4998.4	3002.2
11. Drawings from IMF (Gross)	—	—	—	—	—	—	—	—
12. Allocation of SDRs	—	—	—	—	—	—	—	—
13. Decline (+)/ increase (-) in Reserves	732.2	573.0	956.2	737.5	1449.3	1000.8	1232.4	740.2
TOTAL (10 TO 13)	3788.4	2964.7	5410.1	4172.6	6308.9	4356.5	6230.8	3742.4

Contd.

TABLE 20.7 (*Contd.*)

** Includes loan of Rs. 544.5 crores from the IMF Trust Fund

@ Includes rupee loans under PL-480 Title-I. Figures from 1980-81 onwards are preliminary.

Notes

1. Figures given in this table for some items of capital account do not correspond to the similar statistics published by the Reserve Bank of India. The difference is due to the adjustments made in respect of loan drawings under external assistance and repayment thereof. The presentation of balance of payments statistics in the above table differs from the adjusted balance of payments statistics published in the previous issues of the Economic Survey.
2. The rupee equivalent of all foreign currency transactions has been arrived at by applying the par/central rates upto June 1972 and thereafter on the basis of the average of RBTs spot buying and selling rate for sterling and the monthly averages of cross-rates based on London market for non-sterling currencies.
3. Grants received are covered under item 5 (a).
4. U.S. Embassy expenditures out of PL-480 counterpart funds are included under item 5 (a).
5. Receipts by way of 'loans' by the private sector including loans out of Cooley Fund and amortisation payments thereof are excluded from items 7(a) (i) and 7 (a) (ii) and included under item 10 and 7 (c) respectively.
6. Receipts by way of loans' received by the official sector under the External Assistance programmes including rupee loans out of PL-480 Title-I and corresponding amortisation payments are excluded from item 7 (b) (i) and 7 (b) (ii) and are shown under item 10 and 7 (c) respectively.
7. The movements in PL-480 rupee balances are included under item 7 (b).
8. Since October-December 1986, data on credits under private long term capital and official loans include borrowings made to prepay earlier loans; debits against private long-term capital and official amortization cover such prepayments.

Source: *Economic Survey*, 1991-92.

TABLE 20.8: Direction of Trade

(*Rs. crore*)

	1960-61		1970-71		1980-81		1985-86		1986-87	
	Exports	Imports	Exports	Imports	Exports	Imports	Exports	Imports	Exports	Imports
1	2	3	4	5	6	7	8	9	10	11
I. OECD	**425**	**875**	**769**	**1042**	**3126**	**5740**	**5532**	**10527**	**7004**	**12903**
of which:										
I.1. (a) EEC	232	417	282	320	1447	2639	1929	5234	2736	6549
of which										
I.1.1 (i) Belgium	5	15	20	12	145	296	225	951	343	1096
I.1.2 (ii) France	9	21	18	21	147	280	203	583	271	685
I.1.3 (iii) F.R.G.	20	123	32	108	385	694	513	1544	733	1918
I.1.4 (iv) Netherlands	9	11	14	19	152	215	158	296	226	389
I.1.5 (v) U.K.	173	217	170	127	395	731	524	1251	700	1661
I.2. (b) North America	120	347	235	570	806	1851	2106	2515	2469	2258
I.2.1 (i) Canada	18	20	28	117	62	332	132	451	137	372
I.2.2 (ii) U.S.A.	103	328	207	453	743	1619	1974	2064	2332	1886
I.3 (c) Asia and Oceania	65	80	234	122	708	932	1304	2257	1501	3041
of which:										
I.3.1 (i) Australia	22	18	25	37	92	170	123	442	146	406
I.3.2 (ii) Japan	35	61	204	83	598	749	1164	1774	1334	2592
II. OPEC	**26**	**52**	**99**	**126**	**745**	**3488**	**835**	**3420**	**774**	**1950**
of which:										
II.1 (i) Iran	5	30	27	92	123	1339	95	885	47	140
II.2 (ii) Iraq	3	2	10	3	52	753	34	547	18	126
II.3 (iii) Kuwait	3	0	16	6	97	338	121	340	93	290
II.4 (iv) Saudi Arabia	3	14	15	24	165	540	221	794	214	863

Contd.

TABLE 20.8 (*Contd.*)

1	2	3	4	5	6	7	8	9	10	11
III. Eastern Europe of which	**45**	**38**	**323**	**220**	**1486**	**1296**	**2294**	**2169**	**2390**	**1537**
III.1 (i) G.D.R.	3	3	25	19	49	44	95	85	. 88	84
III.2 (ii) Romania	1	5	14	17	58	97	98	144	80	101
III.3 (iii) U.S.S.R.	29	16	210	106	1226	1014	2006	1678	1867	1006
IV. Developing ountries* of which:	**95**	**132**	**305**	**239**	**1286**	**1966**	**1463**	**3466**	1871	3696
IV.1 (i) Africa	40	63	129	169	350	205	289	593	278	881
IV.2 (ii) Asia	45	64	166	54	900	1431	1156	2344	1563	2469
IV.3 (iii) Latin America and Carribean	10	5	10	16	36	313	18	529	31	406
V.Others	**51**	**25**	**40**	**8**	**68**	**60**	**771**	**75**	**414**	**10**
VI.TOTAL	642	1122	1535	1634	6711	12549	10895	19658	12452	20096

Contd

TABLE 20.8: (*Contd.*)

	1987-88		1988-89		1989-90		1990-91	
	Exports	Imports	Exports	Imports	Exports	Imports	Exports	Imports
1	12	13	14	15	16	17	18	19
I. **OECD**	**8838**	**12380**	**11301**	**16059**	**14743**	**20224**	**17428**	**23310**
of which:								
I.1 (i)EEC	3934	7400	4926	9005	6906	11736	8951	12680
of which:								
I.1.1 (i) Belgium	485	1371	885	2055	1209	2696	1259	2718
I.1.2 (ii) France	379	798	427	806	638	1612	766	1304
I.1.3 (iii) F.R.G.	1059	2159	1236	2458	1778	2750	2549	3473
I.1.4 (iv) Netherlands	279	443	402	536	530	549	644	793
I.1.5 (v) U.K.	1015	1829	1153	2398	1602	2974	2128	2894
I.2 (b)North America	3086	2300	3925	3638	4739	4713	5077	5804
I.2.1 (i) Canada	166	299	197	428	264	454	281	559
I.2.2 (ii) U.S.A.	2920	2002	3728	3239	4474	4260	4797	5245
I.3 (c)Asia and Oceania	1819	2680	2450	3387	3099	3775	3401	4826
of which:								
I.3.1 (i) Australia	180	503	265	707	335	887	321	1464
I.3.2 (ii) Japan	1614	2126	2154	2631	2727	2820	3039	3245
II. **OPEC**	**962**	**2953**	**1193**	**3779**	**1841**	**5074**	**1831**	**7041**
of which:								
II.1 (i)Iran	139	144	89	129	132	390	141	1018
II.2 (ii)Iraq	18	611	53	194	126	461	44	496
II.3 (iii)Kuwait	106	472	144	521	198	1160	74	363
II.4 (iv)Saudi Arabia	278	765	324	1893	429	1448	419	2899

Contd.

TABLE 20.8 *Contd.*

1	12	13	14	15	16	17	18	19
III. Eastern Europe	**2594**	**2126**	**3356**	**1947**	**5336**	**2990**	**5819**	**3377**
of which:								
III.1 (i) G.D.R.	112	93	183	133	216	197	**	**
III.2 (ii) Romania	61	58	38	72	123	106	96	50
III.3 (iii) U.S.S.R.	1963	1608	2609	1258	4463	2038	5255	2548
IV. Developing Countries*	**2204**	**3800**	**3315**	**5260**	**4246**	**6031**	**5465**	**7965**
of which:								
IV.1 (i) Africa	304	626	384	939	521	857	668	959
IV.2 (ii) Asia	1866	2680	2821	3737	3634	4452	4665	6033
IV.3 (iii) Latin America and carribean	33	494	110	584	93	723	132	974
V. Others	**1076**	**985**	**1068**	**1190**	**1515**	**1097**	**2010**	**1500**
VI. TOTAL	**15674**	**22244**	**20232**	**28235**	**27682**	**35416**	**32553**	**43193**

* Excluding members of OPEC.

** Included under F.R.G. (Item I. 1.3 above) with the integration of Germany.

Source: *Economic Survey*, 1991-92.

TABLE 20.9: Exports and Imports with Foreign Countries

		Exports							Imports						
		II 1990	III 1990	IV 1990	I 1991	II 1991	June 1991	July 1991	II 1990	III 1990	IV 1990	I 1991	II 1991	June 1991	July 1991
		Millions of U.S. Dollars							Millions of U.S. Dollars						
1	2	3	4	5	6	7	8	9	10	11	12	13	14	15	16
IFS World Total		**4,290.0**	**4,375.9**	**4,477.1**	**4,946.8**	—	—	—	**5,367.4**	**5,753.3**	**6,851.3**	**6,074.2**	—	—	—
DOTS World Total	**001**	**4,263.7**	**4,273.2**	**4,444.6**	**5,405.8**	**5,023.5**	**1,464.1**	**1,603.6**	**5,352.4**	**5,660.2**	**6,782.9**	**6,150.4**	**4,799.3**	**1,403.5**	**1,766.8**
Industrial Countries	**110**	**2,226.5**	**2,408.8**	**2,441.5**	**3,154.2**	**2,756.6**	**782.0**	**905.5**	**3,019.9**	**3,076.0**	**3,669.9**	**3,724.3**	**2,745.6**	**784.6**	**1,079.0**
United States	111	633.4	714.2	614.3	753.2*	772.5*	240.1*	282.9*	585.4	729.0	714.1	733.7*	496.8*	129.4*	180.6*
Canada	156	42.4	38.3	34.4	46.0*	51.6*	15.4*	16.0*	54.4	86.0	90.9	87.8*	55.9*	14.6*	51.2[E]
Australia	193	38.1	54.4	39.3	45.6*	42.8*	12.9*	20.2[E]	251.4	141.1	203.2	188.2*	112.0*	40.9*	40.3[E]
Japan	158	365.2	375.7	445.3	579.1	513.4*	134.6*	152.5*	421.5	416.5	485.8	452.2*	405.6*	156.2*	148.9*
New Zealand	196	4.8	7.0	4.9	6.3*	4.9*	1.0*	1.8*	11.8	17.8	13.2	23.2*	23.2*	3.4*	3.8*
Austria	122	20.2	14.6	14.0	31.4*	25.9[Y]	7.8*	7.9*	21.0	19.1	19.5	23.0*	19.8[Y]	4.0*	7.1*
Belgium-Luxembourg	126	161.1	157.9	131.7	201.7*	140.3*	42.5*	49.8[E]	325.5	345.2	448.2	393.0*	284.1*	83.8*	148.1[E]
Denmark	128	17.6	17.4	21.3	28.6*	28.5*	6.5*	7.6*	13.9	19.4	15.7	16.5*	10.3*	2.5*	11.7*
Finland	172	22.1	21.6	9.2	24.1*	19.7*	.9*	8.0*	14.1	14.9	26.4	70.6[Y]	47.1*	.5*	1.0*
France	132	94.9	92.6	99.5	194.2*	135.7*	34.0*	38.4*	138.4	114.3	307.5	233.0*	153.0*	50.1*	68.2*
Germany	134	287.5	289.8	356.1	492.0*	319.5[Y]	101.8*	110.1*	403.7	415.1	475.9	481.1*	382.5[Y]	90.9*	131.9*
Greece	174	7.5	5.5	7.3	13.0*	12.1[Y]	7.0*	1.9[E]	1.8	.5	1.6	.2*	.7*	.3*	—[E]
Ireland	178	3.0	5.8	6.0	9.1*	5.3[Y]	.8[E]	1.5[E]	1.0	4.2	3.9	2.2*	.8[Y]	.4[E]	1.3[E]

Contd.

TABLE 20.9: (*Contd.*)

1	2	3	4	5	6	7	8	9	10	11	12	13	14	15	16
Italy	136	84.3	122.3	130.2	167.2*	169.7*	40.4*	50.7E	136.6	162.5	139.9	171.3*	121.7*	46.2*	50.5E
Netherlands	138	44.8	72.2	92.7	94.6Y	61.4Y	15.7*	27.9E	74.1	122.8	114.5	92.8Y	83.7Y	39.2*	29.2E
Norway	142	7.8	7.0	7.8	10.6Y	14.8Y	2.2E	2.6E	5.5	7.5	8.6	9.1Y	7.2Y	2.2E	1.7E
Portugal	182	10.3	9.9	8.8	15.2*	16.7*	4.3*	4.3*	8.1	7.3	1.8	2.6*	1.7*	.3*	.3*
Spain	184	39.5	35.9	50.0	35.8Y	43.4*	12.4E	10.9E	22.3	19.7	38.7	37.8Y	24.6Y	4.9E	5.0E
Sweden	144	23.1	20.3	20.7	28.0*	22.9*	5.1*	5.8*	36.1	39.3	66.6	81.7*	43.4*	8.7*	9.9*
Switzerland	146	51.7	51.5	49.8	49.9*	46.1*	12.8*	15.7*	48.3	57.8	58.6	73.5*	59.8*	17.2*	13.3*
United Kingdom	112	267.4	294.7	298.0	328.3*	309.3*	83.7*	88.9*	445.0	335.8	435.5	548.8*	411.9*	89.0*	174.7*
Developing Countries	**200**	**1,026.2**	**944.0**	**1,100.7**	**1,258.9**	**1,192.0**	**352.5**	**363.5**	**2,082.2**	**2,149.6**	**2,627.2**	**2,095.0**	**1,746.5**	**536.1**	**541.1**
Africa	605	67.3	82.7	99.4	88.9	78.7	25.1	37.4	155.4	204.1	111.5	207.9	167.0	63.0	113.0
Algeria	612	.7	.6	—	1.4Y	.8Y	.2E	.7E	—	.3	.3	—Y	—Y	—E	.2E
Ghana	652	1.7	1.1	1.3	3.7Y	1.9Y	.2E	.3E	.4	.5	1.3	.6Y	.5Y	.3E	.2E
Kenya	664	6.6	9.2	11.0	12.0Y	7.2Y	2.4E	4.0E	4.8	3.4	9.9	4.3Y	5.3Y	1.1E	1.1E
Morocco	686	1.9	2.6	2.7	2.7Y	2.1Y	.4E	.4E	49.1	77.8	14.7	82.2Y	54.0Y	24.3E	32.1E
Nigeria	694	14.6	15.1	15.8	19.7Y	16.0Y	5.2E	5.3E	1.9	7.1	3.9	3.1Y	2.1Y	.5E	3.2E
Sudan	732	1.0	9.7	5.1	.7Y	1.1Y	.3E	3.3E	.4	.4	.7	.4Y	.5Y	.1E	.3E
Tanzania	738	3.3	4.9	12.1	7.5Y	3.6Y	1.2E	1.9E	5.5	9.5	5.4	10.3Y	6.1Y	1.5E	5.2E
Tunisia	744	1.7	1.0	1.8	3.2*	6.4*	4.8*	6.2*	16.3	18.8	1.8	13.2*	14.0*	.8*	38.3*
Zaire	636	.6	.8	.7	1.0Y	.6Y	.3E	.2E	17.8	18.2	13.9	14.8Y	19.6Y	9.3E	6.5E
Zambia	754	5.6	4.0	5.6	6.5Y	6.1Y	1.5E	1.8E	25.9	24.1	26.6	25.9Y	28.5Y	13.7E	13.3E

Contd.

TABLE 20.9: (*Contd.*)

1	2	3	4	5	6	7	8	9	10	11	12	13	14	15	16
Asia	**505**	490.1	501.9	599.5	702.3	624.4	181.6	202.4	654.3	629.6	828.1	884.9	697.4	238.6	197.0
Afghanistan	512	13.6	12.8	12.4	21.9Y	15.0Y	8.0E	7.1E	3.5	4.6	3.4	2.9Y	3.8Y	1.1E	1.0E
Bangladesh	513	68.5	58.6	90.7	87.7Y	75.3Y	22.2E	17.1E	4.8	2.2	3.1	6.6*	11.6*	2.3*	2.7*
China, People's Rep.	924	3.0	6.0	1.0	19.5*	23.6*	9.0*	.1E	4.8	7.8	11.9	45.0*	40.3*	11.1*	2.9E
Hong Kong	532	135.7	119.4	129.3	191.1*	164.6	37.4*	47.5*	39.7	31.1	43.5	77.1*	61.3*	17.5*	19.6*
Indonesia	536	14.7	33.0	29.4	16.8Y	16.1Y	6.8E	12.4E	16.4	9.6	131.6	18.5Y	18.1Y	4.8E	3.4E
Korea	542	40.4	41.3	44.5	41.3Y	44.5Y	191.E	16.3	77.5	91.4	88.0	75.7Y	85.2Y	23.6E	26.1E
Malaysia	548	25.0	32.0	39.9	60.5*	61.6*	20.0*	23.3*	129.8	158.5	137.5	121.7*	56.0*	14.8*	14.3*
Nepal	558	8.0	11.5	14.1	6.5Y	8.9Y	3.1E	3.4E	.3	9.2	5.5	.2Y	.3Y	.2E	.5E
Pakistan	564	9.0	9.2	11.8	15.1Y	7.9*	1.5*	3.6*	7.4	10.3	15.7	10.4Y	3.9	1.1*	1.3*
Philippines	566	4.8	6.1	5.3	16.5Y	15.9*	6.2*	3.7*	.5	1.8	1.3	.6Y	8.4*	.3*	2.7*
Singapore	576	71.3	71.1	87.2	107.6*	88.6	22.3*	25.8*	155.8	143.1	235.0	405.2*	207.8*	70.5*	58.5*
Sri Lanka	524	21.9	24.9	35.7	21.2Y	24.0Y	9.7E	9.1E	6.7	4.5	4.7	6.7Y	7.3Y	1.9E	2.0E
Thailand	578	46.7	44.7	55.5	59.5Y	51.4Y	13.4E	17.4E	16.4	16.3	16.1	19.0Y	18.1Y	5.4E	7.2E
Europe	**170**	111.0	77.0	98.0	108.4	118.8	31.7	30.7	135.8	140.7	154.1	152.5	140.2	36.4	32.2
Czechoslo-vakia	934	30.6	21.4	13.2	50.8Y	33.7Y	6.8E	7.0E	44.8	35.4	39.2	33.1Y	49.3Y	13.3E	9.9E
Hungary	944	12.2	11.2	7.9	11.0Y	13.5Y	3.3E	3.1E	22.3	34.0	20.1	19.3Y	24.6Y	4.1E	4.4E
Poland	964	17.6	10.6	40.2	12.1Y	19.4Y	8.3E	4.2E	17.5	16.5	26.1	25.9Y	19.3Y	5.3E	5.5E
Romania	968	28.7	9.4	3.4	5.7*	24.4*	7.7E	6.6E	10.6	8.8	5.6	7.7*	11.7Y	1.5E	1.6E
Turkey	186	8.1	10.5	15.2	13.6Y	8.9Y	2.2E	5.2E	15.1	26.2	35.8	17.9Y	16.6Y	3.0E	3.4E
Yugoslavia	188	11.5	10.2	10.4	12.1Y	16.4*	2.8*	3.6E	25.1	19.7	26.9	48.5Y	18.5*	9.2*	7.4E

Contd.

TABLE 20.9: (*Contd.*)

1	2	3	4	5	6	7	8	9	10	11	12	13	14	15	16
Middle East	**405**	**343.9**	**264.0**	**282.1**	**346.2**	**337.4**	**107.8**	**88.0**	**947.4**	**1,076.8**	**1,354.8**	**728.1**	**593.1**	**155.4**	**164.1**
Bahrain	419	10.1	8.0	9.3	12.5^{Y}	11.1^{Y}	2.5^{E}	2.9^{E}	27.7	36.7	87.0	53.0^{Y}	30.4^{Y}	8.8^{E}	12.9^{E}
Egypt	469	36.3	25.7	19.0	43.0^{Y}	40.0^{Y}	15.2^{E}	7.3^{E}	2.5	21.9	17.8	3.0^{Y}	2.7^{Y}	.5^{E}	1.1^{E}
Iran, I.R. of	429	14.3	10.1	34.5	19.5^{Y}	15.8^{Y}	7.8^{E}	2.9^{E}	44.2	151.1	219.8	73.1^{Y}	48.6^{Y}	16.4^{E}	16.6^{E}
Iraq	433	13.4	11.4	—	—^{Y}	—^{Y}	—^{E}	—^{E}	247.7	37.1	.5	—^{Y}	—^{Y}	—^{E}	—^{E}
Israel	436	14.8	14.8	11.5	12.8*	16.4*	3.9*	3.3*	20.3	17.9	26.9	14.5*	23.1*	10.8*	6.4*
Kuwait	443	25.0	16.5	.7	—^{Y}	—^{Y}	—^{E}	—^{E}	161.3	46.9	.7	—^{Y}	—^{Y}	—^{E}	—^{E}
Libya	672	.9	.1	2.2	.1^{Y}	1.0^{Y}	—^{E}	—^{E}	—	—	23.3	—^{Y}	—^{Y}	—^{E}	—^{E}
Oman	449	11.9	12.6	16.9	16.3^{Y}	13.1^{Y}	3.8^{Y}	3.4^{E}	3.7	35.0	.5	.5^{Y}	4.1^{Y}	.2^{E}	—^{E}
Qatar	453	5.4	4.6	4.6	7.8^{Y}	5.9^{Y}	1.5^{E}	2.1^{E}	9.1	7.7	4.1	3.8^{Y}	10.0	.2^{E}	4.2^{E}
Saudi Arabia	456	62.8	57.2	57.7	78.4^{Y}	69.1	20.9^{E}	25.0^{E}	213.1	390.1	636.7	258.9^{Y}	234.5^{Y}	63.7^{E}	66.2^{E}
Syrian Arab Republic	463	1.6	2.3	3.8	1.9^{Y}	3.0*	1.7*	.3^{E}	—	—	—	—^{Y}	—*	—*	—^{E}
United Arab Emirates	466	129.0	95.0	101.0	145.1^{Y}	141.9^{Y}	47.4^{E}	39.2^{E}	161.0	273.6	255.2	30.1^{Y}	177.1^{Y}	37.4^{E}	42.0^{E}
Yemen Arab Rep.	474	10.9	3.2	7.5	6.2^{Y}	12.0^{Y}	2.5^{E}	.9^{E}	—	—	31.1	—^{Y}	—^{Y}	—^{E}	—^{E}
Yemen, P.D. Rep.	459	—	.1	.5	.2^{Y}	—^{Y}	—^{E}	—^{E}	.3	.1	—	.3^{Y}	.3^{Y}	.1^{E}	.1^{E}
Western Hemisphere	**205**	**13.9**	**18.4**	**21.7**	**13.1**	**14.7**	**6.2**	**5.0**	**135.3**	**98.3**	**178.8**	**121.5**	**148.8**	**42.7**	**34.9**
Argentina	213	.3	.8	1.7	1.0^{Y}	.4^{Y}	.1^{E}	.1^{E}	17.5	3.3	19.9	15.2	19.2^{Y}	6.22^{E}	1.6^{E}
Brazil	223	.5	1.7	5.6	1.6*	1.0^{Y}	.2^{E}	.4^{E}	52.5	57.0	61.1	63.9^{Y}	57.7^{Y}	21.9^{E}	26.4^{E}
Chile	228	—^{Y}	.5^{Y}	.6^{Y}	—^{Y}	—^{Y}	—^{E}	—^{E}	4.2^{L}	9.0^{Y}	25.6*	8.4^{Y}	4.6^{Y}	—^{E}	—^{E}
Mexico	273	4.9	6.0	5.2	5.5^{Y}	5.4^{Y}	2.0^{E}	2.3^{E}	16.4	21.1	42.1	12.7^{Y}	18.0	9.6^{E}	3.3^{E}
Venezuela	299	1.2	2.4	1.3	1.1^{Y}	1.3^{Y}	.4^{E}	.7^{E}	2.4	3.1	12.8	2.2^{Y}	2.7^{Y}	1.6^{E}	.2^{E}

Contd.

TABLE 20.9: (*Contd.*)

1	2	3	4	5	6	7	8	9	10	11	12	13	14	15	16
U.S.S.R. and selected other countries n.i.e.	**910**	**661.1**	**782.5**	**707.6**	**863.2**	**690.0**	**296.7**	**317.1**	**257.6**	**422.5**	**453.4**	**295.0**	**255.7**	**75.0**	**142.9**
U.S.S.R.	974	617.5	777.9	703.8	847.1Y	679.2Y	295.7E	314.9E	216.2	413.8	434.6	282.9Y	237.8Y	69.8E	140.0E
Memorandum items															
Oil Exporting Countries	999	293.9	258.8	264.3	306.2	281.1	93.7	91.7	860.8	961.6	1,289.4	661.1	497.0	124.8	136.2
Non-Oil Developing Countries	201	732.3	685.2	836.4	952.8	910.9	258.7	271.8	1,167.4	1,187.9	1,337.8	1,433.8	1,249.5	411.3	405.0

Note: To provide guidance regarding the sources of the figures for individual countries, some of the figures are shown with symbols to the right of the figure. These symbols refer only to figures for trade between two partner countries and are not applicable to totals calculated for groups of partner countries, when they refer to trade between two partner countries, figures shown without symbols are data reported from the respective country's own records; symbols indicate figures derived from partner records or by other methods of estimation, as follows:

* = derived solely from partner records
Y = estimated by other methods, sometimes including the use of partner records
E = estimated by other methods
L = 1 month of reported data and 2 months of estimates

Source: *Direction of Trade Statistics*, December 1991.

TABLE 20.10: India's Share in World Exports by Commodity Divisions/Groups

(Value in US million dollars)

Div. Sl.No.	Code Group	Commodity Division/Group	1970 World	1970 India	1970 India's share (%)	1975 World	1975 India	1975 India's share (%)
1	2	3	4	5	6	7	8	9
01		Meat and meat preparations	3584	4	0.1	7378	9	0.1
03		Fish, crustaceans and molluses and prep. thereof	—	—	—	—	—	—
04		Cereals and cereal preparations	6775	9	0.1	25133	16	0.1
	042	Rice	925	6	0.6	1984	12	0.6
05		Vegetables and fruits	1471	17	1.2	10104	154	1.5
06		Sugar, sugar preparations and honey	2700	26	1.0	11663	554	4.8
07		Coffee, tea, cocoa, spices and manuf. thereof	5437	280	5.1	9133	438	4.8
	071	Coffee and coffee substitutes	3205	31	1.0	4580	73	1.6
	074	Tea and mate	587	196	33.4	933	292	31.3
	075	Spices	255	52	20.5	548	73	13.3
08		Feeding stuff for animals	—	—	—	—	—	—
12		Tobacco and tobacco manufactures	1713	43	2.5	3827	124	3.2
	121	Tobacco unmanufactured, tobacco refuse	1058	42	4.0	2357	119	5.0
	122	Tobacco manufactured	655	1	0.2	1470	5	0.4
22		Oilseed and oleaginous fruit	—	—	—	—	—	—
28		Metaliferous ores and metal scrap	7357	193	2.6	13446	253	1.9
	281	Iron ore and concentrates	2373	158	6.7	4601	247	5.4
51		Organic chemicals	6648	9	0.1	20219	22	0.1
52		Inorganic chemicals	—	—	—	—	—	—
53		Dying, Tanning and colouring materials	1615	8	0.5	3642	23	0.6
54		Medicinal and pharmaceutical products	2687	11	0.4	6503	29	0.4
55		Essential oils and perfume materials toilets, polishing and cleaning preparations	916	10	1.1	3059	18	0.6
57		Explosives and pyrotechnic products	—	—	—	—	—	—

Contd.

TABLE 20.10: *Contd.*

1	2	3	4	5	6	7	8	9
58		Artificial resins and plastic materials and cellulose esters and ethers	—	—	—	—	—	—
59		Chemical materials and products n.e.s.	—	—	—	—	—	—
61		Leather, leather mfrs, n.e.s. & dressed furskins	1047	95	9.1	2380	200	8.4
	611	Leather	701	94	13.4	1540	189	12.3
	612	Mfrs. of leather or of composition leather n.e.s.	132	1	0.6	355	4	1.0
	613	Furskins, tanned or dressed etc.	214	—	—	486	8	1.6
65		Textiles yarn, fabrics, made up articles n.e.s.	11371	161	4.1	23798	599	2.5
	652	Cotton fabrics woven	1436	98	6.8	3149	161	5.1
	653	Fabrics, woven of man made fibres	3976	189	4.8	8083	191	2.4
	654	Textiles fabrics woven, other than of cotton or man made fibres	270	2	0.8	547	5	0.9
	667	Pearls, precious and semi-precious stones	2431	53	2.2	5707	128	2.2
67		Iron and steel	14540	132	0.9	40789	116	0.3
69		Manufactures of metals n.e.s.	4328	27	0.6	12053	74	0.6
71		Power generating machinery and equipment	20884	25	0.1	54327	97	0.2
72		Machinery specialised for particular industries	10670	17	0.2	67016	102	0.2
73		Metal working machinery	—	—	—	—	—	—
74		General industrial machinery and equipment n.e.s. and machine parts thereof	—	—	—	—	—	—
75		Office machinery and ADP equipment	—	—	—	—	—	—
76		Telecommunication and sound recording and reproducing apparatus and equipment	—	—	—	—	—	—
77		Electrical machinery apparatus and appliances n.e.s.	—	—	—	—	—	—
78		Road vehicles (including air cushion vehicles)	—	—	—	—	—	—
79		Other transport equipment	—	—	—	—	—	—
84		Articles of apparel and clothing accessories	109	—	—	309	—	—
		Total exports (including others)	313706	2026	0.6	875500	4355	0.5

Source: *Economic Survey*, 1991-92.

Contd.

TABLE 20.10: India's Share in World Exports by Commodity Divisions/Groups (*Contd.*)

(*Value in US million dollars*)

Div. Sl.No.	Code Group	Commodity Division/Group	1980 World	1980 India	1980 India's share (%)	1981 World	1981 India	1981 India's share (%)
1	2	3	4	5	6	7	8	9
01		Meat and meat preparations	17832	67	0.4	15755	61	0.4
03		Fish, crustaceans and molluses and prep. thereof	12258	242	2.0	14335	337	2.4
04		Cereals and cereal preparations	41989	201	0.5	32643	211	0.6
	042	Rice	4355	160	3.7	2916	162	5.6
05		Vegetables and fruits	24018	259	1.1	23606	332	1.4
06		Sugar, sugar preparations and honey	16183	46	0.3	10113	0	0.0
07		Coffee, tea, cocoa, spices and manuf. thereof	22121	879	4.0	20779	971	4.7
	071	Coffee and coffee substitutes	12979	271	2.1	11676	226	1.9
	074	Tea and mate	1631	452	27.7	1973	517	26.2
	075	Spices	1072	156	14.5	1188	229	19.3
08		Feeding stuff for animals	10322	164	1.6	8515	127	1.5
12		Tobacco and tobacco manufactures	3423	151	4.4	7822	140	1.8
	121	Tobacco unmanufactured, tobacco, refuse	3423	151	4.4	3798	113	3.0
	122	Tobacco manufactured	—	—	—	4024	27	0.7
22		Oilseed and oleaginous fruit	9487	30	0.3	7896	20	0.3
28		Metalliferous ores and metal scrap	30239	465	1.5	23137	557	2.4
	281	Iron ore and concentrates	6515	411	6.3	6154	478	7.8
51		Organic chemicals	31841	17	10.1	36923	25	0.1
52		Inorganic chemicals	15491	26	0.2	16318	22	0.1
53		Dying, Tanning and colouring materials	7986	65	0.8	8024	62	0.8
54		Medicinal and pharmaceutical products	13918	109	0.8	15920	130	0.8
55		Essential and perfume materials toilets, polishing and cleaning preparations	7647	86	1.1	8136	56	0.7

Contd.

TABLE 20.10 *Contd.*

1	2	3	4	5	6	7	8	9
57		Explosives and pyrotechnic products	630	1	0.1	840	0	0.1
58		Artificial resins and plastic materials & cellulose esters and ethers	27223	3	—	28456	5	0.0
59		Chemical materials and products n.e.s.	15960	8	—	16613	28	0.2
61		Leather, leather mfrs, n.e.s. and dressed furskins	5967	405	6.8	6444	534	8.3
	611	Leather	3415	342	10.0	4185	331	7.9
	612	Mfrs. of leather or of composition leather n.e.s.	975	62	6.3	1233	202	16.4
	613	Furskins, tanned or dressed etc.	1577	1	0.1	1026	0	0.0
65		Textiles yarn, fabrics, made up articles n.e.s	48884	1145	2.3	48218	1037	2.1
	652	Cotton fabrics woven	6632	351	5.3	6804	327	4.8
	653	Fabrics, woven of man made fibres	9325	44	0.5	9735	20	0.2
	654	Textiles fabrics woven, other than of cotton or man made fibres	3188	204	6.4	3462	167	4.8
	667	Pearls, precious and semi-precious stones	18563	579	3.1	12073	1165	9.6
67		Iron and steel	68231	87	0.1	61891	45	0.1
69		Manufactures of metals n.e.s.	36840	221	0.6	32884	125	0.4
71		Power generating machinery and equipment	35722	88	0.2	38433	59	0.2
72		Machinery specialised for particular industries	58495	65	0.1	54707	97	0.2
73		Metal working machinery	15671	32	0.2	12696	55	0.4
74		General industrial machinery and equipment n.e.s. & machine parts thereof	59443	67	0.1	53954	60	0.1
75		Office machinery and ADP equipment	24750	2	0.0	53604	30	0.1
76		Telecommunication and sound recording and reproducing apparatus and equipment	26799	11	0.0	47318	4	0.0
77		Electrical machinery apparatus and appliances n.e.s.	60947	114	0.2	75739	121	0.2
78		Road vehicles (including air cushion vehicles)	127347	208	0.2	157446	126	0.1
79		Other transport equipment	41291	32	0.1	50709	27	0.1
84		Articles of apparel and clothing accessories	32365	590	1.8	38718	887	2.3
		Total exports (including others)	1989867	8378	0.4	1932387	8750	0.5

TABLE 20.10: India's Share in World Exports by Commodity Divisions/Groups (*Contd.*)

(*Value in US million dollars*)

Div. Sl.No.	Code Group	Commodity Division/Group	1988			1989		
			World	India	India's share (%)	World	India	India's share (%)
1	2	3	4	5	6	7	8	9
01		Meat and meat preparations	25072	39	0.2	27248	92	0.3
03		Fish, crustaceans and molluses & prep. thereof	25005	474	1.9	24854	852	3.4
04		Cereals and cereal preparations	35923	118	0.3	36724	158	0.4
	042	Rice	2762	109	4.0	3377	143	4.2
05		Vegetables and fruits	38276	299	0.8	39292	372	0.9
06		Sugar, sugar preparations and honey	11050	0	0.0	11401	0	0.0
07		Coffee, tea, cocoa, spices and manuf. thereof	22483	507	2.3	24720	832	3.4
	071	Coffee and coffee substitutes	11808	101	0.9	14037	208	1.5
	074	Tea and mate	1646	263	15.9	2214	467	21.1
	075	Spices	1474	144	9.7	1237	156	12.6
08		Feeding stuff for animals	4156	168	4.0	14691	147	1.0
12		Tobacco and tobacco manufactures	11565	65	0.6	13046	99	0.8
	121	Tobacco unmanufactured, tobacco refuse	4067	47	1.2	4390	93	2.1
	122	Tobacco manufactured	7498	18	0.2	8656	6	0.1
22		Oilseed and oleaginous fruit	10229	20	0.2	9149	12	0.1
28		Metalliferous ores and metal scrap	29984	630	2.1	36251	802	2.2
	281	Iron ore and concentrates	6484	561	8.6	8444	673	8.0
51		Organic chemicals	51284	128	0.2	47819	198	0.4
52		Inorganic chemicals	20897	30	0.1	61034	55	0.1
53		Dying, Tanning and colouring materials	13470	90	0.7	13829	143	0.1
54		Medicinal and pharmaceutical products	25101	49	0.2	22127	73	0.3
55		Essential oils and perfume materials toilets, polishing and cleaning preparations	12279	45	0.4	10930	59	0.5
57		Explosives and pyrotechnic products	1018	2	0.2	1043	4	0.3

Contd.

TABLE 20.10 *Contd.*

1	2	3	4	5	6	7	8	9
58		Artificial resins and plastic materials and cellulose esters and ethers	48100	11	0.0	46867	19	0.0
59		Chemical materials and products n.e.s.	23375	17	0.1	22561	27	0.1
61		Leather, leather mfrs, n.e.s. and dressed furskins	9949	566	5.7	9675	590	6.1
	611	Leather	6555	429	6.5	6392	385	6.0
	612	Mfrs. of leather or of composition leather n.e.s.	1826	137	7.5	1705	204	12.0
	613	Furskins, tanned or dressed etc.	1586	0	0.0	1577	0	0.0
65		Textiles yarn, fabrics, made up articles n.e.s.	67968	1374	2.0	103779	1706	1.6
	652	Cotton fabrics woven	9613	319	3.3	9233	430	4.7
	653	Fabrics, woven of man made fibres	12645	38	0.3	11655	45	0.4
	654	Textile fabrics woven, other than of cotton or man made fibres	4764	160	3.4	4509	246	5.5
	667	Pearls, precious and semi-precious stones	2334	2246	9.6	27261	2628	9.6
67		Iron and steel	68115	114	0.2	69998	173	0.2
69		Manufactures of metals n.e.s.	43396	261	0.6	39400	257	0.7
71		Power generating machinery and equipment	54317	68	0.1	79231	117	0.1
72		Machinery specialised for particular industries	76400	60	0.1	72878	78	0.1
73		Metal working machinery	17635	14	0.1	17768	19	0.1
74		General industrial machinery and equipment n.e.s. and machine parts thereof	82725	87	0.1	82728	84	0.1
75		Office machinery and ADP equipment	92846	45	0.0	98882	81	0.1
76		Telecommunication and sound recording and reproducing apparatus and equipment	59823	10	0.0	66280	24	0.0
77		Electrical machinery, apparatus and appliances n.e.s.	137510	81	0.1	142029	115	0.1
78		Road vehicles (including air cushion vehicles)	245204	97	0.0	253165	121	0.0
79		Other transport equipment	44668	4	0.0	44311	6	0.0
84		Articles of apparel and clothing accessories	68712	1546	2.3	70406	2054	2.9
		Total exports (including others)	2832894	13182	0.5	NA	NA	NA

Note: A zero in India's share means negligible or no share at all.
Source: *International Trade Statistics Year Book*, United Nations, New York, 1989.

TABLE 20.11: Index Numbers of Foreign Trade

(*Base; 1978-79=100*)

Year	Exports U.N.I.	Exports Q.I.	Imports U.V.I.	Imports Q.I.	Terms of trade Gross	Terms of trade Net	Terms of trade Income
1	2	3	4	5	6	7	8
1969-70	44.0	55.7	35.2	64.9	116.5	125.0	69.6
1970-71*	45.0	59.0	35.3	67.2	113.9	127.4	75.2
1971-72*	46.0	59.2	32.8	80.6	136.1	140.2	83.0
1972-73*	51.2	59.2	32.8	80.6	136.1	149.2	83.0
1973-74*	62.2	69.5	48.9	87.2	125.4	127.2	88.4
1974-75*	78.0	73.7	84.5	77.2	104.7	92.3	68.4
1975-76*	83.9	81.7	99.1	76.0	93.0	84.7	69.2
1976-77*	89.4	96.8	96.3	76.1	78.6	92.9	89.9
1977-78*	100.3	93.2	88.0	100.0	107.3	114.0	106.2
1978-79	100.0	100.0	100.0	100.0	100.0	100.0	100.0
1979-80	105.4	106.2	114.1	116.4	109.7	92.4	98.1
1980-81	108.5	108.1	134.2	137.9	127.6	80.8	87.3
1981-82	124.1	110.1	133.1	150.6	136.8	93.2	102.6
1982-83	132.0	116.7	136.3	154.6	132.4	96.8	113.0
1983-84	151.0	113.0	125.8	185.4	164.1	120.0	135.6
1984-85	169.8	120.8	161.7	156.1	129.2	105.0	126.8
1985-86	170.8	111.3	158.8	182.3	163.8	107.6	119.8
1986-87	179.4	121.3	139.4	212.3	175.0	128.6	156.0
1987-88	195.4	140.0	160.0	204.8	146.3	122.1	170.9
1988-89	232.2	152.1	195.5	224.4	147.4	125.2	190.4
1989-90	NA	NA	NA	NA	NA	NA	NA
1990-91	**292.5**	**194.1**	**267.7**	**237.7**	**122.5**	**109.3**	**212.2**

* = Converted from the original base with the help of linking factors.
NA = Not available.
U.V.I.= Unit value index.
Q.I. = Quantum index.

Source: *Economic Survey*, 1991-92.

An Overview of India's Imports and Exports

TABLE 20.12: Composition of India's Imports

(*Percentage*)

Sl. No.	Commodity	1989-90	1990-91	1991-92 (April-September)
1.	Petroleum Oil and Lubricants	17.7	25.0	25.6
2.	Capital goods	24.9	24.2	23.1
3.	Pearls and precious stones	12.0	8.7	10.3
4.	Chemicals	7.8	7.4	8.6
5.	Fertilizers and Fertilizer Materials	5.0	4.1	5.5
6.	Iron and Steel	6.5	4.9	5.2
7.	Nonferrous Metals	3.5	2.6	1.6
8.	Cereals and pulses	1.7	1.5	1.0
9.	Edible Oils	0.6	0.8	0.3
	Others	20.2	20.8	18.9
	Total (Rs. in Crores)	35416	43193	21067

TABLE 20.13: Sources of India's Imports

(*Percentage*)

Sl. No.	Country	1989-90	1990-91	1991-92 (April-September)
1.	U.K.	8.4	6.7	1.5
2.	F.R.G.	7.8	8.0	8.0
3.	Other EEC	17.0	14.6	14.3
4.	U.S.A.	12.0	12.1	10.9
5.	Japan	8.0	7.5	8.0
6.	Other OECD	4.0	5.0	4.8
7.	U.S.S.R.	5.8	5.9	5.7
8.	Other East Europe	2.7	1.9	1.3
9.	OPEC	14.3	16.3	16.6
10.	Developing Countries (Non-OPEC)	17.0	18.4	19.8
11.	Others	3.0	3.5	9.2
	Total (Rs. in Crores)	35416	43193	21067

TABLE 20.14: Composition of India's Exports

(*Percentage*)

Sl. No.	Commodity	1989-90	1990-91	1991-92 (April-September)
1.	Agriculture and Allied products	17.6	19.4	19.6
2.	Leather and Leather Manufacturers	7.0	7.9	7.3
3.	Gems and Jewellery	19.1	16.1	16.9
4.	Readymade garments	11.7	12.3	11.5
5.	Engineering goods	11.9	11.9	11.4
6.	Chemicals	7.7	7.8	8.6
7.	Ores and Minerals	4.9	4.6	4.7
8.	Mineral Fuel and Lubricants	2.7	2.9	2.1
9.	Others	17.3	17.0	18.0
	Total (in Rs. Crores)	27682	32553	18711

TABLE 20.15: Destination of India's Exports

(*Percentage*)

Sl. No.	Country	1989-90	1990-91	1991-92 (April-September)
1.	U.S.A.	16.2	14.7	17.0
2.	Japan	9.9	9.3	9.8
3.	U.S.S.R.	16.1	16.1	9.1
4.	F.R.G.	6.4	7.8	7.1
5.	U.K.	5.8	6.5	6.6
6.	Other EEC	12.7	13.1	17.0
7.	Other OECD	2.3	2.0	1.6
8.	Other East Europe	3.2	1.7	2.0
9.	OPEC	6.6	5.6	7.7
10.	Developing countries (Non OPEC)	15.3	16.8	20.2
11.	Others	5.3	6.2	5.8
	Total (in Rs. Crores)	27681	32553	18711

21

MONETARY TRENDS

21.1 Money and Credit

Money supply growth during the current financial year has been faster than in the previous year, even though both the net Reserve Bank credit to the Central Government and bank credit to the commercial sector have expanded at a lower rate. This is primarily because of the substantial build up in foreign exchange reserves.

The stance of the monetary policy in 1991-92 was restrictive to contain the growth of aggregate demand to fight the twin problems of high inflation and adverse balance of payments. Quarterly targets have been set for net domestic assets of RBI, net RBI credit to the Central Government and gross fiscal deficit as also the floor for net official foreign exchange reserves. In addition, indicative targets have been set for broad money (M3) growth and bank credit to Government.

The current financial year is marked by several important changes in monetary policy. The Bank Rate was revised twice and raised from 10 to 12 per cent. Interest rates on term deposits (particularly short-term deposits) were also raised significantly in order to ensure their competitiveness in the market. Interest rates on bank advances of all categories, therefore, underwent upward revision both in keeping with these changes and as an anti-inflationary measure. Higher rates on export credit and larger export credit refinance facilities were introduced to encourage banks in their credit support to exporters.

Among other measures of credit control introduced in 1991-92 are (a) 10 per cent Incremental Cash Reserve Ratio on the increase in net demand and time liabilities of the scheduled commercial banks over May 3, 1991 level; (b) withdrawal of all refinance facilities (except export credit refinance facility, by RBI; (c) imposition of a ceiling on the effective drawing power of big borrowers with aggregate credit limits of Rs. 1 crore and above from May 9 to September 30, 1991 and (d) extension/tightening of selective credit controls on bank advances against price-sensitive essential commodities such as wheat, rice/paddy, cotton and kapas and pulses. The higher minimum cash margin imposed on bank finance for imports in March-April, 1991 came to be reduced in stages with gradual improvement in foreign exchange reserves and also to help exporters in making necessary imports.

The uptrend in the credit sanctioned and disbursed by term lending financial institutions continued in the current financial year. A floor rate of 15 per cent came to replace their fixed lending rate of 14 per cent. Orderly growth of the secondary money market continued to be the concern of the Reserve Bank of India which also took measures to reduce the volatility of call money rates and liberalised the guidelines for issue of commercial paper (CP) and certificate of deposits (CD). The Discount and Finance House of India (DFHI) had large turnover in each major money market instrument. Home Loan Accounts Scheme of

National Housing Bank (NHB) was extended to select Housing Finance Companies (HFCs). NHB also launched National Housing (Voluntary Deposits) scheme to attract black money to social housing schemes.

21.2 Scheduled Commercial Banks

Table 21.1 presents some selected indicators of the operations of the scheduled commercial banks during 1989-90, 1990-91 and up to January 10, 1992 (Table 21.1). The demand deposits recorded much larger expansion than time deposits in the present financial year, relative to their expansion in the last financial year. Non-food credit to deposit ratio stood at 52.6 per cent on January 10, 1992 as against 57.7 per cent on January 11, 1991. Net balances of these banks with RBI improved significantly in the current financial year so far, mainly due to very large increases in their balances with RBI compared to that in 1990-91.

TABLE 21.1: Scheduled Commercial Banks: Variations in Selected Indicators

(Rs. crore)

Items	Variations during			
	1989-90 March 24, 1989 to March 23, 1990	1990-91 March 23, 1990 to March 22, 1991	1990-91 March 23, 1990 to Jan. 11, 1991(P)	1991-92 March 22, 1991 to Jan. 10, 1992(P)
1. Aggregate deposits (a + b)	26809	25583	18184	28384
(a) Demand deposits	5514	4337	2367	9193
(b) Time deposits	21295	21246	15817	19191
2. Borrowings from R.B.I.	—1128	1069	1621	—1346
3. Cash in hand and balances with R.B.I.	2291	554	4006	11047
(a) Cash in hand	204	156	176	174
(b) Balances with R.B.I.	2087	398	3830	10873
4. Net balances with R.B.I. [3 (b) -2]	3215	—671	2209	12219
5. Money at call and short notice	—1172	—489	—443	863
6. Bank credit (a + b)	16734	14848	9721	4422
(a) Public food procurement credit	1237	2500	2398	29
(b) Non-food bank credit	15497	12348	7323	4393
of which: to Priority Sector*	6164	2497	—	—
7. Investments in Government and other approved securities	9707	10696	9278	12080
(a) Government securities	6477	7706	6901	10740
(b) Other approved securities	3230	2990	2377	1340
8. Balances with other banks in current account	247	276	125	479
9. Credit-deposit ratio+	60.8	60.4	60.0	54.6
10. Non-food credit-deposit ratio+	59.6	58.1	57.7	52.6
11. Investment-deposit ratio+	38.6	39.0	39.8	39.4

P = Provisional

— Not available.

\+ Percentage at the end of the period.

* Data relate to 50 banks (49 from March 1990 and 48 from August 1990 due to merger) which account for 95 per cent of bank credit, and variations are based on last reporting Fridays of March.

21.3 External Commercial Borrowing

The country's reliance on external commercial borrowing has been substantial in recent years up to 1989-90 after which there has been a steep decline in this source of external capital. The fall in disbursements coupled with a sharp rise in debt-service payments, resulted in net negative transfer under external commercial borrowing in 1990-91. The situation deteriorated in the first half of 1991-92 (Table 21.2).

Several factors are responsible for the fall in the availability of commercial credit to India in 1990-91 and 1991-92. A major factor has been the overall shortage of capital in the international market due to the low level of savings in some of the major developed countries and the heavy demand on world savings arising from the unification of the Germanys, post-Gulf war reconstruction in West Asia, and restructuring of the East European countries. Banks were also diverting funds from credit expansion towards strengthening their capital base in order to meet capital adequacy requirements of the Bank for International Settlements. The Gulf crisis, political instability, and the erosion of international confidence in the economy resulted in successive downgrading of India's creditworthiness by international rating agencies further constraining India's access to commercial credits.

The fall in fresh borrowing from external commercial sources since 1990-91 is accompanied by a major shift in the composition of ECB approvals. Whereas, the share of bank loans and bonds fell considerably in this period, that of export credits rose. Indeed, in the second half of 1990-91 and first half of 1991-92 there was a spurt in approvals under exports credits partly compensating for the drying up of other sources of commercial credit. This is not surprising as export credits are not that much affected by the loss of creditworthiness as bank loans and bond issues, for the lender in the former case is usually protected by insurance cover offered by credit insurance agency of the concerned country.

The International Finance Corporation, Washington (IFC-W) is the major multilateral agency promoting productive private investment in developing countries by providing long-term loans and risk capital at commercial rates for maturity of 7 to 12 years. Since 1959, the IFC(W) has approved investments in India amounting to about $ 1.0 billion the bulk of which has been in the form of long-term loans. The IFC(W) investments in India have been mainly in sectors such as power, iron and steel, automobiles, chemicals and petrochemicals, and general manufacturing. Approvals for 1990-91 were $ 126 million and for 1991-92 up to November $ 222 million. In the context of deregulation of the Indian economy, IFC(W) is expected to play a more active role in promoting productive private investment, attracting foreign direct investment and also in mobilising resources from international capital markets.

21.4 Non-Resident Deposits

Non-resident deposits which had been a source of considerable support to India's balance of payments over past years received a serious setback in 1990-19 when they registered an accretion of only about $ 250 million against $ 1.3 billion in 1989-90. This reflected the erosion of international confidence in the Indian economy from the latter half of 1990-91 which worsened in the early half of 1991-92 leading to a further outflow of $ 1.5 billion during April-

TABLE 21.2: External Commercial Borrowing

	1985-86	1986-87	1987-88	1988-89	1989-90	1990-91	1991-92**
			(Rs. hundred crore)				
1. Authorisation	17.00	13.96	26.54	43.14	54.79	34.14	15.59
2. Gross disbursements	17.99	24.74	22.52	40.69	41.96	30.50	14.06
3. Debt service payments	11.75	15.65	17.36	22.24	30.41	40.60	21.69
(a) Amortisation	5.65	7.69	8.71	11.03	14.55	21.37	11.12
(b) Interest payments	6.10	7.69	8.65	11.21	15.86	18.69	10.57
4. Net capital inflow [2-3(a)]	12.34	16.78	13.81	29.66	27.41	9.13	2.94
5. Net capital transfer (2-3)	6.25	9.09	5.16	18.45	11.55	—9.56	—7.63
				($ Billion)			
1. Authorisations	1.39	1.09	2.05	2.98	3.29	1.90	0.68
2. Gross disbursements	1.47	1.94	1.74	2.81	2.52	1.70	0.61
3. Debt service payments	0.96	1.22	1.34	1.54	1.83	2.23	0.94
(a) Amortisation	0.46	0.62	0.67	0.76	0.87	1.19	0.48
(b) Interest payments	0.50	0.60	0.67	0.77	0.95	1.04	0.46
4. Net capital inflow [2-3)a)	1.01	1.31	1.07	2.05	1.65	0.51	0.13
5. Net capital transfer (2-3)	0.51	0.71	0.40	1.27	0.69	—0.53	—0.33

* Excludes borrowings upto one year maturity. The estimates are based of ECB Division of the Department of Economic Affairs, Ministry of Finance. External commercial borrowing include loans from commercial banks and other financial institutions, bonds and FRNs, supplies' credit, buyers' credits and credits from export credit agencies of concerned Governments, IFC(W), private sector borrowing from ADB, etc.

** For the period April-September 1991 only.

TABLE 21.3: Stocks and Flows under Non-resident Deposit Accounts

Year	NR(E)R Accounts		FCNR Accounts		Total	
	Outstanding at year end @	Inflow(+)/ Outflow(—)	Outstanding at year end**	Inflow(+)/ Outflow(—)	Outstanding at year end	Inflow(+)/Outflow(—)
1	2	3	4	5	6	7
			(Rs. hundred crore)			
1985-86	34.61	6.16	21.89	11.51	56.50	17.67
1986-87	43.36	4.77	35.11	11.73	78.47	16.50
1987-88	51.07	4.77	49.47	13.63	100.54	18.40
1988-89	58.99	2.35	82.55	22.30	141.54	24.65
1989-90	65.07	—0.04	113.24	21.79	178.31	21.75
1990-91	73.49	1.56	134.05	2.55	207.54	4.11
1991-92*	77.13	—2.02	142.63	—32.45	219.76	—34.47
			($ Billion)			
1985-86	2.81	0.50	1.78	0.94	4.59	1.44
1986-87	3.35	0.37	2.72	0.92	6.07	1.29
1987-88	3.94	0.37	3.83	1.05	7.77	1.42
1988-89	3.77	0.16	5.28	1.54	10.36	1.31
1989-90	2.78	—	6.58	1.31	9.05	1.70
1990-91	3.74	0.09	6.84	0.14	10.58	0.23
1991-92*	3.00	—0.09	5.50	—1.47	8.50	—1.56

@ Inclusive of accrued interest.
* Up to December 31,1991 and provisional.
** Exclusive of accrued interest.

December, 1991 under the FCNR accounts alone against an inflow of $ 397 million in the corresponding period of last year. The NR(E)R deposits also suffered, although marginally, showing an outflow of about $ 90 million during April-December, 1991 against an inflow of $ 30 million in the same period last year. As a result, the total outstanding balances under these two accounts put together declined from $ 10.6 billion at end-March, 1991 to $ 8.5 billion at end-December, 1991 (Table 21.3).

Two additional schemes were introduced to attract foreign exchange sources from non-resident Indians in the second half of 1991-92. On October 1, 1991, the State Bank of India launched its India Development Bonds for non-resident Indians (NRIs) and their overseas corporate bodies (OCBs). The bonds have a five-year maturity period and are denominated in US dollars and pound sterling. The dollar bonds carry an interest rate of 9.5 per cent and the sterling bonds 13.25 per cent. They are freely transferable among NRIs/OCBs as also among Indian residents who receive them as gifts from the former. These bonds are also free from income, wealth and gift taxes in India. The offer which was initially open up to November 30, 1991 was extended up to January 31, 1992. An amount of $ 1085 million and £ 165 million ($ 293 million) had been collected under the scheme as per information available till February 10, 1992.

The second new scheme for mobilising additional foreign exchange resources was entitled 'The Remittances in Foreign Exchange (Immunities) Scheme, 1991'. Under this, the source of funds, purpose and the nature of remittance would not be subject to scrutiny under the exchange control regulations and Direct Tax Laws. However, any income received by the person on the remitted amount would be subject to income tax. A sum of $ 766 million had been received under this scheme as per information available up to February 10, 1992.

21.5 Foreign Investment

Foreign investment has played a very limited role so far in the Indian economy (for example, direct foreign investment approvals in India during 1986-90 had been Rs. 900 crore or about Rs. 180 crore per annum) resulting from a relatively restrictive foreign investment regime followed by the Government till recently. Foreign investment was allowed generally in areas of hi-tech, sophisticated technologies and substantial exports. The normal ceiling for foreign investment was 40 per cent of the total equity capital, but a higher percentage of foreign equity was considered in priority industries if the technology was sophisticated and not available in the country of if the venture was largely export-oriented.

The Government has established a more liberalised foreign investment policy as a part of the new industrial policy announced in July 1991. The new regime of foreign investment contains the following: (i) as against the past policy of considering all foreign investment on a case-by-case basis and that too within the normal ceiling of 40 per cent of total equity investment, the new policy provides for automatic approval of direct foreign investment upto 51 per cent foreign equity holding in 34 specified high-priority, capital-intensive, hi-technology industries provided the foreign equity covers the foreign exchange involved in importing capital goods, and outflows on account of dividend payments are balanced by export earnings over a period of 7 years from the commencement of production; (ii) foreign technology agreements are also liberalised for the 34 industries with firms left free to negotiate the terms of technology transfer based on their own commercial judgement and without the need for prior Government approval for hiring of foreign technicians and foreign testing of indigenously developed technologies; (iii) in order to avail of professional marketing activities for systematic exploration of world markets for foreign products, foreign equity holding up to 51 per cent would be permitted for trading companies as well; and (iv) a special Board (Foreign Investment Promotion Board) has been set up to look into large foreign investment projects where higher foreign equity limits of more than 51 per cent may be permitted.

Although it is too early to expect a substantial inflow of foreign investment resulting from the above changes, the response of the new foreign investment policy measures has been encouraging so far. The overseas investment approvals reached a peak of Rs. 522 crores during 1991 (including approvals given by the Reserve Bank of India up to December 22, 1991) as against only Rs. 128 crores during 1990.

21.6 **Foreign Debt**

India's medium and long-term external debt, consisting of external assistance on Government and non-Government accounts, external commercial borrowings and the IMF liabilities, amounted to Rs. 1,004 hundred crore ($ 51.1 billion) at the end of 1990-91 which constituted about 19 per cent of GDP. Including NRI deposits, the country's external debt (other than short-term debt) stood at Rs. 1212 hundred crore ($ 61.7 billion) constituting about 23 per cent of GDP. Adding the estimates of short-term debt of maturities up to one year, India's aggregate external debt amounted to Rs. 1,307 hundred crore or $ 66.5 billion as on March 31, 1991 which was around 25 per cent of the country's GDP.

It may be noted that short-term debt constitutes a relatively low proportion of India's aggregate debt; the share of short-term debt in total external debt rose from about 4 per cent at the end of 1988-89 to about 7 per cent at the end of 1990-91. The short-term debt is in the nature of suppliers' credits of finance normal import trade as well as bankers' acceptance facilities arranged through Indian banks. India's short-term debt is largely owed by public sector canalising agencies incurred for the import of POL, fertilisers, edible oil and essential raw materials. From the second quarter of 1990-91, Indian banks found it increasingly difficult to raise resources through short-term credit on the one hand, and the cost of alternative sources of short-term credit through suppliers' credits and credits from non-Indian banks rose, on the other.

Drawals from the IMF

In the context of heavy withdrawals from non-resident deposits and the drying up of the source of commercial credits, the much needed support to the country's balance of payments was provided mainly by the IMF. After the completion of the drawings under the extended arrangement in April 1984, India did not take any recourse to the IMF till December 1990. The gross drawings from the fund from January 1991 to January 1992 amounted to SDR 2.2 billion equivalent to $ 3.0 billion or Rs. 65 hundred crore. Details of these drawals are given in Table 21.4.

TABLE 21.4: Drawals from the IMF, January 1991 to January 1992*

Period	Name of Facility	Amount		
		SDR bn.	$bn.	Rs. hun cr.
January 1991	First credit tranche	0.55	0.79	14.50
Jan.-Sep. 1991	Compensatory and contingency financing facility (CCFF)	1.35	1.88	41.08
Nov. 1991— Jan. 1992	Stand-by credit**	0.27	0.38	9.88

* The drawal of SDR 487 million during July-September 1990 of the reserve tranche is not regarded as the use of Fund credit as it is treated as part of the country's external resources which can be drawn up to its full amount at any time without conditions.

** A total of SDR 1,656 billion ($ 2,262 billion) to be disbursed in 8 tranches over a 20-month period from November 1991 to June 1993.

21.7 Narasimham Committee on Financial System

A nine member committee under the chairmanship of Shri M. Narasimham, former Governor, Reserve Bank of India was set up by the Government of India to examine the existing structure of the financial system and its various components and to make recommendations for improving the efficiency and effectiveness of the system, with particular reference to economy of operations, accountability and profitability and for infusing greater competitive vitality into the system so as to enable the banks and financial institutions to respond more effectively to the emerging credit needs of the economy. The committee was also asked to review the existing supervisory arrangement relating to the various entities in the financial sector, in particular the commercial banks and term lending institutions, and to make recommendations for ensuring appropriate and effective supervision. It was also expected of the committee to review the existing legislative framework and to suggest necessary amendments for implementing the recommendations.

The report of the Committee was tabled in both the houses of Parliament on December 17, 1991. The Committee's approach to the subject of financial sector reform was based on three broad and interrelated premises. The first was the perception that the spirit of competitive efficiency that is sought to be brought about in the real sectors of the economy should also cover the financial sector for the exercise to be meaningful and successful. The second premise was that to be able to perform this task effectively in an environment of competitive efficiency, the financial system itself should be healthy and profitable. The third premise was that for the financial sector to operate on an efficient basis it would need to have a measure of operational flexibility and, more importantly, autonomy in decision making and that credit and investment decisions should be based on professionalism and be free from any type of extraneous pressure.

The Committee has, *inter-alia,* recommended, (a) establishment of a four tier hierarchy for the banking structure with 3 or 4 large banks including State Bank of India at the top (which could be international in character) and rural banks (including RRBs) at the bottom (confined to rural areas and mainly engaged in financing agriculture and related activities); (b) hiving off supervisory functions over banks and financial institutions to a separate quasi-autonomous body under aegis of the RBI; (c) a phased achievement of 8 per cent capital adequacy ratio as recommended by the Basle Committee; (d) abolition of branch licensing policy; (e) phased reduction in SLR starting from 1991-92; (f) deregulation of interest rates which are to be related to the Bank Rate on the basis of guidelines given by the Chakravarty Committee; (g) competition among financial instructions which will adopt a syndicating or participating (instead of consortium) approach; (h) retention by IDBI of only its refinancing role and delegation of its direct lending activity to a separate corporate body; (i) prudential guidelines governing the functioning of financial institutions and ; (j) proper classification of assets and full disclosure and transparency of accounts of banks and financial Institutions.

The Committee also made recommendations regarding directed investments and credit programmes and setting up of a separate institution by the Government of India to be known as Asset Reconstruction Fund with the express purpose of taking over a portion of the loan portfolio of banks which has become bad and doubtful and whose recovery is being hampered by the slow legal process. Thus, the recommendations seek to address issues of declining profitability and efficiency and seek to restore the autonomy and flexibility of operations within an overall framework of reasonable monetary stability. They cover policy aspects, organisational issues, accounting practices and operational 'procedures but underlying them all is the central point of qualitative improvement of the advances portfolio and attention to enhancing the inherent strength of the institutions.

21.8 Goiporia Committee on Customer Service in Banks

The improvement in the customer service in banks has long been a concern of the Reserve Bank of India and the Government. In the post bank nationalisation era, this matter assumed greater importance and was examined by both the Banking Commission (chairman: Shri R.G. Saraiya), 1972 and the Working Group on customer service in banks (Chairman : Shri R.K. Talwar), 1975. To oversee the implementation of the recommendations made by the latter, a standing committee on customer service in banks was also set up with representatives from the Government, RBI, banks, and Indian Banks' Association. Special drive was made to record and monitor the disposal of complaints made by the customers against services rendered by their banks.

In September, 1990, a new committee was set up by RBI under the chairmanship of Shri M.N. Goiporia, State Bank of India to look into the causes of below-par customer service in banks, to identify structural and operational rigidities in the banking system, find ways and means to upgrade technology in banks, address deficiencies in bank service and suggest ways to improve work culture among bank employees. The committee submitted its report on 6th December, 1991.

In its report, the Committee has observed that disservice to customer should be treated as delinquency and that an indifferent and casual approach to work should not go unnoticed. The report has identified quite a number of areas of customer service which call for improvement. Among its major recommendations are (i) extension of banking hours for all transactions except cash, (ii) change in the commencement of working hour for bank staff to facilitate timely opening of the bank counters, (iii) immediate credit of outstation cheques upto Rs. 5,000 as against Rs. 2,500 at present, (iv) enhancement of interest rate on

savings account, (v) introduction of tax benefits against bank deposits, (vi) full use of discretionary powers vested in the bank staff at all levels, (vii) expeditious despatch of documents lodged for collection and regular follow-up with the foreign bank to facilitate timely realisation of export proceeds in the case of export finance, (vii) extension of teller's duties, (ix) modernisation of banks, (x) opening of specialised branches for different customer groups, (xi) a new instrument in the form of Bank Orders and (xii) introduction of restricted holidays in banks.

Source: *Economic Survey*, 1991-92.

22

AGRICULTURE

As a result of a good monsoon during 1990-91, foodgrains production reached 176 million tonnes, 3 per cent more than in 1989-90. The production of rice and wheat was 74.6 million tonnes and 54.5 million tonnes respectively. Among the commercial crops, sugarcane and oilseeds reached production levels of 240.3 million tonnes and 18.5 million tonnes respectively.

Due to the erratic behaviour of the monsoon, it is expected that the total production of foodgrains during 1991-92 may fall below last year's level—a setback in production is anticipated for kharif foodgrains and the major oilseed crops, groundnut and soyabean. However, the prospects of rapeseed and mustard are bright. The prospects of sugarcane are excellent. Cotton production during 1991-92 may also be higher. Due to a fall in area, production of jute and mesta during 1991-92 may be a little lower than last year's production.

The irrigation potential estimated to have been created by 1990-91 was about 82.8 million hectares. However, there is a cumulative gap in the utilisation of the potential of about 8.6 million hectares till 1990-91.

Fertiliser consumption reached 12.6 million tonnes in 1990-91 and is expected to about 13.6 million tonnes in 1991-92. Fertiliser subsidy increased from Rs. 3201 crore in 1988-89 to Rs. 4389 crore during 1990-91. As a part of fiscal correction, the Union Budget for 1991-92 increased issue prices of fertilizers by 30 per cent while completely exempting small and marginal farmers from the price increase.

During 1990-91 milk production is estimated to have reached 53.7 million tonnes while egg production has reached a level of 21 billion eggs. As a result of delicensing, dairy industry may face some initial adjustment problems, but it is likely to emerge more competitive and efficient. Fish production in the county has reached 3.8 million tonnes during 1990-91. The performance of agricultural production during 1980 onwards is shown in Table 22.1.

The Eighth Plan has given priority to the growth and diversification of the agricultural sector, which is expected to generate surpluses for exports. The targets and achievements of agricultural production from 1988-89 onwards are given in Table 22.2.

Rice

The area under rice during 1990-91 was 42.60 million hectares. Irrigation coverage is 43 per cent; the remaining area is rainfed. The increase in rice output and productivity in the country owes much to the Integrated Programmes for Rice Development which covers 24 states. Among the major states, Assam, Uttar Pradesh, Karnataka and Bihar showed an increase in rice production during 1990-91. In Andhra Pradesh and Tamil Nadu, production declined owing to a decrease in area coverage; in West Bengal and Punjab, rice production declined owing to lower yield per hectare. A target of 76.50 million tonnes of rice has been fixed for 1991-92.

TABLE 22.1: Agricultural Production

(*Million Tonnes/Bales**)

Crops	1978-79	1979-80	1980-81	1981-82	1982-83	1983-84	1984-85	1985-86	1986-87	1987-88	1988-89	1989-90	1990-91 (P)
Rice	53.8	42.3	53.6	53.2	47.1	60.1	58.4	63.8	60.6	56.8	70.5	73.6	74.6
	(2.1)	(-21.4)	(26.7)	(-0.7)	(-11.5)	(27.6)	(-3.0)	(9.4)	(-5.0)	(-6.3)	(24.1)	(4.4)	(1.4)
Wheat	35.5	31.8	36.3	37.4	42.8	45.5	44.1	47.1	44.3	46.2	54.1	49.8	54.5
	(11.0)	(-10.4)	(14.1)	(3.0)	(14.4)	(6.3)	(-3.1)	(6.8)	(-5.9)	(4.3)	(17.1)	(-7.9)	(9.4)
Pulses	12.2	8.6	10.6	11.5	11.9	12.9	12.0	13.4	11.7	11.0	13.8	12.9	14.1
	(1.7)	(-29.5)	(23.3)	(8.5)	(3.5)	(8.4)	(-7.0)	(11.7)	(-12.7)	(-6.0)	(25.5)	(-6.5)	(9.3)
Coarse grains	30.4	27.0	29.0	31.1	27.8	33.9	31.2	26.2	26.8	26.4	31.5	34.8	33.1
	(1.3)	(-11.2)	(7.4)	(7.2)	(-10.6)	(21.9)	(-8.0)	(-16.0)	(2.3)	(-1.5)	(19.3)	(10.5)	(-4.9)
Kharif Foodgrains	78.1	63.2	77.7	79.4	69.9	89.2	84.5	85.2	80.2	74.6	95.6	101.0	99.9
	(0.5)	(-19.1)	(22.9)	(2.2)	(-12.0)	(27.6)	(-5.3)	(0.8)	(-5.9)	(-7.0)	(28.2)	(5.6)	(-1.1)
Rabi Foodgrains	53.8	46.5	51.9	53.9	59.6	63.2	61.0	65.2	63.2	65.8	74.3	70.0	76.3
	(10.5)	(-13.6)	(11.6)	(3.9)	(10.6)	(6.0)	(-3.5)	(6.9)	(-3.1)	(4.1)	(12.9)	(-5.0)	(9.0)
All Foodgrains	131.9	109.7	129.6	133.3	129.5	152.4	145.5	150.4	143.4	140.4	169.9	171.0	176.2
	(4.4)	(-16.8)	(18.1)	(2.9)	(-2.9)	(17.7)	(-4.5)	(3.4)	(-4.7)	(-2.1)	(21.0)	(0.6)	(3.0)
Groundnut	6.2	5.8	5.0	7.2	5.3	7.1	6.4	5.1	5.9	5.8	9.7	8.1	7.6
	(1.6)	(-6.4)	(-13.8)	(44.0)	(-26.4)	(34.0)	(-9.9)	(-20.3)	(15.7)	(-1.7)	(67.2)	(-16.5)	(-6.2)
Rapeseed and Mustard	1.9	1.4	2.3	2.4	2.2	2.6	3.1	2.7	2.6	3.5	4.4	4.1	5.2
	(11.8)	(-26.3)	(64.3)	(4.3)	(-8.3)	(18.2)	(19.2)	(-12.9)	(-3.7)	(34.6)	(25.7)	(-6.8)	(26.8)
Oilseed @	10.1	8.7	9.4	12.1	10.0	12.7	13.0	10.8	11.3	12.7	18.0	16.9	18.5
	(4.1)	(13.9)	(8.0)	(28.7)	(-17.4)	(27.0)	(2.4)	(-16.9)	(4.6)	(12.4)	(41.7)	(-6.1)	(9.5)
Sugarcane	151.7	128.8	154.2	186.4	189.5	174.1	170.3	170.7	186.1	196.7	203.0	225.6	240.3
	(-14.3)	(-15.1)	(19.7)	(20.9)	(1.7)	(-8.1)	(-2.2)	(0.2)	(9.0)	(5.7)	(3.2)	(11.1)	(6.5)
Cotton (Lint)*	8.0	7.6	7.0	7.9	7.5	6.4	8.5	8.7	6.9	6.4	8.7	11.4	9.8
	(11.1)	(-5.0)	(-7.9)	(12.9)	(-5.1)	(-14.7)	(32.8)	(2.4)	(-20.7)	(-7.2)	(35.9)	(31.0)	(-14.0)
Jute and Mesta*	8.3	8.0	8.2	8.4	7.2	7.7	7.8	12.6	8.7	6.8	7.9	8.3	9.1
	(15.3)	(-3.6)	(2.5)	(2.4)	(-14.3)	(6.9)	(1.3)	(61.5)	(-31.0)	(-21.8)	(16.2)	(5.1)	(9.6)

* 170 kgs. each for cotton and 180 kgs. each for jute and mesta. P = Provisional

@ Nine major oilseeds including groundnut, castorseed, sesamum, rapeseed and mustard, linseed, safflower, nigerseed, sunflower and soyabean

Note: Figures in brackets are per cent increase or decrease over the year.

Agricultural year is from July to June.

TABLE 22.2: Targets and Achievements of Agricultural Production

(Million Tonnes/Bales)

Crop	1988-89		1989-90		1990-91		1991-92	
	Target	Achievement	Target	Achievement	Target	Achievement	Target	Likely Achievement
1	2	3	4	5	6	7	8	9
1. Rice	68.0	70.5	72.5	73.6	73.7	74.6	76.5	70.5—72.5
2. Wheat	52.3	54.1	54.0	49.8	54.5	54.5	56.5	54.0—56.0
3. Coarse Cereals	33.0	31.5	33.8	34.8	33.3	33.1	34.0	29.0—30.5
4. Pulses	13.3	13.8	14.7	12.9	15.0	14.1	15.5	14.0—-14.5
5. Total Foodgrains	166.6	169.9	175.0	171.0	176.5	176.2	182.5	167.5—173.5
6. Sugarcane	195.0	203.0	212.0	225.6	220.0	240.3	230.0	235.0—240.0
7. Oilseeds	15.7	18.0	16.17	16.9	18.0	18.5	18.5	17.0—17.5
8. Cotton*	9.8	8.7	10.0	11.4	11.5	9.8	12.0	10.0—10.5
9. Jute and Mesta**	9.2	7.9	9.5	8.3	9.0	9.1	9.1	8.5—9.0

* Bale of 170 Kgs.

** Bale of 180 Kgs.

Wheat

Wheat production witnessed an increase during 1990-91 in all the major growing Sates of Bihar, Gujarat, Haryana, Madhya Pradesh, Punjab, Rajasthan and Uttar Pradesh. The area covered under the crop has reached 24.0 million hectares.

The productivity of wheat has increased substantially; in 1990-91 it was 3.4 times as compared to the 1950-51 level. A target of 56.50 million tonnes of wheat production has been fixed for the current rabi 1991-92 season.

Coarse Grains

The area covered under coarse grains; namely, jowar, bajra, maize, ragi, small millets and barley, was of the order of 36.55 million hectares during 1990-91. The production of all coarse grains crops, except barley and bajra, declined. There was a fall of 3 per cent in the area covered under coarse grains. For the year 1991-92, a target of 34 million tonnes has been fixed.

Pulses

The production of pulses, reached 14.06 million tonnes in 1990-91, an increase of 9.4 per cent over the previous year. While gram, the major pulse crop, recorded a 23 per cent increase to reach 5.20 million tonnes, the other kharif and rabi pulses also showed marked increases of 8-10 per cent. The output of arhar, however, declined from a level of 2.75 million tonnes in 1989-90 to 2.43 million tonnes in 1990-91.

Pulses are grown mainly under unirrigated conditions; only about 9 per cent of the area under pulses has assured irrigation facilities. The major pulses (arhar and gram) are being produced in the states of Gujarat, Haryana, Madhya Pradesh, Maharashtra, Orissa, Rajasthan and Uttar Pradesh. Gram and arhar are grown in an area of about 7.4 million hectares and 3.6 million hectares, respectively. Gram accounted for 30.4 per cent of total area and 37 per cent of the pulse production during 1990-91; arhar accounted for 14.8 per cent of the area and 17.3 per cent of production in 1990-91.

The production of pulses in 1991-92 has been targetted at 15.5 million tonnes (6.1 million tonnes in kharif and 9.4 million tonnes in rabi season). This is to be achieved through the continuance of National Pulses Development Project (NPDP) and the Special Foodgrains Production Programme (SFPP)—Pulses. The main objective of NPDP is to increase production by adopting location-specific technology. NPDP is supplemented by a special programme under SFPP—Pulses, covering schemes for: (a) plant protection umbrella for gram and arhar crops against pod borers, cut worms and termites in 11 states and (b) the expansion of area under summer moong/urad through the distribution of seeds at concessional rates. Recently, pulses have also been included in the mandate of the Technology Mission on Oilseeds. An integrated approach to crop production technology and price support/market intervention is being adopted to increase productivity.

Oilseeds

The favourable monsoon assisted in increasing the production of nine oilseeds to a level of 18.5 million tonnes during 1990-91. This was achieved despite a 14 per cent decline in the production of kharif groundnut because of adverse weather conditions in Gujarat. The improvement in oilseeds production became possible on account of higher production of the main rabi oilseeds in 1990-91.

Cotton

Cotton is grown in 7.4 million hectares. Only 30 per cent of the crop is irrigated. Cotton production fell from 11.42 million bales in 1989-90 to 9.76 million bales in 1990-91. The area under the crop in Gujarat, Karnataka, Punjab and Tamil Nadu declined considerably. Only Andhra Pradesh recorded substantial increase in production. The pest heliothis attacked the crop at the flowering stage in Punjab, Haryana and Rajasthan. In other states, unfavourable weather conditions led to lower productivity. A target of 12 million bales has been fixed for 1991-92.

Jute and Mesta

Production of jute and mesta increased from 8.29 million bales in 1989-90 to 9.1 million bales in 1990-91. All the major producing states, namely; West Bengal, Assam, Andhra Pradesh, Bihar and Orissa, registered a substantial increase. A target of 9.1 million bales has been fixed for 1991-92.

Sugarcane

Favourable weather and Government measures, such as price incentives raised sugarcane production to 240.3 million tonnes in 1990-91 as against 225.6 million tonnes in 1989-90. Uttar Pradesh contributed 43 per cent. The increase in production was mainly due to an increase in area.

Sugar production in 1990-91 aggregated 11.9 million tonnes as against 11 million tonnes in 1989-90. In 1991-92, sugar production is expected to reach 12 million tonnes. The increase in the availability of sugar led the Government to allow export of 0.56 million tonnes of sugar. The Statutory Minimum Price (SMP) for 1991-92 was increased to Rs. 26 per quintal from Rs. 24 announced earlier. A further increase of the SMP to Rs. 27 has been announced for 1992-93.

Tea

Production of tea increased from 544 million kg in 1979-80 to around 719 million kg in 1990-91. The increase in production was achieved mainly through an increase in yield, from 1490 kg to around 1700 kg per hectare. There has recently been a considerable increase in tea production in South India. The average yield is about 2000 kg per hectare in South India as against about 1600 kg in North India.

Tea production during 1990-91 reached 719 million kg compared to 703 million kg in 1989-90. As tea is one of the main agro-exports, the Government has made vigorous efforts to increase its production. The Tea Board is operating a number of schemes. The target for production in 1991-92 is 735 million kg.

The domestic market takes about two-thirds of the tea output. Domestic demand increased from 328 million kg in 1985-86 to 500 million kg in 1989-90. Although exports of tea declined from 210 million kg in 1989-90 to 199 million kg in 1990-91, export earnings increased from Rs. 905 crore in 1989-90 to Rs. 1045 crore in 1990-91. The average realisation rose from about Rs. 43 to about Rs. 52 per kg. A target of tea exports of 210 million kg valued at Rs. 1200 crore, has been fixed for 1991-92.

Coffee

Coffee production has been fluctuating depending upon weather conditions. Moreover, coffee is a biennial crop. Coffee production increased from 200,000 tonnes in 1984-85 to 215,000 tonnes in 1988-89. In 1990-91, the production was around 173,000 tonnes.

Most of the coffee produced in the country is exported; domestic consumption is stable around 55,000 tonnes. 111,000 tonnes of coffee worth Rs. 278 crore was exported in 1990-91 as against 130,000 tonnes, valued at Rs. 363 crore, in 1989-90. The decline in export earnings was mainly due to a fall in the international prices after quotas were suspended.

Rubber

Government has been making energetic efforts to increase the production of natural rubber. Production of natural rubber is estimated to be 365,000 tonnes in 1991-92 compared to 330,000 tonnes in 1990-91. The increase in production was due to an increase in area as well as an improvement in yield per hectare. It is estimated that around 461,000 hectares will be under rubber in 1991-92. As a result of promotional efforts, in addition to the traditional rubber growing states of Kerala and Tamil Nadu, other non-traditional states have also succeeded in growing natural rubber.

With the growth of the automobile and the road transport industry, consumption of rubber has increased over the years. It is expected to increase from 364,000 tonnes in 199-91 to around 380,000 tonnes in 1991-92. The gap between domestic demand and supply is normally met through canalised imports. In 1990-91, around 31,700 tonnes was imported as against 26,500 tonnes in 1989-90. With the Rubber Board taking continuous measures to improve rubber production, no canalised imports of natural rubber is expected in 1991-92.

Factors Influencing Agricultural Production

Agricultural production depends on a number of factors ranging from weather conditions to input applications and institutional support. Since most of the cropped area does not have assured irrigation, monsoon play a crucial role.

Monsoon

The south-west monsoon during 1991 turned out to be somewhat on the lower side of the normal. In the south-west monsoon season from 1 June to 30 September, 1991 the country-wide rainfall was 92 per cent of the long period average. Eighty per cent of the meteorological sub-divisions (28 out of 35) got normal to excess rainfall. However, the weakening of the monsoon for quite some time from the middle of June, 1991, and its subsequent erratic behaviour, adversely affected agricultural operations, particularly in north and north-western parts of India. Both paddy and groundnut crops were affected.

Reservoir Situation

The weakening of the monsoon for some time and its further erratic behaviour has affected water levels in tanks and reservoirs. The total live storage in 56 important reservoirs monitored by the Central Water Commission in the last week of September 1991 was 2.7 per cent lower than the level of last year: it came down from 100.37 TMC to 97.62 TMC.

Irrigation

Punjab, Haryana, Western Uttar Pradesh, parts of Andhra Pradesh and Tamil Nadu, have assured irrigation facilities. At the end of 1989-90, 32.9 million hectares of land was under major and medium irrigation and 46.8 million hectares under minor irrigation. Another 3.02 million hectares is estimated to have been added in 1990-91 (0.69 million hectares through major and medium and 2.33 million hectares through minor irrigation). Thus the total potential likely to have been created by the end of 1990-91 adds up to 82.8 million hectares. Till the end of Seventh Plan, about Rs. 25,813 crore was spent by the Government for the creation of an irrigation potential of 32.9 million hectares under the major and medium projects. In spite of this massive investment, the utilisation of the created potential is considerably low. The cumulative gap in the utilisation of the potential till the end of 1990-91 is about 8.6 million hectares. The details are given in Table 22.3.

TABLE 22.3: Development of Irrigation Potential and its Utilisation

(*Million hectares*)

Item	Achievement upto Seventh Plan end	Expected achievement during 1990-91	Expected cumulative achievement upto 1990-91	Target for 1991-92
1. Major and medium irrigation Potential	32.91	0.69	33.60	0.64
Utilisation	27.89	0.71	28.60	0.64
2. Minor irrigation				
Potential	46.83	2.33	49.16	2.33
Utilisation	43.53	2.03	45.56	2.06
3. Total Potential	79.74	3.02	82.76	2.99
Utilisation	71.42	2.74	74.16	2.70

The distribution of certified/quality seeds increased from 5.70 million quintals in 1989-90 to 5.71 million quintals in 1990-91. The distribution of certified seeds increased from 3.9 million quintals in 1989-90 to 4.1 million quintals during 1990-91. A target of 4.9 million quintals of certified seeds to be distributed has been fixed for 1991-92.

TABLE 22.4: Area Under High Yielding Varieties of Seeds

(*Million Hectares*)

Crop	Seventh Plan Target	1985-86	1986-87	1987-88	1988-89	1989-90	1990-91*	1991-92 (Target)
1	2	3	4	5	6	7	8	9
Paddy	32.0	23.5 (57.0)	24.0 (58.4)	22.1 (57.3)	25.4 (60.8)	26.2 (62.1)	28.1	30.0
Wheat	22.0	19.1 (83.0)	19.2 (83.0)	19.7 (85.4)	20.2 (83.8)	20.3 (86.4)	20.4	22.0
Jowar	6.5	6.1 (37.6)	5.5 (34.5)	6.1 (38.7)	6.1 (41.8)	6.9 (46.0)	6.7	8.0
Bajra	6.5	5.0 (46.8)	5.3 (46.8)	4.0 (45.4)	5.9 (49.0)	5.6 (51.4)	5.1	6.0
Maize	3.0	1.8 (31.0)	2.2 (37.0)	2.2 (38.8)	2.5 (42.4)	2.3 (39.0)	2.6	3.0
Ragi	—	—	—	—	—	—	1.1	1.0
Total	70.0	55.4	56.2	54.1	60.1	61.2	63.9	70.0

* Provisional

Note: Figures in parentheses give the percentage of HYV area to total area under the crop.

Fertilisers

For improving the yields of different crops, proper application of fertilisers is crucial. Consumption of fertilisers reached 12.6 million tonnes in 1990-91 and is expected to be of the order of 13.6 million tonnes in 1991-92. Trends in fertiliser consumption during the 1980s are given in Table 22.5.

TABLE: 22.5: Consumption of Chemical Fertilisers

(*Million tonnes of nutrients*)

Year	Nitrogenous	Phosphatic	Potassic	Total NPK
1980-81	3.7	1.2	0.6	5.5
1981-82	4.1	1.3	0.7	6.1
1982-83	4.2	1.5	0.7	6.4
1983-84	5.2	1.7	0.8	7.7
1984-85	5.5	1.9	0.8	8.2
1985-86	5.7	2.0	0.8	8.5
1986-87	5.7	2.1	0.9	8.7
1987-88	5.7	2.2	0.9	8.8
1988-89	7.3	2.7	1.1	11.1
1989-90	7.4	3.0	1.2	11.6
1990-91 (Provisional)	8.0	3.3	1.3	12.6
1991-92 (Anticipated)	8.5	3.6	1.5	13.6

Production of fertilisers has shown a gradual increase over the years. During 1990-91 the production of nitrogenous and phosphatic fertilisers was about 9 million tonnes. The gap in the domestic demand is met through imports. As fertiliser is one of the crucial inputs in improving crop yields and its price affects the cost of cultivation, Fertiliser Retention Price and Subsidy Scheme was introduced with effect from 1 November, 1977 under which fertilisers are supplied at a uniform and subsidised prices to the farmers throughout the country. The details of fertiliser production, its imports and subsidies are given in Table 22.6.

TABLE 22.6: Fertilisers: Production, Imports and Subsidies

Year	Production (N+P) (000 Tonnes)	Imports (000 Tonnes)	Subsidies (Rs. Crore)		
			On imported fertilisers	On domestic fertilisers	Total
1979-80	2983	2005	282	321	603
1980-81	3005	2759	335	170	505
1981-82	4093	2041	100	275	375
1982-83	4404	1132	55	550	605
1983-84	4533	1355	142	900	1042
1984-85	5181	3624	727	1200	1927
1985-86	5756	3399	324	1600	1924
1986-87	7070	2310	197	1700	1897
1987-88	7131	984	114	2050	2164
1988-89	8964	1608	201	3000	3201
1989-90	8543	3114	771	3771	4542
1990-91	9044	2758	659	3730	4389
1991-92	10000 @	2793	1100 *	2900 *	4000 *

@ Target

* Budget Estimates.

Source: *Economic Survey*, 1991-92.

Food Procurement

The Food Corporation of India achieved an all-time high in its procurement function by procuring 110.74 lakh tonnes of wheat during 1990-91 rabi marketing season, and 126.56 lakh tonnes of paddy during 1990-91 kharif marketing season.

The Food Corporation of India and the State Governments together operated 7,757 purchase centres during rabi 1990-91 and 3,938 purchase centres during kharif 1990-91. The procurement of wheat during 1991-92 rabi marketing season could, however, be only 77.51 lakh tonnes. The reasons for less procurement were higher open market prices of wheat than the minimum support price of Rs.225 per quintal fixed by the government and large scale purchase by traders and holding back of stocks by farmers in the hope of getting higher prices later in the year. The procurement of rice (including paddy in terms of rice) during 1991-92 kharif marketing season which commenced on October 1, 1991 had been 35.55 lakh tonnes as on 18-11-1991 as compared to 41.49 lakh tonnes during the corresponding period of previous season.

Source: *Yojana,* January 15,1992.

23

ATOMIC ENERGY

General Survey

Unit-1 of Narora Atomic Power Station, the first of the standardised PHWR, commenced commercial operation, and construction work on Unit-2 was nearing completion. Rehabilitation work at the Madras Atomic Power Station Units 1 and 2 also progressed satisfactorily.

The heavy water plants at Baroda, Tuticorin, Thal, and Kota continued satisfactory operation. The Heavy Water Plant at Hazira, and one stream of the Manuguru plant, were commissioned during the year.

The Nuclear Fuel Complex produced sufficient quantities of fuel for meeting the refuelling needs of the operating stations — RAPS-1&2, MAPS-1 and 2, NAPS-1, as well as the first load of NAPP-2.

At Tarapur, the Advanced Fuel Fabrication Facility for the production of mixed oxide fuel commenced operation, the Spent Fuel Storage Facility was commissioned and the Waste Immobilisation Plant was successfully operated.

Some of the facilities commissioned during the year were Sewage Hygienisation Research Irradiator (SHRI) at Baroda, Dredge and Wet Gravity Concentration Project at Chavara, Concentrate Upgrading Plant at Manavalakurichi and Heavy Rare Earths Oxide Plant at Udyogmandal.

Safety surveillance of various nuclear operations of DAE installations continued. The radiological impact was well within the prescribed limits. Personnel monitoring survey covered 37,000 radiation workers in the country.

Emergency preparedness plans of the nuclear installations were found to be satisfactory.

Significant quantities of uranium oxide were added to the uranium resource inventory and samples from Domiasiat (Meghalaya) indicated high uranium contents. Construction of underground mines at Narwapahar and Turamdih, and uranium mill at Turamdih was taken up by UCIL.

The research and development sector witnessed Purnima III attaining criticality. Dhruva, Cirus and Apsara reactors were used for isotope production, research and training.

The radioisotopes and related services offered by the Board of Radiation and Isotope Technology (BRIT) were availed of by 800 user institutions, about 54,000 consignments of various radiopharmaceuticals were supplied for 6 lakh patient investigation, and ISOMED plant at Trombay sterilized 6700 cum of medical products.

Research work in superconductivity, cold fusion, robotics and lasers continued. The high temperature super-conductor with critical temperature close to 92.4K, cold fusion experiments indicating tritium formation in metal phase, a LABOT for laboratory automation and intensive studies in logic and servo-controlled pneumatics were notable developments.

TABLE 23.1: Allocation of Resources 1991-92 (Percentage)

(*Rs. in Crores*)

Name	
Heavy Water Projects*	13.67
Nuclear Fuel Complex*	9.33
Atomic Minerals Division and Uranium Corpn. of India Ltd.*	3.24
Industry and Extension**	2.65
Support Services**	1.06
Nuclear Power Projects*	53.74
Fuel Reprocessing*	2.73
Waste Management*	0.39
Aided Institutions and Miscellaneous*** Research Schemes***	3.67
Indira Gandhi Centre for Atomic Research***	1.69
Centre for Advanced Technology***	0.93
Variable Energy Cyclotron Centre***	0.23
Bhabha Atomic Research Centre***	6.38
Direction and Administration**	0.29

*	Nuclear Power Programme	1776.76
**	Research and Development	275.54
***	Others	85.55

At Trombay, operation of the 30cum/day capacity shipborne thermal desalination plant was demonstrated successfully. In nuclear agriculture certified seed production programme of crop varieties developed at BARC, continued.

AT IGCAR, Kalpakkam, the problems faced by the fast breeder test reactor were solved. The reactor operated at a power level of 500kWt and is now poised for electricity generation.

CAT, Indore, identified as the centre for the national laser programme, achieved development of various types of lasers such as copper vapour lasers, nitrogen lasers and excimer lasers.

The Department of Electronics provided Rs. 66.72 crore by way of grant to its aided institutions namely the Tata Institute of Fundamental Research (Bombay), Tata Memorial Centre (Bombay), Saha Institute of Nuclear Physics (Calcutta), Institute of Physics (Bhubaneshwar), Institute of Mathematical Sciences (Madras), Mehta Research Institute (Allahabad) and National Board of Higher Mathematics (Bombay). The Giant Metrewave Radio Telescope, (GMRT), being set up near Pune under the aegis of TIFR, moved from design stage of construction. Two antennas of 45m diameter were erected. Electronics system and optical fibre links from each antenna to central control room for the GMRT were finalised and prototypes developed. When completed, those would be an unique facility in astronomical research. Upgradation of the Ooty Radio Telescope for improving the sensitivity also continued during the year. TMC took over 60 acres of the land provided by CIDCO for setting up Advanced Centre for Treatment, Research and Education in cancer (ACTREC) at Owe village, New Bombay.

Nuclear Power Generation

The landmarks are, NAPS-1 commencing commercial operation from 1st

January, 1991, NAPP-2 advancing to commissioning stage prior to achieving criticality, and KAPP-1 progressing from construction to commissioning stage. The cumulative generation of electricity from the four operating stations since the commencement of their commercial operation till December, 1990 was 68366 MUs. The stations generated 6182 MUs during the calendar year 1990 — a 54 per cent increase over the corresponding period in the previous year. The Nuclear Power Corporation made a net profit of Rs. 32.84 crores, after providing for appropriations, in the financial year 1989-90. Provisional net profit for the period from 1st April to 31st December, 1990 was estimated at Rs. 53.21 crores. During the financial year 1990-91, NPC raised Rs. 400 crores through market borrowings for investment in its projects.

Tarapur Atomic Power Station: (2x160 MWe BWRs)

The station logged 42 reactor years of commercial operation. From April to December 1990 it generated 1525 MUs with a capacity factor of 72 per cent and availability factor of 88 per cent . An Away-From-Reactor (AFR) spent fuel storage and satellite communication facilities were commissioned.

Rajasthan Atomic Power Station: (2x200 MWe PHWRs)

The unit-2 generated 974 MUs (including 129 MUs of electricity equivalent of steam supplied to nearby Heavy Water Plant) from April to December 1990, with capacity and availability factors of 67 per cent and 83 per cent respectively.

The unit-1 operated at a restricted power level of 100MWe as stipulated by AERB, and the power generated by the Unit from April to December 1990 was 331 MUs.

Madras Atomic Power Station: (2x235 MWe PHWRs)

The station generated 1755 MUs of electricity during April to December 1990 registering capacity and availability factors of 57 per cent and 90 per cent respectively. The capacity factor of the station was not consistent with the availability, as the power levels were restricted to 75 per cent by AERB taking into consideration certain rework to be carried out on the moderator inlet manifold. Rectification of the inlet manifold to enable rehabilitation of the units to perform at full power, is on hand and is progressing satisfactorily.

Narora Atomic Power Station-1: (235 MWe PHWR)

The first unit was declared commercial on 1st January, 1991 and continued to operate with power level reaching upto 80 per cent. During the year 1990, the unit generated 389 MUs with capacity and availability factors of 19 per cent and 42 per cent respectively. The capacity factor was low due to operation at low power levels. The availability remained low due to the teething troubles faced during initial commissioning phase which have been overcome.

Projects under Construction

Narora Atomic Power Station-2 : (235 MWe PHWR)

The commissioning activities reached completion stage. The tests on various systems stipulated by the NAPS Design Safety Committee continued. The Unit is expected to achieve criticality by August, 1991.

Kakrapar Atomic Power Project 1 & 2: (2x235 MWe PHWRs)

The main plant civil works were completed and some of the common service systems were also commissioned. Installation works of unit-1 reached an advanced stage and commissioning activities commenced. Reactor building leak test was carried out and pre- checks and system commissioning for hot conditioning of unit-1 was completed. Four steam generators of unit-2 were erected and installation of piping works continued. Unit-1 & 2 are expected to attain criticality in December, 1991 and December, 1992 respectively.

Rajasthan Atomic Power Projects 3 and 4: (2x235 MWe PHWRs)

Main plant civil works of the project and setting up of site infrastructural works continued. Raft foundation of Reactor Building-3, Turbine Building-3 and 4 and Control Building were completed. Equipment and components pertaining to nuclear and conventional systems of the plant are in procurement, manufacture and delivery stages. Apart from the equipment delivered earlier, three steam generators were received. The target criticality dates for the units are May and November, 1995.

Kaiga Project 1 & 2: (2x 235 MWe PHWRs)

Main plan civil works of the project and setting up of the infrastructural works continued. Concreting of foundation rafts of Reactor Building 1&2 and Turbine Generators-1 and 2 were completed. The works on internal structure, outer containment wall of Reactor Building-1 and other buildings are progressing. Equipment and components pertaining to nuclear and conventional systems of the plant are in different stages of procurement, manufacture and delivery. The calandria, reactor headers for the second unit and end-shields for unit-1 were delivered. The target criticality dates are June, 1995 and December, 1995 for these units respectively.

Tarapur Atomic Power Project 3 and 4: (2x500 MWe PHWRs)

Environmental clearance for the site, was issued by the Union Ministry of Environment and Forests. Subsequently the project financial sanction was accorded by the Government. As part of advance actions, tender for main plant civil works was floated and technical evaluation of bids received was completed. Detailed design engineering and analysis works, and fabrication of calandria and end-shields for the units continued. Activities relating to advance procurement of other long delivery equipment are in progress.

Kaiga Project 3 to 6 : (4x235 MWe PHWRs) and Rajasthan Atomic Power Project 5 to 8: (4x500 MWe PHWRs)

Environmental clearance for the site from State Government and site clearance from AERB were obtained. Environmental appraisal of the site by the Union

Ministry of Environmental and Forests is in progress. Advance procurement of long delivery critical components and equipment for the unit continued.

Kudankulam Project: (2x1000 MWe Soviet VVERs)

Discussion between USSR and India continued on various techno-commercial aspects of setting up the proposed units, and agreement on maximum basic cost of the project was arrived at. Detailed site investigations for establishing design basis and planning and design of site infrastructure works made progress.

Heavy Water

Six heavy water plants are operational at Nangal (Punjab), Baroda (Gujarat), Tuticorin (Tamilnadu), Kota (Rajasthan), Talcher (Orissa) and Thal (Maharashtra).

The heavy water plants at Baroda, Tuticorin, Thal and Kota continued satisfactory operation and production was commensurate with the inputs. Out of the two plants under construction, the Hazira plant was completed and commissioned. At Manuguru, trial production commenced in one of the two streams. Sites were identified for additional heavy water plants.

Due to non-availability of power to the electrolysis plant at Nangal, the National Fertilizers Ltd. put up an alternate unit for generation of pure hydrogen by naphtha reforming and pressure swing adsorption. Operation of the Heavy Water Plan Nangal was switched over to processing feed gas from this new unit. This is expected to improve production of heavy water.

The Baroda Plant produced heavy water on sustained basis consequent upon the improvements carried out so far. Civil works of the facility for upgrading heavy water to nuclear grade was completed. This facility is expected to be commissioned next year. The potassium metal production facility at Baroda also performed well during the year. The plant worked continuously for 430 days without any reportable unusual occurrence.

After improvements, Tuticorin Heavy Water Plant posted good results. It operated continuously for 28 months.

With sustained operation, Heavy Water Plant, Kota performed satisfactorily. However, its capacity utilisation was influenced by the limits on operating pressure stipulated by AERB. During the year, one of the boilers of the captive steam generation unit was commissioned. The second boiler is undergoing commissioning.

The Heavy Water Plant, Thal performed satisfactorily. The problem related to a heat exchanger in one of the main crackers, was solved. This will improve productivity of the plant. Higher concentration of deuterium in the feed synthesis gas was also sustained.

The performance of the Heavy Water Plant, Talcher was not satisfactory for want of inputs from the Fertilizer Corporation of India's (FCI) ammonia plant which remained under annual shutdown for almost 5 months during the year. The Talcher Plant came on stream in September, 1990 and has been operating since then.

The construction work of the Heavy Water Plant, Hazira was completed and various utility systems as well as both the plant streams were also commissioned. Production of heavy water has commenced and operation of the plant is being stabilized.

The civil and structural work for the heavy water upgrading unit at Hazira, were also completed.

The erection work of both the streams of the Manuguru Plant was completed. One stream was commissioned and pre-commissioning activity of the other stream was taken up.

In view of the future demand for heavy water, preliminary work on setting up of new projects was taken up and sites were identified for technical consideration.

Nuclear Fuels

The fuel assemblies and zircaloy core components for the Indian PHWRs, and BWR are manufactured at the Nuclear Fuel Complex (NFC) Hyderabad.

During the year, NFC supplied fuel bundles to the operating power reactors, and zirconium-2.5 per cent niobium coolant tube and garter springs for KAPP-II reactors. A microprocessor controlled vacuum annealing furnace — an import substitution, was put into operation. Fabrication of flow tube assemblies, sparger tubes for MAPS, calandria tubes for Kaiga-I, and fuel bundles for initial criticality of NAPP-II continued.

Under the special materials programmes the production of high purity materials such as gallium, indium, phosphorus and tellurium continued in addition to the production of magnesium granules and zirconium metal powder. The high purity material silver cyanide was a new product developed.

The estimated revenue receipts for the year 1990-91 were Rs. 110 crores.

NFC has envisaged four new projects with a total investment of Rs. 700 crores during Eighth Plan and early Ninth Plan period.

At Trombay, considerable progress was made towards the development of mixed nitride fuel — a candidate fuel for FBTR in place of mixed carbide. The Advanced Fuel Fabrication Facility set up at Tarapur for the production of mixed oxide (MOX) fuel commenced initial operation.

Mineral Exploration

Major achievements were significant augmentation in uranium resource inventory, indication of higher uranium contents in the sandstone samples from Domiasiat (Meghalaya), identification of new surface uraniferous zones and subsurface continuity of uranium mineral, recovery of quality tantalite concentrate from the alluvial placers of Marlagalla, Karnataka, and production of heavy mineral concentrate containing 3-5 per cent xenotime from Siri River, Madhya Pradesh.

Exploration continued for ilmenite and monazite resources in the beach and inland placers of Andhra Pradesh, Maharashtra and Tamilnadu, yttrium oxide in Xenotime in the riverine placers of Gumla district, Bihar and columbite-tantalite in Bastar district, Madhya Pradesh.

Radioactive Waste Management

The radioactive waste management facilities at Trombay, Tarapur and

Rawatbhata continued treating and conditioning the low and intermediate level radioactive wastes. The waste concentrates, such as chemical and solar evaporation pan sludges, were immobilized in cement matrix before disposing them in the solid waste management facility at each site.

The first phase of the waste management facilities at Narora was commissioned and the Waste Immobilisation Plant (WIP) at Tarapur was successfully operated for the vitrification of the high level wastes from PREFRE. The secondary wastes generated in the vitrification process were fixed at the bituminisation plant.

The civil construction work of the process building in WIP at Trombay reached completion stage.

Radiological Safety and Protection

Safety surveillance of various nuclear operations continued at all the DAE installations. Round the clock radiation surveillance and health physics services were provided to the nuclear power plants at Tarapur, Rawatbhata, Kalpakkam and Narora. Environmental survey and monitoring laboratories continuously monitored the environment at these sites.

Radiological impact of nuclear operation was found to be negligible and far below the limit stipulated by the international bodies.

Environmental impact assessment for upcoming plants of NFC, IRE and Kaiga were also carried out.

Under the radiological protection, a national network of environmental radiation monitoring stations is being set up to detect accidental nuclear releases. Five stations of the net work have been in operation at Bombay, Tarapur, Kalpakkam, Calcutta and Indore, since October, 1990. This will be a part of the Global Environment Radiation Monitoring Network (GERMON).

The countrywide monitoring programme for assessment of indoor radon exposure to the population continued. Monitoring of radiation workers, as part of the radiation health surveillance programme continued. To assess occupational health hazards, industrial hygiene surveys were carried out in DAE units. Personnel monitoring service was provided to both DAE and non-DAE institutions and more than 37000 radiation workers, in about 3000 institutions, were monitored.

Regulatory Functions

A countrywide radiological and industrial safety surveillance was carried out by AERB in all the DAE units and the Safety Review Committee for Operating Plants (SARCOP) enforced safety in the units by regulatory stipulations, inspection of facilities/installations and monitoring of reports.

The Board authorised following activities:

* Different operational stages of NAPS-1.
* Operation of heavy water plants at Manuguru and Hazira.
* Operation of Dredge and Wet Gravity Concentration plant at Chavara, Mohur, Helium and Hero Plants at Udyogmandal.
* Operation of irradiation facility at the Shri Ram Applied Radiation Centre, Delhi.

* Sewage Hygienisation Research Irradiator, Baroda.
* Pelletron Accelerator at Nuclear Science Centre, New Delhi.
* Commissioning and subcritical tests of PURNIMA III.

Site authorisation was given of New Uranium Oxide Fuel Plant and New Zircaloy Fabrication Plant at Hyderabad, and New Uranium Oxide Fuel Plant at Turamdih. Other authorisations related to site clearance for locating RAPS-3 to 8, Kaiga-1 to 6 and operation of NAPS-1 up to 100 per cent of the rated power.

AERB was recognised as the nodal agency for reporting nuclear incidents as per the International Nuclear Event Scale Classification System. This programme commenced on a trial basis for one year from September, 1990.

The Task Group of AERB was formed to review and revise the Industrial Radiography (Radiation Surveillance) Procedures. Guides related to Safe transport of radioactive material and allied activities were prepared.

To encourage inter-disciplinary collaboration, AERB funded 5 projects and extended financial assistance to conferences/seminars/symposia.

Emergency Preparedness Plans

A total of eleven plant, six site and two offsite exercises were conducted at the operating power stations. Co-ordination between the nuclear power station staff and district authorities was found to be satisfactory. Efforts to improve communication with public continued.

Research and Development

Three major research centres namely BARC at Trombay (Bombay), IGCAR at Kalpakkam (Tamilnadu), and CAT at Indore (MP), spearhead research in atomic energy, fast breeder technology, lasers and accelerators. Following are the major R&D activities.

Research Reactors

The research reactors at Trombay, namely the 100MW Dhruva, 40MW Cirus, and 1MW Apsara continued satisfactory operation. Purnima III attained criticality and the neutron source reactor Kamini at Kalpakkam approached completion. The year also witnessed Cirus completing three decades of operation and Dhruva becoming the national facility for neutron beam research.

Dhruva operated at its rated power level and was utilized for production of radioisotopes and research. Both Cirus and Apsara reactors continued to operate safely and efficiently, and were used for research, isotope production, and training of personnel. Experiments of operational and safety interest continued with Purnima III.

Accelerator Programme

The 14UD BARC/TIFR pelletron accelerator at Colaba, Bombay logged 3900 hrs. of operation. Research activities were intensified with the availability of energetic heavy ion beams. Research also continued with the Van-de-Graaf accelerator at Trombay.

The VEC at Calcutta was used for production of isotopes for diagnostic purposes. The Variable Energy Cyclotron Centre (VECC) designed and completed the electron cyclotron resonance heavy ion source which will be operational shortly. VECC also entered into a collaboration with the CERN laboratory in Geneva (Switzerland) for research related to quarks.

High Temperature Superconductors

Frontline research work in the development of high critical temperature superconducting materials continued at Trombay. High temperature superconductors were investigated theoretically which resulted in increased understanding of their structure and properties. Development of procedures for the preparation of a bismuth based superconducting material with critical temperature close to the highest critical temperature 92.4K obtained so far elsewhere for this phase of leadfree superconductor, was a notable success.

Work also continued on the synthesis and characterisation of high temperature superconducting oxides and significant findings were made with respect to the influence of impurities, bulk density and grain size on the superconducting properties of a yttrium based superconductor.

Under the programme on low temperature superconductors for indigenous development of niobium-titanium cables for accelerator magnet application, about 160m of 1.85mm dia 7-stand round cable was produced.

Robotics

A remote boring-and-grooving machine for use in MAPS calandria rework, a CNC machine for hot cell use, and a number of systems in the areas of automation, remotisation and robotics were developed.

Notable activities related to the computerised robotic system for laboratory application (LABOT), work on mobile robot mechanisms for survey, inspection, maintenance and waste disposal tasks and computer aided telemanipulation systems. Work continued on the pick-and-place device for use in fuel fabrication. This segment of robotics has good potential in automation of monotonous operations. Studies were intensified in the field of logic-controlled and servo-controlled pneumatics.

Plasma Research

Testing of the prototype plasma cutting torch designed for underwater cutting operations, passing of the technology for plasma spraying of oxide ceramics to the Steel Authority of India for evaluation, and preparation and evaluation of the plasma sprayed superconducting coatings of yttrium based high temperature superconductors were the major activities.

Cold Fusion

The nascent discovery of 'cold fusion' is full of fascinating possibilities. Experiments to study the phenomenon of 'cold fusion' were continued at BARC. These indicated tritium formation in the metal phase.

Nuclear Agriculture

Continuance of certified seed production programme of the crop varieties developed at BARC for distribution to farmers, production of 480 tonnes of improved pulse variety by the Maharashtra State Seed Corporation and 110 tonnes of improved rice variety Hari by the Andhra Pradesh Seed Corporation, were the major achievements of nuclear agriculture research at Trombay. In addition, the spreading groundnut variety Somnath was released for cultivation by the Gujarat State Seed Sub-Committee, and TAG-24 groundnut variety was recommended for release in the Vidharbha region of Maharashtra for both Kharif and summer season.

Food Technology

At Trombay, radiation technology development work for the preservation of economically important agricultural products, continued.

Attempts were made to standardize irradiation for the preservation of onion, potatoes and spices for commercial venture. Electron spin resonance spectroscopy was successfully employed to distinguish irradiated mangoes. Using solar dryer, Bombay Duck (fish) laminates with improved colour and texture were obtained, which were superior to the mechanically dried laminates. The method for preparation of defatted peanuts was also developed.

Desalination

In view of the immense need for good quality water, both for industrial use and human consumption, research continued at Trombay on desalination of water by multistage flash and reverse osmosis (RO) techniques. During the year, operation of the 30cum/day capacity shipborne thermal desalination plant was demonstrated for technology transfer, and evaluation of a 425 cum/day multistage flash (MSF) desalination plant continued. Batch manufacture of polyamide hydrazide polymer for desalination of sea water by RO was an important step towards indigenisation of imported membrane.

Seismology

Seismic arrays at Gauribidanur and Delhi continued to monitor global seismicity. The radio telemetered seismic network at Bhatsanagar collected useful data for seismicity and seismotectonic investigation.

Basic and Applied Research

Signal research activities of BARC related to:

— investigation of materials such as ferrites, ferroelectric ceramics, magnetic alloys etc.
— extensive research work in gamma-ray astronomy at the Nuclear Research Laboratory, Srinagar and the High Altitude Research Laboratory, Gulmarg.
— development of devices for garter spring repositioning in nuclear power reactors, rolled joint detachment and fuel fabrication, and commissioning of

a pulse power system KALI-1000.

— research and development of laser systems for advanced spectroscopy and photo-chemistry studies, deposition of thin oxide film by excimer laser, a computer controlled dye laser spectrometer and an optically pumped ammonia laser.
— commencement of the work on laser induced chemistry and preparation of advanced fuels using sol-gel process.

Other activities related to indigenous development of the electron beam welding machine, recovery of uranium from crude tetrafluoride, successful testing of a process flow sheet for the production of high grade neodymium oxide which will make India as one of the few countries in the world having his knowhow. Several new coordination compounds of uranium, thorium, rare synthesis of earths, tin, titanium, copper, iron, palladium and platinum, were developed at Trombay. A new '3-exit process' for simultaneous recovery of three metals as high purity products, was developed.

The research and development programme in reactor engineering continued its thrust in generation of design information and design details for PHWRs, fuel handling system of 500MWe prototype fast breeder reactor', technology development for performance improvements, repair and maintenance work on operating reactors, and studies for developing a thorium based heavy water reactor.

The work for 500 MWe PHWR made further progress. New facilities were commissioned for evaluating and optimizing designs of various components and subsystems of fuel handling system and spent fuel transfer system.

Development of simple dot blot ELISA technique for the detection of TB antigens and standardisation of an inhibition assay for detection of antibodies to an antigen of leprosy were notable successes.

Technology Transfer

The technologies of microprocessor based electromyograph for use in hospitals, and liquid scintillation counting system were transferred to industry.

The manufacture of four-axis articulated robot is being taken up by ECIL. The know-how of thyristor traction chopper drives for use in locomotives, pneumatic pick-and-place robot, AC drag cup induction servo-motor and AC servo-amplifier are in the process of transfer to industry. The technologies of the 4 and 5 axis articulated robot, variable frequency-variable voltage servo-drives, DC brushless servo motor, 3-phase servo-motors and pneumatic servo-drives, will soon be ready for transfer.

Technical knowhow of the PC-based multipurpose front office posting machines (FOPMA) is being transferred to the Computer Maintenance Corpn., of India.

Radiation Medicine

Over 13000 patients were investigated at the Radiation Medicine Centre (RMC) Bombay. During the year 1.63TBq of radioiodine was handled for therapeutic purposes.

Radioisotopes

Dhruva and Cirus are the major facilities for production of radioisotopes. The Five Year Plan Project on Dhruva Utilization for Isotope Technology was completed during the year. Under this project, updating the shielded facilities for handling multicurie amount of iodine-125, molybdenum-99 and other isotopes, was carried out.

Isotopes were employed by BARC in the study of origin of groundwater and its salinity in some parts of the country.

The Board of Radiation and Isotope Technology (BRIT) continued production and supply of a variety of radioisotope products such as radiochemicals, radiation sources, radiopharmaceuticals and RIA (radioimmunoassay) kits.

TABLE 23.2: Sales Value of Radioisotopes, Related Equipments and Services (1990)
(*Rs. crores*)

Sale value of Radioisotopes										
1980	1981	1982	1983	1984	1985	1986	1987	1988	1989	1990
1.05	1.35	1.50	1.87	2.00	2.3	2.54	3.02	3.96	4.95	5.05

Medicine 243 Lakhs
Research and Agriculture 186 Lakhs
Industry 76 Lakhs

The sale value of radioisotopes and related services offered during the year was Rs. 5.05 crores. About 800 user institutions availed of the services extended by BRIT. Radioisotope products were also exported to Nepal, UK and France.

During the year 220 batches of reactor produced radioisotopes (53.1 TBq) were processed for supply to various users, 2600 consignments of radiation sources were supplied for applications in cancer therapy, non-destructive testing, industrial prices control, radiation processing etc. Other supplies included: Iridium-192 sealed sources (600-TBq) for industrial radiography, 14 sources of cobalt-60 (3607-TBq) for teletherapy and cobalt-60 (1850-TBq) for the radiation sterilisation plant RASHMI at Bangalore. Specially fabricated antimony-124 sources (51-TBq) were supplied for start-up of FBTR at Kalpakkam.

About 54,000 consignments of various radiopharmaceuticals were supplied which are expected to benefit 6 lakhs patients. The regional centres at Bangalore and Delhi processed about 2.44 TBq of ready-to-use Tc-99m products. During the year regular production of Tc-99m column generators was undertaken and work was initiated for the regular production of RIA kits.

4300 consignments of carbon-14 and tritium labelled compounds, and P-32 labelled biomolecules were despatched. Production of P-32 labelled nucleotides continued at the JONAKI laboratory, Hyderabad. These products were supplied to 40 user institutions. Supplies in the field of gamma radiography equipment covered 38 radiography cameras (740 GBq) housing iridium-192 sources, and one cobalt-60 camera.

Radiation Sterilization

Services of ISOMED plant at Trombay were extended to the user industries and over 6700 cum of medical products were sterilized. A total of one million radiation indicator buttons were produced and supplied. The irradiation facility at the Shri Ram Institute of Industrial Research, New Delhi was upgraded and the plant commissioned.

A number of projects such as extension of nuclear medicine and teletherapy facilities, setting up of demonstration plant at Cochin for irradiation of spices for export, upgrading of facilities for radiopharmaceuticals production, and testing of radioisotope equipment and packages were formulated for inclusion in the Eighth Five Year Plan. The financial sanction for the radioisotope equipment production facility project was also received. The project report related to extension of nuclear medicine facilities in the country was prepared.

The NRL, Srinagar provided the gamma ray radiation sterilization facility to one of the local hospitals and to some industrial units in Srinagar.

Fast Breeder Research

The Indira Gandhi Centre for Atomic Research (IGCAR) at Kalpakkam, Tamilnadu, has been working on the development of fast breeder reactor technology.

During the year the Centre successfully overcame the problems faced by Fast Breeder Test Reactor (FBTR). The reactor was operated at power levels upto 500 kWt for 40 days on demonstration run during August-September, 1990. Four reactor physics experiments were conducted and total 1800hrs of operation were logged. The rector is now poised for electricity generation.

The major thrust areas of activities on the 500MWe Prototype Fast Breeder Reactor (PFBR) were the pool hydraulic studies, sodium pump development, safety and instrumentation.

A 316 SS sodium loop for in-sodium material studies was commissioned and an expensive programme for the study of microstructural stability in materials was initiated. For FBTR fuel reprocessing, the Reprocessing Development Laboratory reached completion stage. Phase 1 of the Mini Plant for processing of irradiated fuels from FBTR was completed and Phase II will be ready shortly. Construction of the large plant for reprocessing of FBTR fuel continued. In the project KARP construction of the main process building has been almost completed.

Advanced Technology

The research in advanced technologies such as accelerators, and lasers is spearheaded by the Centre for Advanced Technology (CAT) at Indore (Madhya Pradesh). The Centre was identified as the main Indian Laboratory for developing lasers and systems, under the National Laser Programme. In the laser programme, development of various types of lasers such as copper vapour lasers, nitrogen lasers and excimer lasers were taken up. The Centre also developed a 30 W average power copper vapour laser and a 40 W surgical CO_2 laser for general surgery.

In the field of cryogenics, a closed cycle helium cryorefrigerator was developed by CAT and a prototype of cryoprobe for use in gynaecology was designed and fabricated.

At Trombay, a high power narrow band Rhodamine 6G laser amplifier was set up and significant increase in output power of the axial fast flow CW CO_2

laser resulted in a power level of 650 watts. A Laser Enhanced Ionisation (LEI) Spectrometer with a detection limit of 1 nanogram/millilitre, and an optical data link system for a one kilometre range were developed at BARC.

Indian Rare Earths Limited

During 1989-90, IRE's turnover was Rs. 63.96 crores as against Rs. 60.16 crores in the previous year including Rs. 30.69 crores as foreign exchange earning. The net profit from Southern units was 23.47 crores. However, OSCOM incurred a loss of Rs. 21.17 crores, reducing the total net profit to Rs. 2.29 crores.

The production from the Southern units and OSCOM together was of Rs. 73.61 crores as against previous year's production of Rs. 62.30 crores.

Chavara and Manavalakurichi plants continued to perform well and the mineral production in OSCOM improved substantially. Efforts were made to liquidate the stocks of Orissa ilmenite and rare earths chloride which had accumulated due to adverse market situation and recession in demand. The Thorium Factory at Trombay continued to perform well. The work on the new Thorium Plant at OSCOM is in an advanced stage of completion.

The projects commissioned include the Dredge and Wet Gravity Concentration Project (DWGC) at Chavara, Concentrate Upgrading Plant (CUP) at Manavalakurichi, and the Heavy Rare Earths Oxide (HERO) Project at Udyogmandal. The production of Minerals Separation Plant at OSCOM increased considerably with the commissioning of Concentrate Upgrading Plant. The technical problems at Synthetic Rutile Plant were solved.

Future Plans and Outlook

For 1990-91, the Company's sales target is set at Rs. 60 crores with foreign exchange earning of Rs. 25 crores.

To overcome the sluggish demand for ilmenite and rare earths chloride, efforts are geared towards improving quality, reducing the cost, and developing new products to compete in international market.

Electronics Corporation of India Limited

ECIL executed the Rs. 37 crore order of electronic voting machines, and supplied Rs. 21 crore worth of nuclear and industrial instruments and systems. Technical assistance was extended to a Uganda firm in setting up a TV assembly line and TV sets were exported to Bangladesh and Television Receive Only Systems (TVROS) to Dubai.

The targets for 1990-91 for production and sales are set at Rs. 272 crores and Rs. 321 crores respectively.

Uranium Corporation of India Ltd.

The production of uranium concentrates remained constant. The capacity utilisations of the Jaduguda and Bhatin mines were 83.4 per cent and 55.1 per cent as compared to 89.6 per cent and 76.5 per cent respectively in the previous year. For the Jaduguda mill, the capacity utilisation was 88.63 per cent as compared to 95.7 per cent for the previous year. The production of uranium mineral concentrates from the three uranium recovery plants exceeded the target set for the year but the production of copper and molybdenum concentrates, and magnetite, remained slightly lower as compared to the previous year.

The Corporation took up construction of two new projects — the underground mines at Narwapahar and Turamdih (Singhbhum district, Bihar) and the Uranium mill at Turamdih. To exploit further potential of Jaduguda mines sinking of an auxiliary shaft to 900m continued. An effluent treatment plant was also commissioned at Jaduguda.

At the Bagjata mine underground operations by AMD continued. In the near future the mine will be taken over by UCIL for production and processing of uranium ore.

Financial Support

The Board of Research in Nuclear Sciences (BRNS) of DAE provided financial support for the research projects fellowships, and sponsored symposia, conferences and seminars organised by DAE units and outside agencies. During the year, financial assistance of Rs. 3.2 crores was recommended for 125 ongoing projects and 56 new research projects. Rs. 30 lakhs were provided to various units of DAE and outside agencies for organising symposia/conferences/workshops etc. Rs. 50 lakhs were provided in the budget for award of fellowships. By way of recurring and non-recurring grant to its aided institutions, the Department provided Rs. 35.22 crores to the Tata Institute of Fundamental Research (TIFR), Bombay; Rs. 18.54 crores to the Tata Memorial Centre (TMC), Bombay; Rs. 5.4 crores to the Saha Institute of Nuclear Physics (SINP), Calcutta; Rs. 2.55 crores to the Institute of Physics (IOP), Bhubaneshwar, Rs. 2.06 crores to Institute of Mathematical Sciences, Madras, and Rs. 1.3 crores to the Mehta Research Institute, Allahabad. For the development of mathematics in the country, Rs. 1.65 crores were provided to the National Board of Higher Mathematics, Bombay.

TABLE 23.3: Growth of Manpower

1988-89		1989-90		1990-91	
20109*	10696**	20885*	10366**	22340*	11236**

Note: Does not include staff transferred to NPC
* Scientific and Technical
** Auxiliary and Administrative

International Relations

For the 34th year in succession, India was designated to the Board of Governor of IAEA. The country continued to offer training facility, fellowships, scientific visits and made available the services of its scientists for expert assignments through IAEA and to the countries with which we have entered into bilateral agreements for cooperation in the field of peaceful uses of atomic energy.

Bilateral discussions was held with the delegations of Argentina, Brazil, Vietnam, Egypt, Algeria and other countries for strengthening the cooperation in the field of peaceful uses of atomic energy. The Indian Indo-USSR Working Group on Nuclear Power was held in Moscow. A Working Group was set up under the

Indo-USSR Intergovernmental Agreement of November, 1988 for cooperation in the construction of nuclear power station in the country. A cooperation agreement for the peaceful uses of atomic energy between the Indian Government and Government of the Democratic and Popular Republic of Algeria was concluded.

Atomic Energy Establishments in India

1. Atomic Minerals Division
   Hyderabad

2. Atomic Power Station
   Kaiga
   Kakrapar
   Kalpakkam
   Kudankulam
   Narora
   Rawatbhata
   Tarapu

3. Bhabha Atomic Research Centre
   Bombay

4. Centre for Advanced Technology
   Indore

5. Electronics Corporation of India Ltd.
   Hyderabad

6. Heavy Water Plant
   Baroda
   Hazira
   Manuguru
   Nangal
   Rawatbhata
   Talcher
   Thal
   Tuticorin

7. High Altitude Research Laboratory
   Gulmarg

8. Indian Rare Earths Ltd. : Minerals Division
   Chavara
   Manavalakurichi

9. Indian Rare Earths Ltd.: Rare earths Division
   Alwaye

10. Indira Gandhi Centre for Atomic Research
    Kalpakkam

11. Institute of Physics
    Bhubaneshwar

12. Nuclear Fuel Complex
    Hyderabad

13. Nuclear Research Laboratory
    Bombay
    Srinagar

14. Orissa Sands Complex (OSCOM)
    Chhatrapur

15. Power Reactor Fuel Reprocessing Plant
    Tarapu

16. Saha Institute of Nuclear Physics
    Calcutta

17. Seismic Station
    Gauribidanur

18. Tata Institute of Fundamental Research
    Bombay

19. Tata Memorial Centre
    Bombay

20. Uranium Corporation of India Ltd.
    Jaduguda

21. Variable Energy Cyclotron Centre
    Calcutta

22. Waste Immobilization Plant
    Tarapu

Co-ordinated Research Programmes in India

I. **Food and Agriculture**

1. Nuclear techniques to improve crop production in salt-affected soils, 1985-1993
2. Mutation breeding of oil seed crops, 1988-1993
3. Radiotracer studies to reduce or eliminate pesticide residues during food processing, 1988-1993
4. Development of controlled-release formulations of pesticides utilizing

nuclear techniques, 1988-1993

5. Radiotracer studies of behaviour of DDT in tropical environments, 1988-193
6. Asian regional co-operative project on food irradiation with emphasis on process control and acceptance — RCA, 1989-1993
7. Irradiation with combination with other processes for improving food quality, 1990-1995

II. Life Sciences

8. Research and development in the methods for basic care, preventive maintenance and operative control of nuclear medicine equipment — RCA, 1988-1991
9. Quality control of advanced nuclear medicine equipment in Asia — RCA, 1989-1992
10. Determination of the precision and sensitivity of AFP measurements by RIA as an indicator of malignancy in space occupying lesions of the liver, 1991-1994
11. Evaluation of the imaging procedures for the diagnosis of the liver diseases — PHASE II, 1989-1992
12. Immunodiagnosis of tuberculosis — RCA, 1988-1991
13. Testing of the code of practice for absorbed dose determination in photon and electron beams, 1988-1991
14. Introduction of computerized dosimetry and database in radiotherapy of carcinoma of the cervix in Asian countries — RCA, 1990-1994
15. Use of nuclear and nuclear-related techniques in the study of environmental pollution associated with solid wastes, 1987-1992
16. Assessment of environmental exposure to mercury in selected human populations as studied by nuclear and other techniques, 1990-1995
17. Applications of stable traces in human nutrition research, 1988-1992
18. Isotope-aided studies of the bioavailability of iron and zinc from human diets, 1990-1995

III. Physical and Chemical Sciences

19. Application of personal computers to enhance operation and management of research reactors — RCA, 1990-1993
20. Development of advanced diagnostics for edge plasma studies, 1987-1991
21. Labelling, quality control and clinical evaluation of monoclonal antibodies for scintigraphy, 1990-1993
22. Evaluation of use of bulk reagents for production of ^{99}Tc radiopharmaceuticals and kits, 1991-1994
23. Antibodies immobilized on magnetic particles for radioimmunoassay and immunoradiometric assay of hormones, 1991-1994
24. Production of 99mTC generators based on low temperature sublimation and gel elution, 1991-1994
25. Radiotracers in the development of new separation techniques for trace element analysis by nuclear methods, with special emphasis on environmental research, 1989-1992
26. Isotopes and geochemistry in geothermal exploration in Africa, Asia and the Pacific and the Middle East, 1990-1993

IV. **Seibersdofr Laboratory**

27. Rapid instrumental and separation methods for monitoring radionuclides in food and environmental samples, 1988-1993

V. **Monaco Laboratory**

28. Sources of radioactivity in the marine environment and their relative contributions to overall dose assessment from marine radioactivity, 1988-93

VI. **Nuclear Power**

29. Optimizing of reactor pressure vessel surveillance programmes and their analysis —— Phase III, 1984-1991
30. Acoustic signal processing for the detection of boiling or sodium water reaction in LMFBRs, 1989-1992
31. In-core fuel management code package validation for light-water reactor (LWR), 1988-1991
32. Safe core management with burnable poisons in water-cooled and-moderated reactors (WWERs), 1988-1991
33. Thermophysical properties database for light and heavy water, 1990-1992
34. Benchmark for in-core fuel management programmes of PHWRS, 1989-1992

VII. **Nuclear Safety**

35. Development of probabilistic safety assessment techniques related to the safe transport of radioactive material, 1989-1992
36. Intercomparison programme for individual monitoring, 1988-1993
37. Compilation of anatomical, physiological and metabolic characteristics for a reference Asian man ——, RCA 1989-1994

VIII. **Nuclear Fuel Cycle and Waste Management**

38. Investigations on water chemistry control and coolant interaction with fuel and primary circuit materials in water cooled power reactors, 1987-1991
39. The safety assessment of near-surface radioactive waste disposal facilities, 1991-1995
40. Decontamination and decommissioning of nuclear facilities —— Phase II, 1989-1992

IX. **Department of Safeguards**

Verification of spent fuel without movement, 1988-1991

5 contracts

Argentina, Austria, Hungary, Pakistan, Yugoslavia.

24

DEFENCE

National Security

An analysis of the national security scenario in this region, which has a critical bearing on India's defence policies and plans is given below:

The post-World War structure of Europe, divided into two opposing military alliances and competing ideologies collapsed under pressure of further far-reaching changes in the Soviet Union, Central and Eastern Europe. The onset of the post-Cold War era, however, was overshadowed by the Gulf crisis, involving Iraq and the Multinational Forces led by the US, which snowballed to full-scale military conflict on a scale unprecedented since the Second World War. Hopes that the attenuation of ideological and military confrontation between the NATO and the Warsaw Pact would contribute to the resolution of global and regional problems have not been fulfilled.

Operation "Desert Storm" and its aftermath demonstrated the capability and determination of the US and other participating nations to intervene forcefully to protect their interests. India, together with other like-minded countries, had actively worked for bringing about a cessation of hostilities, restoring peace and promoting durable security in the region. As a close neighbour, India has an abiding interest in the Gulf region and any future regional security arrangement in the area. Any new security arrangements that are put in place should be based upon the initiative of the regional countries themselves, worked out under the overall aegis of the United Nations, guaranteed by the Security Council and UN Peace Keeping Forces and underpinned by disarmament measures that are global in character.

The process of increasing cooperation between USA and USSR continued to gather momentum. Fundamental political changes occurred in the East European countries. Because of these momentous changes, the military role of the Warsaw Pact has ended. The changes in political relations between the USA and USSR have paved the way for the conclusion of an arms reduction agreement under which conventional weapons and forces in Europe will be reduced to significantly lower levels. Progress has also been made in working towards the Strategic Arms Reduction Treaty between the United States and the Soviet Union, though the reduction in strategic nuclear warheads is likely to be significantly lower than the earlier envisaged level of 50 per cent. There is also growing concern about the possibility of delay in the conclusion of START. Besides, the US-USSR disarmament agenda remains confined to particular measures of arms reduction or arms control. Their actions have not so far been guided by a larger commitment to abolish nuclear weapons or to restructure the international order in a manner that progress is made towards a nuclear weapons-free world.

It is a matter of deep concern that the proliferation of nuclear weapons and technology has continued. Failure to move towards a comprehensive treaty to ban nuclear testing has further eroded the commitment to strengthen a genuine non-proliferation regime. Ballistic missile proliferation is another major area of concern, especially since countries in our neighbourhood have been able to acquire this capability through acquisition or transfer of technology from external sources. There has been no recent breakthrough in the negotiations on a Chemical Weapons Convention and such weapons have, in the meanwhile, tended to spread. The decision of the United States and the Soviet Union to retain, while eliminating the bulk of the chemical weapons in their arsenals, two per cent of the stockpiles until such time as, in their judgement, all the chemical weapon-capable countries have acceded to the Convention, has introduced a further complication in the negotiations. It is imperative that a global Chemical Weapons Convention, with universal participation, be quickly finalised and put into effect.

There are certain developments that have cast their shadow on the security environment of our region. Terrorism, religious extremism and ethnic chauvinism have fermented separatist tendencies. In many cases these have received support from external sources, aggravating the problem and complicating the search for political solutions. Traffic in narcotics has markedly increased in our neighbourhood, and its coupling with terrorism has created serious problems for national security, especially where narco-terrorism has sought to exploit religious and ethnic ideological linkages.

India has been making concerted efforts to improve relations with Pakistan. In May 1990 we proposed a package of Confidence Building Measures after which four rounds of Foreign Secretary level talks were held alternatively in Islamabad and New Delhi. The Prime Ministers of the two countries met in Maldives at the SAARC Summit in November, 1990. They agreed that all differences between India and Pakistan should be resolved peacefully and through dialogue. The Foreign Secretaries are scheduled to meet again to carry the bilateral dialogue forward. Several confidence building measures have been agreed upon. The Directors General of Military Operations are in weekly telephonic contact since the beginning of this year. Agreements have been reached on Advance Notification of Military Exercises and Prevention of Airspace Violations by Military Aircraft.

India is seriously concerned at the support that terrorists and subversive elements in Punjab and Jammu and Kashmir continue to receive from across the border. This adversely affects the generation of trust and confidence and hinders a genuine and sustained improvement in our relations. It is also not consistent with the Simla Agreement and universally accepted norms of inter-state conduct.

Pakistan has continued to pursue procurement of military hardware and technology from other countries, far beyond its legitimate defence requirements. In addition, it has continued with its clandestine and weapons-oriented nuclear programme and its efforts to acquire ballistic missiles and technology. In this, it is reported to be availing of Chinese assistance. We continue to monitor developments in this regard in order to take necessary measures to safeguard our security.

India's relations with China registered a perceptible improvement. The exchange of high-level visits and bilateral contacts in various areas of mutual interest contributed to enhanced understanding between the two countries. The Second Meeting of the Joint Working Group on the boundary question resulted in agreement on a mechanism by which border personnel of the two sides would meet from time to time to discuss maintenance of peace and tranquillity in the border areas. The visits of our External Affairs and Commerce Ministers during the year have provided a further impetus to the development of India-China relations.

China's modernisation of the People's Liberation Army continues with special focus on the induction of advanced military technology and the establishment of joint ventures with Western countries and the Soviet Union. Sale of arms to countries in our immediate neighbourhood and elsewhere is likely to hamper the process of de-escalation of regional tensions.

India supports the scrupulous implementation of the Geneva Accords and would like to see a political settlement of the Afghan problem, to be achieved by the Afghans themselves, without external interference or interventions. This should take into account the ground realities and the legitimate interests of all the parties concerned. India favours the preservation of Afghanistan's status as a sovereign, independent and Non-aligned country.

The de-induction of Indian Peace Keeping Forces (IPKF) from Sri Lanka was completed on March 24, 1990. The fragile truce between the Sri Lankan Government and the LTTE, following IPKF de-induction, broke down on June 11, 1990 with LTTE's capture of several police stations in eastern Sri Lanka. The continuing hostilities impinge adversely on the security environment of the region. The resulting influx of around 2 lakh refugees to India continues and has brought in its train a marked increase in smuggling, and affected the law and order situation in India.

The Sri Lankan Government has also made sustained efforts to strengthen and modernise its security forces. This has included acquisition of aircraft, high grade weaponry and arrangements for training from countries in our neighbourhood.

Relations with Maldives were further strengthened through high level visits from both sides. Ongoing cooperation with Maldives includes assistance for infrastructure projects, manpower development and training. President Gayoom visited New Delhi in January 1991 as the Chief Guest for the Republic Day.

The year 1990 was the success of the mass movement in Nepal ushering in a multi-party democracy with a constitutional Monarchy. The misunderstandings that had clouded the traditionally close relations between Nepal and India have to a large extent been dispelled. The visit of the Nepalese Prime Minister to India in 1990 was part of and contributed to normalisation of Indo-Nepal relations. India's security concerns were adequately addressed in the Indo-Nepal Joint Communique of June 1990, signed by the two Prime Ministers. Subsequently, exchanges during the visit of our External Affairs Minister of Nepal in August 1990, the visit of the Nepalese Prime Minister to New Delhi in November 1990, and finally the visit of Prime Minister to Nepal in February 1991, helped the process of enhancing mutual understanding and cooperation with a close and strategically important neighbour.

During the year, high-level exchanges between India and Bhutan were also intensified. However, the situation in Southern Bhutan that caused serious concern to the Royal Government of Bhutan, also had adverse repercussions for India. India has clearly indicated that it will not allow its territory to be used for militant activities against Bhutan and has also expressed the hope that these tensions will be resolved peacefully.

The year witnessed a positive movement in Indo-Bangladesh relations. The Foreign Ministers exchanged visits and the Indo-Bangladesh Joint Economic Commission met at the ministerial level after a gap of seven years. A high-level Defence delegation also visited India during the year. The political turmoil in Bangladesh finally led to a change in Government. A democratically elected Government with Begum Khaleda Zia as Prime Minister assumed office. It is expected that India's relations with Bangladesh will further improve with the democratization of their polity.

Myanmar had its first elections in nearly three decades in May 1990. Power has not, however, been transferred to the elected representatives of the people. India has expressed the hope that this would take place without further delay.

Myanmar has reportedly concluded agreements for obtaining large quantities of military supplies from China. India and Myanmar share a long and sensitive border where constant vigil is required to deal with insurgency-related problems.

While tangible progress has been made in our relations with our neighbouring countries during the period under review, some of the developments in these countries, particularly in Pakistan, continue to cause security concern to India. The international situation is also in a state of flux. The Cold War has ended. The contours of the new world order which might replace it are, as yet, unclear. The developing countries could come under increasing pressure to restrict their access to technologies necessary both for their development and for meeting threats to their security. The rapidly changing external environment necessitates a carefully crafted strategy to safeguard and promote our national security.

National Security Council

The National Security Council was constituted through the Government resolution No. 50/4/18/88-TS of August 24, 1990, with a view to enable consideration of all aspects of national security in a coordinated and comprehensive manner, taking into account linkages between the evolving external situation in the political, military and economic fields and our domestic situation. The Pradhan Mantri is the Chairman of the Council while the Raksha Mantri, Vitta Mantri, Grih Mantri and Videsh Mantri are its Members.

The National Security Council will formulate medium and long-term assessments of the internal and geostrategic environment, which would serve as a tool for shaping Government policy.

Planning for Defence

The planning process for Defence aims at evolving a composite reflection of the requirements of various units of the defence organisation in the context of the security environment, availability of resources and the need for maintaining and modernising the defence apparatus.

The Defence Planning Staff (DPS), an inter-Service organisation, assists the Chiefs of Staff Committee and plays a useful role towards integration of the Defence Planning process. The DPS is a multi-disciplinary group with representatives drawn from the three Services, Ministry of Finance, Ministry of External Affairs and the DRDO. It has conducted several studies and undertaken exercises in connection with medium and long-term plans. For sectoral planning, separate units are functioning in the Departments of Defence Production and Supplies, Defence Research and Development and in the Headquarters of the three Services.

The thrust of the Seventh Defence Plan (1985-90) was towards the modernisation of the country's armed forces to enable them to effectively counter any threat to our security. The Plan aimed at providing the Services with advanced systems of enhanced mobility and fire power, improved surveillance techniques, increased night observation and fighting capability and improved communications.

The Eighth Defence Plan (1990-95) is in the process of being finalised. The planning of defence requirements during this period is being considered against the back-drop of the changes in the regional and global geopolitical situations and the recent Gulf war. The present challenge is to balance the inescapable minimum maintenance requirements of our Defence Forces and the need to modernise them, without unduly straining the national economy.

The perception of the need to optimise resources allocated for Defence led to the constitution of a Committee on Defence Expenditure in June, 1990 under the Chairmanship of Shri Arun Singh. This Committee had the following terms of reference:—

(i) to examine existing expenditures in the Department of Defence and to recommend measures, structures and systems to achieve economy and secure optimal utilisation of available resources;
(ii) to recommend systems for the periodic review and control of expenditure; and
(iii) to examine and report on such further issues as may be referred by Government.

The Committee has since completed its work and its recommendations are under examination, in consultation with the concerned agencies.

Defence Expenditure

The outlays in India's Defence expenditure have generally evolved from the necessity of maintaining a credible defence posture in the light of our long land and sea borders and continuing territorial disputes. Despite these commitments however, the actual quantum of allocations to defence over the years, has remained fairly modest, and in fact, calculated in terms of percentages of the Gross National/Domestic Product, has been lower than the Defence budgets of some of our neighbouring countries.

Table 24.1 and Table 24.2 are representations of : —

(i) Service/Department wise breakup of Defence Expenditure, and
(ii) Service/Department wise expenditure as a Percentage of total Defence expenditure between 1988-89 and 1990-91.

Defence Production

The capacity of a nation to defend itself depends, to a large extent, upon the capability of its defence industry to meet the requirements of arms and equipment of its Defence Forces. In today's security environment, weapons and equipment have not only to satisfy exacting quality standards but have also to be continuously upgraded, to keep pace with the rapidly advancing technological levels. In this context, the Department of Defence Production and Supplies (DDP&S) plays a vital role in the equipping and modernisation of the country's Armed Forces. In particular, it helps the Armed Forces to keep pace with the rapidly changing technological environment.

TABLE 24.1: Service/Department-wise Break up of Defence Expenditure

(*Rs. in crore*)

	Total	Army	Navy	Air Force	Defence Production and Supplies	Defence R & D
1986-87	10477.46	5186.05	1311.20	2245.24	1303.94	431.03
1987-88	11967.49	6738.43	1537.76	2765.47	376.44	549.39
1988-89	13341.02	7512.91	1798.52	3002.74	449.07	577.78
1989-90	14416.17	7995.07	1949.98	3325.27	538.18	607.67
1990-91 (RE)	15750.00	8799.63	1978.00	3730.22	557.15	685.00

TABLE 24.2: Service/Department wise Expenditure as a Percentage of Total Defence Expenditure between 1988-89 and 1990-91

Air Force	Navy	Army	DDR & D	DDP & S
23.12 %	13.16%	55.87%	30%	3.55%

The Department of Defence Production and Supplies has under its direct control, 39 Ordnance Factories and 8 Defence Public Sector Undertakings. These organisations endeavour to meet the growing needs of the Defence Services for new generation of armament systems and equipments in close cooperation with Defence Services and Defence Research and Development Organisation, through licenced production, and with their own in-house R&D. DDP&S, through the Supplies Wing, continuously interacts with the civil sector industry to mobilise its capabilities for undertaking production of equipment, systems, subsystems, components etc., required for the Services. The Department is engaged in a constant endeavour to manufacture or procure the requisite items indigenously, in a cost-effective manner, without compromising on quality and time-frames in which these are required.

The Department of Defence Production was set up in 1962 for organising and expanding the Defence Production base. In 1965, a separate Department of Defence Supplies was set up for mobilising the capabilities in the civil sector industry for Defence production. These two Departments were merged to constitute the present Department of Defence Production and Supplies, in January 1985. The Department has under its control, 5 allied organisations namely (i) Directorate of Planning and Coordination, (ii) Directorate General of Quality Assurance, (iii) Directorate of Technical Development and Production (Air), (iv) Directorate of Standardisation, and (v) Defence Exhibition Organisation.

In the present adverse Balance of Payments situation, DDP&S is making a vigorous effort towards export of Defence items, for earning foreign exchange and for optimally utilising the spare capacities available in the production units after meeting the requirements of the Defence Services. Such exports will be made to friendly countries, subject to periodic assessment of the international situation. Concerted efforts made during the last couple of years, to keep our products internationally competitive, have yielded some results. In 1988-89, the value of Defence exports was Rs. 45 crore (approx). It has gone upto Rs. 80 crore (approx) in 1989-90, thus registering a growth of 75 per cent over the previous year. Exports during 1990-91 are provisionally estimated at Rs. 79 crore. Defence PSUs and Ordnance Factories Board have export orders of Rs. 153 crore in hand for execution.

Self-reliance in the area of ammunition and explosives manufacture has almost been achieved. An indigenously developed field gun is being produced in the Ordnance Factories. The total value of imports in the Ordnance Factories during 1989-90 was only 1.5 per cent of the value of production, as against 2 per cent in 1988-89. These figures, however, are, exclusive of 'A' vehicles, SARATH and AJEYA which are in the completely knocked down phase of indigenous production, wherein presently the indigenous content is only 29 per cent . It is expected that by 1992-93 the indigenous content in AJEYA will go upto 97 per cent and in SARATH to 95.5 per cent .

Indigenisation efforts of Defence Public Sector Undertakings have paid high dividends. In Hindustan Aeronautics Ltd. (HAL), indigenous content for the entire range of production is 60 per cent . In the case of warships, the percentage of indigenisation has been progressively steeped upto about 70 per cent . On an overall basis, the percentage of indigenous content is 70 per cent in Bharat Electronics Ltd. (BEL) and Bharat Dynamics Ltd. (BDL) for the established items of production. MIDHANI aims at 90 per cent indigenisation in their production of super alloys.

Ordnance factories have given high priority to restrict and reduce consumption of key energy items, namely, electricity, petrol, diesel, fuel oil and coke/coal. The Defence Public Sector Undertakings have adopted the following measures aimed at economical use of energy : —

(i) Installation of capacitor Banks in the sub-stations and other load centres, maintaining power factor at 0.95;

(ii) Installation of fluorescent tubes in place of incandescent bulbs resulting in reduced power consumption;

(iii) Introduction of electronic timer switches for facilitating automatic switch on and off of street lights and other adoptable circuits;

(iv) Curtailment in the use of air conditioners in non-essential areas;

(v) Provision of latest heat insulation material and programmable controllers for various furnaces and shells to avoid heat radiation losses; and

(vi) Installation of solar heaters in a big way to meet hot water requirements of canteens and boiler feed water.

The Hindustan Aeronautics Ltd. has saved about Rs. 35 lakh per annum during the last 2 years and GRSE has saved more than Rs. 3.75 lakh during the period under review due to adoption of energy conservation measures.

Ordnance Factories have been consistently endeavouring to preserve the woods in their proximity. Every year a sizable area around these factories is brought under forest cover.

Defence PSUs pay special attention to maintenance of environmental standards through afforestation and pollution control measures. Mazagaon Dock Limited has undertaken to maintain and beautify the Baptista Gardens at Bhandara Hill Reservoir in Mazagaon. Bharat Electronics Limited has taken up beautification of the traffic islands in Bangalore. The Company has also established a large tree nursery. It has been also recognised by the Karnataka Forest Department as one of the centres in the programme for distribution of saplings.

TABLE 24.3: Value of Production and Average Value of Fixed Capital and Manpower for Preceeding Five Years

(*Rs. in crore*)

	Value of Production	Average value of Fixed Capital	Manpower (Nos. in Lakh)
1986-87	1609	585	1.81
1987-88	1846	624	1.78
1988-89	2242	661	1.77
1989-90	2338	749	1.75
1990-91	2570 (Provisional)	800	1.73 (Provisional)

Defence Supplies

The Supplies Wing of the Department of Defence Production and Supplies is responsible for utilising the capacity available in the civil sector for meeting Defence requirements. The rationale for creating a separate Supplies Wing in DDP&S is to optimise the participation of the civil sector in the indigenisation of the imported defence stores and taking up production of stores and equipments developed by Defence Research and Development Organisation (DRDO). This wing also lays down purchase policies for the established items exclusive to Defence, purchase of which is decentralised and dealt with by the concerned Service Headquarters.

Organisation

Supplies Wing functions through Technical Committees, (TCs)— currently 10 in number — headed by senior technical officers having expertise and intimate knowledge of the items/equipments. A Central Technical Committee (CTC) chaired by Secretary (DP&S) provides overall supervision and direction to the Technical Committees. Some of the important functionaries in the CTC are Director General Ordnance Factories (DGOF), Director General Technical Development (DGTD), Director General Quality Assurance and senior representatives of the Department of Defence, Finance, DRDO and the three Services.

Normally, the items selected for indigenisation are those, for the production of which technology is available in the country and the requirement is large enough to make production economically viable. However, indigenisation of items which have strategic importance is taken up irrespective of cost considerations. In respect of imported items, quite often, drawings and specifications are not available. In these cases considerable ground work has to be done by the Technical Committees through preparation of drawings and specifications and trials of prototypes. Bulk production begins only after these stages are successfully gone through. An essential preperquisite for indigenisation is the careful selection of the source. The TCs carry out verification of the capacity of the likely sources in the country through techno-economic surveys. Purchase decisions are taken on the basis of competitive quotations obtained from the 'capacity-verified' firms.

Interaction with Civil Sector

The optimisation of capacity utilisation in the civil sector necessitates a close and continuing interaction between Defence and civil sector. An Apex Body and three discipline-wise Functional Groups provide an institutionalised forum for this purpose. The civil sector industry is represented on these forums through the representatives nominated by the National Federations and Associations of Industry. Senior officials of the DDP&S, Ministry of Industry, Ministry of Finance, Planning Commission, and the three Services constitute the official side. These forums have been found very useful for appreciation of each other's problems.

Seminars and Workshops are organised from time to time to discuss various facets of civil sector participation in Defence production. While permanent Sample Rooms are being maintained in four metropolitan cities to familiarise the civil sector with the type of items needed by the Services, exhibitions on sectoral basis are organised from time to time to give the civil sector a wider exposure to Defence requirements. The interest generated through such exhibitions is used in giving a fillip to indigenisation efforts.

Achievements

The items which the Supplies Wing deals with are those which require *ab initio* development. The value of the orders placed for such items can be taken as an indicator of its performance. The measure of success achieved in this regard can be judged from the fact that the average annual value of orders placed during the Seventh Plan period has been nearly Rs. 225 crore against the annual level of ordering of about Rs. 55 crore and Rs. 100 crore during Fifth and Sixth Plans, respectively. The value of supply orders placed on civil sector for the period April 1, 1990 upto March 31, 1991 is estimated at Rs. 205.11 crore. The value of orders placed by the Supplies Wing on the civil sector—since 1986-87 has been indicated in Table 24.4.

A heartening feature of the civil sector participation in Defence production in the recent years is that, due to the rapid strides made by it in upgrading its technological base, it has been possible to place a greater degree of reliance on this sector for production of critical assemblies/sub-assemblies of sophisticated equipments. It is no longer necessary for Defence production units to manufacture all the assemblies and sub-assemblies in-house. This approach of obtaining assemblies and sub-assemblies from the civil sector with the Defence production units doing the final assembly of the equipment is being progressively implemented.

The first experiment of this kind, namely, the production of AJEYA and SARATH vehicles has been successful. Out of 186 assemblies/sub-assemblies of these combat vehicles given to the civil sector for production. Bulk production clearance (BPC) has already been accorded in respect of 144 items.

TABLE 24.4: Value of the orders placed by the Department of Defence Production and Supplies on Civil Sector

(*Rs. in crore*)

1986-87	1987-88	1988-89	1988-90	1990-91
277.41	245.73	134.02	238.84	205.11

Cooperation Between Armed Forces and Civil Authorities

Apart from discharging their primary responsibility of defending the country, the Armed Forces render assistance to civil authorities whenever called upon to do so, for the maintenance of law and order and in relief and rescue operation. The assistance of the Armed Forces is, however, to be sought and provided only in emergent situations and after all other avenues of assistance have been exhausted. The nature of assistance provided by the Armed Forces during the year under review is briefly outlined hereunder.

(i) *Maintenance of Law and Order*

(a) Army assistance continued to be provided in Jammu and Kashmir to maintain law and order in the Valley;

(b) Army assistance was rendered to the State Governments in Uttar Pradesh, Himachal Pradesh, Rajasthan, Punjab, Haryana, Bihar and Gujarat in the wake of widespread agitations against the implementation of the Mandal Commission recommendations, during September-October, 1990;

(c) Assistance was provided to the Government of Meghalaya in maintaining law and order in Shillong during inter-tribal violence in September, 1990; and

(d) The requisite assistance was extended to the States of Rajasthan, Gujarat, Uttar Pradesh, Haryana, Bihar, Andhra Pradesh, Assam and Jammu and Kashmir during the agitation arising out of the controversy relating to Ram Janma Bhoomi-Babri Masjid dispute. Army also assisted civil authorities in the maintenance of law and order in Uttar Pradesh, Andhra Pradesh and Gujarat during communal riots in December, 1990.

(ii) *Maintenance of Essential Services*

Army assistance was rendered to the concerned authorities in maintenance of essential services during the strikes by employees of the Oil and Natural Gas Commission in April and May, 1990, Uttar Pradesh Provincial Medical Health staff in April, 1990 and Maharashtra State Electricity Board employees in July, 1990.

(iii) *Counter Insurgency Operations*

Following the Presidential proclamation declaring the whole of Assam as a disturbed area and ULFA as an unlawful organisation, the assistance of Army was solicited and OP Bajrang was launched against the activities of the outlawed organisations, in November 1990. The Army also carried out operations against the outlawed National Socialist Council of Nagaland and continued to maintain pressure on the outlawed Peoples Liberation Army in Manipur. Besides, the Army continued to pursue its civil action programmes in Nagaland, Manipur and Assam to wean away misguided segments of the population from the various insurgent groups. During this period, it rendered medical aid, provided canteen facilities and assisted the State governments in their developmental projects.

(iv) *Natural Calamities*

During the period under review, the Army, Navy and Air Force were called upon to assist the civil authorities in combating the ravages caused by floods in many parts of the country and by the cyclone in the coastal districts of Andhra Pradesh. Significant instances where assistance was rendered are recounted below:

(a) Army participated in the rescue and relief operations when a severe cyclonic storm hit the coastal areas of Andhra Pradesh in May, 1990. The Indian Air Force helped the civil administration in providing relief in affected areas by carrying out casualty evacuation of nearly 500 personnel. About 40 tonnes of relief supplies including essential commodities were airdropped. In the aftermath of the cyclonic storm. Naval teams rescued a large number of marooned people and distributed relief material in several affected places;

(b) The Army and Air Force also participated in the rescue and relief operations in flood affected areas of Gujarat, Karnataka, Manipur, Mizoram, Rajasthan, Uttar Pradesh and Maharashtra during July and August, 1990;

(c) In the wake of the devastating earthquake in Iran, the Indian Air Force undertook relief missions to Teheran, airlifting about 90 tonnes of supplies at short notice; and

(d) Subsequent to the annexation of Kuwait by Iraq, 9 IL-76 transport aircrafts were deployed for evacuating about 5,600 Indian nationals from Iraq.

(v) *Diving Assistance*

During the period under review, Naval Divers assisted the civilian authorities in tasks involving underwater operations, namely, search and recovery of contraband goods sunk underwater and salvaging operations. Some notable instances of diving assistance rendered include the underwater clearance of 'MV Thuleland' leased for Antarctica expedition, carrying out repairs of sluice gates of the Yamunanagar Hydel Works and the underwater inspection of the diversion tunnel of the Tehri Dam Project.

National Cadet Corps

The National Cadet Corps (NCC), with its motto of 'Unity and Discipline' was established by an Act of Parliament in 1948. Its principal objectives are : —

(a) To develop leadership, character, comradeship, spirit of sportsmanship and ideals of service;

(b) To create a force of disciplined and trained manpower, which in a national emergency, could be of assistance to the country; and

(c) To provide training for students with a view to develop in them officer such as qualities, thus also enabling them to obtain commissions in the Armed Forces.

The Corps comprises 756 units organised into 91 Groups which are controlled by 16 Directorates. The Directorate General NCC, located at New Delhi, oversees the functioning of NCC through the 16 NCC Directorates. NCC Training Institutes are located at Kamptee and Gwalior.

Youth Exchange Programme

An Indian Team consisting of 8 Officers and 42 NCC cadets went to Canada in July, 1990, under the Indo-Canadian Youth Exchange Programme. They returned to India alongwith 2 Coordinators, 6 Group Leaders and 42 Participants from Canada in November, 1990 and underwent the Indian leg of the programme in the States of Maharashtra and Karnataka. They left India on January 31, 1991.

Four NCC Cadets (2 boys and 2 girls) attended the Annual Training Camp at Singapore from May 26 to June 8, 1990. Eight NCC Cadets (6 boys and 2 girls) attended the Annual Summer Camp in the United Kingdom from July 24 to August 7, 1990. One officer and four NCC Cadets (2 boys and 2 girls) attended the 25th Independence Day Celebrations of Singapore from August 8 to 12, 1990. Eight Cadets (5 boys and 3 girls) attended the Victory Day Celebrations of Bangladesh from December 13 to 23, 1990.

Thirty two Cadets from 7 countries (United Kingdom-8, Bangladesh-8, Singapore-4, Bhutan-4, Nepal-4, Sri Lanka-2, Maldives-2) attended the NCC Republic Day Camp, 1991.

Defence Public Sector Undertakings

The Defence Public Sector Undertakings (DPSUs) were established with a view to building up a strong and diversified production base capable of supplying State-of-the-art technology weapons and equipments to the country's Armed Forces, at economic prices. The Defence technical base that has been built up has also been utilised to meet the critical requirements of non-Defence users in allied fields. The following eight DPSUs have been functioning under the administrative control of the Department of Defence Production and Supplies :

Hindustan Aeronautics Ltd. (HAL)
Bharat Electronics (BE)
Bharat Earth Movers Ltd. (BEML)
Mazagaon Dock Ltd. (MDL)
Garden Reach Shipbuilders and Engineers (GRSE)
Goa Shipyards Ltd. (GSL)
Bharat Dynamics Ltd. (BDL)
Mishra Dhatu Nigam Ltd. (MIDHANI)

Hindustan Aeronautics Ltd.

Hindustan Aeronautics Ltd. (HAL) was set up in 1964 by amalgamating Hindustan Aircraft Ltd., with Aeronautics India Ltd. The Principal business of the Company is to design, manufacture, repair and overhaul various types of aircraft and helicopters and related aero-engines, avionics, instruments and accessories. The company has 13 Divisions located in six States.

HAL is engaged in all aspects of aerospace activity from product conception through design and development to the production and overhaul of aircraft. Its product mix comprises rotary and fixed wing aircraft of indigenous design/licence manufacture, jet and piston engines and matching avionics and accessories.

Highlights

The significant achievements of HAL during the period under review were as follows : —

— MiG-27M aircraft, Dornier-228 aircraft and R-29 B engine were produced from raw material phase during 1989-90 for the first time.
— A contract was signed between HAL and USSR for overhaul of MiG-27 M aircraft, its accessories and systems at various divisions of HAL.
— Aircraft Division of HAL assisted Air India in successful completion of fuselage section 41 structural modification work on Boeing 747-200 aircraft at Bombay. This work was earlier carried out abroad.
— Kanpur Division of HAL has completed structural modification work on Airbus A-300 of Indian Airlines.

Bharat Electronics

Bharat Electronics (BE) was established by the government under the Ministry of Defence in the year 1954 starting with the Bangalore Unit. It is presently the country's premier electronics manufacturing organisation having 9 operating units in various parts of the country. Since its inception, Bharat Electronics has achieved progressive self-reliance in the design, development and production of Radio Communication, Radars and Broadcasting equipments and electronic components of international standards.

Highlights

The noteworthy achievements of BE during the period under review are enumerated below : —

— Major new products delivered by BE to the customers are — Shelterised Radio Relay Equipment — RRE, Hull Mounted Variable Depth (Sonar) — HUMVAD, Radars RAWS/RAWL for Navy, Battlefield Surveillance Radar STENTOR, Secrecy Equipment — BEACON, Stabilizer for T-72 Tank, Electronic warfare Equipments Ajanta (P) and GEM to Defence; Electronic Voting Machine for the Election Commission; communication equipment for DOT; 100W UHF TV Transmitter for Doordarshan.

— To promote export of Computer Software, a business cell software Export Promotion Cell, SOFEX has been set up.
— The Company won the second best Productivity Performance award from the National Productivity Council for 1988-89.
— The Ghaziabad Unit was awarded the National Safety award by the British Safety Council, London for the second consecutive year.

Bharat Electronics is engaged in the production and supply of a very wide range of electronic equipments and components. Its primary job is to design, develop and manufacture the sophisticated state-of-the-art electronic equipments used by the Indian Defence Services. It is notable that there has been very limited import of vital electronic communication equipments by the Indian Defence Services for the last 5 years. The major equipments produced and supplied to the services include HF and VHF Communication Transmitters, Receivers and VHF and UHF and Micro Wave Radio Relay equipments. For the Civil Sector, the equipments supplied include studio and transmitter equipments for sound and TV broadcasting, equipments for Space Research Organisation, communication transmitters and receivers of different frequency and outputs and electronic voting machines.

The components produced by BE include TV Picture Tubes, silicon and germanium semi-conductors, integrated circuits and crystals, transmitting tubes, micro-wave tubes, hybrid micro-circuits, image converters, magnesium manganese dioxide batteries, X-Ray tubes, vacuum capacitors and contractors.

Bharat Earth Movers Limited

Established in 1964 by hiving off the Railcoach Division of the then Hindustan Aircraft Ltd., M/s Bharat Earth Movers Limited (BEML) commenced production in 1965. BEML is at present the leading manufacturer of Earthmoving Equipment, serving approximately 70 per cent of the market. The Company has its Corporate Office and Marketing Division at Bangalore; three production Complexes at Kolar Gold Fields (KGF), Bangalore and Mysore; a Research and Development Division at KGF with unit each at Bangalore and Mysore; and a well knit country-wide net-work of Sales and Service Centres/Regional Offices under its Marketing Division. BEML has a subsidiary company, M/s Vignyan Industries Ltd., Tarikere, (Karnataka) which was taken over in 1984 :

Highlights

Some of the important achievements during the period under review are enumerated below : —

The Company has received the following awards;

— Corporate Excellence award for outstanding performance in 1987-88 was received in August, 1990.
— Certificate of merit for excellence in performance in the achievements of MOU targets for 1989-90.
— All India Special Shield for exporting new products during 1989-90.
— Company Standardisation Commendation Award from the Institute of Standard Engineers for the year 1988-89.

— National Award for the Best Employer of the Handicapped.
— National Safety Award for outstanding performance in industrial safety.

The Company was recognised as an Export House by the Chief Controller of Imports and Exports. The highest ever figure of Rs. 56.12 crore was achieved in respect of exports in 1989-90. BEML's Project for manufacturing the Transmissions and Allied Assemblies for specialised vehicles for Army was completed in 1989-90 as per schedule.

Product Mix

BEML manufactures a wide range of Earthmoving equipment like Electric Rope shovels, Bulldozers, Hydraulic Excavators, Wheel Loaders/wheel Dozers, Dump Trucks, Water sprinklers, Motor Graders of different capacities. For the Railways, the Company manufactures different models of broad-gauge second class passenger railcoaches, postal vans, Motor Vans, parcel Luggage and Brake vans, Overhead Electric Inspection Cars and Track Laying Equipment.

Heavy Duty BEML-Tatra Trucks, Air craft Towing Tractors, Aggregates, Transmissions and Allied Assemblies for specialised vehicles and mine ploughs are some of the specific items manufactured by BEML for the Defence Services.

The Company's Subsidiary M/s. Vignyan Industries Ltd. is engaged in the manufacture of a variety of steel castings.

Mazagon Dock Limited

Mazagon Dock Limited (MDL) has come a long way from being a ship repair yard in 1960 to its current status as a premier builder of warships, submarine, and offshore platforms. As a result of phased programmes of expansion and development, MDL's ship-building capacity has increased to build warships of upto 6000 DWT and merchant ships of upto 27,000 DWT. The East Yard is dedicated to submarine construction.

In 1976 MDL diversified to produce Offshore Platforms for ONGC. To meet these new commitments, the Company developed three production units; in Alcock Ashdown in Bombay adjacent to the main yard, at Nhava Sheva Port and at Mangalore.

Highlights

The important achievements during the period are recounted below : —

— The seventh Offshore Patrol Vessel, CGS VIGRAHA, was commissioned into the Coast Guard;
— The first Missile Boat for the Navy was launched;
— The second Corvette, INS Kuthar, was commissioned into the Navy;
— The keel of the sixth offshore supply vessel for ONGC was laid;
— Work on the seventh offshore supply vessel was commenced;
— The second jack-up Rig, SAGAR UDAY, was delivered to the ONGC.

Garden Reach Shipbuilding and Engineers Ltd.

Garden Reach Shipbuilding and Engineers Ltd. (GRSE) was originally set up in 1884 and was acquired by Government of India in 1960.

GRSE has three well structured divisions; Ship Division, which undertakes construction and repairs of various types of ships and Fibreglass Reinforced Plastic (FRP) Boats; Engineering Division which manufactures portable bridges, deck machinery items, ship-borne equipments, agricultural pumps and other sophisticated equipments for defence and civil use; and an Engine Division which manufactures diesel engines both for marine propulsion and power generation. The Company has 6 units in and around Calcutta and a Diesel Engine Plant located at Ranchi.

Highlights

Salient achievements of the period under review are highlighted below : —

- Keels were laid for landing ship and follow-on Corvette for the Navy and Inshore Patrol Vessel for the Coast Guard and for marine Acoustic Research Ship for Naval Physical Oceanographic Laboratory.
- One Survey Vessel for the Navy and one Inshore Patrol Vessel for the Coast Guard were launched.
- Survey Vessel INS Investigator for the Navy and Inshore Patrol Vessels CGS AKKA DEVI and CGS NAIKI DEVI for the Coast Guard were commissioned.

Goa Shipyard Limited

Goa Shipyard Ltd. (GSL) was established in 1957. Its activities comprise ship construction, repairs to ships and barges as well as associated general engineering works. GSL has undertaken construction of a variety of vessels for the Navy and Coast Guard, including classified vessels, oilers, etc. For the commercial sector, the construction of passenger and Mooring Vessels are in hand, apart from two Fishing Vessels already delivered. Refits to Naval and Coast Guard Vessels as well as repairs to ships calling at the local port are also undertaken.

Highlights

The important achievements of GSL during the period under review are indicated below : —

- Keels were laid for EPV-2 "KAMALA DEVI"
- 20 T TUG BAJRANG, 6 T HU TUG "ANAND" for the Navy and one OPV-2 "VARAHA" for the Coast Guard were launched.
- OPV-1 "VARAD" was delivered to the Coast Guard.

Bharat Dynamics Limited

Bharat Dynamics Ltd. (BDL), Hyderabad was incorporated in July, 1970 as an agency for manufacturing and eventually indigenising the production of guided missiles and allied equipment in the country. The Company has successfully completed the order for the first generation Anti Tank Guided Missile and the 122 mm Grad Rockets. At present, BDL is engaged in the production of the MILAN, a second generation Anti Tank Guided Missile, Production of Konkurs Missile and Konkurs Unified Launcher under licence agreement has commenced in 1989.

Highlights

BDL has established most of the facilities required to undertake the limited series production of Prithvi and Trishul missiles and has produced certain components for conducting their flight trials. As the prime production agency for the manufacture of the 4 missiles systems being developed under DRDO, it is involved in the fabrication of components/assemblies. The Company has also diversified its activities to undertake a number of Naval projects.

A three phased indigenisation programme for Milan was undertaken. 303 items have already been indigenised. BDL has also undertaken an accelerated indigenisation programme for Konkurs which is to be completed by 1992-93.

Mishra Dhatu Nigam Limited

Mishra Dhatu Nigam (MIDHANI) was incorporated on November 20, 1973 as a public sector undertaking of the Department of Defence Production, Ministry of Defence. It went into commercial production in July, 1983. MIDHANI is a unique plant set up to supply special super alloys and special metals requiring high level of technical perfection, to strategic industries such as Aeronautics, Space, Defence Atomic Energy, Chemical Engineering etc.

Highlights

It has been successful in producing alloys to meet the specific requirements of user industries; for instance, MIDHANI has developed the production technology for Maraging Steel for PSLV and GSLV projects of the Space Department. Titanium and Titanium alloys are supplied to Chlor-Alkali industries as substitutes for graphite anodes which is expected to bring down energy consumption by 25 per cent in these industries. The Company continues to meet most of the country's requirement of Molybdenum for the lamp industry and has obtained bulk orders for special type of laminations developed for C-DOT, Significant improvements made by MIDHANI have resulted in improved yields for grades like pure-iron, soft magnetic alloys and controlled expansion alloys.

25

EDUCATION

The 42nd amendment to the Constitution effected in 1976 made education a concurrent subject, thereby empowering the Central Government to legislate on education. However, the Centre, continues to play the role of a co-ordinator and monitor of educational programme and an initiator of innovative programmes. The approach, thus has been to evolve a meaningful partnership between the Central and the State Governments. The Government of India, Ministry of Human Resource Development (Department of Education) appoints Committees and Commissions to examine the state of education in the country and to suggest measures for improvement. It also serves as a clearing house of ideas.

Educational planning in the country is essentially the joint endeavour of the Central and State Governments. At the Central level, planning and monitoring division in the Ministry of Human Resource Development works in close liaison with the education division of the Planning Commission at the Centre and the State Planning Departments.

Actions related to education at the national level including planning and policy-making are guided and coordinated by the Central Advisory Board of Education and a few national level institutions specialising in particular aspects of education.

Department of Education, Ministry of Human Resource Development, Government of India

The Department of Education is one of the constituents of the Ministry of Human Resource Development. The Secretariat of the Department is headed by the Secretary who is assisted by Additional Secretary and Educational Adviser. The Department is organised into Bureaux, Divisions, Branches, Desks, Sections and Units. Each Bureau is under the charge of a Joint Secretary/Joint Educational Adviser assisted by Divisional Heads.

Important functions of the Department of Education are to evolve educational policy in all aspects and to coordinate and determine the standards of higher education and technical education; to develop and coordinate research in social sciences; to coordinate, in partnership with the States, activities aimed at achieving national goals such as Universal Elementary Education (UEE), adult literacy, making education relevant to the world of work, development of scientific temper amongst students, removal of sex bias, provision of access to education for the deprived and disadvantaged etc; to foster and develop study of languages— Hindi, Modern Indian and Classical languages including Sanskrit; to deal with intellectual property; to improve quality of textbooks and develop book industry; to administer scholarships for the deprived and the talented; and to coordinate UNESCO programmes.

Autonomous Organisations and Attached Offices and Allied Organisations connected with Department of Education

1. All India Council for Technical Education, New Delhi for coordinating and setting standards in the area of technical education.
2. Central Advisory Board of Education, Department of Education, Shastri Bhawan, New Delhi.
3. Central Board of Secondary Education (CBSE), Preet Vihar, Delhi; for affiliating schools and conducting examinations.
4. The Kendriya Hindi Sansthan (KHS), Agra, for the promotion of Hindi in India and abroad.
5. The Kendriya Vidyalaya Sanghathan (KVS), New Delhi for running schools for the benefit of transferable Central Government employees.
6. The Navodaya Vidyalaya Samiti, New Delhi, for running schools for the benefit of talented rural children.
7. Indian Council of Advanced Study, Shimla, for research in Higher Education.
8. Indian Council of Historical Research (ICHR), New Delhi, for research in History.
9. Indian Council of Philosophical Research (ICPR), New Delhi, for research in Philosophy.
10. Indian Council of Social Science Research (ICSSR), New Delhi, for research in Social Sciences.
11. The National Council of Educational Research and Training (NCERT), New Delhi, a National level resource institution operating in the school sector.
12. The National Institute of Educational Planning and Administration (NIEPA), New Delhi, also a national level resource institution, specialising in problems of Educational Management.
13. The University Grants Commission (UGC), New Delhi, which coordinates and sets standards in the area of higher education.

Organisation for the Promotion of Books and Languages are :

14. The Bureau for Promotion of Urdu (BPU), New Delhi.
15. The Central Hindi Directorate (CHD), New Delhi.
16. The Commission for Scientific and Technical Technology (CSTT), New Delhi.
17. The National Book Trust, New Delhi.

In the field of Adult Education, following organisations work :

18. Directorate of Adult Education, New Delhi.
19. National Literacy Mission (NLM).
20. National Institute of Adult Education.

In higher education, the following organisation acts as a bureau of information:

21. Association of Indian Universities, New Delhi.

Universal Elementary Education (UEE)

(Classes I to VIII)

Universalisation of elementary education has been one of the most important goals of educational development in India since Independence. Article 45 of the Indian Constitution directed the State to endeavour to provide within a period of 10 years of the commencement of the Constitution free and compulsory education to all children up to the age of 14 years. This resolve to be fulfilled by 1960 was, however, severely hampered by several problems, such as the influx of displaced persons after partition and scarcity of resources, both financial and human. As a result, the target date had to be first revised to 1970, then to 1976, and later to 1990. The present target date according to the National Policy on Education, 1986 is 1995.

Substantial progress has been achieved in the provision of schooling facilities since 1950. The number of primary schools increased from 2,09,671 in 1950-51 to 5,50,700 in 1989-90. During the same period, the number of middle schools increased from 13,596 to 1,43,747. The total enrolment in classes I-V increased from 19.155 million in 1950-51 to 97.3 million in 1989-90. The enrolment in classes VI to VIII increased from 3.120 million to 1950-51 to 32.2 million in 1989-90. The total enrolment of children in classes I-VIII increased from 22.275 million in 1950-51 to 129.5 million in 1989-90. The gross enrolment ratio at the primary stage also registered considerable increase from 42.6 per cent to 99.9 per cent during the period 1950-51 to 1989-90. During this period, the gross enrolment ratio at the middle stage (classes VI to VIII) increased from 12.9 per cent to 59.1 per cent.

Drop-Outs

Despite this level of expansion of education, vast ground is yet to be covered for fulfilling the constitutional mandate of UEE. Dropout rates are significant; retention of children in schools is low; wastage is considerable (in 1986-87 drop out rates were 50.5 in classes I to V and 63.8 in classes I to VIII). There are striking disparities in access to Elementary Education — disparities between regions, rural and urban areas, boys and girls, the affluent and the deprived and the minorities and the others.

Non-formal Education (NFE)

As a part of the effort to provide universal elementary education. Non-formal Education (NFE) Programme introduced during the Sixth Five Year Plan as a Centrally assisted scheme is now implemented in the educationally backward States of Andhra Pradesh, Arunachal Pradesh, Assam, Bihar, Jammu and Kashmir, Madhya Pradesh, Orissa, Rajasthan, Uttar Pradesh and West Bengal. It has also been extended to urban slums, hilly, desert and tribal areas and project for working children in all the other States. Under the revised scheme, assistance is being given to State Governments in the ratio 50;50 and 90:10 for running general NFE centres and girls' NEF centres respectively. Hundred per cent Central assistance is being given to voluntary agencies.

The essential features of the revised scheme are : organisation flexibility, relevance of curriculum, diversity in learning activities to relate them to the learners' needs and strengthened decentralised management. The programme is now being implemented on a project basis.

Operation Blackboard (OB)

The Scheme of Operation Blackboard (OB) started in 1987 aims at bringing about substantial improvement in facilities in primary schools run by Government, Local Bodies, Panchayati Raj and recognised aided institutions. It has three interdependent components, namely,

— Provision of a building comprising/at least two reasonable large all-weather rooms with a deep varandah and separate toilet facilities for boys and girls;
— At least two teachers in every school, as far as possible, one of them a woman; and
— Provision of essential teaching and learning materials including blackboards, maps, charts, toys and equipment for work experience.

Funds for construction of school buildings are to provided mainly under National Rural Employment Programme (NREP) and Landless Employment Guarantee Programme (LEGP), now Jawahar Rozgar Yojana (JRY). Funds for other components are provided by the Department of Education. The scheme seeks to cover the Primary Schools in all the blocks/Municipal areas in the country in a phased manner. The target has been to cover 20 per cent blocks/Municipal areas during 1987-88, 30 per cent of them during 1988-89 and 50 per cent of them during 1989-90.

Navodaya Vidyalayas (NVs)

In order to provide good quality modern education to the talented children predominantly from the rural areas, Government of India launched a scheme in 1987-88 to establish Navodaya Vidyalayas on an average one in each district. Two hundred and sixty one Navodaya Vidyalayas covering 22 States and 7 Union Territories have so far been established in the Country.

Admission to Navodaya Vidyalayas is at the level of Class VI.

Environmental Orientation to School Education

In pursuance of NPE 1986, a Centrally Sponsored Scheme of Environmental Orientation to School Education was brought under implementation from 1988-89. Under the Scheme, 100 per cent financial assistance is provided to States/Union Territories and Voluntary Organisations working in the field of Environment Education. The project activities include review of curricular and extra curricular materials, preparation of general informative books/brochures/postures/audio-visual materials, adoption of monuments by schools for study and upkeep and study of ecological problems in the neighbourhood. One of the preferred activities under the project is setting up of school nurseries. Voluntary Organisations are also involved in innovative projects relating to Environment Education.

Educational Technology (ET) Programme

As a measure of widening access to education and towards bringing about qualitative improvement in education, an Educational Technology Programme was started as a Central Sector Scheme in 1972 and has been continuing as such till 1987-88 when it became a Centrally Sponsored Scheme. However, the Government of India continues to bear 100 per cent expenditure on most of the components of the scheme.

National Population Education Project (NPEP)

The Project was launched with effect from April 1980 designed to introduce population education in the formal education system. The underlying objective is to create in the younger generation adequate awareness of the population problems and realisation in this regard of their responsibilities towards the nation. The programme has been developed in collaboration with the United Nations Population Fund (UNFPA) and with the active involvement of Ministry of Health and Family Welfare which is nodal Ministry for the project. The NCERT provides technical assistance. The expenditure incurred by the implementing agencies in States/UTs and NCERT on this project is reimbursed by UNFPA.

In order to facilitate effective integration of population education elements, the conceptual framework of population education has been revised and Minimum Essential Contents have been identified. A compendium of Lessons on Population Education for selected subjects that are being taught in different classes from I to XII has been developed. A number of prototype curricular and instructional materials including textual and audio visual materials and also evaluation tools, have been developed at the national level and circulated to States/UTs for their use. Four hundred titles of different kinds of material available in 17 Indian Languages have been developed. An evaluation study of curricular and textual materials was conducted. Instructional and training materials, including audio-visual material of 9 Hindi — speaking States and Union Territories were reviewed and screened. About 600 posters and charts prepared in different themes and content of population education were reviewed as also some video cassettes and slide sets. Meaningful guidelines for preparing effective and qualitative audio-visual materials have been developed. The States/UTs developed audio-visual materials used primarily in teacher training programmes. Orientation programmes for textbooks authors, curriculum developers and teacher educators are organised. In States/UTs over a million teachers, teacher educators, key persons, educational administrators and other functionaries have been trained during the last eight years. Painting competition and essay writing competition have been organised at the national level. States/UTs also organise debates, declamation, essay writing and painting competitions, exhibitions, youth parliament and kavi darbars on this subject.

Computer Education in Schools

A Pilot Project on Computer Literacy and Studies in Schools (CLASS) was initiated in 1984-85 in 248 selected Secondary/Higher Secondary Schools jointly by the Department of Electronics and the Department of Education to acquaint students and teachers with the range of computer applications and its potential as a learning medium. By the end of 1988-89, 2080 additional schools had been covered including 380 schools covered during 1988-89. Sixty resource centres have been set up to trained school teachers and provide logistic support to the participating schools. Of these, 7 resource centres were selected during 1989-90. Maintenance of hardware and its installation continued to be the responsibility of Computer Maintenance Corporation Ltd. with the NCERT continuing as the nodal agency to implement the project.

Sources: 1. *Annual Reports 1989-90* and *1990-91*, Department of Education, Ministry of Human Resource Development, Government of India, 1990 and 1991.

2. *Selected Educational Statistics*, 1988-89 and 1989-90.

Examination Reform by Central Board of Secondary Education, Delhi : Court Judgement

The Delhi High Court reluctantly gave green signal to the Central Board of Secondary Education's experiment of multiple sets of question papers in the same hall for class XII and X examinations in Delhi only from March 3 onwards.

The two judges, Mr. Justice D.P. Wadhwa and Mr. Justice R.L. Gupta, said they were "inclined to agree" with the complaints that the board's decision "was arbitrary and discriminatory" but added they were helpless in restraining the Board, as the examination was only three days away (March 3).

"It is impossible to prepare question papers all over again at such short notice", they stated. "The petitioners have come too late in the day", they added.

However, Mr. Justice Wadhwa and Mr. Justice Gupta admitted the petition for detailed scrutiny and even recalled their earlier order of dismissal of a similar writ questioning the new system of examination issued on January 21. "The points now raised were not fully agitated at that time and the petitioner (then) also did not file any further appeal," they observed.

The present petitioners, two class XII students had applied saying that the board's decision of introducing multiple sets of question papers in the ensuing CBSE examination for only Delhi schools was arbitrary and discriminatory. So it be restrained from doing so.

In their order the judges held, "we are, *prima facie*, inclined to agree with the petitioners that the decision to introduce multiple sets of question papers is arbitrary, unreasonable and it has no rational relationship with the object sought to be achieved". The Board said they were doing this experiment in Delhi, as it had the maximum cases of mass cheating during past CBSE examinations. And multiple sets of question papers was one method to combat this. The judges were, however, not convinced with this argument.

The judges even said they will have certainly stopped the Board from going ahead with such an examination but there were even graver considerations at this time.

"There are about 96,000 students appearing for examination for XII class and over 1.5 lakh for X class. Their dates of examination had been announced much earlier. All preparations for the conduct of the examination have been taken. . . to hold an examination for such a large number of students is a Herculean task. The question papers all ready are lying in sealed packets to be sent to various centres", the judges stated.

Source : *Times of India*, February 29,1992.

Panel on School Curricula

The Government has appointed a National Advisory Committee under former UGC Chairman, Prof. Yash Pal to recommend how the school curricula could be modified to reduce the workload on students at all levels, particularly the young ones.

The other members of the committee are Prof. Krishna Kumar of Delhi University, Prof. T.S. Saraswathy of the Baroda-based MS University, Ms Dina Guha, a psychologist from Bombay, Mrs. V. Parthasarathy, principal of the Sardar Patel School, Delhi, Dr. V.G. Kulkarni of the Homi Bhabha Science Centre and Prof. Poromesh Acharya of the IIM, Calcutta. Dr. G.L. Arora, SCERT director, would act as member-secretary.

Higher Education

Growth of Higher Education System

At the beginning of the year 1989-90, the total student enrolment in Universities and Colleges was 39.48 lakhs. This was 1.34 lakhs more than the enrolment in the previous year. The enrolment in the University Departments was 6.55 lakhs and that in the affiliated Colleges was 32.93 lakhs.

Enrolment in the Faculty of Arts constituted 40.3 per cent of the total enrolment. In the Faculties of Science and Commerce the percentage was 19.7 and 21.5 respectively. Enrolment at the first degree level was 34.74 lakhs (88%); at the postgraduate level; 3.75 lakhs (9.5%); at the research level 0.43 lakhs (1.1%); and at the diploma and certificate level 0.55 lakhs (1.4%).

The number of teachers increased to 2.49 lakhs during the year 1989. Of these, 0.55 lakhs were in the University Departments/University Colleges and the rest in the affiliated colleges. Of the 54,973 teachers in the Universities, 6432 were Professors, 13,468 were Readers, 32,764 were Lecturers and 2309 were Tutors/Demonstrators. In the affiliated Colleges, the number of senior teachers was 25,815, the number of Lecturers was 1,59,546 and that of Tutors/Demonstrators was 8734.

Higher Education among Women

The enrolment of women students at the beginning of the year 1989-90 was 12.51 lakhs as against 11.25 lakhs in the previous year. At the post-graduate level, the enrolment of women was 33.0 per cent of the total enrolment. The enrolment of women students was the highest in Kerala (52.1%) followed by Punjab (46.6%), Delhi (44.6%), Haryana (39.7%) and Meghalaya/Nagaland (39.8%). The enrolment of women was the lowest in Bihar (16.0%).

Technical Education

Diploma and Degree Courses

Diploma courses in technical education are offered in about 400 approved polytechnics, with an annual enrolment capacity of about 70,000 students. There are 62 more approved polytechnics meant exclusively for girls with an annual intake of about 5,900. Polytechnics are widely spread in States and Union Territories. They are affiliated to the respective State Boards of Technical Education.

For professional engineers and technologists 200 approved engineering colleges offer courses leading to a bachelor's degree of the respective university. Total admission capacity annually for these courses is about 36,000. Number of institutions offering post-graduate courses is about 115 with an annual capacity of 7,500. Facilities also exist at most of the centres for part time courses at Post-graduate level.

There are 17 regional engineering colleges providing facilities for education in various branches of engineering and technology.

Indian Institutes of Technology

The five Indian Institutes of Technology (IITs) at Bombay, Delhi, Kanpur, Kharagpur and Madras were established as premier centres of education and training in engineering and applied science at the under-graduate level and to provide adequate facilities for post-graduate studies and research. These are Institutes of National Importance. They admit nearly 2,000 students every year to the Post-Graduate courses and research scholars. Their annual provision for under-graduate courses is about 1,600 students.

The IITs conduct four-year under-graduate programmes leading to Bachelor's Degree in Technology (B.Tech.) in various fields of engineering and technology. They also offer integrated Master's Degree Courses in many disciplines.

Literacy

The failure to achieve UEE makes it inevitable to take up Adult Literacy Programme. The National Adult Education Programme was introduced in 1978. As of 30th June, 1990 about 2.7 lakh adult education centres were being operated, in which about 80 lakh illiterate adults are enrolled every year. However, 40 per cent of these enrolled drop out due to a variety of compulsions; about 20 per cent relapse into illiteracy. The remaining 40 per cent who go through the cycle of learning can be said to have acquired some literacy and numeracy though not necessarily of the desired level.

The National Literacy Mission (NLM) was launched in 1988; one of the six technology missions NLM sought to impart functional literacy to about 800 lakh illiterate adults in the age group of 15-35 by 1995. Another landmark was the introduction in 1988 of Jana Shikshan Nilayams (JSNs); the network of JSNs provides an institutional framework for post literacy and continuing education and would help ensure that neoliterates do not relapse into illiteracy. At present, there are over 2.50 lakh AE centres being run through the Rural Functional Literacy Projects, the State Adult Education Programme and voluntary agencies. Out of about 32 thousand JSNs sanctioned so far, over 22 thousand have already become operational. During 1990-91, it is estimated that 84 lakh adults would be enrolled.

Mahila Samakhya

An innovative project entitled 'Mahila Samakhya' (Education for Women's Equity) was launched on a pilot basis in April 1989 in ten districts in the States of Karnataka, Uttar Pradesh and Gujarat. It will continue up to 1995. It is built around the empirical observation noticed in many programmes for women's development that a group of motivated women can be an effective focal point for mobilisation. The project receives 100 per cent assistance from the Government of the Netherlands. The programme is currently operational in 1500 villages in ten districts and is likely to expand to 20 districts in a phased manner.

National Institute of Adult Education (NIAE)

On 4 January, 1991 the Government of India adopted a resolution establishing a National Institute of Adult Education (NIAE) as an autonomous national institution. The main purposes of this Institute are: (1) to provide academic and technical resource support for the National Literacy Mission (NLM) and adult education programmes of every description; (2) to organize training courses designed to meet the needs of the adult education programmes; (3) to work at the improvement of the contents of those programmes and the methods used; (4) to prepare material for the media and to make use of traditional and folk media; (5) to undertake research, evaluation and monitoring activities; (6) to establish links with the different types of institutions and other agencies concerned and co-ordinate their efforts; (7) to establish, develop and administer an institution with these purposes in view.

Although set up in an academic context, NIAE will draw its strength from its close links with field programmes and cultivate team work rather than a bureaucratic hierarchical system.

Marks for Literacy Work

The Central Board of Secondary Education (CBSE) has decided to award marks to students for literacy work under a Special Drive on Adult Literacy. The scheme launched on October 2, 1991 will cover class IX and XI during the current session and will be extended to class X and XII from 1992-93 session.

Under the scheme, five marks will be awarded to a student for each person made literate in a year, 8 marks for two persons and 10 marks for three or more persons made literate in one year. The marks will be awarded by schools in class IX and XI and by the CBSE in class X and XII.

Apart from the students the Board has also worked out a package of incentives for teachers as well as institutions. With the expected target of one literate per student per year in Secondary and Senior Secondary classes, schools will be entitled to Golden Certificate with achievement of 90 per cent and above and Silver Certificate with achievement between 80 per cent and 90 per cent. The Board will award every year Special Trophy for three best schools on the basis of best average of persons made literate.

Similarly teachers will be honoured by the schools with certificates or trophies for commendable work in literacy.

Besides the incentive of marks, certificates will also be awarded to students who make five or more illiterates literate in a year. It is expected that more than

8 lakh illiterates would benefit every year under the Special Drive for Adult Literacy launched by the CBSE.

Source : *Yojana*, December 15, 1991.

Minority Educational Institutions: Supreme Court Judgement on Reservation

In a 4:1 judgement, delivered in the St. Stephen's College case, by a five-judgement constitution bench held that under Article 30 (1) of the Constitution, the minority-aided educational institutions are entitled to prefer their community candidates to maintain the minority character of the institutions subject of course in conformity with the university standard.

The court said that "the state may regulate the intake in this category with due regard to the need of the community in the area which the institution is intended to serve. But in no case such intake shall exceed 50 per cent of the annual admission."

The majority judgement, delivered by Mr. Justice M.H. Kania, Mr. Justice K. Jaganatha Shetty, Ms. Justice M. Fathima Beevi and Mr. Justice Yogeshwar Dayal, said that minority institutions shall make available at least 50 per cent of the annual admission to members of communities other than the minority community. The admission of other community candidates shall be done purely on the basis of merit.

However, Mr. Justice N.M. Kasliwal delivered the dissenting judgement.

Mr. Justice Kania who delivered the majority judgement observed that "the minorities have the right to admit their own candidates to maintain the minority character of their institutions. This is a necessary concommitment right which flows from the right to establish and administer educational institution in Article 30 (1) of the Constitution."

He said, "there is also a related right to the parents in the minority communities. The parents are entitled to have their children educated in institutions having an atmosphere congenial to their own religion."

The judges said that "the collective right is required to be made functional and is not to be reduced to useless lumber. A meaningful right must be shaped, moulded and created under Article 30 (1), while at the same time affirming the right of individuals under Article 29 (2) which says that no citizen shall be denied admission into any educational institution maintained by the state or receiving aid out of State funds on the ground of religion, race, caste, language of any of them.

The court allowed the plea of St. Stephen's College affiliated to the Delhi University that it was entitled to have its own admission programme since it was a minority institutions. The similar plea was made by the Allahabad Agricultural Institute at Naini. The validity of the admission programme and the preference given to Christian students were the issue before the court.

The court rejected an argument that St. Stephen's College after being affiliated to the Delhi University has lost its minority character.

The judges said "we find no substance in the contention. The state or any instrumentality of the State cannot deprive the character of the institution, founded by a minority community by compulsory affiliation."

The judges said "The minority institution has a distinct identity and the right to administer with continuance of such identity cannot be denied by coercive action. Any such coercive action would be void being contrary to the constitutional guarantee".

The right to administer is the right to conduct and manage the affairs of the institution. This right is exercised by a body of persons who the founders have faith and confidence. Such a management body of the institution cannot be displaced or reorganised if the right is to be recognised and maintained, the judges said.

The judges said "reasonable regulations, however, are permissible but regulations should be of regulatory nature and not of abridgement of the right guaranteed under Article 30 (1) of the Constitution.

The judges further said that there was no provision in the Delhi University Act with overriding powers precluding the management of the college from exercising its right to administer the college as a minority institution.

Referring to a circular issued by the Delhi University on June 5, 1980 directing the college to admit students solely on the basis of merit, the judges said that the University cannot direct the college to dispense with its admission programme in the absence of proof of maladministration of the college. The judges concluded that St. Stephen's College is not bound by the impunged circulars of the University.

Referring to minority rights and balancing interests, the judges said the Constitution establishes secular democracy. The animating principle of any democracy is the equality of the people. But the idea that all people are equal is profoundly speculative.

The judges said "we have to recognise a fair degree of discrimination in favour of minorities. But it is impossible to have an affirmative action for religious minorities in religious neutral way. In order to get beyond religion, we cannot ignore religion".

The judges said that it is now an accepted jurisprudence and practice that the concept of equality before the law and the prohibition of certain kinds of discrimination do not require identical treatment. The equality means the relative equality, namely the principle to treat equally what are equal and unequally what are unequal. To treat unequals differently according to their inequality is not only permitted but required.

Source: *Hindustan Times*, December 7, 1991.

Janardhan Reddy Committee on National Education Policy (1986), 1991

The Committee on education policy headed by the Andhra Pradesh Chief Minister, Mr. N. Janardhan Reddy, has recommended that every effort be made to ensure that the constitutional obligation of providing free and compulsory education up to the age of 14 years becomes a reality by the end of the 20th century.

The Committee, which submitted its report to the Human Resource Development Ministry recently, had gone into the implementation of the 1986 National Education Policy, which was formulated when the Prime Minister, Mr. P.V. Narasimha Rao, headed the HRD Ministry. Subsequently, when the National Front government came to power, it appointed a review committee, under the chairmanship of Acharya Ramamurthi, to go into the recommendations of the earlier committee report.

The Reddy Committee was set up by the Congress government in 1991. Besides, looking into the implementation of its own earlier policies, its brief was also to study the Acharya Ramamurthi Committee's recommendations.

In its report, the Reddy Committee has identified several priority areas during the Eighth Plan for attaining the goal of universalisation of elementary education. Among other things, it has emphasised universal enrolment, recommended setting up of primary schools within one kilometre of walking distance for all children and suggested that facilities of non-formal education be provided for school drop-outs, working children and girls, who cannot attend school.

Drop-out Rate

The Committee has called for bringing down the drop-out rate between classes I to V from the existing 45 per cent to 20 per cent and from 60 per cent to 40 per cent for classes I to VIII.

Operation Blackboard should be extended to upper primary level as well and local-level committees, which include women and teachers, be set up to assist in the working of primary educational institutions, the report has recommended.

It has further been suggested that the promotion of universalisation of elementary education and adult literacy should be simultaneous. The Committee described the total literacy campaign approach as a potent and viable one, which could help achieve a significant breakthrough in the literacy scene.

The Reddy Committee has also stressed the need for initiating programmes for post-literacy and continuing education, which, the report suggested, should be planned alongwith literacy campaigns.

Source: *Times of India*, March 2, 1991.

Educational Statistics

TABLE 25.1: Non-formal Education : Achievements

Items	Total for 1988-89, 1989-90 & 1990-91
NFE Centres brought to function	2,70,000
Number of exclusive girls' Centres sanctioned	81,282
Number of voluntary organisations approved for NFE Programmes	410
NFE Centres brought to function by voluntary agencies	27,087
Estimated enrolment (in lakhs)	68
Number of experimental/ innovative projects approved	46
Number of D.R.Us. sanctioned	18
Number of States/UTs covered	17

TABLE 25.2: Operation Blackboard: Achievements

Items	1990-91	Total for 1987-88 to 1990-91
Number of States/UTs covered	25	32
Number of Blocks covered	343	4419
Number of schools covered (in lakhs)	0.39	3.45
Percentage of primary schools covered	7.35	64.21
Post of Primary Teachers sanctioned	14,397	92,871

TABLE 25.3: Vocationalisation of Education: Achievements

Items	Total for 1987-88 to 1990-91
Number of States/UTs covered	27
Number of schools covered	3841
Number of vocational courses approved	10316

TABLE 25.4: Higher Education

Sl. No.	Category	1950-51	1990-91	Increase
1.	No. of Universities, deemed to be Universities, and Institutions of National Importance	27	190	App. 7 times
2.	No. of Colleges (excluding Junior Colleges and those offering Diploma/ Certificate Courses)	695	7,000 (Estimated)	App. 10 times
3.	Enrolment	3,62,323	42,47,000	App. 11 times
4.	Percentage thereof to Total Population in the age group 17—25	0.8%	5%	
5.	Enrolment of Women	43,000	12,92,000	30 times
6.	Autonomous Colleges	Nil	103	—
7.	Curriculum Development Centres	Nil	27	—
8.	Teachers	18,700	2,60,000	App. 14 times

Sources:
1. *Annual Report, 1990-91*, Ministry of Human Resource Development, Department of Education, New Delhi (for data other than number of Universities).
2. *List of Universities*, University Grants Commission, New Delhi.
3. *List of Universities*, Association of Indian Universities, New Delhi.

TABLE 25.5: School Education (1950-51 to 1989-90)

Sl. No.	Category	1950-51	1988-89	Increase
A.	*Primary Education*			
1.	Number of Primary Schools	2,10,000	5,50,700	App. 2.5 times
2.	Enrolment of Pupils in Classes I-V	1,92,00,000	9,73,00,000	App. 5 times
3.	Percentage of Total Enrolment to Total Population in the Age Group 6—11	43.1	99.9	
B.	*Middle Education*			
4.	Number of Middle Schools	14,000	1,43,744	App. 10 times
5.	Enrolment of Pupils in Classes VI to VIII	31,00,000	3,22,00,000	App. 10 times
6.	Percentage of Total Enrolment to Total Population in the Age Group 11—14	12.9	59.1	

Contd.

TABLE 25.5 (*Contd.*)

1.	2	3	4	5
C.	*High and Higher Secondary*			
7.	Number of High/Secondary/ Higher Secondary Schools	7,000	76,114	App. 11 times
8.	Enrolment in Classes IX-XI/XII	14,00,000	2,00,00,000	App. 13 times
9.	Percentage of Enrolment of Girls to Total Enrolment:			
	(a) Classes I-V	28.1	40.1	—
	(b) Classes VI-VIII	16.1	35.4	—
	(c) Classes IX-X, XI, XII	14.3	30.7	—
	Secondary/Hr. Secondary/Intermediate-IX and above			

Source: Ministry of Human Resource Development.

TABLE 25.6: Percentage of Girls, Enrolment to Total Enrolment (1986-87)

Stage	Gross Ratio
Classes I-V	41.16
Classes VI-VIII	34.45
Classes IX-X	31.74
Classes XI-XII	30.71

Source: *Fifth All-India Educational Survey,* NCERT, New Delhi.

TABLE 25.7: Percentage of Enrolment of the Respective Age Group (1985-86 and 1989-90)

Classes/Age Group	1985-86	1989-90
I-V (6-11 Years)		
Boys	108.8	115.5
Girls	77.1	83.6
Total	93.4	99.9
VI-VIII (11-14 Years)		
Boys	65.0	73.0
Girls	38.1	44.6
Total	52.0	59.1

Source: *Selected Educational Statistics, 1989-90,* Ministry of Human Resource Development, Department of Education, New Delhi.

TABLE 25.8: Growth of Educational Institutions at School Level at a Glance (1950-51 to 1989-90)

Year	Number of Primary Schools	No. of Middle Schools	No. of Secondary/ Higher Secondary Schools
1950-51	2,10,000	14,000	7,00
1960-61	3,30,000	50,000	17,000
1970-71	4,08,000	91,000	37,000
1980-81	4,94,000	119,000	51,000
1989-90	5,50,000	1,43,000	76,119

TABLE 25.9: Teachers

Category	Number of Teachers 1950-51	1988-89	Increase
1. Primary Schools	5,37,918	16,03,058	About 3 times
2. Middle Schools	85,491	10,32,534	About 12 times
3. High and Higher Secondary	1,26,504	12,35,530	About 10 times
4. Higher Education	18,648	2,49,000	About 12 times
Total	7,68,561	41,20,122	About 5 times

TABLE 25.10: Percentage of Trained Teachers

Category	1950-51	1989-90
1. Primary Schools	58.8	89.84
2. Middle Schools	53.3	91.74
3. High/Secondary Schools	55.5	92.7

TABLE 25.11: Percentage of Literacy in India (1951 to 1991)

Year	Males	Females	Total
1951	24.9	7.9	16.6
1981	48.89	24.82	36.23
1991	63.86	39.42	52.11

Source: *Annual Report 1990-91*, Ministry of Human Resource Development, Department of Education, New Delhi.

26

ELECTRONICS

Overview

This is the age of electronics. The world has become a global village and one talks about the borderless world. In this borderless world, what are the prospects and attractions of country like India for the electronics industry? India is a huge country with a population of 84.39 crore. There is at least a market of 15 crore people with disposable income and purchasing power. In other words, the potential market in India is almost half the size of the market of Europe. India has, according to one estimate, the world's third largest manpower in science and technology. There are large number of engineers who are English speaking particularly in areas like software and electronics in general. The engineering manpower is cost effective. The engineering man hour cost of India will be 25 per cent of that in Europe or USA or Japan. India has attraction for manufacturers from the market point of view as well as availability of manpower and cost considerations.

Electronics as an industry deserves special attention. It is a meta resource for other industries. There is hardly any sector of industry which is not affected by electronics. Optimum productivity improvements are not possible without the use of electronics. The additional advantages of electronics industry are as following:

- It is relatively pollution free.
- It is footloose and could be used as an instrument for balanced regional development in our country.
- It has a high employment potential for women.
- It is knowledge intensive. With the third largest scientific and technical manpower in the world in our country, we should be able to achieve commanding heights in this industry.

The electronics industry in India is about 30 years old. The period 1960-70 can be described as a pre-liberalisation period. The focus of policy during 1970-80, period was on developing indigenous R&D and capabilities. The next decade of 1980-90 witnessed a pronounced attempt at liberalisation and a series of policy announcements were made towards this.

The Eighth Five Year Plan (draft) prepared in 1990 visualised the development of electronics during the first half of the next decade. A production target of Rs. 300,000 million and an export target of Rs. 65,000 million is to be achieved by 1994-95. These are very small figures compared to the global size of the electronics industry. The Government of India, therefore, have initiated a result-oriented policy package to help the growth of the electronics industry.

Software Development

Computer software has been identified as major thrust area due to abundance of educated and technical manpower available in India. To take advantage of this, special emphasis on software export has been given. Three software technology parks at Pune, Bangalore and Bhubaneshwar have been launched. These technology parks provide the telematic infrastructure for data communication as well as computer infrastructure for software export. In these parks import certification for import of capital goods, software tools, etc. is given by the Department of Electronics and the entrepreneur does not have to approach the Ministry of Commerce. It has been decided in principle to set-up 12 more software technology parks. In addition, the Government have adopted liberal policy decision for promoting software export. This sector has been provided fiscal benefits under Section 80 HHC of the Income Tax Act, removal of double taxation and reduction in import duty of capital goods, etc., ERNET has been made available temporarily to promote software export.

Standardisation

Standardisation and quality control of indigenous electronic products have been receiving major attention. For this purpose 4 regional and 17 state level Test Centres has been set up at present, besides the Centre for reliability, Madras and National Supervising Inspectorate (NSI), New Delhi. India has become the member of International Electro-Technical Commission for quality assessment of electronic components. This would help exports of components to developed countries. A Task Force has been constituted to promote standardisation and production of electronic goods. Major achievements made in standardisation during the year are :

— Updating of the specification of B/W TV receivers has been initiated so as to start a certification scheme of B/W TV receivers on the line of CTV receivers.
— With a view to improve the safety of electronic equipment, a MOU has been signed with TUV Essen, a recognised German Test Laboratory, for mutual cooperation leading to approval of the laboratory for testing as per GS mark requirements of indigenously manufactured mining electronic equipment for exporting to European country.
— Three Indian Test Laboratories located at Delhi, Calcutta and Bombay have been authorised by International Electro-Technical Commission (IEC) for quality assessment of electronic components, Geneva as independent test laboratories which can test and certify electronic components for exports to 24 member countries including USA, Japan, South Korea, Germany, etc.
— The components data in India (CODIN), a computer based system providing necessary information on indigenous electronic component have been started. This will assist Indian electronics industry in the use of standardised electronic components.
— One of the Regional Test Laboratories of the department has been authorised by Underwriters Laboratory (UL), USA to conduct safety test of TV receivers and information technology products.

Industry Promotion

* For promoting export to General Currency Area (GCA), the value addition norm for computer hardware exports to GCA under the advance licensing scheme has been reduced from minimum 33 to 15 per cent.

* Duty drawback on the following items have been fixed :

* (i) CTV receivers using indigenous tubes.
  (ii) Applicability of 20" CTV DEBK rates for 21" CTV receivers.
  (iii) All industry drawback rates for 7 electronic products were announced. These are in addition to 38 electronic items for which rates were fixed earlier.

* A treaty on intellectual property in integrated circuit area was signed by India in Geneva during May 1990.
* A meeting was organised with the representatives of foreign companies dealing in electronics, with a view to promote transfer of technology and establishment of manufacturing operation for both domestic and international markets.
* The Semi-conductor Complex Ltd., Mohali is to be rebuilt with 6" state-of-the-art wafer facility with an annual capacity of 44,000 wafers and to take up research and development work at a total cost of Rs. 1,839 million. Trial production of VLSI at SCL is scheduled to commence within a period of 30 months.

Manpower Development

* A new part-time course has been sponsored at IETE, Delhi for providing diploma in computers for SC/ST, handicapped persons and ex-servicemen.
* A World Bank assisted project with a total amount of Rs. 440 million involving 32 institutions and 5 resource centres for quality improvement of education at engineering colleges, polytechnics, etc. and to develop competence of students at par with the international levels has been initiated.
* For recognising private sector institutions conducting computer courses, a special scheme has been formulated.

Technology Development

* Indigenously developed low energy linear accelerator for treatment of cancer was successfully put to use for treatment of patients at PGIMER, Chandigarh. This was a joint development of SAMEER, CSIO and PGIMER.
* With the commissioning of indigenously developed National High Voltage Direct Current (HVDC) experimental line in October 1989, India achieved a major breakthrough in this technology. On August 20, 1990, this HVDC line had successfully achieved its rated capacity of 100 MW, 100 KV. This national project undertaken at a cost of Rs. 292 million and executed by BHEL, demonstrated the indigenous capability to design, manufacture and test sophisticated system incorporating high technology. Efforts are being made to commercialise this technology.

* As a major step in the direction of India developing contemporary technology in the area of computers, indigenous development of a parallel processing machine with 16 numbers 80386 processing elements based on three different architectures was completed. This technology is now being transferred to the industry.
* A pilot project of ferric oxide for ferrites with a capacity of 2000 TPA mainly for exports has been started.
* A memoranda of technical cooperation was signed with EEC Brussel in 8 specific areas. The scope of cooperation includes training avenue for scientists, bringing expertise from EEC and promoting joint venture between EEC on the one hand and Indian Universities, R&D Centres, Test Industries and Laboratories on the other.

Rural Development and Employment Generation

The Inter-Ministry Electronics Coordination Committee was reconstituted to review the progress and coordinate actual plan among all relevant departments of Central Government for dissemination and use of electronics for rural development, employment generation schemes and weaker section benefits.

The Working Group on Socio-Economic Impact Maximisation under the TDC, was reconstituted with a private sector person as its Chairman for the first time. This group will use voluntary agencies and private/public sector agencies to propose and study electronic application in priority and high-impact sectors of the society.

Application Development

For improving the industrial productivity in the steel sector, a new project on industrial inspection scheme for fault detection in the steel sheets through surface image — a knowledge based technique, has been crystallised.

Annual Plan of the Department of Electronics for 1991-92

The plan proposals are grouped under the following heads:

(a) Corporations (ET&T, CMC and SCL) (b) Societies (C-DAC, SAMEER, ER&DC, NCST, etc.) (c) Departmental projects (STQC, CEDT, KBCS, NHVDC, etc.) (d) Science and Technology programmes.

For the year 1991-92 budgetory support of Rs. 1,216 million for various projects have been provided. Budgetory support is mainly provided this year for ongoing projects/programmes. A very high priority has been given for fast implementation of SCL project for which substantial resources have been provided. For the development of infrastructure such as testing facilities, manpower training, centre for electronic design and technology etc., an allocation of Rs. 180 million has been made. Mission oriented technology project namely Centre for Development of Advanced Computing has also received importance. For giving thrust to technology development efforts and application promotion programmes both through Departmentally run projects as well as through sponsored research activity to be carried out at existing institutions/R&D laboratories, adequate budgetary support has been provided. Six new projects in the areas of

(i) Development of Software Package, (ii) Conference Test Centre for OSI Protocol, (iii) Development of Industrial Robots, (iv) Computer Integrated Manufacturing, (v) Energy Conservation Project using AC Drive and (vi) Advanced Tool Design and Facilities Centre has been initiated.

Licensing Policy and Coordination

There was no change in the industrial licensing policy. Liberalisation measures of 1985 and 1986 led to the influx of large number of applications upto 1987. Further, in June 1988, major sectors of electronics were exempted from the licensing provisions. Judging from the number of investment proposals received, the year witnessed a slackening of enthusiasm of entrepreneurs in setting up electronics industry.

Fiscal and Import Policies

Import-Export Policy for 1990-93 provides a mechanism for providing protection of electronics items having strong indigenous angle. Additional items were added to the list of items restricted for imports. Items not available locally were included in the OGL list. Configuration for import of computer systems under OGL has been modified. Import of spares are permitted to service centres of consumer electronics items. List of office machines permitted for import to certain category of registered exporters was also modified. The Import Replenishment (REP) Scheme was extended to cover software exports as well. REP licences were made fully flexible while the REP entitlement for electronics hardware export was reduced from 30 to 20 per cent. During the year, residual OGL entry was shifted to Appendix 3(A) (*of the document*) and list attestation procedure for electronic components, which was not initially applicable, was introduced and later modified to OGL entitlement certificate. Overall imports were cut by 15 per cent.

Software exports have been included under the new scheme of import of capital goods at 25 per cent import duty with export obligation being equal to 3 times the value of capital goods.

In the Union Budget 1990-91 by and large the *status quo* was maintained in respect of import duty structure. Computer software have been exempted from import duty when imported by research institutions. Excise duty on certain consumer electronics goods was increased.

The Customs duty on electronics raw materials/components and equipment has been increased by 20 per cent. Electronics industry is also facing problems due to raising of L/C margin by the Banks. It is anticipated that the cut on imports, increase in import duty, and raising of L/C margin by Banks would affect the growth of electronics industry.

Custom Workshops held at Ahmedabad and Bangalore, provided a forum for the electronics industries located in Gujarat and Karnataka to discuss day to day customs clearance problems with customs authorities.

The total production of electronics during the year 1990 was worth Rs. 92,000 million compared to Rs. 83,090 million in 1989. The growth rate achieved during 1990 was only 10.7 per cent compared to 31.7 per cent achieved in 1989. The consumer electronics, which account for over 30 per cent of total production has shown only marginal growth. Th production of B/W and colour TV receivers has witnessed negative growth during the last 2 years. The major growth has been in computers and communications sectors. The production and the growth trends for the last 5 yeas has been given in Table 26.1.

TABLE 26.1: Production and Growth, 1986-90

Year	Production (Rs. Million)	Growth (%)
1986	34,600	30.1
1987	47,200	36.4
1988	63,000	33.5
1989	83,090	31.7
1990	92,000	10.7

Consumer Electronics

Being on the fore-front, consumer electronics sector contributed a production of Rs. 29,380 million in the total production of electronics, of Rs. 92,000 million in the country, amounting to 31.9 per cent of the turnover. The growth rate in 1990 works out to 4.9 per cent over the production (Rs. 28,000 million) during 1989. The TV sector is continuing to suffer due to lack of demand but the other products have shown good growth.

The production of major consumer electronics items during past three years is given in Table 26.2.

TABLE 26.2: Production of Major Consumer Electronic Items

(Quantity in million nos.)

Product	1988	1989	1990
1. B/W TV Receivers	4.4	4.0	3.6
2. Colour TV Receivers	1.3	1.2	1.2
3. Radio Receivers	8.0	8.0	6.0
4. Tape Recorders/Radio Cassette Recorders	3.5	4.0	5.0
5. Electronics Watches	1.5	3.5	5.0

To help TV industry, a number of measures have been initiated including the following:

— The TV industry was advised to step up marketing and after sales service networks in semi-urban, rural and remote areas.

— To help the TV industry to export B/W TV sets, REP licences issued against export of these sets has been provided flexibility to import video tape deck mechanism (VIDMs) and populated PCBs.

The country has been operating in the FM transmission arena for sometime now. Frequency Modulated (FM) transmission has the advantage of noise free response and wide band audio spectrum over the conventional Amplitude Modulated (AM) transmission. Indigenous technology for low cost AM/FM radio receivers developed by ER&DC, Trivandrum and ET&T, New Delhi has been offered to the radio industry in the country.

A total indigenously developed domestic microwave oven has been introduced in the market. The only imported components in the products are magnetron and ICs. All other components are being made locally. Apart from this, two more units have come into production.

Digital TV Project

A major project on "System and VLSI Design for Digital TV" was launched as a fore-runner to digital TV fabrication and preparation of a base for taking up HDTV project. The main objectives of the project are development of full customs ASICs (Application Specific ICs) for digital TV receivers based on new ASICs in subsequent phases of the project. This project is being taken up in nine existing institutions which are already having some infrastructure for this kind of activity.

HDTV

A memorandum of technical cooperation has been signed by the Department of Electronics and the Services of the Commission of European Communities in various area including HDTV. The cooperation is envisaged in supply of equipment, components, specialised software packages, training of engineers, visit of technical experts, testing, R&D collaboration, HDTV standards, technical reports and publications, etc.

Public Sector Undertakings

The Department of Electronics has the following three public sector corporations under its administrative control :

(i) Electronics Trade and Technology Development Corporation (ET&T)
(ii) CMC Limited
(iii) Semiconductor Complex Limited (SCL)

The Department also works closer with other PSUs like BEL, ECIL, ITI, BHEL, etc.

Electronics Trade and Technology Development Corporation (ET&T)

Electronics Trade and Technology Development Corporation Limited (ET&T), a Government of India enterprise, was set up in 1974. Till April 1985, the company was a canalising agency for TV picture tubes and a very substantial portion of the business was from this activity. After the decanalisation of the picture tubes since April 1985, the company is operating in fiercely competitive lines of business and is pursuing the above mission to provide value for money to the end consumer. The company, in order to weather the effect of de-canalisation, has diversified its operations in other areas as illustrated by the following economic indicators.

Today ET&T is facing a business crisis as it has to operate within the framework of Government guidelines without having many of the advantages of a private company. Therefore, for the undertaking to turn around at this juncture, policy support from Government has been suggested by ET&T. Turnover during 1985-86 to 1990-91 is shown in Table 26.3.

TABLE 26.3: Turnover, 1985-86 to 1990-91

(*Rs. million*)

	1985-86	1986-87	1987-88	1988-89	1989-90	1990-91 (9 months)
Picture Tubes	1011.9	535.7	546.8	360.0	162.4	108.5
Components and Materials	76.0	124.7	178.1	175.0	181.2	80.0
Equipment	44.5	114.9	153.3	106.5	154.9	108.5
MTB Programmes	73.8	204.3	325.4	400.0	175.1	100.8
Low Cost PC	—	—	—	—	41.9	105.7
Export	20.0	10.0	10.0	07.3	33.5	02.4

CMC Limited

CMC Limited was set up in 1976 to provide users a complete range of services connected with all aspects of computers, that is as a one point computer support company. Today, it is India's largest information technology company. It is a company committed to the creative use of computers and modern communication technology in vital sectors of the economy to improve the quality of life and productivity. The turnover for 1990-91 is expected to be more than Rs. 1,370 million which is 10 per cent more than the turnover in 1989-90. Nearly 2,200 trained staff members have helped CMC to achieve this turnover.

Semiconductor Complex Ltd.

Semiconductor Complex Ltd. (SCL) was set up primarily to design, develop and manufacture LSI/VLSI circuits. SCL commenced commercial production in April 1984 and consistently improved it financial performance every year before an unfortunate fire accident on February 7-8, 1989 destroyed the LSI Manufacturing and R&D facilities.

Organisational, Promotional and Other Matters

Bilateral Trade and International Co-operation

A Memorandum of Technical Cooperation was signed with the Directorate General of Telecommunication and Information Industries in the Commission of the European Communities, Brussels. Eight specific areas have been identified for technical cooperation. Scope of the cooperation includes training of Indian scientists, formulating and implementing projects of mutual benefit, bringing expertise from EEC and promoting joint venture between EEC on the one hand and Indian Universities, R&D Centres, Test Laboratories and Industries on the other.

A six member Chinese delegation visited India during 'Electronics India 90' exhibition and held discussion for identifying areas of cooperation. Department of Electronics participated in bilateral meetings with USSR and Yugoslavian delegations. The possibility of having a data communication facility for computer software export to France was explored.

Eighth meeting of Indo-USSR Working Group on computers and electronics was held on February 18-20, 1991 in New Delhi. USSR was represented by a high level 12 member delegation led by Shri V.M. Neiaman, Dy. Chairman, USSR State Committee on Computers and Informatics. The delegation also visited some electronics industries in Delhi and Bombay and also the Indian Engineering Trade Fair at Pragati Maidan. The four sub-groups under the Working Group, namely, computer techniques including software, electronics, means of communication including consumer electronics, and automation process control instrumentation, met separately to discuss various issues. The protocol of the Working Group was signed on February 20, 1991 wherein potential areas for joint venture, technology transfer and bilateral cooperation have been identified.

Electronics Industry Information System

The data pertaining to licensing, approvals, production, exports, foreign collaborations, manufacturers and product directory and other macro level statistics relating to electronics industry are maintained in a information system called LIPS information System' by the DBID of Department of Electronics. The data bank has up-to-date licensing and foreign collaboration information. The itemwise and unitwise production and export data is available since 1991. The manufacturer and product directory provide up-to-date and reliable information and serve as a Buyer/Seller Guide. It provides manufacturer's information such as address (both office and factory), telephone, telex, gram, name and office of top executive, year of establishment, brand, manpower employed, sector, product range and export product range etc.

The information system is available to public and government officials through Department of Electronics LAN System. It was demonstrated in the Electronics India Exhibition held at Pragati Maidan, New Delhi. Analysis reports highlighting electronics production and exports statistics are brought out and made available to the industry and other users regularly.

Activities with SEDC's

The Fifth All India Conference of State Electronics Development Corporations (SEDCs) was convened in October 1990 to discuss the significant achievements of the SEDCs in implementing innovative projects and in their R&D efforts. The procedure of having for each state and union territory a senior officer of DOE identified as the nodal interface officer has been continued with the nodal officer functioning on the Boards of Directors of SEDCs and in other state level committees for electronics development. In addition, it has been decided that the SEDC will function as the nodal agency for implementation of all electronics manpower development programmes whether from DOE or from the Ministry of Human Resource Development or Ministry of Rural Development, Ministry of Welfare, etc. Recently, Secretary (DOE) convened a meeting of all states' Finance and Industry Secretaries where it was decided to propose a uniform sales tax rate (5%) for electronics goods in consonance with the similar agreement reached at the CM level in the National Development Council (NDC).

TABLE 26.4: Budget Support for Plan Project of the Department of Electronics for 1991-92

(*Rs. Million*)

	Project/Programme	Plan Outlay 1990-91	1991-92
1.	Electronics Trade and Technology Development Corporation Limited	10.00	10.00
2.	CMC Ltd.	1.00	0.00
3.	Semiconductor Complex Ltd.	350.00	510.00
4.	Society for Applied Microwave Electronics Engineering and Research (SAMEER)	43.70	20.00
5.	Centre for Development of Advance Computing (C-DAC)	100.00	50.00
6.	Electronic Research and Development Centres (ER&DC)	20.00	30.00
7.	National Centre for Software Techniques (NCST)	20.00	10.00
8.	Regional Computer Centres (RCC)	2.50	2.50
9.	Centre for Electronic Packaging Technology and Design	4.30	5.00
10.	System Engineering and Consultancy Programme (SECO)	15.00	10.00
11.	Head Quarters (Secretariat and Building)	40.00	10.00
12.	Electronics Materials Development Programme	40.00	30.00
13.	Standardisation, Testing and Quality Control (STQC)	55.50	70.00
14.	Special Manpower Development	15.00	—
15.	Social Electronics and Regional Development	5.00	110.00
16.	Centre for Electronics Design Technology (CEDT)	40.00	—
17.	Computer Literacy and Studies in School (CLASS)	10.00	—
18.	Special Manpower for Computer	20.00	—
19.	Centre for Development of Power Semiconductor Device	5.00	3.00
20.	CAD/CAM Project	10.00	—
21.	Fibre-Optics Application Programme	20.00	5.00
22.	Industrial Electronics Promotion Programme	55.00	30.00
23.	National HVDC Project	22.00	10.00
24.	Fifth Generation Computer System Project	10.00	16.00
25.	Advanced Technology Programme in Computer Networking	10.00	30.00
26.	Software Export Promotion Programme	35.00	30.00
27.	Technology Development Council (TDC) Projects	40.00	60.00
28.	National Radar Council (NRC) Projects	20.00	30.00
29.	National Micro-Electronic Council (NMC) Projects	40.00	60.00
30.	Promotion of Rural Employment in Electronics	10.00	10.00
31.	Technology Development for Indian Languages (TDIL)	20.00	10.00
32.	Photonics Development Programme	10.00	5.00
33.	Electronics for Health Care	7.00	10.00
34.	Research and Development in Agri-Electronics	5.00	6.00
35.	Transportation System Programme	1.00	5.00
36.	Development of Software Packages	—	5.00
37.	Conform. Test Centre for OSI Protocol	—	5.00
38.	Devpt. of Appln. of Indl. Robots	—	5.00
39.	Computer Integrated Mfg. (CIM) Prog.	—	5.00
40.	Energy Conservation Proj. using AC drive	—	3.50
41.	Advanced Tool Design and Fac. Centre	—	5.00
	Total	**1,100.00**	**1,216.00**

Source: *Annual Report*, Department of Electronics, Government of India, New Delhi, 1991.

27

ENERGY

COAL

The Ministry of Coal has the responsibility for the exploration, identification and development of coal and lignite reserves in India. This responsibility is discharged through the Coal India Limited and its seven subsidiaries, the Neyveli Lignite Corporation and the Singareni Collieries Company Limited (A joint undertaking of the Government of India and the Government of Andhra Pradesh).

Additional reserves of about 3.96 billion tonnes of coal were established. As on January 1, 1991, the coal resources in the country (upto a depth of 1200 metres) have been estimated at 192.359 billion tonnes. These reserves are located mainly in the eastern half of the country and are spread over eleven States.

The exploitation of lignite deposits in the country is being done almost exclusively by the Neyveli Lignite Corporation Ltd. The total lignite deposits in the country are estimated at 6.5 billion tonnes of which almost 80 per cent occur in Tamil Nadu. The other States where these deposits occur are Pondicherry, Gujarat, Rajasthan, Jammu and Kashmir and Kerala.

Coal Planning

The coal industry in this country has come a long way since the pre-nationalisation days, in all aspects — production, technology, conservation and labour welfare. From a stagnant figure of 70 million tonnes in the late sixties and early seventies, the production reached a figure of 211.73 million tonnes in 1990-91. During the Seventh Plan period itself the growth in production in absolute terms was 53.4 million tonnes, or about 10.7 million tonnes per year, on an average. This has been made possible by a scientific approach to exploration and exploitation, substantial investments and adoption of new technologies such as opencast mining etc.

In the post-nationalisation phase, in order to increase production, it was essential to modernise the exploration and mining techniques. This imperative gradually led to a process of consultation with, and assistance from, some friendly developed coal producing countries. This has been formalised by the establishment of Joint Working Groups on Coal with USSR, Poland, U.K., France, Germany, Canada and Australia. Protocols executed by these Working Groups provide for assistance in execution of turn-key projects, consultancy, acquisition of equipment and machinery, training of personnel, etc.

Nationalisation of the coal-industry has not only led to an increase in production but has also meant a better deal for the employees. The emphasis on welfare of the coal miners has been increasing year after year, and now encompasses welfare activities such as housing, water supply, medical facilities, family planning, educational facilities, setting up of canteens, cooperative institutions, creches, etc. The cumulative effect of all these measures means better industrial relations. This is reflected in the declining number of man-days and production lost due to strikes in the last few years. In 1986-87, man-days lost were 6.85 lakhs; in 1990-91 this figure was 1.91 lakhs. Loss of production in 1986-87 was 5.70 million tonnes; the figure in 1990-91 was 3.02 million tonnes.

One of the major objectives of nationalisation was to improve the standards of safety, and the working conditions, in the coal industry. Today, the safety of miners is sought to be ensured right from the survey stage, and is a factor also in the choice of appropriate technology, delineation of actual operating conditions and training of personnel. Safety Committees have been established at various levels, from the mine level extending upto the corporate and even the Ministry level. The cumulative result of all these measures is heartening. The rate of fatalities per million tonnes of output has come down from 2.37 in 1973 to 0.74 in 1990 in CIL Companies. Similarly, the rate of serious injuries in the same period has come down from 19.49 to 3.08.

Seventh Five Year Plan

The demand for raw coal by the terminal year of the Seventh Plan (1989-90) had finally been assessed by the Planning Commission at 220 million tonnes. To achieve this level of production, the combined Plan outlay for CIL and SCCL was Rs. 6648 crores, against which the expenditure was Rs. 6185 crores.

Eighth Five Year Plan

The Working Group on Coal and Lignite for the Eighth Five Year Plan had estimated the country's raw coal demand by the terminal year of the Eighth Plan (1994-95) at 315 million tonnes. This was, however, originally scaled down to 285 million tonnes by the Planning Commission. However, in view of the recent developments in the Gulf and their impact on the world oil market, the necessity of using coal as a substitute for oil has assumed importance and urgency. In this context, the demand has again been proposed to be revised to 304 million tonnes, with a production plan of 292.50 million tonnes. An investment of Rs. 16304 crores would be required to attain this level of production.

Annual Plan 1990-91

The production target for 1990-91 for CIL, SCCL and Companies in the private sector was 221 million tonnes. The actual production has been 211.73 million tonnes. The target for 1991-92 has been fixed at 228 million tonnes.

The approved plan outlay for CIL and SCCL for 1990-91 was Rs. 2320.55 crores. The corresponding figure for 1991-92 is Rs. 2390 crores.

The companywise production targets and figures are shown in Table 27.1.

The productivity OMS (output per manshift) in CIL has been improving, as the Table 27.2 shows.

The OMS Target for 1991-92 is 1.37 tonnes for CIL and 1.09 tonnes for SCCL.

Coal Production

During 1990-91, the Coal Production in the Country reached an all time high of 211.73 million tonnes; registering a growth of 5.4 per cent over the previous year. In the current year (1991-92) the all India coal production target is fixed at 228 million tonnes. The sourcewise details of actual production in 1990-91 and anticipated production in 1991-92 are shown in Table 27.3.

TABLE 27.1: Companywise Production Targets

(in Million Tonnes)

	Annual Action Plan Production Target 1990-91	Actual Production Target 1990-91	Production Target 1991-92
ECL	29.00	23.47	24.50
BCCL	28.60	26.70	28.00
CCL	29.17	30.05	31.00
NCL	27.20	27.88	31.60
WCL	23.90	22.78	24.60
SECL	55.33	58.08	62.60
NEC	0.80	0.68	0.70
TOTAL CIL	194.00	189.64	203.00
SCCL	22.50	17.71	20.50
TISCO/ IISCO/DVC	4.50	4.38	4.50
GRAND TOTAL	221.00	211.73	228.00

TABLE 27.2: Productivity Output per Manshift in CIL

(in tonnes)

	OMS Target 1990-91	Actual OMS 1990-91
CIL	1.27	1.31
SCCL	1.16	0.96

TABLE 27.3: Sourcewise Details of Production

(Million Tonnes)

Company	1990-91	1991-92
A. Coal India Limited	189.64	203.00
B. Singareni Collieries Limited	17.71	20.50
C. Others (TISCO, IISCO, DVC)	4.38	4.50
Total	211.73	228.00

Companywise break-up of production in the Seventh Plan period is as Table 27.4 shows.

TABLE 27.4: Companywise Breakup of Production in Seventh Plan

(Million Tonnes)

	Coal Production				
Company	1985-86	1986-87	1987-88	1988-89	1989-90
ECL	24.03	25.62	27.99	30.13	24.49
BCCL	21.08	24.01	25.11	26.30	26.61
CCL	24.13	25.14	27.27	28.07	28.61
NCL	11.61	13.60	16.51	19.63	23.28
WCL	18.17	19.34	21.20	22.06	23.01
SECL	34.25	36.15	39.94	44.41	51.78
NEC	0.84	0.91	1.00	0.90	0.84
TOTAL CIL	134.11	144.77	159.02	171.50	178.62
SCCL	15.66	16.58	16.40	18.61	17.80
Others: TISCO/IISCO/ DVC	4.43	4.44	4.30	4.49	4.47
GRAND TOTAL	154.20	165.79	179.72	194.60	200.89

About 88 per cent of the total coal production in the country comes from CIL Collieries. The situation is unlikely to change in the coming years. The Coal India Ltd. will, therefore, continue to play a dominant role in coal production in this country.

Another important feature to be mentioned is that most of the increase in the total production has been coming from opencast mines. The CIL produced about 18 million tonnes of coal from opencast mines in 1973-74. The production from CIL opencast mines in the previous year *i.e.* 1990-91, has been 132.01 million tonnes. The production from the opencast mines has therefore, been rising at the rate of 3.7 per cent per year. The production in the underground mines of CIL has been, more or less, stagnant and hovering around 60 million tonnes of coal per year.

The situation is same in Singareni Collieries Company Ltd. There the production in the opencast mines has been rising over the years though the SCCL still produces most of its coal from its underground mines.

Coal Productivity

Labour productivity, in terms of output per manshift (OMS), has been improving steadily during the Seventh Five Year Plan and also in the first year (1990-91) of the Eighth Plan, in both CIL and SCCL. While OMS in CIL was only 0.92 tonnes in the first year of the Seventh Five Year Plan, it reached an alltime high of 1.21 tonnes in 1989-90. During 1990-91, CIL achieved an OMS of 1.31 tonnes. An analysis of OMS of the underground and opencast mines of CIL would show that while productivity of opencast mines has been sharply and continuously increasing from 0.76 tonne in 1974-75 to 3.08 tonnes in 1989-90, the productivity of underground mines has almost remained static around 0.52-0.54 tonne during all these years. During 1990-91, CII achieved an OMS of 3.34 tonnes in its opencast mines.

Output per manshift of SCCL mines was 0.81 tonne in 1985-86. At the end of the Seventh Plan, i.e., in 1989-90, SCCL achieved OMS of 0.99 tonne. However, in 1990-91, the OMS of SCCL declined to 0.96 tonne due to production constraints on account of law and order problems.

Demand Satisfaction

With improved availability of coal and effective coordination with the transportation agencies, it has been possible to meet the coal demand of the consumers more adequately during the year under review. The coal requirement of the major sectors, like, power, loco, steel etc. have been almost met in full. Most of these sectors, were given more coal than in the previous year. A comparative position of the satisfaction level achieved during the year 1990-91, as compared to the previous year, is indicated in Table 27.5.

TABLE 27.5: Satisfaction Level Achieved during 1990-91

(Million Tonnes)

Particulars	1989-90	1990-91
Steel & Coke ovens	28.37	30.05
Power Utilities	113.00	116.72
	(2.12)	(2.07)
Railways (Loco)	5.73	5.17
Cement	8.74	9.74
Fertiliser	3.97	3.90
Soft Coke	1.30	1.27
Others (Including Brick kilns, Captive Power etc.)	34.55	39.12
Exports	0.16	0.09
Colliery consumption	3.97	4.01
Total	199.79 + (2.12)	210.07 + (2.07)

Note: Figures in bracket indicate washery middlings.

Pithead Stocks

Coal mining is affected by seasonal factors and while large pithead stocks build up during the winter months, there is drop in production during summer and monsoon periods. During the period April to September each year, part of the requirement of the consumers is met by drawing down of stocks from pitheads. Closing stock in CIL Collieries which was 37.42 million tonnes as on 31.3.1990, declined to 26.16 million tonnes by 30.11.1990. The stocks further started building up with increased production and the closing stock as on 31.3.1991 stood at 41.57 million tonnes.

Producing coal is no doubt the primary task of the coal companies, but reaching coal to consuming points in right time and right quantity is no less important. The coal companies achieve this onerous task by coordinating and interacting with number of transporting agencies; the principal among them being the railways, the roadways merry-go-round systems and conveyor belts. The railways are the major carrier of coal. Of all coal transported about 62 per cent is transported by the railways. Incidentally, coal is also the single largest commodity transported by the railways and constitutes about 40 per cent of the total goods traffic of the railways.

Consumer Satisfaction

A number of steps have been taken by the coal companies to improve quality of their products and keep consumers satisfied. These includes installation of Coal Handling Plants (CHPs) to size lumpy coal and screen out extraneous material at the production stage itself, installation of electronic weigh bridges to ensure correct weighment, down grading of grades, wherever necessary, to ensure that the consumers pay only for that quality of coal which is actually supplied to them. Coal Controller, an independent authority, has been given necessary powers to determine grades of in situ coal reserves and coal supplied to the consumer. He can draw samples and send them for analysis on his own or on complaints from consumers. Coal Controller's decision in the matter is final.

In addition to the big and bulk consumers of coal like, power, steel, cement, loco and fertilizer, there are about fifty thousand consumers who are dependent for their business on coal supplies in one way or the other. Many of them are very small consumers whose requirement of coal is so small that it cannot be moved in trains of 3000 tonnes of load or so. The Ministry of Coal had launched a MISSION to augment availability of coal to the small industries and household sector. In the phase-I of the MISSION the following targets are to be achieved:

(a) 100 new stockyards,
(b) 1000 new briquetting units/SSF Plants,
(c) Supply of 6 m.t. of domestic fuel per year for household.

With a view to making coal freely available to small scale industries and other consumers specially those located near the mines, the liberalised sales scheme for supply of coal had been re-activated and made more effective from September, 1990. The upper limit of quantity of coal that can be lifted by any consumer at a time has been raised from 500 to 1000 tonnes. Further CIL subsidiaries have specified 57 collieries/stockyards from where coal can be lifted under the scheme on cash payment. As on 31.3.1991, 50 stockyards were in operation in ten States and one U.T. Steps are being taken to open 26 more stockyards in the current year.

Coal Price

The pithead price of coal is fixed by Central Government under the Colliery Control Order, 1945. The Central Government revised the average pithead price of Coal India Limited coal from Rs. 219 to Rs. 249 per tonne with effect from 1.1.1989. This was done with a view to compensating the Coal India Limited to meet its increased cost of inputs, upto June, 1988. An additional levy of 10 per cent has been imposed on long flame coal produced in Ranigunj and Central India Coalfields to reflect higher value of this type of coal and also as a measure of conservation of such coal. The prices of soft coke and hard coke have, however, not been revised and these commodities continue to sell at the old rates.

The price of Singareni Collieries Company Limited coal was revised w.e.f. 24.9.88 raising its average pithead price from Rs. 219 per tonne to Rs. 270 per tonne and again w.e.f. 24.1.89 raising it to Rs. 297 per tonne.

Cost Element

Salaries and Wages followed by Stores and Depreciation continue to be the major cost components in unit-cost of production of coal. During the year 1990-91 per tonne cost of production in Coal India Limited was estimated at Rs. 269.82 as against the per tonne cost of Rs. 264.69 in 1989-90. Of the above 47 per cent was spent on wages, 15 per cent on stores, 10 per cent on depreciation, 7 per cent on interest, 7 per cent on power, 5 per cent on administrative expenses, 3 per cent on transport and 6 per cent on miscellaneous expenses.

Coal Royalty and Cess Accruals to State Governments

Considerable revenue accrues to the State Governments where coal is produced, by way of royalty and cesses and taxes on coal levied by the State Governments. The Table 27.6 indicates the payments on these accounts by Coal India Limited and Singareni Collieries Company Limited.

TABLE 27.6: Royalty and Cess Payment by CIL and SCCL

(Rs. in Crores)

	Coal India Limited		Singareni Collieries Co. Ltd.	
Year	Royalty	Cess	Royalty	Cess
1984-85	66.02	432.96	6.09	28.26
1985-86	67.96	547.21	7.66	36.48
1986-87	68.53	661.79	8.09	39.93
1987-88	73.91	818.37	8.09	39.67
1988-89	81.35	1182.95	8.96	45.36
1989-90	80.32	1247.02	8.62	46.65

Mines Safety

Due to the concerted efforts made over the years, the mines have become safer places to work in. The coal companies fully acknowledge that participation of the labour force in implementation of the safety laws is absolutely essential, and they have, therefore, evolved various formats for reviewing the safety conditions in the mines. There are pit-head Safety Committee, Safety Committees at the area and headquarters level, a Safety Board at the level of Coal India in which representatives of workers, the management and the DGMS are associated. Apex forum for this purpose is the Standing Committee on Safety in Coal Mines under the chairmanship of the Energy/Coal Minister. There are independent Workmen Inspectors at the Unit levels who report directly to the DGMS. There is an Internal Safety Organisation headed by a Chief General Manager existing both at the coal company and CIL levels. Many measures have been adopted both in mining operations and establishment of better communication and early warning systems which have added to the safety in working conditions.

Accident in Churcha West Colliery of South Eastern Coalfields Ltd.

The Churcha West Colliery of SECL is located in Sarguja District of Madhya Pradesh. Longwall equipment was installed and commissioned in the colliery in March, 1990. On 2.6.1990 at 00.42 hours, a collapse occurred at the face. A part of the face between Chock Nos. 44 to 88 came under severe pressure and buckled. There was no loss of life but the damage to the longwall equipment and the powered supports have been considerable. Production in the mine has not yet commenced after the accident. Department of Coal appointed an Expert Committee to enquire into the accident in July, 1990. The terms of reference of the Committee included the circumstances leading to the collapse, the support measures required to be taken as also the preventive measures to pre-empt the accident of this type in future. Government has received report of the Committee and the same is being processed for further action in consultation with the manufacturers, consultants and other agencies associated with the supply of the equipment.

Industrial Relations

At the time of nationalisation of the coal mines, industrial relations were quite bad as the welfare of the employees was not a priority item with the managements of the coal mines then. Subsequently, however, with emphasis on welfare, participation in management, etc., the industrial relations have shown a marked improvement. The number of strikes has consistently declined from 428 in 1980-81 to 46 in 1990-91. The position in SECL, however, is slightly worse, this is not due to any inter face problem with the coal company but it is almost entirely owing to the local law and order condition. During 1990-91, there was no general strike by the employees. The Coal Mines Officers' Association of India, however, had resorted to a 2-day strike on 10th and 12th October, 1990 for their demand for pay revision and full neutralisation of D.A. The mandays lost as a result were 32,732 but there was no loss in production.

Neyveli Lignite Corporation Limited

Performance (Production)

Neyveli Lignite Corporation maintained in 1990-91 its high level of performance in all areas of activity. Its performance during the year is given in Table 27.7.

TABLE 27.7: Neyveli Lignite Corporation Performance 1990-91

Unit	Production in 1990-91	
	Target	Actual
Lignite (LT)	110.00	117.59
Power Generation Gross (MU)	7040.00	7462.35
Urea (Tonnes)	1,29,200	1,01,500
Coke (Tonnes)	2,62,000	2,55,457

The shortfall in the production of coke was marginal. In respect of urea, the shortfall was due to waste heat coil choke in Gasifier-B, and outage of Ammonia and gas of Gas Box-II.

Productivity and sales recorded new heights during the year. Lignite output from Mine-I at 75.44 lakh tonnes and coke production at 2,55,477 tonnes were the highest in any year since inception of these units. For the 9th year in a row, the 29 years old First Thermal Power Station achieved over 70 per cent P.L.F. as against the national average of 56.2 per cent .

Financial Performance

The authorised capital of the Corporation is Rs. 1750 crores. The investment by the Government of India upto March, 1991 is given in Table 27.8.

TABLE 27.8: Investment by Government of India in NLC

(*Rs. in Crores*)

	Provisional
Equity	1435.82
Loan from Government of India	435.24
Total	1871.06

In addition, the Corporation had raised resources of Rs. 870.10 crores through market-borrowing till 1989-90. In 1990-91, it has floated fresh bonds for Rs. 400 crores on private placement basis.

The Corporation has been making profits since 1976-77. It earned a net profit of Rs. 92.61 crores in 1989-90. The figure for 1990-91 is Rs. 93 crores (provisional). The reserves and surpluses, which had accumulated to Rs. 545.98 crores upto 31.3.1990 have now gone upto Rs. 639.12 crores (provisional) as on 31.3.1991.

Sales Turnover

The sales turnover has also showed consistent improvement. It was Rs. 468.59 crores in 1990-91 as against Rs. 449.94 crores in 1989-90. The comparative details are shown in Table 27.9.

TABLE 27.9: Sales Turnover of Neyveli Lignite Corporation

(*in Rs. Crores*)

Product	Value	
	1989-90	1990-91 (Prov.)
Lignite Sales	14.91	25.34
Power Sales	323.79	341.21
Urea (including retention price)	64.22	48.72
Tar Products	5.24	6.51
Coke	37.00	41.82
Others	4.78	4.99
Total	449.94	468.59

The contribution of Neyveli Lignite Corporation to the Central and State Exchequers by way of Taxes and Duties during 1990-91 was Rs. 48.32 crores (provisional).

TABLE 27.10: Significant Statistics About Coal and Lignite

	Units	1987-88	1988-89	1989-90	1990-91
1	2	3	4	5	6
I.PRODUCTION					
(a) Coking Coal:					
(i) For Metallurgical Purpose	Million Tonnes	26.29	25.51	24.50	24.17
(ii) For Non-metallurgical Purpose	Million Tonnes	14.72	17.34	19.93	20.09
(b) Total coking coal	Million Tonnes	41.01	42.72	44.43	45.36
(c) Non-coking coal	Million Tonnes	138.71	151.88	156.46	166.37
(d) Total coal production	Million Tonnes	179.72	194.60	200.89	211.73
(e) Lignite-NLC	Million Tonnes	10.15	11.40	11.23	11.76
Gujarat	Million Tonnes	1.01	1.00	1.57	N.A.
Total lignite	Million Tonnes	11.16	12.40	12.80	11.76
(f) Washed coal	Million Tonnes	11.15	11.65	8.37	8.24
(g) Hard coke (CIL)	Lakh Tonnes	4.86	3.97	3.50	3.95
(h) Soft coke (CIL)	Million Tonnes	1.42	1.31	0.98	0.91
(i) Leco (NLC)	Lakh Tonnes	2.34	2.40	N.A.	N.A.
(j) Urea (NLC)	Lakh Tonnes	1.26	1.41	1.43	1.02
(k) Power generation MW (Gross) (NLC)	MW	6465	7580	7385	7462

Contd.

TABLE 27.10 (*Contd.*)

1	2	3	4	5	6
II.OUTPUT PER MANSHIFT					
(a) Coal India Ltd.	Tonne	1.08	1.17	1.21	1.31
(b) SCCL	Tonne	0.95	0.96	0.99	0.96
Despatches					
(a) Coking Coal					
(i) Metallurgical	Million Tonnes	22.10	21.95	22.19	22.88
(ii) Non-metallurgical	Million Tonnes	17.07	19.24	18.85	19.05
Total coking coal	Million Tonnes	39.17	41.19	41.04	41.93
(b) Non-coking coal	Million Tonnes	131.09	142.83	150.89	158.46
III.EXPORT	Million Tonnes	0.32	0.20	0.16	0.09
IV.PIT-HEAD STOCK					
(a) Metallurgical coking	Million Tonnes	5.81	8.32	6.30	7.39
(b) Non-metallurgical	Million Tonnes	4.21	3.92	5.34	7.91
(c) Non-coking	Million Tonnes	22.43	25.06	25.78	27.58
(d) Total coal	Million Tonnes	32.45	37.30	37.42	42.88

TABLE 27.11: All India Figures of Production, Despatches and Stock of Coal From 1960-61 to 1990-91

(Figures in million tonnes)

Year	Production			Despatches			Closing Stocks		
	Coking	Non-Coking	Total	Coking	Non-Coking	Total	Coking	Non-Coking	Total
1	2	3	4	5	6	7	8	9	10
1960-61	15.98	39.69	55.67	15.23	32.55	47.78	1.72	3.84	5.56
1961-62	16.99	38.24	55.23	15.28	35.53	50.81	1.66	2.11	3.77
1962-63	17.32	46.13	63.45	15.92	40.38	56.30	1.66	2.42	4.01
1963-64	17.50	47.63	65.13	15.67	41.30	56.97	1.88	3.31	5.19
1964-65	16.53	46.25	62.78	14.74	40.94	55.69	1.55	3.71	5.26
1965-66	16.96	50.77	67.73	16.05	44.65	60.70	0.73	4.14	4.87
1966-67	15.58	51.98	68.56	14.66	44.85	59.51	1.16	4.85	6.01
1967-68	16.12	52.40	68.52	14.56	46.78	61.34	0.94	4.87	5.81
1968-69	17.19	54.22	71.41	15.36	48.44	63.80	0.89	5.06	5.95
1969-70	18.10	57.62	75.72	15.62	50.55	66.17	1.60	5.48	7.00
1970-71	17.82	55.13	72.95	15.18	47.08	62.26	2.17	7.38	9.55
1971-72	16.75	55.67	72.42	15.31	50.21	65.52	1.64	6.18	7.82

Contd.

TABLE 27.11 (*Contd.*)

1	2	3	4	5	6	7	8	9	10
1972-73	16.62	60.60	77.22	14.63	55.53	70.16	1.43	4.79	6.22
1973-74	15.77	62.40	78.17	14.28	54.31	68.59	0.85	5.80	6.65
1974-75	20.12	68.37	88.49	19.88	65.00	84.88	1.04	5.94	6.98
1975-76	22.19	77.49	99.68	21.16	70.80	91.96	1.67	10.17	11.84
1976-77	23.65	77.39	101.04	22.11	72.91	95.02	2.63	11.85	14.48
1977-78	23.31	77.66	100.87	22.85	76.65	99.50	2.24	9.94	12.18
1978-79	22.52	79.43	101.95	21.48	74.34	95.82	2.73	12.02	14.75
1979-80	23.50	80.45	103.95	21.33	78.25	99.58	3.94	10.07	14.01
1980-81	26.85	87.06	113.91	22.16	83.60	105.76	5.03	13.25	18.28
1981-82	30.25	93.98	124.23	24.54	93.56	118.10	9.07	12.18	21.25
1982-83	30.31	100.19	130.50	27.91	96.15	124.06	8.72	14.95	23.67
1983-84	30.20	108.02	138.22	26.45	104.18	130.63	7.07	16.35	23.42
1984-85	36.50	110.91	147.41	22.49	101.97	135.40	9.58	20.12	29.70
1985-86	35.65	188.59	154.20	34.44	116.58	151.04	9.31	18.47	27.78
1986-87	39.53	126.26	165.79	35.94	122.65	158.70	11.01	17.77	28.78
1987-88	41.01	138.71	179.72	39.17	131.71	170.88	10.02	22.43	32.45
1988-89	42.72	151.88	194.60	41.19	142.83	184.02	12.24	25.06	37.30
1989-90	44.43	156..46	200.89	41.04	150.89	191.93	11.64	25.78	37.42
1990-91	45.36	166.37	211.73	41.93	158.46	200.39	15.30	27.58	42.88

Note: Coking includes Metallurgical and non-Metallurgical coal.

TABLE 27.12: Company-Wise Overall Position of Major/Mini Coal Handling Plants Handling Non-Coking Coal

Company		1986-87		1987-88		1988-89		1989-90		(expected) 1990-91	
		No.	Capacity	No.	Capacity	No.	Capacity	No.	Capacity	No.	Capacity
ECL	Major	6	5.34	7	6.09	7	6.09	7	6.09	8	7.25
	Mini	66	9.90	66	9.90	66	9.90	66	9.90	66	9.90
BCCL	Major	7	2.70	10	4.02	11	4.47	11	4.47	14	8.65
	Mini	36	1.62	36	1.62	36	1.62	36	1.62	36	1.62
CCL	Major	10	7.35	10	7.35	13	10.45	16	10.45	16	10.45
	Mini	4	1.34	4	1.34	4	1.34	4	1.34	4	1.34
NCL	Major	4	9.60	4	14.60	4	14.60	4	14.60	4	15.80
	Mini	—	—	—	—	—	—	—	—		
SECL	Major	22	27.36	22	27.36	27	34.36	29	40.64	29	40.64
	Mini	28	7.05	27	7.05	27	7.05	27	7.05	28	7.12
WCL	Major	12	9.58	13	10.68	16	15.18	17	15.13	17	15.13
	Mini	20	6.09	20	6.09	20	6.09	20	6.09	18	5.64
Total	Major	61	61.93	66	70.10	78	87.41	84	96.38	88	97.92
	Mini	153	26.00	153	26.00	153	26.00	153	26.00	152	25.62
SCCL	Major	11	15.55	11	15.55	11	15.55	13	15.55	14	21.35
Grand Total		225	103.48	230	111.65	244	128.96	250	137.93	256	144.89

TABLE 27.13: Coal Handling Plants of Washeries Dealing with Coking Coal

BCCL	Major	8	13.62	8	13.62	9	14.25	9	14.25	9	14.25
CCL	Major	4	9.31	4	9.31	5	12.31	5	12.31	5	12.31
WCL	Major	1	1.20	1	1.20	1	1.20	1	1.20	1	1.20
Total		13	24.13	13	24.13	15	27.76	15	27.76	15	17.76

TABLE 27.14: Trends in the Power Sector (Utilities only)

Sl. No.	Item	1988-89	1989-90	1990-91#	April-December#		Percentage change		
					1990-91	1991-92	1989-90 / 1988-89	1990-91 / 1989-90	1991-92* / 1990-91
1	2	3	4	5	6	7	8	9	10
1.	**Power generation (Billion kwh)**	**221.4**	**245.4**	**264.6**	**194.0**	**211.4**	**10.8**	**7.8**	**9.0**
	(i) Hydro-electric	57.9	62.1	71.7	54.5	56.8	7.3	15.5	4.2
	(ii) Thermal (incl. nuclear)	163.5	183.3	192.9	139.5	154.6	12.1	5.2	10.8
2.	Plant Load Factor of thermal plants (per cent)	55.0	56.5	53.8	52.0	53.4	—	—	—

Provisional
* April-December

ELECTRICITY

Total electricity generation (total utilities in terms of hydel, thermal and nuclear) at 264.6 billion kwh recorded a growth of 7.8 per cent during 1990-91 but fell short of the target by 2.6 per cent.

Thermal power generation during 1990-91 increased by 4.5 per cent, hydel generation by 15.5 per cent and nuclear power generation by 32.6 per cent. Thermal generation fell short of the target by 7.4 per cent mainly due to loss of generation because of short supply of coal. The other reasons which contributed to the shortfall were low system demand due to excess hydro generation resulting in reduction of irrigation load and for keeping some units under shut-down due to shortage of funds. Low PLF in some of the States also contributed to shortfall in thermal generation. Hydro generation was 13.5 per cent more than the target and nuclear power generation 8.8 per cent below the target due to problems in nuclear power reactors.

Total generation of power in April-December, 1991 was 211.4 billion kwh compared to 194 billion kwh during the same period last year showing a growth of 9 per cent. Hydel power generation at 56.8 billion kwh increased by 4.2 per cent. The thermal (including nuclear) sector at 154.6 billion kwh has registered a growth of 10.8 per cent compared to the same period, last year.

Trends in the power sector are shown in the Table 27.14.

TABLE 27.15: Progress of Electricity Supply (Utilities and Non-utilities)

(Thousand MW)

Year	Installed Plant Capacity					
	Utilities				Non-utilities	Total (5)+(6)
	Hydro	Thermal	Nuclear	Total		
1	2	3	4	5	6	7
1950-51+	0.6	1.1	—	1.7	0.6	2.3
1960-61	1.9	2.7	—	4.6	1.0	5.6
1970-71	6.4	7.9	0.4	14.7	1.6	16.3
1975-76	8.5	11.0	0.6	20.1	2.1	22.2
1976-77	9.0	11.8	0.6	21.5	2.3	23.8
1977-78	10.0	13.0	0.6	23.7	2.5	26.2
1978-79	10.8	15.2	0.6	26.7	2.6	29.3
1979-80	11.4	16.4	0.6	28.4	2.9	31.3
1980-81	11.8	17.6	0.9	30.2	3.1	33.3
1981-82	12.2	19.3	0.9	32.3	3.4	35.8
1982-83	13.1	21.4	0.9	35.4	3.9	39.2
1983-84	13.9	24.4	1.1	39.3	4.4	43.7
1984-85	14.5	27.0	1.1	42.6	5.1	47.7
1985-86	15.5	30.0	1.3	46.8	5.5	52.3
1986-87	16.2	31.8	1.3	49.3	5.7	55.0
1987-88	17.3	35.6	1.3	54.2	6.3	60.5
1988-89	17.8	39.7	1.5	59.0	7.5	65.5
1989-90	18.3	43.8	1.5	63.6	8.2	71.8
1990-91*	18.8	45.7	1.5	66.0	8.4	74.4

(Contd.)

TABLE 27.15 (*Contd.*)

Energy Generated (Gross)

(Billion KWH)

Year	Utilities				Non-utilities	Total (5)+(6)
	Hydro	Thermal	Nuclear	Total		
1	2	3	4	5	6	7
1950-51+	2.5	2.6	—	5.1	1.5	6.6
1960-61	7.8	9.1	—	16.9	3.2	20.1
1970-71	25.2	28.2	2.4	55.8	5.4	61.2
1975-76	33.3	43.3	2.6	79.2	6.7	85.9
1976-77	34.8	50.2	3.3	88.3	7.3	95.6
1977-78	38.0	51.1	2.3	91.4	7.6	98.9
1978-79	47.1	52.6	2.8	102.5	7.6	110.1
1979-80	45.5	56.3	2.9	104.6	8.2	112.8
1980-81	46.5	61.3	3.0	110.8	8.4	119.3
1981-82	49.6	69.5	3.0	122.1	9.0	131.1
1982-83	48.4	79.9	2.0	130.3	10.0	140.3
1983-84	50.0	86.7	3.5	140.2	10.8	151.0
1984-85	53.9	98.8	4.1	156.9	12.3	169.2
1985-86	51.0	114.4	5.0	170.4	13.0	183.4
1986-87	53.8	128.9	5.0	187.7	13.6	201.3
1987-88	47.5	149.6	5.0	202.1	16.9	219.0
1988-89	57.9	157.7	5.8	221.4	19.9	241.3
1989-90	62.1	178.7	4.6	245.4	23.0	268.4
1990-91*	71.7	186.8	6.1	264.6	24.1	288.7

* Provisional + On a calendar year basis.

Note: Figures may not add up to the total owing to rounding off.

Source: *Economic Survey*, 1991-92.

TABLE 27.16: Pattern of Electricity Consumption (Utilities)

(Percentage)

Year	Domestic	Commercial	Industry	Traction	Agriculture	Others
1950-51+	12.6	7.5	62.6	7.4	3.9	6.0
1960-61	10.7	6.1	69.4	3.3	6.0	4.5
1970-71	8.8	5.9	67.6	3.2	10.2	4.3
1975-76	9.7	5.8	62.4	3.1	14.5	4.5
1976-77	9.5	6.2	62.5	3.3	14.4	4.1
1977-78	9.9	6.4	61.6	3.3	14.6	4.2
1978-79	9.8	5.6	61.8	2.8	15.6	4.4
1979-80	10.8	6.0	58.9	2.9	17.2	4.2
1980-81	11.2	5.7	58.4	2.7	17.6	4.4
1981-82	11.6	5.8	58.8	2.8	16.8	4.2
1982-83	12.7	6.1	55.4	2.8	18.6	4.4
1983-84	12.9	6.4	55.8	2.6	17.8	4.5
1984-85	13.6	6.1	55.2	2.5	18.4	4.2
1985-86	14.0	5.9	54.5	2.5	19.1	4.0
1986-87	14.2	5.7	51.7	2.4	21.7	4.3
1987-88	15.2	6.1	47.5	2.5	24.2	4.5
1988-89	15.5	6.2	47.1	2.3	24.3	4.6
1989-90	16.3	5.8	45.6	2.4	25.0	4.4
1990-91*	16.5	6.1	44.9	2.2	26.0	4.3

* Provisional. + On a calendar year basis.

TABLE 27.17: Power Generation Capacity Targets/Achievements

Sector	Commissioned/ Rolled Actual 1990-91		Target 1991-92		April-December, 1991			
					Target		Commissioned/ Rolled	
	No.	Capacity (MW)	No.	Capacity (MW)	No.	Capacity (MW)	No.	Capacity (MW)
Thermal	22	2331.0	24	2586.5	18	1326.5	6	763.5
Hydro	9	445.5	35	754.3	15	383.5	10	91.5
Nuclear	—	—	2	470.0	2	470.0	1	235.0
Total	31	2776.5	61	3810.8	35	2180.0	17	1090.0

Source: *Economic Survey*, 1991-92.

PETROLEUM

Production of crude oil during 1990-91 at 33.02 million tonnes fell short of the target of 35.90 million tonnes and was 3.1 per cent lower than the production of 34.09 million tonnes in 1989-90. The Oil and Natural Gas Commission (ONGC) produced 30.37 million tonnes of crude oil out of which 9.18 million tonnes was from the on-shore areas and 21.19 million tonnes from off-shore areas. The on-shore production by Oil India Limited (OIL) at 2.65 million tonnes in 1990-91 was 0.25 million tonnes short of the target.

The production of crude oil during April-December, 1991 was 22.97 million tonnes against 24.71 million tonnes achieved during the corresponding period last year. The shortfall in crude oil production during the current year is mainly due to the disturbed law and order condition in Assam and on account of technical reasons.

The production of natural gas in 1990-91 was 18 billion cubic metres. This was higher by 6.0 per cent compared to the production of 17 billion cubic metres during the previous year. The utilisation of natural gas during 1990-91 was 12.8 billion cubic metres compared to 11.2 billion cubic metres in 1989-90.

The production of natural gas during April-November, 1991 was 12.2 billion cubic metres which was 5.2 per cent higher than the production of 11.6 billion cubic metres in the same period last year. The utilisation of natural gas upto November, 1991 was 9.4 billion cubic metres compared to 8.2, billion cubic metres during the corresponding period last year.

Flaring of Natural Gas continues to cause considerable concern. However, this has been brought down from about 17 million cubic metres per day a year ago to about 11 million cubic metres per day currently. Further, with the implementation of the Gas Flaring Reduction Project, the flaring of natural gas is expected to be eliminated in the Western Off-shore by 1995. Projects to install compressors and pipelines in the Gujarat region are also under implementation to eliminate flaring in the Western Off-shore region.

Refinery Production

The total refinery crude throughput during 1990-91 at 51.77 million tonnes was marginally lower than 51.94 million tonnes achieved in 1989-90. The average capacity utilisation of all the 12 refineries was 99.8 per cent as compared to

100.2 per cent during the previous years.

The refinery crude throughput during April-December, 1991 at 37.54 million tonnes was marginally lower than the target of 337.99 million tonnes. The target of refinery crude throughput for 1991-92 is 51.65 million tonnes. The achievement upto end-December, 1991 works out to 72.7 per cent of the target. The capacity utilisation of the refineries during April-December, 1991 was 96.4 per cent compared to 98.2 per cent achieved in the same period last year.

Imports

The Gross import of crude oil and petroleum products during 1990-91 at 29.36 million tonnes was 12.7 per cent higher than 26.05 million tonnes imported in 1989-90. The value of POL imports during 1990-91 is Rs. 10,779 crore against Rs. 6,344 crore during the previous year. The import of POL during April-December, 1991 was 23.35 million tonnes valued at Rs. 9,260 crore against the import of 20.47 million tonnes costing Rs. 7,089 crore during the same period last year. The import of crude oil and petroleum products during the current year is likely to be 32.8 million tonnes.

Consumption

During 1990-91, consumption of petroleum products at 55.04 million tonnes showed moderate growth of 1.7 per cent over the previous year. The various demand management measures adopted by the Government in the wake of the Gulf War have helped to curtail the demand for POL during 1990-91. During April-December, 1991 consumption of petroleum products increased by 1.8 per cent over the same period last year. The demand for LPG and Bitumen have showed significant increase, while the demand for HSD and Petrol, has increased by 5.1 per cent and 1.7 per cent, respectively. There has been substantial reduction in the demand for ATF and LDO. It may, however, be added that the demand for petroleum products generally declines in the first half and picks up in the second half of the financial year (Table 27.19).

RENEWABLE SOURCES OF ENERGY

The major programmes launched in the country for the development and utilisation of new and renewable sources of energy areas include programmes relating to bio-energy, solar energy, wind power and micro-hydel. Over 14.03 lakh biogas plants had already been set up in the country till end-March, 1991 under the National Project on Biogas Development with an estimated biogas generation capacity equivalent to about 50 lakh tonnes of fuel wood per year valued at Rs. 200 crore and 5 lakh tonnes of NPK in the form of manure. The target for 1991-92 is fixed at 1.47 lakh plants. During April-December, 1991 88,815 plants have already been installed against the target of 73,500 plants. Under the National Programme for Improved *chullahs*, about 19.87 lakh fuel efficient and smokeless *chullahs* were set up in 1990-91, bringing the total number installed to about 103.77 lakh. These improved *chullahs* are estimated to have the potential of saving 72.6 lakh tonnes of wood valued at Rs. 290 crore per year, in addition to the benefits of preserving the environment. During April-December, 1991, 8.72 lakh *chullahs* had been installed against the target of 9.24 lakh. Appropriate feed-back and monitoring systems have been introduced to ensure the functionality of the installations set up under these programmes.

TABLE 27.18: Trends in the Petroleum Sector

(Million tonnes)

Sl. No.	Item	1988-89	1989-90	1990-91#	April-December#		Percentage change		
					1990-91	1991-92	1989-90 / 1988-89	1990-91 / 1989-90	1991-92* / 1990-91
1	2	3	4	5	6	7	8	9	10
1.	Crude oil production	32.04	34.09	33.02	24.71	22.97	6.4	—3.1	—7.0
	(i) On-shoe	10.93	12.37	11.83	8.78	8.62	13.2	—4.4	—1.8
	(a) ONGC	8.50	9.67	9.18	6.78	6.69	13.8	—5.1	—1.3
	(b) OIL	2.43	2.70	2.65	2.00	1.93	11.1	—1.9	—3.5
	(ii) Off-shore (ONGC)	21.11	21.72	21.19	15.93	14.35	2.9	—2.4	—9.9
2.	Refinery through-put	48.80	51.94	51.77	38.36	37.54	6.4	—0.3	—2.1
3.	Production of petroleum products	45.70	48.69	48.57	35.82	35.10	6.5	—0.2	—2.0
4.	Natural gas (Bn. cub. metres)	13.22	16.98	18.00	11.59@	12.23@	28.4	6.0	5.5@

\# Provisional
* April-December
@ April-November

TABLE 27.19: LPG Production

(Figs in TH.Mt/Yr)

Refinery	1989-90 MOU	OEB	1990-91 PROPOSED OEB	1991-92	1992-93	1993-94	1994-95
Guwahati	7	8	8	9	9	16 *	21 *
Barauni	48	54	55	56	56	61 **	64 **
Gujarat	193	191	201	174 ***	201 ***	217 ***	217 ***
Haldia	30	30	30	30	30	30	30
Mathura	174	176	174	178 ****	178 ****	178 ****	178 ****

* With the completion of facilities for recovery of LPG from coker gases with 60 per cent operation in Ist year and full thereafter.

** With the completion of reformer project with 60 per cent operation in Ist year and full thereafter.

*** Lower in 1991-92 due to lower south Gujarat (ANK/GAN) crude and higher NG Crude considered from 1991-92 onwards. Subsequently LPG production increases from 1992-93 due to operation of Hydrocracker and higher crude intake.

**** Higher due to higher FCC t' put and also higher crude intake.

TABLE 27.20: Refinery, MOU and OEB

(Figs. in % on crude)

REFINERY	1989-90 MOU	1989-90 OEB	1990-91 Proposed OEB	1991-92	1992-93	1993-94	1994-95
MATHURA:							
LT. DIST.	18.5	19.	19.8	19.6	19.6	19.6	19.6
MID. DIST.	51.5	51.2	50.4	50.8	50.8	50.8	50.8
HY. ENDS	24.4	24.5	24.3	24.1	24.1	24.1	24.1
ISD	0.0	—0.3	0.0	0.0	0.0	0.0	0.0

Contued.

TABLE 27.21: Consumption of Petroleum Products@

(Million tonnes)

Sl. No.	Item	1988-89	1989-90	1990-91#	April-December#		Percentage change		
					1990-91	1991-92	1989-90 / 1988-89	1990-91 / 1989-90	1991-92* / 1990-91
1	2	3	4	5	6	7	8	9	10
1.	**Light distillates**	**8.62**	**9.41**	**9.80**	**7.20**	**7.49**	**9.2**	**4.1**	**4.0**
	(a) Naphtha	3.36	3.35	3.45	2.50	2.55	—0.3	3.0	2.0
	(b) LPG	1.96	2.27	2.42	1.77	1.92	15.8	6.6	8.5
	(c) MOgas	3.05	3.49	3.55	2.65	2.70	14.4	1.7	1.9
2.	**Middle distillates**	**29.96**	**32.48**	**33.11**	**24.53**	**24.90**	**8.4**	**1.9**	**1.5**
	(a) Kerosene	7.73	8.24	8.42	6.21	6.18	6.6	2.2	—0.5
	(b) Diesel oil	18.80	20.71	21.14	15.65	16.45	10.2	2.1	5.1
3.	**Heavy ends**	**11.52**	**12.20**	**12.13**	**8..88**	**8.93**	**5.9**	**—0.6**	**0.6**
	Fuel oil	8.46	8.82	8.99	6.64	6.69	4.3	1.9	0.8
	Total	**50.09**	**54.10**	**55.04**	**40.61**	**41.32**	**8.0**	**1.7**	**1.7**

@ Excluding RBF
\# Provisional
* April-December

Physical achievement under the solar thermal extension programme for the period ending March, 1991 includes setting up of a total collector area of 1.74 lakh sq. mts. for purposes such as water heating, distillation of water, timber seasoning, etc. Over 2,00,000 solar cookers have been sold so far. Over 7,000 villages and hamlets have been provided with solar photovoltaic lighting systems and over 50 village legal solar photovoltaic power plants have been installed. The aggregate capacity of photovoltaic systems installed in the country for various applications is about 4 MW. A programme for the development of amorphous silicon solar cell technology has been taken up as a science and technology project in a mission mode and a pilot plant for the production of amorphous silicon solar cells and modules is undergoing trial runs.

Under the wind energy development and demonstration programme, 2,756 wind pumps have been installed and wind farm projects of an aggregate capacity of 38.3 MW have been set up in 7 States. Over 106 million units of electricity have been fed to the respective State grids since the commencement of the Wind Farm Programme in 1986 with a capacity of 3.3 MW. A major wind resource assessment programme is under implementation in 22 States. 848 Biomass gasifier systems, of about 6.4 MW capacity, which can each achieve a diesel replacement of 60-65 per cent have also been installed under a demonstration programme.

Under the demonstration programme of Alternate Fuels for Surface Transportation, 25 buses of the Delhi Transport Corporation have been successfully run over 20 lakh kilometre with ethanol induction to the engine achieving approximately 14 per cent diesel replacement. Battery operated Mini buses for group transportation have also been successfully demonstrated at Delhi. These programmes are being extended to other cities.

The Indian Renewable Energy Development Agency Ltd. (IREDA), set up in March, 1987 had by end-December, 1991 sanctioned a total of 167 projects for about Rs. 63 crore relating to areas such as biomass utilisation for heat, steam and power generation, solar energy thermal energy, generation of biogas/power from industrial effluents, battery powered vehicles as well as for manufacturing equipments needed for various NRSE systems and devices. In 1990-91, IREDA sanctioned a total of 55 projects against 31 projects in 1989-90 involving a total outlay of Rs. 2,629.35 lakh against Rs. 582.87 lakh in 1989-90. The sanctioned projects are expected to result in the additional saving of 3,88,176 million tonnes of coal valued at Rs. 3,598.16 lakh per annum; 8,543.16 kilolitre of furnace oil valued at Rs. 300.09 lakh per annum, 32,202 m.t. of wood valued at Rs. 129.42 lakh and generation of 90.35 million units of electricity valued at Rs. 895.70 lakh per annum.

Solar Energy

A number of technologies for manufacturing solar thermal equipments have been developed and made available to over 150 manufactures, State nodal agencies and voluntary organisations in the country. These include technologies for making solar cookers, low cost solar water heaters, solar huts and solar stills.

For standardisation in production in this field, various material, production and performance standards have been developed and reached the stage of Indian specifications published by Bureau of Indian Standards. A country-wide network of manufacturers and suppliers has also been developed making available quality products which are internationally competitive on energy supply basis.

The Solar Energy Centre is engaged in developing educational and mass media packages for creating large scale dissemination of information on equipment and for ensuring cost competitiveness. The Centre has also been imparting training to solar energy experts on R&D, manufacturing, testing and maintenance.

Source : *Yojana*, January 15, 1992.

28

HEALTH AND ENVIRONMENT

HEALTH

India, being a signatory to the Alma Ata declaration of 1978, is committed to the goal of "Health for All" by the year 2000 A.D. It is with this commitment in the background that the National Health Policy was adopted by the Parliament in 1983 which is a blueprint for action by the Government and voluntary agencies. The health and family welfare programmes have been consistently following the twin goals of "Health for All" and Net Reproduction Rate of 'unity' by 2000 A.D.

Primary Health Care

For providing Primary Health Care and Family Welfare Service to people at their door steps, an integrated Health Care Delivery System with the maximum possible community participation has been developed. Accordingly, a huge network supported by referral institutions has been created throughout the country. During the last four decades considerable progress has been achieved and targets for setting up one sub-centre for 5000 population in ordinary areas and 3000 for hilly and tribal areas and a Primary Health Centre for population of 30,000 in general and 20,000 for hilly and tribal areas have almost been fully achieved. At present there are 3.65 lakh doctors i.e. 4.4 doctors per 10,000 population. The number of beds is 9.4 as against 3.2 per 10,000 of population in 1951.

Control of Communicable Diseases

The National Malaria Eradication Programme (NMEP) is one of the World's biggest programme against a single communicable disease. The programme was modified in 1977 in the context of the resurgence and escalation. Up to the year 1988, there was a gradual downward trend in malaria. However, thereafter the incidence of malaria has been showing an increasing trend. The position is stable since 1990.

Medical Infrastructure

There has been a considerable expansion of institutional facilities for treatment of the sick. The number of hospitals and dispensaries increased from 7,400 in 1947 to 39,971 by 1990. During the same period, the number of beds available went up from 80,163 to 6,49,417. By March, 1991, 1,30,978 subcentres, 22059 Primary Health Centres and 1923 Community Health Centres have been functioning in the country.

Medical education has made rapid progress. There are 128 medical colleges with an estimated 15,000 annual admissions. There are about 3.65 lakh registered MBBS doctors with the Medical Council of India. Besides, 11011 Dentists were registered in 1990 with the Dental Council of India.

Occupational Safety and Health

The International Labour Organisation (ILO) has identified that the accident rate in construction, mining, transport, agriculture and forestry is still high in the Asian Region despite recent development in safety and health in these countries and has asked these countries to build up their enforcement capabilities through each other experience. The Report of the Director General further reveals that small and medium seized enterprises which carry much of the economic activities are barely covered by safety and health regulations.

The report highlights that in construction industry in India an estimated 10 lakh could run the risk of injury in 1991. China has a reported 2,000 fatalities a year in mining industry. Because of increased use of Chemical pesticides in agriculture and forestry, Sri Lanka experienced around 1,000 fatalities and 14,000 persons were hospitalized.

Source : *Yojana*, December 15, 1991.

Health and Family Planning

Health and family Planning gained a lead in the race for a birth control vaccine when a vaccine developed at the National Institute of Immunology (NIIL), New Delhi to produce antibodies against the Human Chronic Gonadotropin (HCG) became the first in the world to reach the efficacy trial stage. Studies so far have proved the vaccine to be completely devoid of any side-effects and reversible.

Centachroman, a once-a-week oral contraceptive pill, developed at the Central Drug Research Institute (CDRI), Lucknow, is claimed to be the first of its kind in the world; it entered the market this year.

Leprosy Programme

A bank funded project of about Rs. 283 crore has been formulated to eradicate leprosy. One hundred and forty three districts in seven States: Madhya Pradesh, Uttar Pradesh, Rajasthan, Himachal Pradesh, Maharashtra and Kerala are covered in this project. During the next five years it will provide treatment to over 20 lakh leprosy cases.

Out of the recorded 25.6 lakh leprosy cases 21.4 lakh were under treatment at the end of March 1990. During the year 1990-91 a total of about 1,22,000 were detected, about 1,20,000 brought under treatment and 1,56,000 cases were discharged. An amount of Rs. 24 crore has been allocated in National Leprosy Eradication Programme this year.

Source : *Yojana*, December 15, 1991.

Aids Control Programme

AIDS Control New Hights in Scientific Field

India became third in the world to make the only known drug for AIDS so far.

Indian Institute of Chemical Technology (IICT), Hyderabad, developed a novel approach to AZT making. The Indian drug is much cheaper than the ones imported so far.

AIDS in India

Official data on AIDS gives cause for serious concern. As on October 31 as many as 6,106 peoples were confirmed to have been infected with HIV virus that causes AIDS.

Though the spread of the infection is found among all States and Union Territories, Maharashtra, Tamil Nadu and Manipur have been identified as the "danger zones".

There are 2,043 HIV-infected persons in Maharashtra, 1,429 in Tamil Nadu and 1,347 in Manipur. Another alarming fact is that more than a million people in the country are found to be practising "high risk behaviour" making them potential candidates for HIV infection. Homosexuals, prostitutes, promiscuous heterosexuals and intravenous drug users are the people among the high risk behaviour groups.

AIDS Day

Recognising the urgency of tackling AIDS the world over the United Nations observed December 1, 1991 as World AIDs Day. The Day was also observed in India.

WHO Project to Control AIDS

The Ministry of Health and Family Welfare has prepared a project on AIDS control and prevention in the country worth $ 65 million to be implemented over a period of three years. The programme is being supported by the external funding agencies such as WHO and US Aid.

The main objective of this project is to secure prevention of HIV transmission and reduction of morbidity and mortality rate of AIDs. The project provides for surveillance to monitor the incidence of HIV infection amongst risk groups.

Another important aspect of this project is to promote safety of blood and blood products by way of establishing 608 blood banks in the country in public sector providing linkages with zonal blood testing centres in all the States.

To prevent AIDs the Government of India in collaboration with the WHO has so far organised 14 training courses for physicians and nurses in the clinical management of AIDs cases in different parts of the country. The medical officers so far trained include 280 doctors and 140 nurses.

Source : *Yojana*, December 15, 1991.

AIDS Bill

Meanwhile, during the year 1991 Government decided to drop a two-year old Bill of AIDS pending before Parliament as it was felt that legislation alone was not enough to control and prevent the disease.

Among the issues which could not be sorted out and led to the dropping of the measure was the policy to be adopted in regulating prostitution. The decision to drop the Acquired Immuno-Deficiency Syndrome Bill, 1989, came during the winter session of Parliament in 1991.

The other contentious issues were how to ensure confidentiality and whether a penalty should be levied on AIDS patients. It was felt that the penalty would be counter-productive as the patient might not be willing to take medical help.

HIV Impact

The spread of the human immuno-deficiency virus, which causes AIDS, via blood and blood products can be controlled. But screening of such products in India leaves much to be desired, leading to a large number of transfusion-related HIV positive cases in many parts of the country, especially in Gujarat.

This was stated by Dr. (Ms.) R.D. Bhattacharya, president, International Society for Research on Civilisation Diseases and on Environment, Ahmedabad, at a Symposium on AIDS at the 48th Bombay Medical Congress held on February 29, 1991.

The HIV is no longer a problem for only high-risk groups like prostitutes and homosexuals but has spread to the general population and its impact will be felt by women and children primarily. Thus, the key factor in HIV prevention would be raising women's status in the country.

There is the need for the Indian Government to launch a countrywide prevention and control programme instead of concentrating only on the four metropolises. It is recognised that prostitutes are a major mode of spread but who are the clients of this group? The migrants from rural areas primarily, who will in turn spread the disease in the remote regions.

Dr. Suniti Solomon, professor of microbiology, Institute of Microbiology, Madras, added that for every one person diagnosed, there were a 100 who went undiagnosed. Thus the exact incidence of this pandemic is yet to be adequately gauged.

The ELISA (enzyme linked immunos sorbant assay) test for the HIV virus, though effective, could give false positive reactions and thus must be repeated for correct diagnosis.

Dr. (Ms.) Prema Ramachandran, additional director, Indian Council for Medical Research (ICMR) announced that India was the first country to really begin serosurveillance to define modes of transmission. ICMR had detected high seropositivity (HIV positivity) in Maharashtra and Tamil Nadu.

Drug addiction-related HIV is still not a major problem in these states as in Manipur where the figures have shot up from two per cent in 1990 to 50 per cent at the end of 1991.

"We need to target our intervention programmes at the right groups, taking into account our scarce resources, and combine intervention with close monitoring."

Dr. J.K. Maniar pointed out there were no facilities at public hospitals for disposing of needles and syringes which should appropriately be incinerated instead of being dumped in the garbage from where urchins and ragpickers could easily be infected.

Besides testing for HIV-1, the government should also look for HIV-2, the latter having been increasingly detected in the last one year. While 10 positive

HIV-2 cases have been detected in this period, there have been 40 cases of combined incidence of HIV-1 and 2.

The arrival of AIDS in India has also initiated the revival of diseases like tuberculosis and kala azar. Colonel V. S. Kolhe, senior advisor (medicine), INHS Asvini, Bombay, said that 40 per cent of the one million HIV patients in India suffer from tuberculosis. "This means that 400,000 tuberculosis cases have been added which is undoubtedly an extra burden on our resources."

Source : *Times of India*, March 3, 1992.

UNDP Workshop on AIDS in North-East India

In view of the increasing problem of HIV infection in the seven North-Eastern States of India, United Nations Development Programme (UNDP), in collaboration with the Government of Manipur, and with assistance from United Nations Drug Control Programme (UNDCP), British Overseas Development Administration (ODA), and World Health Organisation (WHO) organised a week-long workshop on HIV/AIDS in Imphal, Manipur, from 20-24 January 1992. It is one of ten such country workshops to be organised by UNDP under its Regional Project on Development Implications of HIV/AIDS in Asia and the Pacific.

In addition to international consultants from the UK, Hong Kong and Sri Lanka, various international donors were invited to participate, including ODA, UNICEF and the official development agencies of Sweden and Norway. National consultants and active NGOs from each state made presentations of the HIV/AIDS situation in their respective areas.

The workshop focussed on increasing awareness among government policy-makers, State officials and representatives of non-governmental organisations (NGOs) of the effects of HIV transmission and what strategies exist for limiting its spread in the North-Eastern States. It is expected to result in a coordinated and integrated multisectoral plan for AIDS prevention in each of the seven States, including specific interventions for targeted groups to be implemented by Government and selected NGOs. The emphasis will be on stressing that HIV/AIDS is not merely a problems for health sector but one clearly necessitating the involvement of all ministries and parts of society.

Workshop sessions address the legal and ethical issues, and discussed how best to devise an effective information, education and communication plan, and prepare suitable guidelines for helping the individual through community interventions and training. Working sessions defined the goals and needs of each state and outline multisectoral plans for HIV/AIDs prevention.

Source : *UN Newsletter*, January 25, 1992.

ENVIRONMENT

New Pollution Control Policy, 1992

On February 22, 1992, the Government of India announced its new pollution control policy which seeks to tighten the existing regulatory mechanisms and introduce market-oriented price mechanisms to influence people's behaviour to avoid excessive use of natural resources.

Announcing the policy, the Minister of State for Environment, Shri Kamal Nath, said maximum use of legislation and regulation, fiscal incentives, voluntary agreements, educational programmes and information campaigns would play a key role in the policy's implementation.

Preventive Aspects

The policy lays stress on preventive aspects for pollution control and promotion of technological inputs to reduce industrial pollutants. "The emphasis will be on cleean technologies and not clean-up technologies".

Another objective is to integrate environmental consideration into decision-making at all levels. This, the policy says, will be taken up in five steps:

* To initiate prevention of pollution at source;
* To encourage, develop and apply the best available practicable technical solutions;
* To ensure that the polluter pays for the pollution and control arrangements;
* To focus protection on heavily polluted areas and river stretches; and
* To involve the public in decision-making.

Recognising that regulatory measures alone are not enough, the policy says new approaches for considering market choices would be introduced. The aim: to give industries and consumers clear signals about the cost of using environmental and natural resources.

Fiscal Incentives

Also, existing fiscal incentives such as concessional excise and customs tariff for installation of pollution control equipment and shifting of polluting industries from congested areas, would be reviewed to stimulate the advancement of such technologies and create increased demand for them.

Economic instruments would be investigated to encourage shift from curative to preventive measures, internalise the costs of pollution and conserve resources, particularly water. These instruments will also have a distributive effect as the revenues will be used for enforcement, collective treatment facilities, research and promote new investment.

Giving an overview of the problem, the policy sates that there is an increasing trend in environmental pollution. Water is polluted by four kinds of substances: traditional organic waste, waste generated from industrial processes, chemical agents for fertilisers and pesticides for crop protection and silt from degraded catchments.

Total Load

While it is estimated that three-fourths by volume of waste water generated is from municipal sources, industrial waste, though small in volume, contributes over one-half of the total pollutant load, the major portion of this is coming from large and medium industries.

So mechanisms will be evolved to reduce local concentration of pollutants in complex industrial sites. Strategies will be developed for areas with high pollution loads. Existing units in these areas will be targeted for effective action. And new units will be required to comply with location specific standards for stringent environmental quality objectives.

The pollution control norms will be revised to lay down mass-based standards, which will set specific limits to encourage minimisation of waste, promote recycling and reuse of materials, as well as conservation of natural resources.

Local bodies, statutory authorities and public limited companies will have to make annual environmental statements to evaluate the effect of their policies operations and activities on the environment. Ultimately, this will lead an environmental audit which will be compulsory.

Environmental Education Programme (1992-93)

The Government proposes to attach priority to education on environmental issues, both formal and informal, and to all sections of people, children, youth and the old. The Budget proposals for 1992-93, presented in Parliament on February 29, 1992 showed an allocation of Rs. 6.37 crore, as against the revised budget provision of Rs. 5.13 crore for the purpose during 1991-92.

There is, however, an overall drop in the budgetary provision for the Ministry of Forests and Environment for the coming financial year. The provision for the outgoing year was Rs. 339.80 crore, which came down to Rs. 305.80 in the revised estimates, and it is now Rs. 319.37 crore for the next year.

The education programme started at the primary school level and went up to the college. There were several research institutes also, like the one at Dehradun which carried on research in the field of forest and environment.

The Government also proposed to lay great emphasis on pollution control measures in the coming year, and a scheme has also been introduced to make an impact study of those measures in the field of pollution in the air, water and environment. An environment information service has also been introduced for collecting and disseminating environment data. The provision for the Ganga action plan has, however, been proposed to be cut to Rs. 50 crore as against the revised estimate of Rs. 54.50 crore in the revised estimates for the year 1991-92. Special mention was made of the steps to control pollution in the coastal areas.

The Government also proposes to attach much importance to the work of conservation of forest and development of wasteland. Help would be given to the State Governments in protecting forests against armed and organised gangs indulging in illegal activities, including felling of trees and bamboo. Modern fire-fighting devices would also be introduced in the States reserve forest areas.

Source : *Hindustan Times,* March 2, 1992.

Critically Polluted Areas

The Government has identified 17 places in big cities like Delhi, Vishakhapatnam and Howrah which have been declared "critically polluted", where human life faces a threat from large-scale emission of toxic gases from industries.

Notices were being issued to 150 industrial units in various States which had so far failed to comply with the environment standards. Those units had not initiated any steps to combat the pollution created by theme action was being taken by the State pollution control boards under the Environment Protection Act.

State pollution control boards had launched 752 prosecution cases against the defaulting units, which were responsible for causing air and water pollution beyond the permissible limits. Of these, 107 cases were decided in favour of the pollution control boards and 136 went against the prosecution.

Toxic gases were creating havoc in industrial areas in Najafgarh (Delhi), Pali (Rajasthan), Chembur (Maharashtra), Dhanbad (Bihar), Singarauli (UP), and Gobindgarh (Punjab). Suspended particles in the air in some of those cities added to the problem. The Government had taken several other steps to check pollution.

The Ministry had, however, extended the deadline (fixed earlier at December 31, 1991) for taking action against those industrial units which were found to be causing pollution and had not conformed to the environment standards. One more grace period had been given to those industries which had come up between May 1981 and Dec. 31, 1991, to conform to the standards if they had actually initiated action to check pollution at their units. In the case of those industries deadline units which had started production before May 1981, the deadline would be December 1993, but again only in the case of those units which had really started facilities to control pollution.

Source: *Lok Sabha Proceedings*, March 3, 1992, as reported in *Hindustan Times*, March 4, 1992.

29

INDUSTRIES

A major policy reform, substantially deregulating the industrial sector and liberalising foreign investment and technology imports, has been the most significant development during 1991-92. The new package of industrial policy initiatives abandons industrial licensing in all industries except those reserved for the public sector, for the SSI sector and those under compulsory licensing, subject to minimal locational conditions. Lists of industries reserved for the public sector and under compulsory licensing have been pruned. Restrictions on investment by MRTP and FERA companies have been removed. The MRTP Act has been amended to remove threshold limits of assets. Approval for foreign investment up to 51 per cent of equity has been made automatic in specified high priority industries subject to certain conditions regarding the coverage of the import cost of plant and machinery and balancing of dividend payments by export earnings. Approval for foreign technology agreements has been made automatic subject to certain limits on payments. The Phased Manufacturing Programme is abolished and the convertibility clause in the loan agreements with banks/financial institutions removed. Part of the equity holdings of selected public sector enterprises are being divested and placed with mutual funds. Sick public sector enterprises have been brought within the purview of the BIFR.

After consistent high growth in the past three years, industrial production is likely to suffer a setback during 1991-92. The recessionary trend is more pronounced in the manufacturing sector. Factors responsible for this downturn were import compression, rise in the cost of imports due to the cash margin requirement and the downward adjustment of the exchange value of rupee and the tight money policy on the supply side and a perceptible fall in effective demand due to inflationary pressure, reduction in public expenditure, and strict fiscal discipline on the demand side. The setback is transitional, an immediate fall out of the stabilisation measures initiated by the Government for the macroeconomic adjustment of the economy.

However, infrastructure industries performed well, except for crude petroleum and petroleum products. Production of saleable steel and cement increased substantially. There was a deceleration in the production of nitrogenous fertiliser, but phosphatic fertiliser did well. The growth of the small-scale industries decelerated in 1990-91 because of import and credit constraints.

The investment climate continues to be encouraging. There was a significant increase in new capital issues by private sector companies. The stock market has been booming with optimism. Once the key stabilisation measures have been successfully implemented, the overall investment climate is likely to turn brighter in the coming months and years in response to deregulation and liberalisation. Industrial relations were by and large peaceful.

Industrial Policy*

22. The rapid expansion of the industrial sector in the 1980s was induced by reforms undertaken in trade and industrial policies during the early and mid-1980s. The acceleration of the export of manufactured goods during the last four years also bears testimony to the responsiveness of Indian industry to policy changes. A programme of further policy reform is needed to consolidate the gains already achieved and to provide further impetus to industrial growth.

23. The Government of India placed a statement on industrial policy before Parliament on July 24, 1991. This statement marked a major step forward in the government's on going programme of industrial regulatory reform. It announced major initiatives including comprehensive delicensing, abolition of pre-entry controls related to the MRTP Act, and introduction of automaticity in approvals of foreign technology agreements and foreign investments, among others. These measures go a long way toward deregulating entry, which is necessary to provide the competitive stimulus for accelerated industrial growth during the 1990s. The changes in policies concerning foreign technology and foreign investment will enable Indian industry to forge much more dynamic relationships with foreign investors and suppliers of technology than has been possible in the past.

24. The new policy has eliminated investment licensing requirements for all new, expansion and diversification projects except in 18 industries (estimated to account for about 20 per cent of current manufacturing output). Furthermore, the MRTP Act has been amended to remove all requirements for pre-entry approval of large or dominant companies. Thus, except for certain industries related to security and strategic concerns, social aspects, concerns related to safety, overriding environmental issues, and manufacture of chemicals involving hazardous processes, pre-entry regulations governing industrial investment have been removed. In view of serious concerns related to congestion and environmental deterioration, projects within 25 km of the periphery of large cities (23 cities with more than 1 million people) will still require a licence except in prior designated industrial areas. Because of the balance of payments constraint, investors will still need an import licence to import capital goods for projects in which the foreign exchange content is over 25 per cent of total investment of Rs. 20 million, unless foreign exchange supply is ensured through foreign equity capital. The mandatory convertibility clause, under which financial institutions had the right to convert a proportion (up to 20 per cent) of their loans into equity, has been abolished. This will have positive implications for both borrowing companies and the financial institutions. Phased manufacturing programmes, which had involved the enforcement of progressively increasing local content requirements on a case by case administered basis, have been abolished for new projects.

25. Foreign investment and foreign technology agreements in India have hitherto had to obtain specific prior approval from the government. In the case of foreign investment, automatic approval is now available for proposals with a foreign equity share of up to 51 per cent in high priority industries. In view of the

* Para numbers refer to para numbers of the Finance Minister's letter of November 11, 1991.

current balance of payment constraint, this facility is available only to firms that are able to finance their capital equipment imports with the foreign equity contribution. Such firms are also required to balance dividend repatriation with export earnings for a period of 7 years from the commencement of production. This condition has been imposed to provide a signal for foreign investment to be competitive internationally, particularly in the light of expected trade and tariff reforms which will reduce protection within the next 3-5 years. The condition is not likely to impinge on the dividend policy of most companies, since a normal dividend repatriation volume would seldom be higher than one per cent to 2 per cent of sales.

26. Foreign technology agreements where royalties are limited to 5 per cent of domestic sales and 8 per cent of export sales, along with lumpsum payments of up to Rs. 10 million, are now automatically approved. In high-priority industries, free foreign exchange would be available for the payments, whereas in other industries these payments would have to be covered by Eximscrip.

27. Recognising the need to strengthen the incentives for foreign direct investment, the government has set up the Foreign Investment Promotion Board to consider and approve substantial foreign investment proposals. These proposals would be considered in totality, free from pre-determined parameters and procedures. In order to facilitate the financing of large investment requirements, the all-equity requirement for capital goods imports for projects receiving automatic approvals needs to be modified as and when the external payments situation permits. The Government will also endeavour to raise the quantitative limits on capital goods imports or delicensed investment projects as the external payment situation improves. The Government intends to remove the provision linking dividend repayment to export earnings for foreign direct investment projects eligible for automatic clearance, as soon as the external payments situation permits.

28. The Government has been following a policy of releasing industry from price and distribution controls during the 1980s. Such controls were removed for paper, cement and aluminium, among other products. The government intends to continue with similar decontrol in other industries (including steel).

29. The major industrial regulatory reforms already implemented by the government constitute a substantial structural reform of Indian industrial policy. The Government recognizes that the major restructuring of the Indian economy implied by its agenda of macroeconomic adjustment and structural reform will depend on the success of these reforms. Large numbers of sick firms constitute a drain on the Government budget; their unpaid outstanding loan obligations weaken the financial system; and in many cases such firms have closed their doors, leaving labour unemployed without compensation and leaving creditors unreimbursed. Further reforms are needed to formulate a socially acceptable policy to facilitate the restructuring of industrial units in the face of changing technology and the need to modernise. This will prevent sickness in the future. For the restructuring of existing sick and loss making companies in both the public and private sectors, the Government will establish an inter-ministerial working group by November 1991, which will review existing provisions of the various laws governing labour relations, state and local governments' role in industrial restructuring, regulation governing transfer of land, procedures for liquidation under the Companies Act, and other relevant aspects. These reforms will be undertaken along with the efforts to establish adequate safeguards for the

workers, provision of appropriate compensation, and a programme for redeployment and retraining for displaced workers resulting from the winding up of industrial units.

30. The Government is well aware that a prerequisite for a successful policy for industrial restructuring is a "safety net" or social insurance scheme to provide support for displaced workers in the organised sector, through the National Renewal Fund, to be set up by December, 1991. It is our intention to seek the bank's support for the establishment of the facility.

Main Areas of Reforms

A. *Domestic Regulatory Reforms*

1. De-reservation of Industries for Public Sector
2. Abolition of Industrial Licensing
3. Abolition of Phased Manufacturing Programmes
4. Removal of Mandatory Convertibility Clause
5. Removal of Investment Controls on Large Business Houses

B. *Reforms in Regulations Concerning Foreign Investment and Foreign Technology*

1. Automatic approval to industries to make Foreign Technology Agreements within certain Guidelines.
2. No permission required for hiring of foreign technicians and testing of indigenously developed technology abroad.
3. Automatic permission for foreign equity up to 51 per cent equity shares in the high priority industries.

Industrial Production, 1991-92

There has been a mild recession in industrial production in the first eight months of the current financial year. The General Index of Industrial Production (IIP) has shown a decline of 0.9 per cent during April—November 1991 compared with a significant growth of 10 per cent in the corresponding period of last year. The decline in production was much steeper at 2.3 per cent in the manufacturing sector as against a growth of 11.5 per cent last year (Table 29.1) while the production of the mining and quarrying sector fell by 1.6 per cent, that of the electricity sector recorded a lower growth of 7.8 per cent compared with 8.3 per cent last year.

According to the production data at the disaggregated level available upto November 1991, of the 17 major industry groups in the manufacturing sector, 2 groups, viz. beverages and tobacco products and non-metallic mineral products with a combined weight of 4.57 per cent in the IIP recorded accelerated growth, 6 groups of industries (weight : 45.18%) recorded decelerated growth and 9 industry groups (weight : 27.36%) recorded negative growth (Table 29.2). The major industry groups which have been reeling under recessionary pressure were electrical machinery and appliances, non-electrical machinery and machine tools, rubber, plastic, petroleum and coal products, metal products and parts and transport equipment. Some of the major product groups of industries which have shown significant fall (by more than 5 per cent) in production during April-October 1991 are nylon filament yarn, polyester fibre, electric motors, diesel engines, viscose filament yarn, wrist watches, pig iron, telephone instrument, computer systems and peripherals, jeeps, motor cycles, scooters and mopeds, cloth (mill sector), paints and varnishes, petroleum crude and machine tools.

TABLE 29.1: Annual Growth Rates in Major Sectors of Industry

(In percentage)

Year Weight	Mining (11.46)	Manufacturing (77.11)	Electricity (11.43)	General (100.00)
(1)	(2)	(3)	(4)	(5)
1981-82	17.7	7.9	10.2	9.3
1982-83	12.4	1.4	5.7	3.2
1983-84	11.7	5.7	7.6	6.7
1984-85	8.8	8.0	12.0	8.6
1985-86	4.2	9.7	8.5	8.7
1986-87	6.2	9.3	10.3	9.1
1987-88	3.8	7.9	7.7	7.3
1988-89	7.9	8.7	9.5	8.7
1989-90	6.3	8.6	10.8	8.6
1990-91	4.9	9.1	8.7	8.5
April-November				
1990-91	2.5	11.5	8.3	10.0
1991-92	—1.6	—2.3	7.8	—0.9

This decline in the production of the manufacturing sector has come about in spite of a fairly good back up support by the agriculture and infrastructure sectors. Except for petroleum, all other major infrastructure industries like coal, electricity and steel have been performing fairly well.

Steel

Production of saleable steel by the main steel plants excluding Vishakhapatnam Steel Project during April-December 1991 improved substantially (Table 29.3). All the SAIL plants, except Durgapur, increased their production. But there was a decline in the production of pig iron by the SAIL plants. In the case of finished steel, production of the secondary sector (mini-steel plants) which has been growing at an average annual rate of 4 per cent in the past 3 years, suffered a mild setback during the current year because of the inadequate availability of melting scrap due to import constraints. Price and distribution controls on iron and steel items manufactured by integrated steel plants were withdrawn on January 16, 1992. The Freight Equalisation Scheme was also withdrawn. The requirements of defence, railways, small-scale industries, exporters of engineering goods and the North-Eastern region will, however, continue to be met from the priority quota.

TABLE 29.2: Trends in the Output of the Manufacturing Sector: Annual growth rates

(per cent)

Code	Industry group	Weight					April—November	
			1987-88	1988-89	1989-90	1990-91	1990-91	1991-92
1	2	3	4	5	6	7	8	9
20-21.	Food products	5.33	4.4	6.8	1.6	12.5	17.1	1.5
22.	Beverages, tobacco and products	1.57	—13.8	8.5	11.8	1.3	—4.0	9.3
23.	Cotton textiles	12.31	—1.2	—3.1	4.2	14.7	15.6	4.2
25.	Jute, hemp and mesta products	2.00	—10.0	12.0	—4.4	4.4	8.5	1.8
26.	Textile products (including wearing apparel other than footwear)	0.82	5.3	46.3	13.0	—32.0	—31.9	—2.9
27.	Wood and wood products	0.45	—34.3	6.2	2.5	12.7	13.1	—1.5
28.	Paper and paper products	3.23	1.9	3.0	6.0	9.0	7.6	5.0
29.	Leather and fur products	0.49	4.4	—4.4	6.1	3.1	4.1	—5.2
30.	Rubber, plastic, petroleum and coal products	4.00	3.7	8.5	3.1	—0.1	0.9	—2.4
31.	Chemicals and chemical products	12.51	14.5	16.2	6.1	2.7	5.9	1.0
32.	Non-metallic mineral products	3.00	—1.4	16.8	2.9	1.7	2.9	8.0
33.	Basic metals and alloys	9.80	6.9	6.9	—0.8	10.8	10.2	7.9
34.	Metal products and parts	2.29	4.1	3.0	6.8	0.4	4.3	—7.6
35.	Machinery and machine tools	6.24	—1.8	15.8	6.6	8.4	12.0	—2.7
36.	Electrical machinery and appliances	5.78	31.6	3.2	32.7	22.4	29.8	—18.1
37.	Transport equipment	6.39	4.8	12.8	5.7	6.3	10.2	—3.3
38.	Other manufacturing	0.90	15.6	12.6	8.8	—2.9	—0.2	—18.9
Div. 2-3	Manufacturing	77.11	7.9	8.7	8.6	9.1	11.5	—2.3
Div. 1	Mining and quarrying	11.46	3.8	7.9	6.3	4.9	2.5	—1.6
Div. 4	Electricity	11.43	7.7	9.5	10.8	8.7	8.3	7.8
	General	**100.00**	**7.3**	**8.7**	8.6	8.5	10.0	—0.9

TABLE 29.3: Output of Iron and Steel

(*Million tonnes*)

Item	1988-89	1989-90	1990-91	April—December		Percentage change		
				1990-91	1991-92£	1989-90 / 1988-89	1990-91 / 1989-90	1991-92* / 1990-91*
1	2	3	4	5	6	7	8	9
1. Production of saleable steel by main producers								
(a) SAIL	7.26	7.06	7.38	5.21	5.83	—2.8	4.5	11.9
(b) TISCO	1.95	1.97	1.95	1.40	1.48	1.0	—1.0	5.7
Total	9.21	9.03	9.53**	6.61	7.31	—2.0	5.5	10.6
2. Production of finished steel								
(a) Main producers	7.09	7.00	7.20	5.09	5.75	—1.3	2.9	13.0
(b) Secondary producers	5.75	6.00	6.21	4.64	4.54	4.3	3.5	—2.2
Total	12.84	13.00	13.40	9.73	10.29	1.2	3.1	5.8
3. Production of pig iron by main producers	1.01	1.23	1.39	1.02	1.08	2.18	13.0	5.9

£ Provisional

* Relates to April—December

** Includes 200,000 tonnes by VSP

Cement

The cement industry has been doing well during the current year. Production of cement during April-December 1991 recorded a growth of 10.7 per cent compared with 7 per cent in the corresponding period of last year. The bulk of the increase during the current year has come from the large plants in the private sector which contributed more than 80 per cent of total cement production (Table 29.4). This better performance of private sector cement plants can be partly attributed to the firm trend in cement prices since the decontrol of the industry in March 1989.

Textile Industry*

Highlights

The textile industry in India is the largest single industry accounting for around 20 per cent of the total industrial output and employs, in the aggregate, around 15 million people. It is also the largest single contributor to India's exports. The industry is extremely complex and varied in its structure, with the handspun, hand woven sector at one end of the spectrum, and the sophisticated capital-intensive high-speed operations at the other. There is also an intermediate segment consisting of decentralised small scale powerloom units. By the very nature of its structure, the problems besetting the industry are complex and interrelated, and expectedly different both in magnitude and in nature from those that are observed in relatively homogenous systems.

Prior to 1976, there was no independent Department of Ministry of Textiles. Textile Industry was then looked after by the Department of Export Promotion in the Ministry of Commerce. With a view to giving undivided attention to the development of the textile industry at the government level, a full-fledged Department of Textiles was created in the Ministry of Commerce in March, 1976. This arrangement continued upto November, 1977 when the work relating to the development and regulation of the textile industry was transferred to the Ministry of Industry (Department of Industrial Development) and that relating to textile exports was retained in the Ministry of Commerce. The Department of Textiles that was created in 1976, ceased to exist from December, 1977. The Department was however, revived in April, 1980 in the Ministry of Commerce and the work relating to the development and regulation of the textile industry was transferred back from the Ministry of Industry to the Ministry of Commerce. An independent Ministry of Textiles came into existence with effect from 15-11-1985. From November, 1989, the Ministry of Textiles has been separated from Ministry of Commerce with separate common services and with its own staff. However, the cadre continues to be common for both the Ministry of Commerce and the Ministry of Textiles.

---

* *Annual Report*, Ministry of Textiles, Government of India, New Delhi.

TABLE 29.4: Cement Output

(*Million tonnes*)

Sl. No.	Plants	1988-89	1989-90	1990-91	April—December		Percentage change		
					1990-91	1991-92£	1989-90 / 1988-89	1990-91 / 1989-90	1991-92* / 1990-91*
1	2	3	4	5	6	7	8	9	10
1.	Large plants:								
(i)	Public sector	5.29	5.29	4.96	3.55	3.70	No ch.	—6.2	4.2
(ii)	Private sector	36.47	37.68	40.82	29.31	32.89	3.3	8.3	12.2
2.	White/mini cement plants	2.53	2.82	3.26	2.38	2.42	11.5	15.6	1.7
	Total	44.29	45.79	49.04	35.24	39.01	3.4	7.1	10.7

£ Provisional
* Relates to April—December

The most significant Government intervention in this sector in the recent years has been the announcement of the Textile Policy Statement of 6th June, 1985. This Policy provides a framework for the integrated and balanced development of the three sectors of the industry, namely, the organised mill sector, the powerloom sector and the handloom industry as a whole to increase the production of cloth of acceptable quality at reasonable prices to meet the clothing requirements of the growing population, keeping in view the employment and export potential of the industry.

Considering that the Textile Policy of June, 1985 had been in force for three years, Government set up in May, 1988 a Committee under the Chairmanship of Shri Abid Hussain to assess the impact of the Policy on various sectors of the textile economy, particularly its effectiveness in protecting the handloom sector and in maintaining the pre-eminent role of cotton as the main raw-material of the textile industry. The Committee submitted its Report in February, 1990. The Committee firmly believed that the 1985 Policy was anchored on the right principles although no policy frame is immutable. The Committee came to the conclusion that the Textile Policy did not address itself to the institutional, financial and other means required to achieve the objectives it had set for itself. The Committee has made far-reaching recommendations in respect of raw-materials (cotton and synthetic fibre and yarn), spinning sector, weaving sector (handloom, power-looms and mills), exports, fiscal levies and modernisation. The Report of the Committee has been forwarded to the various organisations/Federations of the industry representing various sectors and to the State Governments for furnishing their views. Meetings have been held with State Governments and industry for obtaining their views and further action is being taken.

Consistent with the Government's thrust on creation of more employment and providing a fair deal to the workers and farmers, the new Policy initiatives will have to be taken to strengthen the infrastructural support to the handlooms and handicrafts sector in the areas of raw-material supply and marketing and to achieve higher value addition to increase the wages of the weavers and craftsmen and the returns to the jute and the cotton farmers.

New Schemes

Two major schemes in the textile sector were launched during 1991.

The first one aims at providing skill, upgradation and organisational support for weavers below the poverty line. This has helped many weavers, particularly those from Andhra Pradesh, who were on the verge of starvation due to hike in inputs and stiff competition from the synthetic fabric, according to official sources.

The second scheme is intended for selected handloom villages which excel in craftsmanship. It would provide greater organisational support, further skill upgradation and improved infrastructure relating to both handloom and non-handlooms that would improve the quality of life of the weavers.

With the weaver population of about 15 million having around 38 lakh looms, the handloom sector occupies an important place in the country's economy, producing roughly 30 per cent of the total textile production.

Production

As far as the production of cloth and yarn is concerned, this has been steadily increasing. In 1990-91 the total production of yarn and cloth was of the order of 1795 million kgs and 17818 million metres respectively against the production of 1454 million kgs of yarn and 15148 million metres of cloth in 1985-86. It is significant to note, however, that while yarn production takes place almost entirely in the organised mill sector, 77 per cent of the total cloth production was in the decentralised sectors (power-looms and handlooms) in 1989-90. The organised mill sector thus contributed only 15 per cent of the total cloth production in that year. Eight per cent of the total cloth production was accounted for by hosiery sector.

During the recent past, the price trends of most of the textile items have remained relatively stable and some textile items have even displayed a declining trend in prices. The price situation continues to present a somewhat mystifying pattern of unrelated upsurges and falls in different sectors of cotton, yarn, fabrics which are all organically inter-related and inter-dependent.

A study of the wholesale index numbers shows that raw cotton prices declined by 13.9 per cent between March, 1989 to March 1990 and increased by 36 per cent (provisional) between March, 1990 and March, 1991. At the same time, the prices of cotton yarn have shown a sharp increase of 14.4 per cent and a marginal increase of 0.1 per cent during the same periods. A separate study of hank yarn indices shows that their prices increased by 15.8 per cent and 1.5 per cent while cone yarn prices increased by 13 per cent and 1.9 per cent in these two years.

In the case of cotton cloth, mill cloth prices indices have increased by 14.5 per cent and 5.4 per cent during these two years. The percentage increase of handloom fabrics during the same two periods are 29 per cent and 0.1 per cent respectively. There has been some hike in the prices of viscose staple fibre, while the prices of PSF declined by 4.3 per cent in 1989-90 and increased by 5.4 per cent in 1990-91. The prices of partially oriented yarn (POY) and texturised yarn have increased whereas the prices of other filament yarns have declined. The index numbers of all commodities increased by 8.6 per cent during 1989-90 and by 12.3 per cent during 1990-91. It is seen that as compared to the increase in the prices of all commodities, the price indices of textile items show a mixed trend.

The Nodal Agency set up pursuant to the Textile Policy to evolve rehabilitation packages for potentially viable sick mills, has so far examined 177 sick closed textiles mills of which 51 were found to be viable. Likewise, the Board for Industrial and Financial Re-construction had till February 1991 registered cases of 176 textile companies. Out of these 134 had been disposed of, and the remaining 42 cases are in different stages of consideration.

The response to the Textile Modernisation Fund of Rs. 750 crores set-up under the Textile Policy of 1985 to encourage modernisation of textile units has been encouraging. Till the end of February, 1991 a total number of 478 applications amounting to Rs. 1920.45 crores were received, of which 342 applications for an amount of Rs. 1265.31 crores have been sanctioned, of which Rs. 685.13 crores have already been disbursed in 264 cases.

The Textile Workers Rehabilitation Fund Scheme introduced under the New Policy to provide interim relief to the workers rendered unemployed as a consequence of permanent closure of mills also picked up during the year under report. Under the scheme an assistance of Rs 35.03 crores has been paid to 19418 workers of 19 closed mills so far.

The cotton monopoly procurement scheme of the Government of Maharashtra, operated through the Maharashtra State Coop. Cotton Grower's Marketing Federation has been extended for a period of three years with effect from July 1, 1990 to June 30, 1993 subject to the condition that guaranteed prices under the scheme shall be the same as the support prices for different varieties of cotton approved by the Government of India.

The Ministers of GATT member countries met in Puntadel-Este (Uruguay) in September, 1986 and declared launching of Multilateral Trade Negotiations (popularly known as Uruguay Round of Negotiations)* with the mandate to halt and reverse the protectionism and restrictiveness which has been growing under successive MFAs. They proposed to develop a more open, viable and durable multilateral trading systems. In the Uruguay Round, GATT Ministers also approved the eventual integration of textile sector into GATT on the basis of strengthened GATT rules and disciplines, thereby also contributing to the objective of further liberalisation of trade. A separate Negotiating Group on Textiles and Clothing has been set-up for negotiating the future of international trade in textiles and clothing, presently under MFAIV. India has been taking active part in the negotiations. After several rounds of negotiations, a draft agreement has been prepared which will be further discussed in Geneva in 1991.

Eight Five Year Plan Proposals

The Approach Paper for the Eighth Five Year Plan lays emphasis on employment generation exports, decentralisation angles and backward area development. The textile industry, particularly the decentralised sectors of handlooms and powerlooms and also the handicrafts sector are highly employment oriented, particularly in rural areas. Ministry of Textiles have formulated proposals and furnished them to the Planning Commission. The proposals include schemes for supporting garment sector which is highly employment oriented. In the exports sector, a scheme has been included for providing infrastructural facilities in export intensive areas. The outlay proposed for the Eighth Five Year Plan is of the order of Rs. 2058.74 crores. The outlay for the year 1991-92 proposed is Rs. 500.47 crores. However, the Planning Commission have allocated an outlay of Rs. 314.65 crores, comprising Rs. 234.54 crores as budgetary support and Rs. 80.11 crores as internal and extra budgetary resources.

Computer for MIS

The need of introducing the Computerisation for providing support to the Management in Decision-Making has been realised long ago. National Informatics Centre (NIC), Planning Commission has been entrusted with the responsibility of implementing the Comprehensive Integrated Computerised Management Information Systems (MIS) in the Ministry and its attached/subordinate offices. To achieve the objective, NIC is already in the advanced stage of im-

---

* *See also* Appendix II.

plementing the plan. Computer Centre having the various machines like Super-AT, IBM compatible PC-AT/XT alongwith team of computer professionals has been established in the Ministry. A mini-computer has been installed in the Office of Textile Commissioner, Bombay to process the data on various aspects of textile industry. This will also form an information bridge between Ministry and Industry. A super-AT machine is after in the process of installation at the Office of Jute Commissioner, Calcutta. Software is already developed and ready for implementation. Office of Development Commissioner (Handicrafts) and (Handlooms) are also taken up for Computerisation. Areas are identified and softwares are under development.

MIS in the following areas is made operational in the Ministry:

1. *Data Base* : Data Base on textiles and garment exports to various countries, textiles industry and its growth, jute industry, silk industry, handicraft export to various countries, man-made fibre industry etc. has been created. The system provided details on various parameters such as country, year, items, quantity, value etc. on exports and management, state, year, licensed/installed capacity etc. on textile industry. System also provided the details on production, stock, consumption import and export etc. on jute industry. This also facilitates trend analysis and its study.
2. *Monitoring Systems* : Various monitoring systems on textiles price sickness of industry, powerloom, mill sector etc. are developed which help in increasing efficiency. In powerlooms sector system monitors the status of registration of powerlooms, availability of yarn and production of cloth by the sector. Various graphical representations are made through Computer as an aid to decision-making.

Industrial Sickness

An outstanding credit of Rs. 9353 crore which constituted about 9.2 per cent of the total bank advances and 17.4 per cent of the outstanding bank credit to industries was locked in about 2.2 lakh sick industrial units (excluding 125571 non-existent and non-traceable SSI units with an outstanding bank credit of Rs. 240 crore) on the rolls of commercial banks as at the end of March 1990. If the non-traceable and non-existent units are also taken into account, total bank credit locked in sick and weak units as at the end of March 1990 at Rs. 9593 crore was 24.5 per cent higher than the Rs. 7705 crore outstanding at the end of December 1988, which constituted 9.4 per cent of the total outstanding bank advances (Table 29.5). There was a slight abatement in the increasing incidence of sickness, which is a welcóme trend signalling some positive results of the measures taken by the banking system to improve and strengthen the mechanism for an early detection of the symptoms and prevention of sickness among the assisted industrial units as well as for the rehabilitation of such units. The share of the SSI sector in the aggregate bank credit locked in sick/weak units (including non-traceable and non-existent units) had come down from 28.7 per cent at the end-December, 1987 to 27.8 per cent at the end of March 1990. According to RBI data, about 74 per cent of the bank credit locked in non-SSI sick and weak units at the end of March 1990 was in the private sector. Industry group-wise, the incidence of sickness and weakness in the non-SSI sector, in terms of credit outstanding, was the highest in textiles (27.7%) followed by engineering (19.9%), chemicals (6.9%), iron and steel (5.8%) and paper (5.2%).

TABLE 29.5: Industrial Sickness

(*Rs. crore*)

	Number of units			Amount outstanding		
	End-December 1987	End-December 1988	End-March 1990	End-December 1987	End-December 1988	End-March 1990
1	2	3	4	5	6	7
1. SSI sick units	204259 (40.1)	240573 (17.8)	218828* (—9.0)	1797.31 (37.6)	2141.00 (19.1)	2426.94 (13.3)
2. Non-SSI sick units	1119 (—43.0)	1241 (10.9)	1455 (17.2)	2801.79 (—21.5)	3887.30 (20.9)	4538.82 (34.0)
3. Non-SSI weak units	720 (N.A.)	770 (3.9)	814 (5.7)	1657.30 (N.A.)	2177.00 (31.4)	2386.77 (9.6)
Total	206098 (39.5)	242534 (17.7)	221097* (—8.8)	6256.40 (22.3)	7705.30 (23.2)	9352.53 (21.4)

* The figure does not include sick SSI units which are not traceable/not in existence.

Note: Figures in parentheses indicate the percentage change over the previous year.

Small-Scale and Village Industries

Small-Scale Industries

The estimated number of small-scale units at the end of 1990-91 was 19.38 lakh including 5.6 lakh unregistered units. Value of production is provisionally estimated at Rs. 155340 crore and employment at 124.30 lakh. Direct exports from the sector during 1990-91 are provisionally estimated at Rs. 9,100 crore. The growth of the sector during 1990-91 was relatively low because of the adverse impact of certain factors like import destructions, credit squeeze and hike in interest rates. The combined adverse effects of these factors are likely to aggravate further during the current year. Production in the small scale sector is expected to go up only by about 3 per cent this year as against 8.5 per cent in 1990-91. The growth in employment is also likely to be only marginal.

The new policy measures for promoting and strengthening small, tiny and village enterprises were laid in Parliament on 6 August, 1991. The main thrust of the new policy is to impart more vitality and growth to employment and exports. The salient features of the new policy are:

(i) De-regulation, de-bureaucratisation and simplification of statutes, regulations and procedures;
(ii) Increase in the investment limit in plant and machinery of tiny enterprises from Rs. 2 lakh to Rs. 5 lakh, irrespective of the location of the unit;
(iii) Inclusion of industry-related services and business enterprises, irrespective of their location, as small-scale industries;
(iv) Ensuring both adequate flow of credit on a normative basis and quality of its delivery for viable operation of the SSI sector;
(v) Setting up of a special monitoring agency to oversee the genuine credit needs of the small-scale sector;
(vi) Introduction of suitable legislation to ensure prompt payment of small industries bills;
(vii) Introduction of a scheme of Integrated Infrastructural Development (including technological back-up services) for small-scale industries;
(viii) Setting up of a Technology Development Cell in the Small Industries Development Organisation;
(ix) Market promotion of SSI products through co-operative/public sector institutions, other specialised professional/marketing agencies and the consortia approach;
(x) Setting up of an Export Development Centre in the Small Industries Development Organisation.

The scope of the National Equity Fund and Single Window Scheme being implemented by the Small Industries Development Bank of India for the benefit of the smaller among small-scale units was further widened during 1991-92 by enhancing the limit of the project cost of eligible units from Rs. 5 lakh to Rs. 10 lakh and from Rs. 10 lakh to Rs. 20 lakh, respectively. The limit of working capital assistance under the Single Window Scheme was also enhanced from Rs. 5 lakh to Rs. 10 lakh.

Khadi and Village Industries

Units under the Khadi and Village Industries Commission produced Rs. 2225 crore worth of goods in 1990-91 and provided employment to 47.93 lakh persons. During 1991-92, the production level is expected to go up to Rs. 2460 crore and employment to 50.01 lakh.

Investment Climate

The approval of Letters of Intent, SIA registrations, DGTD registrations, etc., are the conventional indicators of investment intentions. After the announcement of the New Industrial Policy, all registrations have been abolished but the issuance of Letters of Intent for still licensed industries continues. The filing of Industrial Entrepreneurs' Memoranda has replaced the system of registrations. The response to the New Industrial Policy is shown by the filing of 3095 memoranda since this system began in mid August. Thus the aggregate indication of investment intentions increased from 2763 during April-December, 1990-91 to 4699 in April-December, 1991-92. The funds raised in the capital market and the flow of institutional credit to the industrial sector broadly indicate the trend of actual financial investment in the sector. Approvals for new capital issues granted to non-Government companies during April-December 1991 at Rs. 7309 crore have shown an increase of 59 per cent over Rs. 4604 crore in the corresponding period of last year. Actual issues also increased by 44 per cent indicating the highly optimistic outlook of the capital market in spite of a recessionary trend in industrial production. According to the provisional data available, assistance sanctioned by all-India financial institutions in the first six months (April-September) of the current financial year, shows an increase of 9.6 per cent over corresponding period of last year. Actual disbursements also have gone up by 39.8 per cent. Approvals for the import of capital goods granted by the Capital Goods (Main) Committee during April—December 1991 was two and a half times more than the approvals granted in April-December, 1990. Approvals for foreign investment proposals and foreign technology agreements also showed an increase. A full picture of the investment behaviour during the current year, particularly in the post-deregulation period, would be available only after the recalibration of the data reporting system. However, the overall prospects of investment during the current year is expected to turn brighter, responding to the liberalisation measures initiated under the new Industrial Policy announced in July 1991.

Handicrafts Exports

Exports of handicrafts reached a record level of Rs. 1220 crore during 1990-91 exceeding the target by Rs. 20 crore. During 1989-90 it was 1084.64 crore and in 1988-89 it was Rs. 770.42 crore. A growth of over 20.95 per cent has been registered during 1990-91. Exports of handknotted carpets and other handicrafts recorded a growth rate of 20.69 per cent and 21.14 per cent respectively for the same period. Keeping in view the favourable trend the target for this year has been fixed at Rs. 1584 crore. Indian handicrafts are exported to more than 100 countries including Germany, U.K., U.S.A., France, Switzerland, USSR, Saudi Arabia, Italy, Netherlands, Australia, Japan and Canada. The main items of export include handknotted carpets, art metalware, woodware, handprinted textiles, embroidered and crocheted goods, shawls, zari and zari goods and imitation jewellery.

Source : *Yojana*, December 15, 1991.

30

INFORMATION AND BROADCASTING

The objective of the Ministry of Information and Broadcasting is to inform, educate as well as entertain the people with a view to creating awareness among them about the nation's potential for development, its problems and soliciting their participation in the implementation of Government's policies, plans and programmes.

The aforesaid objectives of the Ministry are achieved through its media units, namely, Akashvani (All India Radio), Doordarshan, Press Information Bureau, Publications Division, Research and Reference Division, Directorate of Advertising and Visual Publicity, Registrar of Newspapers for India, Directorate of Field Publicity, Photo Division, Song and Drama Division and Films Division. The Ministry is also associated with the National Film Development Corporation, the Children's Film Society, the Film and Television Institute of India, the Indian Institute of Mass Communication, the Press Council of India and the Central Board of Film Certification.

Non-Aligned News Agencies Pool

Non-Aligned News Agencies Pool (NANAP) is a system of news exchange based on professional co-operation and co-ordination among the News Agencies of Non-Aligned Countries. To co-ordinate the activities of the Pool, there is an elected body known as the Coordinating Committee of the Pool. For a close review and monitoring of the Pool operations, there is a small group known as the Monitoring Group. Ever since the inception of the Pool in 1976, India is a member of NANAP. Indian News Pool Desk (INPD) is being operated by the Press Trust of India. India is a leading member of the Pool. The volume of outgoing Pool file carries on an average 50 items (10,000 words) a day. The Pool desk handled around 50,000 words a day on an average from other Pool participants.

Committee on Film Industry

The High Powered Committee set-up in February 1989 to study the problems of Film Industry and make suitable recommendations to Central/State Governments submitted its report in January 1990. In all, the Committee made 59 recommendations, recommending number of concessions/reliefs for the industry in the matter relating to entertainment tax, excise duty, customs duty on the wine equipment/cine raw stock, concessional institutional finance, increased royalty for telecast/broadcasting of films/songs, licensing and regulation of video exhibition for combating video piracy etc. These recommendations were intensively deliberated at the Conference of State Ministers for Information and Cinematography in April 1990 and the same were accepted. Seven recommendations have already been implemented and action is being taken on 24 other recommendations. Twenty-two recommendations fall within the jurisdiction of State Governments/Union Territory Administrations and are to be implemented by them. On five recommendations action is to be taken by the film industry. One recommendation on reconsideration has been rejected.

News Index

The 'News Index' maintained by the Research and Reference Division of the Ministry of Information and Broadcasting includes articles from 18 major periodicals. Significant news items, articles and editorials from 10 metropolitan and mofussil dailies were clipped and classified for reference.

Reference Library

The Division has a Reference Library with a large collection of books on various disciplines of mass media. The Library serves over 700 accredited correspondents and a large number of Government's own mediamen. It is also a one-point depository of the reports of various commissions and committees. The Library receives around 150 Indian and foreign journals.

National Documentation Centre on Mass Communication

The National Documentation Centre on Mass Communication (NDCMC) was set-up in this Division in 1976. It collects and disseminates information relating to agencies, events and trends in mass communication. The Centre documents a large volume of news items, articles and other information material relating to mass communication and media in the country.

The NDCMC disseminates the collected information through eight popular services — 'Current Awareness Service', 'Reference Information Service', 'Bibliography Service', 'Who's Who in Mass Media', 'Honours Conferred on Mass Communicators,' 'World Media Service,' 'Media Memory' and 'Bulletin of Film'. The Centre also has a newspaper clipping service. During April-December 1990, the Centre released 30 papers under its various services. It plans to bring out 16 papers between January and March 1991.

Computerisation

The Division is in the process of computerising its documentation and retrieval services. This would not only impart speed and efficiency to the Division's research and reference activities, but also prove helpful to the users including Press Correspondents who visit the Division's library for their professional work.

Indian Institute of Mass Communication

The Indian Institute of Mass Communication, set-up in August, 1965, as a Centre for advanced study, training and research in Mass Communication, is an autonomous body registered under the Societies Registration Act, 1860. It gets funds from the Ministry of Information and Broadcasting and is managed by a

Society which is reconstituted biennially.

The Institute conducts a number of training and teaching programmes in the field of mass communication. It also organises seminars and symposia for the development of communication infrastructure suitable for India and other developing countries. The Institute provides its expertise and services to other Institutions in the country and to international organisations like UNESCO, UNICEF and WHO.

The Institute has a printing press, well-equipped sound and TV studio and other audio facilities. An editing U-matic Console has been installed in the TV control room. The Institute has a library with more than 21,000 books. It brings out two journals—*Communicator* (English) and *Sanchar Madhyam* (Hindi).

Plan Performance

The main thrust of the Broadcasting and Information media (including Films) of the Ministry has been extensive dissemination of information relating to Government policies and programmes and motivating people to participate in the national endeavour for integrated development of the country. A skilful combination of traditional and folk forms of inter-personal communication and modern audio-visual media using satellite communication was successfully used for achieving the communication objectives. The programmes and messages were designed with a view to benefit the people in general and the rural, tribal and weaker sections in particular. Developmental schemes for the SCs and STs in different occupational categories, especially the poverty prone groups like landless labourers and marginal and small farmers continued to receive coverage in the Plans of this Ministry.

The seventh plan sector-wise outlay/allocation/utilisation are indicated below:

TABLE 30.1: Seventh Plan Sectorwise Outlay/Allocation/Utilization

(*Rs. in crores*)

Sector	Outlay	Actual allocation	Utilisation
Sound Broadcasting	700.00	660.50	588.20
Doordarshan	753.29	740.97	716.07
Information Media	30.00	25.66	11.58
Film Media	41.51	47.39	44.32
Total	1,524.80	1,474.52	1360.17

The Eighth Plan (1990-95) recommendations of the Working Group set up by the Planning Commission for the Ministry of Information and Broadcasting were sent to the Planning Commission for discussions and finalisation.

Annual Plan 1990-91

The plan outlay for 1990-91 and anticipated expenditure (RE) is given below:

TABLE 30.2: Plan Outlay for 1990-91 and Anticipated Expenditure (RE)

(*Rs. in crores*)

Sector	Outlay	Anticipated Expenditure (R.E.)
Doordarshan	215.00	166.99
All India Radio	185.00	146.98
Information Media	8.00	4.50
Films Media	16.00	13.66
Total	424.00	332.13

TABLE 30.3: Yearwise Utilization of Seventh Plan Outlay in the Broadcasting Sector

(*Rs. in crores*)

	1985-86	1986-87	1987-88	1988-89	1989-90
Doordarshan	57.75	122.19	143.08	184.50	208.55
Air	41.92	105.70	124.08	145.37	171.10

TABLE 30.4: Utilization of Plan Outlay in the Films and Information Sector

(*Rs. in crores*)

	1985-86	1986-87	1987-88	1988-89	1989-90
Films	6.72	6.50	7.78	11.37	11.89
Information	1.87	1.10	1.50	2.24	4.87

TABLE 30.5: Seventh Plan Allocation/Utilization

Allocation	Doordarshan	Air	Films	Information	Total
	740.97	660.50	47.39	25.66	1474.52
Utilization	1985-86	1986-87	1987-88	1988-89	1989-90
	108.28	343.77	620.22	963.70	1360.17
Financed from M/I&B's Resources	1985-90				
	333.21	—	—	—	—

Annual Plan 1991-92

The Plan outlay for the year 1991-92 for the four sectors is as under:

TABLE 30.6: Plan Outlay for 1991-92

(*Rs. in crores*)

Sector	Outlay
Doordarshan	250.80
Sound Broadcasting	215.00
Information Media	007.50
Films Media	015.50
Total	488.80

The outlay includes internal resources of Rs. 183.94 crores, out of which Rs. 180.37 crores is to be met from the Akashvani and Doordarshan Commercial Revenues Fund (NLF) and Rs. 3.57 crores by NFDC from its internal resources.

Doordarshan

The targets for 1991-92 include commissioning of the Studio Centres at Aizawal, Itanagar and Bhubaneshwar; Programme Generation Facility Centres at Port Blair, Bareilly and Daltonganj; a Studio Centre at Calcutta for Second Channel service and High Power Transmitter at Bareilly (10 KW), Tirupati (10 KW) and Dharwad (10 KW), Gangtok (1 KW), Mokokchung (1 KW) and Churachandpur (1 KW). In addition, 38 Low Power Transmitters and Very Low Power Transmitters and Transposers will also be commissioned. Civil works for the Studio building at Patna (permanent set-up) and Madras (Second Channel service), TV Centre building at Shimla, Programme Generation Facility building at Siliguri and High Power Transport building at Lunglei are expected to be completed. Civil Works will be in progress for the studio at TV Centre at Bombay. Civil works for RCC Towers at Rameshwaram, Barmer and Fazilka as also the Programme Generation Facility building at Gangtok are expected to be taken up during 1991-92.

New schemes for News Rooms Automation, Satellite News Gathering and Regional Maintenance Centres will also be taken up during 1991-92. Satellite-based Regional Service is likely to be introduced in Orissa during 1991-92.

All India Radio

Continuing projects envisaged for completion during 1991-92 include setting up of 25 FM Stations; nine Short Wave Transmitters at Lucknow, Jaipur, Imphal, Kohima, Calcutta, Bhopal, Panaji (2 × 250 KW SW), Trivandrum and Madras; six Medium Wave Transmitters of different powers at Bikaner, Srinagar, Lucknow, Calcutta, Gangtok and Trichur, seven fulfledged stations at Pauri, Bhawanipatna, Kokrajhar, Ziro, Diphu, Ahwa and Ootacamund; three replacements at Passighat, Tezu and Tawang; additional studios at Guwahati, Type IV studios at Pune; Type I (R) studios at Jabalpur and refurnishing of studios at Bombay.

There are 52 projects of different entities that were shown as replacement schemes in the Eighth Plan and are to be taken up in the Annual Plan 1991-92. SFC has been issued for about 50 per cent of these projects and orders have been placed for delivery of equipment. The works envisaged on these projects during 1991-92 would be, issue of SFC for remaining projects, taking up of civil works and placing orders for equipment.

Information Media

Press Information Bureau

During 1991-92, 20 FAX machines will be provided at various branch offices under the scheme 'Computerisation of PIB activities'. Three Branch Offices will be opened. Six staff cars will be purchased for greater mobility in the Bureau's Branch Offices.

Publications Division

A Sales Emporium at Bhopal and a Mobile Book Shop at Bombay are to be set up. An Internal Inspection Cell is to be created.

Directorate of Advertising and Visual Publicity

Audio-visual equipment will be acquired for the Exhibition Division. Field Research Cell will be created. Audio-visual Cell will be strengthened in addition to the Administration and Accounts infrastructures and computerisation. National Awards for Printing will be restored to improve the quality of printing.

Photo Division

Modern computerised equipment including automatic colour processor and auto printer are to be procured.

Registrar of Newspapers for India

The three Regional Offices are to continue and computerisation of records at Headquarters will go on.

Indian Institute of Mass Communication

Work on the second phase of building will be started. One or two text books and journals will be published.

Soochna Bhavan

Work on Phase-III will be completed and Phase-IV work will be initiated.

Song and Drama Division

The Division proposes to mount special publicity campaigns in disturbed and border areas. 400 programmes will be given by the tribal troupes in tribal areas by the unit at Ranchi.

Directorate of Field Publicity

The plan schemes include construction of office and residential accommodation in the North-Eastern States, strengthening of administration at Headquarters and Regional Offices, conducted tours, and procurement of equipment.

Films Media

Films Division

Storage facilities for technical equipment in the second phase of the building will be completed. Two Production Centres are to be opened and 10 featurette films will be produced during the year. It is proposed to produce two animated films and one documentary film. One featurette film with the SCs/STs and backward classes as target audience will be produced under the new scheme 'Production of Special Films'. An increase of prints in colour is proposed for release to theatres. Cinematographic equipment will be procured for Division's offices at Bombay and Delhi. Preliminary work for setting up a Film Archival/Library Complex will be completed under the scheme 'Preservation and Retrieval of Archival Film Material'. A marketing and sales promotion cell is to be created to explore possibilities of earning revenue in foreign exchange. An International Festival for Documentary and short films will be organised at Bombay.

National Film Archive of India

The work of air-conditioning plant, fixing up furniture in the auditorium and preview theatre, and procurement of equipments and other fixtures for the new building are to be completed. It is also proposed to acquire a proper site for the construction of specialised vaults for storing nitrate films. 500 films including prints and video cassettes of about 100 tele films, 1,000 books, 200 periodicals, 500 disc-records, 1,200 stills and 1,000 scripts will be acquired. Indian Film Annuals 1986, 1987, 1988, and 1989 are proposed to be published. Two more Regional Offices at Madras and Hyderabad are to be set-up and the manpower of the existing three will be augmented.

Film and Television Institute of India

Machinery and equipment for the Direction, Cinematography and Production Departments and Printer for Film Laboratory are to be acquired.

Children's Film Society of India

Feature, featurette and short films will be produced as usual in addition to the purchase of Indian and foreign films, dubbing in language versions and subtitling. The Seventh International Children's Film Festival will be held in November, 1991.

Directorate of Film Festivals

The Directorate proposes to hold six Indian Film Weeks abroad and will participate in six Foreign Film Weeks in India. It also proposes to participate in 45 Foreign Film Festivals. IFFI-92 and National Film Festival, 1991 will be held during the year 1991-92. Strengthening and computerisation of the Directorate is also proposed.

National Film Development Corporation

Besides providing loan assistance for films production and theatre construction, the NFDC proposes to produce four feature films and to import about 45 films.

Central Board of Film Certification

It proposes to strengthen the Headquarters and continue maintenance of its Regional Offices.

TABLE 30.7: Budget

(*Rupees in thousands*)

S.No.	Demand No. 54—Ministry of Information and Broadcasting Name of Media Unit	Budget Estimates 1990-91 Plan	Non-Plan	Total	Revised Estimates 1990-91 Plan	Non-Plan	Total	Budget Estimates 1991-92 Plan	Non-Plan	Total
	Revenue Section Major head—"2251"—Secretariat—Social Services									
1.	Main Secretariat	—	2,37,50	2,37,50	—	2,66,35	2,66,35	—	2,61,23	
2.	Composite PAO	18,00	1,23,50	1,41,50	1,00	1,25,65	1,26,65	—	1,31,77	
	Total	18,00	3,61,00	3,79,00	1,00	3,92,00	3,93,00	—	3,93,00	
1	2	3	4	5	6	7	8	9	10	
	Major head—"2205"—Art and Culture Certification of Cinematographic films for public exhibition									
3.	Central Board of Film Certification	7,00	52,00	59,00	7,00	49,00	56,00	—	53,80	
4.	Film Certification Appellate Tribunal	—	2,00	2,00	—	2,00	2,00	—	2,20	
	Total — Major head "2205"	7,00	54,00	61,00	7,00	51,00	58,00	—	56,00	
	Major head—"2220"—Information and Publicity									
5.	Films Division	1,83,00	14,06,09	15,89,09	72,50	13,43,90	14,16,40	-	14,85,15	
6.	Directorate of Film Festivals—Establishment	15,50	27,90	43,40	6,50	27,60	34,10	—	30,41	
7.	International Film Festivals in India	90,00	—	90,00	90,00	—	90,00	—	—	
8.	Film Festival under cultural exchange	84,28	—	84,28	79,12	—	79,12	—	—	
9.	National Awards for Films	35,00	—	35,00	35,00	—	35,00	—	—	
10.	Regional Film Festivals	27,00	—	27,00	27,00	—	27,00	—	—	

Contd.

TABLE 30.7 (Contd.)

1	2	3	4	5	6	7	8	9	10
11.	Participation in Foreign Film Festivals	11,22	—	11,22	5,00	—	5,00	—	—
12.	Maintenance of Film Festival Complex	—	1,56,00	1,56,00	—	1,65,00	1,65,00	—	1,15,00
13.	National Film Archive of India	46,00	28,25	74,25	53,00	25,09	78,09	—	28,65
14.	Grants-in-aid to Children's Film Society	1,65,00	23,58	1,88,58	1,23,68	24,28	1,47,96	—	27,00
15.	Grants-in-aid to Film & Television Institute of India	60,00	1,89,22	2,49,22	47,50	1,73,88	2,21,38	—	1,87,71
16.	Grants-in-aid to Film Societies	3,00	—	3,00	2,70	—	2,70	—	—
17.	Research and Reference Division	7,00	28,55	35,55	1,50	29,20	30,70	—	30,60
18.	Grants-in-aid to IIMC	1,10,00	89,37	1,99,37	72,00	82,85	1,54,85	—	94,14
19.	Directorate of Advertising and Visual Publicity	25,00	19,60,70,	19,85,70	12,50	25,33,50	25,46,00	—	26,91,00
20.	Press Information Bureau	2,10,00	5,94,74	8,04,74	1,22,99	5,99,26	7,22,25	—	6,37,81
21.	Press Council of India	—	26,25	26,25	—	23,72	23,72	—	27,24
22.	Subsidy in lieu of interest on loan to PTI	—	4,29	4,29	—	3,33	3,33	—	2,86
23.	Payment for Professional & Special Services	—	39,22	39,22	—	35,72	35,72	—	39,22
24.	Directorate of Field Publicity	1,00,00	7,90,54	8,90,54	78,42	7,53,28	8,31,70	—	8,18,43
25.	Song and Drama Division	60,00	4,74,78	5,34,78	43,60	4,48,33	4,91,93	—	5,03,95
26.	Publications Division	35,00	4,25,72	4,60,72	2,00	4,32,44	4,34,44	—	4,54,44
27.	Employment News	—	5,64,04	5,64,04	—	5,68,50	5,68,50	—	6,52,10
28.	Reimbursement of losses to STC	—	3,03,00	3,03,00	—	3,03,00	3,03,00	—	3,18,00
29.	Subsidy to Small & Medium Newspapers on indigenous Newsprint	—	1,60,00	1,60,00	—	60,00	60,00	—	1,00
30.	Registrar of Newspaper for India	15,00	56,56	71,56	5,42	57,10	62,52	—	57,14
31.	Photo Division	80,00	82,35	1,62,35	23,57	77,52	1,01,09	—	83,15
32.	Contribution to International Programme for the Development of Communication	—	16,85	16,85	—	18,50	18,50	—	19,00
	Total Major head—"2220"	13,62,00	74,48,00	88,10,00	9,04,00	77,86,00	86,90,00	—	83,04,00
	Total-Revenue Section	13,87,00	78,63,00	92,50,00	9,12,00	82,29,00	91,41,00	—	87,53,00

(*Rupees in thousand*)

S.No.	Capital Section Major heads—"4220"—Capital outlay on Information and Publicity Machinery & Equipment	Budget Estimates 1990-91			Revised Estimates 1990-91			Budget Estimates 1991-92		
		Plan	Non-Plan	Total	Plan	Non-Plan	Total	Plan	Non-Plan	Total
1	2	3	4	5	6	7	8	9	10	11
1.	Acquisition of equipment for Films Division, Bombay	96,00	—	96,00	1,16,00	—	1,16,00	—	—	
2.	Acquisition of equipment for NFAI, Pune	34,00	—	34,00	34,00		34,00	—	—	
	Buildings									
3.	Multistoreyed building for Films Division—Major Works	15,00	—	15,00	2,00	—	2,00	—	—	
4.	Construction of office building for NFAI—Major Works	20,00	—	20,00	9,00	—	9,00	—	—	
5.	Film Festival Complex—Additions and alterations—Major Works	80,00	—	80,00	49,50	—	49,50	—	—	
6.	Soochna Bhavan Buildings—Major Works	1,00,00	—	1,0,00	47,85	—	47,85	—	—	

Contd.

1	2	3	4	5	6	7	8	9	10	11
7.	Construction of Office and Residential Accommodation for Field Publicity—Major Works	35,00	—	35,00	31,15	—	31,15	—	—	
8.	National Press Centre	5,00	—	5,00	8,00	—	8,00	—	—	
	Investments in Public Sector and other undertakings									
9.	National Film Development Corporation	1,50,00		1,50,00	1,43,50	—	143,50	—	—	
	Total—Major head—"4220"	**5,35,00**	**5,35,00**	**4,41,00**	**4,41,00**					
	Major head—"6220"—Loans for Information Publicity									
	Loans to Public Sector and other undertakings									
	National Film Development Corporation Ltd.	1,50,00	—	1,50,00	1,35,00	—	1,35,00	—	—	
	Total—Major head—"6220"	1,50,00	—	1,50,00	1,35,00	—	1,35,00	—	—	
	Total—Capital Section	6,85,00	—	6,85,00	5,76,00	—	5,76,00	—	—	
	Total—Demand No. 54	20,72,00	78,63,00	99,35,00	14,88,00	82,29,00	97,17,00		87,53,00	

Broadcasting Services

Revenue

(*Rs. in thousands*)

Sl. No.	Description	Budget Estimates 1990-91			Revised Estimates 1990-91			Budget Estimates 1991-92		
		Plan	Non-Plan	Total	Plan	Non-Plan	Total	Plan	Non-Plan	Total
1	2	3	4	5	6	7	8	9	10	11
	Revenue Section									
	(A) Major Head—"2221"									
	ALL INDIA RADIO									
1.	Direction & Administration	2,00,00	7,29,40	9,29,40	1,56,00	7,29,00	8,85,00	3,76,22	8,29,00	12,05,22
2.	Operation & Maintenance	10,19,00	23,88,01	34,07,01	13,25,00	27,99,00	41,24,00	13,20,79	29,08,00	42,28,79
3.	Commercial Services	8,00	9,61,52	9,69,52	1,00	9,81,00	9,82,00	14,94	10,93,00	11,07,94
4.	Programme Services	24,34,00	81,31,59	1,05,65,59	10,46,00	82,53,00	92,99,00	38,28,86	89,85,00	1,28,13,86
5.	News Services	54,00	8,16,15	8,70,15	8,00	9,98,00	10,06,00	1,32,05	9,42,00	10,74,05
6.	Listeners' Research	18,00	62,42	80,42	5,00	63,00	68,00	31,98	67,00	98,98
7.	External Services	20,00	2,03,04	2,23,04	5,00	2,04,00	2,09,00	42,93	2,18,00	2,60,93
8.	Planning & Development	1,10,05	3,52,82	4,62,87	1,12,00	3,62,00	4,74,00	1,60,41	4,01,00	5,61,41
9.	Research & Training	1,01,95	1,83,05	2,85,00	75,00	1,78,00	2,53,00	1,29,82	2,07,00	3,36,82
10.	Suspense	—	74,55,00	74,55,00	—	60,32,00	60,32,00	—	50,02,00	50,02,00

Contd.

TABLE 30.7 (*Contd.*)

1	2	3	4	5	6	7	8	9	10	11
11.	Transfer to Akashvani & Doordarshan Commercial Revenues Fund	—	22,25,00	22,25,00	—	21,79,00	21,79,00	—	21,71,00	21,71,00
	Total: AIR (Revenue)	39,65,00	2,35,08,00	2,74,73,00	27,33,00	2,27,78,00	2,55,11,00	60,38,00	2,28,23,00	2,88,61,00
DOORDARSHAN										
1.	Direction & Administration	10,00	4,39,00	4,49,00	1,00	4,80,00	4,81,00	15,00	5,82,00	5,97,00
2.	Operation & Maintenance	11,00,00	35,45,00	46,45,00	10,99,00	33,29,00	44,28,00	15,89,00	43,54,00	59,43,00
3.	Commercial Services	—	30,12,00	30,12,00	—	34,65,00	34,65,00	—	34,84,00	34,84,00
4.	Programme Services	30,70,00	93,59,00	1,24,29,00	20,62,00	97,30,00	1,17,92,00	45,90,00	1,11,92,00	1,57,82,00
5.	Listeners' Research	10,00	55,00	65,00	1,00	43,00	44,00	6,00	50,00	56,00
6.	Suspense	—	72,00,00	72,00,00	—	65,00,00	65,00,00	—	80,67,00	80,67,00
7.	Transfer to Akashvani & Doordarshan Commercial Revenues Fund	—	1,63,53,00	1,63,53,00	—	1,86,41,00	1,86,41,00	—	1,86,03,00	1,86,03,00
	Total: Doordarshan (Revenue)	41,90,00	3,99,63,00	4,41,53,00	31,63,00	4,21,88,00	4,53,51,00	62,00,00	4,63,32,00	5,25,32,00
	Total: (A) Major head—"2221"	81,55,00	6,34,71,00	7,16,26,00	58,96,00	6,49,66,00	7,08,62,00	1,22,38,00	6,91,55,00	8,13,93,00
	(B) Major head—"3606" Gift Equipment for TV Centres	—	—	—	—	—	—	—	—	—
	Total Revenue Section (A+B)	81,55,00	6,34,71,00	7,16,26,00	58,96,00	6,49,66,00	7,08,62,00	1,22,38,00	6,91,55,00	8,13,93,00

Capital

(*Rs. in thousand*)

S.No.	Description	Budget	Estimates	1990-91	Revised	Estimates	1990-91	Budget	Estimates	1991-92
		Plan	Non-Plan	Total	Plan	Non-Plan	Total	Plan	Non-Plan	Total
1	2	3	4	5	6	7	8	9	10	11
Capital Section—Major Head "4221"										
ALL INDIA RADIO										
1.	**Machinery & Equipment**	1,27,20	—	1,27,20	32,95	—	32,95	1,26,40	—	1,26,40
2.	**Studios**	49,98,10	6,00	50,04,10	40,04,95	25,00	40,29,95	42,66,65	8,00	42,74,65
3.	**Transmitters**	76,61,70	—	76,61,70	61,93,90	—	61,93,90	76,01,75	—	76,01,75
4.	**Suspense**	—	5,88,30	5,88,30	—	5,19,00	5,19,00	—	4,89,00	4,89,00
5.	**Other Expenditure (Estt. & Misc. Works Schemes)**	17,48,00	5,88,70	23,36,70	17,33,20	6,28,00	23,61,20	34,67,20	—	34,67,20
	Total: All India Radio	1,45,35,00	11,83,00	1,57,18,00	1,19,65,00	11,72,00	1,31,37,00	1,54,62,00	4,97,00	1,59,59,00

Contd.

TABLE 30.7 (*Contd.*)

1	2	3	4	5	6	7	8	9	10	11
DOORDARSHAN										
1.	Machinery & Equipment	61,00	—	61,00	43,88	—	43,88	1,04,00	—	1,04,00
2.	Studios	73,28,40	32,56	73,60,96	63,50,91	74,39	64,25,30	84,80,56	1,66	84,82,22
3.	Transmitters	72,02,59	1,08,59	73,10,83	55,34,48	1,10,55	56,45,03	70,69,01	1,34	70,70,35
4.	Suspense	—	11,51,90	11,51,90	—	8,21,00	8,21,00	—	7,96,00	7,96,00
5.	Other Expenditure (Estt. Misc. Works Schemes)	27,18,01	3,03,30	30,21,31	16,06,73	2,78,06	18,84,79	32,26,43	1,05,00	33,31,43
	Total: Doordarshan	1,73,10,00	15,96,00	1,89,06,00	1,35,36,00	12,84,00	1,48,20,00	1,88,80,00	9,04,00	1,97,84,00
	Total: Major Head "4221"	3,18,45,00	27,79,00	3,46,24,00	2,55,01,00	24,56,00	2,79,57,00	3,43,42,00	14,01,00	3,57,43,00
Major Head "6250"										
1.	Loans by Air to APSEB	—	—	—	—	—	—	—	—	—
2.	Loans by Television to APSEB	—	—	—	—	—	—	—	—	—
	Total Major Head "6250"	—	—	—	—	—	—	—	—	—
	Total Capital Section	3,18,45,00	27,79,00	3,46,24,00	2,55,01,00	24,56,00	2,79,57,00	3,43,42,00	14,01,00	3,57,43,00
	TOTAL DEMAND NO. 55	4,00,00,00	6,62,50,00	10,62,50,00	3,13,97,00	6,74,22,00	9,88,19,00	4,65,80,00	7,05,56,00	11,71,136,00

Sanctioned Budget Grant, Revised Estimates 1990-91 and Budget Estimates 1991-92 Under Capital Grant of Doordarshan

(*Rs. in thousands*)

Demand No. 55 **Broadcasting Services**	**Budget Estimates**		**1990-91**	**Revised Estimates**		**1990-91**	**Budget Estimates**		**1990-91**
Major Head "4221"	Plan	Non-Plan	Total	Plan	Non-Plan	Total	Plan	Non-Plan	Total
DOORDARSHAN									
1. Machinery & Equipment	61,00	—	61,00	43,88	—	43,88	1,04,00	—	1,04,00
2. Studios	73,28,40	32,56	73,60,96	63,50,91	74,39	64,25,30	84,80,56	1,66	84,82,22
3. Transmitters	72,02,59	1,08,24	73,10,83	55,34,48	1,10,55	56,45,03	70,69,01	1,34	70,70,35
4. Suspense	—	11,51,90	11,51,90	—	8,21,00	8,21,00	—	7,96,00	7,96,00
5. Other Expenditure	27,18,01	3,03,30	30,21,31	16,06,73	2,78,06	18,84,79	32,26,43	1,05,00	33,31,43
Major Head "6250"									
Loans to Andhra Pradesh, State Electricity Board (APSEB)	—	—	—	—	—	—	—	—	
Total: Doordarshan	173,10,00	15,96,00	189,06,00	135,36,00	12,84,00	148,20,00	188,80,00	9,04,00	197,84,00
Voted:	173,05,00	15,96,00	189,01,00	135,31,00	12,84,00	148,15,00	188,70,00	9,04,00	197,74,00
Charged:	5,00	—	5,00	5,00	—	5,00	10,00	—	10,00

Sanctioned Budget Grant Revised Estimates 1990-91 and Budget Estimates 1991-92 Under Revenue Grant of Doordarshan

(Rs. in thousands)

Demand No 55. Broadcasting Services Major Head "2221"	Budget Estimates 1990-91			Revised Estimates 1990-91			Budget Estimates 1991-92		
	Plan	Non-Plan	Total	Plan	Non-Plan	Total	Plan	Non-Plan	Total
DOORDARSHAN									
1. Direction & Admn.	10,00	4,39,00	4,49,00	10,00	4,80,00	4,81,00	15,00	5,82,00	5,97,00
2. Operation & Maintenance	11,00,00	35,45,00	46,45,00	10,99,00	33,29,00	44,28,00	15,89,00	42,54,00	59,43,00
3. Commercial Services	—	30,12,00	30,12,00	—	34,65,00	34,65,00	—	34,84,00	34,84,00
4. Programme Services	30,70,00	93,59,00	124,29,00	20,62,00	97,30,00	117,92,00	45,90,00	111,92,00	157,82,00
5. Listeners' Research	10,00	55,00	65,00	1,00	43,00	44,00	6,00	50,00	56,00
6. Suspense	—	72,00,00	72,00,00	—	65,0,00	65,00,00	—	80,67,00	80,67,00
7. Transfer to Reserve	—	163,53,00	163,53,00	—	186,41,00	186,41,00	—	186,03,00	186,03,00
Total	41,90,00	399,63,00	441,53,00	31,63,00	421,88,00	453,51,00	62,00,00	463,32,00	525,32,00
Major Head "3606" Aid Material and Equipment	—	—	—	—	—	—	—	—	—

ALL INDIA RADIO

Radio Stations Likely to be Commissioned During 1991-92

FM Transmitters		Medium Wave/Short Wave Transmitters	
1	2	3	4
1. Bhatinda	20. Godhra	1. Calcutta (10 KW MW)	20. Madras C
2. Kathua	21. Satara	2. Tura	21. Hyderabad
3. Banswara	22. Nanded	3. Tiruchirapally	22. Bikaner
4. Nagpur	23. Bilaspur	4. Suratgarh	23. Srinagar
5. Chittorgarh	24. Yeotmal	5. Jammu	24. Lucknow (10 KW MW)
6. Sawai Madhopur	25. Shivpuri	6. Jalandhar	25. Lucknow (50 KW SW)
7. Patiala	26. Nagpur	7. Srinagar	26. Pauri
8. Jhalawar	27. Bhopal	8. Gorakhpur	27. Jaipur
9. Jalandhar	28. Indore	9. Varanasi	28. Bhawanipatna
10. Kasauli	29. Hospet	10. Guwahati	29. Calcutta (2×10 KW MW)
11. Baripada	30. Chitradurg	11. Jabalpur	30. Imphal
12. Purnea	31. Cannaro	12. Bombay	31. Gangtok (2×10 KW MW)
13. Jorhat	32. Hassan	13. Bhopal (10 KW MW)	32. Jeypore
14. Hazaribagh	33. Hyderabad	14. Barmer	33. Kokrajhar
15. Sasaram	34. Obra	15. Gangtok (10 KW MW)	34. Passighat
16. Patna	35. Chaibasa	16. Itanagar (100 KW SW)	35. Tezu
17. Betul	36. Kailashahar	17. Calcutta (100 KW MW)	36. Tawang
18. Chindwara	37. Haflong	18. Itanagar (50 KW MW)	37. Ziro
19. Ahmednagar	38. Nowgong	19. Panaji (100 KW MW)	38. Diphu

Contd.

TABLE 30.8 (*Contd.*)

1	2	3	4
39. Belonia	58. Jaisalmer	39. Kohima	
40. Shahdol	59. Bhadarwah	40. Calcutta (50 KW SW)	
41. Raigarh	60. Hamirpur	41. Bhopal (50 KW SW)	
42. Balaghat	61. Poonch	42. Panaji (2×50 KW SW)	
43. Chanderpur	62. Daltonganj	43. Ahwa	
44. Kolhapur	63. Berhampur	44. Bangalore	
45. Dhule	64. Lungleh	45. Trivandrum	
46. Guna	65. Churachandpur	46. Trichur	
47. Pune	66. Mokokchung	47. Ootacamund	
48. Kurnool	67. Bolangir	48. Madras	
49. Mercara	68. Rourkela		
50. Raichur	69. Sagar		
51. Anantpur	70. Nasik		
52. Kurukshetra	71. Osmanabad		
53. Churu	72. Surat		
54. Bareilly	73. Idukki		
55. Faizabad	74. Karwar		
56. Jhansi	75. Karaikal		
57. Jammu			

31

LAW AND JUSTICE

IMPORTANT SUPREME COURT JUDGEMENTS

Antulay Case

The verdict in the Antulay case brought to an end the uncertainties and legal obfuscations that have marked the trials of former Maharashtra Chief Minister, who has been accused of misusing his office to collect crores of rupees for the Indira Gandhi Pratibha Pratishthan Trust, which he had floated.

Cauvery Disputes

The court declared as "unconstitutional" the Karnataka Cauvery Basin Irrigation Ordinance, 1991 paving the way for implementation of the interim order of the Cauvery Water Dispute Tribunal directing Karnataka to release 205 TMC ft of river water to Tamil Nadu.

Union Carbide and the Nadiad Cases

The court ruled that it has very wide powers under Article 142 of the Constitution to ensure due and proper administration of justice. "This power must necessarily be sparingly used only in exceptional circumstances for furthering the ends of justice", the judges observed.

Bofors Case

The verdict in an aspect of the Bofors case gave the kiss of life to the tardy investigations into the Rs. 64 crore kickbacks scandal which for four years had been mired in political intrigue and legal tangles.

The judgement was of significance from two points of view. First, it scotched the last major legal effort to stall the probe, by rejecting contentions that neither was the CBI legally constituted nor the FIR legally valid. The court ruled that the *suo motu* action of Justice M.K. Chawla of the Delhi High Court was based on "convoluted and stained reasoning". The court also ruled that no third person, except accused, had locus standi in the matter.

Secondly, the judgement prevented the possible salting away of the money from the kickbacks, believed to be kept in six code-named accounts in Swiss Banks by suspected beneficiaries of the deal. The accounts were frozen by a Swiss court on India's request.

In the Antulay case, the court had laid down detailed guidelines for speedy trial of the accused in a criminal case, but declined to fix any time limit for trial of offences. The judges said "the guidelines are not exhaustive. It is difficult to foresee all situations. Nor is it possible to lay down any hard and fast rules".

Mandal Case

A nine-judge Constitution bench declined to pass any order on a plea to vacate stay on the V.P. Singh Government order reserving 27 per cent jobs to backward classes in Central Government and public sector undertakings. The matter was referred by a five-judge Constitution bench to a nine-judge Constitution bench in view of the court's ruling in the Thomas case, decided by a seven-judge Constitution bench, that the reservation in Government jobs should not exceed 50 per cent.

"Minority aided educational institutions may reserve 50 per cent seats for their community candidates and are entitled to give them preference in admission as it is necessary to maintain the minority character of the institutions", was another significant judgment pronounced by the court. The court also ruled that in the matter of admission to college or any public employment, the oral interview test should not be relied upon as the exclusive test.

"But this may be resorted to only as additional or supplementary test and great care must be taken to see that persons who are appointed to conduct the oral interview test are men of high integrity, calibre and qualification", Justice N.M. Kasliwal who delivered his dissenting judgement in the St. Stephen's College case said.

Justice Ramaswami Case

A five-judge Constitution bench clarified that the constitutional protection to judges is not for "their personal benefit" but for protecting the judiciary. The court had demarcated the jurisdiction of the judiciary and legislature in impeachment proceedings. There were allegations of "financial irregularities" against Justice Ramaswami, a sitting apex court judge, when he was the Chief Justice of the Punjab and Haryana High Court.

The bench while ruling that the court is not empowered to either direct the Chief Justice of India or the judge concerned to stop work, has placed the onus of establishing a desirable precedent on the concerned judge, hoping that his sense of judicial propriety would persuade him to abstain from work during inquiry.

Justice K. Veeraswami Case

The court also ordered prosecution of the former Chief Justice of Madras High Court K. Veeraswami, who has been charged by the CBI with amassing wealth disproportionate to his known sources of income when he was a public servant during 1969 and 1976. The court had dismissed an appeal of Mr. Veeraswami against the Madras High Court judgement which rejected his plea to quash the FIR field by the CBI in 1979.

L&T Mega Issue Case

The court upheld the Rs. 820 crore mega issue by the Larsen and Toubro and also the order of the Controller of Capital Issues approving the mega issue.

Foreign Matrimonial Judgement

The court laid down fresh guidelines to recognise foreign matrimonial judgement by Indian judiciary. The court made it clear that the Indian court would not recognise a foreign judgement if it has been obtained by the fraud which need not be only in relation to the merits of the matter but may be in relation to jurisdictional facts.

The court ruled that the jurisdiction assumed by the foreign court as well as the grounds on which the relief was granted must be in accordance with the matrimonial law under which the parties were married.

Anti-Defection Cases

The court ruled that para 7 of the 10th Scheduled of the Constitution, which takes away powers of the courts to review the decision of the Speaker disqualifying a legislator, was "unconstitutional". The court quashed the orders of the Speakers of the Meghalaya and Manipur Legislative Assemblies disqualifying five and 15 MLAs, respectively on the ground of defection.

ONGC Case

The court ruled that dispute between various Government departments and public sector undertakings should be first screened by a committee of Secretaries headed by the Cabinet Secretary and only after clearance by the committee the cases could be filed in a court.

Nadiad Case

The court for the first time sent five police officials, including an IPS officer, to the Tihar Central Jail here as they were found responsible for harassing and handcuffing the then Chief Judicial Magistrate of Nadiad N.L. Patel.

Ram Janmabhoomi-Babri Masjid Case

The court directed the Uttar Pradesh Government not to put any permanent structure on the land acquired by it near the disputed site.

Compulsory Retirement of Government Employees

The Supreme Court ruled that the Government can compulsory retire its employees without assigning any reason or following the principles of natural justice.

In a judgement, a three-judge bench comprising Mr. Justice L.M. Sharma, Mr Justice V. Ramaswami and Mr. Justice B.P. Jeevan Reddy laid down the following principles governing compulsory retirement:

(1) An order of compulsory retirement is not a punishment. It implies no stigma or any suggestion of misbehaviour.
(2) The order has to be passed by the Government on forming the opinion that it is in the public interest to retire a Government servant compulsorily.

The order is passed on the subjective satisfaction of the Government.

(3) Principles of natural justice have no place in the context of an order of compulsory retirement.

The judges said that this did not mean that judicial scrutiny was excluded altogether. While the High Court or the Supreme Court would not examine the matter as an appellate court, they may interfere if they are satisfied that the order is passed mala fide or that it is based on no evidence or that it is arbitrary in the sense that no reasonable person would form the requisite opinion on the given material; in short, if it was found to be a perverse order.

(4) The Government (or the Review Committee, as the case may be) shall have to consider the entire record of service before taking a decision in the matter, of course attaching more importance to record of and performance during the later years.

(5) An order of compulsory retirement is not liable to be quashed by a court merely on the showing that while passing it uncommunicated adverse remarks were also taken into consideration. That circumstance by itself cannot be a basis for interference.

Source : *Hindustan Times,* February 22, 1992.

Operation Resurrection for District Judiciary

The Supreme Court on November 13, 1991, directed the Union and State Governments to implement a time bound 12-point programme to evolve a viable, independent and enlightened district judiciary for deciding the civil and criminal cases of citizens.

This 12-point programme, given by Chief Justice R.N. Misra, Justices A.M. Ahmadi and P.B. Sawant on the petition of the All India Judges Association, is as follows: An All India Judicial Service, unlike the present State-wise service, should be set-up and the Union of India should implement this direction "as early as possible". By March 31, 1993 all States and Union Territories should bring about uniformity in the designation of judicial officers of both the civil and criminal services, and the monitoring towards this deadline must be done by the Union Government and especially its Ministry of Law and Justice.

On the civil side, the Judicial Service of each State will be classified as District or Additional District Judge, Civil Judge (Senior Division) and Civil Judge (Junior Division).

On the criminal side there should be a sessions judge or additional sessions judge and below him Chief Judicial Magistrate and magistrates as provided for in the Criminal Procedure Code. Appropriate adjustment if any may be made of existing posts by indicating their equivalence with any of the categories.

The definition of the higher district judiciary in Article 236 is only inclusive and in simplifying uniformly the designations as directed no amendment of the Constitution is required.

With effect from December 31, 1992 the retirement age for all district judicial officers shall be 60. All States and Union Territories must amend their rules on this score within this deadline.

The question of appropriate pay scales, taking into account all the "relevant aspects", shall be determined by the pay commissions or committees likely to be set-up in another three or four years by the Government of each state and union territory.

Every civil judge, junior or senior division must by given a residential office allowance of Rs. 250 per month. Judicial officers above this will get it at the rate of Rs. 300 per month.

By June 30, 1992, every judicial officer in the country must have, on a uniform pattern, a small residential library. Every district judge must have a provision made in his budget for providing judicial officers under his control with such a library and the respective high courts will monitor this aspect effectively.

From April 1, 1992 every district judge will get a monthly sumptuary allowance of Rs. 300 and every chief judicial magistrate Rs. 200 for holding a weekly meeting of judicial officers to assess problems and performance.

This allowance is to be used "to the full extent for entertaining judicial officers" and hence is not an income of the recipient. The judges have "commanded" suitable enhancement in the sumptuary allowance of Rs. 300 per month being given by the Union Government presently to the high court judges. By December 31, 1992, every judicial officer must be given, by the State Government concerned, residential accommodation, having provision for a residential office. The accommodation, according to the entitlement of each judicial officer, shall be either State accommodation or in its absence requisitioned accommodation. For this the maximum recovery will be 12.5 per cent of the judicial officer's salary.

The balance shall be met by the state exchequer. In case the Planning Commission does not come forward to take up the matter before January 1992 of constructing state accommodation at the respective stations of judicial officers, the Chief Justice of every High Court will set-up under his chairmanship a committee. This committee will consist of two senior High Court judges and the secretaries of finance, law and works for annual planning of construction of residences.

By March 31, 1993, every district judge must be given a state car. By September 30, 1992 every Chief Judicial magistrate must be given a State vehicle. By March 31, 1993, every station with more than four judicial officers must have a pool State vehicle, under the control of the seniormost officer of the pool, for travel from home to court and other official purposes.

The pool car is entitled to 60 litres of petrol per month. State Governments must "immediately" provide for loans to judicial officers in outlying areas where there are not more than five judicial officers, for buying a two wheeler automobile. Such officers would be entitled to an allowance of Rs. 200 per month.

Latest by December 31, 1992, and preferably within a year from today, an All India Institute of In-service Training for higher officers of the judiciary, including the district judges, shall be set-up. In the same time frame a state level institute for training of the other members of the subordinate judiciary within each of the states or union territories or, one common institute for more than one State or Union Territory will be set-up. This has to be organised by the respective high courts.

The amount collected as court fee should be spent on the administration of justice instead of being utilised as a source of general revenue of the states. The income from court fees is more than the expenditure on the administration of justice as shown by the figures of the Union Ministry of Law and Justice.

High courts must take greater interest in the proper functioning of the district judiciary under their control. Inspection should not be a matter of casual attention.

The Union Government, the State Governments, the Union Territories and the High Courts, are all bound to carry out these directions within the time limits specified because Article 141 of the Constitution states: The law declared by the Supreme Court shall be binding on all courts within the territory of India", and Article 144 requires all authorities to act in aid of the Supreme Court.

All these binding directions in what have been termed by the court as operation "resurrection" have been given on the basis of four principles. Firstly, under the Constitution the judiciary is a class separate from the executive. The efficient functioning of the rule of law so that the democratic polity can exist requires an efficient, strong and enlightened judiciary in which the trial judge is the "kingpin in the hierarchical system of administration of justice".

To have such a judiciary the nation has to pay a price. Hence the plea that the other wings in the states would demand improvement in their scales of pay is not a relevant feature at all. Article 50 of the Constitution clearly postulated separation of the judiciary from the executive.

Secondly, judicial officers with an LLB qualification enter the judicial service at a much older age than the civil service officers, and the nature of judicial work is entirely different in terms of the reading and application of mind required as compared to civil servants. Hence this approach of comparing the judiciary with the administration must be given up in the matter of conditions of service.

Thirdly, judges are human beings and their function of justicing is "divine". A great change has overtaken today's society. Life has become competitive, demands of life have increased and attitudes have changed. Therefore, today a judicial officer looks at life in a comparative way with administrative officers of his age.

Professional income at the bar has tremendously swelled and very often a counsel's fee per day equals the salary of the judicial officer for a full month or even a longer period. "This great disparity affects peace and equilibrium in the judicial operation".

Fourthly, austerity and utter probity both in personal and public life of every judge is expected by the public.

The Supreme Court ended over 30 years of inaction on the Law Commission reports concerning the district judiciary.

The petition for the All India Judges Association had been filled by Mr. A.T.M Sampath. It was argued by its chairman, Mr. Sriramulu, a former judge of the Andhra Pradesh High Court with the help of Mr. Ashok Srivastava, President of the Association, and others. Mr. Raju Ramachandran acted as amicus curiae at the request of the court.

Source : *Indian Express,* November 14, 1991.

32

PERSONNEL POLICIES

The Ministry of Personnel, Public Grievances and Pensions consists of three separate departments. These are:

— Department of Personnel and Training.
— Department of Administrative Reforms and Public Grievances.
— Department of Pension and Pensioners' Welfare.

The Ministry is under the charge of the Prime Minister.

The Ministry is the chief formulator of policy in the field of personnel management for all organisations of the Government of India. It coordinates the implementation of different aspects of the personnel management policy including administrative vigilance, reservation in the services and posts for the Scheduled Castes (SCs), Scheduled Tribes (STs) and other specified categories, joint consultation and compulsory arbitration, staff welfare, pension administration, administrative reforms and public grievance redressal.

The Department of Personnel and Training—the biggest unit of the Ministry—is the cadre-controlling authority for the Indian Administrative Service and the three Central Secretariat Services. It looks after all administrative matters relating to the Central Bureau of Investigation (CBI), Administrative Tribunal (A.T.), Union Public Service Commission (UPSC), Staff Selection Commission (SSC) and the Indian Institute of Public Administration (IIPA). It is also part of the department's responsibility to oversee the functioning of the Lal Bahadur Shastri National Academy of Administration, Mussoorie and the Institute of Secretariat Training and Management, New Delhi.

The Ministry took several important steps for improvement of personnel management, review and re-organisation of the cadre structure for several services, improvement in the pension payment dispension, better application of Government's policy for reservation for the members of the Scheduled Castes and the Scheduled Tribes and so on. The following specific steps are worth noting:

(i) A UNDP project was launched in the Lal Bahadur Shastri National Academy of Administration (LBSNAA) at Mussoorie in June, 1990. The project is to cover a period of three years and aims at strengthening the content and methodology of training in specific disciplines, development of the faculty of the Academy in certain areas through participation of its members in courses in overseas institutions, enhancement of the use of the computer, training in computer application for administrators and upgradation and modernisation of the training infrastructure of the Academy.

(ii) A special recruitment drive was launched to fill up, through an open examination during 1990, the backlog and current vacancies for members of the Scheduled Castes and the Scheduled Tribes in the grades of LDC, Stenographer Grade 'D' and Assistant. As a result of this special drive 412 LDCs and 90 Assistants have been recommended to different ministries/departments.

(iii) The upper age limit for appointment of widows, divorced women as well as women judicially separated from their husband and not remarried, which was hitherto applicable for appointment to Group 'C' and 'D' posts, has been raised to 35 years (40 years in the case of the members of the SCs and STs) and has also been extended to cover appointment to Groups 'A' and 'B' posts, except for cases in which recruitment is made through open competitive examinations.

(iv) It has been decided to allow, as a one time measure, age relaxation for casual employees to the extent of the period of service rendered by them in duties normally prescribed for Group 'C' staff in order to enable them to appear in the Clerks/Stenographer's Grade Examinations conducted by the Staff Selection Commission and to appear in other selection tests conducted by other agencies. They have also been allowed relaxation obviating their sponsorship by employment exchanges.

(v) A Special Recruitment Drive covering all the ministries/departments, public sector undertakings, public sector banks and insurance corporations was launched during the current year to fill up the backlog of vacancies reserved for members of the Scheduled Castes and the Scheduled Tribes as it prevailed on 31-3-90 including the reserved vacancies left unfilled under the drive carried out during 1989. The number of vacancies identified under the drive and the number of candidates recruited up to March, 1991 were 31,928 and 19,096 respectively.

(vi) The Union Public Service Commission held special examinations at specified centres for recruitment of the Visually Handicapped (VH) and Hearing Handicapped (HH) persons to Groups 'C' and 'D' posts in the Central Government departments and public sector undertakings. As a result of this, 46 vacancies for the VH and 77 for the HH categories have since been filled up.

(vii) At a meeting of the National Council of Joint Consultative Machinery (JCM), the Government announced its decision to provide at least one promotion to such Groups 'C' and 'D' employees as have stagnated at the maximum of their pay scales for one year.

(viii) A child born to/of a parent who is a retired government servant has also been made eligible for grant of family pension. It has also been decided to extend the benefit of family pension to the spouse of a government servant who marries after his or her retirement. These benefits have also been extended to past cases in which life-time family pension was not admissible due to the operation of the restrictions under the rules.

(ix) The ceiling on the insurance amount payable under the Contributory Provident Fund Deposit-Linked Insurance Scheme to eligible members of a deceased subscriber's family has been raised from Rs. 10,000 to Rs. 30,000.

PERSONNEL MANAGEMENT

Personnel management involves, amongst other things, the placement of officers at the middle and senior management levels in the Government of India so as to match skill and experience with job requirements. Planning for career development and offering the services of expert for foreign assignments are some of the other important areas of its responsibility.

Placement

All posts in the Secretariat from the level of Under Secretary and above in the various ministries, departments and other offices of the Government of India (except in the Ministries of Railways and External Affairs) are filled up on the basis of tenure deputation under the Central Staffing Schemes. The Establishment Officer obtains the names of the eligible officers from the State Governments and other cadre controlling authorities and a list is drawn up keeping in view the suitability of officers in terms of their qualification and experience vis-a-vis the job requirements. Panels of names for the posts of Under Secretary and above, up to the level of Joint Secretary, are circulated by the Establishment Officer to the departments and ministries concerned. Approval of the Appointments Committee of the Cabinet (ACC) is obtained for posting at the level of Deputy Secretary and above. Approval of the ACC is required also for all important, non-secretariat senior appointments to positions such as Chairman, Managing Directors, Functional and Executive Directors and other Directors on the boards of all public sector undertakings, nationalised banks, statutory authorities as well as government-owned companies and enterprises. For posts above the level of Joint Secretary, proposals for placement are initiated by the Cabinet Secretary.

Career Development

As part of the programme for the development of the potential of the officers of the Indian Administrative Service, certain steps have been taken in consultation with the State Governments to ensure that officers acquire adequate field experience at appropriate stages of their career. All State Governments have been advised to make individual career plans for the direct recruits. The executive records of all IAS officers have been computerised to facilitate the monitoring of their career patterns.

Foreign Assignments

Assignment of Indian experts to various developing countries of Asia, Africa and Latin America is done by the department in the following areas:

(a) bilateral assignment to other developing countries;
(b) international assignment to the United Nations and its allied agencies;
(c) assignments under the Indian Aid programme to friendly countries; and
(d) assignments under the Indian Technical and Economic Cooperation Programme.

The Foreign Assignment Section of the Department maintains a panel of experts in various fields like public administration, economic administration etc. Experts who are registered with the department are sponsored for bilateral assignments on request received from developing countries. The panel of experts is drawn up after inviting applications from central ministries/departments, State Governments, universities, etc. through correspondence. The Department of Personnel and Training maintains a panel of experts and offers suitable persons from these panels. The panels are revised every three years, the current one being valid up to December, 1992. During the year 1990, 511 and during the period from January to March 1991, 72 experts were sponsored by the Department for assignment with the UN and its allied agencies.

The Department of Personnel and Training frames the policy for deputation of experts to the United Nations, its allied agencies and other international organisations and coordinates the steps for the implementation of this policy. The nodal ministries/departments dealing with specific subjects process the vacancy notices issued by the UN agencies concerned.

The services of Indian experts are also offered to some developing countries under the Indian Technical and Economic Cooperation (ITEC) programme administered by the Ministry of External Affairs. The Foreign Assignments Selection Committee (FASC), chaired by the Establishment Officer, makes selection for this purpose. During 1990, 17 and during the period from January to March 1991, 11 experts were selected under this programme.

All information regarding foreign assignments has now been computerised thereby making its retrieval easy.

CADRE MANAGEMENT

All India Services

Cadre Strength

The authorised strength of the Indian Administrative Service Cadre for all the States put together and the number of officers in position as on 1-1-1991 are 5334 and 5021 respectively. The triennial cadre review of the IAS cadres of Arunachal Pradesh, Goa, Mizoram and Union Territories, Jammu & Kashmir, Kerala, Andhra Pradesh and Karnataka was conducted during the year.

Amendment to Rules

The IAS/IPS/IFS (Pay) Rules have been amended to the effect that the first increment in the Senior Time Scale would henceforth be admissible to an officer on his completion of 5 years of service. Earlier the first increment used to be allowed to an officer only after his completion of the 6th year of service.

District Planning Unit

The Planning Commission has recognised the need for IAS officers to act as team leaders for all the functionaries involved in the exercise of decentralised planning at the district level and, therefore, of the need to treat the LBSNAA as a leading institution for training in the techniques and skills required for District Planning. "The District Planning Unit" has been started and its staff strength augmented. For this purpose the LBSNAA is also processing a design for the preparation of a multi-volume training manual with the assistance of the Food and Agricultural Organisation. Proposals for this have been sent to the Ministry of Agriculture. The Research Unit of the Academy has provided significant assistance in submitting an exhaustive report on Bonded Labour in the country.

UNDP Project

A UNDP project was launched in LBSNAA in June 1990 for a period of three years. The salient features of the project are:

1. Strengthening the content and methodology of training in specific disciplines.
2. Development of the faculty of the LBSNAA in certain areas through short and medium term courses in overseas institutions.
3. Enhancement of the use of the computer, computer aided instructions and training in computer application for administrators.
4. Upgradation and modernisation of the training infrastructure of the LBSNAA.

Central Secretariat Services

The Central Secretariat has three services:

(i) Central Secretariat Service (CSS) comprising four grades, namely:
  (a) Selection Grade;
  (b) Grade I;
  (c) Section Officers' Grade; and
  (d) Assistants' Grade.

(ii) Central Secretariat Stenographers' Service (CSSS) comprising four grades, namely:
  (a) Private Secretary's Grade;
  (b) Grade A and B (merged);
  (c) Grade C; and
  (d) Grade D.

(iii) Central Secretariat Clerical Service (CSCS) comprising two grades, namely:
  (a) Upper Division Grade; and
  (b) Lower Division Grade.

Except for the Selection Grade, Grade I of the CSS and the Private Secretary's Grade in the CSSS, all other grades in the three Secretariat Services constitute decentralised cadres i.e. all appointments to promotions in these grades are made by each cadre comprising posts in a ministry/department and its participating attached offices or in groups of ministries/departments.

The Selection Grade and Grade I of the CSS and the new Private Secretary's Grade of the CSSS are centralised cadres and appointments to and promotions in these are made on an all-secretariat basis. In respect of decentralised cadres, the Department of Personnel and Training performs the role of a monitor assessing the overall requirement of different cadres, fixing zones of promotion, arranging centralised recruitment through open competitive examinations and organising Limited Departmental Competitive Examinations, wherever stipulated.

Grade I of CSS and Selection Grade

All appointments to Grade I of the CSS and Selection Grade are made according to the Central Staffing Pattern. Cases of eligible Grade I officers of the CSS for promotion to Selection Grade are under process. The panel for Grade I of the CSS could not be prepared for the years 1987, 1988, 1989 and 1990 on account of a dispute between directly recruited Section Officers and promoted Section Officers regarding their seniority. This has become a subject matter of litigation. Decision on the Special Leave Petition (SLP) on this issue, filed in the Supreme Court against the judgement of the Central Administrative Tribunal, is awaited. However, in accordance with the observations of the Supreme Court made in its interim order dated the 20th January 1989, ad hoc promotion has been given to 76 officers with effect from 31-3-89 on the basis of the 1987 eligibility list. Further ad hoc promotions have been made on the basis of cadre-wise seniority lists. An application seeking further promotions on the basis of the 1988/1989 eligibility lists is pending in the Supreme Court.

Zones for Promotion in Decentralised Grades

With a view to minimising disparities in promotion in the decentralised grades of CSS/CSSS/CSCS, zones of promotions are reviewed and refixed annually. The zones of promotion for the grades of UDC and Stenographers of Grades A and B (merged) have been so delineated as to include all the existing long term appointees in the respective Select Lists. In the grade of Assistants, where the prevalence of long term appointees is large, necessary steps are being taken to regularise all the long-term appointees. Candidates who are found suitable within the prescribed zones, but are not accommodated in their own cadres for want of vacancy, are nominated to other cadres for promotion to higher grades subject to their willingness to move to another cadre on promotion.

Steps have been taken to closely monitor the management of various cadres with a view to ensuring that the ad hoc recruitment/appointments are minimised and that it is only in exceptional or unavoidable circumstances that ad hoc promotions/appointments are made from amongst the employees in the cadre concerned.

Cadre Training Plan

A comprehensive Cadre Training Plan for the officers of CSS/CSSS/CSCS, both direct recruits and promotees, to be conducted at the Institute of Secretariat Training and Management, was drawn up. However, because of financial constraints, the necessary infrastructural facilities and faculty back-up could not be provided. Efforts are being made to provide them so that the training could commence early.

CADRE REVIEW

Periodical review of the cadre strength of a regularly constituted Service/Cadre is an important element of cadre management which aims at rationalisation of the existing cadre structure based on manpower projections.

Cadre review proposals in respect of the Geological Survey of India, Group 'A' were processed and a detailed 'brief' containing the views of the Department of Personnel and Training on these proposals was prepared for consideration of the Cadre Review Committee. The revised briefs for cadre review of the Indian Supply Service and Indian Inspection Service were prepared in the light of the proposals for decentralisation of certain purchase activities and were placed before the Cadre Review Committee for consideration. The recommendations of the Cadre Review Committee were communicated to the concerned cadre controlling authorities for necessary action.

Groups B and C cadres of the Directorate of Accounts, Cabinet Secretariat were restructured so as to fall in line with the other organised Accounts Services.

Review in Hand

Cadre review proposals in respect of the following Services/Cadres were received from the cadre-controlling authorities and are being processed:

1. Military Engineering Service—Engineers' Cadre
2. Military Engineering Service—Architects' Cadre
3. Military Engineering Service—Surveyors' Cadre
4. Central Engineering Service (C.P.W.D.)
5. Central Electrical and Mechanical Engineering Service (C.P.W.D.)
6. Indian Broadcasting (Engineers') Service
7. Central Water Engineering Service.

These cadre reviews are expected to be finalised shortly.

PERSONNEL POLICIES

Central Civil Service (Conduct) Rules

(a) Rule 20 of the CCS (Conduct) Rules, 1964 provides that no government servant shall bring any political or outside influence to bear upon any superior authority to further his interest in respect of service matters. To curb the increasing tendency among the government servants to approach the Ministry of Urban Development for allotment of out-of-turn residential accommodation, instructions have been issued clarifying that allotment of government accommodation to a government servant is a matter related to his service under the government and therefore, canvassing for out-of-turn allotment with Members of Parliament etc. constitutes violation of Rule 20 of the CCS (Conduct) Rules, 1964.

(b) The limit for intimation to the government in respect of minor repairs to immovable property belonging to a government servant has been raised from Rs. 1000 to Rs. 10,000. The government servant would now be required to intimate the government only if the estimate of repairs exceeds Rs. 10,000.

(c) The monetary limits prescribed under Rule 13 of the CCS (Conduct) Rules, 1964 for giving intimation of or seeking permission for acceptance of gifts by a government servant, members of his/her family or any other person acting on his/her behalf, have been reviewed. While the existing limits for acceptance of gifts from near relatives or personal friends have been doubled, the limit for acceptance of gifts from foreign dignitaries etc. has been reduced from Rs. 3000 to Rs. 1000 so as to bring it in line with the provisions of the Foreign Contribution (Regulation) Act.

Leave Travel Concession (LTC)

(a) Earlier LTC Rules used to provide that where both husband and wife were government servants and resided together, they constituted one family unit for the purpose of LTC and only one of them could claim this concession for the family. The Department has since issued instruction to liberalise LTC so as to remove this disadvantage to either of the spouses. Now husband and wife, both of whom are government servants, can at their option choose to declare separate home towns and both of them can claim the concession separately under the normal provisions of CCS (LTC) Rules, in respect of members of their respective families subject to the condition that if the husband or wife avails himself/herself of the facility as a member of the family of the other, he or she will not be entitled to claim the concession for himself or herself, independently. This decision will be applicable to journeys performed under LTC against the block year 1990 onwards.

(b) In view of the prevailing financial constraints caused by the situation in the Gulf, the Leave Travel Concession facility available to the government servants under the CCS (LTC) Rules, 1988 was suspended from the 23rd January 1991 till the 31st March, 1991. However, government servants retiring during the period were allowed to avail themselves of the facility provided it was otherwise admissible to them.

Central Civil Services (CCA) Rules

It has come to notice that the administrative authorities sometimes take disciplinary action against representatives of the staff for minor lapses of a technical nature in their day to day work mainly to victimize them for their role as office bearers of staff organisation. In this connection, instructions have been issued clarifying that if a government servant is penalized for an act done by him which is directly or indirectly connected with his position as an office bearer of an association, he can prefer an appeal against such action directly to the President in accordance with the Rule 24(3) of the CCS (CCA) Rules. This would ensure examination of the grievances of the office-bearer concerned at the highest level and thus, provide him/her adequate protection against undue victimization.

Judgements of the Courts/Tribunals, etc.

This Department has been scrutinizing regularly the judgements pronounced by the Supreme Court/High Courts and various Tribunals like the Central Administrative Tribunal so that wherever necessary rule can be modified so as to bring them in consonance with the court's decisions.

The following judgements have been circulated to the ministries/ departments:

(a) Judgement of the Supreme Court in the case of Shri Parma Nanda vs. State of Haryana and others (1989 (2) SC 179) in which the court held that the Tribunal could exercise only such powers which the Civil Courts or High Courts could have exercised by way of judicial review. The Tribunal cannot interfere with the findings of the enquiry officer where it agrees that the findings are not arbitrary or perverse. If there has been an enquiry consistent with the rules and according to the principles of natural justice, a decision on what punishment would meet the ends of justice is a matter exclusively within the jurisdiction of the competent authority. However, one exception to this is where a person is dismissed or reduced in rank without an inquiry, solely on the basis of a conviction in the criminal court. In such a case the Tribunal may examine the adequacy of the penalty imposed in the light of the conviction and sentence inflicted on the person.

(b) The judgement of the full bench of the Central Administrative Tribunal in the case of Amarjit Singh Vs. Union of India (AIR 88(2) CAT 637) where it was held that the institution/continuance of proceedings relating to serious acts of misconduct/negligence is not dependent upon a pecuniary loss being occasioned to the government. Under Rule 9 of the CCS (Pension) Rules even in the absence of any pecuniary loss, the pension of a pensioner can be withheld or withdrawn in whole or in part, after following the prescribed procedure for an act of misconduct or negligence committee by him or her while in service.

Departmental Committee Procedures (DPC); Revised Zone of Consideration for Selection Posts

For promotion by selection on merit with due regard to seniority, the zone of consideration for officers to be considered by the DPC was prescribed as being three times the number of vacancies. Keeping in view the need for avoiding excessive suppression in the event of a large number of vacancies being filled up, instructions were issued on 12-10-90 modifying the zone as indicated below:

TABLE 32.1: Zone of Consideration by DPC

No. of vacancies	No. of officers to be included in the zone
1	5
2	8
3	10
10	10+Twice the number of vacancies in excess of 3 vacancies.

Recognition of Educational Qualifications

The Government recognised the following qualifications for the purposes of employment under the government.

TABLE 32.2: Qualifications, Examination and Equivalence for Employment

Institution	Examination	Equivalence
Rashtriya Sanskrit Sansthan, Delhi	Poorva Madhyama	Secondary School Certificate Exam. (effective from 1983)
	Uttar Madhyama	Certificate Examination/Intermediate (effective from 1985)
	Prak Shastry	Uttar Madhyama Intermediate (effective from 1985)
State Council for Vocational Courses, Haryana	Vocational Education Courses.	Higher Secondary (10+2) Examination
Gurukul Mahavidyalaya Jawalpur, M.P.	Vidya Vibhusan	Class VIII (effective from 1980)
	Vidya Ratna	10 years High School Examination (effective from 1982)
	Vidya Nidhi	12 years Sr. Sec. Examination (effective from 1984)
	Vidya Bhaskar	B.A. (effective from 1986)

Appointment to Non-functional Selection Grade in Group A: Case of Scheduled Castes and Scheduled Tribes

It has been decided that SC/ST officers considered for being appointed in their turn to posts in the non-functional Selection Grade against available vacancies, may be included in the select list even if they do not fulfil the criteria laid down for such appointment, provided they are not considered unfit by the Selection Committee.

Age Relaxation for Widows, Divorced Women and Women Separated from their Husbands, etc.

For the purpose of appointment to Groups C and D posts under the Central Government filled through the Staff Selection Commission (SSC) and Employment Exchanges, the upper age limit in the case of widows, divorced women and judicially separated from their husbands and not remarried are relaxed up to the age of 35 years (up to the age of 40 years for members of SC & ST). This age relaxation which was hitherto valid for appointment to Groups C and D posts only, was extended to cover appointment to Groups A and B posts too, except where recruitment is made through open competitive examinations.

Posting of Physically Handicapped Employees

The Government has issued instructions that physically handicapped employees in Groups C and D posts, who have been recruited on a regional basis, may be given posting as far as possible near their native place within the region subject to administrative consideration.

Measures to Improve Representation of Scheduled Castes and Scheduled Tribes in Government Services

On the basis of recommendations of a Committee of Members of Parliament which examined various matters relating to representation of the SCs and STs in government services, instructions have been issued to the effect that where recruitment to a grade is made both by promotion and by direct recruitment i.e. where separate quotas for promotion and direct recruitment are prescribed in the Recruitment Rules, reserved vacancies falling in the promotion quota, which cannot be filled up due to non-availability of eligible persons belonging to SCs and STs in the feeder cadre, may be temporarily diverted to the direct recruitment quota and filled in by recruitment of candidates belonging to the SCs or STs, as the case may be. In the subsequent years when reserved vacancies in the direct recruitment quota become available, they may be diverted back to the promotion quota to make up for the vacancies diverted earlier and filled up from among the SC and ST candidates in the feeder cadre who may, by now, have become eligible for promotion. The exchange of vacancies in this manner will ensure that the structure and composition of the cadre remains unaffected over a period of time.

Promotion of Peons to the Posts of Senior Gestetner Operator

In order to fill up the post of Senior Gestetner Operator when it cannot be filled up on the ground that no eligible Group D employee is available or willing to be considered for promotion to the post, revised instructions have been issued enabling various offices to fill up the lone post of Senior Gestetner Operation from amongst peons by temporarily down-grading the post to the level of Junior Gestetner Operator.

Regularisation of Casual Workers Recruited to Perform Duties of Group C Posts: Relaxation of Age and Employment Exchange Procedures

On the basis of a request of the staff side in the National Council (JCM) it was decided to allow age relaxation to the extent of the period of service rendered by the casual employees performing the duties normally prescribed for Group C staff, in order to enable them to appear in the Clerks/Stenographer's grade examinations conducted by the SSC and to appear in other selection tests conducted by agencies other than the SSC. These casual employees have also been allowed exemption from being sponsored by the employment exchanges.

Decision on Matter Relating to Leave, Pay and Allowance of the Central Government Servants

(a) *Leave*

- (i) The maximum study leave in combination with other kinds of leave is now allowable up to 36 months for the Central Government employees undergoing courses of study leading to the Ph.D. degree, subject to the fulfilment of various other conditions regarding the grant of study leave.
- (ii) The period of earned leave that a government servant can take at a time has now been raised to 180 days' as against 120 days in the past.
- (iii) Officers appointed on contract to the various posts under the Central Government are now allowed to encash earned leave to the extent of 30 days to 240 days, depending on the period of their contract. For contract

of two years or less, no encashment is permissible. The maximum limit of 240 days is inclusive of the encashment facility enjoyed by such an employees in his previous employment.

(iv) Employees whose duties involve risks and who draw a Risk Allowance while performing their duties, have now been allowed to draw this allowance even when they are on leave. The Risk Allowance will also form part of their leave salary.

(b) *Allowances*

(i) All the government servants, irrespective of their pay limits, whose children are studying in recognised schools are now eligible to get children's education allowance, reimbursement of the tuition fee and hostel subsidy. Assistance is admissible to a maximum number of 3 children at any time if they were born on or before 31-12-87, and for only two children born thereafter.

(ii) The scheme for engagement of consultants was reviewed by a Committee of Secretaries. In order to make the scheme more effective, it has now been decided that in respect of consultants engaged from outside, their period of engagement should not exceed 2 years. In respect of retiring employees being engaged as consultants in the same department, the maximum number of consultants is two and the post held by the retiring employee should be kept vacant until he completes his work as a consultant. For the Planning Commission the maximum number of consultants has been restricted to 25.

(c) *Pay*

(i) The period of training undergone by a government servant before he formally takes over charge of the post for which he has been selected for a regular appointment, whether on remuneration or otherwise, is to be treated as duty and will be counted for the purpose of his/her drawing increments.

(ii) Restrictions under FR 35 are not to apply when a government servant, holding a post in a substantive or temporary or officiating capacity is promoted or appointed in a substantive or temporary or officiating capacity, as the case may be, to another post carrying duties and responsibilities of greater importance, if he has fulfilled the eligibility conditions as prescribed in the relevant recruitment rules.

(iii) Employees who were promoted after 1-1-1985 but before 1-1-1986 and whose next increment in the lower posts fell due on or after 1-1-1986, are allowed another option to get their pay fixed under FR 22 C in the posts to which they have been promoted either from the date of promotion or the date of the next increment due in the lower post.

(iv) In case a junior government officer, promoted after 1-1-1986, gets a higher pay than a government servant who is senior to him because of the benefit of the Rs. 25 added to the pay of the lower post for fixation of his pay in the scale for the higher post under FR 22-C, the pay of the senior government servant may be stepped up with reference to the pay of his junior, subject to the fulfilment of the other conditions laid down in the CCS (RP) Rules, 1986.

Central (Surplus Staff) Cell

A scheme for disposal of the surplus staff was brought into force in February, 1966. It provided for the deployment of the staff who are rendered surplus as a result of the work measurement studies conducted by the Staff Inspection Unit of the Ministry of Finance and the Internal Work Study Units of the ministries or winding up or abolition of the Central Government departments/subordinate offices as well as various administrative reform measures introduced in the Central Government offices. The scheme was reviewed, particularly in the context of the proposal for introduction of the Zero-Base Budgeting system and a revised scheme came into force from the 1st of April, 1989, superseding the earlier one. Unlike the original scheme, the revised scheme did away with the provision for time-bound termination of services of the surplus personnel who remain unredeployed for six months, and further makes a provision for (i) the training of the surplus staff where necessary and (ii) for the re-adjustment of the surplus staff who had to be redeployed in the first instance, to posts carrying a lower scale of pay or having a lower classification or in the case of low-paid staff, in a State different from that of their choice or their last posting. Statutory rules were, from time to time, made to regulate the redeployment of various categories or surplus staff. After the adoption of the revised scheme, a set of consolidated rules, namely 'The Central Civil Services (Redeployment of Surplus Staff) Rules, 1990' has been brought into force with effect from 28-2-1990 superseding the earlier rules.

While redeployment and readjustment of surplus employees belonging to Groups 'A', 'B' and 'C' is handled in the Central (Surplus Staff) Cell located in the Department of Personnel and Training, the redeployment, as also readjustment of Group 'D' surplus staff continue to be managed by the Special Cell in the Directorate General of Employment and Training, Ministry of Labour.

Redeployment/Absorption of Retrenched Temporary/Central Government Employees

The temporary or quasi-permanent Groups 'C' and 'D' employees, recruited through the employment exchange or appointed on compassionate grounds, who have put in not less than three years of regular continuous service, are in the event of their retrenchment, given the facility of being considered for re-employment on certain specific terms. The primary responsibility for arranging alternative employment for such surplus employees, rests with the administrative ministry/department concerned, but where it is unable to do so, it can refer such cases to the Department of Personnel and Training with a view to obtaining their re-employment.

Allocation of Staff and Integration of Services as a Result of Reorganisation of States

The States Reorganisation Act, 1956, and the subsequent laws which deal with reorganisation of States and Union Territories vest powers in the Central Government to allocate the staff to the successor States and Union Territories. The responsibility for integration of the allocated staff has also been entrusted to the Central Government under these laws.

Advisory committees have been constituted in each of the reorganised states to examine the representations of the affected employees and to make recommendations thereon for the consideration of the Central Government. In Andhra Pradesh, the Central Government has also been reviewing promotions of the allocated staff with the assistance of the Advisory (Review) Committees. Besides, if any State Government wants to make any changes in the conditions of service as admissible to the allotted employees, which are to their disadvantage, they are required to obtain the prior concurrence of the Central Government.

The work pertaining to allocation of staff, done by this Department, has already been completed. Similarly, the work pertaining to the integration of services of the various reorganised States and Union Territories and review of promotion of the integrated staff in Andhra Pradesh has also been completed except where it is required to be redone under the orders of the courts of law.

TABLE 32.3: Strength of Central Government Employees As on January 1, 1990

	Group A	Group B	Group C	Group D		Total Employees	
Total	No.%age	No.%age	No.%age	Excluding Sweepers No.%age	Including Sweepers No.%age	Excluding Sweepers No.%age	Including Sweepers No.%age
Total Emp.	61686	92968	2217234	1105165	101281	3477053	3578334
*	5331 (8.64)	10497 (11.29)	336880 (15.19)	237400 (21.48)	84395 (83.33)	590108 (16.97)	674503 (18.85)
**	1593 (2.58)	2222 (2.39)	107103 (4.83)	74327 (6.73)	3026 (2.99)	185245 (5.33)	188271 (5.26)

*Scheduled Castes
**Scheduled Tribes

TABLE 32.4: Progress of Representation of SC & ST From 1971 to 1990 As on Ist January

	Group A		Group B		Group C		Group D	
	No.	%age	No.	%age	No.	%age	No. (Excluding	%age Sweepers)
1	2	3	4	5	6	7	8	9
				Scheduled Castes				
1971	741	2.58	1794	4.06	136259	9.59	221248	18.37
1972	860	2.99	1850	4.13	143830	9.77	224038	18.61
1973	972	3.14	2110	4.52	115221	10.05	222635	18.37
1974	1094	3.25	2401	4.59	161775	10.33	230203	18.53
1975	1201	3.43	2695	4.98	174119	10.71	230864	18.64
1976	1287	3.46	2956	5.41	186719	11.31	230723	18.75
1977	1662	4.16	3421	6.07	198662	11.84	237718	19.07
1978	1940	4.50	3618	6.44	203192	12.13	239963	19.13
1979	2204	4.75	4150	7.37	215762	12.55	245596	19.32
1980	2375	4.50	5055	8.54	235555	13.44	247607	19.46
1981	2883	5.46	5298	8.41	243028	12.95	238985	19.35
1982	2980	5.49	5970	9.02	255730	13.39	256261	23.41
1983	3574	6.72	6368	10.17	276690	14.57	249405	19.74
1984	3829	6.92	7015	10.36	278133	13.98	240596	20.20
1985	4228	7.30	6932	10.07	298065	14.87	257931	20.80
1986	4475	8.00	7718	10.39	306842	14.43	232126	19.36
1987	4752	8.23	7857	10.41	308119	14.45	234743	20.09
1988	4886	8.67	8864	11.18	309041	14.80	221114	19.88
1989	5204	8.51	10021	11.65	330330	14.85	223045	20.41
1990	5331	8.64	10497	11.29	336880	15.19	237400	21.48

Contd.

TABLE 32.4 (*Contd.*)

1	2	3	4	5	6	7	8	9
				Scheduled Tribes				
1971	117	0.41	192	0.43	23732	1. 7	43916	3.65
1972	144	0.50	196	0.44	25282	1.72	45947	3.82
1973	155	0.50	227	0.49	29366	1.95	47543	3.92
1974	192	0.57	258	0.49	33383	2.13	47679	3.84
1975	218	0.62	322	0.59	36893	2.27	49464	3.99
1976	253	0.68	402	0.59	41405	2.51	48332	3.93
1977	309	0.77	434	0.77	46603	2.78	54206	4.35
1978	366	0.85	494	0.88	48731	2.86	58461	4.66
1979	435	0.94	579	1.03	53460	3.11	65975	5.19
1980	506	1.06	763	1.29	55334	3.16	68401	5.38
1981	590	1.12	824	1.31	59228	3.16	62672	5.07
1982	633	1.17	947	1.43	66278	3.47	81496	7.45
1983	761	1.43	922	1.47	75858	0.04	89822	5.53
1984	943	1.07	1200	1.77	75353	3.79	71895	6.04
1985	1001	1.73	1089	1.57	84153	4.02	70668	5.07
1986	1079	1.93	1323	1.73	89717	4.22	66539	5.55
1987	1182	2.05	1450	1.92	90160	4.23	68220	5.84
1988	1295	2.03	1668	2.01	93627	4.48	67869	6.01
1989	1373	2.24	1720	0.02	100425	4.52	70583	6.46
1990	1593	2.58	2222	2.39	107103	4.83	74327	6.73

TABLE 32.5: Salient Recommendations of Important Management Studies of 1990-91

No.	Name of Study		Salient Recommendations
1	2		3
1.	DESU (procedure/practice for new connection and issue of the first bill)	(i)	The application form for a fresh connection is not well designed. It needs revision so that intending consumers can fill up the form easily without professional help. The DESU separately has issued a booklet containing general guidelines for consumers. In this booklet, instructions for filling the application form could be added and the booklet could be given alongwith the form. At present the application form is priced at Re. 0.10 and the booklet at Re. 0.50. After suitable revision if the two are given together, a consolidated fee of Re. 1 could be charged.
		(ii)	There is a great deal of common information between the form of application and the prescribed test report which has to be submitted alongwith the application. When the application form is revised, care should be taken to exclude such information from it, which is already contained in the test report and need not be duplicated in the application form.
		(iii)	The document relevant to the inspector in the office of the Zonal Assistant Engineer is the prescribed test report. There appears, therefore, to be no need to send any other papers to the Zonal Office. When the application of the intending consumer is found in order and the requisite security money has been deposited, a "K" number could be allotted and noted on a copy of the test report submitted with the application. The application could then be permitted to take this test report alongwith the noted. "K" number for submission to the Zonal Office. This could lead to a reduction in the delay in transmission of papers through dak. It may be noted, however, that if the intending consumer does not wish to carry the test report himself to the Zonal Office, it should be transmitted in normal course by the DESU itself.
		(iv)	The possibility of giving a fixed date to the intending consumer for inspection of premises together with an alternative date in case the first one is inconvenient, should be explored. There are many ways of doing this. It could be done either at the district level or by the Zonal Office. Intimation could be given by post or at the time the application is accepted. The advantage of such an intimation is that the chances of the premises being found locked or similar circumstances where the Inspector cannot carry out his inspection due to the absence of a responsible person at the premises are reduced. This will also help in making the process of energisation a more definitive one in terms of a time schedule.
		(v)	It is observed that usually the material used for providing a new connection is known and there does not appear to be any good reason why such items should be out of stock in the district store, if the availability of materials is at all the problem in providing new connections expeditiously. The store

Contd.

TABLE 32.5 *Contd.*

1	2		3
			being located in the district office provides an easy opportunity to the Executive Engineer of the district to supervise its functioning and to see that the necessary materials are at hand. The Executive Engineers already have access to the information pertaining to the number of application for fresh connections.
		(vi)	The Inspectors could maintain a diary of the work done by them so that some supervision could be exercised over them in relation to the energisation of new connections.
2.	Streamlining the procedure for employment on compassionate grounds	(i)	The Department of Personnel and Training should revise its instructions so as to define the term near relative and to include a wife or husband or brother or sister of the deceased government servant as a beneficiary of the scheme of compassionate appointment.
		(ii)	The ministries/departments should ensure that the compassionate appointments are made on means-cum-merits basis.
		(iii)	The Welfare Officer in each ministry/department should meet the members of the family of the deceased government servant immediately after his death to advise and assist them in getting appointment on compassionate grounds.
		(iv)	A time norm of 6 to 8 weeks should be fixed for the making compassionate appointment.
		(v)	Wherever the cases are screened by a board/committee of officers, the frequency of the meeting of such board/committee should be increased to once a month so that the applications do not remain unattended for long.
		(vi)	The Ministry of Defence should allow candidates selected for compassionate appointment to join on a provisional basis pending detailed verification of their character antecedents.
3.	An organisational study of the National Cooperative Development Corporation (NCDC)	(i)	Territorial jurisdiction of the Regional Directorates may be readjusted and the number of the Directorates may be brought down from 7 to 6.
		(ii)	A provision may be made in the NCDC General Regulations to the effect that the Board shall meet atleast once every quarter.
		(iii)	The Regional Directors may indicate the likely allocation of NCDC funds to a State for the ensuing year.
		(iv)	The Regional Directors should offer their recommendations/comments on proposals from cooperative societies within a specific time limit, say, a fortnight.
		(v)	The Corporation may adopt issue of cheques with 'at par' facility instead of the present system of despatching bank drafts.
		(vi)	The MIS Division may get the cheque printed on computer.

Contd.

TABLE 32.5 (*Contd.*)

1	2		3
		(vii)	Not more than 50 per cent of the staff and officers may be retained in the Head Office and the remaining staff and officers may be redeployed to the Regional Directorates and Project Offices.
		(viii)	An exercise may be carried out for a proper layout plan for seating officers in head office to enhance their functional efficiency.
		(x)	The scheme of NCDC may be sent to taluk offices/district offices for wider circulation among cooperative societies.
4.	Problems faced by people living in trans-Yamuna colonies	(i)	Municipal authorities should mark the presence of their *safai karamacharis* who have been designated to clean the bye-lanes, only if they produce the signatures of atleast 5 residents of the area certifying that they had performed their duty satisfactorily.
		(ii)	A multi-pronged programme should be adopted to increase public awareness of the importance of cleanliness. Publicity measures should be taken to educate the people on the use of public toilets. The forum of *anganwadis* should be used for imparting such education to children. Voluntary organisations should be encouraged to take up programmes of making people aware of the basics of hygiene.
		(iii)	The Municipal Corporation should take steps to repair the drains around public toilets. The septic tanks of these toilets should be cleaned every year.
		(iv)	For the proper disposal of household refuse, the Municipal Corporation should place mobile garbage bins at the corners of each byelane. These bins should be wheeled by *safai karamcharis* every day to the main site earmarked for dumping garbage in the colony from where it could be periodically removed to municipal garbage during sites.
		(v)	Cleanliness campaign should be undertaken every year before the onset of the rainy season.
		(vi)	The functions and responsibility of the Municipal Corporation and the Delhi Development Authority (DDA) in respect of the *Jhuggi Jhopri* clusters should be clearly demarcated. The Slum Wing of the DDA should provide permanent assets like lanes, drains, handpumps and toilets while the work of scavenging, pumping out of the accumulated water etc., should be done by the Municipal Corporation.
		(vii)	Additional toilets should be constructed in the *Jhuggi Jhopri* clusters.
		(viii)	The Municipal Corporation should post their *safai karamacharis* immediately to clean the *Jhuggi Jhopri* clusters everyday.
		(ix)	The DESU should work out a scheme for providing lighting for the *Jhuggi Jhopri* dwellers.
		(x)	Such instructions as make it obligatory on the part of parents to produce registration or birth certificates for obtaining admission of their children to primary schools should be withdrawn.

Contd.

TABLE 32.5 (*Contd.*)

1	2		3
		(xi)	Welfare programmes like ICDS and Adult Literacy should be started for the benefit of the people residing in *Jhuggi Jhopri* clusters.
		(xii)	Anti-mosquito measure like pumping out of stagnant water and spraying of chemicals should be undertaken regularly.
		(xiii)	Temporary trenches should be dug which could be used as soakage pits for dirty water.
		(xiv)	An effective check on the sale of unhygienic foodstuffs should be maintained.
5.	Procedure for processing of applications/project reports under the Self-Employment Scheme for Educated Unemployed Educated Unemployed Youth (SEEUY)	(i)	The eligible age group for beneficiaries should be 25 to 40 years rather than 18 to 35 years.
		(ii)	The limit on the maximum amount of loan for an industrial unit should be raised from Rs. 35,000 to Rs. 50,000
		(iii)	The maximum eligibility limit of income of the beneficiary together with the income of his or her spouse from all sources should be raised to Rs. 15,000 per annum instead of Rs. 10,000 per annum as at present. The beneficiary should be considered as unemployed for the purpose of the scheme, if his income is within this suggested limit.
		(iv)	DICs with the assistance of banks and the Small Industries Service Institutes should select a variety of projects suitable for the district concerned and conduct baseline surveys to gather detailed and upto date information about the sources of raw materials, markets, existing units, etc. These data are expected to be helpful to entrepreneurs in project formulation.
		(v)	DICs should conduct short training course for entrepreneurs selected by the task force for the grant of loans and separately for persons belonging to the SCs/STs to encourage them to come forward to participate in the scheme.
		(vi)	The task force at the district level should be discontinued. Instead, several task forces at sub-district levels should be set-up, incorporating representation, particularly of the banks, at the local level.
		(vii)	The RBI should advise banks participating in the scheme that the applications for loans should be processed in about a month's time at the latest.
		(viii)	The mandatory quota of SCs/STs representation under the scheme can be better utilised if the targets in this respect are distributed to the districts keeping in view the proportion of SCs/STs population to the total population in the district.
6.	Evaluation of Adult Literacy Programme	(i)	The priorities of the Adult Education Programme should be re-arranged so as to give more weightage to the awareness and functionality components.
		(ii)	Social phenomenon like seasonal migration should be taken into account while planning for adult education.
		(iii)	Topics of interest to the learners like their occupation, functional skills, environment, culture should be given wider coverage.

Contd.

TABLE 32.5 *(Contd.)*

1	2	3	
		(iv)	The use of folk music, songs, plays and theatres should be increased. There should be more discussions and demonstration than simple lecturing at the Adult Education Centres.
		(v)	The programme should be integrated with other development schemes of government.
		(vi)	The educated villagers should be encouraged to take upon themselves the responsibility of making their fellowmen literate.
		(vii)	The involvement of other development agencies of government in the programme should be improved.
		(viii)	There should be some short duration in-service training courses to supplement the initial training given to the instructors.
		(ix)	There is a need to make the villagers aware of the objectives of the Jan Shikshan Nilaams (JSNs) so that this institution is recognised by them as an institution of continuing post literacy education.
		(x)	Parallel existence of the separate preraks for the JSNs and for supervising the Adult Education Centres should be brought to an end.
		(xi)	Post literacy education should be formalised by conducting short duration course (2-3 months) at the JSNs for the neo-literates.
		(xii)	The State Resource Centre should bring out more learning and teaching materials in the tribal and other spoken languages of Maharashtra.

33

PUBLIC SECTOR UNDERTAKINGS

Public Enterprise Reform*

35. India's severely constrained budgetary circumstances create both the need and opportunity for rationalising the scope of public sector activity, and for placing greater reliance on the private sector for resource mobilisation and investment. Public enterprises have absorbed large amounts of budgetary support for their expansion or operations, but in many cases they have failed to generate adequate returns on the investments of public money and contributed significantly to the public sector saving gap and fiscal deficit. Many public enterprises fail to cover the cost of capital they employ and incur cash losses. Central government public enterprises as a whole impose a burden on the exchequer. Since 1985-86, annual budgetary support, net of royalties, taxes, interest and dividend payments, to Central Government Public Enterprises (CPEs) has averaged more than Rs. 30 billion.

36. Public enterprises provide many of the basic and critical inputs in India, and it is a matter of serious concern that for a variety of reasons there has been inadequate attention to improving their efficiency. As a result, many basic industrial inputs have become high-priced, contributing significantly to the high cost structure of the economy. The government recognizes that actions taken in the area of public enterprise reform will be central to the near term growth performance of the economy, as well as to its medium term transformation. To support rationalisation of the scope of the public sector, the government does not propose to create new central public enterprises except in industries reserved for the public sector and essential infrastructure, exploitation of oil and mineral resources and strategic-related activities. The government also reaffirms its policy against nationalisation or takeover of sick private firms, which has already been in effect for the past five years.

37. There are currently 244 autonomous CPFs and 845 state-level public enterprises (SPEs) covering multiple areas of activity (from mining and manufacturing to trading and welfare services). In 1989-90, there were 20 highly profitable units in steel, oil, power, minerals and metals, coal and lignite, heavy engineering, protochemicals, transportation services, financial services and telecommunication services; 74 units providing various services with modest overall profitability; 11 units still under construction; 4 units in a no-profit no-loss situation, and 135 units, concentrated in chemicals and pharmaceuticals, engineering, consumer goods, textiles and various service sub-sectors, with an aggregate negative net profit. Forty-seven of this latter group have in fact been incurring chronic cash losses for a number of years. Specifically, these 47 CPE units can be characterised as sick, with a negative net worth totalling Rs. 46 bil-

---

* *Note* : Paras refer to paras of Finance Minister latter of November 11, 1991.

lion, a total labour force of 310,000 persons, and annual cash losses of Rs. 12 billion which are covered by the budget. The units that fall under special provision of the Sick Industrial Companies Act (1985) will be referred to the Board for Industrial and Financial Reconstruction (BIFR) for restructuring or winding up. The budgetary stringency faced by the government underlines the importance of quickly formulating provisions for restructuring and closing sick and unviable public enterprises, and opening up selected units and sectors to private capital. In this context, the government will formulate an action programme to initiate restructuring and closure procedures for units in the public sector that are patently unviable by May 1992. In the context of public enterprise restructuring, it will be important to assess the social costs associated with the closure of sick units and to develop options and measures for compensation of retrenched labour and alleviation of the social costs.

38. In the context of improving the incentives and policy framework in which CPEs remaining under the government's control operate, and in order to achieve better financial performance and enhanced economic efficiency, regulatory and protection policies are being reviewed. The government has already taken measures in the following areas bearing on the performance of public enterprises; industrial reservations; competition and regulatory polices; and pricing and procurement policies.

39. Enterprises in areas where continued public sector involvement is judged appropriate will be provided a much greater degree of managerial autonomy and made to face a much harder budget constraint through the progressive reduction of budgetary transfers and loans. Specifically, the government intends to establish a schedule of quantitative targets for the elimination of all budgetary transfers and loans to CPEs beginning from 1992-93, and complete elimination of government loans and equity to non-infrastructural PEs over three years. In the same vein, the existing system of monitoring enterprises through Memoranda of Understanding (MoU) will be strengthened, to ensure greater autonomy to management, with their primary accountability toward profitability and the rate of return on capital.

40. Sales of selected firms or partial divestment in specific sectors is increasingly being pursued. The 1991-92 budget confirmed the government's decision to sell partial equity interest (up to 20 per cent) in central public enterprises, totalling Rs. 25 billion, through mutual funds. The objective is for the mutual funds to seek a listing for the shares on the stock market and to dispose of them gradually so as to finally ensure wider holding of shares. Over the course of the next three years, the government intends to raise a total of up to Rs. 75 billion from partial divestment. A more comprehensive programme of divestment of public holdings is under formulation, with the objective of increasing the scale of divestiture from 20 to 49 per cent of equity through a mix of sales of shares to mutual funds, stock market flotation, labour buy-outs and joint ventures with private investors.

Role of Public Sector

The public sector will continue to perform an important role in the coming years.

(i) The role envisaged for it would mainly be in areas where investment is of an infrastructural nature and where private participation is not forthcoming to an adequate extent within a reasonable time. Thus, the public sector will continue to play a dominant role in areas like energy, transport, communications and irrigation. However, if private initiative comes forward to participate in creating such infrastructure on reasonable terms, including full protection of people's interests, such initiatives would be encouraged.

(ii) The public sector would play a useful role in augmenting basic resources of the country like land, forest, water, ecology and science and technology. The public sector will have responsibility for meeting social needs and for regulation of long-term interests of the society like population control, health, education, etc.

(iii) In large parts of its operations where commodities or services are produced and distributed, the principle of market would be applied as basic operating guideline, unless it is necessary to protect the interests of the poorest in the society. This implies recovery of costs and efficiency in operations.

Central Government Public Enterprises

There were 246 Central Government public enterprises as on March 31, 1991, out of which 236 enterprises were in operation. Net profits of these enterprises declined from Rs. 3,789 crore in 1989-90 to Rs. 2,368 crore in 1990-91 (Table 33.1). The rate of return, as measured by the ratio of net profits to capital employed, declined from 4.5 per cent in 1989-90 to 2.3 per cent in 1990-91, the lowest since 1984-85. As in the previous years, the petroleum sector accounted for the bulk of the net profit—Rs. 2,299 crore out of the total of Rs. 2,368 crore. However, there was a decline in the net profits of both petroleum and non-petroleum sectors. The fall in the net profit during 1990-91 is marked in the case of Oil and Natural Gas Commission (Rs. 576 crore), Bharat Coking Coal Ltd. (Rs. 148 crore), Export Credit Guarantee Corporation (Rs. 141 crore) and Mahanagar Telephone Nigam Ltd. (Rs. 96 crore). Rashtriya Ispat Nigam Ltd. had incurred a net loss of Rs. 478 crore in 1990-91, the very first year of its operation. National Thermal Power Corporation and Indian Railway Finance Corporation had improved their net profits by Rs. 164 crore and Rs. 98 crore respectively in 1990-91. During the year 1990-91, 146 Central public enterprises generated gross internal resources to the extent of Rs. 11,372 crore.

As on March 31, 1991, 23.05 lakh people including about 88,000 casual/daily rated workers were employed in 246 Central public enterprises. The total number of regular employees of public enterprises had gone up from 17.03 lakh in 1978-79 to 22.2 lakh in 1990-91.

State Governments' Commercial Undertakings

The working results of departmentally run commercial undertakings of States and Union Territories have continued to be poor. Of all departmentally run enterprises, only forest and mines have been generating net surpluses. While the profits from forest and mines registered a modest increase between 1985-86 and 1991-92, the losses of non-profit making enterprises more than doubled during this period. On the whole, the losses of departmentally run enterprises are estimated at a staggering level of Rs. 1827 crore during 1991-92. The unsustainable nature of the operations of those enterprises is mainly attributable to uneconomic pricing. In the context of the on-going process of fiscal adjustments, it is essential that urgent measures are taken to improve the performance of State-run enterprises. Economic pricing, coupled with increase in productivity, could be starting point (Table 33.2).

The two major non-departmental undertakings, namely, the State Electricity Boards (SEBs) and the State Road Transport Corporations (SRTCs) continued to incur substantial losses in their operations. The commercial losses of all SEBs taken together amounted to Rs. 4104 crore in 1989-90 and Rs. 4169 crore in 1990-91. These are estimated to increase to Rs. 4858 crore in 1991-92. The performance in terms of rate of return on capital (after depreciation and interest) was negative, being (—) 16.4 per cent in 1989-90 and (—) 13.8 per cent in 1990-91.

The rate of return is estimated to deteriorate to (—) 14.8 per cent in 1991-92. The Electricity Supply Act, 1948 enjoins on the SEBs to earn a return of not less than 3 per cent by way of net surplus after providing for depreciation and interest. An important factor contributing to the high level of commercial losses of SEBs is the requirement to supply electricity to the rural/agricultural sector at lower tariff. The losses of SEBs shown above do not take into account the claims of SEBs for subsidies for rural electrification from the State Governments.

The performance of SRTCs was equally unsatisfactory. The commercial losses at Rs. 470 crore in 1990-91 (RE) were higher as compared with Rs. 359 crore in 1989-90. The losses are estimated at Rs. 362 crore for 1991-92. At the time of the formulation of Seventh Plan, it was envisaged that State Road Transport Corporations would generate internal resources of the order of Rs. 1789 crore after taking into account the gross yield of Rs. 2200 crore from fare revisions. Though the yield from fare revisions was around Rs. 2213 crore, which marginally exceeded the Seventh Plan target, the internal resources amounted to only Rs. 60 crore. This was mainly due to sharp increase in operational expenses.

Source: *Economic Survey*, 1991-92.

Loss Making Public Sector Undertakings

Of the 244 PSUs in the Central Sector, 98 are loss-making. Based on 1989-90 figures, the analysis shows that the 98 suffered a net loss of Rs. 1,959 crore during the year. Their cumulative losses add up to over Rs. 10,000 crore.

Of the 98 units, the Department of Public Enterprises (DPE) has picked up 58 and classified them as "chronically-sick". Of the chosen 58, eight units are not being referred to the Board of Industrial and Financial Reconstruction (BIFR) since they are deemed to be "enterprises rendering services". The eight includes for instance, the Delhi Transport Corporation, which with 41,000 workers has the dubious distinction for running up losses of Rs. 448 crore.

The 50 PSUs to be referred to the BIFR have a total of 3.40 lakh employees. The sick textile mills of the National Textiles Corporation (NTC) lead the way both in number employed and losses incurred. In these 50 PSUs, the annual loss per employee works out to Rs. 38,714 as of 1989-90. And the accumulated losses per employee is of the order of Rs. 2.09 lakh.

TABLE 33.1: Profile of Centre's Public Enterprises

	Units	1980-81	1983-84	1984-85	1985-86	1986-87	1987-88	1988-89	1989-90	1990-91
1	2	3	4	5	6	7	8	9	10	11
1. Number of running Public Enterprises	Number	163	201	207	211	214	211	226	233	236
2. Capital Employed	Rs. Crore	18207	29851	36382	42965	51835	55554	67629	84869	101797
3. Turnover	Rs. Crore	28635	47272	54784	62360	69088	81271	93137	106069	118355
4. Gross Margin (Profit before depreciation, interest and tax)	Rs. Crore	2401	5771	7386	8230	9897	11134	13438	16412	18510
5. Depreciation*	Rs. Crore	983	2205	2758	2983	3376	4150	4866	5790	7151
6. Gross profit before interest and tax	Rs. Crore	1418	3565	4628	5287	6521	6984	8572	10622	11359
7. Interest	Rs. Crore	1399	2086	2529	3115	3420	3595	4167	5329	7539
8. Net Profit before tax	Rs. Crore	19	1480	2099	2172	3101	3389	4405	5293	3820
9. Tax	Rs. Crore	222	1239	1190	1000	1330	1329	1411	1504	1452
10. Net Profit after tax	Rs. Crore	—203	240	909	1172	1771	2060	2994	3789	2368
11. Internal Resources generated (Gross)	Rs. Crore	1225	3278	4251	5068	6014	6947	8915	10774	11372
12. Net Profit (after tax) to capital employed	Per cent	—1.1	0.8	2.5	2.7	3.4	3.7	4.4	4.5	2.3

* Includes deferred revenue expenditure.

TABLE 33.2: Financial Results of Departmental Commercial Undertakings of State & UTs

(Rs.Crore)

	1985-86	1986-87	1987-88	1988-89	1989-90	1990-91 (R.E.)	1991-92 (B.E.)
1. Depart, Comm. Undertakings*							
(i) Forest	497.70	516.21	543.69	414.35	540.24	372.46	528.33
(ii) Power project	—75.04	—93.81	—116.40	—84.19	—34.83	—54.56	—42.98
(iii) Road	—25.65	—36.59	—110.76	—56.51	—93.21	—75.78	—64.10
(iv) Dairy Development	—99.29	—40.45	—43.91	—52.38	—106.99	—72.23	—77.18
(v) Industries	—14.10	16.46	—20.51	—10.09	159.66	—112.91	—40.04
(vi) Mines & Minerals	40.06	35.05	27.02	51.83	60.62	60.43	75.26
(vii) Irrigation Projects (Commercial)	—871.60	—1225.95	—1344.50	—1840.79	—1916.85	—2002.63	—2206.66
(viii) Multipurpose River Projects							
2. Profit of Profit making Undertakings	537.76	51.26	570.71	466.18	600.86	432.89	603.59
3. Loss of Loss making Undertakings	—1085.68	—1413.26	—1636.08	—2043.96	—2311.54	2318.11	—2430.96
4. Net Financial Results of Departmental Undertakings	—547.92	—862.00	—1065.37	—1577.78	—1710.68	—1885.22	—1827.37

* These do not include State Electricity Boards and State Road Transport Corporations.
[Profit (+)/Loss (—)]

TABLE 33.3: Some of the Chronically-sick PSUs

Sl. No.	Name	Accumulated Losses (Rs. in Crore)	No. of employees
1.	Indian Iron & Steel Company	601.71	36,226
2.	Fertiliser Corporation of India	1,217.02	10,975
3.	Hindustan Fertiliser Corporation	949.69	10,592
4.	Indian Drugs and Pharmaceuticals Ltd.	345.82	12,225
5.	Scooters India Ltd.	212.48	3,116
6.	Hindustan Shipyard Ltd.	273.20	7,282
7.	National Jute Manufactures Corporation	445.46	31,618
8.	NTC (Maharashtra North)	222.01	16,133

Source: *Hindustan Times*, January 20, 1992.

Public Enterprises Survey Report

The overall net profit of public enterprises fell sharply by about 38 per cent from Rs. 3,788.87 crore in 1989-90 to Rs. 2,367.74 crore in 1990-91, showing a decrease of Rs. 1421.13 crore even as the government took steps to bring about structural changes, in this vital sector.

The 1990-91 Public Enterprises Survey tabled in Parliament on March 5, 1992 attributed the fall to the low production to crude oil, rise in cost of wages and other inputs, the Gulf crisis and general poor economic situation during the year. The survey said the government had disinvested a part of the shares in 30 selected public sector undertakings (PSUs) in favour of public sector investment institutions and mutual funds.

The number of enterprises signing memoranda of understanding was expected to go up from 23 in 1990-91 to about 130 in 1992-93.

The production and services enterprises together contributed to the total decrease of Rs. 1421.13 crore in net profits.

Major Sectors

Petroleum, steel, coal and lignite, heavy engineering, transportation and telecommunication services were the major sectors contributing to the decreased profits.

On the other hand power, industrial development, and technological consultancy services and trading and marketing showed substantial favourable variation compared to the previous year.

A detailed analysis of the enterprise-wise profitability reveals that during 1990-91, 124 enterprises earned a net profit of Rs. 5431.42 crore compared with the net profit to Rs. 5750.47 crore earned by 131 enterprises during the previous year, showing a decline of Rs. 319.05 crore.

The losses of loss making enterprises have also increased. In 1989-90, 99 enterprises incurred a net loss of Rs. 1961.60 crore which went up to Rs. 3063.68 crore incurred by 109 enterprise during 1990-91.

Gross Profits

The survey said in absolute terms, the gross profits of public enterprises have shown an increase of Rs. 737.76 crore from Rs. 10,621 crore in 1989-90 to Rs.

11358.76 crore in 1990-91 — an increase of 6.94 per cent.

The survey said after taking into account the tax provision of Rs. 1,451.93 crore, the net profit for the year worked out to Rs. 2,367.74 crore against Rs. 3,788.87 crore for 1989-90, showing a decrease of Rs. 1,421.13 crore.

The survey, however, said that during the last ten years, there had been an impressive improvement in the quantum of gross margin which had progressively increased from Rs. 4,012 crore in 1981-82 to Rs. 18,510 crore in 1990-91, showing an increase of 361.35 per cent.

The ratio of gross margin to capital employed has, however, decreased from 18.29 per cent in 1981-82 to 18.20 per cent in 1990-91.

After providing for depreciation, amortisation and deferred revenue expenditure written off, the gross profit of the group as a whole also recorded impressive upward movement from Rs. 2,654 crore in 1981-82 to Rs. 11,359 crore in 1990-91, an increase of 327.93 per cent.

In terms of overall net profit, the survey said the picture was rather worse. From a net profit of Rs. 445 crore in 1981-82, the PSUs had recorded an overall net profit of only Rs. 2,368 crore in 1990-91.

Profitability

The survey said about 15 enterprises including the Steel Authority of India, the Indian Oil Corporation and the National Thermal Power Corporation registered an improvement in profitability from Rs. 1,399.16 crore in 1989-90 to Rs. 2,112.80 crore in 1990-91.

The Oil and Natural Gas Commission and the Indian Oil Corporation continued to occupy the first and second positions during 1990-91. The companies that have changed their positions included Indian Railway Finance Corporation, Shipping Corporation and Neyveli Lignite.

The survey said the top ten loss making enterprises accounted for 56.43 per cent of the total loss of Rs. 3,063.68 crore incurred by 109 enterprises from 1990-91.

During 1990-91, export earnings of public enterprises had improved by Rs. 730.03 crore — 11.47 per cent — compared to the previous year.

Source: *Times of India,* March 6, 1992

TABLE 33.4: Growth of Public Sector Undertakings

Year	No. of PSUs	Investment (in Rs. Crores)
1951	5	05
1956	21	81
1961	47	948
+		
1966	73	2,410
1969	84	3,897
1974	122	6,237
1979	169	15,534
1985	215	42,673
1989	238	85,628
1990	244	99,315

Source : *Indian Express*, October 22, 1991.

34

SPACE APPLICATIONS

The primary objective of the Indian space programmes is to establish operational space services in self-reliant manner. The main thrusts are satellite based telecommunication, TV broadcast and radio networking, and satellite based remote sensing for resources survey and management, environment monitoring and meteorological services.

The Indian space programme was formally organised in 1972 when the Government of India set-up the Space Commission and Department of Space (DOS) to promote the development and application of space technology and space science for the socio-economic benefit of the nation. DOS is responsible for implementing the policies framed by the Space Commission. The activities are carried out through the Indian Space Research Organisation (ISRO), the National Remote Sensing Agency (NRSA), the Physical Research Laboratory (PRL) and other agencies. DOS is also the nodal agency for the establishment of the National Natural Resources Management System (NNRMS) with the participation of various Central and State agencies.

ISRO, with its headquarters in Bangalore, has the following Centres/Units:

* Vikram Sarabhai Space Centre (VSSC), Thiruvananthapuram, specialising in launch vehicle technology
* ISRO Satellite Centre (ISAC), Bangalore, specialising in satellite technology
* Space Applications Centre (SAC), Ahmedabad, specialising in space applications technology
* SHAR Centre, Sriharikota (Andhra Pradesh), with facilities for supporting ISRO launch missions

TABLE 34.1: Areawise Distribution of Funds

(*Rs. in lakhs*)

	Actuals 1989-90	Revised Estimates 1990-91	Budget Estimates 1991-92
Direction and Administration	1050.82	1358.00	1423.00
INSAT Operational	14816.55	2498.00	6915.00
Pocket Development	14740.70	17028.00	23410.00
Satellite Development	13892.24	12150.00	12119.00
Space Applications	4507.35	5120.00	5533.00
Space Sciences	848.29	980.00	1530.00
Grand Total	39855.95	39136.00	50930.00

INDIAN NATIONAL SATELLITE (INSAT) SYSTEM

The Indian National Satellite (INSAT) system is a joint venture of the Department of Space (DOS), Department of Telecommunications (DOT), India

Meteorological Department (IMD), All India Radio (AIR) and Doordarshan. DOS is responsible for establishment and operation of the INSAT space segment. INSAT is a multipurpose operational satellite system for domestic telecommunications, meteorological observation and data relay, nationwide direct satellite TV broadcasting to augmented community TV receivers in rural and remote areas and nationwide TV programmes distribution for rebroadcasting through terrestrial transmitters.

The first generation INSAT-1 satellites have the following capabilities.

* Twelve national coverage telecommunications (Fixed Satellite Service — FSS transponders of 36 MHz bandwidth each operating in 5935-6425 MHz (earth to satellite) and 3710-4200 MHz (satellite to earth) frequency bands, with 32 dBW (min) End of Life (EOL) effective isotropic radiated powered (eirp) over the primary coverage area.
* Two high power national coverage TV broadcast (Broadcast Satellite Service — BSS) transponders operating in 5855-5935 MHz (earth to satellite) and 2555-2635 MHz (satellite to earth) frequency bands, each capable of handling one direct broadcast (community reception) TV channel and five low level carriers for services like radio programme distribution, disaster warning, etc. with a 42 dBW (min) EOL eirp over the primary coverage area. These transponders also support the dissemination of disaster warning and standards time and frequency signals.
* A Very High Resolution Radiometer (VHRR) for meteorological earth imaging in visible (0.55-0.75 micrometre) and infrared (10.5-12.5 micrometre) band, with resolutions of 2.75 km and 11 km respectively, having half hourly full earth coverage and sector scan capability.
* A data relay transponder having global receive coverage with a 402.75 MHz earth to satellite link for relay of meteorological, hydrological and oceanographic data from unattended land and ocean based automatic data collection cum-transmission platforms.

INSAT-1B

INSAT-1B, launched in August 1983, completed its designed life of seven years in August 1990. It is located at 74 degree East longitude. All the four service payloads on board the satellite, except for one of the twelve FSS C-band transponder channels, are still operating satisfactorily. The satellite is now used without controlling the inclination and it is serving as a standby for INSAT-1D.

INSAT-1C

INSAT-1C, launched on July 22, 1988 on board the European Ariane vehicle, lost earth lock on November 22, 1989 and is inoperable now.

INSAT-1D

INSAT-1D is the last satellite of first generation INSAT-1 series. It slightly differs from the other satellites of this series, in that it has higher battery capacity and 3:2 redundancy for output devices (TWTs) of CXC transponder channels 11 and 12. INSAT-1D was launched on June 12, 1990 on board the US Delta launch vehicle. The orbit raising operations were successfully carried out from the

Master Control Facility (MCF) at Hassan in Karnataka. INSAT-1D commenced operational services on July 17, 1990 after a series of checkout and commissioning tests.

INSAT-2

The INSAT-1 satellites are to be gradually replaced by indigenously developed second generation INSAT-2 satellites. Two INSAT-2 test satellites, INSAT-2A and 2B, will be launched during 1991-92 and 1992-93 respectively to demonstrate and flight test the indigenous design and engineering of the satellites. Launch services agreements have already been signed with Arianespace of Europe for the launch of both the satellites.

The INSAT-2 space segment and the associated spacecraft configuration were defined under the umbrella of the interministerial INSAT Coordination Committee (ICC) based on the requirements for satellite services during 1990s as envisaged by the user agencies, namely, DOT, IMD, AIR and Doordarshan. The INSAT-2 space segment will have three multipurpose satellites, two of them collocated at the primary orbital position and one at the major path orbital position. The two collocated satellites at the primary orbital position will be maintained in the orbit so as to appear as a single large capacity spacecraft in terms of their total FSS in conventional and upper extended C-band using orthogonal polarisation.

INSAT-2 satellites will have enhanced capabilities and consequently are about 50 per cent heavier than INSAT-1. Each of the INSAT-2 satellites in the three-spacecraft space segment will have 18 FSS transponders (12 in normal C-band and 6 in extended C-band) with a capability to provide 32 dBW Edge of Coverage (EOC) eirp from 16 transponders for communication and television distribution services and 34 dBW from 2 high power transponders for specialised telecommunication requirements. For BSS, INSAT-2 will use two high power (42 dBW eirp) S-band transponders. INSAT-2 has a VHRR with 2 km resolution in the visible and 8 km resolution in the infrared band for meteorological applications. It also has a Data Relay Transponder (DRT) with global receive coverage in UHF band for receiving meteorological, hydrological and oceanographic data from unattended land and ocean based platforms and transmit them to a central facility. INSAT-2 also carries a payload for Satellite Aided Search and Rescue (SAS&R) mission which is an addition to the INSAT system. This payload will provide instantaneous emergency alert capability in this part of the world and is an important contribution to the international satellite aided search and rescue programme.

INSAT-2 weighs about 1,900 kg at lift-off and about 860 kg after positioning in geosynchronous orbit. It measures about 23 m with the fully deployed solar array and solar sail. The solar array generates a minimum power of 1,180 W at the End of Life (EOL). The array consists of three full panels and two half panels and, unlike in INSAT-1, is configured in such a way as to avoid partial deployment during the transfer orbit. The satellite has two 1.77 m diameter deployable antennae on the east and west faces for providing C-band and S-band transmit function. Another 0.9m diameter fixed antenna on the earth viewing face is provided for all 6 GHz receive and VHRR, DRT and SAS&R data transmit functions. Thus the spacecraft configuration allows a greater mission function savings in case of antenna deployment anomalies. To provide improved coverage for TTC during on-orbit phase a global horn is provided apart from the TTC omni antenna.

During the year, the Structural Model (SM) of the INSAT-2 spacecraft, simulating all mechanical elements of the final flight configuration but with mechanical dummies (simulating mass and moment of inertia) of electronic packages, was integrated and subjected to qualification level sinusoidal vibration tests in all the three axes and qualification level acoustic environment tests. Subsequently, all the deployment mechanisms have been successfully tested. Based on the SM tests, clearance for the final assembly of the flight structure was given to Hindustan Aeronautics Limited (HAL), the main contractor for the structure. The flight structure has since been delivered.

The Electrical Thermal Model (ETM) of the spacecraft, simulating all the electrical packages of the flight model but using commercial parts instead of space qualified parts, was integrated during the year and has undergone extensive integrated spacecraft level tests. The model has also undergone thermal and thermovacuum tests in the 4m diameter thermovacuum chamber at ISAC simulating space thermal and vacuum environment for about one month. Minor modifications are to be made on some units based on the results of these tests. Most of the flight electronic packages have already been fabricated and are in the final stages of assembly and testing. The integration of the flight model has started in January 1991.

All the necessary test and operation facilities, including the Large Space Simulation Chamber (LSSC) for solar simulation tests on the flight model and augmentation of Master Control Facility (MCF) at Hassan, are in the final phases of commissioning.

INSAT-2 Operational Spacecraft

In order to establish the operational INSAT-2 space segment in the time frame 1993-95, using one of the test satellites (INSAT-2A or 2B) and operational satellites, fabrication of three operation satellites under INSAT-2 series, namely, INSAT-2C, 2D and 2E was approved in May 1990. Inclusion of a Ku-band payload in INSAT-2C has also been envisaged in place of the meteorological payload depending upon the functioning of INSAT-2A and 2B satellites at that point of time.

INSAT-3

The definition of the third generation INSAT spacecraft (INSAT-3) has been initiated. The user departments have projected their requirements in terms of space segment capacity which are now being analysed.

INSAT Master Control Facility (MCF)

The performance of the INSAT-MCF at Hassan is satisfactory. MCF availability for INSAT-1B and 1C TTC operation has been cent per cent.

MCF has been augmented for INSAT-2 with an additional 11 m diameter limited steerability antenna and associated earth station equipment, Satellite Control Centre (SCC) and computer facilities, civil works, etc. As per the contract, the 11 m diameter antenna, all C-band equipment, tracking receiver, etc, were provided by Electronic Corporation of Indian Limited (ECIL) on a turnkey basis. The equipments in the extended C-band have been built inhouse. Both the 11 m diameter antennae for INSAT-2 programme (one with limited steerability) have been installed. These antennae provided support during INSAT-1D launch also. The total complement of antennae now available at MCF is as follows.

* Two 14 m diametre fully steerable antennae
* Two 11 m diameter antennae (one with limited steerability)
* One 7.5 m diameter limited steerability antenna
* One 4.5 m diameter antenna

INSAT Utilisation

As of November 1, 1990 a total of 105 telecommunication terminals of various sizes and capabilities (excluding NICNET microterminals) were operating in the INSAT telecommunication network providing 4,366 two-way speech circuits or equivalent over 120 routes. These include, among others, 65 fixed, 17 transportable and 23 captive networks (ONGC, ITI, NFL, Master Earth Stations of NICNET and Government). Use of satellite capacity on Madras-New Delhi route by *The Hindu* newspaper for facsimile transmission of fully composed pages for printing of its Delhi edition has continued. Over 100 additional earth stations, including 50 for Rural Telegraphy Networks (SBRTN) pilot project in the north-eastern region, are under various stages of implementation in the DOT network. In the National Informatics Centre Network (NICNET), at present, over 450 microterminals are operating and the plan is to eventually have one NICNET microterminal in every district headquarters. Various other networks for dedicated use are under implementation. Under the Remote Area Business Message Network (RABMN) a total demand for 927 microstations has been registered and 41 micro-earth stations supplied.

As of September 30, 1990 INSAT-1D satellite has been commanded to give 958 meteorological images — 911 full earth and 47 sector scans. The Meteorological Data Utilisation Centre (MDUC) of IMD processes and disseminates the INSAT-1 meteorological images. Upper winds, sea surface temperature and precipitation index data products are regularly generated by MDUC/IMD. The 0600 hours GMT VHRR image-derived wind data are regularly put on the Global Telecommunications System (GTS) of the World Meteorological Organisation (WMO). The 0300 hours GMT full disk IR picture are being transmitted as radio facsimile broadcast every day for reception in the neighbouring countries.

Till September 30, 1990 INSAT-1B provided 30,826 meteorological images — 30,707 full earth and 119 sector scans. Now in its eighth year of satisfactory operation, INSAT-1B VHRR is one of the very few geostationary VHRR instruments to have completed long term satisfactory space operation without exercise of any redundancy. The INSAT, VHRR imageries are regularly used on Doordarshan's night news coverage and by newspapers for weather reporting. At present, repetitive and synoptic weather systems observations over the Indian Ocean from geostationary orbit are available only from the INSAT system.

The INSAT-1 VHRR data is now available in near realtime at 22 Secondary

Data Utilisation Centres (SDUCs) in various parts of the country. Two of these are provided with processed data over a CXs direct satellite retransmission facility. With the commissioning of this direct satellite retransmission facility, which also uses INSAT-1, it is now possible to provide SDUC type of data at any location in the country irrespective of its distance from Delhi (MDUC/IMD) and availability of point-to-point terrestrial transmission circuits. After INSAT-2 launch, it will be necessary to process meteorological data from both satellites simultaneously in view of the overlapping life spans of INSAT-1 and INSAT-2. The INSAT-2 VHRR data processing facility at MDUC/IMD has been defined and the implementation of the earth station segment of this facility has been taken up. The earth station which will work in the extended C-band is expected to be completed in 1991.

100 Data Collection Platforms (DCPs) have been installed. DCP data are processed and disseminated by MDUC/IMD. One of the INSAT DCPs is deployed at the Indian base station, Schiramacher Hills, Antarctica. The Central Water Commission (CWC) has deployed 14 DCPs in the Yamuna catchment area for flood forecasting. DCP service is being provided by INSAT-1B as the Data Relay Transponder in INSAT-1D is not operational.

100 Disaster Warning System (DWS) receivers have been installed in selected cyclone-prone coastal areas of Andhra Pradesh and Tamil Nadu with DWS upline from Madras. DWS receivers are selectively addressable. IMD is also planning deployment of additional units of receivers in other cyclone-prone coastal areas of the country. The cyclone that hit the Andhra coast on May 9, 1990 was monitored using VHRR imageries and the warnings sent through the DWS were quite effective in taking precautionary measures.

One of the two high power S-band transponder channels on board INSAT-1D is used by Doordarshan for the national TV channel. The second S-band channel is earmarked for regional TV services. The S-band transponders are also supporting a six channel radio networking service, DWS standard time and frequency signal dissemination and a direct satellite retransmission facility for processed INSAT meteorological (VHRR) images.

The C-band transponders on board INSAT-1D and the leased transponders provide regional networking services. Regional service in Karnataka was started on November 1, 1990. Regional networking services are expected to start shortly in Orissa, Gujarat and the north-eastern States.

There are at present 44 high power transmitters, ten 1 kW transmitters, 373 low power transmitters, 71 unattended very low power transmitters and 18 TV transposers in the INSAT TV network. The TV transmitters are provided with S-band TV receive-only and C-band TV receive-only facility for reception of national channel as well as regional network programmes besides providing a back-up for the national programme. The national programme is transmitted both in S-band and C-band using leased transponders. There are about 35,000 direct reception TV sets in the country.

It is now possible to cover important events in any part of the country using transportable earth stations. Five such transportable TV uplinking earth stations are available.

The radio networking service through INSAT provides reliable, high fidelity, six-channel national/regional feeds for retransmission by AIR stations. At present all the 102 intended centres of AIR have been equipped with five channel S-band receive terminals in the INSAT radio network. In addition to a five-channel Radio Net-working (RN) uplink capability from Delhi, single channel uplinking capabilities are also available from Calcutta, Bombay and Madras. Twelve more uplinking stations are being added. AIR is adding certain captive transportable RN uplinking terminals also. The utilisation of the five RN channels is about 2,400 hours per month. A sixth radio networking channel, for programme feed to the national service channel radio transmitter, at Nagpur has been operational for over a year now. This channel supports programme feeds to other radio transmitters as and when they get introduced in the national service channel network. It will also be used later for synchronisation of transmitters in the national channel network.

A Standard Time and Frequency Signal Dissemination Service (STFSDS) using a radio networking such as CXS carrier on INSAT-1, commissioned by National Physical Laboratory (NPL), New Delhi, is available round the clock in a broadcast mode in the S-band downlink frequency and is receivable on a system consisting of a 2.44 m diameter chicken mesh antenna, a front end converter, FM demodulator and a microprocessor controlled signal decoder.

The Press Trust of India (PTI) has implemented a project to provide its news and information services at higher speed and increased volume and variety directly to a wide range of media and other users across the country by utilising the broadcast facilities of INSAT-1 satellite. The project will utilise a radio networking type channel on one of the broadcast (CXS) transponders. The project is operational with 13 terminals (12 of PTI and 1 shared with AIR). The main features of the project are:

* time division and frequency division multiplexing and demultimplexing of news and newsphoto carrying communication channel to enable PTI to simultaneously broadcast its English, Hindi and other Indian languages and commercial news services, Newsscan and Comscan (video text) and other services as well as its newsphoto service directly to media and other users all over the country as required.
* dynamic time-sharing of the RN channel by multiple uplinks which will enable PTI to transmit its news and newsphoto services simultaneously from its four main news bureaux at New Delhi, Calcutta, Bombay and Madras.
* sharing of All India Radio and Doordarshan direct reception facilities for parallel reception of PTI news services along with their own signals.

Development of Satellite News Gathering (SNG) service in CXS band and CXC band using ultra portable vehicle mounted terminals for TV/Radio has been initiated.

Lease of Transponders

As a back-up to INSAT system two transponders of INTELSAT spacecraft are available on lease. To further augment and back up INSAT space segment capacity, twelve C-band transponders are on lease from ARABSAT-1B spacecraft located at 26 degree East longitude for two years effective from October 1, 1989. Also, one transponder was leased from INTERSPUTNIK Statsionar-13 satellite located at 80 degree East longitude for a period of nine months from December 1989 to end August 1990 to provide back-up for national TV services. The Delhi Earth Station (DES) has been used extensively to uplink Doordarshan TV programmes to INTELSAT and Statsionar-13 satellites.

Satellite Aided Search and Rescue Programme

India has signed an agreement with the international COSPAS-SARSAT council for the use of systems and operation of Local User Terminals (LUT). The first LUT and the Mission Control Centre (MCC) at Bangalore were established in 1989, collected with ISTRAC station. The second LUT at Lucknow has been commissioned during the year. A 406 MHz Satellite Aided Search and Rescue (SAS& R) payload is being incorporated on broad INSAT-2. They are funded by the participating agencies, namely, Services, Shipping, Civil Aviation and Coast Guard.

The establishment of LUT and MCC as a part of COSPAS-SARSAT network is a significant milestone in the Indian satellite aided search and rescue programme. The Indian MCC/LUT provide realtime coverage to a large part of the Indian Ocean area covering Bangladesh, Indonesia, Kenya, Malaysia, Maldives, Singapore, Somalia, Sri Lanka, Tanzania and Thailand.

The Indian MCC operations are routed through National Airport Authority (NAA) of India which has Rescue Coordination Centres (RCC) at Bombay, Calcutta, Delhi and Madras. The search and rescue activities are carried out by Coast Guard, Navy and Air Force and coordinated by RCCs. The MCC is linked with the RCCs through automatic teletext mode. As an alternative the MCC is also being provided with the Aeronautical Fixed Telecommunication Network (AFTN) linkage with the Indian RCCs and other international RCCs and MCCs.

India is regularly taking part in the COSPAS-SARSAT operations, technical working groups and coordinating committee meetings to ensue that the Indian inputs are reflected properly in the procedures under evolution.

Radio Determination, Navigation and Mobile Satellite Communication Services

ISRO has an active mobile satellite communication programme. An Inter Agency Steering Committee (IASC) oversees the development of this programmes under which ISRO is developing INMARSAT Standard-C terminal with the involvement of electronic industries. The primary function of the terminal is text and data transmission to and from ships/remote locations and terrestrial subscribes through a variety of public networks. The terminal development is in an advanced stage.

Under IASC on Radio Determination Satellite Services (RDSS) and Mobile Satellite Services (MSS), a task team was constituted to laydown specifications and standards for development of Global Positioning System (GPS) receiver in India. ISRO has taken up the development of a sequential GPS receiver capable of receiving the Coarse Acquisition code from the US GPS satellites meant for satellite aided navigation globally. Development of this GPS receiver is in an advanced stage.

To estimate the requirements of different sectors in India for Land Mobile Satellite Services (LMSS) and to identify the space segment requirements for meeting the potential demand in a phased manner, a task team under the aegis of the IASC has been constituted. This team will work out the details of possible LMSS demonstrations in India.

Frequency Management

The frequency management in ISRO ensures that the frequencies used by the space programme in the country follow the guidelines set out at the national and international levels. It also enables to find ways and means for overcoming technical compatibility problems. The frequency management office of ISRO projects the frequency requirements to the national agency responsible for frequency allocation and carries out suitable coordination activities required for national and international frequency clearance in consultation with ISRO Centres and Units.

During the year, actions have been initiated for registration of frequencies for IRS-1C and INSAT-2 Ku-band operations. Protection of operations of the space projects and programmes from intersystem interference point of view is an important activity. The frequency management activities include participation in the work of International Telecommunication Union (ITU/CCIR) study groups and other international fora such as Space Frequency Coordination Group (SFCG).

Preparations in regard to the WARC-1992 dealing with the Mobile Satellite Services frequency allocations, Sound Broadcasting Satellite Services frequency allocation, etc, are going on.

National Natural Resources Management System (NNRMS)

The Department of Space, as the nodal agency for establishment of the National Natural Resources Management System (NNRMS), is responsible for ensuring availability of remote sensing data to the users, integration of remotely sensed data with conventional data through collaborative studies, establishment of infrastructure, manpower training and conducting application studies towards evolving a National (Natural) Resources Information System for the country.

Space Segment

The first indigenous operational Indian Remote Sensing Satellite, IRS-1A, completes three years of successful operation on March 17, 1991. The state-of-the-art satellite has become the mainstay of NNRMS. IRS-1A has covered the entire country about fifty times and provided about three lakh imageries.

The 975 kg satellite carries two types of cameras, Linear Imaging Self-scanning Sensors, LISS-I and LISS-II, working in four spectral bands and with spatial resolutions of 72.5 m and 36.25 m respectively. LISS-I provides a swath of 148 km and the two LISS-II cameras provide a composite swath of 145 km. The satellite incorporates advanced technologies like driven deployable sun tracking solar panels, three-axis body stabilisation using dry tuned gyros and reaction wheels, scanning earth sensors and reaction control system, high bit rate image transmission, automatic payload operation, etc. It is maintained in the specified 904 km polar sunsynchronous orbit through a set of on-orbit manoeuvers at regular intervals. The satellite returns to its original orbital trace every 22 days enabling repeated collection of data over the same place and at the same local time.

The second satellite in the IRS series, IRS-1B, identical to IRS-1A, is scheduled for launch by the middle of 1991.

On August 29, 1991 India's second remote sensing satellite, IRS-1B, shot into space on Soviet rocket notching its eighth success in space in 16 years.

The indigenously designed state-of-the-art remote sensing satellite, was successfully launched from Baikonur cosmodrome in the Soviet Union on Soviet rocket "Vostok" at 9.48 a.m. Moscow time (12.18 p.m. IST).

It was the fifth launch of an Indian satellite from the Soviet Union.

The second generation IRS satellites, namely, IRS-1C and 1D, will have better spatial and spectral resolutions, more frequent revisits, stereo viewing and on-board data recording facility. IRS-1C and 1D sensors will have spatial resolutions of 20 m in multispectral bands and better than 10 m in the panchromatic band. A new sensor in the short wave infrared band with a spatial resolution of 70 m and a wide field sensor with 180 m spatial resolution and a swath of 770 km are also included for vegetation monitoring. IRS-1C and IRS-1D are scheduled for launch during 1993-94 and 1996-97 respectively.

Ground Segment

The Spacecraft Control Centre (SCC) at Bangalore is responsible for monitoring and control, mission analysis, operations planning and tracking network coordination for IRS. The ground stations at Lucknow, Mauritius and Weilheim in Germany, support SCC in the mission management. Payload operations are carried out on a routine basis during day time passes and the payload calibration activities are carried out once in every repetitivity cycle.

Data Reception, Processing and Dissemination

The NRSA data reception station at Shadnagar near Hyderabad receives data from IRS-1A both in S-band and X-band. The station has provisions for quick-look display of data from any one of the selected spectral bands of any of the selected imaging sensors.

IRS-1 A data products generation and dissemination is carried out both from NRSA, Hyderabad, and SAC, Ahmedabad. Photographic and digital data products at various levels are generated routinely and supplied to the users.

During the year NRSA continued to receive, process and disseminate data from the US Landsat and French SPOT and METSAT satellites besides IRS-1A. An integrated information management system has been developed by NRSA to efficiently manage the acquisition, archival, processing and dissemination of remote sensing data and to optimally utilise the data processing capability. About three lakh imageries from IRS-1A, collected over 50 cycles, are now available in the archive. NRSA Data Centre (NDC) has supplied around 14 thousand data products during the year (73 per cent from IRS-1A, 11 per cent from Landsat, 9 per cent from SPOT and 7 per cent from METSAT). The data products are supplied in the form of floppies and cartridge tapes, apart from photo products and computer compatible tapes. The major users of the data include Geological Survey of India, Central Ground Water Board, Oil and Natural Gas Commission, Atomic Minerals Division, Forest Survey of India, National Bureau of Soil Survey and Land Use Planning, Survey of India, Department of Ocean Development, Department of Agriculture and Co-operation, Wasteland Development Board, Department of Environment, State remote sensing application centres and State Departments of geology, ground water and agriculture, town planning and irrigation.

The NRSA data reception station has been augmented for receiving data from IRS-1B. The raw data archival system and realtime quick-look system are also being augmented to process data simultaneously from IRS-1A and 1B. Augmentation of the station for acquiring higher resolution data from IRS-1C/1D has commenced and preliminary design and system engineering have been completed.

Aerial remote sensing operations by NRSA continued during the year for ground truth collection and to supplement satellite data. 138 hours of flying had been logged till November 1990. An additional Beechcraft has been procured during the year and will join the existing fleet comprising an Avro, a Dakota and a Beechcraft.

Microwave Remote Sensing

The Avro aircraft of NRSA has been modified for installation of Side Looking Airborne Radar (SLAR) for carrying out snow hydrology studies over Kulu-Manali valley. The flights were completed and SLAR data products successfully generated.

The dissemination of Synthetic Aperture Radar (SAR) data acquired over Andaman and Nicobar, Cauvery and Godavari basins and Orissa coast (using X-band SAR system during October 1988) has been completed. The data are being analysed for eleven projects in ocean application, geology, soil moisture, crop type discrimination, forestry, landuse and vegetation studies, textural parametres for land cover, human settlement, and irrigation command inventory. The X-band air borne SAR data covering parts of West Godavari district has also been analysed.

Ground based scatterometer, mounted on a cherry picker, has been developed for collecting data under field conditions. An experiment is being conducted for collection of data on different soil moisture conditions and paddy crop during its growth cycle.

The Landsat/SPOT data reception system at NRSA is being augmented to receive SAR payload data from the European ERS-1 satellite.

Remote Sensing Applications

The task force on disaster management and landuse, with representatives from various user agencies/departments, has deliberated in detail on the application of space technology towards rural development and proposed a number of application projects for ground water development, wasteland reclamation, landuse/land cover mapping for agro-climatic zonal planning, fisheries development, flood monitoring and management, disaster warning system, etc. Specific pilot project on wasteland reclamation, integrated planning, development of ground water and marine fisheries have been identified.

Several application areas with high visibility and encouraging results have been enlarged to national level mission project during the year. These include ground water potential zone mapping, large area crop acreage and yield estimation, urban sprawl mapping, landuse mapping, saline/alkaline soil mapping, drought monitoring, flood mapping, wasteland mapping, geological mapping and integrated land and water resources studies.

The highlights of activities in remote sensing applications in various areas are as follows:

Agriculture

* Landuse/Land Cover Mapping for Agro-climatic Zonal Planning

A nationwise project on landuse/land cover mapping for generation of operational plans for 15-agro-climatic zones of India has been taken up. Interpreted thematic maps on 1:2,50,000 scale using IRS data for 15 agro-climatic zones covering 442 districts are being prepared. Of these, 274 districts will be visually interpreted and the remaining,digitally. The work is being carried out in 26 work centres under the overall coordination of NRSA. 184 final maps have been already generated.

* Drought Monitoring

Under the National Agricultural Drought Assessment Monitoring System (N-ADAMS), biweekly drought bulletins were issued during 1989 Kharif season for 246 districts in Andhra Pradesh, Gujarat, Haryana, Karnataka, Madhya Pradesh, Maharashtra, Orissa, Rajasthan, Tamil Nadu and Uttar Pradesh. Messages on drought occurrence are also sent to affected districts.

* Integrated Study to Combat Drought

A pilot project for integrated drought management to evolve a permanent solution through a set of development activities in agriculture, water management and forest development has been taken up in 18 districts in 13 States. DOS is providing managerial and technical guidance while the State remote sensing centres are executing the project. Thematic maps in the areas of soils, landuse, forest cover, wasteland, ground and surface water are being prepared using IRS data on 1:50,000 scale by the work centres in conjunction with the socio-economic data, ground truth, etc. The All India Soil and Landuse Survey (AIS&LUS) of the Ministry of Agriculture is assisting the project by carrying out soil survey for 12 districts. The National Bureau of Soil Survey and Landuse Planning (NBSS&LUP) of Indian Council of Agricultural Research (ICAR) and State centres are carrying out soil mapping for the remaining six districts.

* Saline/Alkaline Soil Mapping

Preliminary digital analysis and visual interpretation of Ahmedabad district in Gujarat has been completed and final digital analysis on 1:50,000 scale is in progress. Saline/alkaline soil maps of Punjab, Haryana and Uttar Pradesh on a 1:2,50,000 scale have been prepared. Ground truth data collection of parts of Rajasthan and Bihar and chemical analysis of soil samples have been completed. Final soil maps of parts of Mahanadi delta and adjacent areas in Orissa have been prepared on 1:2,50,000 scale. Soil erosion maps on 1;2,50,000 scale and 1:50,000 scale have been prepared for parts of Manipur, Tripura and Arunachal Pradesh.

* Crop Acreage and Production Estimation

A project, jointly with the Department of Agriculture and Co-operation, has been taken up for operationalisation of crop acreage and production estimation procedures using remotely sensed data. Preharvest acreage estimates have been made for wheat in Punjab, Haryana and parts of Uttar Pradesh, Madhya Pradesh and Rajasthan and for rice in Orissa and Tamil Nadu. Similar studies for sorghum in central Maharashtra and for mustard in parts of Rajasthan and Gujarat have also been carried out using IRS data. Districtwise yield forecasts for Punjab and Haryana have been made. Growth profiles for wheat have been generated using NOAA data and different profile parameters were related to yield. Use of middle IR band data to improve yield prediction has been attempted in parts of Karnal test sites.

A project on cotton acreage estimation and condition assessment has been initiated for the Ministry of Textiles covering major cotton growing districts of Maharashtra, Punjab, Haryana, Madhya Pradesh, Andhra Pradesh and Gujarat. Acreage estimation has been completed for four districts each in Punjab and Maharashtra. A data base is being generated for condition assessment.

* Fisheries Development

A project has been taken up for mapping for coastal landuse and inland water bodies for aquaculture development. Coastal landuse maps have been prepared for West Bengal, Orissa and Andhra Pradesh on 1:50,000 scale for brackish water. Mapping of surface water bodies on 1:2,50,000 scale has been taken up for Bihar, Orissa, Andhra Pradesh, Assam, Uttar Pradesh and West Bengal.

Forest and Environment

* Forest Type

Methodology developed to estimate vegetation parameters in teak plantations at Yellapur in Karnataka has been extended to teak plantations in parts of Mercara, Hunsur and Mysore forest divisions of Karnataka. The parametres amenable to remote sensing technique have been identified in dry deciduous forests and regression equations are being developed.

* Wildlife Habitat

Impact of floods during August 1990 in the Kaziranga national park was studied using multidate satellite data. It is observed that the extent of water bodies inside the park increased by a factor of 1.6 between October 1984 and May 1989. A data based on land cover, terrain and water resources has been prepared using 0.5 km grid for Kanha national park in Madhya Pradesh.

* Grassland Mapping

Grassland mapping for 2,000 square km area of Banni region in Rajasthan has been taken up and analysis of satellite data of 1980 and 1988 has shown significant increase in salinity and prosopis juliflora growth.

* Environmental Impact of Mining and Thermal Power Complexes

A project for studying environmental impact in various test sites for mining has been taken up. In Dehra Dun-Mussoorie limestone mine belt, it is found that forest area has dwindled by 2.8 square km between 1972 and 1988. Some of the river courses have shown variation due to mining wastes and the debris brought down by landslides. In case of thermal power stations, the impact has been studied within a radius of 16 km from the mid-point of power plants. In Korba, forest area has been reduced by about 25 per cent, mainly near the coal mines between 1972 and 1989. It is seen that the coal mining and fly-ash deposition have adversely affected about 537 square km area during the same period. In Talcher, forest area has decreased by 34 per cent between 1975 and 1989. River Brahmani is found to be highly polluted as effluents from the industries are being discharged into it and these could be seen well beyond a distance of 25 km.

Water Resources

* National Drinking Water Mission

District-wise hydro-geomorphological maps have been prepared for the entire country on 1:2,50,000 scale based on visual interpretation of satellite imageries. The task was completed on schedule in March 1990. An atlas of hydro-geomorphological maps of India, based on the inputs from participating organisations was handed over to Department of Rural Development, the nodal agency for National Drinking Water Mission, in July 1990.

Detailed mapping of Jaisalmer and Bikaner districts of Rajasthan on 1:50,000 scale to identify ground water prospective zones has been initiated. 24 base maps have already been prepared and preliminary interpretation completed for 22 maps.

* Flood Mapping

The estimation of crop area damaged during the 1989 floods in Brahmaputra river and their value assessment have been made using multi-date satellite data and ground based data. Flood risk zone maps for Kosi and Brahmaputra rivers have been prepared using satellite data taking into account the floods during the past few years. Flood control works like embankments and spurs along Kosi river have been mapped on 1:50,000 scale for Ganga Flood Control Commission. Data pertaining to Andhra Pradesh cyclone in June 1990 have been analysed and interpreted maps prepared showing flood affected areas.

As a part of the Subansiri watershed study, the investigation on migration of channels has been taken up in parts of Brahmaputra basin. Channel pattern changes have been identified in the Subansiri river basin through visual analysis of multidate satellite data.

* Snow Mapping

Development of simulation model for predicting short term snow-melt run-off in Beas basin is in progress. A data base has been created for all the basins in western and central Himalayan region for development of run-off models. Operational procedure for snow mapping has been finalised.

Snow covered area in Sutlej basin was monitored during the 1989-90 snowfall season and the snow-melt run-off forecast of Sutlej basin into Bhakra reservoir has been found to be accurate upto two per cent of the actual flow. Analysis of NOAA data to determine maximum seasonal snow-melt for forecasting inflows into Bhakra reservoir from Sutlej river has been completed.

* Glaciers

Glacier mapping for Uttar Pradesh, Sikkim and Arunachal Pradesh was completed on 1:2,50,000 scale with details on accumulation/ablation area, ice/basin divide, snow equalisation line, glacier lakes, etc. A detailed inventory of Himachal Pradesh indicated 125 glaciers covering an area of 1896 square km with a water equivalent of 165 cubic km. Inventory in Sikkim indicated 22 glaciers covering an area of 426 square km and six glacier-dammed lakes which have caused catastrophic floods in Tista valley in the past.

Land Use

* Urban Sprawl

Urban landuse mapping on 1:50,000 scale for Bombay Metropolitan Region Development Authority (BMRDA), Calcutta Metropolitan Development Authority and Ahmedabad Urban Development Authority has been completed. Mapping on 1:25,000 scale for urban complexes of Bombay, Calcutta and Ahmedabad has been completed. Urban sprawl mapping of Bombay, Calcutta and Ahmedabad and zoning map of BMRDA for regional planning purpose have also been made. Hydro-geomorphological and construction material mapping for Bombay metropolitan region on 1:50,000 scale has been carried out.

Urban sprawl map, urban landuse map and urban landuse zoning map for Madras and its environs on 1:50,000 scale, along with area estimates, have been prepared and an atlas, "Urban Sprawl of Madras", generated. Interpretation and preparation of urban landuse maps for Hyderabad, Delhi, Lucknow and Jaipur have been completed. Interpretation work for mapping of urban sprawl of Nagpur and Bangalore has been taken up.

* Wasteland Mapping for Critically Affected Districts

The national wasteland mapping project covering 146 districts had been completed in the previous years. A project proposal for the next phase, submitted to National Wasteland Development Board (NWDB), envisages mapping in 84 districts in 17 States having five to 15 per cent wasteland immediately and later 34 border districts with wasteland in excess of more than 15 per cent area. The mapping will be carried out using IRS data on 1:50,000 scale.

Meteorology and Oceanography

* Ocean Related Applications

A national remote sensing programme for ocean related applications, funded by the Department of Ocean Development (DOD), has been taken up. The programme, planned for three years starting from July 1990, is focused on four independent projects for specific tasks. NRSA is the focal agency for the entire programme.

The four projects are the following: (i) ocean related remote sensing applications addressing Sea Surface Temperature (SST) retrieval and dissemination, SST applications (eddies and heat budget), coastal zone mapping and management, microwave applications for wind/wave parameters as well as for natural wave, coastal bathymetry, etc., (ii) national ocean information system covering development of thematic information system on remotely sensed data, physical/chemical oceanographic data, biological oceanography data and coastal zone management data, (iii) sea truth collection for remote sensing applications, and (iv) ocean modelling studies for understanding and prediction of ocean processes as well as their interaction with the climate.

The first two projects will be carried out with the involvement of National Institute of Oceanography (NIO), Central Marine Fisheries Research Institute (CMFRI), Orissa State Remote Sensing Applications Centre (OSRSAC) and Institute of Ocean Management of Anna University while the third project will be carried out by NIO and concerned agencies and the ocean modelling project will be carried out by National Aeronautical Laboratory (NAL) and other academic institutions. Operational dissemination of SST maps and photo products is planned shortly.

* Climate/Geosphere-Biosphere Studies

Using a simple two-dimensional model, role of clouds in greenhouse warming process has been studied and it is found that cloud albedo produces a significant perturbation in the greenhouse warming. Radiative heating rate profile of the atmospheric layers has been estimated from satellite data and radiation transfer theory. Determination of marine geoid from satellite altimeter data has been taken up. Using a matched filter technique with the GEOSAT altimeter data, Arabian seamounts have been detected.

* Retrieval of Meteorological and Oceanographic Parameters

The SST data from NOAA have been determined to an accuracy of $\pm$ 0.75 K. In a joint project with NIO and ONGC, sea surface wave parameters — wave height, swell height and swell period — over Indian ocean have been mapped from the GEOSAT altimeter data. Methodology has been developed for determining sea surface wind field from simulated ERS-1 scatterometer data to an accuracy of $\pm$ 2 m/s in speed and $\pm$ 30 degree in direction with a 50 per cent better match-up than before. An algorithm has been developed for determining significant wave height from the altimeter pulse. Internal waves have been detected and studied from NOAA imageries. Under a joint verification programme for Japanese MOS-1 satellite, the data from microwave scanning radiometer have been analysed and data quality report submitted to NASDA, Japan.

* Coastal Environment

A manual is being prepared for mapping wetland and shoreline changes, funded by Ministry of Environment and Forest. The wetland and shoreline change maps of Gujarat, Kerala, Tamil Nadu, Andhra Pradesh, Orissa, West Bengal and Lakshadweep have been completed with classification accuracy of 85 per cent. Detailed mapping for Kerala and Tamil Nadu on 1:50,000 scale has been initiated under funding by Department of Ocean Development.

* Evaluation of Littoral Processes

Based on the correlation reflectance of TM sensor and depth variation in coastal waters, an algorithm for the retrieval of depth contours has been developed. The comparison of 1985-86, -87 and -88 depth contour data (near shore profile) was done to find the sediment drift.

* Marine Fisheries

A total of 78 fishery prospect charts were generated for different maritime States, based on location of thermal fronts using NOAA-AVHRR. At the end of 1989-90 fishing season, a detailed feedback from Gujarat reported a poor catch in about 12 per cent cases as against fair-to-excellent catches in 88 per cent cases. Also it was noted that the maximum number of high catches were observed to have occurred during March and April (considered to be the off season) as also observed during Phase-I (February — April 1989). A possible reason for this was the general warming conditions seen off the Gujarat coast on SSt images of March-April.

National (Natural) Resources Information System (NRIS)

Evolution of a comprehensive National (Natural) Resources Information System (NRIS) to help decision-makers ensure environmentally benign development while optimally utilising the natural resources, is one of the main objectives of NNRMS. DOS is the convener of the interagency expert committee set-up by the Planning Commission towards establishing NRIS.

Several pilot projects on various disciplines to develop Geographical Information System (GIS) have been taken up. The pilot projects include the following:

* urban and regional information system
* application of GIS for wasteland development
* watershed management
* regional mineral targeting
* wasteland development
* topographic modelling
* district level planning

Significant progress has been made by SAC and RRSSCs in arriving at a PC-based GIS package.

Regional Remote Sensing Service Centre (RRSSC)

The five Regional Remote Sensing Service Centres (RRSSCs) at Bangalore,

Nagpur, Kharagpur, Jodhpur and Dehra Dun have become operational. The digital image processing systems at the RRSSCs are being used in the fields of geology, forestry, hydrology, agriculture, etc. In addition, specific software to meet the requirements of application projects related to crops, landuse, soil, water quality, surface water, forest change detection, volume estimation and biomass estimation have been developed. The following are the major projects carried out by the RRSSCs:

* preparation of district level landuse/land cover maps on 1:2,50,000 scale using digital techniques for 115 districts
* data base creation and operationalisation of Indian National Geographical Information System (INGIS)
* wheat acreage estimation for Punjab, Haryana and selected districts of Madhya Pradesh and rice acreage and production estimation in Orissa for 1989-90 Kharif season
* soil mapping of Akola district in Maharashtra and Datia district in Madhya Pradesh
* forest fire mapping of Melghat reserved forest, Maharashtra, and forest density categorisation of Bhamragad reserved forest in Maharashtra
* environmental impact assessment in Jharia-Raniganj coal mines, Cochin refinery, Assam refinery near Goalghat, mining project near Kuhi (Nagpur district), nuclear power plants at Kaiga in Karnataka, etc.
* geology/minerals project including geological mapping of Bhopal, geological study of atomic minerals in Sarguja area, imaging by airborne radiometer to identify new target areas for atomic mineral deposits, lineament and glacier study in Tehri area and lineament study of the Himalaya
* landuse/land cover projects for alignment of an outer ring road for Bangalore city, Delhi urban utility project, capacity evaluation of Malaprabha and Ghataprabha reservoirs, mapping of suspended sediments and other oceanographic surface features along the west coast, watershed response analysis of Thungabhadra catchment area, flood mapping of Luni River in Rajasthan and updating of topomap of Bangalore on 1:50,000 scale
* acreage estimation and condition assessment of cotton, tobacco and mulberry crops in Karnataka and identification and acreage estimation of sugarcane.

State Remote Sensing Application Centres

Twenty-one States in the country have set-up remote sensing application centres as part of NNRMS with visual interpretation equipment. Tamil Nadu, Uttar Pradesh, Orissa, Punjab and Haryana have digital image processing facilities also. The State centres carry out projects of direct relevance to the States and actively participate in national level projects such as mapping of wasteland, ground water potential zone, landuse mapping, etc.

NNRMS Standing Committees

The six Standing Committees of NNRMS, chaired by the Secretaries of the concerned user departments and including representatives of other concerned user agencies at Central and State levels, met regularly and provided directions for remote sensing applications.

The Standing Committee on Agriculture reviewed the crop acreage and production estimation project in December 1990 and made recommendations for extending the project to cover all major crops including dry land crops, providing yield estimates at district level, improvement in turnaround times for yield estimates and better accuracy.

The Standing Committee on Bio Resources has met five times so far and the eleven projects identified by the Committee are progressing well. New projects in the fields of wetland mapping, mangroves mapping, identification and mapping of coral reefs, grassland mapping, forest cover type mapping and development of LIDAR system for atmospheric studies have been recommended.

The Standing Committee on Geology and Mineral Resources met during July 1990. Under the project Vasundhara, a prognostic model is being developed to correlate the integrated data base to the mineralised zones. An Indian Geographical Information System has been developed under this project.

The Standing Committee on Ocean and Marine Resources has initiated a programme for ocean remote sensing funded by Department of Ocean Development. The four themes covered by the programme include ocean related remote sensing application, sea truth data collection, ocean modelling studies and national ocean information system. All major user organisations are participating in this programme.

Five regional workshops/training programmes were organised under the Standing Committee on Water Resources to apprise users at State level on remote sensing applications for water resources. The Committee identified a set of projects for management of major river basins, water management in command areas, surface water monitoring of selected reservoirs, snow melt runoff model development and information system for water resources.

The Standing Committee on Training and Education has initiated several actions towards introduction of remote sensing courses in academic institutions.

Remote Sensing Training and Education

Nearly 4,000 scientists and engineers have been trained so far in the application of aerial and satellite remote sensing. The demand for trained manpower is increasing due to the number of projects at National/State/District levels, especially after the setting up of State remote sensing application centres and remote sensing cells in various user departments. NNRMS is pursuing with government and academic institutions the starting of remote sensing courses and training. The Indian Institute of Remote Sensing, Dehra Dun, National Remote Sensing Agency, Hyderabad, Space Applications Centre, Ahmedabad, all the five Regional Remote Sensing Service Centres, Centre for Studies in Resources Engineering, IIT, Bombay, and the Institute of Remote Sensing at Anna University, Madras, are offering training in remote sensing. User departments and organisations such as Geological Survey of India, National Bureau of Soil Survey and Land Use Planning and Forest Survey of India are also offering training in their respective fields.

Anna University, Roorkee University, Indian Institutes of Technology, Indian School of Mines, Aligarh Muslim University, Jamia Millia Islamia, BM Birla

Science and Technology Centre, Bharathidasan University and Andhra University are offering postgraduate courses in remote sensing. Other universities have included remote sensing as part of their curricula under geology, geography, civil engineering, hydrology, geophysics, forestry, architecture and computer science. With the initiatives taken by Standing Committee on Training and Education, the University Grants Commission and National Council of Educational Research and Training are now preparing syllabus and providing guidance and support to the universities to introduce remote sensing courses.

Sponsored Research

Sponsored Research (RESPOND) programme is supporting research projects in space science, technology and application in universities and academic/research institutions in the country. Collaborative projects in the areas of advanced space technology and applications are also undertaken. RESPOND provides assistance to academic activities, national/international conferences, symposia, etc. which are of direct relevance to the space programme. The main objective of RESPOND is to strengthen the co-operation between ISRO and academic institutions for the furtherance of the space programme in the country.

The following new research projects have been initiated during 1990-91 under RESPOND:

* establishment of R&D planning and data processing cell at R.V. College of Engineering, Bangalore.
* preparation of advanced aluminium haematite particulate composite and evaluation of its mechanical, machinability and corrosion properties at R.V. College of Engineering, Bangalore.
* river migration studies in Tamil Nadu at Bharathidasan University, Tiruchchirapalli.
* studies on problem of pollution in the Anchuthengu Kadinamkulam estuarine system with reference to retting of cocoanut husk at University of Kerala.
* identification of prospective sites for detailed ground water exploration using remote sensing technique at Manipur University.
* assessment of phytoplankton productivity by remote sensing application at Berhampur University.
* study of trace gas emission from agricultural eco-system and its impact on stratospheric ozone chemistry at Gujarat University.

The following three projects were completed during the year:

* analysis of elastic and elasto-plastic fracture under static and impact loading at Bengal Engineering College, Howrah.
* synthesis, characterisation and application studies on bonding agents for composite propellants, at Indian Institute of Science (IISc), Bangalore.
* studies on the evolution of transition metal enzyme at the University of Roorkee.

Five new projects under the ISRO-IISc Space Technology Cell have been approved in addition to the ongoing 15 projects after a review. The topics include characterisation and application of various polymers and composites, integrated fibre optic gyro, baffle configuration for suppression of sloshing, space grade solar cells, etc.

The ongoing research activities at the ISRO-IIT (Madras) Space Technology Cell include study of development of hologram interferometry and speckle methods for crack detection, interference effects in spray combustion, expert system for space programme, effects of ultrasonic vibration on heat treatment of some hardenable alloys and supersonic combustion phenomenon. The Space Technology Cell at IIT (Bombay) continued the research activities in the field of remote sensing application.

Source: *DOS Annual Report*, 1990-91.

TABLE 34.2: Major Indian Space Missions, 1985-96

Missions	Seventh Plan					Eighth Plan					Ninth Plan
	1985-86	1986-87	1987-88	1988-89	1989-90	1990-91	1991-92	1992-93	1993-94	1994-95	1995-96
SROSS/ASLV			D-1	D-2			D-3/C-1	C-2			
IRS	1A Procured Launch					IE IB Procured Launch		1C Procured launch			
PSLV						D-1	D-2 Space Science SAS & R Piggy Back			D-3/01	
INSAT				1-C Procured S/C Procured Launch		1-D Procured S/C Procured Launch	2A Indigenous S/C Procured Launch	2B Indigenous S/C Procured Launch		2C Indigenous S/C Procured Launch	2D Indigenous S/C Procured Launch
GSLV											

Source: *DOS Annual Report*, 1990-91.

35

SPORTS

South Asian Federation (SAF) Games

India took part in SAF Games held in Sri Lanka in December 1991 and won 64 gold, 59 silver and 41 bronze medals as against won 61,43 and 20 at Islamabad (Pakistan) India emerged at the top in swimming pool competition. India's performance was very poor in boxing.

Federation Cup

Defending Champions. India regained the title in the men's finals.

Athletics

Services retained the title in the 26th National Cross Country Championship in Jabalpur on December 2, 1991.

TABLE 35.1: Hockey

	1984 Olympics	1986 World Cup	11th Champions Trophy (Berlin)	1990 World Cup
India vs Australia	2:4	0:6	2:3	2:3
India vs Germany	0:0	2:2	3:2	1:1

Archery

What Şachin Tendulkar is to cricket and Vishwanath Anand to chess, is Limba Ram to archery. The sharpshooter (Limba Ram) finished 11th out of 12 archers at Shri Jinshan ranges in the western hills of Beiging in the 1990 Asian Games, has come a long way in this totally — neglected sport.

Source : C.S. Rao, *Hindustan Times.*

TABLE 35.2: Olympic and World Records

MEN

Event	Olympic			World		
100m	9.92	Carl Lewis (U.S.)	Seoul 88	9.86	Carl Lewis (U.S.)	Tokyo 91
200m	19.75	Joe Déloach (U.S.)	Seoul 88	19.72	P. Mennea (ITA)	Mexico 79
400m	43.86	Lee Evans (U.S.)	Mexico 68	43.29	B. Reynolds (U.S.)	Zurich 88
800m	1:43.00	J. Cruz (Brazil)	Los Angeles 84	1:41.73	S. Coe (GBR)	Florence (ITA) 81
1,500m	3:32.53	S. Coe (GBR)	Los Angeles 84	3:29.46	S. Aouita (MOR)	Berlin 85
5,000m	13:05.59	S. Aouita (MOR0	Los Angeles 84	12:58.39	S. Aouita (MOR)	Rome 87
10,000m	27:21.46	B. Boutayeb (MOR)	Seoul 88	27:08.23	A. Barrios (MEX)	Berlin 89
3,000m SC	8:05.51	J. Kariuki (KEN)	Seoul 88	8:05.35	P. Koech (KEN)	Stockholm 89
110m	12.98	R. Kingdom (U.S.)	Seoul 88	12.92	R. Kingdom (U.S.)	Zurich 89
400m H	47.19	A. Phillips (U.S.)	Seoul 88	47.02	Edwin Moses (U.S.)	Koblenz (GER) 83
FIELD EVENTS:						
High jump	2.38m	G. Avdeyenko (USSR)	Seoul 88	2.44	J. Sotomayor (Cub)	San Juan 89
Pole vault	5.90m	Sergei Bubka (USSR)	Seoul 88	6.11	S. Bubka (UKRA)	Dijon 92
Long jump	8.9m	Bob Beamon (U.S.)	Mexico 68	8.95	Mike Powell (U.S.)	Tokyo 91
Triple jump	17.61m	Khristo Markov (BUL)	Seoul 88	17.97	Willie Banks (U.S.)	Indianapolis 85
Shot put	22.4m	Ulf Timmermann (GDR)	Seoul 88	23.12	Randy Barnes (U.S.)	Westwood 90
Discus	68.82m	Jurgen Schult (GDR)	Seoul 88	74.08m	Jurgen Schult (GDR)	Neubrandenburg (GER) 86
Hammer	84.80m	Sergei Litvinov (USSR)	Seoul 88	86.74	Yuriy Syedikh (USSR)	Stuttgart 86
Javelin	85.90m	Jan Zelemy (CZECH)	Seoul 88	94.74	Jan Zelemy (CZECH)	Oslo 92
Decathlon	8847	Daley Thompson (GB)	L A 84	8847	Daley Thompson (GB)	Los Angeles 84

Event	Olympic			World		
RELAYS						
4 x 100m	37.83	U.S.	Los Angels 84	37.50	U.S.	Tokyo 91
4 x 400m	2:56.16	U.S.	Mexico 68	2:56.16	U.S.	Mexico Games 68
	2:56.16	U.S.	Seoul 88			

OTHER EVENTS

Event	Olympic			World		
20km Walk	1:19.57	Jozef Pribilinec (CZECH)	Seoul 88	1:18.13	Pavol Blazek (CZECH)	Hildesheim 90
50km Walk	3:38.29	Vyacheslav Ivanenko USSR	Seoul 88	3:37.41	Andrey Perlov (USSR)	Leningrad 89
Marathon	2:09.21	Carlos Lopes (POR)	Los Angeles 84	2:06.50	B. Densimo (ETH)	Rotterdam 88

WOMEN

Event	Olympic			World		
100m	10.62	Florence G. Loyner (U.S.)	Seoul 88	10.49	Florence Joyner	Indianapolis 88
200m	21.34	Florence G. Joyner (U.S.)	Seoul 88	21.34	Florence Joyner	Seoul 83
400m	48.65	Olga Bryzgina (USSR)	Seoul 88	47.60	Marita Koch (GDR)	Canberra 85
800m	1:53.43	N. Olizarenko (USSR)	Moscow 80	1:53.28	J. Kratochvilova (Czech)	Munich 83
1500m	3:53.96	Paula Ivan (ROM)	Seoul 88	3:52.47	Tatyana Kazankina (USSR)	Zurich 80
3000	8:26.53	Tatyana Samolenko (USSR)	Seoul 88	8:22.62	Tatyana Kazankina (USSR)	Leningrad 84
10,000m	31:05.21	Olga Bondarenko (USSR)	Seoul 88	30:13.74	Ingrid Kristiansen (NOR)	London 85
100m H	12.38	Yordanka Donkova (USSR)	Seoul 88	12.21	Yordanka Donkova	Stara Zagora 88
400m H	53.17	Debble Klintoff-King (AUS)	Seoul 88	52.94	Marina Stepanova (USSR)	Tashkent 86

Event	Olympic			World		
High Jump	2.03m	Louise Ritter (U.S.)	Seoul 88	2.09m	Stefka Kostadinova (BUL)	Rome 87
Long Jump	7.40m	Jackie J. Kersee (U.S.)	Seoul 88	7.52m	Galina Chistyakova (USSR)	Leningrad 88
Shot Put	22.41m	Ilona Slupianek (GDR)	Moscow 80	22.63m	Natalya Lisovskaya (USSR)	Moscow 87
Discus	72.30m	Martina Helmann (GDR)	Seoul 88	76.8m	Gabriela Reinsch (GDR)	Neubrandenburg 88
Javelin	74.68m	Petra Felke (GDR)	Seoul 88	80.00m	Petra Felke	Potsdam 88
Heptathlon	7291 pts	Jackie Kersee (U.S.)	Seoul 88	7291	Jackie J. Kersee	Seoul 88
Relays						
4 x 100m	41.60	GDR	Moscow 80	41.37	GDR	Canberra 88
4 x 400m	3:15.18	USSR	Seoul 88	3.15.17	USSR	Seoul 88 (Jan)

OTHER EVENTS	Olympic			World		
10km walk				41.30	Kerry Saxby (AUS)	Canberra 88
Marathon	2:24.52	Ioan Benoit (U.S.)	Los Angeles	2:21.06	Ingrid Kristiansen (NOR)	London 85

TABLE 35.3: Performance Gap in Olympics

	1988 Olympics	Barcelma	Current World Best
Women			
400 m	-5.28	-5.77	00:48:13
800 m	-7.16	-8.00	01:57:00
1600 m	-18.28	-24.5	03:17:00
Men			
800 m	-5.16	-6.10	01:42:50
1500 m	-12.84	-15.10	03:32:00
3000 m (Steeplchase)	-44.49	-29.0	08:00:00

Source : *Hindustan Times*, July 25, 1992

36

TRANSPORT AND COMMUNICATIONS

TRANSPORT

Railways

The size of the Railway network during 1990-91 increased to 62,366 route kilometres, an increase of 155 route kilometres over 1989-90. The electrified network increased to 10,083 route kilometres with electrification of additional 831 route kilometres in 1990-91. By the end of 1990-91, three trunk routes, namely, (a) New Delhi-Howrah, (b) Delhi-Kota-Bombay, and (c) New Delhi-Madras, had been fully electrified. During 1991-92, two trunks, namely, (a) New Delhi-Bhusawal-Bombay and (b) Bombay-Howrah, are scheduled to be electrified. Track renewal was completed on 3,611 kilometres against as target of 3,500 kilometres.

The originating freight traffic in the year 1990-91 was 341.4 million tonnes, comprising 318.4 million tonnes of revenue earning traffic and 23.0 million tonnes of non-revenue earning traffic. The freight transport effort in 1990-91 was 242.7 billion tonne kilometres comprising 235.8 billion tonne kilometres of revenue earning traffic and 6.9 billion tonne kilometres of non-revenue traffic. The freight traffic carried in 1990-91 in terms of tonne kilometres was about 2.4 per cent more than the traffic carried in 1989-90. In terms of tonnage, it was 2.1 per cent more than in 1989-90 (Table 36.3).

During April-December, 1991 the freight traffic carried was 244.9 million tonnes against 227.8 million tonnes in the same period last year, implying as increase of 7.5 per cent. The traffic measured by freight transport output was 185.9 billion tonne kilometres against 176.0 billion tonne kilometres last year, implying an increase of 5.6 per cent.

The passenger traffic in 1990-91 was 3,854 million as against 3,653 million during 1989-90, implying an increase of 5.6 per cent. The volume of passenger traffic in terms of passenger kilometres was 295.7 billion as against 280.8 billion in 1989-90, implying an increase of 5.3 per cent. During April-December, 1991 the passenger traffic was 3,062 million against 2,835 million in the same period last year which was higher by 7.3 per cent.

RAILWAYS

Railway Budge for 1992-93

Salient Features

Increases

— Freight rates of all items, except 15 essential commodities up by 7.5 per cent and for coal by 4 per cent.

— Minimum charge for fresh fruit and vegetables Rs. 20 and for parcels and luggage up from Rs. 17 to Rs. 30.
— Minimum fare for AC Sleeper, First Class, AC Chair Car up by 20 per cent for all distances.
— Fares for Rajdhani, Shatabdi, Delhi-Bombay AC Express trains to be suitably increased.
— IInd Class Mail, Express fares up by Rupee one at the lowest distance slab, going up to Rs. 25 per ticket for distances beyond 1,300 km.
— IInd Class ordinary fares up by 50 paise per ticket in the lowest slab, going up to Rs. 5 per ticket for beyond 250 km. travel.
— IInd Class sleeper surcharge for 501 km. to 1,000 km. up from Rs. 20 to Rs. 25.

Unchanged

— Freight rates of essential commodities like foodgrains pulses, salt, sugar, tea, fruit and vegetables, edible oils, kerosene, diesel, oilseeds, livestock and fodder.
— IInd Class ordinary fares up to 10 km. sleeper surcharge up to 500 km. and platform ticket.

New Trains

— Fifteen new trains to be introduced from July 1 this year.
— A weekly Rajdhani Express from New Delhi to Secunderabad/Bangalore to be introduced during 1992-93.

TABLE 36.1: Budget at a Glance

(Figures in crores in rupees)

		Actuals, 1990-91	Budget 1991-92	Revised 1991-92	Budget 1992-93
1	2	3	4	5	6
(a)	Gross Traffic Receipts	12096.49	13319.00	13586.00	15884.00
(b)	Ordinary working expenses	8233.90	9180.00	9205.00	10460.00
(c)	Appropriation to Depreciation Reserve Fund	1950.00	2000.00	2000.00	2300.00
(d)	Appropriation to Pension Fund	969.96	1050.00	1090.00	1200.00
(e)	Total working expenses (b)+(c)+(d)	11153.86	12230.00	12295.00	13960.00
(f)	Net Traffic Receipts (a)-(e)	942.63	1089.00	1291.00	1924.00
(g)	Net Miscellaneous Receipts	171.15	183.00	183.00	206.00
(h)	Net Railway Revenue (f)+(g)	1113.78	1272.00	1474.00	2130.00
(i)	Dividend Payment to General Revenues	926.14	1037.00	1039.00	1150.00
(j)	Payment of Deferred Dividend	11.97	—	—	416.46
(k)	Excess/Shortfall (h)-(i)-(j)	+175.67	+235.00	+435.00	+563.54
(l)	Appropriation to Railway Development Fund:	175.67	235.00	435.00	563.54

Contd.

TABLE 36.1 (*Contd.*)

1	2	3	4	5	6
	(a) Repayment of Loan & Interest	53.44	110.00	310.00	281.82
	(b) Development Works	122.23	125.00	125.00	145.00
	(c) Balance for Plan Finance	—	—	—	136.72
(m)	Operating Ratio	92.0%	91.8%	90.3%	87.7%
(n)	Percentage of Net Revenue to Capital-at-Change	6.9%	7.2%	8.3%	10.9%

Note: Budget was presented by the Railway Minister C.K. Jaffer Sharief in the Lok Sabha on February 25, 1992.

Items of Railway Income and Expenditure, 1990-91

Rupee comes from	in paise
1. Goods earnings	67
2. Passenger earnings	25
3. Other coaching earnings	03
4. Miscellaneous and other earnings	05
Total	100

Rupees goes to	
1. Staff wages and other allowances	33
2. Depreciation Reserve Fund	16
3. Fuel	13
4. Stores	08
5. Pension fund	08
6. Dividend	07
7. Development Works	02
8. Miscellaneous	13
Total	100

TABLE 36.2: Financial Performance of Indian Railways

(Rs. crore)

	1980-81	1983-84	1984-85	1985-86	1986-87	1987-88	1988-89	1989-90	1990-91 (RE)	1991-92 (BE)
1	2	3	4	5	6	7	8	9	10	11
1. Gross traffic receipts	2624	4986	5359	6428	7506	8435	9259	10739	12038	13319
(i) Passenger coaching	827	1354	1459	1720	1941	2060	2455	2669	3130	3493
(ii) Other coaching	16	166	179	210	293	255	271	313	350	369
(iii) Goods	1618	3353	3603	4376	5133	5982	6343	7624	8380	9222
(iv) Other earnings	82	119	125	133	142	162	225	226	226	255
(v) Suspense account	—19	—6	—7	—11	—3	—24	—35	—93	—48	—20
2. Working expenses	2537	4661	5142	5823	6901	7803	8633	9887	11091	12230
(i) Ordinary working expenses	2233	3629	4071	4643	5301	6003	6583	7444	8241	9180
(ii) Appropriations to Depreciation Reserve Fund	220	850	850	920	1250	1350	1500	1715	1950	2000
(iii) Appropriation to pensions	84	182	221	260	350	450	550	728	900	1050
3. Net traffic receipts (1-2)	87	325	217	605	605	632	626	852	947	1089
4. Net miscellaneous receipts	40	54	53	81	76	91	111	130	135	183
5. Net revenues (3+4)	127	379	270	686	681	723	737	981	1082	1272
6. Payments to general revenues	325	424	466	507	579	639	716	809	927	1037
7. Surplus (+) or deficit (-)	—198	—45	—196	179	102	84	22	173	155	235
8. Capital at charge	6096	7568	8286	9078	10373	11622	12988	14629	16091	17620
9. Item 5 as % of Item 8	2.1	5.0	3.3	7.6	6.6	6.2	5.7	6.7	6.7	7.2
10. Item 7 as % of Item 8	—3.2	—0.6	—2.4	2.0	1.0	0.7	0.2	1.2	1.0	1.3

Source: *Economic Survey*, 1991-92.

TABLE 36.3: Performance of Railway Sector

(Million tonnes)

Sl. No.	Item	1988-89	1989-90	1990-91$	April-December$		Percentage change		
					1990-91	1991-92	1989-90 / 1988-89	1990-91 / 1989-90	1991-92* / 1990-91
1	2	3	4	5	6	7	8	9	10
1.	Total revenue earning freight traffic (million tonnes)	302.05	309.97	318.40	227.79	244.91	2.6	2.7	7.6
(i)	Coal	128.01	130.15	135.16	96.66	106.56	1.7	3.8	10.2
(ii)	Raw Materials for steel plants (excl. coal)	26.97	27.43	25.90	18.93	20.93	1.7	—5.6	11.2
(iii)	Pig iron and finished steel from steel plants	10.18	10.15	10.01	7.13	7.96	—0.3	—1.4	11.6
(iv)	Iron ore for export	13.64	14.76	13.14	9.48	9.52	8.2	—11.0	0.4
(v)	Cement	25.91	27.45	28.78	20.33	21.51	5.9	4.8	5.8
(vi)	Foodgrains	24.88	23.66	25.35	18.46	19.39	—4.9	7.1	5.0
(vii)	Fertilizers	16.10	16.97	18.36	13.79	14.08	5.4	8.2	2.1
(viii)	POL	22.60	24.31	25.06	18.35	18.89	7.6	3.1	2.9
(ix)	Balance (other goods)	33.76	35.09	36.64	24.46	26.07	3.9	4.4	6.6
2.	Net tonne kilometre (million)	222.37	229.60	235.78	171.13	181.30	3.3	2.7	5.9
3.	Net tonne kilometre per wagon per day (BG)	1453	1428	1455	1361 @	1431 @	—1.7	1.9	5.1
4.	Passenger traffic originating (million)	3500	3653	3858	2855	3062	4.4	5.6	7.2
5.	Passenger kilometres (billion)	263.7	280.8	295.7	218.5	235.1	6.5	5.3	7.6

$ Provisional
* April-December
@ April-November

Roads and Road Transport

The road net work increased steadily during the Seventh Plan. In the terminal year of the Sixth Plan (1984-85) the road network which had a total length of 16.9 lakh km increased to 19.7 lakh km by the end of the Seventh Plan showing an increase of 17 per cent. The total length of national highways increased from 31.7 thousand km to 33.6 thousand km during the same period registering a growth of about 6 per cent. The Seventh Plan also witnessed spectacular growth in the number of registered vehicles. The number of such vehicles increased from 90 lakh in 1984-85 to about 190.7 lakh in 1989-90 and further to about 214.9 lakh in 1990.91.

Ports

Cargo handled at major ports during 1990-91 at 152.6 million tonnes exceeded the target of 151 million tonnes and was also higher than the throughout of 148.1 million tonnes in the preceding year. The re-assessed cargo handling capacity at major ports at the end of 1990-91 was 163.5 million tonnes. No increase in port capacity is scheduled to materialise during 1991-92.

During April-December, 1991 the major ports handled 114.1 million tonnes of cargo against the target of 112.8 million tonnes, which was also higher than the throughput of 110.5 million tonnes handled in the corresponding period last year. Major increases over traffic handled were in the traffic of POL (23.8 lakh tonnes) iron ore (10.3 lakh tonnes) and coal (24 lakh tonnes). However, general cargo traffic declined as compared to the same period last year.

Shipping

During 1991-92, acquisition of Indian shipping tonnage has declined. The fleet strength at the end of December, 1991 was 415 vessels of 5.94 million GRT compared with 418 vessels of 6.03 million GRT in the same period last year. The overseas trade during 1990-91 was about 110.35 million tonnes against 106.75 million tonnes in 1989-90. The share of Indian flag in the total traffic has decreased marginally from 35.8 per cent during 1989-90 to 35.6 per cent in 1990-91.

Largest Indigenous Ship Launched

Eighty-six thousand tonnes capacity vessel, the largest ship ever manufactured so far, named after Jawaharlal Nehru was formally launched at Cochin on March 1, 1992.

As the ship docked out of the yard, hundreds of workers who toiled for nearly five years to fulfil their dream this day joyfully clapped amidst chanting of songs and religious hymns. Mrs. Kalyani Karunakaran placed garland at the rear end of the ship before it slowly moved out of the ship dock. The oil vessel with a cargo tank capacity of 105,949 cubic metres and overall length of 237.60 metres has been built for the Shipping Corporation of India. This is the second biggest ship built by the Cochin Shipyard which apart from undertaking repairs of not only Indian ships but also foreign vessels. Recently, the Cochin Shipyard Ltd. earned foreign exchange to the tune of the one crore by repairing a foreign ship.

According to Cochin Shipyard Chairman and Managing Director the ship Jawaharlal Nehru, has been built out of 15,750 tonnes of steel and more than 390 km. of welding material. 86 kms. of electric cables, two lakh litre of paint and 2,300 valves have been used in the ship which is the second largest in the country. The ship's generators would produce 3,440 KW of electric power.

Speaking on the occasion, Minister of Surface Transport said the manufacturing of the ship was the greatest achievement of the ship manufacturing industry in the country and it proved that India was sincerely following the concept of self-reliance taught by Jawaharlal Nehru. The 86,000 tonnes capacity vessel also clearly suggested that the country was fastly acquiring high technology needed for the ship building industry.

The Minister said the improvement in the productivity was key to making the shipyard financially viable. This had assumed importance in view of the constraints of budgetary resources and the need to meet the emergent requirements of priority sectors. He said he would like that the Shipyard should be self-sufficient and not dependent upon the budgetary support. As a matter of fact, he would like to go a step further and say that the objective in the long run should not only be to achieve a break even level but to provide some return for the investment already made in the shipyard.

The Shipyard should not only improve its productivity but concentrate on profit-generating activities. In this regard he was happy that the turnover in the ship-repair sector had shown tremendous improvement.

The Government was also considering a proposal for augmentation of ship-repair facilities at an estimated cost of about Rs. 20 crore. With the augmentation of these facilities, the shipyard would be able to increase the ship-repair turnover manifold and thus contribute towards saving the precious foreign exchange.

Source : *Hindustan Times*, March 2, 1992.

Civil Aviation

The Civil Aviation sector consists of two distinct segments — Operational and Infrastructural. Indian Airlines and Air India provide domestic and international services on the operational side. In addition, Pawan Hans provides Helicopter services to ONGC and to inaccessible areas and difficult terrains. Infrastructural facilities are provided by the International Airports Authority of India (IAAI) and the National Airports Authority (NAA).

Air India

During 1991-92, the recession of the western economies deepened having its impact on Air India's traffic. On the other hand, with the resolution of crisis in Kuwait outlook for Gulf traffic improved. However, opening up of the Indian economy, which is expected to boost international business traffic, has not yet had a significant impact. The Available Seat Kilometres (ASKMs) deployed by Air India is expected to increase by 4.2 per cent. However, the Passenger Kilometres (PKMs) is expected to increase only marginally by 1.5 per cent. In view of the discontinuance of leasing of aircraft, the total capacity offered by Air India in 1991-92 is expected to decline. Cargo operations of Air India have become uneconomical consequent to the devaluation of Indian Rupee as the freighter lease charges are denominated in hard currency but most of the freight revenue is received in Rupees. Air India operates in a competitive international market and therefore, has to match its competitors in pricing and there is no element of subsidy as available to some other public sector undertakings.

Indian Airlines

The capacity of Indian Airlines in terms of ATKMs increased from 959.6 million tonnes in 1984-85 to 1100 million tonnes in 1991-92. The traffic in terms of RTKMs increased from 664 million to 800 million during the same period. Compared to the last year the performance in terms of ATKMs and RTKMs is expected to be higher by 19 per cent and 14 per cent, respectively.

COMMUNICATIONS

Postal System

India ranks foremost among the postal systems of the world in terms of number of post offices. Besides the vastness of the country and large population, this is attributable to the conscientious efforts made by Government since independence to develop postal network as a means of social integration and as an instrument of economic development and rural re-generation. Apart from the basic objective of extending communication, the expansion of postal network has also significantly contributed to other socio-economic goals of the Government such as, rural development, employment, promotion of small savings and setting up industries in backward areas.

By the end of the Seventh Plan, the National Postal Network had touched the 1,47,236 mark of which 16,249 post offices were in the urban sector and 1,30,987 in the rural sector. The all-India averages with regard to population served per post office and the average area served by a post office as on 1-4-1991 were 4607 persons and 22.10 sq. km., respectively. The long-term objective is to strive for location of a post office in a radius of 3 km. in a village without a post office at present. Upgradation and consolidation of postal services is also proposed to be accorded due attention.

Telecommunications

The performance of telecom sector during 1990-91 in creating additional switching capacity, providing new telephone and telex connections and production of switching equipment was good. Net additional capacity added during 1990-91 was 5.57 lakh lines which is 16.5 per cent higher than 4.78 lakh lines in 1989-90. About 25.9 per cent of this capacity expansion was in metro telecom districts of Delhi, Bombay, Calcutta and Madras. Progress for 1991-92 is medicated in the Table 36.4.

TABLE 36.4: Performance of the Telecommunications Sector

Group/Total	1988-89	1989-90	1990-91$	April-December$		Percentage change		
				1990-91	1991-92	1989-90 / 1988-89	1990-91 / 1989-90	1991-92* / 1990-91
1	2	3	4	5	6	7	8	9
I. Net additional switching capacity: (Lakh lines)								
(i) Metro District	1.19	1.45	1.44	0.60	1.25	21.8	—0.7	108.3
(ii) Others	3.49	3.33	4.13	1.11	2.01	—4.6	24.0	81.1
Total (All India)	4.68	4.78	5.57	1.71	3.26	2.1	16.5	90.6
II. Net telephone connections provided: (DELs) (000 Nos.)								
(i) Metro. Districts	102.83	122.45	133.09	52.98	91.52	19.1	8.7	72.7
(ii) Others	272.11	293.77	352.67	121.58	186.10	8.0	20.0	53.1
Total (All India)	374.94	416.22	485.76	174.56	277.62	11.0	16.7	59.0

Contd.

TABLE 36.4 *Contd.*

1	2	3	4	5	6	7	8	9
III. Telex service:								
(i) Telex capacity (lines)	2358	1020	2051	1665	1744	—56.7	101.1	4.7
(ii) Telex connections (Nos.)	3900	3080	2156	1201	1167	—21.0	30.0	—2.8
IV. Production of switching equipment: (000 lines)								
(i) Strowger	213.2	175.8	85.8	53.5	39.2	—17.5	—51.2	—26.7
(ii) Crossbar	86.5	63.5	57.9	25.9	37.3	—26.6	—8.8	44.0
(iii) Electronic	483.3	735.1	800.3	444.4	496.6	52.1	8.9	—11.7
Total (All India)	783.0	974.4	944.0	523.1	573.1	24.4	—3.1	9.4
V. Laying of telephone cable: (lakh Conductor KMs)								
(i) Metro, Districts	23.36	22.37	19.48	11.2	13.6	—4.2	12.9	21.4
(ii) Others	35.90	42.33	51.37	28.2	42.3	17.9	21.4	50.0
Total (All India)	59.26	64.70	70.85	39.4	55.9	9.2	9.5	41.9
VI. Addition in Rural Communications:								
(i) No. of exchanges	747	484	2727	362	1122	—35.2	463.4	209.9
(ii) No. of LDPTs	2631	1633	1742	203	7663	—37.9	6.7	3674.9

$ Provisional
* April-December

TABLE 36.5: Financial Performance of the Department of Posts and Telecommunications

(Rs. crore)

	1980-81	1983-84	1984-85	1985-86	1986-87	1987-88	1988-89	1989-90	1990-91	1991-92 (RE)
1	2	3	4	5	6	7	8	9	10	11
1. Gross receipts	910	1463	1635	1786	1788	2344	3101	3544	4246	4490
(i) Posts	278	435	444	477	558	643	742	703	841	920
(ii) Telecommunications	632	1028	1191	1309	1230	1701	2359	2841	3405	3570
2. Networking expenses	821	1189	1368	1582	1779	2081	2287	2569	2890	3080
(i) Posts	346	508	557	640	774	834	912	966	1033	1145
(ii) Telecommunications	475	681	811	942	1005	1247	1375	1603	1857	1935
3. Net receipts (1-2)	89	274	267	204	9	263	814	975	1356	1410
(i) Posts	—67	—73	—113	—163	—216	—191	—170	—263	—192	—225
(ii) Telecommunications	156	347	380	367	225	454	984	1238	1548	1635
4. Dividend to General Revenues	37	97	135	170	213	0	161	180	220	204
5. Surplus/deficit (3-4)	52	177	132	34	—204	263	653	795	1136	1206
(i) Posts	—72	—82	—125	—163	—216	—191	—170	—263	—192	—255
(ii) Telecommunications	124	259	257	197	12	454	823	1058	1328	1431

Source: *Economic Survey*, 1991-92.

37

WELFARE PROGRAMMES

Including Welfare of Scheduled Castes, Scheduled Tribes and Other Backward Classes and Weaker Sections

Family Welfare and Planning

One of the most critical problems facing the nation today is the rapid growth of population. The 1991 Census estimated India's population at 844 million. The population is increasing by about 16 million every year. If the growth continues at the present rate, the country will have about 1000 million people by 2000 A.D. and 1700 million by 2024 A.D. It would become difficult to provide even basic necessities of life to such large population. All the additional production and facilities will be utilised by the additional population and there would not be any improvement in the quality of life. Such a relentless population growth would also wreak havoc on our environment, lead to ecological crises and social tension. It is, therefore, imperative that the highest priority is accorded to population control.

The National Family Planning Programme was started in 1951 with a clinical approach. An extension education approach was adopted in mid-sixties and since late seventies the family planning has gradually expanded into a community oriented service network. The programme has made a significant impact on fertility. The birth rate declined from 41.7 per 1000 in 1950s to 34 in 1979, then it was stable around 34 till 1984. In 1985 it came down to a level of 33 and declined further to 29.9 in 1990-91. The average annual growth rate of population which rose from a level of 1.25 per cent in the 1940s reached a plateau at 2.22 per cent in the 1970s and has now declined to 2.11 per cent during 1981-1991. During the Seventh Plan, the total number of family planning acceptors rose consistently from a level of 18.92 million in 1985-86 to 27.26 million in 1990-91. An overall couple protection rate of 44.1 per cent was achieved by March, 1991 as against the target of 60 per cent by 2000 A.D. However, the birth rate has not declined as much as the death rate and the rate of population growth has remained high.

The long-term goal is to reach Net Reproduction Rate of "Unity: (NRR = 1) by 2000 A.D. with a birth rate of 21, death rate of 9, and an infant mortality rate below 60 per thousand.

Welfare of Weaker Sections

Uneven economic growth and development tend to lead to imbalances in the socio-economic structure. Accordingly, a conscious effort has been made through special schemes and programmes to provide for equitable distribution and provision of welfare services for weaker sections such as Scheduled Castes and Scheduled Tribes, Backward Classes and the handicapped.

Scheduled Castes

The Special Component Plan strategy for Scheduled Castes is, at present, in operation in 21 States and 3 UTs. There are 21 Scheduled Caste State Development Corporations which extend assistance for economic development to Scheduled Castes. Special Central Assistance is paid to States/UTs as an additive to their Special Component Plans. There are several Centrally Sponsored Schemes for the educational and economic development of Scheduled Castes. Under Point 11-A of the 20-Point Programme, economic assistance was provided to 103 lakh Scheduled Caste families during Sixth Plan, 120 lakh families in Seventh Plan and 22.40 lakh families during 1990-91, to enable them to cross the poverty line.

The target fixed for 1991-92 was 25.56 lakh families. However, only 3.91 lakh families were reported to have been assisted up to September 1991.

Scheduled Tribes

The total sub-plan strategy is in operation in 18 States and 2 UTs and is being implemented through 193 Integrated Tribal Development Projects (ITDPs). This strategy aims at socio-economic development of Scheduled Tribes.

Special central assistance is provided by Government of India to States/UTs to supplement their efforts for tribal development. There are several Centrally Sponsored Schemes for the economic and educational development of STs. For marketing of tribal produce, especially the minor forest produce, a Tribal Cooperative Marketing Development Federation (TRIFED) set-up in August, 1987 is expanding its activities. During the Seventh Plan, 52.89 lakh ST families were given economic assistance. In 1990-91, against the target of 8.24 lakh ST families, 8.93 lakh ST families were economically assisted. The target fixed for 1991-92 is 8.04 lakh families. Against this, 2.48 lakh families were assisted up to September, 1991. The achievement up to September, 1991 is approximately 103 per cent of the target of 2.40 lakh families.

National Scheduled Castes and Scheduled Tribes Finance and Development Corporation (NSFDC)

To accelerate the pace of economic development of Scheduled Castes and Scheduled Tribes, the National Scheduled Castes and Scheduled Tribes Finance and Development Corporation (NSFDC) was set-up in February, 1989 with an authorised capital of Rs. 75 crore and paid-up capital of Rs. 50 crore. Since its inception, the Corporation has sanctioned 125 income generating projects/schemes which are likely to benefit about 1.25 lakh SC and ST beneficiaries. The disbursements made till December, 1991 reached Rs. 20.08 crore. Further, the Corporation has to far also spent Rs. 5.59 lakh for providing training to upgrade the knowledge and skills of SCs and STs to make them self-employed.

Backward Classes

In order to provide an additional channel of finance for economic development of the Socially and Educationally Backward Classes (SEBCs), Government of India has decided to set-up a National Backward Classes Finance and Development Corporation (NBFDC) with an authorised capital of Rs. 200 crore.

The Corporation was registered on 13-1-1992 as a Company under Section 25 of the Companies Act, 1956 and paid-up Capital of Rs. 25 crore was provided in the budget for 1991-92. The objects of the Corporation include, *inter alia*, promotion of self-employment and other ventures, extension of loan for pursuing general/professional/ technical education or training at graduate and higher levels and upgradation of technical and entrepreneurial skills of people belonging to Backward Classes. The Corporation will work as an apex institution for coordination and monitoring the work of all Corporations/Boards set-up by the State Governments and UT Administrations for the welfare of Backward Classes.

Recruitment

The Union Public Service Commission (UPSC) and the Staff Selection Commission (SSC) are the two designated recruitment agencies, the former for Group 'A' and Group 'B' services/posts and the latter for recruitment to non-technical Group 'C' posts. The Assistants' Grade and Grade 'C' Stenographers' Open Examination, both for Group 'B' posts, have also been entrusted to the Staff Selection Commission.

Recruitment of Teachers for Municipal Corporation of Delhi (MCD)

For the last two years, the SSC has been conducting separate examinations for recruitment of Primary Teachers, Assistant Teachers (Primary) and Nursery Teachers for the MCD. It has now been decided to hold a common examination for recruitment of teachers for the MCD.

Special Recruitment Drive for SC & ST

A Special Recruitment Drive was carried out in 1989 to fill up the backlog of reserved vacancies existing as on 30-4-89. The drive covered all ministries/departments, public sector undertakings, public sector banks and insurance corporations. The number of vacancies identified and the number of candidates who were offered appointment in the Central Government under the 1989 drive were 35647 and 31243 respectively.

Another drive has been launched during the current year in order to fill up the backlog of reserved vacancies prevailing as on 31-3-90 including the reserved vacancies left unfilled under the drive carried out last year. Every effort is being made to fill up all the reserved vacancies. The number of vacancies identified under the drive and the number of candidates recruited according to the reports received up to March, 1991 were 31928 and 19870 respectively.

As on October, 1990 there were 6161 vacancies reported for posts reserved for SCs/STs. These included a backlog of 2007 vacancies. Nearly 1400 reserved vacancies out of the backlog have been cleared by the Commission. In addition 1990 more vacancies, subsequently reserved for SCs/STs, have also been filled up. This leaves about 2900 vacancies to be filled up through examinations which have either been held already or are yet to be held.

Pre-recruitment Training for SCs/STs

Pre-recruitment Training Programmes for members of the SCs/STs were conducted not only to improve their competitiveness but also to boost their confidence and motivate them to compete in larger numbers in the SSCs examinations.

The Governments of Kerala, Tamil Nadu, Karnataka, Orissa, West Bengal and Madhya Pradesh came forward in a big way to assist the Commission in conducting training programmes for SC/ST candidates. The North Eastern Regional Council also rendered substantial assistance in organising training programmes in all the 7 States of the North Eastern Region. About 12000 SC/ST candidates were given training at about 80 centres spread all over the country.

Special Recruitment of the Blind and the Deaf

The Commission held special examinations at specified centres for recruitment of the Visually Handicapped (VH) and Hearing Handicapped (HH) persons for Groups 'C' and 'D' posts in the Central Government departments and public sector undertakings. As a result of this 46 vacancies for VH and 77 for HH candidates have since been filled up.

Workshops on Interviewing Skills

The Commission continued its efforts aimed at further refining the interviewing techniques and skills so as to make them more scientific and result oriented. Four workshops on interviewing skills were held during the year at Pune, Cochin, Bangalore and New Delhi bringing the total number of workshops held by the Commission in this field to 21.

Lodestar: a quarterly journal

There is a growing demand for the Commission's quarterly journal, *Lodestar/Dhruvatara.* The guidance materials published therein for the use of the candidates appearing in the major examinations held by it have been well received. There has been a substantial increase in the circulation of the journal.

Reservations and Concessions

Various concessions like relaxation in the upper age limit, unlimited number of chances available within the relaxed age limit for appearing at the competitive examinations, full exemption from the payment of examination fee, relaxation in standard of suitability have been prescribed to further improve the representation of Scheduled Castes and Scheduled Tribes in services. Reservation in promotion has been extended to those grades in which the element of direct recruitment, does not exceed 75 per cent (as against the limit of 66-2/3 per cent prevailing earlier).

Reservation for Socially and Educationally Backward Classes

The Central Government issued orders on the 13th August, 1990, providing for reservation for Socially and Educationally Backward Classes (SEBCs) in direct recruitment to all Groups of services at the rate of 27 per cent of the total vacancies in the group concerned. These orders are at present inoperative, due to a stay order given by the Supreme Court.

Reservation for Ex-servicemen

Initially reservation for ex-servicemen was provided for a period of two years from 1-7-66. It was extended from time to time and has been in force on a permanent basis from 1-7-1979. Ten per cent of the vacancies in posts of the level of Asstt. Commandant in all Para Military Forces, 10 per cent of the vacancies in Group C services and posts and 20 per cent of the vacancies in Group D services and posts meant to be filled up by direct recruitment in any year are reserved for ex-servicemen provided that the percentage of reservation to specified for a category of post can be increased or decreased to the extent to which the total number of vacancies reserved for ex-serviceman, SC/ST and other categories taken together falls short or is in excess of 50 per cent of the vacancies in that category of posts filled in that year. The DG (Resettlement), in the Ministry of Defence monitors the implementation of this policy in the Central Government.

Reservation for the Physically Handicapped

A provision for reservation of three per cent of the vacancies in Groups C and D posts/services under the Central Government, meant to be filled up by direct recruitment, was introduced for the physically handicapped persons in November, 1977 and has been in operation since then. The categories of handicapped persons who benefited from this scheme are the blind, the deaf as well as the orthopaedically handicapped, each category being entitled to one per cent of the total three per cent reservation. This reservation holds good for identified posts in Groups C and D which are suitable for the physically handicapped and are filled in by direct recruitment. Reservation in promotion within the Group D, from Group D to Group C and within the Group C has also been introduced with effect from November, 1989.

Housing

National Housing Policy (Draft)

The Draft National Housing Policy was placed before both the Houses of Parliament in May, 1988. The document was approved by the Rajya Sabha in November, 1988. The document was forwarded to all the States and Union Territories for initiating necessary steps for the implementation of the policy.

The draft National Housing Policy envisages an increase in the dwelling units in rural and urban areas. It is proposed also to undertake the construction of 1000 night shelters per year for the pavement dwellers in urban areas. The availability of housing finance for different income groups will be expanded through housing finance institutions under the overall supervision of National

Housing Bank while Housing and Urban Development Corporation (HUDCO) will be assisted in expanding the provision of finance for the economically weaker sections and target groups. Under the policy, the Housing Programme will form part of the citywide programme of poverty alleviation, employment support and skill upgradation under Nehru Rozgar Yojana and other schemes for basic services to the poor. In order to reduce the cost of construction as well as promotion of appropriate technology and materials including those based on the utilisation of industrial and agricultural waste, a systematic programme of technology transfer and commercial application of appropriate technology has been taken up through Building Materials and Technology Promotion Council (BMTPC).

Housing and Urban Development Corporation (HUDCO)

An important role is being played by Housing and Urban Development Corporation (HUDCO) for meeting the housing needs of the poorer sections and vulnerable groups in urban and rural areas through various State and local agencies. It has so far financed over 48 lakh dwelling units in the last 21 years including 21.91 lakh units in rural areas, of which 90 per cent have gone to the poorer and vulnerable groups. HUDCO plans to expand its lending for various forms of housing activities and urban infrastructure during Eighth Plan period. It is also operating a network of building centres for extension of appropriate housing technology and skill-promotion.

National Housing Bank (NHB)

For meeting the requirements of housing finance, a National Housing Bank (NHB) was established in 1988. The bank is providing assistance through a number of schemes. These include: Home Loan Account Scheme, liberalised lending by commercial banks and refinance facilities. Refinance for land development and shelter programmes of public/private agencies and cooperatives in order to increase the supply of serviced land in urban and rural areas have been undertaken. Till December, 1991 the NHB had advanced refinance amounting to Rs. 770.38 crore to various Commercial Banks and other housing finance institutions and cooperatives, out of which it had provided loans amounting to Rs. 45.93 crore to various public and private agencies for undertaking land development and shelter scheme. Over 5.44 lakh accounts (estimated) have been opened with various commercial banks under the Home Loan Account Scheme of NHB whereby household savings to the extent of Rs. 100 crore (estimated) have been mobilised by December, 1991.

National Housing Bank also announced a Voluntary Deposit Scheme for mobilisation of black money and its partial use for construction of houses for the poor. As on 20th January, 1992, a total sum of Rs. 80.74 crore had been mobilised. The banking sector has been involved substantially in housing finance in recent years. Revised interest rates have been fixed by the Reserve Bank of India and National Housing Bank for the loans advanced by the commercial banks and housing finance institutions. It is recognised that increased supply of serviced land and housing finance for various income groups, with due regard to the needs of lower income groups to the informal sector are desiderata of larger supply of dwelling units.

Urban Basic Services and Slums

The Urban Basic Services Programme was introduced as a centrally sponsored scheme with the assistance of UNICEF. The scheme envisages support for basic services such as water supply, low cost sanitation, health care, pre-school education and programmes designed to promote cooperative group action. The scheme aims at reducing the morbidity and mortality rates of children, improving the health of women and enhancing their ability to supplement their incomes. It also envisages improving the capacity of voluntary organisation to manage programmes for the urban poor. During the Seventh Plan period, 169 towns in 37 districts were covered in 21 States/UTs.

The Environmental Improvement of Urban Slums (EIUS) was identified as a need of the slum population since the commencement of the Fifth Five Year Plan. The EIUS scheme was made an integral part of the Minimum Needs Programme (MNP) and was transferred to the State Sector. The scheme aimed at ameliorating the living conditions of urban slum dwellers and envisages provision of drinking water, sewerage, storm-water drains, community baths, community latrines, widening and paving of existing lanes, and street lighting.

Water Supply and Sanitation

Water supply and sanitation is a State subject. It is the responsibility of the State Governments and urban local bodies to plan, implement, operate and to maintain urban water supply and sanitation schemes. The rural water supply and rural sanitation schemes are implemented under the State Sector Minimum Needs Programme as well as under Centrally Sponsored Schemes. The 1981-90 decade was designated as the "International Drinking Water Supply and Sanitation Decade". India is a signatory to the Resolution thereof and has pledged its full support to the Action Plan under the Programme.

The drinking water supply problem in the rural areas is a matter of high priority. The Seventh Plan target was to cover all the remaining 1,61,722 identified problem villages. However, 1,53,357 villages could be provided with at least one safe source of drinking water supply, leaving a balance of 8365 hardcore 'No Source' problem villages. Out of this, 3032 villages were covered during 1990-91. A special allocation of Rs. 250 crore was approved during the current year for coverage of these residual 'No Source' problem villages by 31 March 1993. However, up to December 1991, only 591 villages could be covered. Besides, around 15 lakh partially covered villages and habitations also require augmentation for full coverage. The percentage of population with drinking water supply and sanitation facilities by the end of the year 1990-91 *vis-a-vis* the position at the end of the Sixth and Seventh Plans is given in Table 37.1.

TABLE 37.1: Percentage of Population Drinking Water and Sanitation Facilities

		Sixth Plan (1980-85)	Seventh Plan (1985-90)	1990-91*
(i)	Rural water supply	54	74	88
(ii)	Rural sanitation	1	2	3
(iii)	Urban water supply	72	84	84
(iv)	Urban sanitation	28	46	47

* Provisional

Source: *Economic Survey*, 1991-92.

National Drinking Water Mission (NDWM)

The Government of India is making a determined effort to raise the standard of living of the people, especially of those living in rural areas and the economically weaker sections. The Government of India, in its statement to the Lok Sabha on 27th February, 1986 had declared: 'We are setting up a number of scientific missions and thrust to see that funding, proper scientific management and all the resources that are required in these areas are available. . . . One of the areas we have chosen is drinking water.'

The National Drinking Water Mission was launched in October, 1986. Prior to Independence India's progress in the field of Rural Water Supply was very slow and sporadic. A recent analysis has revealed that plan outlay on Rural Water Supply and Sanitation has been stepped up from 0.18 per cent of the total Public Sector Plan Outlay during the First Plan (1951-56) to 1.97 per cent during the Seventh Plan (1985-90). 0.27 per cent of the GDP on an average (at current market prices) has been spent on Rural Water Supply and Sanitation Sector in the current decade (1980-81 to 1989-90).

Currently Rural Water Supply Programme is implemented under:

(a) State Sector — Minimum Needs Programme (MNP).
(b) Central Sector — Accelerated Rural Water Supply Programme (ARWSP) — National Drinking Water Mission (NDWM).

At the beginning of the Seventh Plan, 1,61,722 problem villages (out of 5,83,003 villages in the country) and about 211,90 million rural population (40 per cent) remained uncovered with safe drinking water facilities.

The main objectives of the NDWM are:

(a) Scientific Source Finding and Development.
(b) Water Harvesting and Conservation of Water.
(c) New Rigs and Equipment for Water Prospecting.
(d) New Dimensions by Application of Science and Technology Inputs in an Integrated Manner.
(e) Provision of safe drinking water to prevent a host of water-borne diseases and reduce the burden on those who traditionally fetch water: Women and children.

The target of the project is to:

(i) Cover 98,746 residual problem villages by March, 1990 (62,008 hard core uncovered problem villages and 36,738 villages partial to full).
(ii) Supply 40 litres per capita per day in all areas for human beings and in addition 30 litres per capita per day in desert areas for cattle.
(iii) Evolve cost effective technology.
(iv) Take conservation measures for sustained supply of water.
(v) Improve the performance and cost effectiveness of the on-going programmes.

The methodologies so far devised by the NDWM are:

(i) Scientific source finding and development

(ii) Improvement of traditional methods
(iii) Purification of water
(iv) Improvement of materials and design
(v) Improvement of maintenance methods
(vi) Computerized management information system
(vii) Continuous monitoring and evaluation
(viii) Community involvement — village panchayats, voluntary agencies
(ix) Awareness campaign.

The NDWM has identified five problem areas of immediate concern and five Sub-Missions have been set up. Some operational targets of the Sub-Missions include:

(i) Conservation of water and recharging of aquifers by providing Remote Sensing Technique followed by Hydrogeological and Geophysical survey with the participation of SAC/SCIR, CGWB, SGWB, SGWD, etc. in areas where no sustained water source is available.
(ii) Eradication of guinea worm (8,811 villages) with the participation of NICD and NEERI by 1990.
(iii) Control of fluorosis (8,700 villages) by application of appropriate technological input like Nalgonda technique by 1990 with the participation of NEERI and AIIMS.
(iv) Control of brackishness (17,500 villages) by reduction to tolerable limits by application of appropriate technological inputs like reverse osmosis, electro dialysis, solar stills with the participation of CSIR and BHEL by 1990.
(v) Removal of excess iron (2,900 villages) to tolerable limits by application of appropriate technological inputs with the participation of NEERI by 1990.

The problems of supplying drinking water in the villages are many and vary from region to region. Based on the problems associated with the supply of drinking water 55 Mini Mission Project areas have been taken in 25 States and three Union Territories.

Achievements of the NDWM can be stated thus:

(a) Potable water is now available to about 75 per cent of the rural population (3936.17 lakhs out of 5254.57 lakhs as per 1981 census) as on 1-4-1988.
(b) Only 22,000 villages of the target 98,746 residual problem villages remain to be covered as on 1-4-1989.
(c) Water sources for 7779 problem villages have been located through scientific source finding where earlier efforts have failed.
(d) Science and technology inputs have increased the success rate of drilling from 60 to 90 per cent in certain areas.
(e) In April 1988 there were only 3,111 villages affected with guinea worm, down from 8,811 in 1985.
(f) Computerized Rig Monitoring system as developed by UNICEF has been extended to 18 States and one U.T. Administration in the country.
(g) Water Quality Assessment has been given its due importance, 2 Nos. mobile water testing laboratories have been developed (one each by ITRC and NEERI):

100 Nos. water testing laboratories (85 Nos. stationary and 15 Nos. mobile) are being established during 1989-90. Laboratory Manuals on Water Analysis have been prepared as a part of the Mission activity.

For areas that have no water to desalt and cannot import water, application of new technology of an old method of water harvesting has been advocated. It is being used not only in India but also in Australia. Israel, USA and some of the arid regions. It consists of collecting and storing water from sloping land rendered impervious. The catchment can be of any size.

A Council for Social Audit of the Six National Technology Missions including National Drinking Water Mission is a people's forum composed of socially committed citizens. It has been set-up to :

(i) Independently evaluate official claims
(ii) Provide reliable feedback on the quality of services
(iii) Respond to citizens concerned.

We hope the Drinking Water Mission will remove the long-standing difficulties of drinking water in different parts of our country.

Source : Datta, M.M., *Prabuddha Bharata*, February, 1990.

38

PROGRESS MADE AND TASKS AHEAD

The following excerpts from President R. Venkataraman's address to the joint session of Parliament on February 24, 1992 reflect the progress made and tasks ahead.

The Government had given an assurance that elections would be held in Punjab in February, 1992. Despite many serious problems, this assurance has been fulfilled. Members are aware that the State of Punjab has been facing terrorist violence for the past decade and many innocent lives have been lost. The brave people of Punjab deserve to be congratulated for the courage they have displayed in reaffirming their faith in the democratic process and in the abiding values of secularism and nationhood. The Government is committed to finding a just and amicable solution to all the outstanding issues in Punjab. The Rajiv-Longowal Accord was a step in this direction. The presence of elected representatives will strengthen a meaningful dialogue and the participation in the process of all sections in the State.

The involvement of forces across the border in aiding, arming and providing logistic support to the terrorists in Kashmir is now well-known. Pakistan has continued its massive propaganda and disinformation campaign to defame India and to divert world attention from its overt and covert support to terrorism. Terrorist action has taken a heavy toll of innocent lives. For over two years the normal life of the people in the State has been dislocated. A section of the population has been forced to flee the State and take shelter outside. No doubt all efforts are being made to take care of the needs of those who have migrated, but the solution to the problem lies in their return to their own homes where they can be resettled safely.

Government has launched a massive operation against the terrorists with the help of the Army. All out efforts have been made to stop border infiltration. The recent efforts by terrorists to make massive intrusions across the Line of Control create a serious threat to peace in that area.

Assam

In the eastern part of the country, the Army had to be deployed in Assam from September 1991 to restore peace and normalcy. The security forces have apprehended a number of ULFA activists and seized their weapons. Some activists have also surrendered voluntarily. ULFA has released all hostages and has unilaterally declared the suspension of its agitations. ULFA has shown willingness to hold negotiations with the Government to find an amicable solution to the problems of Assam within the framework of the Constitution. The Army operations in Assam have been suspended, pending a dialogue with the ULFA.

Ayodhya issue

A close watch is being kept on the situation arising out of the Ram

Janmabhoomi-Babri Masjid dispute. Government has enacted legislation to maintain the status quo of the other places of worship as existed on August 15, 1947.

Action has been completed to set-up a Foundation for Communal Harmony to take care of children of families affected by communal violence. One of the commitments of the Government was to establish a composite rapid action force to quell communal riots. All necessary decisions in this regard have been taken. The Force has been raised.

Economy

In my last address, I had spoken of the need to take hard decisions to overcome the grim economic situation confronting the country. The Government has moved swiftly to deal with the crisis. The balance of payments problem has been successfully handled. Our reserves of foreign exchange today stand at over Rs 10,000 crore. We have redeemed the gold we had pledged, and arrested the outflow of capital. International confidence is being restored. At the same time, the Government has initiated steps to restructure the economy for greater productivity and growth, changes have been made in industrial, fiscal and trade policies. This process of change will continue and will have to be extended to other important sectors of the economy.

The new industrial policy aims at consolidating the gains of the past decade, and imparting a fresh impetus to Indian industry for enhancing its efficiency and productivity. Along with changes in the industrial policy, a policy package for support to small-scale industry has been announced.

We place great emphasis on exports. Despite an unavoidable import compression of about 20 per cent exports to general currency area countries have shown a modest growth of 6 per cent in dollar terms. External obstacles on exports to rupee payment area have, however, affected overall export growth. Efforts are being made to restore trade with the republics of the former Soviet Union, and framework agreements are being entered into with all of them.

The Government is fully conscious of the need to protect the interest of all those workers who may be affected by restructuring as contemplated by the new policies. A programme of retraining and re-deployment will be taken up, for which necessary funds will be provided.

Price rise

The rise in prices is a matter of grave concern. Inflation is being caused, to a large extent, by the fiscal deficit. Once the fiscal deficit is reduced and brought under control, inflation can be expected to come down to reasonable levels. Other possible administrative steps like dehoarding measures and increase in release of foodgrains have been taken. The inflation rate has come down from over 16 per cent in August 1991 to about 12 per cent at present. The Government will continue to monitor prices and take steps to reduce these further.

The economic policy changes initiated recently will form the basis for the Eighth Plan which envisages a growth rate of 5.6 per cent. This growth target is to be achieved by a proposed total outlay of Rs 400,000 crore. The foremost objective of the plan will be to generate increased employment. Other priorities of the plan are eradication of illiteracy, universalisation of elementary education and providing drinking water and primary health facilities. The emphasis will be on people's involvement and in reaching out to the poorest and the most needy sections of our people. The Eighth Plan will also focus on strengthening infrastructure.

Growth encouraging

Growth rates have been encouraging in several critical infrastructure areas like electricity, coal, steel and cement. Government is committed to further strengthening infrastructure. Every effort will be made to step up power supply and make it more stable. The development of atomic energy and non-conventional energy sources will receive high priority. The importance of effective communication systems for the country's development cannot be over stated. These will be strengthened. Every effort will be made to increase the capacity and transport capability of the railway network. A new shipping policy is being initiated. A major restructuring of Indian Airlines and Air India is envisaged.

The progress made by the country in the field of science and technology is a matter of pride. To cite only a few, the indigenous fabrication of the second generation Insat-2 series of satellite is proceeding according to schedule. Insat-2A is expected to be launched next month. With the planned launching of satellite launch vehicles, in the next one year, India will join the ranks of those few countries which have their own launch capability.

While doing everything possible to accelerate the pace of progress, there must be environmental accountability all-round on the part of Government, industry and people. A scheme of financial incentives and disincentives would supplement the normal regulatory measures to achieve this purpose.

One of the world's worst industrial tragedies took place in Bhopal on 2nd December, 1984. The aftermath of this event has scarred the lives of thousands of people. The Government of India has taken upon itself the responsibility to secure compensation for those affected and provide them relief. The legal processes have been completed by the directive of the Supreme Court on 3rd October, 1991. Government will ensure maximum relief to the victims.

The tourism sector has emerged as one of the largest foreign exchange earners providing employment to many. The Government has launched a major initiative to accelerate growth of tourism in cooperation with the State Governments, travel trade and hotel industry. This has already started yielding results and the tourist arrivals have picked up, recording the highest level of international tourist arrivals in December 1991.

The foundation of our future security and progress lies to a great extent in agricultural growth. The dramatic progress we have made in agriculture, including in food crops, horticulture, fisheries, animal breeds and poultry, has a lot to do with progress in our research laboratories, but more than all else, it is the story of the life of the Indian farmer, his grit and determination. 1990-91 was the third agricultural year in succession when a new record in foodgrains production was achieved.

Water disputes

Recently issues associated with the sharing and allocation of waters between

States have been generating passions and tensions. It will have to be ensured that water, one of nature's precious gifts, is shared in an equitable manner in the larger national interest. Water is a flowing entity, variable in quantity from year to year and season to season. It should be managed in harmonious manner in a spirit of understanding and cooperation between the areas served by it. Rivers should be a binding force for the people of different regions rather than a matter of discord. Every effort should be made to resolve through dialogue all disputes relating to the use of waters of any inter-State river. Should this not be possible, Government will ensure expeditious settlement of the disputes through the adjudication machinery set-up by law for the purpose.

Effective measures are being taken to generate greater employment opportunities for the most disadvantaged sections through the integrated rural development programme and the Jawahar Rozgar Yojana. Special efforts will be made to expand employment opportunities for Scheduled Castes, Scheduled Tribes and women. No effort would be spared to provide safe drinking water to our people, on which depends the state of their health.

Poverty is no less acute in the urban areas. Employment generation and poverty alleviation schemes in the urban sector will be continued. A new national housing policy is on the anvil. The main objectives of the new policy will be to create an enabling environment for housing activity and to assist people, in particular the vulnerable sections, to secure for themselves affordable shelters through access to developed land, building materials, finances and technology.

Government is committed to the eradication of the dehumanising practice of manual scavenging through low cost sanitation schemes through a time bound programme.

Dalits

The Government is acutely conscious of the problems of the Scheduled Castes and Scheduled Tribes, in respect of repeated incidents of atrocities against Scheduled Caste and Scheduled Tribes. A special conference of Chief Ministers was held in October 1991 in order to focus on the need for the State Governments to pay special attention to deal with this problem.

In my last address I had mentioned that steps would be initiated for the effective implementation of the 15-point programme for the welfare of minorities which seeks to ensure that minorities are protected and that they are not discriminated against in the matter of employment in public services and benefits from development schemes. To realise this objective the 15-point programme is now being recast to make it more effective.

Government will give very high priority to the needs of children and women, the most vulnerable of groups in our society. Government will expand the ICDS programme during the Eighth Plan so as to cover the entire country. The girl child will receive particular attention with focus on her nutrition, health and educational needs.

Government attaches the highest priority to ensuring that no uncertainty whatsoever exists in the people getting their basic daily necessities. To this end, Government will make allout efforts to strengthen the public distribution system.

The Essential Commodities Act, 1955, is being strictly enforced against hoarders and black marketeers to enhance and sustain availability of essential commodities and this drive will continue. The Government looks upon the public distribution system as the centre of a new social development focus to be imparted to its various antipoverty programmes. Appropriate linkages will be forged with other programmes like the Jawahar Rozgar Yojana and the ICDS.

Population

The rate at which our population is growing will put tremendous pressure on our resources. The Government has taken steps in recent months to evolve an integrated and holistic approach to achieve a marked decline in the birth rate. Towards this end an action plan has been drawn up which seeks to improve the quality and outreach of services. It is now proven that birth rates have remained high in areas with low female literacy, low age of girls at marriage and high infant and maternal mortality. It is in these areas that social efforts will be concentrated under the action plan. Particular attention will be given to 90 districts in the country which have a crude birth rate of over 39 per thousand.

A national policy on education was adopted by Parliament in 1986 and its implementation commenced soon thereafter. Several developments in the sphere of education, and the report of the NPE review committee, made it necessary to examine the need for modifications in the education policy. The process of examination is soon to conclude and I am confident that the uncertainty in respect of the policy will now be set at rest reiterating the main thrusts of the 1986 policy. The national literacy mission, which was launched by the late Shri Rajiv Gandhi in May 1988, has made significant strides. I share with you a sense of pride in the fact that all the districts of Kerala and Pondicherry, as well as several in other States, have succeeded in eradicating illiteracy. Total literacy campaigns are at present being implemented in nearly 70 districts in the country. The campaigns in these districts will cover nearly 30 million illiterates in various age groups and would cost Rs. 210 crore.

We also need to effectively delink degrees from jobs and to give to the entire educational system a work and vocational orientation. A decision has already been taken to set-up a central institute of vocational education.

World Events

Events on the world scene have continued to unfold at an amazing pace since I last addressed Parliament in July last year. The intervening period has been an extremely active one in India's foreign policy.

The Government's foreign policy priorities are to maintain the unity and territorial integrity of India, to ensure our geo-political security by creating a durable environment of stability and peace in our region and to build up a framework conducive for the economic well-being of our people by encouraging a healthy external economic environment.

The recent visits of the Prime Minister of Nepal has ushered in a qualitatively new era of relations between the two countries resulting in opening very important areas of cooperation which will fortify the unique closeness of our ties, strengthened by the emergence of multi-party democracy in Nepal.

The recent visit of the Chinese Premier has been an important milestone in the further development of our relations. We have enhanced our mutual understanding through exchange of views on bilateral, regional and international issues at the highest level.

We are keen that the traditional friendly relations with Bangladesh are further expanded in the changed context with the advent of democracy in Bangladesh becoming an additional bond between the two countries.

We are committed to the strengthening and consolidation of bilateral relations with Sri Lanka in keeping with the traditional and historical ties between the two countries. The voluntary return of Sri Lanka refugees back to their homeland, based on assurances received from Sri Lanka Government commenced on January 20, 1992 and is continuing.

Pak Approach

Pakistan's negative approach towards India and its support to terrorism in Punjab and Jammu and Kashmir continue to be the main impediments to normalisation of relations. The dangers inherent in its actions in violation of the Simla Agreement and universally accepted norms of inter-State conduct have been repeatedly pointed out to Pakistan. We have nevertheless continued with our effort to carry the confidence-building process and bilateral dialogue forward. Unfortunately, in the recent past, the Government of Pakistan and the Pakistan National Assembly have chosen to associate themselves with statements and actions that have vitiated the atmosphere. We hope that the Government of Pakistan will join us in serious endeavours to establish tension-free and good neighbourly relations between the two countries.

Ties with Russia

On December 26, 1991, we announced our decision to accord formal recognition to the Russian Federation and to all the other republics of the erstwhile Soviet Union. Russia has assumed the role of a successor state and has taken over the seat of the erstwhile Soviet Union in the United Nations Security Council. We have sought to maintain our traditionally close relations not only with Russia but with the other republics as well. In addition to our embassy in Moscow, we plan to open embassies in Ukraine, Kazakhstan and Belarus and upgrade our consulate general in Tashkent in Uzbekistan.

The values of democracy, individual liberty and respect for human rights which we share with the United States of America provide a strong basis for close cooperation between the two largest democracies of the world. Our expanding consultations in both bilateral and multilateral fora encompass a wide range of issues including peace, security and threats emanating from terrorism and drug-trafficking. The United States is our largest trading partner and a major source of technology. It has been supportive of our efforts to overcome our temporary economic difficulties and launch a far-reaching programme of economic reform. We look forward to a long-term and mutually rewarding economic partnership with the United States.

West Asia

We attach special importance to our relations with countries of West Asia and North Africa. We have over the years extended consistent and unequivocal support to the Arab cause, particularly to the Palestinian struggle for their just and inalienable rights. India has welcomed the reactivation of the West Asian peace process and the ongoing dialogue between Arab States and Israel to find a just and equitable settlement to the Arab-Israeli dispute.

Given the changed political realities in the region, India has decided to establish diplomatic relations with Israel. We look forward to establishing a comprehensive and multifaceted relationship with Israel.

Non-aligned

At the multilaterally level, our participation has similarly been within our overall framework of priorities. The Non-aligned movement is readjusting in a dynamic manner to the breathtaking pace of global developments. We have re-affirmed our faith in its continued relevance. The independence of national decision-making that is enshrined in its philosophy is today more relevant than ever before.

In other multilateral fora such as the G-15 and the Commonwealth summit, the Prime Minister not only articulated our views on important issues but re-emphasised the need to restore the centrally and criticality of development issues on the multilateral agenda. The Uruguay Round of negotiations was reached a crucial stage. We shall continue to defend our vital interests and seek improvements as we work towards the establishment of a fair and balanced multilateral trading system.

We believe that given the global reach of nuclear weapons we need to follow a global approach.

Source: *Hindustan Times*, February 29, 1992.

39

SIGNIFICANT NATIONAL EVENTS

April, 1991

3 Shri V.C. Shukla, former Union Minister rejoins Congress.
4 U.P. Assembly is dissolved after the withdrawal of Congress support to Shri Mulayam Singh's Ministry of SJP.
— Shri Chimanbhai Patel forms Janata Dal (G) in Gujarat.
5 Kerala Assembly is dissolved.
12 Election Commission announces poll dates.
13 Shri Arun Nehru and Shri Arif Mohammad Khan quits Janata Dal.
17 Election Commission allow BJP to use Lotus symbol in elections.
19 President promulgates Ordinance announcing Tenth General Elections and issues poll notification.
24 Poll dates for Punjab and Assam are announced.

May

18 Shri Morarji Desai gets Pakistan's highest civilian honour, Nishan-e-Pakistan, at his Bombay residence.
19 Fifty persons are killed in violence in first phase of polling.
21 Shri Rajiv Gandhi is assassinated by a woman wearing 'belt bomb' at Sriperumbudur in Tamil Nadu.
22 Second and third phases of polling are postponed by 20 days to June 12 and 15.
— Veteran Communist leader Shri S. Dange is dead.
23 Smt. Sonia Gandhi declines Congress (I) Presidentship.
24 Shri Rajiv Gandhi is cremated in New Delhi.
27 Shri P.V. Narasimha Rao emerges as Congress (I)'s consensus choice for party presidentship.

June

6&8 Polling is held in Assam.
17 Shri Rajiv Gandhi and Sardar Patel are awarded Bharat Ratna posthumously.
20 Tenth Lok Sabha is formed with Chief Election Commissioner's notification.
— President invites Shri P.V. Narasimha Rao to form government.
21 Narasimha Rao Cabinet is sworn in Punjab elections are postponed.
22 Punjab Governor, General O.P. Malhotra resigns.
23 Saikia Government is sworn in Assam.

July

1 Government announced devaluation of rupee by 8.7 to 9.7 per cent against four international currencies.
3 Rupee is again devalued by 10.58 per cent to 12.31 per cent.
4 Government announces new trade policy.
10 Shri Shivraj Patil is elected as Lok Sabha Speaker.
15 Narasimha Rao Government wins vote of confidence in Lok Sabha.
16 Railway budget proposes 10 per cent hike in freight rates.
18 Reserve Bank of India admits sending 46.91 tonnes of gold to England to tide our Balance of Payment (BOP) crisis.
24 Union Budget for 1991-92 is presented. New Industrial Policy is announced.
28 President seeks Supreme Court's opinion on Cauvery issue.

August

5 Shri Surendra Nath is appointed Punjab Governor.
6 Government cuts down fertiliser subsidy and exempts small farmers from hike.
9 Supreme Court upholds Chief Election Commissioner's decision to postpone Punjab polls.
10 Shri S. Malikarjunaiah of BJP is elected Deputy Speaker of Lok Sabha.
29 India's second remote sensing satellite IRS-1B is launched successfully from Baikanour Cosmodrome.

September

10 Lok Sabha passes Places of Worship Bill seeking to maintain status quo as on August 15, 1947 at all places of worship except the Ayodhya Shrine.
12 Rajya Sabha passes Places of Worship Bill.
15 Army is deployed in Assam to curb ULFA activities.
25 Narasimha Rao Government issues notification amending the National Front Government's proposed 27 per cent reservation for SEBC, adding ten per cent more for economically backwards.

October

1 Supreme Court declines to lift stay on implementation of Mandal Commission's recommendations.
2 Election Commission announces by-election for the 16 Lok Sabha and 58 Assembly seats to be held on November 15.
10 BJP Government of U.P. issues notification acquiring land at the Ram Janmabhoomi Shrine.
11 President's rule is imposed in Meghalaya.
20 Major earthquake rocks Uttarkashi area killing about 500 people.

November

15 Supreme Court orders U.P. Government to maintain status quo at

Ayodhya.

17 Shri P.V. Narasimha Rao, Prime Minister wins election from Nandyal with a record 5.8 lakh votes margin.

22 Supreme Court quashes Cauvery Ordinance of Karnataka Government.

December

5 Central Government announces Legislative Assembly and Council of Ministers for Delhi and envisages election within six to eight months.

6 Janata Dal formally splits in Uttar Pradesh.

11 Chinese Premier Shri Li Peng arrives in New Delhi.

12 BJP President Shri M.M. Joshi begins *Ekta Yatra* from Kanya Kumari.

21 Parliament approves the Delhi Assembly Bill.

26 India recognises 12 Soviet Republics.

— Shri Ajit Singh is expelled from the Janata Dal for six years.

31 The National Integration Council welcomes the Government's decision to hold elections in Punjab on February, 1992.

January, 1992

1 Prime Minister P.V. Narasimha Rao launches a nation-wide Public Distribution System (PDS).

— Non-Attack Pact on nuclear installation comes into force between India and Pakistan.

3 The Finance Minister, Dr. Manmohan Singh, said that India would continue to need the support of the multinational agencies like the International Monetary Fund (IMF) for three more years when enough direct foreign investment would not be coming.

4 President R. Venkataraman issues an Ordinance amending the Representation of the People's Act to restrict countermanding of elections only on the death of the candidate of a recognised political party and not that of an independent. It applies to the whole of the country and comes into effect immediately.

6 Punjab poll schedule soon, says Election Commissioner T.N. Seshan.

7 President's rule imposed in Manipur and the State Assembly kept in animated suspension since the ruling United Legislative Front (ULF) had lost its majority with the resignation of seven Janata Dal legislators.

8 Personal baggage carried in the railways in excess permitted limits to cost passengers 30 per cent more from January 16.

12 Noted vocalist musician Kumar Gandharva's death takes place.

15 Punjab polls to 13 Lok Sabha, 117 Assembly seats to be held on February 19, according to the announcement made by the Election Commission.

16 Iron and steel price decontrolled. India and U.K. agree to have a treaty on extradition and confiscation of the properties of the people involved in terrorism.

— One million tonnes of wheat to be imported in order to bring down the price of this essential commodity.

17 Four Akali Groups (Akali Dal — Badal; Akali Dal —Mann; Akali Dal — Baba Joginder Singh; and Babbar Akali Dal) and three Sikh Student Federations (Babbar Vidyarthi Jathebandi; AISSF (Manjit Group) and Sikh

Student Federation (Mehta Chawla) decide to boycott Punjab elections.

19 President issues ordinance, campaign period reduced to 14 days.

20 The Government of India increases the sugar price from Rs. 6.10 to 6.90 per kilogram with effect from Jan. 21. This was necessitated by the enhancement in statutory minimum price of sugarcane from Rs. 23 per quintal to Rs. 26 per quintal (October 1991 to September 1992).

— Saraswati Samman from K.K. Birla Charitable Foundation, for renowned Hindi poet and author Dr. Harivansh Rai Bachhan. The award of Rs. 3 lakh was on his autobiography titled *'Deshdwar se Sopan tak'* (1985).

— Akalis not keen on Chandigarh — Home Minister S.B. Chavan (*Hindustan Times* Jan. 21).

21 Home Minister S.B. Chavan's appeal to BJP to stop *Ekta Yatra*. B.J.P rejects Chavan's appeal. Army asked to provide security to 'yatris' once they enter Doda district on Jan. 25 and move towards Srinagar on Jan. 26.

— Shri Jiwan Singh Umranangal forms a new political party called the Shiromani Jagat Akali Dal and decides to contest elections under the banner of the newly formed party.

23 Bharat Ratna for Maulana Abul Kalam Azad and Netaji Subhash Chandra Bose.

— *Ekta Yatra* is at BJP's own risk — Home Minister S.B. Chavan.

24 BJP agrees to reduce the size of the contingent of the *Ekta Yatra* to hoist the National Flag at the Lal Chowk on Jan. 26.

— Punjab militants fire at the advance party of the *Ekta Yatra* near village Mehton on the Phagwara-Jallandhar highway and kill six and injure 40 yatris.

— Chief of the Panthic Committee Shri Sohan Singh asks the militants to stop militancy and seek the support of the public through democratic means.

— Director General of Jammu and Kashmir police, J.N. Saxena and three other senior police and paramilitary forces critically wounded in a rocket attack at police head-quarters building in Srinagar.

25 Punjab poll notification issued by the Election Commission.

— Bharat Ratna conferred upon the noted industrialist Shri J.R.D. Tata and Padma Vibhushan on BJP leader Shri A.B. Vajpayee.

26 BJP President Murli Manohar Joshi unfurls tricolor at Lal Chowk Srinagar.

27 The Union Cabinet approves a proposal for setting up a fresh delimitation commission to readjust the Lok Sabha and State Assembly constituencies on the basis of the latest Census.

29 India and Israel decide on full diplomatic ties.

— Government lifts curbs on Foreign Exchange Regulation Act (FERA).

30 Prime Minister Narasimha Rao appeals to all political leaders and parties to contest Punjab polls.

February

1 Samajwadi Janata Party MP H.D. Deva Gowda sends his resignation on Cauvery issue to Lok Sabha Deputy Speaker to be handed over to the Speaker.

— Russian President Boris Yeltsin backs India on Kashmir issue. Nominations ends in Punjab.

— Akali Dal (Mann) President Simranjit Singh Mann urges the Government to call off the Feb. 19 polls in Punjab as there could be post-poll "communal tension and bloodshed" (*Hindustan Times*, February 3, 1992).

3 Speaking at a congregation of world leaders at Davos (Switzerland), the Prime Minister P.V. Narasimha Rao states that economic reforms in India will continue.

— Kapil Dev becomes the second bowler in Test cricket to take 400 wickets.

— Chief Election Commissioner Shri T.N. Seshan orders inquiry into the allegations made by the Akali leaders regarding preventing some of their candidates to file their nominations to make the contest easy for the Congress.

4 Sukhjinder Singh Akali Dal (S) decides to withdraw from elections, alleges, unfair means and directs all the 31 candidates who filed nominations to withdraw.

5 Shri Prakash Singh Badal, President Akali Dal (Badal) asks Punjabis to boycott elections and prepare for a struggle.

— *Hartal* in Kashmir to general call strike by Pakistan.

— Split in Janata Dal and Shri Ajit Singh chosen president of the split Janata Dal.

— Congress Ministry headed by D.D. Lapang, sworn in Meghalaya.

— Oil struck at Bombay Offshore.

8 Foreign Minister Madhav Singh Solanki warns Pakistan on the proposed JKLF march on the Lines of Actual Control (LAC) on February 11.

10 All-party meet support Government in its efforts to resist by all means any violations of the Line of Control or the border in Jammu and Kashmir.

11 JKLF attempt to cross LAC foiled.

12 Twelve JKLF activists killed in Pak firing.

13 Open General Licences (OGL) import curb withdrawn.

— Thirty-nine Bhumihars were killed and several injured in an attack in Bara village of Gaya district by extremists of the Maoist Communist Centre (MCC).

— Total strike in Central Universities against the proposed UGC (Amendment Bill).

— The Supreme Court Bar Association votes against Justice Ramaswami.

17 Tripura Chief Minister Sudhir Ranjan Majumdar submits the resignation of his ministry as coalition breaks and recommends the dissolution of Assembly.

18 65 pilgrims killed in a stampede as over 25 lakh people crowded around the Mahamaham tank in Kumbakonam to take a holy dip.

21 Congress bags 12 Lok Sabha seats in Punjab. Congress scores a record victory in Punjab Assembly elections by winning 86 seats out of total 117 seats.

22 EC derecognises 3 National parties — Janata Dal Samajwadi, Lok Dal and Indian Congress (Socialist). It also derecognises 10 State parties.

24 Economic reforms in more areas — President Shri R. Venkataraman addressing the joint session of Parliament.

— Shri Beant Singh unanimously elected leader of the 87 member Congress Legislative Party of Punjab.

25 Railway Minister C.K. Jaffer Sharief presents the railway budget in the Lok

Sabha.

— Beant Singh Ministry sworn in by the Punjab Governor.

26 Finance Minister Manmohan Singh places the controversial letter of November 11, 1991 written to the World Bank on the table of Parliament.

27 The pre-budget Economic Survey for 1991-92 presented to Parliament paints a grim picture of economy.

— Shri P.V. Narasimha Rao declared elected unopposed as the president of the All India Congress Committee.

28 Estimate Committee cautions Government against hasty steps.

29 Finance Minister Manmohan Singh presents the Annual Budget 1992-93 to Parliament.

March

22 Federico Mayor Director General of UNESCO arrived in New Delhi and discussed with Prime Minister Narasimha Rao on UNESCO's role in developing basic education as well as science and technology through technical cooperation.

23 It was stated in the Rajya Sabha that the educated unemployed constituted around 40 per cent of the total unemployed in the country in 1987-88 as per the survey conducted by the National Sample Survey Organisation.

— A one-week course (23-28 March) on "Environmental Impact Assessment of Thermal Power Plants" was sponsored by the Ministry of Environment and Forests, Government of India.

APPENDIX I

POPULAR INFORMATION

I. NATIONAL INFORMATION

(i) India comes within the First Ten Countries in . . .

	1	2	3	4	5	6	7	8	9	10
Area	0	0	0	0	0	0	*	0	0	0
Atomic Technology	0	0	0	0	0	*	0	0	0	0
Bicycles	*	0	0	0	0	0	0	0	0	0
Cardamom	*	0	0	0	0	0	0	0	0	0
Caustic Soda	0	0	0	0	0	0	0	0	*	0
Cement	0	0	0	0	0	0	0	0	*	0
Chillies	*	0	0	0	0	0	0	0	0	0
Cigarette	0	0	0	0	0	0	0	0	0	*
Coal	0	0	0	0	0	0	*	0	0	0
Cotton Fabrics	*	0	0	0	0	0	0	0	0	0
Cotton Lint	0	0	*	0	0	0	0	0	0	0
Cotton Yarn	0	0	0	*	0	0	0	0	0	0
Feature Films	*	0	0	0	0	0	0	0	0	0
Fish-catching	0	0	0	0	0	0	*	0	0	0
GNP	0	0	0	0	0	0	0	0	*	0
Groundnuts	*	0	0	0	0	0	0	0	0	0
Irrigated Areas	0	*	0	0	0	0	0	0	0	0
Jute Cultivation	0	*	0	0	0	0	0	0	0	0
Population	0	*	0	0	0	0	0	0	0	0
Rice	0	*	0	0	0	0	0	0	0	0
Salt	0	0	0	0	*	0	0	0	0	0
Soda Ash	0	0	0	0	0	0	0	*	0	0
Sugar	0	0	0	0	*	0	0	0	0	0
Tea	*	0	0	0	0	0	0	0	0	0
Tobacco Cultivation	0	0	*	0	0	0	0	0	0	0
Turmeric	*	0	0	0	0	0	0	0	0	0
Wheat	0	0	0	*	0	0	0	0	0	0

* indicates position of India.

(ii) **General Information**

States/Union Territories	Main Language	Preferable Season to Visit
Andhra Pradesh	Telugu	Nov. to Mar.
Arunachal Pradesh	Tribal	Oct. to May
Assam	Assamese	Oct. to May
Bihar	Hindi	Oct. to Mar.
Goa	Konkani, Marathi	Oct. to May
Gujarat	Gujarati	Oct. to Mar.
Haryana	Hindi	Oct. to Mar.
Himachal Pradesh	Hindi, Pahari	Apr. to Oct.
Jammu and Kashmir	Kashmiri	Dec. to Mar (winter)
Jammu and Kashmir	Kashmiri	Apr.to Oct. (summer)
Karnataka	Kannada	Nov. to Apr.
Kerala	Malayalam	Oct. to Apr.
Madhya Pradesh	Hindi	Sep. to Mar.
Maharashtra	Marathi	Nov. to May
Manipur	Manipuri	Sep. to Apr.
Meghalaya	Tribal	Nov. to Mar.
Mizoram	Mizo	Oct. to May
Nagaland	Angami	Oct. to Mar.
Orissa	Oriya	Oct. to Mar.
Punjab	Punjabi	Oct. to Mar.
Rajasthan	Hindi	Oct. to Mar.
Sikkim	Bhutia	Mar. to May
Tamil Nadu	Tamil	Nov. to Mar.
Tripura	Tripuri	Sep. to Mar.
Uttar Pradesh	Hindi	Oct. to Mar.
West Bengal	Bengali	Oct. to Mar.
Andaman and Nicobar Islands	Tribal	Dec. to Apr.
Chandigarh	Punjabi, Hindi	Oct. to Mar.
Dadra and Nagar Haveli	Gujarati, Marathi	Sep. to Oct.
Daman and Diu	Gujarati, Marathi	Oct. to Mar.
Delhi	Hindi	Oct. to Mar.
Lakshadweep	Malayalam	Oct. to May
Pondicherry	Tamil	Nov. to Apr.

II. INTERNATIONAL INFORMATION

(i) Dimensions of Continents

Africa	11,500,000	square miles
Asia	17,000,000	square miles
Europe	3,750,000	square miles
North America	8,000,000	square miles
Oceania	4,000,000	square miles
Polar Regions	6,205,000	square miles
South America	6,800,000	square miles

The latest estimates of the earth's area place the fertile regions at 33,000,000 square miles; steppes at 19,000,000 square miles; deserts at 5,000,000 square miles.

Asia, the largest continent, is about 6,000 miles from East to West, and over 5,300 miles from North to South. Africa is 5,000 miles from North to South. Europe is 2,400 miles from North to South, and 3,300 miles from East to West. South America is 4,600 miles from North to South and 3,200 miles from East to West. North America is 4,900 miles from North to South and over 4,000 miles from East to West.

(ii) Dimensions of the World

Equatorial Diameter	7,926.68	miles
Polar Diameter	7,899.99	miles
Difference	26.69	miles
Mean Diameter	7,918.00	miles
Equatorial Circumference	24,902.37	miles
Meridional Circumference	24,860.44	miles
Difference	41.83	miles
Area of Surface	196,950,284.00	square miles
Water Area	139,950,284.00	square miles
Land Area	57,000,000.00	square miles
Volume of Land	29,300,000.00	square miles
Volume of Water	320,000,000.00	cubic miles

(iii) Areas and Depths of the Ocean

Oceans	Area (Square Miles)	Greatest Depth (Feet)
Pacific	68,634,000	30,000
Atlantic	41,321,000	27,366
Indian	29,340,000	18,582
Antarctic	7,500,000	25,200
Arctic	4,000,000	9,000

(iv) **World Currencies**

Country		Currency
Argentina	Peso	= 100 Centavos
Australia	Dollar	= 100 Cents
Austria	Schilling	= 100 Groschen
Belgium/Luxembourg	Franc	= 100 Centimes
Brazil	Cruzeiro	= 100 Centavos
Bulgaria	Lev	= 100 Stotikni
Canada	Dollar	= 100 Cents
Czechoslovakia	Koruna	= 100 Haleru
Denmark	Krone	= 100 Ore
Finland	Markka	= 100 Pennia
France	Franc	= 100 Centimes
Germany, DR	Ostmark	= 100 Plenning
Germany, FR	Deutschemark	= 100 Plenning
Greece	Drachma	= 100 Lepta
Hong Kong	Dollar	= 100 Cents
Hungary	Forint	= 100 Filler
India	**Rupee**	**= 100 Paise**
Indonesia	Rupiah	= 100 Sen
Iran	Rial	= 100 Dinars
Ireland, Republic of	Pound	= 100 Pence
Israel	Pound	= 100 Agorot
Italy	Lira	= 100 Centisimi
Japan	Yen	=
Korea	Won	= 100 Jeon
Kuwait	Kuwait Dinner	= 1,000 Fils
Libya	Libyan Dinar	= 1,000 Dirhams
Malaysia	Dollar	= 100 Cents
Mexico	Peso	= 100 Centavos
Netherlands	Guilder	= 100 Cents
New Zealand	Dollar	= 100 Cents
Nigeria	Naira	= 100 Kobo
Norway	Krone	= 100 Ore
Philippines	Peso	= 100 Centavos
Poland	Zloty	= 100 Groszy
Portugal	Escudo	= 100 Centavos
Romania	Leu	= 100 Bani
Saudi Arabia	Riyal	= 100 Halalas
Singapore	Dollar	= 100 Cents
South Africa	Rand	= 100 Cents
Spain	Peseta	= 100 Centimos
Sweden	Krone	= 100 Ore
Switzerland	Franc	= 100 Centimos
Turkey	Lira	= 100 Kuru
United Kingdom	Pound	= 100 Pence
U.S.A.	Dollar	= 100 Cents
U.S.S.R.	Rouble	= 100 Copocus
Venezuela	Bolivar	= 100 Centimos
Yugoslavia	New Dinar	= 100 Paras

(v) **Country: Capital and Area**

Country	Capital	Area in sq. km.
Africa		
Algeria	Algiers	2,381,741
Angola	Luanda	1,246,700
Botswana	Gaborone	600,372
Burundi	Bujumbura	27,834
Cameroon	Yaounde	475,442
Central African Republic	Bangui	622,984
Comoro Islands	Moroni	2,171
Congo	Brazzaville	342,000
Egypt	Cairo	1,001,449
Equatorial Guinea	Maiabo	28,051
Ethiopia	Addis Ababa	1,221,900
Gabon	Libreville	267,667
Ghana	Accra	238,537
Guinea	Conakry	245,857
Kenya	Nairobi	582,646
Liberia	Monrovia	111,369
Libya	Tripoli	1,759,540
Madagascar	Antananarivo	587,041
Mauritania	Nouakchott	1,030,700
Mauritius	Port Louis	2,045
Morocco	Rabat	446,550
Mozambique	Maputo	783,030
Namibia (S. Africa)	Windhoek	824,292
Niger	Niamey	1,267,000
Nigeria	Lagos	923,768
Senegal	Dakar	196,722
South Africa	Pretoria (Admn.) Cape Town (Leg)	1,221,037
Sudan	Khartoum	2,505,813
Tanzania	Dodoma	945,087
Tunisia	Tunis	163,610
Uganda	Kampala	236,036
Upper Volta (Burkina-Fasco)	Ouagadougou	274,200
Zambia	Lusaka	752,614
Zimbabwe	Harare (Salisbury)	390,580
Asia		
Afghanistan	Kabul	647,497
Bahrain	Manama	622
Bangladesh	Dhaka	143,998
Bhutan	Thimphu	47,000
China	Peking (Beijing)	9,561,000
India	**New Delhi**	**3,287,590**
Indonesia	Djakarta	1,904,345
Iran	Tehran	1,648,000
Iraq	Baghdad	434,924
Israel	Jerusalem	20,770
Japan	Tokyo	372,313
Jordan	Amman	97,740
Kampuchea	Phnom Penh	181,035

(contd.)

(contd.)

Country	Capital	Area in sq. km.
Korea (North)	Pyongyang	120,538
Korea (South)	Seoul	98,484
Kuwait	Kuwait	17,818
Laos	Vientiane	236,800
Lebanon	Beirut	10,400
Malaysia	Kuala Lumpur	329,749
Maldives	Male	298
Mongolia	Ulan Bator	1,565,000
Myanmar	Rangoon	676,552
Nepal	Kathmandu	140,797
Pakistan	Islamabad	803,943
Philippines	Manila	300,000
Qatar	Doha	11,000
Saudi Arabia	Riyadh	2,149,690
Singapore	Singapore	581
South Yemen	Aden	332,968
Sri Lanka	Colombo	65,610
Syria	Damascus	185,180
Taiwan	Taipei	35,961
Thailand	Bangkok	514,000
U.A.E.	Abu Dhabi	83,600
Vietnam	Hanoi	332,559
Yemen	Sana	195,000
Australia and Oceania		
Australia	Canberra	7,686,848
Fiji	Suva	18,274
New Zealand	Wellington	268,676
Papua-New Guinea	Port Moresby	461,691
Vanuatu	Vila	14,760
Eurasiap		
Cyprus	Nicosia	9,251
Turkey	Ankara	780,576
Europe		
Albania	Tirana	28,748
Austria	Vienna	83,853
Belgium	Brussels	30,513
Bulgaria	Sofia	110,912
Czechoslovakia	Prague	127,877
Denmark	Copenhagen	43,075
Finland	Helsinki	337,032
France	Paris	547,026
Greece	Athens	131,944
Hungary	Budapest	93,033
Iceland	Reykiavik	103,000
Ireland (Fire)	Dublin	70,283
Italy	Rome	301,225

(contd.)

(contd.)

Country	Capital	Area in sq. km.
Luxembourg	Luxembourg	2,586
Malta	Valletta	316
Monaco	Monaco	1.5
Norway	Oslo	324,219
Poland	Warsaw	312,677
Portugal	Lisbon	92,082
Romania	Bucharest	237,500
Spain	Madrid	504,782
Sweden	Stockholm	449,964
Switzerland	Bem	41,293
The Netherlands	Amsterdam	40,844
U.K. Britain	London	244,103
Yugoslavia	Belgrade	233,804
North and Central America		
Bahamas	Nassau	13,935
Barbados	Bridgetown	431
Belize	Belmopan	22,965
Bermoda	Hamilton	53
Canada	Ottawa	9,976,139
Costa Rica	San Jose	50,700
Cuba	Havana	114,524
Dominica	Roseau	751
Dominican Republic	Santo Domingo	48,734
El Salvador	San Salvador	21,041
Guatemala	Guatemala City	108,899
Haiti	Port-Au-Prince	27,750
Honduras	Tegucigalpa	112,088
Jamaica	Kinston	10,991
Mexico	Mexico City	1,972,547
Nicaragua	Managua	130,000
Panama	Panama City	75,650
Trinidad & Tobago	Port-of-Spain	5,128
U.S.A.	Washington	9,363,123
South America		
Argentina	Buenos Aries	2,776,889
Bolivia	La Paz	1,098,581
Brazil	Brasilia	8,511,965
Chile	Santiago	756,945
Colombia	Bogota	1,138,914
Ecuador	Quito	283,561
Guyana	Georgetown	214,969
Paraguay	Asuncion	406,752
Peru	Lima	1,285,216
Uruguay	Montevideo	176,215
Venezuela	Caracas	912,050

(vi) **Standard of Living**

Countries	Per Capita Daily Intake			Population Per			
	Fat (gm)	Protein (gm)	Calories	Passenger Car	TV Set	Telephone	Physician
Australia	137	97	3389	2	2	2	500
Bangladesh	15	40	1899	2065	1111	—	9700
Brazil	51	61	2633	14	8	13	1300
Canada	156	98	3432	2	2	1.5	550
China	35	61	2602	4189	143	200	1730
Egypt	65	82	3263	53	23	67	760
France	162	108	3359	3	3	2	460
India	**34**	**51**	**2189**	**533**	**250**	**250**	**3700**
Iran	—	—	3122	467	18	19	2900
Israel	111	103	3060	7	4	3	400
Italy	139	106	3538	3	4	2	750
Japan	83	92	2856	4	1.8	2	740
Kenya	39	56	2151	160	250	77	10140
Mexico	75	76	3177	15	9	11	1200
Myanmar	37	65	2547	751	10000	—	4900
Pakistan	46	59	2159	266	83	167	2910
Phillippines	33	55	2341	148	38	67	6710
Singapore	68	73	2771	11	5	3	1100
South Korea	40	77	2841	87	6	6	1390
Sri Lanka	50	43	2485	110	303	143	7460
Sweden	148	95	3097	3	3	1.1	410
U.K.	143	87	3131	3	2	2	680
U.S.A.	167	106	3663	2	1.3	1.3	500
W. Germany	153	91	3474	2	3	2	420

(vii) **International S.T.D. Codes**

City	Country Code	City/area Code
Abu Dhabi (Town)	971	2
Adelaide	61	8
Ajman	971	6
Amsterdam	31	20
Athens	30	1
Auckland	61	9
Baghdad	964	1
Bahrain	973	—
Bangkok	66	2
Belgrade	36	11
Berlin, East	37	2
Berlin, West	49	30
Birmingham	44	21
Bombay	**91**	**22**
Bonn	49	2221
Boston	1	617
Brisbane	61	7
Brussels	32	2
Budapest	38	1
Hague, The	31	70
Hamburg	4940	—
Helsinki	358	0
Hong Kong	852	5
Houston	1	713
Istanbul	90	11
Jakarta	62	21
Jaddah	966	21
Johannesburg	27	11
Kampala	256	41
Kowloon	852	3
Kuala Lumpur	60	3
Kuwait*	265	—
Lisbon	351	19
London	44	1
Los Angeles	1	213
Madras	**91**	**44**
Madrid	34	1
Manchester	44	61
Manila	63	2
Makkah	966	22
Melbourne	61	3
Mexico City	52	5
Milan	39	2
Montreal	1	514
Moscow	7	095
Munich	49	89
Muscat*	968	—
Nairobi	254	2
Nandi	679	—
New Territories (Hong Kong)	852	12
Buenos Aires	54	1
Calcutta	**91**	**33**
Cape town	27	21
Chicago	1	312
Colombo (Central)	94	1
Copenhagen (Inner Area)	45	1
Copenhagen (Outer Area)	45	2
Dalias	1	214
Delhi	**91**	**11**
Detroit	1	313
Doha*	974	—
Dubai (Town)	971	4
Dublin	353	1
Frankfurt (Main)	49	069
Fujairah	971	91
Geneva	41	22
Glasgow	44	41
New York City	1	212
Osaka	81	6
Oslo	47	2
Ottawa	1	613
Paris	33	1
Perth (W.A.)	61	9
Port of Spain	1	809
Prague	42	2
Ras Al Khaimah	971	**7
Rio de Janeiro	55	21
Riyadh	966	1
Rome	39	6
San Francisco	1	415
Seoul	82	2
Seychelles*	248	—
Sharjah	971	5
Singapore*	65	—
Stockholm	46	8
Suva	679	—
Sydney	61	2
Taipei	86	2
Tehran	98	21
Tokyo	81	3
Toronto	81	416
Trinidad and Tobago	1	809
Umm al Quwain	971	6
Vancouver	1	604
Vienna	43	222
Warsaw	48	22
Washington D.C.	1	202
Zegreb	38	41
Zurich	41	1

* City/area code not required.
** all points.

International Subscriber Dialling Codes

Most countries are continuously extending the facilities for direct international subscriber dialling. The 'dial-in' code generally remains the same, internationally, whilst the access code or 'dial-out' code vanes from country to country. It is necessary to dial this code first, as it provides connection to the international exchange and is generally followed by a changed dial tone. One must then dial the country code followed by the city/area code, and the required subscriber's telephone number.

Lisbon — the city/area code. If dialled from outside Portugal is 19; if dialled from within Portugal it is 01.
Secondly, international country codes for nearby regions may vary; for instance, Ireland — the international 'dial-in' code is 353. However, if dialled from the UK the code is 000.
or, Mexico City — the 'dial-in' code from the USA and Canada is 905, whilst the international code for Mexico is 52. Within Mexico the national city/area code for Mexico City is 5, which corresponds to the international city/area code.

Please note, international city/area code may be sometimes at variance with the national city/area code; for instance,

(viii) **International Airports**

Country/City	Airport	From city	
		Miles	km.
Argentina			
Buenos Aries	Ezeiza	22	35
	Aeroparque in the city		
Australia			
Melbourne	Tullamarine	12	19
Sydney	Kingsford Smith	7	11
Austria			
Vienna	Schwechat	11	18
Belgium			
Brussels	Zaventem	7	11
Brazil			
Rio	Galeao	14	23
Sao Paulo	Viracopos	60	97
	Congonhas in the city		
Canada			
Montreal	Dorval	14	23
	Mirabel	34	55
Toronto	Int'l	15	24
Chile			
Santiago	Arturo Merino Benitez	12	20

(Contd.)

(Contd.)

Country/City	Airport	From city	
		Miles	km.
China			
Peking	Beijing	16	26
Colombia			
Bogota	Eldorado	8	13
Denmark			
Copenhagen	Kastrup	6	10
Egypt			
Cairo	Cairo	14	23
Finland			
Helsinki	Helsinki	12	19
France			
Paris	Orly	9	14
	de Gaulle	14	23
Germany (W)			
Berlin	Tegel	6	10
Frankfurt	Frankfurt	6	10
Hamburg	Fuhlsbuttel	8	12
Munich	Munchen Riem	6	10
Greece			
Athens	Hellenikon	9	14
Hong Kong	Kaitak	2	3
India			
Bombay	**Sahar**	**22**	**35**
Calcutta	**Dum Dum**	**10**	**16**
Madras	**Meenambakam**	**10**	**16**
New Delhi	**Palam**	**9**	**14**
Indonesia			
Jakarta	Helim Perfanakusumah	6	10
Irish Republic			
Dublin	Dublin	5	8
Israel			
Tel aviv	Ben Gurion	12	19
Italy			
Milan	Malpensa	35	56
	Linate	10	16
Rome	de Vinci	22	35
Japan			
Tokyo	Narita	41	66

(Contd.)

(Contd.)

Country/City	Airport	From city	
		Miles	km.
Kenya			
Nairobi	Kenyatta	12	20
Korea			
Seoul	Kimpo	10	16
Lebanon			
Beirut	Khalde	10	16
Malaysia			
Kuala Lumpur	Subang	13	21
Mexico			
Mexico City	Central Int'l	8	13
Netherlands			
Amsterdam	Schiphol	10	16
New Zealand			
Auckland	Int'l	16	26
Wellington	Wellington	5	8
Nigeria			
Lagos	Murtala Mohammed	14	23
Norway			
Oslo	Fornebu	5	8
Pakistan			
Karachi	Karachi	10	16
Phillippines			
Manila	Int'l	7	12
Portugal			
Lisbon	Portela	5	8
Saudi Arabia			
Jeddah	Jeddah in the city		
Riyadh	Riyadh in the city		
Singapore	Changi	6	10
South Africa			
Jo'burg	Jan Smuts	15	24
Cape Town	DF Malan	12	19
Spain			
Madrid	Barajas	3	13
Sweden			
Stockholm	Arlanda	24	41

(Contd.)

(Contd.)

Country/City	Airport	From city	
		Miles	km.
Switzerland			
Geneva	Cointrin	2	4
Zurich	Kloten	7	12
Taiwan			
Taipei	Chiang Kai-shek	27	45
Thailand			
Bangkok	Don Muang	20	32
Turkey			
Istanbul	Yesikoy	15	24
UK			
London	Heathrow	15	24
	Gatwick	27	43
USA			
Atlanta	Hartsfield	9	14
Boston	Logan	3	5
Chicago	O'Hare	21	34
Cleveland	Hopkins	27	43
Dallas	Dallas/Fort Worth	17	27
Detroit	Metropolitan	25	40
Houston	Houston	25	40
Los Angles	Int'l	18	29
New York	Kennedy	15	23
Philadelphia	Philadelphia	7	11
S. Francisco	S.Francisco	14	22
Washington	Dulles	30	48
Russia			
Moscow	Sheremetyevo	18	29
Venezuela			
Caracas	Maiquetia	13	21
Yugoslavia			
Belgrade	Surcin	$7^1/_2$	12

(ix) **International Air Distances/Flying Times**

	Amsterdam	Bangkok	Buenos Aires	Cairo	**Delhi**	Frankfurt	Geneva	Hong Kong	Johannes-burg
1	2	3	4	5	6	7	8	9	10
Amsterdam	—	6058/15	8570/5	2042/5	**5737/10**	228/1	424/1	5767/18	6733/14
Bangkok	6058/16$^1/_2$	—	14910	4510/12	**1815/4**	5619/14$^1/_2$	5831/15	1064/3	7797
Buenos Aires	8570/17	14910	—	9912	**12367**	8571/17$^1/_2$	8264/17$^1/_2$	15546	6807
Cairo	2042/5	4510/11$^1/_2$	9912	—	**2738/7$^1/_2$**	1815/5	1755/5	6099	3912
Delhi	**5737/13**	**1815/4**	**12367**	**2738/8**	—	**5463/9$^1/_2$**	**5391/9$^1/_2$**	**2345/7**	**6260**
Frankfurt	228/1	5619/13$^1/_2$	8571/9$^1/_2$	1815/5	**5463/9**	—	287/1	8277/17	6480/14$^1/_2$
Geneva	424/1	5831	8264/9	1755/5	**5391/9**	287/1	—	8205/17	6289/14
Hong Kong	5767/17	1064/3	15546/34	6099	**2345/7**	8205/18	8277/18	—	8760/16
Johannesburg	6733/15	7797	6807	3912	**6260**	6480/14$^1/_2$	6289/14	8760/15$^1/_2$	—
Karachi	3726/11	2302/5	12285	2212/6$^1/_2$	**665/2**	3539/9	3633/9	3596/7$^1/_2$	4526
London	230/1	5929/15$^1/_2$	6910/18	2185/5	**4180/11$^1/_2$**	406/1$^1/_2$	457/1$^1/_2$	5989/15$^1/_2$	5634/13$^1/_2$
Manila	7069/20$^1/_2$	1368/3	16388	5780/15	**3656/8**	6851/19	7063/19	702/2	9165
Moscow	1330/4	4396/13	10056	1796/15$^1/_2$	**2708/6$^1/_2$**	1253/3	1493/3	6063	6849
New York	3639/7	11401/25	5302/15	6730/14	**9550/19**	3851/9	3859/9	10279/22$^1/_2$	9712/16
Paris	26/1	7810/15	8268/18	1995/5	**5679/10**	289/1	250/1	8493/18	6584/13
Rio de Janeiro	5945/13	10025	1232/4	1649	**11263**	5948/13	5684/13	13429	4441/9
Rome	809/3	7011/13	8317/16	1329/3	**3679/9**	598/2	439/2	7694/15$^1/_2$	4802/13$^1/_2$
Sydney	10306/25	5774/12	11240	10855	**7795**	10033/26	10961/26	4586/9$^1/_2$	9121/19
Tokyo	9522/20	2849/8	14091	8245/20	**4959/12$^1/_2$**	9776/21	10029/21	1788/5	10905/21$^1/_2$

Contd.

(ix) International Air Distances/Flying Times Contd.

	Karachi	London	Manila	Moscow	New York	Paris	Rio de Janeiro	Rome	Sydney	Tokyo
1	11	12	13	14	15	16	17	18	19	20
Amsterdam	3726/11	230/1	7069/19	1330/3½	3639/7	261/1	5945/13	809/2	10306/24	9522/20
Bangkok	2302/5	5929/16½	1368	4396/13	11401/26	7810/16	10025	7011/14	5774/11½	2849/7½
Buenos Aires	12285	6910/17	16388	10056	5302/14	8268/16	1232/3½	8317/15	11240	14091
Cairo	2212/6	2185/5½	5780/15½	1796/4½	6730/15	1995/5	6149	1329/4	10855	8245/20
Delhi	**665/2**	**4180/13**	**3656/8**	**2708/8½**	**9550/22**	**5679/11**	**11263**	**3679/10½**	**7795**	**4959/11½**
Frankfurt	3539/9	406/1½	6851/19	1253/3	3851/9	289/1	5948/14	598/2	10033/24	9776/20
Geneva	3633/9	457/1½	7063/19	1493/3	3859/9	250/1	5684/14	439/2	10961/24	10029/20
Hong Kong	3596/7½	5989/17	702/2	6063	10279/20½	8493/19	13429	7694/16½	4586/9½	1788/4½
Johannesburg	4526	5634/14½	9165	6849	9712/17	6584/14	4441/10½	4802/13½	9121/16	10905/21
Karachi	—	3935/11	3670/10	2608/6	9104/22	3810/11½	8082	3307/10½	8269	5742/12½
London	3935/10½	—	6686/19	1557/3½	3456/7	209/1	5746/13	892/2½	10568/24½	5955/20
Manila	3670/10	6686/20½	—	6906	10368/2½	9336/21	15128	8536/17½	3892/8	1862/4½
Moscow	2608/6	1557/4	6906	—	5620/10	1533/4	8606	1476/4	11044	4667/10
New York	9104/20	3456/6½	10368/24½	5620/9	—	3628/6½	4816/10	4280/8	12052/25	8133/16
Paris	3810/11	209/1	9336/9½	1533/4	3628/7	—	5697/12	688/2	10249/29	9771/17
Rio de Janeiro	8082	5746/12½	15128	8606	4816/9½	5697/11½	—	5707/12	12741	13512/31
Rome	3307/10	892/3	8536/17	1476/4	4280/9	688/2	5707/13	—	10450/25	9840/20
Sydney	8269	10568/25	3892/8	11044	12052/21	10249/28	12741	10450/26	—	6904/9½
Tokyo	5742/13½	5955/20	1862	4667/10	8133/14½	9771/17	13512/26½	9840/21	6904/9	—

The figures after the oblique stroke(/) represent the flying times in hours.

CONVERSION FACTORS

(i) Linear Measure

Inches	Feet	Yards	Metres	Kilometres
1	0.08333	0.02778	0.0254	0.0000254
12	1	0.3333	0.3048	0.0003048
36	3	1	0.9144	0.0009144
39.37	3.2808	1.0936	1	0.001
39,370	3,280.8333	1,093.6111	1,000	1
63,360	5,280	1,760	1,609.3472	1.6093

(ii) Square Measure

Square Inches	Square Feet	Square Yards	Square Metres	Acres	Hectares
1	0.006944	0.0007716	0.0006452	$1.594 X 10^{-10}$	$6,452 X 10^{-11}$
144	1	0.1111	0.09290	$2,296 X 10^{-8}$	$9,290 X 10^{-9}$
1,296	9	1	0.8361	$2,066 X 10^{-7}$	$8,361 X 10^{-8}$
1,549,9969	10.7639	1,1960	1	$2,471 X 10^{-7}$	0.0001
6,272,640	43,560	4,840	4,046.9543	1	0.4047
15,499,969	107,638.6736	11,959.8526	10,000	2.4710	1
1,549,996,900	10,763,867,361	1,195,985.2623	1,000,000	247.1054	100

(iii) Cubic Measure

Cubic Inches	US Liters	Cubic Gallons	Cubic Feet	Cubic Yards
1	0.01639	0.004329	0.0005787	0.00002143
61.0234	1	0.2642	0.03532	0.001308
231	3,7853	1	0.1337	0.004951
1,728	28,3163	7.4805	1	0.03704
46,656	764.5401	201.9740	27	1
61,023.3779	999.972	264.1729	35.3144	1.3079

(iv) Weight

Grams	Kilograms	Quantals	Tonnes (Metric)	Pounds
1	0.001	0,00001	0.000001	0.002205
1,000	1	0.01	0.001	2.2046
100,000	100	1	0.1	220.462
1,000,000	1,000	10	1	2,204.62
453,5929	0.4536	0.004536	0.0004536	1
50,802	50,802	0.50802	0.050802	112

(v) **Conversion Formula**

Multiply	By	To obtain	Multiply	By	To obtain
Acres	0.404686	Hectares	Litres	0.22009	Gallons (U.K.)
Acres	40467.00	Square Metres	Litres	1.76072	Pints
Acres	0.001562	Square Miles	Metres	3.2808	Feet
Centimetres	0.393701	Inches	Metres	1.093614	Yards
Cubic Centimetres	0.061024	Cubic Inches	Metric Tonnes	0.98421	Tons (U.K.)
Cubic Feet	6.228	Gallons	Miles	1.609343	Kilometres
Cubic Feet	0.02832	Cubic Metres	Millimetres	0.03937	Inches
Cubic Inches	16.3871	Cubic Centimetres	Ounces	28.34953	Grams
Cubic Metres	35.31445	Cubic Feet	Pints	0.56795	Litres
Cubic Metres	1.30794	Cubic Yards	Pounds	0.4536	Kilograms
Cubic Yards	0.76456	Cubic Metres	Sq. Centi-metres	0.15500	Square Inches
Feet	0.3048	Metres	Square Feet	0.09290	Square Metres
Gallons	0.1337	Cubic Feet	Square Inches	6.45163	Sq. Centi-metres
Gallons (U.K.)	4.5461	Litres	Square kilometres	0.386102	Square Miles
Grams	0.03527	Ounces	Square Metres	0.0002471	Acres
Hectares	2.47105	Acres	Square Metres	10.76387	Square Feet
Horsepower	0.7457	Kilowatts	Square Metres	1.19599	Square Yards
Inches	2,539998	Centimetres	Square Miles	640.00	Acres
Inches	25,39998	Millimetres	Square Miles	2.58999	Square Kilometres
Kilograms	2.204620	Pounds	Square Yards	0.83613	Square Metres
Kilograms	0.0009842	Tons (U.K.)	Tons (U.K.)	1.01605	Metric Tonnes
Kilometres	0.621372	Miles	Tons (U.K.)	1016.0470	Kilograms
Kilowatts	1.341	Horsepower	Yards	0.914399	Metres

(vi) **Temperature**

°C	°F	°C	°F	°C	°F
-100	-148	+0	+32.0	+31	+87.8
-90	-130	+1	+33.8	+32	+89.6
-80	-112	+2	+35.6	+33	+91.4
-70	-94	+3	+37.4	+34	+93.2
-60	-76	+4	+39.2	+35	+95.0
-50	-58	+5	+41.0	+36	+96.8
-45	-49	+6	+42.8	+37	+98.6
-40	-40	+7	+44.6	+38	+100.4
-35	-31	+8	+46.4	+39	+102.2
-30	-22	+9	+48.2	+40	+104.0
-25	-13	+10	+50.0	+41	+105.8
-20	-4.0	+11	+51.8	+42	+107.6
-19	-2.2	+12	+53.6	+43	+109.4
-18	-0.4	+13	+55.4	+44	+111.2
-17	+1.4	+14	+57.2	+45	+113.0
-16	+3.2	+15	+59.0	+46	+114.8
-15	+5.0	+16	+60.8	+47	+116.6
-14	+6.8	+17	+62.6	+48	+118.4
-13	+8.6	+18	+64.4	+49	+120.2
-12	+10.4	+19	+66.2	+50	+112.0
-11	+12.2	+20	+68.0	+51	+123.8
-10	+14.0	+21	+69.8	+52	+125.6
-9	+15.8	+22	+71.6	+53	+127.4
-8	+17.6	+23	+73.4	+54	+129.2
-7	+19.4	+24	+75.2	+55	+131.0
-6	+21.2	+25	+77.0	+56	+132.8
-5	+23.0	+26	+78.8	+57	+134.6
-4	+24.8	+27	+80.6	+58	+136.4
-3	+26.6	+28	+82.4	+59	+138.2
-2	+28.4	+29	+84.2	+60	+140.0
-1	+30.2	+30	+86.0	+61	+141.8

Temperature equation

°C = (F—32) X 5/9 °F = 9/5 C + 32

PAST AND PRESENT EXECUTIVE HEADS OF THE UN SYSTEM

Organ			
UN	Trygve Lie	Norway	1946-1953
	Dag Hammarskjold	Sweden	1953-1961
	U Thant	Burma	1961-1971
	Kurt Waldheim	Austria	1972-1981
	Javier Perez de Cuellar	Peru	1982-
UNICEF	Maurice Pate	USA	1947-1965
	Henry Labouisse	USA	1965-1979
	James Grant	USA	1980-
UNCTAD	Raul Prebisch	Argentina	1965-1969
	Manuel Perez-Guerrero	Venezuela	1969-1974
	Gamani Corea	Sri Lanka	1974-1986
	Kenneth Dadzie	Ghana	1986-
UNDP	Paul Hoffman	USA	1966-1972[1]
	David Owen	UK	1966-1969[1]
	Rudolph Petersen	USA	1972-1976
	Bradford Morse	USA	1976-1986
	W.H. Draper	USA	1986-
UNEP	Maurice Strong	Canada	1972-1976
	Mustafa Tolba	Egypt	1976-
UNFPA	Rafael Salas	Phillippines	1969-1987
	Nafis Sadik	Pakistan	1987-
UNRRA	Herbert Lehman	USA	1943-1946
	Fiorello LaGuardia	USA	Apr.-Dec. 1946
UNRWA	H. Kennedy	Canada	1950-1951
	J. Blanford	USA	1951-1953
	Henry Lahouisse	USA	954-1958
	John H. Davis	USA	1959-1963
	Laurence Michelmore	USA	1964-1971
	Sir John Rennie	UK	1971-1977
	T. McElhiney	USA	1977-1979
	Olof Rydbeck	Sweden	1979-1985
	G. Giacomelli	Italy	1985-
UNCHS	A. Ramachandran	India	1978-
UNDRO	F. Berkol	Turkey	1972-1982
	M. Essafi	Tunisia	1982-
UNHCR	G.J. van H. Goedhart	Netherlands	1950-1956
	A.R. Lindt	Switzerland	1956-1960
	F. Schnyder	Switzerland	1960-1965
	Sadruddin Aga Khan	Iran	1965-1977
	P. Harting	Denmark	1978-1985
	J. Hocke	Switzerland	1985-1989
	T. Stoltenbery	Norway	1990-
WFC	John Hannah	USA	1975-1978
	Maurice Williams	USA	1978-1986
	G.I. Trant	Canada	1986-
WFP	A.H. Boerma	Netherlands	1962-1967
	F. Auquino	El Salvador	1968-1976
	T.C.M. Robinson	USA	1976-1977
	G.N. Vogel	Canada	1977-1981
	B. de A. Brito Azevedo	Brazil	1981-1982
	J.C. Ingram	Australia	1982-
ILO	E.J. Phelan	Ireland	1941-1948
	David A. Morse	USA	1948-1970
	Wilfred jenks	UK	1970-1973
	Francis Blanchard	France	1973-1989

Contd.

	Michel hansenne	Belgium	1989-
FAO	Sir John Boyd Orr	UK	1945-1948
	Norris E. Dodd	USA	1948-1954
	Philip V. Cardon	USA	1954-1956
	B.R. Sen	India	1956-1967
	A.H. Boerma	Netherlands	1968-1975
	Edouard Saouma	Lebanon	1976-
UNESCO	Julian Huxley	UK	1946-1947
	Jaime T. Bodet	Mexico	1948-1952
	John W. Taylor	USA	1952-1953
	Luther H. Evans	USA	1953-1958
	V. Veronese	Italy	1958-1961
	Rene Maheu	France	1961-1974
	Amadou M. M'Bow	Senegal	1974-1987
	Federico Mayor	Spain	1987-
ICAO	Albert Roper	France	1946-1951
	E.C.R. Ljungberg	Sweden	1952-1959
	R. McDonnell	Canada	1959-1964
	Bernard T. Twight	Netherlands	1964-1970
	Assad Kotaite	Lebanon	1970-1976
	Yues M. Lambert	France	1976-1988
	S.S. Sidhu	India	1988-
WHO	Brock Chisholm	Canada	1946-1953
	Marcolino T. Mahler	Brazil	1953-1973
	Halfdan T. Mahler	Denmark	1973-1988
	Hiroshi Nakajima	Japan	1988-
UPU	Alois muri	Switzerland	1945-1949
	Fritz Hess	Switzerland	1950-1960
	Edouard Weber	Switzerland	1961-1966
	Michel Rahi	Egypt	1967-1973
	A.H. Ridge	UK	1973-974
	M.I. Sobhi	Egypt	1975-1984
	A.C. Botto de Barros	Brazil	1985-
ITU	Franz van Ernst	Switzerland	1947-1950
	Leon mulatier	France	1950-1953
	M.A. Andrada	Argentina	1954-1958
	Gerald C. Cross	USA	1959-1965
	M.B. Sarwate	India	1965-1967
	Mohamed Mili	Tunisia	1968-1982
	R.E. Butler	Australia	1983-1989
	P.J. Tarjanne	Finlan	1989
WMO	G. Swoboda	Switzerland	1948-1955
	David A. Davies	UK	1955-1980
	A. Wiin-Nielsen	Denmark	1980-1983
	G.O.P Obsai	Nigeria	1984
IMO	O.H. Nielsen	Denmark	1959-1961
	J. Roullier	France	1962-1967
	Colin Gond	UK	1968-1973
	C.P. Srivastava	India	1974-1989
	W.A. O'Nell	Canada	1990
WIPO	Arpad Bogsch	USA	1973
IFAD	A.M. Al-Sudeary	Saudi Arabia	1980-1984
	Idriss Jazairy	Algeria	1984
UNIDO	Domingo Siazon	Phillippines	1985
IAEA	Sterling Cole	USA	1957-1961
	Sigvard Eklund	Sweden	1961-1981
	Hans Blix	Sweden	1981
GATT	Eric W. White	UK	1948-1968
	Olivier Long	Switzerland	1968-1980

Contd.

	Arthur Dunkel	Switzerland	1980
IBRD	Eugene Mayer	USA	June-Dec.1946
	John McCloy	USA	1947-1949
	Eugene R. Black	USA	1949-1962
	George De. Woods	USA	1963-1968
	Robert McNamara	USA	1968-1981
	A.W. Clausen	USA	1981-1986
	Barber Conable	USA	1986
IMF	Camille Gutt	Beligium	1946-1951
	Ivar Rooth	Sweden	1951-1956
	Per Jacobsson	Sweden	1956-1963
	Pierre-Paul Schweitzer	France	1963-1973
	H. Johannes Witteveen	Netherlands	1973-1978
	J. deLarbosiere	France	1978-1986
	Jean-Michel Camdessus	France	1987
UNITAR	J.M. Hester	USA	1975-1980
	Soedjatmoko	Indonesia	1980-1987
	H.G. de Souza	Brazil	1987

Notes:

The most striking fact is that among 136 executive heads appointed since 1946 only one woman has headed an organization—Dr. Nafis Sadik, the Executive Director of UNFPA since 1987.

[1] Paul Hoffman was head of the UN Special Fund from 1959 to 1966; David Owen was Chairman of the UN Technical Assistance Board from 1950 to 1966 when these two bodies were merged into the new UNDP; the two men served as co-Administrators of UNDP from 1966-1969 until David Owmn retired from the UN, and Paul Hoffman continued as sole Administrator unitl 1972.

Source: *Development Dialogue*, 1990, 1-2.

URUGUAY ROUND :
Dunkel Proposals

Backgrounders

General Agreement on Tariffs and Trade (GATT) is a binding contract between 103 governments which together account for around 90 per cent of world merchandise trade. The objective of the contract is to provide a secure and predictable international trading environment for the business community and a continuing process of trade liberalisation in which investment, job creation and trade can thrive. In this way, the multilateral trading system contributes to economic growth and development throughout the world.

General Agreement on Tariffs and Trade (GATT)

General Agreement on Tariffs and Trade (GATT) made in 1948 was meant to be a temporary arrangement pending the establishment of the Internationl Trade Organisation (ITO).

The idea was to build a multilateral institution that would allow countries to settle amicably who gets what share of world trade — by determining both tariff rates and quantitative restrictions on imports and exports globally.

But in order to protect its own sovereignty in U.S. withdrew from this plan and the ITO consequently never came into being. Thus, for 44 years GATT has remained a provisional treaty — a sort of contractual agreement — which allows for successive rounds of 'agreements' on tariff rates and other trade matters but has few institutional structures. The 102 countries in GATT are known as 'contracting parties' and not 'members'.

The conventional western view holds that GATT has made the world a better place to do business in by allowing a more free and fruitful flow of goods and services across the seven seas. But 'free' and 'fruitful' for whom? By and large the developed countries have managed mutually to lower their tariff rates and other trade barriers but relatively much less so in the case of exports from the Third World.

Mr. Arthur Dunkel is presently the Director-General of GATT and Chairman of Trade Negotiations Council (TNC).

Concepts and Terms

GATS — General Agreement on Trade in Services in its present draft demands total freedom of movement for transnational corporations in the service sector, such as banking and insurance, without putting any demands on their behaviour.

TRIPs — Trade Related Intellectual Property Rights would create a globally uniform system on patents with the burden of proof shifted to the alleged violator of a patent law. It would also allow for 'product patents' in many areas, instead of process patents which have till now prevailed in most countries. A product patent prevents others from making the same product through any other process, thus giving the patent holder an absolute monopoly. The patent periods would also be almost doubled.

TRIMs — Trade Related Investment Measures would allow the developed countries to invest freely in the Third World without any sector restrictions or controls over how much equity is retained by the nationals of that country.

Since the end of the Second World War, seven rounds of multilateral trade negotiations have been launched and successfully completed, under the auspices of GATT. The eighth, known as the Uruguay Round, was formally begun in September 1986, shaped by the objectives set forth in the January 1986 Punta del Este Ministerial Declaration.

Multilateral Trade Negotiations

1. Geneva negotiations, 1947
2. Annecy negotiations, 1949
3. Torquay negotiations, 1950-51
4. Geneva negotiations, 1955-56
5. Geneva negotiations ("Dillon Round"), 1959—62
6. Geneva negotiations ("Kennedy Round"), 1963—67
7. Geneva negotiations ("Tokyo Round"), 1973—79
8. Geneva negotiations (Uruguay Round"), 1986—

The broad goal of all the rounds has been the same — to promote growth and development through the removal of trade distortions, and the development of a more open, predictable, and durable multilateral trading system — although the focus of the negotiations has sometimes differed. This first six rounds concentrated almost exclusively on reducing tariffs, while the Tokyo Round (1973—79) moved on to tackle nontariff barriers, and the Uruguay Round embraces new areas such as services, intellectual property rights, and trade-related investment. The breadth of this latest round, originally scheduled to be concluded at a ministerial meeting in Brussels in December 1990, required important political breakthroughs to resolve obvious difficulties, a task that could not be completed in the time available. As a result, talks were suspended in Brussels; however, a basis for their resumption was found in early 1991, reviving hopes that before too long, a successful conclusion would be forthcoming.

Source: *Finance and Development*, 1991.

Excerpts from Two Reports

The following are excerpts from two reports on the state of play in the Uruguay Round, given by the TNC Chairman, Mr. Arthur Dunkel, to senior negotiators on 7 and 29 November respectively:

TNC MEETING, 7 NOVEMBER 1991

The basic elements of the Uruguay Round package

Let us avoid the trap of looking at the negotiating process solely in terms of the negotiating structure. In other words, attention should be more and more addressed to the basic elements of the global package which is our goal. These elements are:

* market opening, a traditional and central part of all multilateral trade negotiations;
* rule-making, which in this Round means (a) establishing multilateral rules and disciplines in areas of increasing trade importance; (b) strengthening existing rules in order to underpin and secure the higher levels of market opening and competition which will be achieved; and (c) putting in place a dispute settlement system capable of dealing with future challenges to the multilateral system;
* bringing agriculture and textiles and clothing under improved multilateral rules and disciplines; and
* the institutional support necessary for implementing and securing the results of the negotiations.

The Uruguay Round offers us, an historic opportunity to establish a strengthened multilateral trading system, broader in scope and more universal in membership.

Market access

Market access cuts across virtually the entire negotiating agenda: manufactured products, tropical products, natural resource-based products, textiles and clothing and agriculture. Market access negotiations involve not just the reduction and elimination of tariffs and non-tariff measures at the border, but also corresponding commitments at the level of domestic policies that distort trade and competition. It is, therefore, central to the balance that every government would like to achieve in the overall package.

The immediate problem is to set the scene for an effective negotiating process involving broad-based exchanges of concessions on the basis of the most-favoured-nation principle, taking into account the particular needs of developing countries.

One trigger to start the process lies in an early agreement on modalities, including tariffication, for negotiating market access as part of the reform programme being negotiated in agriculture.

A second trigger is agreement on modalities for liberalizing trade in textiles and clothing, and for integrating this sector into the GATT.

The opening up of markets through the reduction of existing barriers is a key element of the negotiations in services. This is the purpose behind the initial commitments negotiations which will be an integral part of the General Agreement on Trade in Services (GATS).

Rule-Making

The establishment of multilateral rules and disciplines in areas of increasing trade importance brings me to two key subjects of the Uruguay Round-Services and Trade-Related Aspects of Intellectual Property Rights, including Trade in Counterfeit Goods (TRIPS).

In services, governments must adhere to the application of unconditional most-favoured-nation treatment as a general obligation and sharply restrict exemptions. This applies especially to such important service sectors as maritime transport, basic telecommunications, and audiovisual services, as well as to the movement of personnel related to the supply of a service.

Technology and creativity have become, like services, a critical factor in international economic relations and competition. The TRIPS negotiations have brought within grasp an international consensus on a very wide range of issues concerning the impact of protection and enforcement of intellectual property rights on international competition. To bring this work to fruition three basic decisions have to be made. First, the level of protection must be adequate; this will require significant changes in national legislation in all countries. Second, governments must be convinced that the new consensus will be operational; this will require an effective multilateral dispute settlement mechanism and a commitment to use it as the means of settling disputes on TRIPS matters. Third, for a number of governments which are mainly importers of technology, the commitments in this area will have to be viewed in the context of the overall results of the Round.

A central part of the negotiating agenda concerns strengthening of existing rules and disciplines in the GATT system. In anti-dumping, the main task is now to find an acceptable compromise between the objective pursued by many governments of strengthening existing rules in such areas a the determination of the existence of dumping and injury, and the objective pursued by others of introducing new rules to ensure that the enforcement of legitimate anti-dumping measures is not circumvented.

In the area of subsidies and countervailing measures the key question is whether the negotiators are ready to accept, in return for improved disciplines on the use of subsidies in general, that some subsidies which are not meant to have any trade distorting effects may be non-actionable (i.e., neither countervailing measures nor multilateral counter-measures will normally be taken against them). The second key question is the scope of special treatment for developing countries. If a satisfactory solution is found to these two issues, participants will have got parameters indispensable for resolving other outstanding problems.

In the safeguards negotiations, the three main outstanding issues are: "quota modulation" (i.e., whether in an overall import quota, the share allocated to countries found to be contributing more to global injury could be lower than the share allocated to them on the basis of recent trade patterns); the time period allowed for phasing out "grey area" measures such as voluntary export restraints and orderly market arrangements; and the provision which would preclude the use, for safeguards purposes, of measures other than those provided for in the agreement.

Texts of revisions to seven GATT Articles are awaiting adoption — on Articles II: 1(b), XVII, XXIV, XXV:5, XXVIII, XXXV - as well as a revised text for the

Protocol of Provisional Application. These would contribute greatly to the strengthening of the GATT system. With the same objective in view, governments also have before them proposals to improve the functioning of the provisions relating to measures taken for balance-of-payments purposes.

Concerning Trade-Related Investment Measures (TRIMS), though there are different opinions on a TRIMS agreement, the questions which must be addressed are: the specification of measures inconsistent with Articles III and XI of the GATT; the establishment of disciplines on export-performance requirements; the transitional arrangements needed in respect of measures to be eliminated; and the institutional support for any further work in this area.

Still in the broad area of rule-making, and effective implementation, governments have to put in place a reinforced and credible dispute settlement system for dealing with future challenges to the multilateral trading system. The degree to which the dispute settlement process should be automatic and binding, and the linked question of doing away with unilateral measures, are two major questions to be resolved. A third key question is the application of the dispute settlement process across the board to the package of the Uruguay Round results, particularly if all the results must be accepted as a single undertaking. . . .

Agriculture, Textiles and Clothing

Let me now turn to agriculture. At the TNC, in February this year I noted participants' agreement to negotiate specific binding commitments in each of the three areas of domestic support, market access and export competition, and to reach an agreement on sanitary and phytosanitary issues. Major elements of the reform programme have emerged through the intensive work carried out since then, including broad consensus on the product coverage of the agriculture negotiations. As agreed, special and differential treatment will apply in respect of developing countries. In addition to the fundamental point concerning market access to which I have already alluded, three further political decisions are key to bringing all the elements together and finalizing the package:

* the direct payments to be exempted from reduction commitments on domestic support;
* the policy coverage of reduction commitments in the export competition context; and
* the amount, base period and duration of commitments to reduce support and protection.

In textiles and clothing, the central problem is the so-called "economic package", consisting of the product coverage of the agreement, the percentages for integration of products in stages, growth percentages for quotas on products not yet integrated, and the duration of the agreement. Successful conclusion of the textiles and clothing negotiations will bring this sector within GATT rules and disciplines after decades of managed trade. Trade in this sector amounts to almost a tenth of world trade in manufactures and is of crucial importance to a large number of participants.

Institutions

I now come to the last of the four elements of the negotiations — the institutional support necessary for implementing the results. A very well coordinated approach is essential in respect of the infrastructure that will be put in place to fulfil the requirements of notification, monitoring, surveillance, and dispute settlement arising from a large number of Uruguay Round agreements. Agriculture, textiles and clothing, TRIPS, TRIMS and services come immediately to mind and there are others as well.

HEADS OF DELEGATION MEETING, NOVEMBER 29, 1991

Continuous Bargaining

The market access negotiations have now moved into a continuous bargaining process with a view to developing the substantive political package. There are, however, important political breakthroughs to be made before a meaningful overall market access deal can emerge.

Among the positive developments, there has been:

* A renewed political commitment among a wide range of participants that a substantial and balanced trade liberalization package is a central element for a successful Round;
* Development in the negotiations in agriculture—these have been helpful in removing doubts on product coverage and negotiating links with access issues in this key area;
* Systematic efforts in the last two weeks to advance bilateral negotiations across the whole range of tariff and non-tariff measures issues; and
* Informal plurilateral stock-taking exercises held on tropical products, resource-based products and other sectoral issues, as well as on other tariff and non-tariff measure issues.

Source: *Finance and Development*, June, 1991.

GOVERNMENT OF INDIA NOTE ON DUNKEL DRAFT TEXT ON GATT

The Uruguay Round of Multinational Trade Negotiations was launched by a Ministerial meeting at Punta del Este in Uruguay in September 1986. What distinguished the Round from the previous GATT negotiations was its scope. As against discussions on tariff and non-tariff measures regulating trade in goods, in the previous round of negotiations, in the Uruguay Round, the Agenda included trade in Services, Trade Related Aspects of Intellectual Property Rights (TRIPs), and Trade Related Investment Measures (TRIMs). A significant feature of the negotiations was an attempt made by the participating countries to make progress in liberalisation of trade in agriculture. The negotiations were scheduled to be concluded in December, 1990, but this did not happen mainly because of differences on trade in agriculture between the major industrial economies.

In the latest phase of the negotiations which ended on 20 December, 1991, a serious attempt was made to resolve the differences which have divided the

108 participating countries on the extent of liberalisation of world trade to aim at and the trade rules that should govern the trade relationships between nations in future. As a result, many differences were narrowed down while others remained outstanding, particularly in the crucial areas of trade in agriculture, trade in textiles, rules on anti dumping and TRIPs. To break the impasse, Mr. Arthur Dunkel, Director General of GATT and Chairman of the Trade Negotiations Committee at the official level has drawn up proposals for consideration of Governments. In a 436 page document presented by Mr. Dunkel, the progress made so far in the negotiations has been captured and solutions have been offered in areas in which the negotiations were blocked by difference. Mr. Dunkel had requested Governments to give their views at a meeting of the Trade Negotiations Committee which began on 13th January, 1992. The Government has been scrutinizing various elements of the Dunkel package and its examination has not been concluded. The Indian representative at Geneva has been instructed to inform the trade Negotiations Committee that we would take more time to give our definitive view.

This note gives the outline of Mr. Dunkel proposals. The negotiations encompass seven broad areas, namely, (i) Market Access; (ii) Agriculture; (iii) Textiles; (iv) GATT Rules including TRIMs; (v) TRIPs; (vi) Trade in services; and (vii) Institutional Matters. The following paragraphs describe the contents of the Dunkel package under these seven headings.

(i) Market Access

Negotiations in past five years have been aimed at reduction of tariff and non-tariff barriers on goods. While negotiations are taking place on the basis of across-the-board reductions of tariff, groups of countries have been stressing on achieving maximum reduction in product groups of interest to them, e.g., tropical products, natural resource-based products, agricultural products, textiles, etc. In this area, Mr. Dunkel has not made any proposals other than suggesting that bilateral, plurilateral and multilateral negotiations for reduction of tariff and non-tariff should be concluded in the first two months of 1992. Earlier, various participating countries including India have made conditional offers for reduction of tariffs and during the negotiations that will take place in the next few weeks, it is expected that the participating countries will try to ensure that the offers made by them are balanced. It may be mentioned that India has offered a reduction by 30 per cent of its basic customs duty on raw materials, intermediates and capital goods, with a few exceptions.

(ii) Agriculture

In trade in Agriculture, existing GATT rules lack rigorous discipline on the use of subsidies and quantitative restrictions. Taking advantage of this, the industrialised countries have been heavily subsidising and protecting their agriculture, completely distorting world production and trade of temperate zone agricultural foodstuffs. Due to competitive subsidisation of cereals, dairy products, meat, sugar, oilseeds etc. world prices of these products have been depressed for many years, reducing market opportunities for the efficient producing countries. The focus of attention in the Uruguay Round is on the policies of the industrialised countries on agricultural trade and production. While all the industrialised countries have agreed on reduction subsidy and protection, differences have persisted till the end on the extent of reduction that could be committed during the negotiations.

The Director General's proposals for reform in agricultural policies envisage special and differential treatment for developing countries. The proposals for general application are:

(a) All domestic support in favour of agricultural producers with the exception of certain measures which have been exempted (in view of their non-distortive effect) shall be reduced for the year 1993 to the year 1999 by 20 per cent.
(b) Export subsidies which are in the nature of direct subsidies shall be subject to commitments for reduction of budgetary outlay and quantities by 36 per cent and 24 per cent respectively from the year 1993 to the year 1999.
(c) There shall be comprehensive tariffication. Ordinary customs duty, including those resulting from tariffication shall be reduced from the year 1993 to the year 1999 on a simple average basis of 36 per cent with a minimum rate of reduction of 15 per cent for each tariff line.

The proposals for developing countries envisage the following special treatment:

(a) Countries which have aggregate support levels of up to 10 per cent for individual agricultural products shall not be require to make reductions.
(b) Investment subsidies which are generally available to agriculture and agriculture input subsidies provided to low income or resource poor farmers have been exempted from the purview of reduction commitments.
(c) In addition to the above; the developing countries which have Balance of Payments restrictions (such as India) have been exempted from the purview of tariffication of non-tariff measures. Further, they have been given the facility of offering ceiling bindings of tariffs.

(iii) Textiles and Clothing

In textiles and clothing, world trade is governed by the Multi-Fibre Arrangement (MFA) which enables importing countries to deviate from the general GATT rules and impose discriminatory restrictions on imports from exporting countries which are able to export cheaper products by virtue of lower wages. The Director-General, GATT's proposals on textiles contains the following elements:

(a) The MFA will be phased out during the 10-year period 1993-2002. On 1 January, 2003, textiles and clothing sector shall stand integrated in GATT, with all restrictions under this agreement having been eliminated.
(b) The 10-year period will be divided into three stages of 3:4:3. At the commencement of the first stage, effectively 16 per cent of the total volume of imports for 1990 shall be integrated into GATT. The percentages of integration at the commencement of the 2nd and 3rd stages would be 17 and 18 respectively. Thus, 51 per cent of the total imports, shall be integrated into GATT on 1 January, 2000; leaving the remaining 49 per cent to be integrated on 1 January, 2003. Thus, the effective integration in the

first seven years is low. The position is even less satisfactory than what might appear *prima facie* because in the first two stages (1993-1999), EEC and USA which are our major markets, can achieve the prescribed integration percentages, if they so choose, by integrating products whose imports from India are not under restraint.

(iv) GATT Rules

In the rule making area, a common aim widely shared by the participating countries was to strengthen and preserve the multilateral trading system by reaffirming the principle of non-discrimination and by removing ambiguities and scope for arbitrary action in the administration of rules governing non-tariff measures. At the same time, developing countries wanted to retain maximum flexibility for use by them of commercial policy instruments such as quantitative restrictions and export subsidies, except for anti-dumping and one aspect of the safeguards agreements, agreement was reached on all the rule making areas. The main features of the text presented by Mr. Dunkel are given below:

(a) in anti-dumping, it has been provided, inter-alia, that there shall be immediate termination of proceedings, where the authorities determine that the volume of dumped imports from a particular country is less than one per cent of the domestic market unless the cumulative total of imports from these exporters is 2.5 per cent of the market.

(b) In countervailing duties, developing countries have been exempted from investigations if the volume of subsidised imports represents less than 4 per cent of the total imports, unless the cumulative total share of such suppliers comes to 9 per cent of the total imports.

(c) Countries with a per capital income of less than US $1000 per annum have been exempted from the obligation to phase out export subsidies on products in which they have attained a share of at least 3.25 per cent in the world trade of that product for two consecutive years. It is important to note that for the purposes of calculation, a product is defined as a section head of the Harmonised System of Nomenclature. At present, India's share of world exports of only one item, namely diamonds and jewellery is around 10 per cent. Other exports are less than the cut-off limit.

(d) Indirect taxes borne by the exported products were earlier reimbursable only if they had been imposed on an input which was physically incorporated into the exported product. Now duties and taxes on inputs consumed in the production process such as fuel, oils, energy and catalysts have also been made reimbursable.

(e) In safeguards, grey area measures such as voluntary export restraints, orderly marketing arrangements, have been banned. The principle of non-discriminatory treatment in the use of safeguard measures for protecting domestic industry from serious injury has been reaffirmed and selectivity has been prohibited except for minor departures by way of quota modulation. It has been provided that safeguard measures shall not apply if the share of imports of a developing countries does not exceed 3 per cent provided that the cumulative share of imports from such countries is not more than 9 per cent of the total imports.

(f) The Balance of Payments provisions have been renegotiated in a way which substantially preserves the freedom of developing countries to use these measures and to vary the incidence of restrictions on various imported goods to reflect national needs and priorities. The rules will make it possible for developing countries such as India to facilitate import of capital goods and inputs needed for industrial and agricultural production while maintaining restrictions on consumer goods.

(g) The TRIMs agreement has been limited to interpreting the rules of GATT on national treatment and quantitative restrictions in relations to investment measures. There is no new obligation and export obligations have been totally excluded from the purview of the agreement. Developing countries are able to continue with import balancing requirement as long as they experience balance of payments problems. There is no obligation whatsoever on whether foreign direct investment should be permitted or whether ceiling can be imposed on foreign direct investment.

(v) TRIPs

The following are the main features of the Dunkel package in respect of intellectual property rights:

(a) Copyright protection will be given in accordance with the Berne Convention. It shall extend to expression and not to ideas, procedures, methods of operation or mathematical concepts as such. Computer programmes whether in source or object code, shall be protected as literary works. Compilation of data or other material, whether in machine readable or other form, which by reason of the selection or arrangement of their contents constitute intellectual creations shall be protected as such.

(b) In respect of at least computer programmes and cinematograph works, authors and their successors in title shall be provided the right to authorise or to prohibit the commercial rental to the public of originals or the copies of their copyright works. The provisions of rental rights shall apply to producers of phonograms and any other right holders in phonograms as determined in domestic law.

(c) In respect of fixation of their performance on a phonogram, performers shall have the possibility of preventing the following acts when undertaken without their authorisation: The fixation of unfixed performance. Performers shall also have the possibility of preventing the following acts when undertaken without their authorisation: the broadcasting by wireless means and the communication to the public of their live performance. Producers of phonograms shall enjoy the right to authorise or prohibit the direct or indirect reproduction their phonograms.

(d) Trade marks shall be made registerable whether on goods or services. The use of a trade mark shall not be unjustifiably encumbered by special requirements, such as use with another trade-mark, use in a special form or use in a manner detrimental to its capability to distinguish the goods or services of one undertaking from those of other undertakings. The nature of the goods or services shall in no case form an obstacle to registration of the trademark.

(e) In respect of geographical indications, legal means shall be provided for interested parties to prevent the use of any means in the designation or presentation of a good that indicates or suggests that the goods in question originates in a geographical area other than the true place of origin in a manner which misleads the public as to the geographical origin of the goods.

(f) Protection shall be provided for independently created industrial designs that are new or original.

(g) patents shall be available for any invention, whether products or processes, in all fields of technology, provided that they are new, involve an inventive step and are capable of industrial application. In general, patents shall be available and patent rights enjoyable without discrimination as to the place of invention, the field of technology and whether products are imported or locally produced. Apart from standard exclusions relating to public order, morality, including protection of human, animal or plant life or health, the proposals provide for exclusion of diagnostic, therapeutic and surgical methods for treatment of humans or animals and plant and animals and essential biological processes from the production of plant or animals, however, micro-organisms and non-biological and micro-biological processes have been proposed to be made patentable. Further, it has been recommended that protection of plant varieties shall be afforded either by patents or an effective *sui generis* system or by any combination thereof.

(h) The term of the patent has been proposed to be for a uniform period of at least 20 years.

(i) No grounds for grant of compulsory licence have been proposed leaving Governments somewhat free to make provisions in their law on such licensing. However, there are strict conditions for such authorisation. Each case will have to be considered on individual merit and compulsory licence shall be granted only if the proposed user has made efforts to obtain authorisation from the right holder on reasonable commercial terms and conditions and such efforts have not been successful within a reasonable period of time. The legal validity of any decision relating to the authorisation of such use shall be subject to judicial review or other independent review by a distinct higher authority. Further any decision relating to the remuneration provided in respect of compulsory licence shall be also subject to similar review.

(j) In respect of the process patents, it has been suggested that at least in one of the following circumstances, any identical product when produced without the consent of the patent owner shall, in the absence of proof to the contrary, be deemed to have been obtained by the patented process: (a) If the product obtained by the patented process is new: (b) if there is a substantial likelihood that the identical product was made by the process and the owner of the patent has been unable through reasonable efforts, to determine the process actually used.

(k) It has been suggested that protection shall be provided to lay-out designs of integrated circuit only in so far as it continues to contain an unlawfully reproduced layout design.

(l) Protection shall be afforded to undisclosed information by providing natural and legal persons the possibility of preventing information lawfully within their control from being disclosed to, acquired by, or used by others, without their consent in a manner contrary to honest commercial practices.

(m) All countries have been given a transitional period of one year and developing countries of additional four years. To the extent that a developing country was not extending product patent protection to areas of technology on the general date of application of the agreement, it has been provided that the developing country concerned may delay the application of the obligations in respect of patents to such areas of technology for an additional period of five years. Thus, in respect of food, chemicals, pharmaceuticals and bio-technological products, India will have the possibility of delaying the application of the obligations till 1.1.2003. However, after the date of entry into force (envisaged as 1.1.1993), such countries will have to provide means by which applications for patents for such inventions can be filled. These applications for patents for such inventions can be filled. These applications shall be examined only when the obligations on patent protection of these products become effective. There is provision also for exclusive marketing rights for a period of five years, after obtaining market approval for new products.

(vi) Trade in Services

The General Agreement on Trade in Services (GATS) sets out the framework under which governments can negotiate market access negotiations. The only important disciplines which would apply across the board to the entire universe of services are Most Favoured Nation Treatment (MFN) and transparency. There is no general obligation imposed on the need to provide access to foreign services enterprises or for granting to them national treatment, i.e., same treatment as to national enterprises. These have been made subject to negotiations on a request and offer basis. Dunkel has recommended that negotiations shall take place in the next few weeks for obtaining a better balance in these offer. The framework provides scope to participants to seek concession on movement of personnel as well as on investments in the service sector.

(vii) Institutional Matters

(a) An important area of negotiations was that of dispute settlement. The Dunkel package contains an understanding on rules and procedures on dispute settlement whereby these rules have been time-bound, automatic and judicial in approach. Specific provisions have been made on joining countries to follow the dispute settlement provisions in considering retaliation against other contracting parties. A feature of the GATT rules on dispute settlement is that before any retaliatory step is taken by a contracting party, it has to take authorisation from the full membership. The new rules that have been developed thus have implications for those countries whose domestic law contains provisions for unilateral retaliation.

(b) One of the results of the negotiations incorporation into the Dunkel package is the establishment of the Multilateral Trading Organisation (MTO) to provide the common institutional framework for the conduct of trade relations between the members of the MTO in matters relating to

GATT, GATS and TRIPs agreements. MTO will be a successor agreements to GATT. The main organs of the MTO will be the Ministerial Conference, the General Council, a Goods Council, a Services Council, and a TRIPs Council.

(c) An element of the MTO will be the integrated dispute settlement system. The implication of this will be that while GATS and TRIPs agreements will have separate legal status from GATT and in this GATS and TRIPs agreements will be on an equal footing, a common dispute settlement procedure would apply to all the three agreements. While cross retaliation has been permitted as a last resort, a number of safeguards have been provided. First such cross retaliation will be possible only after following a hierarchical structure, whereby for rights infringed in a sub-sector, redressal has to be obtained in that sub-sector only. Only if there is no trade in that sub-sector, can a winning party go to other sub-sectors within the same agreements. As a last recourse, if the case is serious, the winning party can cross retaliate across agreements. However, authorisation of retaliation across agreement is subject to arbitration and the arbitrator's findings are final.

(d) The DG's proposals include the draft of a Final Act embodying the results of the negotiations. Such a documents has been drawn up with the intention of establishing the results, authenticating the instruments and indicating the intention of the participating Governments to present the text to their authorities for acceptance. A feature of the draft is that the whole package has been presented for acceptance as a whole, i.e., as a single undertaking.

Source: *Third Concept,*, February 1992.

DIVERSE SIGNIFICANT MATTERS

(Not Reported Elsewhere in Main Text)

(i) Indo-Nepal Affairs

The Indo-Nepal summit held in New Delhi in December 1991 marked a positive turning point in the delicate ties between the two countries. The success of the Nepalese Prime Minister, Mr. Girija Prasad Koirala's visit to India is a happy reminder of the fact that it is never beyond well-meaning neighbours to resolve bilateral issues if they display the necessary political will.

In an epoch making efforts to strengthen age-old friendship, India and Nepal signed on December 6, 1991 five agreements including on trade and transit and reached far reaching understanding to tap enormous potential of water resources for mutual benefit.

Among the projects on which an agreement was reached, following deliberations of the Indo-Nepal joint commission, are the Karnali multipurpose project, Pancheshwar multipurpose project, the Kosi-Bhimnagar barrage, the Baghmati-Kamala scheme, the Sapta-Kosi high dam and the Burhi Gandak scheme. The only pending water-sharing scheme now is the Tanakpur scheme on which the Nepalese side came up with new suggestions on details of power sharing. The matter was referred back to the joint commission.

India agreed to enter into separate treaties on trade and transit with Nepal thereby removing one of the irritants between the two countries. The treaty on transit is valid for seven years and includes procedures to encourage Nepalese imports and exports. The treaty on trade is valid for five years and is renewable for the same period. Besides the elements included in the earlier treaty, India has agreed to giver several new facilities and concessions for Nepalese exports to India.

The visiting Nepalese Prime Minister and India's Prime Minister, Mr. P.V. Narasimha Rao, jointly decided to set-up an Indo-Nepal foundation in the name of late Nepalese leader, Mr. B.P. Koirala.

(ii) Indo-China Affairs

The five-day official goodwill visit of Chinese Premier Li-Peng to New Delhi from December 11 to 16, 1991, was the first ever at that level after 31 years. The previous visit by Premier Chou en Lai had taken place in 1960 at a time when tensions were high on account of the mounting differences in regard to the Sino-Indian boundary question.

The two countries have committed themselves to reaching an "early and mutually acceptable" solution to the 30-year-old border problem with both sides agreeing to maintain peace and tranquility along the Line of Actual Control through periodical meetings of military personnel in the border area on a regular basis. A joint communique issued on December 16 said the Joint Working Group (JWG) should step up its work to find an "earliest-possible" solution to the boundary question. It was decided that the next JWG meeting would be held in New Delhi in early 1992.

On Tibet, the two countries stated their respective position. China said that Tibet was an "inalienable part of the Chinese territory" and it was "firmly opposed to any attempt and action aimed at splitting it bringing about independence of Tibet." On the other hand, India, while reiterating its long standing and "consistent position" on Tibet, said Tibet was an autonomous region of China and it "does not allow Tibetans to engage in anti-China activities in India." While China, anticipating troubles in the coming years in Tibet, wanted India to endorse its old position to Tibet, India showed no desire that China should comment or state its position on Kashmir.

(iii) **Indo-Pak Affairs**

The Line of Actual Control (LAC) is a live wire that has claimed hundreds of lives ever since it came into existence.

The LAC, known as the ceasefire line before the 1972 Simla agreement between India and Pakistan, came into being as an aftermath of armed conflict between these two countries over Kashmir in 1947-48.

Following the accession of Jammu and Kashmir to India by the last Dogra King, Maharaja Hari Singh, there was tribal attack on the State which was repulsed by the Indian Army. The ceasefire line was a creation of the United Nations that intervened to halt the armed conflict between the armies of India and Pakistan.

This 600-km-long borderline from Chhamb to Siachen Glacier is different from the international border. While the international border is guarded by the paramilitary forces—Border Security Force (BSF) on this side and Rangers on Pakistan side—the LAC is guarded by the regular armies on both sides. This border which is yet to graduate to the status of international border has witnessed many skirmishers and till the Kashmir issue is resolved and it gains the status of the international border, such mini-wars that it has been witnessing for over four decades are unlikely to halt.

If it was Siachen Glacier, the highest battleground of the world in late eighties which made news after the secessionist militancy broke out in Kashmir, the LAC in Uri, Kupwara, Teetwal Sadhna picket, Chokibal, Poonch and Rajouri sectors became live in August-September last year. The Poonch sector had been converted into a full-fledged war zone in which both Indian and Pakistan sides suffered losses. Besides scores of casualties among the troops, there was loss of civilian lives as well. It was prompt action taken by the Director-Generals of the military operations of both the countries which saved the war spilling out to other sectors along the LAC.

Since 1986, when the two countries started their massive military exercise—first Brasstacks by India then Zarbe-Momin by Pakistan—the two armies have come close to a confrontation. In early 1990 also a similar situation arose and war seemed inevitable. Once again, a similar situation has arisen on the eve of the Jammu and Kashmir Liberation Front's (JKLF) proposed march to this side of Kashmir from Pakistan occupied Kashmir (PoK) after crossing the LAC on Feb 11. Troops have moved to forward positions and night curfew imposed.

Since 1990 there have been at least half a dozen attempts by the civilians from across to come over to this side. Those were mainly protest demonstrations against India. Those were unscheduled and fully backed by the Pakistan Government. It first happened on Jan. 19 in Ranbirsinghpura sector. Then in Poonch sector on Jan. 31. On Feb. 4 in Uri sector, again in the first week of March in the same sector. In all, over a dozen persons died when the Indian troops repulsed their attempts to cross over to this side. This was in 1990 when the secessionist militancy was gaining ground support in the Valley and Pakistan was making determined efforts to internationalise the issue.

But the Kashmiri youth crossed the LAC at will to receive training in arms and ammunition. They returned, most of the time unchecked, for any amount of vigil along the LAC, marked by dense jungles, deep ravines and treacherous mountain posses, cannot check the crossing. Aerial patrolling was mooted to check the movement on the LAC but that also did not help.

According to an official estimate more than 1,400 militants have died on the LAC while trying to cross the border.

Militants have in the past surrendered mostly in Kupwara and Poonch sectors, when challenged by the security forces. However, the militants have dodged the security forces and sneaked into this side of the LAC and reached their destination unchallenged.

The situation as of today is that more than 400 families of Baramulla, Kupwara, Poonch and Rajouri districts have gone across besides a number of militants—the number is always a baffling question for the authorities. But this movement does not present any extraordinary picture. Even in the past, what the uniformed men term as "peacetimes", families from the two sides have been crossing and meeting their friends and relatives. In early eighties when PoK was witnessing a rise in prices and other problems, more than 3,000 families had crossed over to this side in Rajouri and Poonch district alone. They could not be detected; neither their physical features nor their language is different from the natives.

Source: *Hindustan Times,* February 9, 1992.

(iv) **Nag Missile Test**

The third generation anti-tank missile, "Nag" was successfully flight-tested at Chandipur test range in November 1990.

According to an official Press release, the missile was manoeuvred smoothly during its controlled flight and thus it fully met the objectives of the present trials. Further tests would be carried out in the coming months.

Flight tests had been carried out in the same range as well as the long range artillery rockets last month, meeting the technical objectives of the present campaign. This system will be further tested and the lethality fully assessed before beginning the operational trials, the release said.

Defence scientists were over-joyed in achieving yet another success after the successful test firing of the country's intermediate range missile Akash and surface-to-surface missile Prithvi.

The scientific adviser to the Defence Minister, Dr. V.S. Arunachalam, has described Nag as more than matching any comparable missile in the armoury of

NATO or the Warsaw Pact.

The test flight of the Nag was preceded last month, according to defence officials, by successful test firing of the indigenous long-range artillery rockets christened Pinacha. These tests were also carried out at the Chandipur range, they added.

India, which hitherto had been deploying the Russian-made multi-barel rocket system, recently faced immense difficulties in acquiring spare parts for these close range infantry support weapons as suppliers in Eastern Europe and Soviet Union demanded payment on convertible currencies.

The Nag, the third generation anti-tank missile system, according to DRDO sources, has a "fire and forget and top attack capability". They said the Nag missile would overcome the present disadvantages and was designed to pierce all futuristic armour, including reactive armour.

The missile, which can be launched both from land-based missile carriers as well as helicopters, has a range of four kilometers. The missile's target acquisition system includes thermal sight operating, carbondioxide ranger finder with range accuracy and day sight and other vision aids for the crew.

Source: *Indian Express*, November 29, 1990.

(v) **Indigenous Submarine Commissioned**

The first-ever India-made world-class diesel-electric submarine, comparable to the best anywhere, joined the Indian Navy's submarine fleet on February 7, 1992 raising the submarine strength to 18.

The Rs. 180 crore SSK-type submarine, christened "INS Shalki" was commissioned by Defence Minister Sharad Pawar. "Shalki" was an expressive symbol of efforts towards indigenisation and self-reliance. It was absolutely necessary to have a viable Navy to protect the maritime interests of the nation.

Source: *Hindustan Times*, February 7, 1992.

(vi) **National Science Centre, New Delhi**

Prime Minister P.V. Narasimha Rao on January 9, 1992 dedicated to the nation the National Science Centre set-up at the cost of Rs. 15 crore and named it after late Mr Rajiv Gandhi.

Located at Bhairon Road, adjacent to Pragati Maidan and overlooking the Old Fort, the National Science Centre is the latest and largest in the chain of such centres set up in the country by the National Council of Science Museums. Spread over an area of 17,000 sq. feet, it is also the largest of its kind in Asia and acclaimed as one of the best by the international museum community.

The Centre has about 1,200 exhibits meant to portray India's 5,000-year-old heritage and provide an insight into some basic concepts of science.

Speaking on the occasion, the Prime Minister referred to ancient India's achievements in the field of science and stated that today's scientist must seek inspiration from these. These should be applied to the modern conditions.

To discard outright something done in India long ago is not acceptable. And to copy something blindly is equally unacceptable.

He also stressed upon the need for the technology to be such as to keep the environmental aspect in view. To strike a balance between environment and development was a tough task, he said.

It was tougher still to evolve a common approach towards environmental problems by the developed and developing countries due to their differing views on the subject, Mr. Rao felt. A common approach on the issue was unlikely to emerge in the near future as it appeared to be tougher than achieving disarmamentor removal of nuclear weapons, the Prime Minister pointed out.

Emphasising upon the need for self reliance in solving the country's enormous problems, he expressed the belief that if the nation's scientists and intellectuals worked together they would be able to meet the challenges facing it.

Union Minister for Human Resource Development Arjun Singh stated on the occasion that during the days of the British Raj, an impression was created that all scientific achievements came from the West. However, now the National Science Centre would provide an opportunity to get direct knowledge of India's achievements in the field of science and technology.

(vii) **New Heights in the Scientific Field**

During 1991 Indian scientists sent a Remote Sensing Satellite, put into operation atomic power plant units, emerged third in the world to make the anti-AIDS AZT drug, gained an early lead in the race for birth control vaccines and made inroads into defence technology.

Their counterparts around the world discovered a new planet, produced energy from nuclear fusion for the first time, turned female mice into males and traced the "father of us all" to a pygmy who lived many million years ago in Africa.

Indian space scientists found reason for cheer as the second Remote Sensing Satellite IRS-1B shot into space to join its sister IRS-1A, marking the country's eight space success in 16 years.

Put into orbit from the Baikonur cosmodrome in the USSR in August, IRS-1B will send data on agriculture, land use, forestry, geology, and marine and water resources.

The flight version of the liquid propulsion, second stage of the Polar Satellite Launch Vehicle (PSLV) was successfully ground tested in Mahendragiri in Tamil Nadu in June.

Atomic scientists too were upbeat as the second unit of the Narora atomic power plant became critical in October—another milestone in India's nuclear power programme. The plant design incorporates safety features enabling it to withstand tremors and shut down automatically in case of emergencies.

For the first time since the Fast Breeder Test Reactor (FBTR) at Kalpakkam reached critically in 1985, it began operating at one mega watt thermal power from April, thanks to scientists of the Indira Gandhi Centre for Atomic Research.

(viii) **Comparative State of Development**

Following six Tables, based on the data collected by UNICEF from various international and national agencies provide a comparative state of development of more than one hundred countries. In some sectors, data covers as many as one hundred and twenty-nine countries developed, developing and least developed.

TABLE 1: Demography

	Item	Year	India	Best country/ Countries		No. of countries for which data available	India's position in the world
1.	Population Annual Growth Rate %	1980-90	2.1	Austria Hungry German Democratic Republic	—0.1	129	51
2.	Crude Death Rate	1990	11	Kuwait	2	129	67
3.	Crude Birth Rate	1990	32	Italy Denmark G.F.R. Japan	10 11 11 11	129	61
4.	Life Expectancy	1990	59	Japan	79	129	84
5.	Total Fertility Rate	1990	4.2	GFR Italy	1.5 1.4	129	59
6.	% Population Urbanised	1990	27	Singapore Belgium Kuwait	100 97 96	129	99

TABLE 2: Economy

	Item	Year	India	Country at the top		Countries for which data available	India's position in the world
	1	2	3	4	5	6	7
1.	G.N.P. Per capita (U.S. Dollars)	1989	340	Switzerland	29880	127	105
2.	% Rate of Inflation	1980-89	8	Oman	7	111	51
3.	% Population Below Poverty Line	1980-89					
	(a) Urban		29	N.A.		49	29
	(b) Rural		33	N.A.		53	
4.	% Expenditure on						
	(a) Health	1986-90	2.0	Bhutan	42	84	69
	(b) Education		3	Algeria	25	80	68
	(c) Defence		19			76	11

TABLE 3: Education

Item	Year	India	Country with best position		Countries to which data available	India's position in the world
1. Adult literacy	1990		Jamaica	98	90	59
(a) Male		62	Greece	98		
(b) Female		34	Italy	98	90	62
2. Primary School Enrolment Ratio (Gross)						
(a) Male	1986-89	114	China	142	118	16
(b) Female (Net not available)		83	China	126	118	80
3. % of Grade I Enrolment Completing Primary School	1985-87	40	Norway	100	110	91
			Japan	100		
4. Secondary School Enrolment Ratio (Gross)	1986-89		Denmark	106		60
			Netherlands	105		
(a) Male		50	Canada	104		
(b) Female		29	Denmark	107		77
			Spain	107		

TABLE 4 : Health

Item	Year	India	Country with best position		Countries to which data available	India's position in the world
1. % of Population with Access to Drinking Water	1989-90	75	Hongkong	100		
			Kuwait	100	91	25
			Singapore	100		
2. % of Population with Access to Health services	1985-90	N.A.	Kuwait	100	84	—
			Mauritius	100		
			Singapore	100		
3. % Fully Immunized One Year Old Children	1981 / 1989-90					
(a) TB		12/97	Hungry	99/99	114	20
(b) DPT		31/92	Sweden	99/99	129	23
(c) Polio		7/93	Denmark	97/100	129	26
(d) Measles		/87	Hungry	99/99	129	26
4. % Birth Attended by Trained Health Personnel	1983-90	33	Bulgaria, USA		116	91
			Belgium, Norway, Sweden, Japan		100	
5. Maternal Mortality Rate	1980-90	460	Norway	03	110	90
			Ireland	02		
			Sweden	05		

TABLE 5: Nutrition

	Item	Year	India	Country with best position		Countries for which data available	India's position in the world
1.	% of Children with Low Birth Weight	1982-88	30	Ireland Hongkong Sweden Spain	4 4 4 1	101	100
2.	% Children Suffering from Malnutrition (a) Mild-Moderate (b) Severe	1980—91	 61 09	Figure available for a few countries only			
3.	Average Index of Food Production Paper Capita (1979-81=100)	1990	118	Saudi Arabia	252	124	15
4.	Daily Per Capita Calorie Supply as % of Requirements	1988	95	Ireland Greece	147 148	126	88
5.	% of House-hold Income Spent on All Food	1980-85	52	Canada Hongkong U.K. Sweden Austria	11 12 12 13 13	83	70

(ix) **Micro Planning for Population Control**

There is need for area specific planning within the general directional framework of a national policy aimed at generating a people's movement with the total and committed involvement of community leaders, irrespective of denominational affiliation and linking population control with larger programmes of female literacy, women's employment, social security, access to health services, immunisation and mother and child care.

There is a need to classify the 90 districts identified by the Health Ministry for concentration on the basis of 1991 Census (the Health Ministry's action plan is based on the 1981 Census) into different groups where the relevant parameters are fairly homogenous, and adapt policies and programmes to the specific characteristics of each group.

Such data analysis clearly underscored the need of area specific planning. Although there is likely to be commonalities of approach in the general contours of any population policy for the country, it is critical that the programme content must relate to area specific planning at district, and the panchayat levels. There is also a need for coordination of programmes meant for women's development and also by making population control and child care an important component of all such programmes.

The health care systems must have an inbuilt resilience but a sharply defined accountability. Till such time that the panchayats reach an optimally operational mode, existing institutions shall have to be strengthened to provide a thrust to the population control programme.

A major emphasis on health manpower planning along with a review of the education and training programmes of all categories of health care. Involvement of practitioners of all systems of medicine (besides the 360,000 practitioners of modern medicine there are more than 510,000 practitioners of Indian systems of medicine and Homoeopathy). Exploitation of voluntary organisations for spreading the message is also required. Major investment in bio-medical research for development of new contraceptive methods including regulation of fertility in the male and vaccines for fertility regulation both in the male and female is called for.

There should be continuous monitoring, review and evaluation for successful implementation of population programme. While the political will and community commitment transcending denominational affiliations, must provide the requisite leadership, the administration should play a critical fasilitatory role for generating the necessary momentum for population control movement by the people.

Source: Document prepared by Planning Commission, under supervision of Prof. J.S. Bajaj, Member-in-charge Health as reported in *Hindustan Times,* January 6, 1992.

CONCEPTS AND DEFINITIONS OF TECHNICAL TERMS

Absolute Poverty Level: Income level below which a minimum nutritionally adequate diet plus essential non-food requirements is not affordable.

Access to Health Services: Percentage of the population that can reach appropriate local health services by the local means of transport in no more than one hour.

Adult Literacy Rate (ALR): Percentage of persons aged 15 and over who can read and write.

Births Attended: Percentage of births attended by physicians, nurses, midwives, trained primary health care workers or trained traditional birth attendants.

Breast-Feeding: Percentage of mothers either wholly or partly breast-feeding.

Child Malnutrition: *Mild or Moderate* — between 60% and 80% of the desirable weight-for-age. *Severe* — less than 60% of the desirable weight-for-age.

Children Reaching Final Grade of Primary School: Percentage of the children entering the first grade school who eventually reach the final grade.

Contraceptive Prevalence: Percentage of married women aged 15-49 currently using contraception.

Crude Birth Rate: Annual number of births per 1,000 population.

Crude Death Rate: Annual number of deaths per 1,000 population.

Debt Service: Sum of interest payments and repayments of principal on external public and publicly guaranteed long-term debts.

DPT: Diphtheria, pertussis (whooping cough) and tetanus.

Gross National Product (GNP): Annual GNP's per capita are expressed in current United States dollars. GNP per capita growth rates are average annual growth rates that have been computed by fitting trend lines to the logarithmic values of GNP per capita at constant market prices for each year of the time period.

Income Share: Percentage of household income received by the highest 20 per cent and lowest 40 per cent of households.

Infant Mortality Rate (IMR): Annual number of deaths of infants under one year of age per 1,000 live births. More specifically this is the probability of dying between birth and exactly one year of age.

Life Expectancy at Birth: Number of years new-born children would live if subject to the mortality risks prevailing for the cross-section of population at the time of their birth.

Low Birth Weight: 2,500 grammes or less

Maternal Mortality Rate: Annual number of deaths of women from pregnancy related causes per 100,000 live births.

Mean: Sum of all the items divided by the number of items. In cases where the range is not very extensive, the most commonly used average is the mean. However, when we are dealing with countries of very different sizes and population, we would immediately encounter the problem of weighting if we used the mean.

Median: Middle value of a data set arranged in order of magnitude. It is the average commonly used where there are a large number of items of data with a great range; it has the advantage of not being distorted by the very small or the very large countries.

ODA: Official Development Assistance.

ORS: Oral Rehydration Salts.

ORT Use: Percentage of all cases of diarrhoea in children under five years of age treated with ORS, or an appropriate household solution.

Primary and Secondary Enrolment Ratios: The gross enrolment ratio is the total number of children enrolled in a schooling level — whether or not they belong in the relevant age group for that level — expressed as a percentage of the total number of children in the relevant age group for that level. The net enrolment ratio is the total number of children enrolled in a schooling level who belong in the relevant age group, expressed as a percentage of the total number of children in that age group.

Stunting: *Moderate and Severe* — below minus two standard deviations from median height for age of reference population.

Total Fertility Rate: Number of children that would be born per woman, if she were to live to the end of her child-bearing years and bear children at each age in accordance with prevailing age-specific fertility rates.

Under Five Mortality Rate (U5MR): Annual number of deaths of children under five years of age per 1,000 live births. More specifically this is the probability of dying between birth and exactly five years of age.

Underweight: *Moderate and Severe* — below minus two standard deviations from median weight for age of reference population; *Severe* — below minus three standard deviations from median weight for age of reference population.

Urban Population: Percentage of population living in urban areas as defined according to the national definition used in the most recent population census.

Wasting: *Moderate and Severe* — below minus two standard deviations from median weight for height of reference population.

APPENDIX V

INSTITUTIONS OF NATIONAL IMPORTANCE IN INDIA

Agriculture

Central Inland Fisheries Research Institute, Calcutta.
Nautical Engineering Training, Cochin.
Forest Research Institute and Colleges, Dehradun.
Indian Agricultural Research Institute, New Delhi.
Indian Agricultural Statistics Research Institute, New Delhi.
Indian Council of Agricultural Research, New Delhi.
Indian Society of Agricultural Economics, Bombay.
Indian Veterinary Research Institute, Izatnagar.
Indira Gandhi National Forest Academy, Dehradun.
National Dairy Research Institute, Karnal.
National Sugar Institute, Kanpur.
Rubber Board and Rubber Research Institute of India, Kottayam.

Culture — Art and Architecture

Allahabad Museum, Allahabad.
Anthropological Survey of India, Calcutta.
Archaeological Survey of India, New Delhi.
The Asiatic Society, Calcutta.
Central Board of Film Certification, Bombay.
Central Institute of Buddhist Studies, Leh (Ladakh).
Central Institute of Higher Tibetan Studies, Varanasi.
Centre for Cultural Resources and Training, New Delhi.
Gandhi Smriti and Darshan Samiti, New Delhi.
Indian Museum, Calcutta.
Indira Gandhi National Centre for Arts, New Delhi.
Indira Sangeet Vishwavidyalaya, Khairagarh.
Jallianwala Bagh National Memorial Trust, Amritsar.
Lalit Kala Academy (National Academy of Fine Arts), New Delhi.
National Council of Science Museum.
National Gallery of Modern Art, New Delhi.
National Museum of India, New Delhi.
National Research Laboratory for Conservation of Cultural Property, Lucknow.
National School of Drama, New Delhi.

Nehru Memorial Museum and Library, New Delhi.
Rashtriya Manav Sangrahalaya (National Museum of Man), Bhopal.
Sahitya Akademi (National Academy of Cultures), New Delhi.
Salarjung Museum, Hyderabad.
Sangeet Natak Akademy (National Academy of Music, Dance and Drama), New Delhi.
Sarnath Museum, Varanasi.
School of Buddhist Philosophy, Leh (Ladakh).
Sikkim Research Institute of Tibetology, Gangtok.
Victoria Memorial Hall, Calcutta.

Defence

Air Force Academy, Hyderabad.
Air Force Administrative College, Coimbatore.
Armed Forces Medical College, Pune.
College of Combat, Mhow.
Defence Institute of Physiology and Allied Sciences, New Delhi.
Defence Scientific Information and Documentation Centre, New Delhi.
Defence Services Officers Institute, New Delhi.
Indian Military Academy, Dehradun.
I.N.S. Chilka, near Bhubaneswar.
Institute of Defence Studies and Analysis, New Delhi.
National Defence Academy, Khadakvasala.
National Defence College, New Delhi.
Naval Academy, Cochin.
Officers Training School, Madras.
Rashtriya Indian Military College, Dehradun.

Employment and Training

Central Institute of Research and Training in Employment Services, New Delhi.
Institute of Secretariat Training and Management, New Delhi.
Public Enterprise Selection Board, New Delhi.
Staff Selection Commission, New Delhi.
Union Public Service Commission, New Delhi.

Health

All India Institute of Medical Sciences, New Delhi.
B.M. Institute of Mental Health, Ahmedabad.
Central Council of Indian Medicine, New Delhi.
Indian Council of Medical Research, New Delhi.
Indian Medical Association, New Delhi.
National Institute of Communicable Diseases, Delhi.
National Institute of Health and Communicable Diseases, New Delhi.
National Institute of Health and Family Welfare, New Delhi.
National Institute of Nutrition, Hyderabad.

Vallabhbhai Patel Chest Institute, Delhi.

Languages

Anjuman-i-Islam Urdu Research Institute, Bombay.
Bureau of Promotion of Urdu, New Delhi.
Central Hindi Directorate, New Delhi.
Central Institute of English and Foreign Languages, Hyderabad.
Central Institute of Indian Languages, Mysore.
Kendriya Hindi Sansthan, Agra.
Rashtriya Sanskrit Sansthan, New Delhi.

Libraries/Archives

Adyar Library and Research Centre, Adyar, Madras.
Central Library, Bombay.
Central Reference Library, Calcutta.
Central Secretariat Library, New Delhi.
Connemara (State Central) Public Library, Madras.
Delhi Public Library, Delhi.
Government Oriental Manuscript Library, Madras.
Khuda Baksh Oriental Public Library, Patna.
Library of Tibetan Works and Archives, Dharamsala.
National Archives of India, New Delhi.
National Library, Calcutta.
Oriental Research Library, Pune.
Oriental Research Library, Vadodara.
Raja Ram Mohan Roy Library Foundation, Calcutta.
Rampur Raza Library, Rampur.
Tamil Nadu Government Oriental Manuscripts Library, Madras.
Thanjavur Maharaja Serfoji's Saraswati Mahal Library, Thanjavur.
Visheshwarananda Vedic Research Institute Library, Hoshiarpur.

Social Sciences (and allied disciplines)

Administrative Staff College of India, Hyderabad.
Ahmedabad Textile Industries Research Association, Ahmedabad.
Anthropological Survey of India, Calcutta.
Archaeological Survey of India, New Delhi.
Asiatic Society, Calcutta.
Association of Indian Universities, New Delhi.
Bhandarkar Oriental Research Institute, Pune.
Central Board of Secondary Education, New Delhi.
Centre for Economic and Social Studies, Hyderabad.
Development and Educational Communication Unit (ISRO), Ahmedabad.
Directorate of Adult Education, New Delhi.
Economic Botany Information Service (NBRI), Lucknow.
Gandhian Institute of Studies, Varanasi.

Gokhale Institute of Politics and Economics, Pune.
India International Centre, New Delhi.
Indian Council of Applied Economic Research, New Delhi.
Indian Council of Historical Research, New Delhi.
Indian Council of Philosophical Research, New Delhi.
Indian Council of Social Science Research, New Delhi.
Indian Council of World Affairs, New Delhi.
Indian Law Institute, New Delhi.
Indian Statistical Institute, Calcutta.
Indian Institute of Public Administration, New Delhi.
Indian Institute of Advanced Study, Shimla.
Indian National Commission for Cooperation with UNESCO, New Delhi.
L.N. Mishra Institute of Economic Development and Social Change, Patna.
Kendriya Vidyalaya Sangathan, New Delhi.
Madras Institute of Development Studies, Madras.
National Book Trust, New Delhi.
National Council of Applied Economic Research, New Delhi.
National Council of Educational Research and Training, New Delhi.
National Institute of Basic Education, New Delhi.
National Institute of Educational Planning and Administration, New Delhi.
National Institute of Public Cooperation and Child Development, New Delhi.
National Institute of Rural Development, Hyderabad.
National Productivity Council, New Delhi.
National Labour Institute, New Delhi.
National Research Development Council, New Delhi.
Navodaya Vidyalaya Samiti, New Delhi.
Oriental Institute, Vadodara.
Oriental Research Institute, Mysore.
Tata Institute of Social Sciences, Bombay.
University Grants Commission, New Delhi.

Science and Technology

Bhabha Atomic Research Centre, Bombay.
Biological Control Centre (ICAR), Bangalore.
Birla Research Institute for Applied Sciences, Birlagram, Nagda.
Central Electronic Engineering Research Institute, New Delhi.
Central Leather Research Institute, Madras.
Central Mining Research Institute, Dhanbad.
Central Road Research Institute, New Delhi.
Central Tobacco Research Institute, Rajahmundry.
Centre for Advanced Technology, Indore.
Council of Scientific and Industrial Research, New Delhi.
Directorate of Cocoa, Arecanut and Spices Development, Calicut.
Gujarat Fisheries Aquatic Science Research Institute, Okhaport (Gujarat).
High Altitude Research Laboratory of BARC, Gulmarg.
Indian Academy of Sciences, Bangalore.
Indian Institute of Remote Sensing, Dehradun.

Indian Institute of Science, Bangalore.
Indian National Science Academy, New Delhi.
Indian National Scientific Documentation Centre, New Delhi.
Indian Space Research Organisation, Ahmedabad.
Institute of Mathematical Sciences, Madras.
Institute of Physics, Bhubaneshwar.
ISRO Satellite Centre, Bangalore.
Institution of Electronics and Telecommunication Engineers, New Delhi.
International Commission on Irrigation and Drainage, New Delhi.
Madhya Pradesh State Forest Research Institute, Jabalpur.
Maharashtra Association for the Cultivation of Science, Pune.
Meteorological Data Utilisation Centre, New Delhi.
National Aeronautical Laboratory, Bangalore.
National Atlas and Thematic Mapping Organisation, New Delhi.
National Botanical Research Institute, Calcutta.
National Environmental Engineering Research Institute, Nagpur.
National Geophysical Research Institute, Hyderabad.
National Institute of Oceanography, Goa.
National Institute of Virology, Pune.
National Research Development Council, New Delhi.
National Physical Laboratory, Delhi.
Nuclear Atomic Power Station, Tarapur.
Nuclear Research Laboratory, Sri Nagar.
Physical Research Laboratory, Ahmedabad.
Raman Research Institute, Bangalore.
Saha Institute of Nuclear Physics, Calcutta.
Solar Observatory, Udaipur.
Tata Institute of Fundamental Research, Bombay.
Tata Institute of Social Sciences, Bombay.
Variable Energy Cyclortorn Centre, Calcutta.
Vikram Sarabhai Space Centre, Trivandrum.
Zoological Survey of India, Calcutta.

APPENDIX VI

RELEVANT READING

Agriculture and Industry Survey, 1990-91, Vadamalai Media (P) Ltd. Coimbatore, 1991.

Census of India 1991: Historical and World Perspective, by J.C. Aggarwal and N.K. Chowdhry, Chand and Company Ltd., New Delhi, 1991.

Census of India 1991: Provisional Population Totals, Registrar General and Census Commissioner of India, New Delhi, 1991.

Directory of Trade between India and the East European Countries, ed. by Ajeet Kaur, India International Publication, New Delhi, 1990.

Drought-prone India : Problems and Perspectives, by Kathakali S. Bagchi, Agricole Publication Academy, New Delhi, 1991.

Economic Survey 1991-92, Government of India, Ministry of Finance, New Delhi, 1992.

Educational and Social Uplift of Backward Classes : At What Cost and How? Mandal Commission and After, by S.P. Agrawal, and J.C. Aggarwal, Concept Publishing Company, New Delhi, 1991.

Essays on Poverty, Equity and Growth, by George Psacharopoulous, Pergamon, Elmsford, New York, 1991.

Famines in India: A Study in Some Aspects of the Economic History of India with Special Reference to Food Problem, 1860-1990, by B.M. Bhatia, 3rd rev. ed., Konark Publishers, Delhi, 1991.

Geography of Marketing and Commercial Activities in India: Documentation on Research Information, by R.S. Dixit, Concept Publishing Company, New Delhi, 1990.

Gulf Crisis : Pre-War and Post-War Scenario, by J.C. Aggarwal, S. Chand and Company Ltd., New Delhi, 1991.

Human Resources Development Report 1990, Oxford University Press, New York; UNDP, 1990.

Human Resources Development Report 1991, Oxford University Press, New York; UNDP, 1991.

India, by Stanley A Wolepert, University of California Press, 1991.

India : The Emerging Challenges, Sage, New Delhi, 1991.

India 1991, A Reference Manual, Publications Division, Ministry of Information and Broadcasting, Government of India, New Delhi, 1991.

Indian Development Planning and Policy : An Alternative View, by Yoginder K. Alagh, Vikas Publishing House, New Delhi, 1991.

Indian Social and Economic Development, 1990 : An Index to the Literature, Sage, New Delhi, 1991.

Indian Writings on Education, 1979 to 1986, by S.P. Agrawal and J.C. Aggarwal, Concept Publishing Company, New Delhi, 1992.

Information India 1981-91 : Global View, by S.P. Agrawal and J.C. Aggarwal, Concept Publishing Company, New Delhi, 1992.

International Monetary Fund (IMF), by C.V. Brown, Deep and Deep, New Delhi, 1990.

Islamic Studies in India, by Mohammed Taher, Concept Publishing Company, New Delhi, 1991.

Lok Sabha and Vidhan Sabha Election in India 1989 and 1990: Process and Results with Comparative Study of Manifestoes, by S.P. Agarwal and J.C. Agarwal, Concept Publishing Company, 1990.

Nation in Crisis : Achievements, Failures and Non-Function of the Government, by S.P. Agrawal and J.C. Aggarwal, Concept Publishing Company, New Delhi, 1991.

National Accounts Statistics, 1990, United Nations, New York, 1990.

Panchayati Raj : Annotated Resources Guide, by N.B. Inamdar, N.G. Satish and Anil Takalkar, Concept Publishing Company, New Delhi, 1991.

The Political Economy of Sugar in India, by Sanjaya Baru, Oxford University Press, New York, 1990.

Ramamurti Report, 1990, on National Policy on Education in India : Major Recommendation, Evaluation and Corrective Measures, by J.C. Aggarwal, Doaba House, New Delhi, 1991.

Ramjanmabhoomi through the Ages, by J.C. Aggarwal and N.K. Chowdhry, S. Chand and Company Ltd., New Delhi, 1991.

Rise and Fall of Non-Congress Government of India, by S.P. Agrawal and J.C. Aggarwal, Shipra Publications, Delhi, 1991.

Rural Poverty and Unemployment, by Bepin Behari, Vikas Publishing House, New Delhi, 1991.

Second Educational Survey of Educational Developments in India : Select Documents 1985-1990, by S.P. Agrawal and J.C. Aggarwal, Concept Publishing Company, 1991.

The State of the World Children, UNICEF (United Nations Children's Fund), 1992.

Towards an Enlightened and Human Society : NPE, 1986 : A Review, Ministry of Human Resource Development, Government of India, New Delhi, 1990.

Unemployment and Inflation, by C.V. Brown, Disha Publications, Delhi, 1990.

Wealth and Poverty : An Economic History of the Twentieth Century, by Sidnery Pollord, Oxford University Press, New York, 1990.

Women's Education in India: Historical Review, Present Status, Perspective Plan with Statistical Indians, by S.P. Agarwal and J.C. Aggarwal, Concept Publishing Company, 1992.

World Culture in the Indian Context, by Jai B.P. Sinha, Sage Publications, New Delhi, 1990.

World Development Report 1991 : The Challenge of Development, Oxford University Press, New York, 1991.

World Economic Outlook, International Monetary Fund (IMF), Washington, April 1991.

World Population Trends and Policies : 1990 Monitoring Report, United Nations, New York, 1991.

INDEX

CICIL-25 First Handbook of Psychological and Social Instruments
Udai Pareek and **T. Venkateswara Rao** Rs. 500

CICIL-26 Educational and Social Uplift of Backward Classes: At What Cost and How? Mandal Commission and After
S.P. Agrawal and **J.C. Aggarwal** Rs. 275

CICIL-27 Mass Media and New Horizons: Impact of TV & Video an Urban Milieu
H.R. Trivedi Rs. 180

CICIL-28 Indian Writings on Education : An Indicator to Indian Educational Journals Grouped by Subject Deseriptors 1979 to 1986 (in two parts)
S.P. Agarwal Rs. 900 (per set)

CICIL-29 Nation in Crisis
S.P. Agrawal and **J.C. Aggarwal** Rs. 200

CICIL-30 Information India 1990-91: Global View
S.P. Agrawal and **J.C. Aggarwal** Rs. 500

CICIL-31 Development of University Libraries in India after Independence
O.P. Gupta Rs. 270

CICIL-32 Handbook on Child : With Historical Background
Pramila Pandit Barooah Rs. 320

CICIL-33 Weaker Section in Indian Society : Undiscovered Past, Uncertain Present and Unpredictable Future : Index to Writings in Indian Scholarly Journals and 10 National Newspapers Classified under 1500 Descriptors 1886-1990
S.P. Agrawal and **Rajeev Kumar Sharma** Rs. 600

CICIL-34 Communication Informatics and Librarianship in India : An Introductory Guide to Publications Based on a Survey of Libraries in Capital City of India
S.P. Agrawal and **Pushpa Rani Sharma** Rs. 720

CICIL-35 Problems of Collection Development in Special Libraries
M.S. Sridhar Rs. 225

CICIL-36 National Information Resources for Social Sciences in India : Mobilisation, Dispersal and International Enhancement
S.P. Agrawal Rs. 225

CICIL-37 Modern History of Punjab : A Look Back into Ancient Peaceful Punjab Focusing Confrontation and Failures Leading to Present Punjab Problem, and a Peep Ahead : Relevant Select Documents
J.C. Aggarwal and **S.P. Agrawal** Rs. 400

CICIL-38 India Information Sources : Economics and Business
Kyllikki Ruokonen and **Manohar Lal** Rs.

CICIL-39 Educational Planning in India : With a Slant to Educational Financing and Administration, Vol. 1, Reports of Committees and Commissions, Five Year Plans, Statistical Tables
J.C. Aggarwal and **S.P. Agrawal** Rs. 650

CICIL-40 Integrated Library System : Two Case Studies : Latin America and India
Maria Luiza Rigo Pasquarelli, Rosaly Favero Krzyanowski, Ines Maria M. Imperatriz and **S.P. Agrawal** Rs. 160

CICIL-41 Social Science Information in India: Effort towards Bibliographical Control
S.D. Vyas Rs. 300

CICIL-42 Higher Education in India Since Independence: U.G.C. and Its Approach
O.P. Gupta Rs. 360

CICIL-43 Government and Politics in India: A Bibliographical Study of Contemporary Scenario Chronicling Rajiv Gandhi Era
S.P. Agrawal and **Rajeev Kumar Sharma** Rs. 500

CICIL-44 Second Handbook of Psychological and Social Instruments
D.M. Pestonjee Rs. 300

CICIL-45 Development/Digression Diary of India; 3D Companion Volume to Information India: 1990-91
S.P. Agrawal Rs. 200

CICIL-46 Development/Digression Diary of India; 3D Companion Volume to Information India: 1991-92
S.P. Agrawal Rs. 300

CICIL-47 Information India 1991-92: Global View
S.P. Agrawal and **J.C. Aggarwal** Rs. 500